MW01031592

Beyond the Score

Beyond the Score

Music as Performance

NICHOLAS COOK

OXFORD
UNIVERSITY PRESS

Oxford University Press is a department of the University of Oxford.
It furthers the University's objective of excellence in research, scholarship,
and education by publishing worldwide.

Oxford   New York
Auckland   Cape Town   Dar es Salaam   Hong Kong   Karachi
Kuala Lumpur   Madrid   Melbourne   Mexico City   Nairobi
New Delhi   Shanghai   Taipei   Toronto

With offices in
Argentina   Austria   Brazil   Chile   Czech Republic   France   Greece
Guatemala   Hungary   Italy   Japan   Poland   Portugal   Singapore
South Korea   Switzerland   Thailand   Turkey   Ukraine   Vietnam

Oxford is a registered trademark of Oxford University Press
in the UK and certain other countries.

Published in the United States of America by
Oxford University Press
198 Madison Avenue, New York, NY 10016

© Oxford University Press 2013

All rights reserved. No part of this publication may be reproduced, stored in a
retrieval system, or transmitted, in any form or by any means, without the prior
permission in writing of Oxford University Press, or as expressly permitted by law,
by license, or under terms agreed with the appropriate reproduction rights organization.
Inquiries concerning reproduction outside the scope of the above should be sent to the
Rights Department, Oxford University Press, at the address above.

You must not circulate this work in any other form
and you must impose this same condition on any acquirer.

Library of Congress Cataloging-in-Publication Data
Cook, Nicholas, 1950–
Beyond the score: music as performance / Nicholas Cook.
    pages; cm
ISBN 978-0-19-935740-6 (hardback)—ISBN 978-0-19-935741-3 (website)—
ISBN 978-0-19-935742-0 (online content)—ISBN 978-0-19-935743-7 (electronic text)
1. Music—Performance.   2. Music—Philosophy and aesthetics.   3. Musical analysis.   I. Title.
ML457.C75 2015
781.1'7—dc23
                        2013027060

This volume is published with the generous support of the Donna Cardamone Jackson Endowment of
the American Musicological Society, funded in part by the National Endowment for the Humanities and
the Andrew W. Mellon Foundation.

9 8 7 6 5 4 3 2 1
Printed in the United States of America
on acid-free paper

CONTENTS

FIGURES

MEDIA EXAMPLES

3.1 Schubert, op. 90 no. 3, bars 1–48, played by d'Albert. The line graph represents duration, the silhouette pattern dynamics. All media files of op. 90 no. 3 are based on the 2/2 barring used in editions such as Liszt's. Sound and Sonic Visualiser session files 63

3.2 Schubert, op. 90 no. 3, bars 1–48, played by Sapellnikoff. Reproduced by permission of the Pianola Institute. Sound and Sonic Visualiser session files 66

3.3–3.8 Schubert, op. 90 no. 3, bars 1–48, played by Fischer (3.3), Rubinstein (3.4), Sauer (3.5), Schnabel (3.6), Perahia (3.7), and HP (3.8, bars 1–32 only). 3.8 reproduced by permission of the pianist. Sound and Sonic Visualiser session files 81

4.1–4.7 Mozart, Sonata K 332, 1st mvmt. exposition, played by Landowska (4.1), Casadesus (4.2), Gould (4.3), de Larrocha (4.4), Bilson (4.5), Lancaster (4.6), van Oort (4.7). Sound and Sonic Visualiser session files 102

4.8–4.14 Mozart, *Rondo alla turca*, played by Reinecke (Welte-Mignon, 4.8 and Hupfeld, 4.9), Pachmann (4.10), d'Albert (4.11), Sauer (4.12), Friedman (4.13), van Oort (4.14). 4.8 reproduced by permission of the Pianola Institute and 4.9 by permission of Julian Dyer. Sound and Sonic Visualiser session files 112

4.15 Mozart, Sonata K 332, 1st mvmt. exposition, played by Reinecke. Reproduced by permission of Paul Tuck. Sound and Sonic Visualiser session files 123

5.1 Chopin, op. 33 no. 2, bars 1–72, played by Friedman. Sound and Sonic Visualiser session files 167

6.1 Chopin, op. 63 no. 3, bars 1–32, played by Gornostaeva. Sound file 176

6.2 Schubert, op. 90 no. 3, bars 1–32, synthesised version by Windsor and Clarke (based on Todd's model). Reproduced by permission of Eric Clarke. Sound file 178

6.3–6.10 Chopin, op. 63 no. 3, bars 1–32, played by Friedman (6.3), Rachmaninoff (6.4), Pachmann (6.5), Niedzielski (6.6), Földes (6.7), Horowitz (6.8), Czerny-Stefańska (6.9), Neuhaus (6.10). Sound files 189–197

8.1 Beethoven, Quartet op. 59 no. 2, 2nd mvmt., bars 11–21 (Léner Quartet). Sound file 263

ACKNOWLEDGEMENTS

This book has been a long time in the making and in the course of it I have incurred many debts. The most conspicuous are to the Arts and Humanities Research Board (later Council), whose funding of CHARM (the AHRC Research Centre for the History and Analysis of Recorded Music) provided a research base for much of the work in this book; to Royal Holloway, University of London, which not only hosted CHARM but also provided financial support; and to Craig Sapp, a Research Fellow at CHARM, without whose expert input the quantitative studies presented in this book would have been impossible. CHARM's Coordinator, Carol Chan, also supported my research in innumerable ways.

I owe much to the input of the CHARM co-directors (Eric Clarke, Daniel Leech-Wilkinson, and John Rink), whose input is reflected in the many cited publications by each but actually extends much further. I also received valuable advice from John Butt. I would like to acknowledge the contributions of Georgia Volioti, Melissa Wong, and Marcelle Pierson, who respectively helped with preparing the text for submission, music setting, and copyright clearance. I am also grateful to those who read the draft manuscript and made helpful comments, among them Daniel Leech-Wilkinson, David Trippett, Matt Pritchard, David Patmore, Sheila Guymer, and Myles Eastwood. The last two are among a succession of graduate students who gave me useful ideas, or feedback on mine, at Royal Holloway, the University of Cambridge, and Chicago University.

I owe debts of other kinds to Denis Hall, who not only provided me with transfers of piano rolls in his collection but also shared some of his vast knowledge of the subject with me; to Paul Tuck and Julian Dyer, who also provided me with transfers of rolls in their collections; to Donald Manildi (of the International Piano Archives at Maryland), Nick Morgan, Salve Márquez, and Janos Cegledy, who provided me with copies of early recordings; to Timothy Day, Mike Gray, and others who were generous with discographic advice; and to more scholars than I can list who provided me with pre-publication copies of their research or otherwise shared their knowledge with me. Finally I would like to express my gratitude to Suzanne Ryan, Music Books Editor at Oxford University Press, for her encouragement and knowledgeable help; and to Jessen O'Brien, Molly Morrison, and Thomas Finnegan, thanks to whose efforts the book went through production with unusual speed.

Although it incorporates some even earlier ideas, this book essentially has its origins in an article entitled 'Between Process and Product: Music and/as Performance', which appeared during 2001 in *Music Theory Online*; an abridged version was published under the title 'Music as Performance' in *The Cultural*

Study of Music: A Critical Introduction, ed. Martin Clayton, Trevor Herbert, and Richard Middleton (London: Routledge [2003], 204–14; 2nd ed. [2012], 184–94). Thereafter parts of the ongoing research appeared in a number of conference papers and publications. None of this material appears in the same form in this book, but the publications that are most relevant and not referenced in the book are 'Off the Record: Performance, History, and Musical Logic', in *Music and the Mind: Essays in Honour of John Sloboda*, ed. Irène Deliege and Jane Davidson (Oxford: Oxford University Press, 2011), 291–310; 'A Bridge Too Far? Musical Performance Between the Disciplines', in *Gemessene Interpretation: Computergestützte Aufführungsanalyse im Kreuzverhör der Disziplinen*, ed. Heinz von Loesch and Stefan Weinzierl (Mainz: Schott, 2011), 1–14; 'Against Reproduction', in *Music Semiotics: A Network of Significations—In Honor of Raymond Monelle*, ed. Esti Sheinberg (Farnham: Ashgate, 2012), 173–83; 'Bridging the Unbridgeable? Empirical Musicology and Interdisciplinary Performance Studies', in *Music as Performance: Interdisciplinary Perspectives*, ed. Nicholas Cook and Richard Pettengill (Ann Arbor: Michigan University Press, 2013), 70–85; and 'Scripting Social interaction: Improvisation, Performance, and Western "Art" Music', in *Improvisation and Social Aesthetics*, ed. Georgina Born, Eric Lewis, and Will Straw (Durham, NC: Duke University Press, forthcoming).

ABOUT THE COMPANION WEBSITE

www.oup.com/us/beyondthescore

The companion website to this book contains relevant extracts from the recordings that are discussed in detail in Chapters 3–6, 8, and 12. There is also a video clip for Chapter 10. These are referenced as Media Examples and cued in the text by the symbol shown at right.

All audio materials are provided as mp3 files, but those for Chapters 3–5 are accompanied by Sonic Visualiser session files (.sv). These are to be used with the playback and visualisation program Sonic Visualiser, which is available for all major platforms and operating systems and is freely available on the web. While the mp3 files may be played directly using any audio playback program, Sonic Visualiser allows more flexible navigation of the recordings. In particular, the associated session files include bar numbers, making it easy to go to any particular point in the recording and hence follow the argument in the text. The session files for Chapter 3 also include tempo graphs which move as the music plays. Brief instructions for downloading and installing Sonic Visualiser, and for playing the sound and associated session files, may be found on the website.

In addition the website includes colour versions of Figures 6.5–6.13, which are more informative than the black-and-white versions provided in the text. These are cued in the text by the symbol shown at right.

Beyond the Score

I have said it requires talent, emotion, intelligence and technique to make an artist; what then would be the result if one or more of these four requisites were wanting?

The following table will suggest such probable results:

Talent.	Emotion.	Intelligence.	Technique.	The Highest Obtainable Result would be:
1	2	3	4	Executive artist, of highest order.
1	2	3	..	Non-executive artist; probably first-class teacher.
1	2	..	4	Natural artist, without musical training; for instance, Hungarian gypsy musicians.
1	..	3	4	Executant musician; probably scholarly and critical, but dry.
1	2	..	..	Enthusiastic music-lover; more impulsive than discriminating.
1	..	3	..	Probably a good teacher.
1	..	..	4	A virtuoso, without being either an artist or a musician.
1	..	..	..	An individual possessing the key to a treasure-chamber, without ever having opened the door.
..	2	3	4	An ever-laboring artist, whose life is too short to attain the perfection he aims at.
..	2	3	..	Artistic connoisseur; probably a good art-critic.
..	2	..	4	Spasmodic executant; for instance, certain lady pianists with more sentimentality than judgment.
..	2	..	..	Music-lover by instinct; a good listener.
..	..	3	4	Scholarly executant, but cold.
..	..	3	..	Musical theorist.
..	..	..	4	Virtuoso of the music-box kind.

Adolph Christiani, *The Principles of Expression in Pianoforte Playing* (1885: 15-16)

Introduction

Attempting to compare the singing of Dietrich Fischer-Dieskau and his former teacher Charles Panzéra, Roland Barthes complained about language's incapacity to articulate the things that matter about music. And he continued: 'rather than trying to change directly the language on music, it would be better to change the musical object itself, as it presents itself to discourse' (Barthes 1977: 180). This book is an attempt to change the musical object from the perspective of musicology. In a nutshell, musicology was set up around the idea of music as writing rather than music as performance. To think of music as writing is to see its meaning as inscribed within the score, and accordingly to see performance as the reproduction of this meaning. That turns performance into a kind of supplement to the music itself, an optional extra, rather like reading poetry aloud (because isn't the meaning already there on the printed page?). Even if that is a satisfactory way of thinking of poetry—which critics such as Stanley Fish would deny—it is not a satisfactory way of thinking of a performing art like music. The experience of live or recorded performance is a primary form of music's existence, not just the reflection of a notated text. And performers make an indispensable contribution to the culture of creative practice that is music. My claim is that in order to build this deeply into our thinking about music—in order to think of music *as performance*—we need to think differently about what sort of an object music is, and indeed how far it is appropriate to think of it as an object at all.

Interdisciplinary performance studies, which developed from theatre studies into a general approach to the performative dimensions of culture, understands meaning as created in the act of performance, or to put it more longwindedly but also more accurately, it focusses on how performances afford the production of meaning. This idea is fundamental to my book. At the same time, my approach is more conservative than much of the writing on music that has been carried out within, or influenced by, performance studies. My aim is not to displace traditional musicology but rather to rethink it from the inside. I want to address the issues of culture and meaning that concern most musicologists, but to build performance deeply into their formulation, and make it possible to bring the specifics of individual performances—often in the form of recordings—to bear upon them. I want to go beyond the score, as my title puts it, but at the same time I suggest that it is only once you think of music as performance that you can start to make sense of scores. Seen in the context of performance culture, scores are much more like theatrical scripts than the literary texts as which musicology has traditionally understood (or misunderstood) them, and that is just one of several ways in which thinking of music as performance means rethinking basic assumptions of the music-as-writing approach. As all this may suggest, the book is centred on performance within the tradition of Western 'art' music (hereafter WAM), and to a considerable degree on common-practice repertories such as nineteenth-century piano music. I talk about other repertories too, ranging from Corelli's violin sonatas to 'New Complexity' composition, and from jazz improvisation to rock, but in general my purpose in doing so is to throw light on performance within the core WAM repertories on which musicology has traditionally been based. Naturally I hope that some of what I say will extend to the study of musical performance more generally.

I talk about rethinking musicology because I attribute its failure to engage fully with music as performance to habits of thought that are deeply entrenched in the discipline. By this I do not mean musicologists are uninterested in performance, although that claim is sometimes made. On the contrary, plenty of musicologists write about performance, just as do ethnomusicologists, sociologists, psychologists, and philosophers—not to mention the emerging literature in which performers feed their experience as practitioners into research, just as they feed research into their performances. And you don't get to be a musicologist without performing. A significant number of musicologists started as performers, and a few maintain serious performing careers alongside their musicological work. By contrast, although I have at one time or another had experience of performing on a range of instruments and in a range of genres, it has been at a strictly amateur level. In some ways, then, I approach the topic as an outsider, a stance that comes with both advantages and disadvantages. (The main advantages are independence and freedom of interpretation, the main disadvantage the likelihood of missing the point or not even realising there is a point to be missed.) What motivates the book is less a personal experience that I wish to share with others than a longstanding belief that the study of music has from the beginning been skewed, and its relevance to most people outside academia diminished, by its orientation towards music as writing. Such a belief might have been viewed as eccentric or plain silly thirty years ago. Nowadays the explosion of research in musical performance, and the burgeoning field of practice as research, show that it is widely shared. My aim is to add what weight I can to this belief, underline its radical implications for this discipline, and bring together a wide range of concrete proposals for how we might study music as performance and what we might learn from it.

The fact that there are so many and such different directions from which to engage with music as performance is one of the joys of working in this area. Adolph Christiani's table, reproduced at the beginning of this Introduction, makes the point—though at the expense of music theorists, who, it transpires, do not need talent, emotion, or technique in order to succeed. In reality, of course, established theoretical approaches based on score analysis have a part to play in the study of music as performance, though they need to be placed in context and weaned from their traditional fixation with structure. Approaches based on the signifying body figure prominently on the contemporary musicological agenda and are essential to performance analysis. Again, music subsists in the collaborative action of people playing and working together, so that performances can be thought of as complex social interactions, and scores as scripting them. And at the same time the acoustic traces of real or fictitious performances—sound recordings—lend themselves to quantitative analysis, creating an opportunity to work empirically with large quantities of data, in contrast to the data-poor approaches characteristic of most musicology. Through such work, style opens up as a domain of musical meaning that complements the individual musical work (since the middle of the twentieth century the almost exclusive focus of music-theoretical attention). Such research raises the question of how far such data-driven methods can be reconciled with the issues of culture and meaning that motivate musicologists, myself included. I hope to convince you that working with as complex and slippery a phenomenon as music requires the deployment of a wide variety of analytical methods.

Then there is the issue of history. Most so-called histories of music are really histories of composition, or even of compositional innovation. This ignores the fact that, for the past two centuries, the culture of WAM has largely consisted of the performance of old music. It is partly a matter of aesthetic ideology, but it is also because histories of music are written on the basis of documents, ranging from scores and transcriptions to treatises and criticism. Performance, however, is an art of telling detail—detail that falls between the notes of musical texts and the words of literary ones. This means we have remarkably little idea how music sounded before the development of recording. (If the singing style of Alessandro Moreschi, as recorded in 1902, is altogether foreign to present-day norms, how can we possibly imagine what performances were like in 1802 or 1602?) And the result is that present-day performance style is projected back into the past. The post-war modernists who proclaimed the values of authenticity to the musical text presented themselves as reinstating a classical performance style that had been perverted by the excesses of nineteenth- and early twentieth-century performance. It is easy to invoke the support of history in the absence of historical facts and hence the possibility of contradiction. It seems much more likely that the literalist performance style that became dominant after 1945 is a relatively recent invention. Yet its stylistic features have been erected by practitioners, teachers, and theorists into universally applicable principles of articulate performance, further impinging on performers' ability to make creative choices.

This book is not intended as an attack on modernist performance, but it does show how modernist assumptions have boxed in both performance and thinking about performance, and it illustrates some of the fundamentally different performance options that have accordingly been ruled out. The key point does not have to do with playing this way or that way. It is that music affords an apparently unlimited variety of interpretive options, and we could be much more adventurous in our exploration of them if our thinking about performance was more flexible. The idea of music as sounded writing gives rise to what in this book I call the paradigm of reproduction: performance is seen as reproducing the work, or the structures embodied in the work, or the conditions of its early performances, or the intentions of its composer. Different as these formulations are—and the last can serve as a justification for almost anything—they all have one thing in common: no space is left for the creativity of performers. Or at least, if creativity should slip in, it must do so unannounced and untheorised. And then the same thinking is applied to recording. Classical producers aim to reproduce the experience of listening to live music, at the same time as live music seems increasingly to reproduce the experience of listening to a CD or mp3 download. I see this as a vicious circle that is largely responsible for WAM's diminishing role in the modern world. Live and recorded music can offer very different experiences that engage with contemporary lifestyles in very different ways, but each needs to be developed in light of its particular potential. That is not going to happen as long as thinking about music is constrained by the paradigm of reproduction. At one level, I am concerned in this book with musicology and with practices of performance across the last century or so. At another level, however, I would like to think that it could have some impact on current and future practice.

The book begins, then, by tracing the history and consequences of dominant ways of thinking about the performance of music. The opening chapter, 'Plato's Curse', sets out the textualist paradigm around which musicology has traditionally been configured—in other words, the idea that music is sounded writing, that it consists of texts or works reproduced in performance. I see that approach as having driven a wedge between the real-life experience of music and the academic discipline based on it. The second chapter, 'Page and Stage', develops this critique in relation to established music-theoretical and analytical approaches to performance. I argue that their structuralist orientation embodies far too narrow an understanding of the many ways in which performances afford the production of meaning. They treat as a paradigm of what performance is—or should be—what is in reality a specifically modernist practice.

Thereafter the books falls into pairs of chapters. The next two chapters put flesh on the bones of this critique, focussing in part on the early twentieth-century theorist Heinrich Schenker, whose work was particularly influential in the formation of today's music-theoretical approaches to performance. Chapter 3, 'What the Theorist Heard', is built around a piano roll of Schubert's Impromptu op. 90 no. 3 by Eugen d'Albert: this is one of very few pieces of which we have both an analysis by Schenker, including detailed prescriptions for how it should be played, and a contemporary recording by a performer whom Schenker admired. I show how Schenker's performance prescriptions fit closely with the principles underlying what I call d'Albert's 'rhetorical' playing but have remarkably little relationship to his own analysis. Even as he was developing the theory on which today's performance pedagogy is based, Schenker continued to conceive music in terms of a very different, premodern performance style, one based less on the idea of structure than on that of rhetoric. To that extent, we have been misreading and misimagining Schenker's analyses all along.

Chapter 4, 'Beyond Structure', goes more deeply into the idea of rhetorical performance, using the topics (stylised musical references) of the classical repertory as its starting point. I compare modern, or modernist, performances of two movements by Mozart (the *Rondo alla turca* from K 331 and the first movement of the Sonata K 332) to those of today's fortepianists; I relate the idea of rhetorical performance as appropriated by the historically informed performance

(HIP) movement to its presence in Schenker's and other late nineteenth- or early twentieth-century writings, where it figures much more prominently than is generally recognised; and on the basis of this I examine early recordings of these works, in particular by Carl Reinecke, whom Schenker regarded as the greatest living Mozart interpreter. I theorise the relationship between rhetorical and what by contrast I term 'structuralist' performance in terms of opposed conceptions of time, but I argue that these should not be seen as representing incommensurable mentalities or demarcating separate historical periods. Just as we slip from one metaphorical construction of everyday experience to another, so the rhetorical and structuralist approaches represent complementary ways of construing music as both theory and practice, and to that extent permanently available options, even though one or the other may predominate at any given time or place. That is why structuralist performance is not a model of performance in general—which is how established music theory presents it—but a stylistic option.

Chapter 5, 'Close and Distant Listening', continues with piano music but focusses on comparative analysis of performance style. Its first half is methodological in orientation. I begin by contrasting structural and stylistic analysis, asking why the latter went out of favour at the same time that comparative musicology was transformed into ethnomusicology; then I discuss issues of close listening, what might be termed computer-assisted listening, and the quantitative approaches to performance analysis that I call 'distant listening'. I also outline significant issues in discographical source criticism, in other words what one can and can't deduce about period performance styles from recordings, and how far the aim should be to analyse recordings or to analyse performance practices *through* recordings. This clears the way for the second half of the chapter, which focusses on recordings of Chopin's mazurkas from across the twentieth century, with Ignaz Friedman's recordings of Chopin's Mazurka op. 33 no. 2 occupying stage centre: my analysis extends from the role of accentuation in the creation of this style to the manner in which it has come to signify Polish national identity. Chapter 6, 'Objective Expression', continues with Chopin's mazurkas but approaches them from the perspective of distant listening. Its specific focus is on phrase arching, the practice of getting faster and louder as you play into a phrase, and slower and softer as you come out of it. I explore this across a large corpus of recordings of the Mazurkas op. 17 no. 4 and op. 63 no. 3, develop a computational model of it, and suggest that the kind of fully coordinated phrase arching seen by music psychologists as a permanent dimension of expressive performance is in reality a historically situated phenomenon, achieving its modern form only after the Second World War. Again my aim is to link technical and cultural analysis, and the chapter concludes with an extensive discussion of issues of streamlining, standardisation, and sentimentality that relates musical performance to a range of contemporaneous cultural practices, in particular architecture and design.

The second half of the book moves away from close analysis of recordings of eighteenth- and nineteenth-century piano music to a broader cultural purview featuring a wider range of musics. Chapter 7, 'Playing Somethin', picks up from my earlier critique of the traditional approach to performance as the reproduction of works and develops a model of what I call the work as performance: this is less a thing than a network of signifiers, and in order to formulate it I generalise theoretical approaches to jazz improvisation drawn from the work of Jeff Pressing and Keith Sawyer. An essential dimension of this is seeing music as not just a social activity but one that generates specific socialities, and this is central to my understanding of performance as a semiotic and creative practice. Whereas the focus of Chapter 7 is broadly theoretical, Chapter 8, 'Social Scripts', ties down the idea of the work as performance by focussing on specific interactions between performers, and how scores serve to script them. I draw my examples largely from contemporary 'art' music, showing how the ostensively mathematical notations used by 'New Complexity' composers function in performance as what I call social scripts.

Chapters 9 and 10 remain in the social and cultural domain but introduce a focus on the performing body. Chapter 9, 'The Signifying Body', is structured round a case study of Jimi Hendrix's stage performances of 'Foxy Lady': I focus in particular on how Hendrix's embodied practices construct a range of subject positions for the audience, and the rich cultural connotations on which they draw, including traditions of blackface minstrelsy. I argue that critical concepts developed within the context of black cultural studies, such as Henry Louis Gates Jr's 'signifyin(g)', articulate practices and values that are relevant to performance culture more generally. Chapter 10, 'Everything Counts', uses the issue of embodiment to pursue an argument concerning the relationship between contrasted approaches to performance analysis. Focussing on pianistic gesture, I develop a performance studies approach to the construction of meaning through embodied practice in filmed performances of Chopin's op. 63 no. 3 by Grigory Sokolov and others, and then I ask how it might be possible to reconcile this approach with the sound-based, style-analytical approach developed in Chapter 6. My conclusion is that the performance studies approach enhances awareness of the meanings constructed through performance, while the empirical approach provides a foundation for understanding how these meanings are constructed.

Whereas the argument of the first ten chapters is largely based on recordings, it is in the final two that I thematise the relationship between performance and recording. This enables me to further develop what I like to think of as the commonsensical semiotic perspective that runs through the book: I argue in Chapter 11 ('The Ghost in the Machine') that just as performances are not adequately understood as reproductions of works, so recordings are not adequately understood as reproductions of performances; rather, they represent performances though complex processes of cultural signification. We hear recordings as performances, in other words diegetically, even when we know that the performance represented by the recording never took place. To listen to a recording is therefore to experience music as performance, and in this way I see recorded and live performance as together constituting a single, though complex and varied, cultural domain. Seen this way, producers and sound engineers become performers, and the scope of performance is massively expanded, as are the sites and modes of its consumption.

Within the WAM tradition, however, the potential of technologically mediated experiences of music has been drastically curtailed by the paradigm of reproduction. Classical recordings set out to reproduce the acoustic traces of live performance, just as live performances have come to resemble recordings, not least by downplaying the dimensions of the visual and the embodied. The result is creative practice in both performance and recording that is not as creative as it might be. In the final chapter ('Beyond Reproduction') I explore approaches to classical production based on specifically phonographic ways of experiencing music. Equally I return to the social dimension of performance, including the traditions of participatory music making that largely fell victim to the professionalisation of classical performance after the Second World War: the many contemporary contexts within which making music together serves as an agent of personal or social transformation epitomise the capacity of performance to afford meaning that lies beyond reproduction. Theorising music as performance—as a social event in which meaning is produced, rather than as sounded writing that reproduces pre-existing meaning—helps to open up possibilities for both creating and experiencing music that outmoded thinking has closed off.

1

Plato's Curse

We call it music, but that is not music: that is only paper.
—Leopold Stokowski[1]

For generations musicologists have behaved as if scores were the only real thing about music.
—Nicholas Kenyon[2]

SOUNDED WRITING

'Basically', wrote the *fin-de-siècle* Viennese pianist, critic, and teacher Heinrich Schenker (2000: 3), 'a composition does not require a performance in order to exist…. The reading of the score is sufficient'. What makes this negative assessment of the performer's role so striking is that it is the first sentence of his unfinished treatise *The Art of Performance*; how many other books start with a statement that their topic is redundant? What Schenker was actually saying, however, bordered on the commonplace. According to Dika Newlin (1980: 164), Arnold Schoenberg—who himself had ideas of writing a book on performance—once remarked that the performer was 'totally unnecessary except as his interpretations make the music understandable to an audience unfortunate enough not to be able to read it in print'. Rudolph Kolisch, the violinist and quartet leader who was closely associated with Schoenberg—and who at one time planned to co-author a book on performance with T. W. Adorno—echoed this as late as 1978: 'the entire need for performance disappears if one can read music'.[3] One might think that such off-the-cuff remarks shouldn't be taken seriously. But in another sense,

1. In Gould (1987: 264).

2. Kenyon (2012: 11).

3. Transcribed and translated by David Trippett from a recorded interview with Berthold Türcke, 18 April 1978 (Houghton Library, Harvard University, b MS Mus 195-2211, no. 32). For Kolisch's co-authorship see Adorno (2006: 12).

just because they are unconsidered, they reveal deeply embedded assumptions or prejudices with particular clarity. And what Schoenberg apparently said to Newlin ties in with other things that he set down on paper, for example in an essay of 1934 where he talks about the 'freedom in the manner of expression' of the old-fashioned fantasia, and adds that such freedom is

> permissible in our own day only perhaps in dreams; in dreams of future fulfilment; in dreams of a possibility of expression which has no regard for the perceptive faculties of a contemporary audience; where one may speak with kindred spirits in the language of intuition and know that one is understood if one uses the speech of the imagination—of fantasy. (Schoenberg 1975: 274–75)

This may be no more than a daydream, but it still powerfully articulates the ideal of a music that travels instantaneously from mind to mind, in the manner of telepathy, or perhaps of what was in 1934 the still recent technology of radio. At the same time it resonates with Ludwig van Beethoven's famous inscription in the autograph of the *Missa Solemnis*: 'From the heart—may it go straight to the heart'. In this vision of an ideal music, performers are conspicuous by their absence.

Discourses around musical performance, both academic and vernacular, are strangely conflicted. On the one hand, music is one of the heartlands of the star system, not only in pop but across the range of the classical tradition, from Claudio Abbado to Hayley Westenra, and this has been the case since the days of Enrico Caruso—the first star created by sound recording—and before that Niccolò Paganini, the virtuoso violinist whose achievement Franz Liszt set out to emulate. (Earlier still, the eighteenth-century opera world revolved around stars in much the same way as twentieth-century Hollywood.) And a survey carried out in 2002 by Classic FM, the UK radio station, showed that while only 65% of children between six and fourteen could name a single classical composer, 98% could name a classical performer.[4] On the other hand the official publications of the classical music establishment tell a different story. The 1983 edition of the *New Oxford Companion to Music*, edited by Denis Arnold, included highly obscure composers but had no entries for performers. And what are sold as histories of classical music represent music as something made by composers rather than performers. The twentieth century emerges as dominated by atonality, Schoenbergian serialism, post-war serialism, and a variety of postmodern reactions against it; depending on the market, there may be a few chapters on jazz and popular music. You could not tell from this that most classical music making in the twentieth century consisted of the performance, recording, and consumption of earlier music. It is like telling the story of the car purely in terms of successive refinements of the internal combustion engine rather than in terms of the innumerable ways in which cars changed people's lives,

---

4. As cited by Howard Goodall in an unpublished interview conducted as part of the research for Victoros (2009).

not to say the physical environment, in the course of the twentieth century. And the worst thing about this skewing of musicological discourse is it cuts academic studies off from precisely the dimension of music that touches most people's lives.

I originally voiced my complaint about the *New Oxford Companion to Music* more than fifteen years ago (Cook 1996: 33): the 2002 edition of the *Companion*, completely overhauled by Alison Latham, gives proper representation to performance. And during that period there has been a steady, even spectacular, increase in academic studies of musical performance from a wide range of complementary directions, to the extent that today there are perhaps more conferences about performance than about any other area of music studies. Many aspects of the network of interconnected aesthetic assumptions I set out in this chapter have come under scrutiny in recent decades. So it might seem decidedly late in the day to be voicing complaints about the neglect of music as performance. But the claim I would now advance is rather different from the one I made in 1996. It is that this new consciousness of the role and importance of performance has for the most part been grafted onto traditional ways of thinking about music, or squeezed in as a new specialist area, whereas thinking about music as performance should prompt a fundamental rethinking of the discipline as a whole. It is that rethinking to which I hope to contribute.

There is an obvious comparison with theatre studies, which broke away from the mainstream of literary studies as a consequence of a fundamentally different attitude towards the dramatic text. I shall shortly discuss these matters at greater length, but in brief, the literary studies approach is to see meaning as inherent in a written text, whether dramatic or otherwise. The theatre studies approach, by contrast, is to see the dramatic text as one of many inputs into a performance, and to see meaning as something that emerges in the course of performance. In other words, though literary studies and theatre studies both deal with dramatic texts, they do so in terms of different methods and, more important, different epistemological assumptions. Seen this way, traditional musicology is like literary studies: it sees meaning, of whatever kind, as embodied in musical notation, from which it follows that performance is in essence a matter of communicating that meaning from the page to the stage. The performer's work becomes a supplement to the composer's. The musicological approach, then, has been to study music *and* performance, in contrast to studying music *as* performance—a term which in recent years has started to be used within musicology, but has a specific provenance within the field of performance studies.[5] The difference between 'and' and 'as' stands for the fundamental rethinking to which I referred.

The disconnect between the discourses around music and its performance has a long history: assumptions about the nature of music that marginalise performance go back at least as far as the early middle ages. And this goes beyond a simple contrast between some ideal, philosophical *musica mundana* and a merely practical *musica instrumentalis*. From his study of ninth-to-eleventh-century

5. Frequently abbreviated to MAP, 'Music as Performance' is the name of one of the working groups set up by the (North American) Association for Theatre in Higher Education to forge relationships with neighbouring disciplines.

discussions of chant, Sam Barrett concludes that 'neumatic notation served not simply as a pragmatic *aide-memoire*, but as a reflexive tool for disciplined knowing': it 'mirrors a higher order of being' (2008: 93, 90). Music is in other words conceived platonically, as an abstract and enduring entity that is reflected in notation, with the notation itself being reflected in singing (since mistakes in singing can be corrected by reference to the notation). As Barrett (92) comments, 'The primary melodic reality is suprasensual, an ongoing, unfolding celestial round of praise: the equivalent performance in the world of sense is at best a mere transcription and at worst a deviation'. And he adds: 'between the two domains lies the cognitive domain of memory'. From here it would be possible to trace the idea of music as an abstract and enduring entity through a variety of later sources, though its relationship to notation changes. As Bojan Bujić (1993: 134) says, 'the whole subsequent course of Western notation represents a move away from memory towards the state in which a written document can stand on its own, as it were, representing the work as such and offering to the performer clear indications how to recreate it in musical sounds'.

My purpose is not to trace a history but merely to identify a recurrent idea, so I will use another medieval source as a launching pad from which to jump to the early modern era and beyond: Aurelian of Réôme's account of a Frankish monk who 'heard a choir of angels singing the response that is sung on the birthday of the apostles', and 'carried it back with him to Rome' (Barrett 2008: 92). The idea of genius as a kind of divinely inspired authorship emerged in the sixteenth century, as exemplified in the artist and biographer Giorgio Vasari's account of Giotto, the painter and architect whose work contributed crucially to the Italian Renaissance: this marked a decisive shift towards what become the dominant paradigm of appreciating artistic products as the work of their author. And the idea of inspiration from a higher authority continued to inform the idea of genius until well into the twentieth century. The connection with Aurelian is made explicit in Karl Bauer's painting of the composer Hans Pfitzner (Figure 1.1), who wrote extensively on both inspiration and genius, and whose opera *Palestrina* revolves around the vision of angelic singing that supposedly inspired the Italian composer's *Missa Papae Marcelli*. Pfitzner's opera was first performed in 1917, but the picturesque thinking that informs it survives to the present day. According to the liner, a 2005 CD by the healer and holistic practitioner Celeste, recorded over a sequence of full moons, consists of 'angelic healing harmonies sung through Celeste'.[6]

At the same time, ideas of authorship, genius, and inspiration were fundamental to the development in the late nineteenth and early twentieth centuries of formalistic approaches to music, which transformed ideas of divine authority into those of aesthetic autonomy, and in this way gave a modernist gloss to an older conception. An obvious example is the approach developed by Schenker, who

6. Celeste, 'Celestial Sounds: A Harmonic Embrace for the Soul', Celestial Sounds 5060115940078 (2005).

Figure 1.1 Karl Bauer, 'Hans Pfitzner', from *Jugend* (1918). Photo: akg-images

represented musical works as the unfolding of a basic structural idea that can be expressed in notational terms: if for Schenker the structural idea represented the inspiration of the work, then the ability to unfold it was the mark of genius, and it was a basic principle of Schenker's thought that composers were frequently unaware of the means by which they achieved this. Schenker's thinking bears the traces of the late-nineteenth-century context from which it sprang, but was reshaped in line with the values of post-war American academia by his ex-pupils and followers—it was at this point that Schenker was transformed from the pianist, critic, and teacher as which I described him at the beginning of this chapter to the theorist as which he is known now—and it is in this modernised form that his ideas exerted a wide influence on post-war approaches to musical structure. Meanwhile a parallel development took place in philosophical approaches to the musical work and its performance. Despite their different perspectives, debates between writers such as Peter Kivy, Stephen Davies, Jerrold Levinson, and Julian Dodd have been framed within a conception of the musical work as the ontological basis of musical culture that embodies the two ideas I have described: first, that the musical work is an abstract and enduring entity, conceived in a more or less platonic manner; and second, that it is grounded in notation.

What does all this have to do with performance? In one sense, nothing; in another, everything. Under the shadow of what I call Plato's curse, music is embraced within a communicative chain. Music goes from heart to heart, as Beethoven had it, but—as Schoenberg glossed it—unless you are fortunate enough to be able to read what Beethoven wrote for yourself, it has to go via the performer. To repeat Barrett's words, the performer's role is at best to transcribe the work from the domain of the abstract to that of the concrete, and at worst to deviate from it. The performer becomes a mediator, and as in the case of all middlemen, this involves a kind of contractual relationship: it is the performer's obligation to represent the composer's work to the listener, just as it is the listener's obligation to strive towards an adequate understanding of the work itself. And it is here, in a conception of the relationship between composer, performer, and listener that extends from E. T. A. Hoffmann and Adolph Bernhard Marx to Schoenberg and Pierre Boulez, that the ethically charged language that has surrounded WAM (Western 'art' music) performance emerges: I am talking of the language of 'authority', 'duty', and 'faithfulness', as well as the overall tone of, for example, Schoenberg's reference to 'the Sodom and Gomorrha of false interpreters' (1975: 328). The entire early music revival was built around the claim that certain performance practices were authentic while others were not. Even in the more pluralistic culture of the early twentieth century the moral dimension retains a currency in music for which it is hard to find parallels in other arts. In the theatre, and even in the opera house, it is taken for granted that old works should be reinterpreted for modern audiences and that a director should express his or her own vision. If issues of historical accuracy are raised, then they are likely to be seen as just one of a number of competing desirables. With WAM it is different. I shall come back to these issues at the end of the book.

The idea of the performer's duty has traditionally come in two distinct versions: on the one hand duty to the composer, on the other to the work (sometimes referred to as *Werktreue*). But in practice there is slippage between these. In mainstream repertory composers are safely dead, and various parties may seek to appropriate their authority. When Schenker explains the principles governing Beethoven's compositions—principles of which Beethoven may well have been unaware—and draws conclusions for how they should be performed, he is laying claim to the composer's authority. Performers, too, invoke Beethoven's authority in negotiating interpretations. Robert Martin (1994: 117–18), who was cellist in the Sequoia Quartet, imagines a rehearsal in which this exchange takes place around Beethoven's notoriously problematic metronome markings:

> 'Beethoven's marking for the slow movement is perfect (60 to the quarter)—so why should we doubt his marking for the *Allegretto*?'
> 'Look, we play the slow movement around 60 because that feels right to us—our reaction to the metronome marking is that he got it right! In the *Allegretto* he gives a tempo that feels wrong.'
> 'It may feel wrong to you. I think we will get used to it, and anyway, it's what he wanted! You're not denying that, are you?'

The absent Beethoven is invoked as a kind of rhetorical construct: the performers do not express their opinions directly but rather ventriloquise them. Faithfulness to the composer is tempered by the essential unknowability of his intentions, which enables them to function as a vehicle for the performers' own judgements about the music.

In practice, then, it makes little difference whether duty is owed to the composer or to the work. In either case two consequences follow, both of which I have mentioned but on which I now expand. The first consequence is that meaning is understood as laid down by the composer, deposited in the work. If, in the words of Nicolai Listenius (the sixteenth-century writer often credited with the first clear formulation of the concept of the musical work), the composer's labour results in 'a perfect and absolute *opus* [*opus perfectum ed absolutum*]' (Goehr 1992: 116), then all that remains for the performer is to reproduce it in sound. This was explicitly stated by Eduard Hanslick (1986: 29), whose *On the Musically Beautiful* was first published as long ago as 1854 ('the performer can deliver only what is already in the composition'), and it still underpins the philosophical approaches I mentioned earlier. 'Reproduction' became a standard term in the discourse of twentieth-century composers, critics, and theorists: it was routinely used (alongside several other German terms normally translated as 'performance') by Schoenberg, Adorno, and Schenker, who approvingly cited Johannes Brahms's statement—as quoted by his biographer Max Kalbeck—that 'whenever I play something by Beethoven, I have no individuality whatsoever, insofar as the piece is concerned: instead I strive to reproduce the piece as Beethoven prescribed, and I then have enough to do' (Schenker 2005: 31). And Laurence Dreyfus (2007: 254) has shown that even the apparently more generous term 'interpretation' draws on biblical and legal contexts where it refers to the clarification of existing content rather than the generation of new insights.

My concern is, however, not so much with the words as with the musical ontology that they express—an ontology that is still influential in discourses around WAM. It is expressed in the legal concept of the musical work, which, as Anne Barron (2006) has shown, developed in parallel—though not always in step—with the aesthetic concept. Perhaps the clearest illustration is provided by the American case *Newton* v *Diamonte et al.* [2002], in which the jazz flautist James Newton sought recompense for the use in a Beastie Boys song of a six-second sample from his album *Axum*. Newton's claim was refused on the grounds that 'a musical composition consists of rhythm, harmony, and melody, and it is from these elements that originality is to be determined'.[7] Seen this way, the sample in question consisted merely of Newton singing the notes C-Db-C while fingering a C on the flute. That was not, of course, the reason the Beastie Boys used the sample: they did so because of the highly distinctive aural effect resulting from Newton's idiosyncratic performance technique. Despite this, the judge took it for granted that meaning inheres in the composition and not its performance.

The second consequence of this way of thinking follows directly on the first and was repeatedly stated throughout the nineteenth and twentieth centuries: as a mediator, the performer's highest ambition should be self-effacement. This point is best made by quotation. 'The true artist,' writes E. T. A. Hoffmann (1989: 103), 'lives only in the work that he conceives and then performs as the composer intended it. He disdains to let his own personality intervene in any way; all his endeavours are spent in quickening to vivid life, in a thousand shining colours, all the sublime effects and images the composer's magical authority enclosed within his work'. Hoffmann's image of the painting resonates with the brusque claim, by Hector Berlioz (1918: 101–2), that performers are only there to shine a light upon the canvas, but what is particularly revealing about this quotation is the idea of meaning having been enclosed within (another translation renders it 'sealed in') the work. Again, in the notes for his unfinished book on performance, for which one of his working titles was 'Reproduction Theory: A Music-philosophical Investigation', Adorno copied out a quotation from Proust's *In Search of Lost Time*: 'the playing of a great musician [is] so transparent, so replete with its content, that one does not notice it oneself, or only like a window that allows us to gaze upon a masterpiece' (Adorno 2006: 119). The organ composer Marcel Dupré concurs, but spells out the hierarchy and ramps up the imperative tone: 'The interpreter must never allow his own personality to intrude. As soon as it penetrates, the work has been betrayed. By concealing himself sincerely before the character of the work in order to illuminate it, even more so before the personality of the composer, he serves the latter and confirms the authority of the work' (Hill 1994: 44). Maybe it is not irrelevant that organists, unlike most other performers, are generally invisible to their audiences. At all events, with this image of the self-effacing performer whose highest aspiration—like that of high-class servants—should be invisibility, we are more or less back at the sentiments of the Schenker and Schoenberg quotations with which I began this chapter.

What Schoenberg was saying was that, in practice, performers (like servants) are a necessity, except of course for those who can read the printed score for themselves, and it is on the role of the score that I would now like to focus. It

7. Quoted by Judge Nora Manella from the standard legal textbook Nimmer and Nimmer (1997). It should be stressed that this case concerned rights in the work, rather than subsidiary rights in the performance, which the Beastie Boys had cleared; the point of the case was that the former are much more valuable than the latter. Further discussion may be found in Toynbee (2006), Lewis (2007), and Cook (2013a).

is a recurring complaint—prominently articulated by James Winn (1998)—that humanities disciplines are driven by textualist values, driving a wedge between text and performance, and Winn traces this back to the disciplining of music by text in ancient Greece. But musicology's version of the text-performance split has more specific foundations. As we have seen, there was a long tradition of seeing music as some kind of abstract entity, closely (though often not very clearly) linked to notation. According to Gary Tomlinson, it was in the late eighteenth century, and specifically with the writings of Johann Nikolaus Forkel, that a decisive impetus developed to identify notation with cultural value: for Forkel, a society's position on the spectrum from musical primitiveness to perfection depended on the sophistication of its notation, so that 'the history of European musical development could be plotted as a story of the progress of writing' (Tomlinson 2012: 65). This view of music as text resonated perfectly with the context in which the modern discipline of musicology first into came into being during the nineteenth century, the politically motivated programme of documenting—or inventing—national origins through culture. The retrieval, editing, and criticism of national literary canons lay at the heart of this project, and so it was natural that the nascent musicology should model itself on philology.

That may be sufficient to explain musicology's traditional orientation to source studies and textual criticism. But its orientation to text rather than to performance draws on other sources too. The idea of the text as a repository of meaning goes back to early modern conceptions of authorship and was also deeply embedded in religious thought, particularly that of the Reformation: that is the context of the conception of interpretation that Dreyfus discussed. Charles Rosen (2003: 17) provides a telling example of how such ideas work out in the context of music. He quotes Giovanni Maria Artusi, at the beginning of the seventeenth century, criticising the compositional innovations of Claudio Monteverdi and his circle. 'These composers', Artusi wrote,

> seek only to satisfy the ear and with this aim toil night and day at their instruments to hear the effect which passages so made produce; the poor fellows do not perceive that what the instruments tell them is false and that it is one thing to search with voices and instruments for something pertaining to the harmonic faculty, another to arrive at the exact truth by means of reasons seconded by the ear.

The references to falsity and truth reflect the platonic epistemology I have described, while the idea that composition proper proceeds through the exercise of reason, rather than through experimentation with instrument in hand, still survives in conservative critical circles. And in this context the exercise of reason corresponds to the manipulation of notation. It is then the same textualist mentality that motivates Artusi's criticism and Schoenberg's claim (1975: 319), in an unpublished typescript headed 'For a treatise on performance', that 'The highest principle for all reproduction of music would have to be that what the composer has written is made to sound in such a way that every note is really heard'. Seen this way, performed music is notation made audible.

It did not escape Schoenberg's notice that the most direct way in which to achieve this would be through the use of mechanical instruments. In an essay published in 1926 (probably two or three years after his notes for a treatise on performance), Schoenberg writes that 'the true product of the mind—the musical idea, the unalterable—is established in the relationship between pitches and time-divisions'. But under today's conditions, he explains, it is all but impossible to secure adequate performance of anything except the most conventional music, and so he concludes that 'mechanical production of sounds and the definitive fixing of their pitch, their length, and the way they relate to the division of time in the piece would be very desirable' (1975: 326). Adorno thought the same. While reading Frederick Dorian's *The History of Performance: The Art of Musical Interpretation from the Renaissance to Our Day* in preparation for his own unfinished treatise on performance, he made a note headed 'Elimination of the interpreter as "middleman"', and continued: 'We have only to think of the possibility of an apparatus that will permit the composer to transmit his music directly into a recording medium without the help of the middleman interpreter' (Adorno 2006: 23).

I would like to draw three points out of this. The first is that the identification of musical substance with what can be notated—from which it follows that anything attributable only to the performer is insubstantial—is an assumption built deeply into discourses that surround WAM: it might be described as ideological, in the sense that it presents itself not as an assumption at all but just as the way things are. Again the point is made by the way the law treats this principle as self-evident. It is implicit in the judgement on *Newton* v *Diamonte*, and it also explains why the British fair dealing exceptions for study and research apply to musical scores but not recordings: in the words of MacQueen, Waelde, and Laurie (2008: 172), 'If I want to study the music or lyrics embodied in a sound recording, I will have to do so in ways other than copying the sound recording: for example, by making copies of the musical notation or the text of the words'. The implication is that there is nothing to study in a recording, over and above what is already in the score. The second point emerges from Schoenberg's identification of notational relationships with 'the true product of the mind'. Just as in his telepathic fantasy, music is assumed to be something in people's heads. Once again perpetuating the platonic tradition, social dimensions are eliminated from the understanding of music. It is on the one hand an abstract structure optimally represented in notation, and on the other a paradigmatically subjective experience, transcending its physical surroundings; in Figure 1.2 the performer's presence is reduced to a hand, matched by the hand with which the listener covers her eyes, as it were channelling her gaze inwards. I will have much to say in this book about these missing social dimensions.

The third, and most obvious, point is the denigration of performers that emerges as much from the tone as the substance of Schoenberg's and Adorno's discussions of the desirability of replacing them by machines. In advocating the

Figure 1.2 Fernand Khnopff, 'Listening to Schumann' (1883), oil on canvas, Brussels, Musées Royaux des Beaux-Arts de Belgique. © Royal Museums of Fine Arts of Belgium, Brussels / photo: J. Geleyns / Ro scan

development of what she calls a 'performer's discourse', the pianist and scholar Mine Doğantan-Dack (2008: 302) speaks of performers' 'notorious image as inarticulate musicians'. (If this echoes Christiani's 'lady pianists with more sentimentality than judgement', it is still a more desirable category than 'musical theorist'.) There is a long tradition of disparaging performers, of which—perhaps because he never had occasion to tone them down—Adorno's notes towards his unfinished book constitute something of a storehouse. 'Most reproducing musicians', he asserts, 'have the perspective of the bumble bee' (2006: 126); by this he means much the same as Schenker (1996: 3) did when he complained that performers 'drag themselves along from moment to moment, with the laziest of ears, without any musical imagination'. Again, Adorno (2006: 10, 78) complains that 'there has been a downward trend as regards what the average musician must know', and that most performers 'know only two characters: the brilliant (allegro) and the lyrical cantabile (adagio)'; Schenker's writings, too, are full of references to the decline in performance standards, and in particular the loss of nuance. But what is most revealing is when Adorno (159) notes that his wife Gretel has asked him 'how actors, who are mostly of questionable intelligence and always uneducated,

Figure 1.3 Carl Johann Arnold, 'Quartet Evening at Bettina von Arnim's in Berlin' (1856), water colour. Used by permission of bpk, Berlin / Frankfurter Goethe-Museum with Goethe-Haus, Freies Deutsches Hochstift, Frankfurt am Main, Germany / Lutz Braun / Art Resource, New York

can represent people and deliver lines that convey the most difficult of ideas'. He records his convoluted answer to the question, the conclusion of which is that 'it is a *prerequisite* for an actor not to "understand", but rather to imitate blindly'. And he adds: 'Perhaps include in the theory of musical reproduction'.

Carl Johann Arnold's painting of a musical evening at the home of the writer, social activist, and patron of the arts Bettina von Arnheim depicts a performance taking place under the watchful eyes of the great composers (Figure 1.3). What is puzzling is the extent to which performers have connived in the hierarchy so graphically represented by Arnold. Alongside the proclamations of writers such as Hoffmann and Proust, and of composers such as Dupré and Schoenberg, may be set those of performers such as Sviatoslav Richter ('if [the performer] is talented, he allows us to glimpse the truth of the work that is in itself a thing of genius and that is reflected in him. He shouldn't dominate the music, but should dissolve into it' [Monsaigneon 2001: 153]). Or there is Leonard Bernstein (1959: 56), one of the most charismatic figures in twentieth-century music, who enjoined that the conductor 'be humble before the composer; that he never interpose himself between the music and the audience; that all his efforts, however strenuous or glamorous, be made in the service of the composer's meaning'. And if such asseverations of faith to dead composers or metaphysical entities sound too quaint to be taken seriously, it should be remembered that they still circulate within performers' discourse (recall Martin's rehearsal discussion). They are taken for granted in the discourses of classical record production, too.

As long ago as 1922 Paul Bekker, the German music theorist and critic whose ideas strikingly anticipate a number of major currents in contemporary musicology, launched a full-scale attack on this entire system of ideas, in particular targetting the idea of performance as reproduction. 'The goal of today's reproducing artist', he wrote, is 'to place himself fully at the service of the composer, only following his directions in order to give a true likeness or rather reproduction of the will of the creator. This sounds both attractive and virtuous', he continues, 'but is in reality unrealizable'. And warming to his theme, he speaks of

> the monstrous presumptuousness that lies behind the concept of an objectively correct, note-faithful reproduction.... This sham objectivity meant in fact the diminishing of decisive values of personality in favor of an imaginary ideal of objectivity, the mechanization of the methods and goals of performing art, the subversion of concepts of quality, the advancement of mediocrity, the insinuation of artistic immorality and a suspicion of the extraordinary.

He pins the blame on 'the luxuriantly flourishing conservatory business', before concluding that 'today's ruling paradigm of objective reproduction... is a philistine self-deception and in the realm of music, preposterous' (Hill 1994: 57–58). And what was in 1922 an isolated challenge to the hegemony of composers and works has become increasingly prevalent in writing about music. Extreme examples range from Christopher Small's claim (1998: 51) that *performance does not exist in order to present musical works, but rather, musical works exist in order to give performers something to perform* (the italics are Small's) to the philosopher Stan Godlovitch's assertion (1998: 96) that works should be understood as 'vehicles and opportunities' for performance. And Robert Martin (1993: 123), who is a philosopher as well as a cellist, concurs: 'musical works', he writes, 'are fictions that allow us to speak more conveniently about performances'. He even adds that as far as listeners are concerned, 'musical works... simply do not exist'.

But in practice, of course, the regime of the musical work and its reproduction never quite conformed to its representation in the writings of musicians, critics, and aestheticians. There are a number of reasons for this. One of the many problems in trying to reconstruct historical performance practices from documentary sources is performers who say one thing but do another. In his exhaustive study of early piano recordings, Neal Peres da Costa (2012) cites numerous examples of performers who advocate performance practices based strictly on the musical text—fully synchronised hands, avoidance of unnotated arpeggiation, avoidance of tempo modification—but then, on record, disregard their own prescriptions. And there is a more basic problem. What looks like a description of what people do is often really a prescription of what people *should* do, in other words a description of what they *don't* do; the imperative tone that I referred to in connection with Dupré should act as a warning of this. Then again, there survived into the early twentieth century—and, in music pedagogy, arguably still survives—a less formalised conception of the musical work that did not identify it with the notation but rather positioned it *beyond* the notation: as Doğantan-Dack (2012b: 7–12) argues, this more liberal approach, which is implicit in the practices of early recorded pianism, has received far less recognition from musicologists than the textualist model of the aestheticians. In all these ways, what might be termed the official discourses around performance are out of kilter with practice. Sometimes this is quite glaringly the case. For example, the discursive framework of composer worship and *Werktreue* is almost completely irrelevant to the major stream of nineteenth-century pianism that centred around the cult of virtuosity and culminated in the 'piano wars' of the second quarter of the century: rival performers mainly played their own compositions, which were often variations on popular operatic arias of the day, and sometimes they improvised them, but in all cases the focus was on the athletic skill and competitive display of the performance. In this context, Small's and Godlovitch's iconoclastic claims are simple statements of fact.

There are also deep contradictions within what, borrowing Bekker's term, I call the paradigm of reproduction. For one thing, the idea that one can conceive a musical work independently of specific assumptions as to how it might go in performance, which is built into the concept of the autonomous musical work, is highly questionable. Peter Johnson (2007) has shown how, when British critics of the interwar and early post-war years talked about Beethoven's op. 135, they were largely talking about features of the famous Busch Quartet recording from 1933, and not about the work as such at all. Anthony Pryer (forthcoming) makes a similar point in relation to the music criticism which formed the core of Hanslick's professional writing: 'whenever Hanslick was reviewing or assessing work', he says, 'he was also, by aesthetic default, reviewing or assessing real (or imagined) performances. And it is this unspoken *performance postulate* that seems to hold the key to the apparent oddities and contradictions of his theory'. Among the contradictions to which Pryer refers is that on the one hand, as we have seen, Hanslick claimed with his aesthetician's hat on that 'the performer can deliver only what is already in the composition', but on the other his critical writings are full of demonstrations of the opposite. As Pryer points out, Hanslick (1963: 167) says of the famous soprano Adelina Patti that 'If we go today to hear operas such as *Linda, Sonnambula, I Puritani*, etc., we do not go to hear the works themselves—all dull—but to hear Patti. It is her talent and her voice which breathe new life into these empty and ineffectual melodies'. In other words, what Patti delivers is precisely what is not in the composition.

Hanslick's aesthetic theory underpins the philosophical discourses to which I referred, framed within the idea of the musical work as a more or less platonic entity grounded in notation. (The vagueness reflects significant disagreements within this framework.) Aestheticians working within this tradition take seriously the discourses of duty, and attempt to identify the essential aspects of the musical work on the basis of which a given performance of it can be shown to be (or not to be) faithful or authentic. In other words their approach is basically an ontological one: How can we know that a performance is indeed a performance of the work? It is obviously problematic for this approach if Hanslick the critic blatantly ignores the prescriptions of Hanslick the aesthetician. But it is all the more problematic if it turns out that the work concept, which these philosophers treat as in effect an aesthetic universal, applies to some streams of WAM performance culture but not others—especially in the nineteenth century, when the regime of the musical work is supposed to have been at its height. It is not surprising then that, within the larger philosophical community, a number of assaults have been aimed at this entire edifice, of which I shall mention two. The first is the devastating attack on the ontological approach to performance launched by Aaron Ridley, which turns on a simple question: 'When was the last time you came away from a performance of a piece of music—live or recorded—seriously wondering whether the performance had been of *it*?' (2004: 113). His point is that issues of ontology simply do not bear upon how listeners engage with or value performances, and so he concludes that 'the whole move to ontology in thinking about musical performance is a mistake' (111).

The second assault on traditional philosophies of music, which has perhaps been more influential in musicological circles than philosophical, is Lydia Goehr's attempt (1992) to reformulate the musical work in more realistic and sensible terms. Goehr's crucial move was to think of the musical work not as a set of essential features or compliance classes determining whether or not, in Ridley's words, a given performance is a performance of *it*, but rather as a regulative concept: a way of thinking about music, and structuring its practice, that fulfils a normative function. Built into this approach is the expectation that, at different times or places, or in relation to different genres, music may conform to a greater or lesser degree with the regulative concept. Goehr developed her thesis through historical analysis, concluding that while it was anticipated in many earlier sources (including Listenius), the concept of the musical work achieved its present form and role around 1800, remaining in place from then until the present day. Many musicologists quibbled over Goehr's chronology, putting forward examples of the work concept from before 1800, or cultural practices that were not regulated by it after then: I have already mentioned the nineteenth-century piano virtuosi, and the desire to contradict Goehr's philosophical incursion deep into musicological territory probably stimulated research into WAM traditions that were not regulated by the work concept but embodied different aesthetic assumptions. But in quibbling over the details, these musicologists were accepting the broad framework that Goehr was proposing, and in a way such objections might be seen as precisely making her point: if the musical work is a regulative concept subject to historical change rather than a timeless ontological principle, then the pattern of exceptions and variations documented by musicologists is exactly what you would expect. And in any case, if Goehr's formulation of the work concept does not map effortlessly onto the historical practices of music, that in no way diminishes its penetration as a critique of received discourses about music and its performance, as well as of the institutions that have been built on these discourses.

The issue of discourse is essential. My concern in this chapter is less with performance than with the discourses around it, and in particular the way they constrain and channel thinking. One might speak of a grammar of performance that inheres in the transitive mode. You don't just perform, you perform *something*, or you give a performance *of* something, and the grammar of performance deflects attention from the act of performance to its object. More specifically, the conceptual system I have been outlining construes the object as something that endures, and as such exists on a different plane from ongoing, experienced time. In other words, performance is seen as the translation into ongoing, experienced time of something that is not in itself temporal. Scores represent pieces of music as spatial configurations (you can flip the pages forwards or backwards), and music theory mainly consists of the elaboration of non-temporal models. Obvious examples are Schenkerian theory, which conceives of music as the unfolding in time of the 'chord of nature' or major triad, or neo-Riemannian theory, which understands compositions as individuated temporal trajectories across pitch space.

To think of a performance as simply the performance of a particular work—or of the structures into which it may be analysed—excludes all sorts of other possibilities as to what is being performed (I shall come back to this, particularly in Chapter 10). But it is not just that. It is that this underlying grammar makes it impossible to see performance as an intrinsically temporal, real-time activity through which meanings emerge that are not already deposited in the score. Not least as a result of Goehr's intervention, musicologists are aware of the shortcomings and distortions inherent in the work concept and the reifying vocabularies that derive from it. But their words still run away with them. The issue is what received discourses *allow* us to think, for—as I said in the Introduction—it is not my contention that musicologists are uninterested in performance. That accusation is frequently made. Bruce Johnson (2002: 103) cites, as if representative of the discipline, the 'eminent Sorbonne musicologist André Pirro', who supposedly said 'I never go to concerts any more. Why listen to music? To read it is enough'. Yet anyone who works with musicologists must know that many are passionately interested in and knowledgeable about performance; some are distinguished performers in their own right. The problem is that there often seems to be an almost schizophrenic dissociation between the discursive, academic knowledge with which they deal as musicologists and the tacit, action-based knowledge that they rely on as performers. The excessively black-and-white aesthetic ideologies I have been describing militate against effective translation between these quite different domains of musical experience. And the trouble with ideologies is that they represent themselves as just the way things are, suppressing the possibility of alternative views and even the fact that views are involved at all. In short, under the shadow of Plato's curse, received discourses frustrate musicologists' natural inclination to do justice to music as the performing art we all know it is.

PERFORMATIVE TURNS?

Traditional aesthetic and musicological ways of thinking about works and performances, then, reflect an assumption that meaning resides in the former at the expense of the latter. But this is precisely the way of thinking that came under sustained scrutiny across the humanities under the impact, from the 1960s, of reception theory. This was in origin a product of German-language scholarship, and early musicological work in this area, such as that of Hans Heinrich Eggebrecht on Beethoven, adopted an essentially Hegelian framework: processes of reception were seen as the unfolding of meanings that were already latent within the work, so revealing its true value. (The resonance with Schenkerian theory is not accidental but reflects the strong Hegelian component in Schenker's thought.) Understood this way, the study of reception might be seen as perpetuating the platonic model of the musical work, only by other means. But the approach was subsequently developed in a fundamentally different direction by anglophone musicologists, largely influenced by reader response criticism—a field linked (through Wolfgang Iser) to German reception theory, but given a strongly postmodern twist at the hands of French and American literary theorists such as Roland Barthes and Stanley Fish. Barthes (1977: 148) summarised the entire approach in the final sentence of a famous essay ('the birth of the reader must be at the cost of the death of the author'); in the same way, Fish saw meaning as produced through processes of interpretation, whether by readers or critics. In this way literary works came to be seen as sites for the production of meaning, and the process through which this happened became the prime focus of study.

There is an obvious parallel between this and the development of theatre studies—or at least a certain strain within theatre studies, for no academic discipline is monolithic. The basic premise of W. B. Worthen's *Shakespeare and the Force of Modern Performance* (2003: 29) is the 'misunderstanding' that 'a performance "of *Hamlet*" is a reproduction of textual meanings in some straightforward way'. Worthen (12) explains: 'Dramatic performance is not determined by the text of the play: it strikes a much more interactive, *performative* relation between writing and the spaces, places, and behaviors that give it meaning, *force*, as theatrical action'. In other words, attention is relocated from the dramatic text to the manner in which it interacts with an indefinite number of other factors to produce meaning in the real time of performance. Equally, responsibility for the production of meaning is shifted from authors to interpreters, whether directors, actors, or viewers. And this is the basic approach that performance studies (which in this book I sometimes refer to as 'interdisciplinary performance studies', to distinguish it from musical performance studies) extended far beyond the traditional domain of artistic practice. There is a probably apocryphal story that the new discipline owed its origin to a chance conversation between the theatre director and drama theorist Richard Schechner and the cultural anthropologist Victor Turner, whose work centred on ritual. (The point of such stories is not that they are true, but that they express disciplinary self-identity.) The two supposedly realised that combining the methods of theatre studies with the purview of anthropology could give rise to what Schechner (1988a), in the title of a brief but influential essay, termed the 'broad spectrum approach'. Like Barthes, Schechner (2006: 38) compressed his thinking into a single sentence: 'Just about anything can be studied "as" performance'.

But there was a further ingredient in the mix: J. L. Austin's theory of the performative. As a philosopher of language, Austin (who died in 1960) was concerned to define what he termed 'speech acts'. By this he meant the use of language not to describe some external reality, but rather to intervene in that reality. An obvious example is the point in the marriage ceremony where you say 'I do': this is a speech act, and it is by virtue of saying it—as well as filling out numerous forms—that you become in fact married. (Other examples include curses, christening, or the bestowing of knighthood.) Putting all this together, one might as readily talk about the performance of the Bourbon kingship as about that of *King Lear*, and indeed many of the strategies employed by Louis XIV to construct and maintain royal power are amenable to analysis in theatrical terms (including the design of royal palaces as stage sets). One might also as readily talk about the performance of gender as about that of *Carmen*, and Judith Butler's book *Gender Trouble* greatly increased the profile of such performative approaches by interpreting gendered behaviour as not the expression of biological difference but rather a social performance: in a much quoted phrase, she spoke of performative attributes of gender that 'effectively constitute the identity they are said to express or reveal' (Butler 1990: 98). These approaches converged in the so-called performative turn that swept across the humanities and social sciences in the years around 1990.

What was the impact of reception theory and the performative turn on musicology? Reception theory, and the historical approaches that derived from it, were a major influence, reaching musicology rather later than other subjects but developing into a fast-flowing disciplinary stream by the early 1990s. Such work focussed on the critical, social, and ideological meanings constructed through the totality of the discourses that surround music, and through the institutions that mediate musical values. For example, a major focus within the more historical wing of the 'New' musicology that reshaped the discipline during the 1990s was the formation of canons: it was shown that the Beethovenian canon came about through the interpretation of some (but only some) of the composer's works as embodying particular values, and those values were then reinforced through the impact of this increasingly closed repertory on concert practices, criticism, historiography, and education. Performance, then, appeared on the agenda, but only as considered in terms of its social, institutional, or aesthetic contexts. The discipline consistently shied away from serious engagement with what might reasonably have been considered the most obvious and salient acts of musical interpretation: actual performances, particularly as represented by the now-century-old heritage of sound recordings.

Why was this? One reason may have been a hostility to traditional practices of close reading that had quite different origins, but was widespread within the same progressive musicological circles that took up reception theory. A probably more significant reason was that sound recordings had not yet become established as sources for music-historical research: there was no equivalent to the source-critical skills for written documents that are routinely taught to graduate students, and so nobody knew quite what to do with them. Whatever the explanation, the consequence was that while the 'New' musicology did a great deal to enlarge and modernise disciplinary agendas, the fundamental rethinking at which it aimed was severely compromised. It continued to adhere to the textualist paradigms shared by traditional musicology and by literary studies, from which 'New' musicologists drew many of their more innovative approaches. The same might be said of the sociological approaches on which they drew through Adorno, and I shall come back to this in Chapter 8.

The difference in intellectual climate between musicology and other disciplines—which I see as reflecting the failure of established musicological discourses to engage with the concept of performance—can be measured by comparing the interdisciplinary performance studies approach with two developments that brought together academic research and performance practice in music: the historically informed performance movement, generally abbreviated to HIP, and the music-theoretical approach that works from page to stage. I will discuss each in turn. HIP has long historical roots, in the British context going back through the Arts and Crafts environment, within which the scholar and instrument builder Arnold Dolmetsch worked, to the origins of musicology in the nineteenth-century quest for national origins. But it took its modern form, beginning in the late 1960s, as a reaction against the established mainstream of post-war performance, and as such was in many ways comparable to the roughly contemporaneous 'real ale' movement, a reaction against the standardised products of the big breweries. And like many oppositional movements, it adopted the discourses of what it was opposing, but turned them to different ends. The ideologues of HIP, among whom were some of the most prominent performers of the day, built on traditional discourses of duty. Indeed, just as in the case of faithfulness to the composer as against *Werktreue*, so one can distinguish two strains of faithfulness within HIP: one, as before, to the composer's intentions, and a second, more tangible one to the circumstances and practices of original performances. (Kivy [1995] identifies a third conception of authenticity in HIP: period sound.) While the second is more open to historical evidence, there is still room for interpretive freedom: it is perfectly clear that for a multitude of reasons, not least inadequate rehearsal, original performances were often far from what composers would have wished, an obvious example being Beethoven's Ninth Symphony. In this way the various criteria for faithfulness could be conveniently played off against one another to legitimise a wide range of desired performance options.

It could be argued that the discourses which emerged round HIP—and formed an integral part of it—represented an intensified disciplining of performance, a subordination of practice to the written word. In the first place, period treatises were invoked as authoritative prescriptions for authentic performance practice. But since, as specifications of such practice, words tend to be vague or ambiguous at best and unintelligible at worst, musicologists also played an essential role as interpreters of period documents: in this way they acquired an unaccustomed degree of authority in matters of performance. And as these references to authority might suggest, the imperative tone to which I have already referred was a conspicuous element of HIP culture, generally directed against mainstream performance and building on an anti-romantic rhetoric that was already under way: Robert Hill (1994: 46) refers to the 'moral imperative to "cleanse" the performance practice of "classicist" works in order to restore to them a purity of which they had allegedly been deprived by late-romantic distortions'. He reinforces his claims with a specific example: 'Repugnantly self-righteous, anti-romanticism reached a grotesque institutional extreme with the formation of a *Stilkommission* at the Academie für Musik und darstellende Kunst Vienna [i.e. Vienna Conservatory] in the early 1960s'. Appropriately grisly details are provided.

It is obvious that, as I have described it, the relationship between academic research and performance practice in HIP was about as far removed as could be from the basic approach of interdisciplinary performance studies. Instead of seeing performance as a context for meaning production and seeking to understand its operation, the role of scholarship in HIP was to discipline practice. Yet at the same time, when considered in purely scholarly terms, HIP was at best controversial, and at worst obviously flawed. The basic problem is that, to expand on what I said before, written documents are highly problematic as sources of information on performance practice. In addition to the issues of prescription versus description to which I referred, words are capable of any number of interpretations: Robert Philip (1992: 220) quotes a treatise from 1823 that enjoins the performer to maintain 'an equilibrium between the feelings that hurry him away, and a rigid attention to time', and adds, 'One can imagine musicians from the eighteenth to the late twentieth centuries nodding their heads in agreement with this carefully worded advice, without having the least idea how much tempo fluctuation the authors really had in mind'. Then again, it is a truism that scores do not convey unnotated nuance, and even when they do embody specific performance information, as for instance in the case of written-out ornamentation, there are problems as to the purpose and therefore interpretation of the notations. (Were they models for beginners? guides to good practice? pedagogical exercises? demonstrations of skill? attempts to reproduce actual performances?) Similar problems apply to such other sources as drawings and paintings (can we assume the painters were realistically depicting what they saw?) and, where they exist, old instruments: Have they been rebuilt or adapted? How has the ageing of their materials affected their operation and sound? What about perishables, such as felts and strings? What about tuning?

Given the interaction between these multiple uncertainties, not to mention fundamental interpretive questions such as how far there was such a thing as a consistent performance practice at any given time or place, the effect of scholarship was less to contribute to certainty than to create an arena for contested practice. It is no wonder, then, that the view of HIP proposed by Daniel Leech-Wilkinson (1984) and Richard Taruskin (1995)—that its authentic value was not as scholarly reconstruction but as a distinctively late-modernist performance style—is nowadays widely accepted; Kivy (1995: 232) similarly refers to 'the refreshing quality of novelty' that 'opacity of medium lends to even the most overworked warhorses in the concert repertory'. One might then conclude that the traditional, ethically charged discourses of performance were invoked in order to sweep away the established style of the post-war mainstream, just as that style had invoked them to sweep away the remnants of Romantic performance style. Seen this way, HIP represented a brilliant exercise in image management, giving credibility and profile to a generation of up-and-coming performers in opposition to an institutionalised performance establishment at that time strongly supported by major record companies and government subsidy. Leech-Wilkinson (2009a: chapter 4, paragraph 47) observes that 'the HIP phenomenon was...probably the first occasion in the history of music when a change of style was intentionally manufactured by performers'. Under such circumstances style change was not just an aesthetic matter, but one of career advancement, and indeed of financial opportunity, most obviously for small record labels seeking niche markets overlooked by the majors.

But if HIP wasn't quite what it made itself out to be, neither do the last two paragraphs really do justice to it. In particular, whereas scholarly pronouncements were certainly invoked for their rhetorical force, the relationship between scholars and performers was by no means the one-way street that talk of disciplining performance might suggest. By this I do not just mean that HIP had twin sources in scholarship and performance, which did not always pull together, or that in the end HIP was forged by the performers who decided what to take from the scholars and what to leave. I mean that one of the motors behind HIP was continuous two-way interaction between scholars and performers: scholarly interpretations based on period sources were trialled in performance, leading to revised or refined interpretation of the sources, renewed experimentation, and so on in a virtuous circle. Again, the aggressively authenticist rhetoric that marked the early years of HIP, and that formed the principal source of contention, grew progressively less strident as instrument builders became better at copying period instruments and performers played them better. And leading directors such as Nikolaus Harnoncourt and Philippe Herreweghe increasingly worked with mainstream orchestras (both, for instance, have been guest conductors with the Amsterdam-based Concertgebouw and the Vienna Philharmonic), bringing to them what they had learned from working with period-instrument ensembles.

The result was a process of hybridisation, with the former opposition between HIP and mainstream performance being replaced by a more diverse performance environment. Perhaps most important, HIP revealed that post-war mainstream performance did not simply embody how music went, but was itself a style, an option among other options. In this way it returned responsibility for decision making to the performer, licensed the consideration of an unlimited range of historical, hermeneutical, and other perspectives in arriving at a personal interpretation, and in this way might be seen as a means through which performance was liberated rather than disciplined. In all these respects, HIP can be said to have had a transformative effect on the culture of WAM performance as a whole: the conductor Sir Charles Mackerras claimed that 'the insights of period-instrument performance changed certain things beyond recall, and as a result the tradition of performance has been completely altered' (Lawson and Stowell 2012: 829). And in that sense, as documented by the practitioner and commentator John Butt (2002), it can be said to have had a transformative effect on performers' thinking. At the same time, the grounding of HIP in the historical positivism of its early ideologues served to graft new performance practices onto old discursive paradigms, in this way giving them a further lease of life.

I said the second development that brought together academic research and performance practice was in the field of music theory, and because this is particularly relevant to my book, it is the focus of the next chapter. However, theoretical approaches to musical performance are closely linked with, and drew on, developments in cognitive psychology, and so I will start there. From around 1970 there was a remarkable convergence of music theory and psychology, cemented with the establishment in 1983 of the journal *Music Perception*. The basis of this convergence was that on the one hand psychologists saw music as an area that was both culturally meaningful and exceptionally amenable to quantitative investigation, while on the other hand theorists saw psychological methods as offering new approaches to existing problems. At first, as the title of the journal indicates, the focus was on perceptual issues, but in the 1980s studies of performance became increasingly popular. One reason was the difficulty of conducting ecologically valid research into the perception of music (because the process of gathering responses may easily perturb the perceptual process). By contrast, it was much easier to collect performance data without disrupting the phenomenon under investigation. This was particularly the case after the introduction—also, as it happens, in 1983—of MIDI: all that was now necessary to start conducting empirical research on performance was a cheap MIDI keyboard, a standard computer, and a MIDI interface (in those days they were not built in). And while cheap MIDI keyboards were not a good basis for studying the detail of expert performance, weighted keyboards and acoustic pianos with MIDI sensors, such as the Yamaha Disklavier, appeared before the end of the decade. By comparison, previous work in this field had required complex, purpose-built equipment: examples include a system of rubber tubes placed under piano keys and connected to a cylinder recorder, developed by Alfred Binet and Jules Courtier as early as the 1890s (Judd 1896); Carl Seashore's 'Iowa piano camera' from the 1930s (Henderson, Tiffin and Seashore 1936); and Henry Shaffer's use (1980) of photocells to interface the action of a Bechstein grand piano to a DEC PDP-11 minicomputer in the late 1970s.

Although certainly pioneering, both Binet and Courtier's work and Seashore's are of little more than curiosity value today, and for essentially the same reason. Binet and Courtier claimed for their system that it would enable the identification of faults in piano performance, that is to say deviations from the nominal values represented in the score—according to which each beat has the same duration, each crotchet lasts two quavers, and so forth. This is the most extreme form of musical textualism imaginable, according to which the point of performance is literally to reproduce the score. Seashore and his co-workers studied not only piano but also vocal and violin performance, and aimed to replace 'the jargon of arm-chair theories' by 'an adequate scientific aesthetics' (Seashore 1936: 5). What this means becomes clear when, two pages later, Seashore writes, 'One of the first revelations in the laboratory record-ing of music is the demonstration of an extraordinary disparity between the actual physical performance and the music we hear....We hear but little of what actually exists, and that little is greatly distorted in hearing'. It is the ideas of 'what actually exists' and 'distortion' that are revealing. Seashore conceives of music having an objective existence which is represented rather inaccurately in perceptual experience. In effect this is the old platonist model in scientific clothing.

By contrast, Shaffer's approach arose from a much more appropriate and pro-ductive conceptual framework, that of cognitive psychology. His work on piano performance developed out of his previous work on typing: his primary concern was with the mechanisms underlying skilled motor control of whatever nature. In collecting and analysing data from piano performance, then, his aim was to explain it in terms of relatively persistent abstract schemata (what you build up as you learn a piece), seen as organising the motor actions of performance through some kind of hierarchy of increasingly complex specifications. The question was what, in music, such schemata and hierarchies might look like. This is where the link between music theory and the psychology of performance was forged, and it came about largely through the presence in Shaffer's laboratory at this time of Eric Clarke, who had a background in music theory and completed a PhD on piano performance under Shaffer's supervision.

Music theory provided precisely the kind of schemata and hierarchies Shaffer was looking for. Schenkerian analysis, for example, can be well described as based on an abstract schema (the basic linear and harmonic progression known as the Ursatz or fundamental structure), elaborated through a succession of increas-ingly detailed levels that converge upon the music as composed. In other words, it represents music as a hierarchy of increasingly complex specifications. From this perspective, it became a question of how such a representation might be inter-nalised, and how it might be translated into real-time motor performance. As I shall explain in Chapter 3, Schenker himself worked in the vastly different cul-tural and intellectual context of fin-de-siècle Vienna. But his theoretical approach was repackaged and supplemented at just this time by Fred Lerdahl and Ray Jackendoff: their Generative Theory of Tonal Music (1983) expressed Schenker's basic method in a more or less scientific manner that could hardly have differed more from the original, but made it much more accessible to music psychologists, and indeed to many music theorists of that time.

Lerdahl and Jackendoff borrowed the term 'generative' from Noam Chomsky's structural linguistics, and though they were not specifically concerned with performance, it corresponded directly to the central insight of Shaffer and Clarke's approach. It seemed clear that pianists did not memorise by precisely encoding every specific finger or wrist movement involved in playing a given piece: not only would that necessitate the storage of impractical amounts of information, but it would also—for example—make it impossible to change fingerings on the fly. (Rudolf Serkin told Dean Elder [1986: 57], 'I change fingers constantly, at the spur of the moment sometimes, according to the piano, the hall, my disposition, how I slept, and so on'.) The guiding ideas underlying Shaffer and Clarke's work were then that, through practice, pianists build up a relatively stable cognitive representation of the music, that there is some system of rules that generates the physical actions of performance in real time, and that these cognitive structures and processes leave their mark on what is played, in the form of the unnotated but apparently systematic and evidently meaningful nuances of expressive performance. The arresting prospect that this opened up was that a common analytical approach could make sense of cognitive structure, motor control, and expressive meaning.

All this meant that, by around 1990, the theory and psychology of music had come to share three characteristics that were inherited from the more traditional discourses of music I have described in this chapter, together with a fourth that was not. The first of these characteristics might be seen as Plato's curse in a mentalistic guise: in the music psychologist Caroline Palmer's words, 'The listener's and performer's experience of a musical piece can be described as a conceptual structure, an abstract message that specifies the relevant musical relationships in a piece' (1996: 25). As in Schoenberg's telepathic fantasy, music is understood to be something inside people's heads, so losing its social dimension. The second characteristic also emerges from Palmer's formulation: as in the formalist version of nineteenth-century idealism, music is understood to subsist in structure, where structure can be more or less resolved into notational categories. Third is the conception of music in terms of a communicative chain that passes from the composer via the performer (Adorno's 'middleman interpreter') to the listener, as epitomised in Beethoven's 'from the heart...to the heart'.

As for the fourth characteristic, this is a slippage between two senses of 'expression': on the one hand its ordinary-language meaning, where it refers to mood, affect, or emotion, and on the other the idea of performance 'expressing' structure. I said this fourth characteristic was not inherited from traditional discourses of music, but it is found in Schenkerian theory, in which it is normal to refer to structure being expressed by compositional parameters such as dynamics or orchestration. And Schenker himself highlighted the reduction of emotional properties to structure when in 1925 he quoted a passage from C. P. E. Bach's *Essay on the True Art of Playing Keyboard Instruments*. While speaking about the fantasy, Bach makes a reference to 'the

passions'. Schenker (1994: 5) takes immediate action to tame Bach's theoretically unruly term:

> One must not seek in Bach's word 'passions' what certain aestheticians
> of the doctrine of affections bring to it....He means by it simply the
> consequences of a change of diminution: pure musical effects which
> have nothing in common with the amateurishly misunderstood and so
> grossly exaggerated ideas of the aestheticians. For Bach, even the indi-
> vidual motives of diminution are really distinct affects, distinct passions,
> so greatly does he feel their unifying and characteristic properties, and at
> the same time their contrast to one another....Bach will have wanted to
> say nothing more than that the creator of a fantasy must have taken pains
> to alternate motives, in order to produce tension and transmit it to the
> listener. Nothing more.

It is hard not to read Schenker's excessive, repetitive denials as betraying a certain
unease with the tradition of erasing emotion from musical discourse that goes
back to Hanslick, and I shall return to this in Chapter 3.

In this way the convergence between music theory and psychology in the
years around 1990 gave rise to an approach that drew on key assumptions of
the traditional discourses around music, but—as I argued of HIP—gave them
a new lease of life. It repackaged them for the knowledge industry of the late
twentieth and early twenty-first centuries. But from this point on there is something of a divergence between the two disciplines. As represented by the work
of English-language writers such as Caroline Palmer, Bruno Repp, and Luke
Windsor, and in other languages of Alf Gabrielsson, Johan Sundberg, Henkjan
Honing, and Peter Desain, psychological work on performance has built
steadily on, which is also to say that it has developed away from, these foundations: recent work by John Sloboda and Patrik Juslin has put emotional meaning firmly back on the performance analysis agenda, the work of Jane Davidson
and Eric Clarke has stimulated rapidly growing interest in the embodied
dimensions of performance, and in his own work Clarke has sought alternatives to what he terms the 'information processing' paradigm of cognitive psychology. (In this book I will make repeated references to these developments.)
Meanwhile, particularly in North America, the majority of music-theoretical
work on performance has continued to be based on the assumptions I outlined
in the previous paragraphs. Since this book is at the same time an attempt to
build on and a reaction against that approach, the next chapter will examine it
in some detail.

2

Page and Stage

THEORIST'S ANALYSIS

Hanslick's aesthetics of music, as set out in his *On the Musically Beautiful*, underpins not only much subsequent philosophising about music, as I said in Chapter 1, but also what in the course of the twentieth century became the discipline of music theory. Now it has so frequently been claimed that Hanslick denied music could have emotional or expressive properties, insisting instead on a formalism based solely on abstract structure, that it has almost become true. In fact it is not. What Hanslick claimed was that emotional properties fell outside the purview of musical aesthetics. In this way he firmly redirected attention from those properties to their structural underpinnings: structure became identified with the music itself, or the purely musical, so creating through opposition the category of the extra-musical. (All these terms commonly attract scare quotes.)

We saw in Chapter 1 how, when he took up his critical pen, Hanslick played fast and loose with his own formalist principles, ascribing to Patti the power to bring life to empty melodies even when in principle his own formalism turned performance into reproduction. We also saw Schenker's apparent unease as he insisted that C. P. E. Bach's 'passions' could be reduced to purely structural properties. Nevertheless it is the idea of music being definable as structure, and of whatever further meaning it may have being predicated on such structure, that gives music theory its disciplinary identity. I do not mean by this that theorists are *only* interested in structure, or that they believe (as Schenker tried to persuade himself) that all musical meaning can be translated into structure. Just as Sloboda and Juslin have put emotion and expression back onto the music-psychological agenda, so a number of music theorists—most notably Robert Hatten—have put them firmly onto the music-theoretical agenda. But there has been a tendency to construe such meanings as in effect a superstructure, the topping on the structural pizza.[1] The issue with which I am concerned in this chapter is how far the structuralist paradigm, as developed by music theorists, can be an adequate basis for understanding performance, however many toppings are piled onto it.

---

1. I argued this, with reference to Hatten's earlier work, in Cook (2001: 175).

My discussion of this issue centres around Schenkerian theory and analysis, for a number of reasons. In the first place, as I mentioned, while the Schenkerian approach originated in *fin-de-siècle* Vienna, it was imported into North America in the late 1930s by his disciples (who formed part of the Jewish diaspora that did so much to reshape musicology). During the post-war period Schenkerian theory was disseminated to the extent that, by the last decades of the twentieth century, it had become the dominant theoretical approach to music of the 'common practice' era (say, from Bach to Brahms) across the anglophone world. Moreover issues of the relationship between analysis and performance, which already play a significant if problematic role in Schenker's own writings, received a great deal of attention within the Schenkerian community, so that it makes sense to speak of a Schenkerian performance pedagogy: the longstanding association of Schenkerian analysis with the Mannes College of Music (now officially Mannes College The New School for Music) played an important role in this. Not only are a number of professional Schenkerian theorists gifted performers, such as Carl Schachter, but there are also professional performers who are strongly committed to Schenkerian analysis: today the outstanding example is Murray Perahia, while in Schenker's day it was Wilhelm Furtwängler.

It is worth pointing out that while, in its post-war American form, the teaching of Schenkerian theory was absorbed into the structures and practices of institutionalised higher education, in Schenker's own hands it much more resembled the personally oriented practices of traditional performance teaching. Never employed by an institution, Schenker had many private pupils, but he did not teach them theory or analysis as such: he aimed at a holistic musical education in which theory and analysis were integrated with performance and composition, the goal being as much the development of ear and mind as manual dexterity. While this was entirely unlike the conservatory style of performance training which had come into existence in the course of the nineteenth century (Schenker [1979: xxiii] spoke contemptuously of 'the teaching of music in condensed courses, as languages are taught for use in commerce'), it had features in common with an older teaching pattern that survived almost into the twentieth century: Sergei Rachmaninoff's training with Nikola Zverev, for example, was an immersive experience which encompassed all aspects of music, attendance at concerts and the theatre, and literary education (Harrison 2006, chapter 3). Although Zverev's emphasis was on performance, it is significant that two of his pupils, Alexander Scriabin and Rachmaninoff himself, developed into major composers.

Schenker explained the basic principles of his performance pedagogy in his last book, *Free Composition* (1935). What is necessary, he explains, is to penetrate beneath the obvious surface features of the music:

> The *performance* of a musical work of art can be based only upon a perception of that work's organic coherence. Interpretation cannot be acquired through gymnastics or dancing; one can transcend 'motive', 'theme', 'phrase', and 'bar line' and achieve true musical punctuation only by comprehending the background, middleground, and foreground. As punctuation in speech

transcends syllables and words, so true punctuation in music strives toward more distant goals....Consequently, the concept of background, middleground, and foreground is of decisive and practical importance for performance (1979: 8).

But Schenker's thinking on performance long predates the graphical analytical technique for which he is known today. In 1911 Schenker drafted extensive materials for a treatise on performance. But although he returned to these materials on numerous subsequent occasions, he never finished it. Knowledge of it circulated widely among Schenkerians, mainly through being quoted in writings by those who had access to Schenker's papers, but it was not until 2000 that it appeared in print under the title *The Art of Performance*, in an English translation that structured the materials in such a way as to give the whole the appearance of being an essentially complete, if short and oddly balanced, book. There is an instructive comparison to be made with Adorno's also unfinished treatise on performance, to which I referred in Chapter 1, and which was published in German the year after *The Art of Performance* (and in English translation five years after that): this is presented frankly as what it is, a series of notes that Adorno made, largely in the course of reading other books on performance, together with a continuous fifty-page draft of one section, in which ideas that are often highly tentative in the notes take on a startlingly confident and authoritative form. Whereas the chronological presentation of the Adorno materials documents an unfinished project, the effect of *The Art of Performance* is to construct a book that Schenker never actually wrote. (And if he had, he might not have started with that first sentence.)

Right up to his 1930 essay on Beethoven's 'Eroica' Symphony, Schenker's major analytical essays included sections on performance, which offer detailed, sometimes bar-by-bar directions for interpretation. For reasons that will become clear in Chapter 3, modern Schenkerians have taken remarkably little notice of these directions. Instead they have drawn almost exclusively on two sources: the book fragments from 1911, the unrealised aim of which was to set out a coherent theory of performance, and the writings from the 1920s and 1930s in which Schenkerian theory and analysis take on the form in which we know them today, but are only sporadically linked to performance. However, Schenker's thinking in 1911 was very different from what it later became, and that means these sources are very much out of kilter with one another. The consequence is that today's Schenkerian performance pedagogy is in essence the work of post-war Schenkerians from Charles Burkhart and Edward Laufer to Carl Schachter and William Rothstein. Some clues could of course be found in Schenker's later publications. In the paragraph from *Free Composition* that I quoted, for instance, Schenker follows up his comparison between performance and punctuation by saying, 'This, of course, does not mean that the tones of the fundamental line need to be overemphasised, as are the entrances in a poor performance of a fugue. The player who is aware of the coherence of a work will find interpretive means which allow the coherence to be heard'. The second sentence is too vague to be helpful for pedagogical purposes, and as for the first, the 'of course' might be seen as another of Schenker's unwitting self-revelations. In the middle 1920s he had actually developed the idea of giving dynamic emphasis to structural notes into 'a theory that explicit dynamic levels could be deduced with certainty from the level of the pitch structure', as Burkhart (1983: 112) describes it: he even illustrated its operation in two published analyses of Bach's solo violin music, before quietly dropping it.[2] The basic question facing the creators of Schenkerian performance pedagogy, then—the problem that Schenker himself had not solved—was how to find ways of mapping structure to performance that were not naively literal.

As a key early text of this pedagogy, Burkhart's 1983 article takes this as its starting point: 'it would clearly be tasteless to overemphasise the tones of the framework itself' (107). Having quoted Schenker's own statements to this effect, Burkhart continues, 'For Schenker, . . . it is not so much the "main" tones that the player should expressly bring out, but the diminutions thereof'. (In saying 'For Schenker', Burkhart is arguably indulging in the same sort of ventriloquising as the performers in Robert Martin's imagined rehearsal, cited in Chapter 1.) Or to put it another way, the aim should be to bring out not the structure itself but rather its consequences, in terms of the sometimes complex and occasionally contradictory relationships between levels. In *Free Composition*, Schenker (1979: 100) discusses what later Schenkerians termed motivic parallelisms, meaning that the same patterns of notes appear at—and sometimes serve to link—different structural levels. He comments, 'In view of the fact that the masters based their syntheses mainly upon such relationships, there can be no doubt of the importance of projecting them—it remains only to find the specific means of achieving such projection'. Burkhart enlarges on this hint, analysing examples of motivic parallelism from Beethoven and Chopin, and suggesting how the parallelism may be brought out: in one place, he says, lifting the right hand before the initial note of the motif will help to project it, in another he recommends giving a different quality of tone to different elements (Burkhart 1983: 102, 104). He also suggests that, where a motive is on too large a scale to be literally performed (such as the motive that embraces the entire middle section of Chopin's F♯ Impromptu op. 36), awareness of it will 'inevitably if ever so subtly influence the way the performer shapes the large dimensions of the composition' (104). The implication is that knowledge seeps into interpretation even when its mechanisms cannot be precisely defined.

Burkhart is clearly concerned not to intrude excessively upon the performer's freedom. He discusses the structural implications of the fingerings Schenker provided in his edition of the Beethoven piano sonatas, urging his readers to consider them carefully 'before replacing his fingering with their own' (Burkhart 1983: 99). And on the final page of his article he writes that 'The particular means of execution—be it articulation, rhythm, tone colour, dynamics, or a combination of these—that the player employs to interpret the diminutions on the surface will depend ultimately on his personal style'. But, Burkhart continues (112), 'he cannot

---

2. See the essays on BWV 1005 and 1006 in Schenker (1994).

even recognise the diminutions, much less interpret them, until he knows what is being "diminuted"—has a clear conception of the underlying levels. In other words, only when he is aware of the "main" tones can he perceive the diminutions and perform them in the light of the main tones'. The fine line that Burkhart treads between freedom and constraint has its origins in Schenker's 1911 writings. According to Schenker, composers' scores represent the effects they wish to create, not the manner in which these effects are to be created: to take the simplest possible example, a sequence of minims with marcato signs 'does not at all show the way the sequence should be played but indicates the effect the composer desires—leaving it up to the performer to find the means' (2000: 5). Therein lies the performer's freedom. But it is contained within an inflexible framework, for as Schenker also explains, the effects are defined by the work's 'linear progressions, neighboring tones, chromatic tones, modulations', in short its structural formations, and 'about these, naturally, there cannot exist different interpretations'.[3] In other words, the performer's freedom is restricted to the means through which compositional effects are to be realised in the contingent circumstances of particular performances: the effects themselves are off limits, and it is in this sense that, as Schenker says elsewhere in these materials, 'Each work of art has only *one* true rendition' (77).

Since it is precisely the analyst's business to reach the correct interpretation of the compositional effects, the whole process is unambiguously one in which understanding is derived from the score and applied to the performance. It is to designate this that I borrow the term 'page-to-stage' from theatre studies (Melrose 1994: 215). As usual with Schenker, however, things are a little more complicated than that might imply. Schenker sees scores as authoritative except when they are wrong. He attributes particular importance to autographs as evidence of composers' intentions, but does not hesitate on occasion to overrule them: in Chopin's Etude op. 10 no. 5, for example, there is an e♭³ that Schenker (1994: 98) confidently treats as a slip of the pen, on the grounds that the voice leading demands g♭³ ('voice-leading is a higher entity than Chopin', he remarks). So properly speaking we should say that it is the understanding of the work as an ideal entity—as a set of compositional effects correctly deduced from the score—that is applied to the performance. This is an illustration of the mentality that in Chapter 1 I described as deeply embedded in the discourses around WAM.

Other examples of the writing about performance through which a Schenkerian pedagogy developed also sought ways of softening the fundamental authoritarianism of the approach. Rothstein, himself a pianist as well as a theorist, took his cue from the idea of dissembling, which appears frequently in Schenker's 1911 materials: as presented in the published version, there is a even a section entitled 'Ways of dissembling', which discusses how pianists can create effects corresponding to legato (not literally achievable on a percussive instrument such as

---

3. Quoted in Rothstein (1984: 10); I have been unable to locate this quotation in *The Art of Performance*, which however does not include all of the 1911 materials.

the piano) or portamento. Rothstein (1995: 218) critiques the general assumption that analysis is useful for performers 'because, knowing what a piece of music contains in terms of structure, the performer can proceed to "bring it out" ': he describes this as 'a dangerous half-truth' (218). Instead, he uses Schenkerian and other analytical techniques to identify situations in which the performer's aim should be *not* to bring out structure, whether to avoid pedantic over-clarification, to create dramatic effects, or simply because some things cannot be brought out. 'It is one thing to be convinced that something is true analytically', he says, 'quite another to decide how—or even whether—to disclose such information to one's listeners in a performance' (238).

While still emphasising the value of analytical understanding, Rothstein returns freedom to the performer by turning the disclosure of structure into an interpretive decision, where less sophisticated page-to-stage approaches presuppose it, and this creates a resonance between Rothstein's way of thinking and Schenker's. The idea that structure should as a matter of course be brought out, disclosed to listeners, reflects the aesthetics of Bauhaus or international modernism, as embodied in the slogan 'form follows function' and seen in the modernist architecture of the interwar and post-war periods. To the extent that Schenker can be regarded as a modernist at all, his modernism was of the Viennese variety, of which the idea of concealment is a much more characteristic trope.[4] (Near the beginning of *Free Composition*, Schenker [1979: 6] quotes the 'ingenious words' of the *fin-de-siècle* playwright Hugo von Hofmannsthal: 'One must conceal the depths. Where? On the surface.') And this is directly reflected in Schenker's views on performance. In his monograph on Beethoven's Ninth Symphony, which is almost precisely contemporaneous with the 1911 materials on performance, Schenker (1992: 86, 70) wrote of the 'clarification-mania' that led Wagner, in his retouching of Beethoven's orchestration, to uncover everything that the composer had artfully camouflaged, and this is one of his most frequently recurring complaints about performances.[5]

Another pianist, Janet Schmalfeldt, sought to subvert the authoritarianism of the page-to-stage approach through the literary form in which she framed her contribution. Like Rothstein, she drew a contrast between the activities and priorities of the analyst and those of the performer: anticipating Rothstein's words of ten years later, she wrote that 'It is one thing to consider how we might some day realize a score, and it is quite another thing to perform the work' (Schmalfeldt 1985: 19). So she structured her 1985 article, which focusses on two bagatelles from Beethoven's op. 126, as a dialogue between analyst-Schmalfeldt and performer-Schmalfeldt. This is an attractive format, and the idea is that the two Schmalfeldts will trade insights to the mutual benefit of

---

4. For further discussion see Cook (2007b, chapter 2).

5. Wagner's modifications were incorporated in his 1872 performance of the symphony to mark the laying of the foundation stone for the Bayreuth Festival Theatre, and described in his essay 'The rendering of Beethoven's Ninth Symphony' (Wagner 1895: 229–53).

both. As a number of commentators observed, however, it doesn't quite work out like that. The two Schmalfeldts tend to lecture one another rather than engage in dialogue, and the relationship between them seems very unequal: Lawrence Rosenwald (1993: 61) points out that performer-Schmalfeldt behaves rather as if she is analyst-Schmalfeldt's student, and Joel Lester (1995: 198n) makes a similar observation. Mine Doğantan-Dack (2008: 300) goes further. She draws attention to the rather fawning account of herself that performer-Schmalfeldt offers to analyst-Schmalfeldt ('If I succeed in finding confidence for the performance of the Second Bagatelle, it will be because I have tried more than ever to find an analytic basis for performance decisions'), and comments acidly, 'such statements represent wishful thinking by analysts rather than the conditions of success on stage'. Partly in response to such criticisms, Schmalfeldt revisited the issue in a recent book chapter, and this provides an opportunity to assess my claim (at the end of Chapter 1) that there has been rather little development in mainstream music-theoretical thinking about performance since then. Schmalfeldt disagrees: 'studies about the performance/analysis relationship have come a long way since 1985' (2011: 114).

One of her aims in the 1985 article, Schmalfeldt now says, was 'to bring two facets of myself into dialogue with one another' (2011: 114), and it had been her intention 'to give both characters equal authority within their exchange. But', she continues, 'the Analyst fails to clarify that many of her analytic views had in fact been inspired by the Performer. Nor does the Performer grasp the opportunity to demonstrate that performances can, and usually do, influence and even determine analytic interpretations, just as much as analyses can, and often do, inform performances'. The aim of her new study, which focusses on Schubert's A minor Sonata op. 42, is to demonstrate this. The monograph in which it appears is on the idea of form as process, as illustrated by early nineteenth-century music, and Schmalfeldt writes, 'I have been led to the central topic of this book... by the performer in me as much as by my analytic and theoretic concerns' (114). The bulk of the chapter consists of demonstrating how Schubert has created the potential for musical processes without fully determining their exact nature: the performer is frequently 'in charge' of the musical process, as she puts it, and is in that sense a co-creator of the music alongside Schubert. Much of the time 'the performer' is obviously Schmalfeldt herself, but she also makes detailed reference to recordings by Richard Goode, Maurizio Pollini, András Schiff, and Andreas Staier.

The result is a richly interpretive approach based in established theory, drawing on Schmalfeldt's own experience as a performer, and engaging with other performers. The overall approach, however, remains within the page-to-stage framework. While it is no doubt the case that aspects of Schmalfeldt's interpretation derive from her performance experience, the linkage of performance and critical interpretation remains largely invisible: one has to take it on trust. The presentation of the chapter takes the traditional form in which ambiguities or other forms of under-specification are identified in Schubert's score, and interpretive options derived from them. And although, when Schmalfeldt discusses the four pianists' recordings, her approach is descriptive and interpretive, it is fair to detect a more prescriptive undercurrent: it is evident that Schmalfeldt has clear views about how the piece should be performed. That is fair enough, but arguably brings her within range of Doğantan-Dack's challenging claim (2008: 302) that 'for any present-day researcher who wishes to prescribe performance decisions by relying on the authority of analytical findings based on the score, there is no excuse for not demonstrating through a recorded performance of her own how exactly such analytical knowledge is translated into a sounding performance of the piece'.

As illustrated by Schmalfeldt's work, then, work on the relationship between analysis and performance has in some respects come a long way since 1985, but in others rather little has changed. And here a variety of socially and culturally entrenched factors come into play. The fact that, both in 1985 and in 2011, the relationship between analysis and performance is being negotiated on the printed page is a metonym of the more general situation of performance within the discourses and institutions of academia: as long as the mechanisms of research accreditation and career advancement remain wedded to the written word, interactions between analysts and performers will be away fixtures for the latter. It is true that significant numbers of performers do write about what they do, but as Doğantan-Dack observes, 'most of this literature does not involve disciplinary concerns...and consequently does not find acceptance in musicological circles as presenting a legitimate knowledge producing perspective' (2008: 303). But in any case it is perverse that performers should be valorised for their writing rather than for their performing. When he advocated that theorists should take account of actual recordings, rather than just talking about ideal, imaginary performances, Lester (1995: 214) made the point that in this way 'performers could enter analytical dialogue *as performers*—as artistic/intellectual equals, not as intellectual inferiors'. Lester's point is sharpened by the language of some theoretical writing on performance, at least in the early days. A 1988 essay by Eugene Narmour, for example, which evaluated commercial recordings of a variety of music on the basis of Narmour's own theoretical approach, illustrated a striking readiness to rubbish performers: Glenn Gould 'ruins the form', Julius Katchen's performance 'lacks insight and therefore perceptual consistency', and 'sometimes conductors do utterly inexplicable things that make no sense at all' (1988: 321n, 319, 333n). There is no suggestion that, where a performer does something that doesn't make sense in theoretical terms, it might be the theory that is at fault.

There is a sense in which what Lester calls for is exactly what Schmalfeldt provides through her engagement with Goode, Pollini, Schiff, and Staier—except that the idea of dialogue loses much of its force when someone else is speaking for you, and you have no opportunity to reply. And the unequal relationship of theorists and performers within the academic firmament is conditioned by real-world issues such as employment. It has traditionally been common for universities to hire performers on fixed-term, fractional contracts—in contrast to the permanent, full-time contracts normal for academic staff. This explains the kind of analyst-performer interactions at one time frequently encountered at North American conferences, where a theorist (usually male and tenured) would talk about the piece in question, and then his points would be illustrated by an instrumentalist (as likely as not female and on a fixed-term contract), with the theorist fielding most of the questions and the performer interpolating a few comments. Such an inequitable relationship might be in place in a coaching studio, but outside music it is not typical of interaction among academic colleagues. Other issues of disciplinary politics have played a role, too. Composition is well established in music academia on both sides of the Atlantic, and in North America often linked to theory, with composition and theory sometimes being combined in one post. Many of those who were instrumental in the development of page-to-stage theory came from this background. For example Edward T. Cone, whose book *Musical Form and Musical Performance* (1968) was an important early contribution to this field, became professionally known as a theorist, as well as a fine pianist, but he thought of himself as primarily a composer. From that perspective both the self-evidence of the page-to-stage orientation and the authority attached to composers' intentions and notations become easier to understand.

Larger cultural and philosophical factors are at play too. By this I mean the general discursive framework of Plato's curse, of course, but there are some specific features I would like to emphasise. One is the persistent influence of Cartesian dualism, with the body being subordinated to the mind. In her chapter on Schubert's op. 42, Schmalfeldt stresses that 'the processes of thinking, feeling, and using the body to perform interact inseparably for performers who also analyze' (2011: 114), and at one point she draws an analytical insight from how 'the fifth finger of the pianist's left hand' (evidently her own, and maybe it's an unhelpful vestige of traditional analytical discourse that she doesn't say so) wants to linger on a particular F♮. But once again that is not how the field was originally set up. The pianist and theorist Erwin Stein, who was much influenced by Schoenberg and whose 1962 book *Form and Performance* was an even earlier contribution to the field than Cone's similarly named volume, clearly expressed a dualist conception when he referred to the need for the performer to have 'a whole piece of music in a nutshell in his mind' (71). The page-to-stage approach transforms such dualism into a means of disciplining the performing body, subjecting it to a mentalistic construal of the musical work.

But it is not just a matter of the page-to-stage approach. The same Cartesian mentality is expressed in the very idea of an all-purpose virtuoso technique, which developed in the course of the nineteenth century and the aim of which was to enable any interpretive option to be put into practice; this was in turn associated with the contemporaneous standardisation of pianos, in particular their actions (Winter 1990). Given the extent to which I have presented Schenkerian performance pedagogy as an expression of the traditional discourses about music that I discussed in Chapter 1, it is worth noting that Schenker himself deplored both these developments. He was scathing about virtuosos and practice regimes based on the cult of velocity, insisting that there could be no such thing as an all-purpose system of fingering: 'Every piece has its own special fingering', he argued, 'its own special dynamics' (2000: 77). This fits with Burkhart's characterisation of Schenker's fingerings (1983: 111) as oriented toward 'bringing out what he saw as the *musical* gesture rather than to being as physically easy as possible'. Schenker also criticised the English action originally introduced by Broadwood, which supplanted the Viennese action over the course of the century, and with which, as Schenker put it,

> perfect evenness of touch has arrived. Simultaneously, music training has for decades striven for perfect evenness also of the fingers. Thus we are faced with evenness of fingers and keys. We could be pleased by this development if—what irony!—precisely the opposite were not the crux of the matter: unevenness! The fingers, by nature uneven, must play unevenly: all effort in practicing is in vain if it does not aim at unevenness in performance (2000: 77).

And finally, a reductive dualism of mind and body maps onto an equally reductive dualism between theory and practice, with the former in either case taking precedence over the latter. I mean this in terms of both importance and sequence. It is implicit in Stein's formulation that first you get the piece into a nutshell in your mind, and then you perform it. It becomes explicit in the introduction which Benjamin Britten wrote for Stein's book: 'after the intellect has finished work, the instinct must take over. In performance the analysis must be forgotten' (Stein 1962: 8). And one of the key characteristics of the page-to-stage approach, as illustrated by Wallace Berry's *Musical Structure and Performance* (which appeared in 1989 and marked the coming of age of the page-to-stage approach within music theory), was that the 'to' denotes a one-way street. Near the beginning Berry says his aim is to show 'how...a structural relation exposed in analysis can be illuminated in the inflections of edifying performance'; he abbreviates the same idea in such formulations as 'the findings of analysis and consequent outlets in performance', or 'the path from analysis to performance' (x, x, 10). This is not because Berry was an ivory-tower academic: on the contrary, his book drew on his extensive experience as a composer (with two ASCAP awards) and performer (pianist and conductor), as well as an eclectic theorist who drew on a wide variety of methods. It is in part because of the entrenched factors to which I referred, coupled to the larger discursive framework of Plato's curse. One might say the whole field was set up in a way that militates against attempts to reverse the one-way flow from page to stage, from performance to analysis—not only Schmalfeldt's 2011 book but also, for example, a collaborative article on Ravel's *Concerto pour la main gauche* by the theorist Daphne Leong and the concert pianist David Korevaar (2005: para 1), the aim of which was to reverse the usual direction and 'explore the value and limitations of performance for analysis'. But there was also a problem that has to do with the nature of the analysis in question, to which I now turn.

PERFORMER'S ANALYSIS

A particularly influential critique of Berry's *Musical Structure and Performance* came from John Rink (1990), yet another pianist, but one whose trajectory was significantly different from those I have so far described. His work proceeded in two linked but distinct directions, on the basis of which I organise the remainder of this chapter. The first is the attempt to formulate what Rink terms 'performer's analysis', as opposed to trying to apply what one might correspondingly term 'theorist's analysis' to performance. This needs unpacking. There is a small, and—as Doğantan-Dack pointed out[6]—in general theoretically unacknowledged, body of analytical writings by performers that directly address performance concerns. A prominent example is Alfred Brendel's *Thoughts and Afterthoughts*, in which he sets out what he calls Beethoven's technique of 'foreshortening'. This looks like standard theorist's analysis, in that it is based on the score and involves the addition of square brackets showing how Beethoven constructs his themes so that they embody a quickening pace of harmonic, motivic, and rhythmic change: the first eight bars of op. 2 no. 1, for example, consist of 'two two-bar units, two one-bar units, three half-bar units' (1976: 43). What makes the analysis different is the way it is used.

As Jennifer Tong (1994, chapter 4) has argued, from a theoretical point of view the puzzling thing about Brendel's approach is not so much the analysis itself, but the way he thinks about it. Instead of seeing foreshortening as one of many factors which condition Beethoven's style, as a theorist might, it is as if Brendel was obsessed by it: he describes it as '*the* driving force of [Beethoven's] sonata forms and a basic principle of his musical thought'. It is at this point that Tong makes the crucial observation that this is not an unbalanced or unprofessional example of theorist's analysis (a genre for which Brendel has little use[7]), but something basically different. It is a means of identifying and conceptualising the building and dissipation of tension, the convincing handling of which is fundamental to the performance of repertory such as this. It is in other words a means of facilitating the control of pacing, comparable (as Tong also observes) to Rachmaninoff's shadowy conception of the 'culminating' or 'peak point' around which he said he structured his performances—a point which may be 'at the end or in the middle, it may be loud or soft; but the performer must know how to approach it with *absolute calculation*, absolute precision, because if it slips by, then the whole construction crumbles' (Norris 1993: 78).

6. To avoid misunderstanding, I should say that Doğantan-Dack (2008: 305) uses the term 'performer's analysis' to designate representations that embody personal interpretation, which means that many of the examples I discuss in the following paragraphs would not meet her definition. I deal more specifically with the kind of performer's analysis she means in my Chapter 4.

7. 'I feel that few analytical insights have a direct bearing on performance, and that analysis should be the outcome of an intimate familiarity with the piece rather than an input of established concepts' (Brendel 1990: 249).

As performer's analysis, what is unusual about Brendel's theory of foreshortening is the extent to which (unlike Rachmaninoff's culminating point) it is theoretically developed, and more than this, the fact that he has published it: indeed, in the preface to *Thoughts and Afterthoughts*, Brendel 'invite[s] colleagues whose time is less limited than my own to test and pursue more thoroughly Beethoven's technique of foreshortening' (1976: 9), an invitation which has not been much taken up. For in other respects Brendel's approach shades into the many informal and largely non-discursive analytical strategies that performers use to support aspects of performance ranging from memorisation to pacing and other interpretive issues. Belonging to oral rather than written culture and disseminated largely through one-to-one teaching, these practices have recently been documented by the multidisciplinary team of Roger Chaffin, Gabriela Imreh, and Mary Crawford (Chaffin and Crawford are psychologists, while Imreh is a professional pianist). An audit by Imreh and Crawford of material mainly derived from published interviews brought to light a number of distinct memorisation strategies used by pianists, involving visual, aural, and 'muscle' memory, but many mentioned what the researchers term 'conceptual' memory, based on an awareness of structure.

The major element in the research process, however, was what I shall call an ethnographic investigation of the stages through which Imreh went in preparing her repertory for performance.[8] On the basis of this, the researchers developed a theoretical model according to which a variety of structural features are used in order to build up the cognitive schemata that control performance: there is an obvious comparison between this approach and that of Henry Shaffer and Eric Clarke, which I mentioned in Chapter 1. Memorisation strategies include 'switches' (points where a number of continuations are possible and it is essential to know which is the right one), and a series of performance cues that Chaffin and Imreh term 'basic', 'expressive', and 'interpretive'. The purpose of these is to support performance at a number of levels, from simple continuity (what Chaffin and Imreh call the 'security blanket') to the idiosyncratic qualities that identify the personal interpretation of a particular piece. According to the authors, 'structure is so important because it is the key to memorization as well as interpretation'. For this reason, while not all the pianist interviews mention the use of conceptual memory, Chaffin and Imreh conclude that it is in fact universal among professional pianists, claiming that that 'if the artists in these interviews had been asked about it directly they would have acknowledged this' (Chaffin et al 2002: 205, 236).

---

8. The terms 'ethnography' and 'ethnographic' are used in different ways by different people. Some reserve them for anthropological research in the tradition of Bronislaw Malinowski, the aim of which is to understand how the cultural practices of a given society inter-relate; central to such research is fieldwork conducted over an extended period. (Big-E ethnography, as this might be called, is the basis of the post-war discipline of ethnomusicology.) Others use it to designate a set of research methods—such as observation, participant observation, interviews, and questionnaire-based approaches—that may be incorporated within projects in a range of fields from sociology and social psychology to communication studies and history. In this book I use these terms in the second sense.

At the same time they comment that this kind of memory seems to be poorly understood by the pianists themselves: there is a lack of common terminology ('artists talked variously about form analysis, harmonic structure, analytic memory and structural memory'), and the pianists seemed curiously reticent about their use of it (235). Interestingly, while the aim of Chaffin and his co-workers was to document and theorise what performers do, there are already examples of pianists drawing on their work as a source of new strategies (Gerling 2011).

What the strategies adopted by all these pianists have in common is that they are directed at real-time action, and it is here that there is a fundamental distinction between theorist's analysis and performer's analysis. Theorists can ponder alternative options at their leisure, or debate them with colleagues: there is always time for second (or third) thoughts about whether the primary tone of the first movement of Mozart's Sonata K 331 is really $\hat{5}$ or $\hat{3}$. It has often been observed that the situation of performers is as different as could be: they have to commit themselves to one interpretation or the other, meeting their obligations alone and in real time (Gritten 2005: 138–39). In Chapter 1 I argued that most theorist's analysis does not construe music as intrinsically temporal, in the way that performance is, but treats it as some kind of non-temporal structure that is unfolded through time. But even if we concede the metaphorical equivalence between time and space, such that the one can be mapped unproblematically onto the other, there are very different perspectives from which the resulting topography can be viewed.

Mark Johnson and Steve Larson (2003) distinguish the perspective of the observer, who as it were flies above the landscape and can see the whole at once, from that of the participant, who is located on the ground and follows 'the path that defines a particular musical piece' (72). The observer's perspective, Johnson and Larson say, is predominantly that of the analyst, and from here all relationships within the piece can be seen at once: it is in this sense that they are spatial. In his essays from the 1890s Schenker several times invoked such a bird's-eye view, but in terms of his later theory a better image would be a series of hierarchically arrayed containers. This is an equally spatial conception, and it carries quite specific implications for the experiencing of time. At a structural break, you don't go directly from one moment to the next, but indirectly: it is necessary to traverse several levels of the hierarchy, resulting in a motion that is more vertical than horizontal. By contrast, the pedestrian perspective of the participant means experiencing the music as a continuous unfolding from one moment to the next, horizontally as it were: this is what Levinson (1997) calls the concatenationist position. Johnson and Larson associate the participant's perspective with the listener, but as Leslie Lewis (2006: 2) has pointed out, performers also work from note to note.

Now the point I am driving at is that, whether we are talking about motifs, phrases, or formal sections, the observer's or analytical perspective throws the weight of interpretation onto the segments as wholes. Conversely it de-emphasises the transitions between successive segments, which become invisible in rather the same way as those shadowy passages in scores that are split up between first- and second-time bars. From the concatenationist perspective, by contrast, a succession of transitions is what music *is*. And my claim is that performance (and listening too, but I shall not pursue that here) is to a very large extent an art of transitioning—in other words, it is oriented to precisely the horizontal dimension of music that the spatialised, hierarchical models of theorist's analysis de-emphasise. It is this dimension of real-time transitioning that performer's analysis foregrounds, from the switches and cues identified by Chaffin and Imreh to the series of points of high emotion that emerged from a study by John Sloboda and Andreas Lehmann (2001): the peak emotional points identified by listeners to performances of Chopin's E minor Prelude (op. 28 no. 4) often clustered around musical phrase boundaries, and as interviews with the pianists revealed, they had often been deliberately planned as part of an interpretive strategy. Again, superimposed tempo profiles from multiple performances tend to show the greatest variance at points of transition. In short, transitions are places where meaning is both concentrated and open to performers' intervention: there is a parallel with Lawrence Kramer's observation that meaning 'is not diffused evenly throughout a work of music or anything else, but distributed unevenly in peaks and valleys. The peaks are the points of endowment from which meaning extends to "cover" the work as a whole' (2011: 182). Theorist's analysis, by contrast, assumes that meaning is concentrated in coherent wholes rather than the transitions between them, and that is one of the reasons it often seems irrelevant in performance.

The nature of performer's analysis now falls into place. Read as theorist's analysis, Brendel's foreshortening looks crudely reductive. But redescribed in terms of performer's analysis, it facilitates real-time pacing through summarising such musical dimensions as harmony, motive, and rhythm) into a single representation: for Brendel, at least, it is what from the theorist's perspective seems like crude reduction that makes the approach valuable. And to return to Rink, with whom this discussion started, his own version of performer's analysis can be characterised in the same way. He employs, among other things, what he calls 'intensity curves': these are adapted from Wallace Berry's earlier book *Structural Functions in Music* (where however they are applied to scores rather than performances), and Rink describes them as 'a graphic representation of the music's ebb and flow, its "contour" in time, determined by all active elements (harmony, melody, rhythm, dynamics, etc.) working either independently, in sync, or out of phase with one another to create the changing degrees of energy and thus the overall shape' (1999: 234).

In a publication now almost fifteen years old, I complained that you couldn't decompose such intensity curves into their parts, or as I put it, 'there is no way in which the reader, or performer, can disassemble the contribution of the various musical parameters to the summary graph and so reconstruct the experience of the music that motivates it' (Cook 1999a: 15). In saying that, I now think I was treating these curves as if they were theorist's analysis. After all, Rink offers them not as insightful interpretations of the music in their own right, but as a model of how it is possible to set about creating an interpretation and handling a performance. The question of decomposition does not arise because the curve is not meant to contain information about each individual parameter in a form that could be communicated to someone else: rather it articulates or provides a handle on knowledge that has been developed through practice and is held as much in the performer's body as his mind—or hers, since Rink offers this as a technique for other performers to try for themselves. Rink also situates the use of intensity curves within a set of other approaches that range from the identification of formal divisions to rhythmic reduction: the toolbox approach reflects the fact that in performance, as in most walks of life, people need to find and customise approaches with which they are personally comfortable. As an example of performer's analysis that is published in a widely disseminated, student-friendly handbook, Rink's approach can be seen as an attempt to bridge the normally distinct domains of public, music-theoretical discourse and the essentially private activity documented by Chaffin and his co-workers.

Seen in this light, the prescriptiveness of dominant music-theoretical approaches to performance results from trying to make too direct a link between two domains, writing and playing, that have common elements but are in key respects epistemologically incommensurable. A few commentators, recognising this, have sought principled ways of bringing the two domains into alignment. Bethany Lowe (2003), for example, posits the existence of a third domain which she calls the Interpretation: she imagines it as the apex of a triangle, of which the Analysis and the Performance form the other two corners, with the Interpretation feeding into both, but without there being any direct contact between the latter. This is an attractive approach, in that it puts performance and analysis 'on an equal level, thus diffusing any power relationships that might be thought to exist—or that scholars might attempt to assert—between them' (93). The difficulty as I see it is one that Gilbert Ryle might have diagnosed: embodied neither in the practice of performance nor in the symbols of analysis, the Interpretation becomes a metaphysical construct, a kind of phantom force field generated by the actual domains of analysis and performance. In short, the approach creates a spurious stability out of what I see as an inherently dynamic and unstable relationship between analysis and performance.

Another search for a principled way to bring analysis and performance into alignment was conducted by Jerrold Levinson (1993), though one does not get the impression he ever intended to find one. He expressed it rather differently: his question is whether any performance interpretation (PI) can unambiguously specify a corresponding critical interpretation (CI). And his answer is that it cannot, because PIs invariably under-specify CIs, so that for any PI, there must always be another CI that it could equally well be specifying. His approach betrays its textualist grounding in the exclusive focus on how PIs under-specify CIs (why not the other way round?), and it doesn't help that the CIs he has in mind are commentaries of the Anthony Hopkins variety, intended for the musically unlettered reader, whereas more technically specified interpretations—such as those discussed by Joel Lester in his 1995 article 'Performance and analysis'—might have produced quite different results. (In a sense what Levinson is arguing is that you can't make the kind of associations between analyses and performances that

Lester in fact does make.) But I do not see these issues as invalidating Levinson's overall conclusion: 'Though ideally there should be, and often is, substantial inter-action between critical-analytic and performative-practical notions about a piece of music, the former are not equivalent to the latter, nor are they strictly implicit in them' (1993: 57).

Rink sometimes uses the heavily loaded term 'translate' for the relationship between structure and performance: for instance a paper of which he is lead author describes some structural features that are likely to condition performance and refers to the 'ways in which musicians apprehend, translate into action, and ultimately subsume [them] within broader expressive strategies' (Rink, Spiro, and Gold 2011: 271). The use of this term might suggest the kind of easy mapping from analysis to performance against which I have been arguing, but this is not what is intended: indeed in the review of *Musical Structure and Performance* to which I referred, one of Rink's criticisms (1990) was that Berry's approach involved 'too simplistic a translation from analysis to performance' (321). In this context the idea of translation, then, has to be understood in the complex or strong sense in which Walter Benjamin theorised it: Lawrence Rosenwald, himself a translation theorist, cites this as the right way of thinking about the relationship between scores and performances, summarising it as 'we do not know the original, do not and cannot know it in se, and...come to know it precisely by means of reflect-ing on its translations'. When Rink (2002) says the aim of performer's analysis is 'to discover the music's "shape", as opposed to structure' (39), then, this could be glossed as the need to translate structure to shape in the strong sense of rethinking or re-understanding it. And after warning against simplistic mappings from anal-ysis to performance, Rink and his co-authors comment, 'That does not mean that musical structure as conventionally understood is wholly irrelevant to performers or listeners—only that the relationship is far more complex and less exclusive than some have assumed' (Rink, Spiro, and Gold 2011: 268).

Such a conclusion, which is in effect a restatement of Levinson's, identifies a middle path between the equally absurd propositions that musical structure as understood by theorists has nothing to do with performance, and that it has every-thing to do with performance. It means that on the one hand we don't have to be as sweeping about the usefulness of theorist's analysis to performers as Brendel is, while on the other we can expect that—for those performers who do find it useful—its application will be to a greater or lesser degree individualistic, idiosyn-cratic, and contingent. Even for a performer-theorist such as Schmalfeldt, on the evidence of her 2011 chapter, the analysis of the theory classroom and research article constitutes just one element in the arsenal of interpretive approaches. Similarly Rothstein's article 'Like falling off a log' (2005: paras 23, 20), which extracts some principles from the way he handles rubato in playing Chopin's A major Prelude, is an eclectic mix of established theory, quasi-theoretical impro-visation (at one point he invents the concept of 'temporal viscosity'), and graphic metaphor: the 'falling off a log' of his title is intended to convey the idea of 'sliding or falling in response to gravity', and at one point the log develops 'a protruding bit of bark' that slows the fall. One might say that these are examples of theorist's analysis being rethought as performer's analysis, as well as combined with quite different approaches. All this is consistent with Doğantan-Dack 's claim that 'a particular performer's perspective... will involve many different kinds of assumptions, information, images and associations, which will contribute in unique ways to the formation of her performance interpretations, and performance signature' (2008: 303). And she adds: 'the different kinds and modes of knowledge... do not necessarily form a hierarchy of importance'.

PERFORMANCE ANALYSIS

Rink's efforts to formulate performer's analysis as something distinct from theorist's analysis has been complemented by a second approach, which has been and perhaps still is as characteristic of British scholarship in this field as the analysis-to-performance approach has been of North American scholarship. (Rink is himself American but has been based in the UK since his postgraduate days.) Instead of being seen as the beneficiary of analysis, performance is now seen as an object of analysis, and this is the approach which the remainder of my book focusses on. The difference between the two approaches is profound: at a stroke, performance analysis—as I shall term this approach—removes the authoritarian prescriptiveness of the analysis-to-performance approach, since performers now appear in the role of informants, consultants, or co-researchers. And as that suggests, one of the main research methods that this opens up is the ethnographic study of live performance. Such work ranges from questionnaire-based and interview approaches to a wide variety of observational studies involving situations ranging from teaching to rehearsal and performance: performer-researchers carry out autoethnographic (self-observational) work, as well as what in ethnomusicology is known as participant observation. Indeed all such work might until recently have been described as the ethnomusicology of WAM: it is a sign of the changes being wrought by the heightened profile of performance studies that it now seems more appropriate to think of it as musicological work that draws on ethnographical techniques.

I will have more to say in Chapter 8 about ethnographic approaches, but the work with which I am here concerned draws more heavily on another approach: the analysis of recorded performances. Given the existence of well over a century's worth of recordings, which have become increasingly accessible in recent years (through a combination of generally small companies reissuing old recordings, Amazon resellers, eBay, online sound archives, and YouTube), there is clearly a huge field of investigation to be opened up here. Doing so, however, involves solving, or at least finding a way round, a number of significant problems. I have already mentioned one: recordings are like any other historical documents in that they provide selective and incomplete information, and knowing what can be deduced from them depends on knowing about the circumstances of their production and circulation. In short, there are issues of discographical source criticism. A second problem is that it is in the nature of sound reproduction technology that it divorces sounds from their social and historical contexts: the same might be said of scores, and one of the main criticisms made of music theorists is that they attempt to interpret music without taking sufficient account of context. Recordings, then, provide an opportunity to make the same mistakes all over again. Both of these issues will recur in this book. But there is a third that I would like to address now, and this is the role of approaches derived from score-based analysis in analysing recorded performances. In essence my claim is that, given the embeddedness in the discipline of the page-to-stage or analysis-to-performance approach, it is all too easy to fall into its mirror image: a stage-to-page or performance-to-analysis approach in which 'analysis' is still conceived as theorist's analysis, resulting in the replication of many of the problems I have been discussing in this chapter. And since my intention is to criticise, I shall set out what is at issue in relation to a publication of my own that goes back to 1995.

This was a study of two of Furtwängler's recordings of the first movement of Beethoven's Ninth Symphony, dating from 1951 (with the Bayreuth Festival Orchestra) and 1953 (with the Vienna Philharmonic); like all of Furtwängler's recordings of this piece, they were live, not studio recordings (Shirakawa 1992: 482). My project was prompted by what I felt was the peculiar and compelling quality of Furtwängler's tempos, which surge and ebb, sometimes over immensely long time spans, resulting in a very characteristic quality of monumentality. Given Furtwängler's known admiration for Schenker, my hunch was that there was a connection to be made here, and so my approach was to chart the constantly changing tempos in the chosen recordings, and match them up with Schenker's 1912 monograph on the symphony. (The vintage of the article is betrayed by the fact that I explained how I had played the CDs using my computer's CD-ROM drive, tapping a key at every half bar while I listened and using a short, custom-written program to log the times of the taps.) I noted, for instance, how Schenker segmented the development into four sections or subdivisions, which he saw as the necessary basis for performance interpretation. On the one hand, he says, 'the performance of the Development will be the better the more its subdivisions…are given clear expression as such'. But on the other, the subdivisions must be integrated into a continuous temporal flow. It is necessary, Schenker writes,

> to summon all powers to direct one's consciousness immediately, exactly upon entering the first subdivision—thus as early as bars 180–181!—, toward the cadence of bar 192ff., which awaits beyond the 'mountain pass' of bars 188–194; that is, one must organize the performance of the subdivision according to a kind of bird's-eye view, a premonition of the overall course of the subdivision from its first tonic up to its last cadence. Only then will the cadence be performed as a cadence to the whole subdivision and not, as we unfortunately hear all too often, as a new unit in itself (1992: 97).

While his 'bird's-eye view' corresponds again to what Johnson and Larson called the observer's perspective, Schenker is in effect asking the performer to

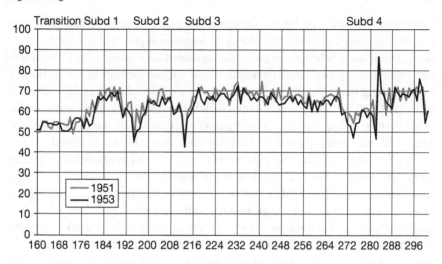

Figure 2.1 Tempo graph of Furtwängler's 1951 and 1953 recordings of Beethoven, Symphony no. 9, 1st mvmt. development section (Cook 1993: 111)

combine aspects of the participant's and the observer's perspectives. (Schmalfeldt [2011: 215] does the same: 'why should we not imagine that it is possible for performers and analysts alike to experience the present and the past simultaneously within a musical work, even when thinking about its future goals?…Singers and instrumentalists cannot help but remember where they have been musically and where they will be going, because their vocal cords, their fingers, their breathing will remind them'.) The reader will be less than astonished to learn that what Schenker asked for is exactly what I found in Furtwängler's two recordings—which, incidentally, were very similar at everything except the most local level, thereby refuting Paul Henry Lang's claim that Furtwängler's 'inability to keep to a steady tempo' was not 'the result of deliberate intention'; rather, Lang insisted, it resulted from the 'lack of the sort of orchestral discipline we expect from our conductors' (1978: 22).

The article came with a series of tempo graphs covering the whole movement, of which that for the development is shown in Figure 2.1: the length of each minim beat is represented on the vertical axis, and as this is a tempo graph—as opposed to a duration graph—higher on the chart means faster tempo and hence shorter duration. (I used an arbitrary scale for the vertical axis, but such graphs often employ metronome marks.) As may be seen, the beginning of each subdivision, as also of the following recapitulation, is preceded by a rallentando or caesura (bars 195, 213, 274, 300), with Furtwängler regaining speed as each subdivision starts. Actually there is nothing surprising about this, given that Beethoven has marked the first two 'ritenuto' in the score, while the third coincides with a new theme. But it can also be seen that, for each section, Furtwängler either maintains the tempo or creates a pattern of accelerando followed by rallentando, in other words an arch-shaped profile, so subsuming each section within a single, continuous gesture. This means he avoids the trap into which less analytically informed performers fall, seduced by the variegated surface of Beethoven's composition into creating form-defining rallentandi or caesurae at points that have no structural significance. Schenker in particular censures Sir George Grove, the author of a handbook on Beethoven's symphonies as well as founder of the dictionary, for describing bar 253 as the beginning of a new section: 'such hearing', Schenker sniffs (1992: 103). That, however, is exactly where Mengelberg slams on the brakes in his 1940 recording with the Concertgebouw, just as he also does at bars 192 and 210, in this way creating precisely the bitty effect that Schenker deplored.

My claim, then, was that there is a correlation between Furtwängler's large-scale tempo profiles and the spans of Schenker's analysis: the term 'span' invokes the later theory, of which Schenker had no coherent conception in 1912, but equally expresses the kind of long-range vision vividly conveyed by Schenker's talk of mountain passes. (Furtwängler [1985: 3] himself spoke of Schenker's *Fernhören*, or long-range listening.) If one thinks of Schenker's analysis in terms of the traditional analytical representations based on nested slurs (sometimes called 'umbrella diagrams'), then there is a visual resemblance to the shapes in the tempo chart. To think of the relationship as an iconic one, however, is not really correct. Furtwängler conveys the structure of the subdivisions through a combination of caesurae, which are traditional signifiers of points of division, and the kind of continuous profiles that Eric Clarke had in mind when, in a ground-breaking article from 1988, he listed the 'generative sources of expression' in performance: the first was 'graduated timing changes... used to indicate the group structure of the music, group boundaries being marked by maxima in the timing profile' (17). I went further than that, arguing that since an arch profile is a regular pattern, creating an expectation of continuation, it is possible to distinguish structural spans from purely local, or rhetorical, divisions, and that this enabled Furtwängler to convey the operation of distinct hierarchical levels in a way that, in 1912, Schenker was unable to represent theoretically. That may have been a display of excessive structuralist enthusiasm, but in any case I have explained enough to support the points I now want to make about this work.

I felt, and continue to feel, that my analysis supported the hypothesis that there was a relationship between Schenker's analysis and Furtwängler's performance: in matters of detail Furtwängler often did something different from what Schenker specified, but in terms of large-scale structure the correlations are strong. However I would now wish to offer two major qualifications. The first is the extent to which my entire approach was pervaded by structuralist values. I argued that far from being the 'dyed-in-the-wool romantic, favoring arbitrary and highly subjective procedures in tempo, dynamics and phrasing' as which Lang depicted him (1978: 17), Furtwängler was himself a structuralist: at one point I described his performances as 'analyses in sound' (Cook 1995: 120). I structured my article as a confirmation of Peter Pirie's unsupported claim (1980) that 'his interpretation analyzed the structure' (49). Moreover I cast Mengelberg in the role of fall guy: whereas 'Furtwängler is structuring tempo hierarchically', I wrote, Mengelberg 'treats tempo modification as principally a means for creating nuance' (1995: 120), and I concurred with Pirie's judgement (1980: 10) that 'whereas in every Furtwängler modification of phrasing or tempo there was a purpose, in Mengelberg's they seemed often to be merely ornamental or even pointless'. (At least I then added a footnote: 'But also refreshingly playful, I would add, precisely because of the way they contradict expectations'. The telling thing, of course, is that this remark could not be accommodated in the main argument.) The article offers no justification for the structuralist methodology, or for the unstated but ubiquitous identification of structure and value. It simply takes both for granted.

The other qualification is less self-criticism and more statement of fact. The relationship between Schenker and Furtwängler is very much a special case. Furtwängler read Schenker's monograph on the Ninth Symphony shortly after it was published, probably in 1913, and was so impressed that in 1919 he sought Schenker out in person, leading to regular meetings at which they would discuss repertory Furtwängler was preparing (Federhofer 1985: 106–7; Jonas 2003: 134). Given this, it is not surprising that there are many resonances between the two men's thinking on music generally, or in their approach to the Ninth Symphony in particular: Furtwängler, for whom rubato was the key to Beethoven interpretation and a barometer of the performer's sincerity,[9] must have repeatedly asked himself how he could translate (Rink's word again) Schenker's insights into performance. My project, then, was to retrace Furtwängler's footsteps. The point, however, is that this is a highly unusual situation in the analysis of performance.

I have already mentioned that, in an important contribution that appeared in the same collection as mine, Lester encouraged theorists to take more notice of actual performances instead of delivering prescriptions for imaginary ones. Interestingly, he presented this not as a matter of changing the musical object but rather of bringing a new resource to music theory: 'acknowledging that performances are relevant to analysis', he wrote, will 'dramatically broaden the repertoire that theorists call upon when making analytical assertions', since there are many more recordings than published analyses (1995: 213). And he did what Levinson says can't be done: he examined published analyses by Schenker, Schachter, and Rothstein of a range of core repertory items in order to identify interpretive options, and then matched these up to alternative commercial recordings. Alan Dodson employed a similar approach in a much more recent article on recordings of Beethoven's Sonata op. 81a, identifying alternative strategies on the basis of Schenker's analyses and then correlating them with seven recordings ranging from the 1930s to the 1990s. Dodson (2008: 110) is careful not to claim too much for his approach, emphasising that he is talking about 'correlation rather than causation'. In neither his work nor Lester's, then, is there any suggestion that the performers played as they did because they knew the analyses in question. But that is exactly the point. It is taken for granted that Schenkerian and other structuralist methods are directly applicable to performance in general, so that historicising

9. Furtwängler (1991: 35–36 and 1977: 52), where he writes, 'it is possible to tell from the treatment of the so-called *rubato*, as from a barometer reading, whether or not the impulses provoking it...are genuine'.

questions about who knew what become unnecessary. Otherwise there would be no rationale for the approach.

In any specific instance, this approach may well be productive. That is true of both the articles I have just cited. It is also true of a more recent article in which Dodson (2009) uses Harald Krebs's theory of metrical dissonance, along with other approaches, to analyse recordings of Chopin mazurkas by Ignacy Paderewski, who during his lifetime was supposedly the highest-earning of all pianists (and briefly prime minister of Poland) but is not generally considered to have recorded well. Dodson's approach is to identify metrical layers and dissonances based on composed accents, whether specifically marked or implied, and then to match this analytical framework to the recordings: the aim is to determine how far Paderewski's playing conforms to the composed structure as an analyst might interpret it, or alternatively undermines it, or achieves a parallel effect but through different means—or, for that matter, creates a quite new effect that has no correlate in the score. The analytical approach makes many aspects of Paderewski's playing interpretable, and Dodson is open to the variety of relationships that may hold between structure and performance, as well as to their creative potential. Indeed his aim is to vindicate a performer who has been widely disparaged on grounds similar to those on which Lang disparaged Furtwängler. But how Dodson does this tends to reinscribe the structuralist paradigm: just as with Furtwängler—but not Mengelberg—Paderewski's apparently arbitrary mannerisms turn out after all to be structurally grounded. Like my account of Furtwängler, Dodson's account of Paderewski rehearses one of the most characteristic music-theoretical tropes: it is the prodigal son's apparently transgressive behaviour that makes his reclamation for the structuralist canon so satisfying.

The danger with the structuralist approach is that it becomes so entrenched as to be circular or self-validating. A particularly overt example comes from an article by Robert Wason on Webern's Piano Variations op. 27, which attempts to reconcile an analysis based on the composition's serial organisation with the performance indications in Peter Stadlen's copy of the score: Stadlen premiered the piece in 1937, and marked up his score while being coached by the composer. (Universal Editions published a facsimile of the marked-up score in 1979.) Wason's problem is that serial structure and performance markings frequently do not match up. At the beginning of the first movement, for example, Webern wanted the top line brought out as an expressive melody, yet it cuts across the serial organisation. In short, seen from the serial perspective, Webern was asking for a non-structural, or anti-structural, performance. One response to this might be to change the perspective. There are many traditional aspects to the Piano Variations—melody, harmonic and textural build-up, even regular patterns of phrasing in the first movement—and these are much easier to relate to Webern's prescriptions: to see these as the structural correlates of performance, however, would be to settle for a much looser, less coherent analytical interpretation than serialism offers, and Wason does not consider such an option. Instead he adheres unflinchingly to the assumption that serial structure and performance must be linked, and he puts forward a number of ways in which the offending facts might be explained away.

First, Wason suggests, the fact that we can't at present explain that melody line in serial terms doesn't preclude the possibility that one day we will: 'the derivation of these "melody" notes is itself an interesting phenomenon for future study, although…it has so far eluded systematic explanation' (1987: 95). Second, he argues that the structure is so explicit that it doesn't much matter how you play it: 'The music is so clear that the interpreter may occasionally phrase *against* formal segmentations of the music without placing that dimension of the music in jeopardy of total loss (although obviously one must have a clear understanding of just what one is "playing against")'. Similarly he refers to performance indications that 'produce a tension against the structural segmentations, while certainly assuming their existence' (102–3). The final clauses of both these quotations invoke the third and most telling strategy, which might be summarised as 'heads I win, tails you lose'. If the performance corresponds to the structure, then that confirms the need to understand performance in terms of structure. If it doesn't, then this deviation confirms the need to understand performance in terms of structure.

The basic problem is that, instead of approaching the performance inductively and drawing out of it those dimensions that help to make sense of it, Wason is thinking in terms of theorist's analysis: he is attempting to map Webern's performance indications onto a prefabricated structural conception that is based on the score. But if your analytical approach is to map score and performance onto one another, and to ascribe significance to what maps, then by definition you are filtering out everything that won't map. You gain a fast track to getting publishable results, but you rule out far too much of what you are investigating and diminish your chances of making unexpected discoveries. That is an unwise thing to do with a musical field of study as young as performance analysis. The conclusion I draw from this is that seeking answers to existing questions that arise out of the structuralist paradigm may be less important for the development of the field than seeking new questions, as well as new ways of answering them. That is what the remainder of this book is about.

3

What the Theorist Heard

AFFECTING THE SENTIMENT

I said that Schenkerian performance pedagogy is primarily the creation of post-war Schenkerians, and that it does not have a straightforward relationship to Schenker's own thinking. In this chapter I address this issue head on, my purpose being not to undermine Schenkerian performance pedagogy—its value does not depend on its genealogy—but to introduce what I see as the elephant in the room, the dimension that is missing from analysis-to-performance theory: the dimension of style. In essence my claim is that what analysis-to-performance theory presents as a paradigm, a foundational way of thinking about performance in general, is more correctly seen as a stylistic approach to performance that has long historical roots but that became the norm only in the second half of the twentieth century. And I make that claim by arguing that Schenker's own views about how music should go in performance, which reflected the stylistic universe of Vienna at the turn of the twentieth century, were quite different from what modern Schenkerians have read into his writings. How then did the performances that Schenker heard go? When he analysed music, how did he imagine it going?

Born in 1868 in the far-flung Habsburg province of Galicia, Heinrich Schenker entered the University of Vienna in 1884 to study law. He found time however to study in parallel at the Vienna Conservatory between 1887 and 1889, and on graduating from the university in 1890 threw himself into a reasonably successful musical career as a critic, composer, and pianist specialising in accompaniment. The highlight of his performing career was when he toured with the Dutch baritone and Bach specialist Johannes Messchaert in 1899, filling in for Messchaert's usual accompanist Julius Röntgen, and one can gain a sense of Schenker's allegiances as a performer from his critical writings: essays dating from 1895 and 1896 contain listings of great contemporary performers, including—for example—the baritone Francesco de Andrade, the violinist Joseph Joachim, the cellists Hugo Becker and Julius Klengel, the clarinettist Richard Mühlfeld, and the pianists Anton Rubinstein, Eugen d'Albert, Emil von Sauer, Josef Hoffmann, Moriz Rosenthal, and Alfred Grünfeld (Federhofer 1990: 130, 326).

This is a roll call of what are sometimes called 'old school' performers, some but not all of them associated with the Brahms circle to which Schenker had distant connections, and they stand for a kind of musicianship that was on the decline after the First World War and defunct after the Second. In 1894 Schenker wrote essays about two of them, Rubinstein and d'Albert (Federhofer 1990: 82–84, 103–9, 115–21): both were composers as well as pianists, and in Rubinstein's case that is what Schenker mainly focusses on. But it was only later that d'Albert's career as a composer took off, and so in this case Schenker's main focus is performance. And from the essays we learn, for example, that in comparison to Rubinstein's highly subjective playing, that of d'Albert is objective. This is possibly the last word a modern critic would apply to d'Albert, but Schenker puts a little flesh on the bones. Rubinstein, he says, plays mercurially, as if creating the music in the moment of performance, whereas in d'Albert's playing there is a quality of reflection: the heat of the moment has cooled, creating a 'well-tempered, balanced mood that dissolves, sucks in all changing moods' (118). And in an essay from two years later Schenker draws a similar comparison between d'Albert and Röntgen, who 'views the events too much in isolation' (328): d'Albert, by contrast, understands 'purely musical' relationships much better, and in this way has a more secure grasp of the music's 'higher poetic function'. But it is hard to know quite how any of this might translate into sound.

The best way to understand how Schenker thought music should go, of course, would be to hear a recording of his own playing—but though there was at one time talk of it, no such recording was ever made.[1] There is a contemporary description of his playing by Herman Roth, who again used the term objectivity, along with lack of vanity, strong conception of the whole, intellectual penetration, and artistic intuition.[2] (Roth wrote this in 1931 but had known Schenker since 1912.) However this presents the same problem as with Schenker's contrast between Rubinstein's and d'Albert's playing: how can you translate such vocabulary into any real sense of performance effect? I would even say the same of William Rothstein's attempt (1984) to characterise Schenker's playing on the basis of the copious performance markings written into personal copies of piano music, largely for teaching purposes: illuminating though these markings undoubtedly are in terms of Schenker's thinking, interpretive values, and pianistic allegiances, what they cannot convey is the quality of sound as experienced, the balancing of a chord or nuancing of a melody, in short, the things that cannot be captured on paper yet lie at the heart of performance style. In this way, if we are to gain a concrete sense of how Schenker thought that music should go, the evidence of what he wrote has to be supplemented, despite the limitations of early technology, by that of contemporary recordings. Most of the performers on Schenker's lists left recordings, whether in the form of piano rolls or the acoustic media of cylinders and discs, but in order to gain a better sense of how such recordings might have related to Schenker's own experience, we need to line up recordings by performers

1. Federhofer (1985: 100, 138).

2. Herman Roth, 'Bekenntnis zu Heinrich Schenker', *Hamburger Nachrichten*, 17 September 1931 (Ernst Oster Collection, New York Public Library, File 2, 84).

whom Schenker admired with pieces about whose performance Schenker wrote in detail.

This is not hard as regards orchestral music—indeed my comparison of Schenker's writing on the Ninth Symphony with Furtwängler's recordings is an illustration of it—but here I am concerned less with issues of large-scale interpretation than with a close-grained sense of how the music goes from moment to moment, the makeup of its fabric as sound. And if we turn to the more intimate medium of piano music as the obvious source for this sort of comparison, then there are two possibilities, and as it happens they both involve piano rolls by d'Albert.[3] One is Beethoven's Sonata op. 101, the subject of Schenker's 1921 *Erläuterungsausgabe*, which includes extensive commentary on performance; d'Albert recorded the sonata twice, on 2 June 1913 for Welte-Mignon (issued as rolls 2972–2973), and around 1927 for Aeolian Duo-Art (rolls 0273–0275). We also have Schenker's own extensively annotated playing copy of this sonata,[4] not to mention his edition of the Beethoven sonatas, so these materials could together support a far more extended study than there is room for in this chapter. Accordingly I focus only on the second: Schubert's Impromptu op. 90 no. 3 (D 899), which d'Albert recorded on 19 May 1905 for Welte-Mignon (roll 422).

Musicologists tend to be on the one hand insufficiently critical of sound recordings, not appreciating the limitations in what can be deduced from them about past performance culture, but on the other hand over-critical of piano rolls, dismissing them as intrinsically unreliable. In both cases the basic problem is ignorance. I shall come back to source-critical issues in sound recordings in Chapter 5, but will briefly consider piano rolls now. In the first place, it is necessary to distinguish what I shall refer to as the standard pianola (the terminology is applied loosely) from the much more sophisticated reproducing piano. Pianola rolls are the pre-digital equivalent of MIDI files: they were manufactured in factories on the basis of scores, using nominal timing values—with each crotchet twice as long as each quaver—and with no dynamic information. The pianola is better thought of as a musical instrument than as an equivalent to the gramophone: you played it, operating pedals, sliders, or levers in real time to control the speed of playback and dynamic levels and so supply the missing expression. ('Simple as they are to manipulate, the expressive devices of the Pianola-Piano are intensely susceptible to the temperament of any true music-lover', read an advertisement by the Orchestrelle Co. in the March 1914 issue of *Strand Magazine* [p. 81]. 'The emotions with which the music inspires you are reflected in your interpretation and give you an individuality that is impossible with any other piano-playing instrument'.) Pianola rolls accordingly have nothing to tell us about period performance

3. In principle the list could be extended to include Bach's Chromatic Fantasy and Fugue and Beethoven's Sonata op. 111, which d'Albert recorded using the Duca system, but I have been unable to source these rolls, and even if they could be obtained, playback would be a major problem.

4. Oswald Jonas Memorial Collection, University of California, Riverside, Box 26, Folder 4.

practices—except, of course, insofar as playing the pianola was itself a performance practice, a participatory mode of musical consumption that musicologists
have generally ignored.

By contrast, the rolls used by reproducing pianos were created through real-time
performance, and the aim of the technology was to provide an exact reproduction
of the original performance when the roll was played back. There were, of course,
compromises of various kinds, and it is here that differences between brands of
reproducing piano—or the same brands at differing stages of development—
become crucial. In some cases, such as the Hupfeld Phonola system, dynamic
values were recorded but not played back automatically: as with the pianola,
you controlled dynamics by means of a slider, using a wavy line printed on the
roll as a guide. In other systems, including the later Hupfeld Triphonola as well
as the Welte-Mignon and Duo-Art systems, dynamic playback was automated,
but represented a simplified version of what had originally been played: in the
Welte-Mignon system, for example, there was one dynamic level for the bottom
half of the keyboard and another for the top, sometimes resulting in a remarkably
convincing effect. And whereas, until the LP era, sound recordings were limited to
a playing length of around four minutes—which is why many early pianists, like
Grünfeld, are represented only by their encore pieces—piano rolls made it possible
to record extended sonata movements, such as Beethoven's op. 101. That makes it
ironic that Schubert's op. 90 no. 3 was one of d'Albert's favorite encores: he played
it in Liszt's version, transposed up a semitone from G♭ major to G♮, and rebarred
from 4/2 to 2/2, with the tune coming back in octaves in the final section.

Early sound recordings advertise their distance from the present day through
the snaps, crackles, and pops that have become potent symbols of nostalgia. By
contrast reproducing pianos sound deceptively life-like: as they play, the automatic depression of the keys creates an uncanny sensation that d'Albert's ghost is
seated at the keyboard. But there are in fact many source-critical problems. One
is that, as with sound recordings following the introduction of magnetic tape,
piano rolls could be cleaned up. Fortunately d'Albert's recording of Schubert's
op. 90 no. 3 was made when the Welte company had just introduced their new
system and embarked on a major programme of recording the leading European
pianists of the day: the production schedule evidently did not permit much editing, for—unlike later Welte-Mignon rolls—those from 1905 contain many wrong
notes. Another promising research project, then, might be European pianism in
1905, as recorded by Welte.

Other problems, however, are insoluble. You are recording on a piano that has
a particular tonal quality, in a room that has its own acoustic quality, and these
things are not captured by a piano roll. All the same, they leave their mark on the
dimensions of the performance that *are* captured: timing, articulation, and (to
whatever degree) dynamics. You then play the roll back on an instrument that has
its own tonal qualities and is located in a quite different acoustic space. As a result,
you end up hearing something that corresponds only in part to the original performance. It is perhaps more than anything these problems, coupled with poorly
maintained playback instruments and a failure to distinguish the best systems

from the not-so-good ones, that result in complaints such as Charles Rosen's: 'I have always disliked…piano rolls as they never seemed to me to represent the variety of tone quality that I have always admired in the finest playing' (2003: 147). That may be fair comment, but it is here that the issue of source criticism comes in. If your aim is to learn about past piano performance practices, then you should not listen to a piano roll in the way you might listen to a CD, as if piano rolls allowed some kind of time travelling. As with other historical sources, a more informed and analytical approach is required. The aim is to extract the evidence that is reliable, and discard what is not. We know that nuance based on tonal effect is unreliable, and that dynamics are simplified; by contrast the evidence of relative timing should be reliable, within bounds of temporal resolution that are variable but generally good enough, and though the interactions between timing, dynamics, tonal qualities, and room acoustic mean that we are working with incomplete information, that is in the nature of doing historical research.[5] It is for this reason that my discussion of d'Albert's playing of Schubert's op. 90 no. 3 is based almost exclusively on tempo.

In the last chapter I mentioned Rothstein's comparison of Chopin's rubato and falling off a log. The idea that there is some kind of relationship between musical performance and gravity is an old one; in the 1880s, for example, the piano pedagogue and denigrator of music theorists Adolph Christiani (1885) wrote that 'the accentuation of a slurred phrase may be exemplified by the throwing of a stone' (160) and illustrated his point by a little diagram consisting of a typographer's hand symbol and two notes, which look remarkably like stones, separated by dots. He continued, 'The opening extreme has the energy of throwing; the terminal note, that of contact; and the *legato* motion within should be as smooth and even as the flight of a stone'. And though few music theorists are probably familiar with Christiani's work, his image entered the theoretical mainstream through its appropriation by Edward T. Cone in his *Musical Form and Musical Performance*, which in Chapter 2 I cited as an important early contribution to analysis-to-performance theory. Again it is employed to describe the musical phrase, which—in the tradition of Riemannian theory, of which more in Chapter 6—Cone described as 'a microcosm of the composition' (1968: 26): he divided the phrase into an initial downbeat (in Cone's image it is a ball rather than a stone that is thrown), a period of motion, and a cadential downbeat as the ball is caught.

Cone applied this model not only at the level of the four-bar phrase but at higher levels too. For example, he analyses the sixteen bars of Chopin's A major Prelude as a single ball-throwing motion that encompasses a series of smaller ball-throwing motions. He does not translate this directly into directions for performance: rather he says how the music is, as theorists do, and implies that this must be the basis of

5. Musicologically informed discussions of piano rolls as historical sources may be found in Leech-Wilkinson 2009a (chapter 3, paragraphs 69–81) and Peres da Costa (2012: 9–13, 24–40). As Peres da Costa explains, there are aspects of piano roll technology—including Welte's recording of dynamics—that are likely to remain unclear: manufacturers viewed such details as industrial secrets, and the Welte factory was bombed during the Second World War.

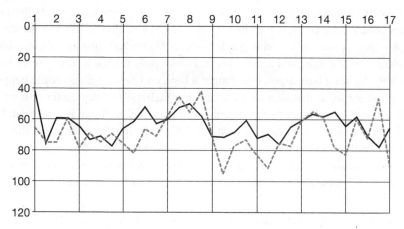

Figure 3.1 Duration graphs of d'Albert's (solid line) and Sapellnikoff's (dotted line) 1905 piano rolls of Schubert, op. 90 no. 3, bars 1–16

articulate interpretation. 'The arrival of a strong measure', Cone writes, 'must be heralded by careful temporal adjustment rather than by simple accentuation' (1968: 42). This is a typical formulation of the analysis-to-performance approach in three respects: its imperative quality ('must'); the assumption that principles of performance can be deduced from the score, rather than involving performers' agency; and the fact that Cone is not describing any particular performance, but simply saying how the music goes. (In reality, of course, he is saying how he would play the piece.) Coupled to the invocation of gravity, a natural and universal physical principle, the result is a built-in resistance to seeing performance in terms of stylistic options or even historical change. And if it is in the nature of much music theory to de-emphasise both individual agency and history, then the same is true of music psychology, where the analogy between performance and gravity is again deeply embedded. An obvious example is Neil Todd's theory of phrase arching, the tendency to get faster and louder as you play into a phrase, and slower and softer as you come out of it: Todd (1985, 1992) modelled this as in effect a nested hierarchy of ball-throwing trajectories (four bars, eight bars, etc.), expressed in both tempo and dynamics. His model can be used to simulate the expressive performance of pieces such as Schubert's op. 90 no. 3, and in Chapter 6 I shall return to it, as well as to the issues concerning historical change that such naturalistic models pose, or rather mask.

I raise these issues of performance and gravity because they are relevant to d'Albert's playing of Schubert's op. 90 no. 3, and indeed to the study of tempo in general. Figure 3.1 graphs the opening of d'Albert's performance, together with a performance from another Welte-Mignon roll (950), recorded on 1 December 1905 by Wassily Sapellnikoff;[6] it is based on the 2/2 barring adopted by Liszt and many

6. Figure 3.1 is based on the Dal Segno transfer of d'Albert's roll (on *The Great Pianists*, vol. 6, Dal Segno 022 [2008]), and a private transfer of Sapellnikoff's by Denis Hall from a roll in his collection. I would like to thank Denis not only for this and other transfers but also for his generous advice on piano rolls more generally.

nineteenth-century editors, so for convenience Figure 3.2 reproduces bars 1–49 from Liszt's version (the equivalent of bars 1–24 in today's editions). This is a duration graph—the opposite of a tempo graph (such as Figure 2.1). Just as a thrown ball decelerates as it climbs and accelerates as gravity pulls it back to earth, so in this graph the higher a beat appears the longer it lasts, and hence the slower the tempo. The graph shows us that after an expansive but metrically unclear initial two bars, d'Albert gently accelerates to the downbeat of bar 5, where there is a reversal: he gradually decelerates to the second beat of bar 6, at which point there is one shorter beat before the deceleration continues. This culminates on the first beat of bar 8, after which d'Albert accelerates into the second eight-bar phrase, and so the process continues. But these two sentences are like the wrong sort of score description: they

Figure 3.2 Liszt's edition of Schubert, op. 90 no. 3, bars 1–49 (Cotta, ca. 1870)

Figure 3.2 Continued

describe the graph rather than meaningfully evoking the quality of d'Albert's performance, and it is questionable whether anybody listening to the recording would be likely to notice that the second beat of bar 6 is shorter than the neighbouring notes, unless perhaps they were making a special mental effort to evaluate beat lengths. It is graphs and descriptions of this sort that have got the analysis of recordings a bad name in some musicological circles.

Nevertheless the graph does cue some of the palpable experiences that emerge when the music is heard, and that are intensified in an integrated playback environment such as Sonic Visualiser, where the graph—itself generated through use of the program—scrolls as the music plays. (I shall discuss Sonic Visualiser more systematically in Chapter 5.) Media Example 3.1 contains the first section of d'Albert's recording, with duration and dynamic graphs. And as will become obvious if it is downloaded and played in Sonic Visualiser, we can now redescribe this passage using language in which gravity plays a central role.[7] The first note, defined only by the quaver figuration, is so long as to be effectively unmeasured (it goes off the scale of the Sonic Visualiser graph), and it is only with the repeated melody notes in bar 2 that any clear sense of metre emerges. D'Albert freewheels into the middle of the first phrase, as we might now say, until the downbeat of bar 5: now it is as if he commences to trudge uphill (pushing his bike?), with a slight lightening of gravitational force before the final ascent to the 'mountain pass' that is reached in bar 8. The impression of effort connoted by 'trudge' is particularly clearly audible in the crotchets of bar 6, which take longer than arithmetic says they should: it is almost as if the air, rather than thinning at this altitude, was becoming thick and sticky (recall Rothstein's semi-serious concept of 'temporal viscosity'), or more plausibly, as if you were walking through snow.

After that, d'Albert freewheels down into the second phrase, where the process is renewed, with an ascent from the second beat of bar 12 that peaks at bar 14: this time d'Albert's freewheeling takes him far into the third eight-bar phrase. Again it is in the retarded motion of the crotchets (bar 14) that the effect is most pronounced. And here, for once, there is evidence that a contemporary listener, the pianist and writer Paul Roës, heard d'Albert's playing in the same way. Roës wrote a semi-fictionalised account of his own accidental encounter with d'Albert at the Bösendorfer studios in Vienna. D'Albert engaged Roës in conversation, we are told, and then played him Schubert's op. 90 no. 3: according to Roës 'he played the eighth notes of the melody relatively slower than the quarter notes, thus giving to that melodic line a superhuman tranquillity'.[8] The story ends with Roës and d'Albert playing concerts at the same time in neighbouring halls. At the end of his concert, having played several encores and received visitors in his dressing room, Roës visits the other hall, where he finds it 'filled to capacity, a public bursting with enthusiasm, and Eugene d'Albert in the process of playing his "nth" encore: the Impromptu in Gb major by Schubert'.

Now my language of trudging ascents and mountain passes is clearly not mandated by the score: it was in fact prompted by Schenker's description of bars 188–94 from the first movement of the Ninth Symphony, quoted in Chapter 2. But such imagery is a commonplace of nineteenth-century discourses of performance.

---

7. In Sonic Visualiser session files that include duration graphs (Media Examples 3.1 and 3.2), duration values are aligned with the end of the note to which they belong, in contrast to printed graphs (such as Figure 3.1), where duration values are aligned with the beginning of the note. This means that, as a given note scrolls, the graph is moving towards its duration value, which comes into existence only at the point when the note ends: though it may sound confusing, this divergent practice for static and moving graphs will be found intuitive in practice.

8. Actually there are no quavers (eighth notes) in the melody of op. 90 no. 3; the smallest note values, to which I assume Roës is referring, are crotchets. References to Paul Roës's *Music, the Mystery and the Reality*, which was published in French in 1955 and in English translation in 1978, are based on the liner notes to *The Centaur Pianist: Complete Studio Recordings, 1910–28* (Arbiter 147, 2005).

In a passage from his *Traité de l'expression musicale* (1874) that seems to bear the impress of his native landscape, the Swiss piano pedagogue and theorist Matthis Lussy wrote that ascending means

> raising one's self to a superior elevation, against the tendency of our being. The more the ascent is steep, bristling with obstacles and asperities, the more force is required, the more rapidly our pulses beat, the greater becomes our animation; but, also, the sooner we are exhausted. Once the summit being attained, we experience a certain well-being; we breathe with ease—the victory makes us happy. This comparison furnishes us with a simple and rational explanation of the inclination, which musicians have, of hastening, at the commencement of ascending phrases, and retarding towards the end. Descending, on the other hand, is reaching an inferior degree, physically as well as morally. It is following one's natural bent. And the impetus is in proportion to the length and uniformity of the descent. From this arises, with the musician, the inclination to accelerate, and the necessity to retard, on uniformly descending passages.[9]

In this way real or imagined physical action, pictorial imagery, and morality, all predicated on the metaphor or conceptual framework of gravity, combine into a kind of semantic network that is cued by d'Albert's constantly mobile tempo.

But we can also explain the effect more technically. In Chapter 2 I detailed the first of Eric Clarke's generative sources of performance expression; the second is that 'a note may be lengthened so as to delay a following note, the function of the delay being to heighten the impact of the significant delayed note' (1988: 19). What d'Albert is doing could be considered an extension of this principle from an individual note to a group of notes, but with the same effect of creating an expressive accent. Or to generalise further, it is an example of unanticipated change resulting in a particular point or passage becoming 'marked for consciousness', to borrow Leonard Meyer's and Grosvenor Cooper's useful definition of the accent (1960: 4); as Daniel Leech-Wilkinson (2009a: chapter 6, paragraph 35) observes, 'change in tempo and/or loudness, it seems, is more significant than the kind of change (louder or softer, faster or slower)'.[10] In short, the basic principle of d'Albert's performance is the identification of certain locations as particularly salient, and the shaping of tempo around them. In terms of the music-theoretical approach represented by Cone, the question becomes one of how we can see the patterning of d'Albert's changing tempo as specified by the structure of Schubert's composition, resulting in the tight linkage of composition and performance that provides the rationale for the analysis-to-performance approach.

At this point it is helpful to compare d'Albert's performance of the opening of op. 90 no. 3 with that of Sapellnikoff, a Russian pianist who was an intimate

---

9. Translated from Lussy's *Traité de l'expression musicale* in Christiani (1885: 276).

10. Kullak (1893: 277) makes the same point: 'the *decrescendo* may just as well be regarded as an intensification as its opposite'.

associate of Tchaikovsky's and enjoyed considerable success in England (Media Example 3.2). Sapellnikoff uses as much rubato as d'Albert; a rough and ready measure of this is the standard deviation between beats, normalised for average tempo, and computed this way Sapellnikoff employs almost 9% more rubato than d'Albert. But this totalised value counts for much less than the way the rubato is applied. For example, as can be seen and heard in Media Example 3.2, Sapellnikoff clearly articulates the junction between the eight-bar phrases at bars 8–9 and 16–17, and in each case he does so in the same way. On the second beat of bar 7 he lengthens the melody note B, and then slows down again in the second half of bar 8 (here the figuration defines the tempo). In this way he marks the beginning of the new phrase at bar 9, at which point he reverts to what one might regard as his basic, underlying tempo for this section, around minim = 75–80 MM. And the same happens at bars 16–17.

D'Albert's approach is rather more roundabout. He lengthens the cadential A in bar 8, so—like Sapellnikoff—acknowledging the phrase break, though the effect is weaker because of the preceding rallentando to bar 6. In the following phrase the pre-cadential A at bar 15 is emphasised as the target of the preceding rallentando (from bar 12), but from there d'Albert follows an accelerating trend that continues up to bar 18, cutting right across the phrase break. To the extent that the beginning of the new phrase is acknowledged at all, it is by hand breaking (the left hand anticipates the right at the first beat of bar 17) and, if the roll can be trusted, dynamics. And d'Albert's tempo is so constantly on the move that it is not clear that the idea of a basic tempo—as opposed to a purely statistical average—could be usefully applied to his performance at all. Where Sapellnikoff treats these junctions between phrases in the same manner, then, d'Albert treats them quite differently, in effect swallowing the second.

And the same applies to other aspects of what Schenkerian theorists call design, such as the melodic and harmonic sequences at bars 17–20 and 21–24. There are many similarities in d'Albert's and Sapellnikoff's shaping of tempo during these passages, which shows how a common framework of practice may be shared between easily distinguishable performers. Yet the differences are crucial to the effect. Sapellnikoff shapes each sequence around the expressive appoggiatura (the d^2 at bar 19 and the $f\sharp^2$ at bar 23): the main difference is that he also prolongs the second beat of bar 24, in order to mark the beginning of the third eight-bar phrase at bar 25. By contrast, d'Albert plays the two sequences quite differently. Like Sapellnikoff, he shapes the first around the appoggiatura at bar 19. But the second time, as the duration graph shows clearly, he de-emphasises the appoggiatura at bar 23, instead subsuming it within a prolonged rallentando that reaches its peak on the downbeat of bar 25.

This is a complex moment. At bar 19, d'Albert used the rallentando to accentuate the appoggiatura; by not doing the same at bar 23 but instead prolonging the rallentando to the downbeat of bar 25, he builds tension that is discharged at this moment, so strongly marking it for consciousness. This is then an accent, yet its effect is not to bring out the beginning of the new phrase, as Sapellnikoff does, but rather the opposite. And here d'Albert is working with an unusual feature of the composition. Elementary tonal composition manuals tell you not to sustain the same harmony across structural divisions, and in particular not to do so using the same chord inversion and melody note. But that is exactly what Schubert has done: his *decrescendo* hairpin in bar 23 and *pianissimo* marking at the beginning of bar 25 suggest an effect of sinking onto the theoretically strong beat. (Liszt's edition adds a 'dim' marking in bar 24 to underline the effect.) D'Albert builds on this. By making bar 25 the culminating point of a sustained rallentando, and through the audible faltering of his quaver figuration there, he makes it seem for a moment as if time might stand still. It could be argued that this magical effect has already been composed into Schubert's score and that d'Albert is merely bringing it out. I would however argue that it is through performers such as d'Albert that we discover what effects scores are capable of affording, and that there is no reason to privilege Schubert's own knowledge of what might be created out of what he wrote. This is an example in miniature of what it means to think of music as performance.

Hans Gál (1974) once said that 'Schubert's phrase cannot stand the restriction of a stiff collar' (33). Neither d'Albert nor Sapellnikoff gives it that: they share what might be termed the 'language' of turn-of-the-twentieth-century rubato, but apply it to very different effect. Though there is nothing modernist about Sapellnikoff's playing (and I hope it does not seem as if I am setting him up as a structuralist fall guy, the reverse of the anti-structuralist Mengelberg), his performance of the first twenty-four bars of op. 90 no. 3 in essence conforms to the Cone approach: he projects the composed phrase structure and treats parallel passages in the same way, resulting in a more or less regular and self-explanatory shaping of Schubert's music. (From bar 33, however, where the passage beginning at bar 17 is repeated in slightly varied form, his playing becomes less regular: in particular his handling of bar 41, which corresponds to 25, is almost closer to d'Albert's than to his own performance of the earlier passage.) As for d'Albert, there are occasions when he projects phrase junctions quite strongly, as at bars 8–9, but more often he de-emphasises them, as when he rushes through bars 16–17 or almost comes to a stop at bar 25. His performance seems rather to be organised around a series of expressive accents whose locations have little or nothing to do with structure, as it might be defined in terms of Cone's ball-throwing theory, Todd's model of phrase arching, or indeed the analysis-to-performance approach more generally.

That could of course be because such approaches have embodied too narrow a concept of structure. Prompted by what he sees as the limited success of computer simulations of expressive performance, the systematic musicologist Richard Parncutt promises in a 2003 article a new angle on the concept of structure, focussing on precisely what is at issue here: 'the relationship between accents and expression' (163). The basic principle of Parncutt's approach is that, as he puts it, 'performed accents reinforce immanent accents' (175). By 'immanent' accents he means any points of emphasis that are inherent in the composition, so in a sense this is an example of the analysis-to-performance approach. And his concept of accent includes the features that analysis-to-performance theorists normally talk about, ranging from phrase or hypermetrical structure to the linear-harmonic structures of Schenkerian theory. But it also includes aspects of design, or what Schenkerians might call purely surface features, such as melodic contours (Parncutt refers to 'turns' and 'skips'), points of harmonic change, dissonances, or aspects of texture. This more generous interpretation of structure affords much enlarged possibilities of linking immanent and performed accents, and might therefore be seen as promising the tight linkage of composition and performance to which I referred: the combination of Parncutt's model and a set of principles for translating accent into performance practice, such as Clarke's 1988 listing, would constitute a theory of expressive performance.

But now there is another difficulty, and it is the very generosity of Parncutt's model that is responsible for it. As he says,

> The hypothesis that performed accents reinforce immanent accents allows for a wide variety of interpretations of a given piece of piano music. Musical scores typically include many different kinds of immanent accents, of varying strengths. The performer is thus presented with a wide variety of accents, occurring both individually and in various combinations. It would appear to be a matter of artistry to decide which of these accents should be emphasized in performance, and which of the various possible means of expression should be used for this purpose (2003: 175).

In essence Parncutt is saying that music is so rich in potentially expressive moments that simply to identify them explains little. That underlines the performer's freedom of interpretation, but in calling it a matter of 'artistry', he repackages the original problem rather than solving it. The tight linkage that provides the rationale for the analysis-to-performance approach remains elusive. And in truth this is not surprising. After all, both d'Albert and Sapellnikoff, in their different ways, play what is in immanent terms the same music quite differently—and within their performances, each plays the same music quite differently when it comes back. Perhaps then—as Rothstein suggested—there is a problem with the basic idea of a piece of music embodying a structure that performers can bring out.

Parncutt's formulation, as well as d'Albert's and Sapellnikoff's practice, suggests a more radical but at the same time rather obvious alternative that has been articulated in a recent article by Mitchell Ohriner: 'Performers do not passively transmit structure in a one-to-one mapping, but neither do they "interpret" structure, layering inessential details over something determinate and fixed. Performers create structure in much the same way that readers create poems' (2012: para 38). And if the reference to Stanley Fish jars with Ohriner's—and more generally music theory's—structuralist vocabulary, the solution may be to think of performers as more broadly creating meaning within the structural affordances of compositions, meaning that cannot itself be encompassed within a purely structural description. Though Parncutt does not mention it, that would be in line with a long theoretical and pedagogical tradition of formulating criteria for the identification of immanent accents, though it was not the terminology these writers employed. As even a cursory examination of books by Richard Hudson (1994) and Clive Brown (1999) will show, the eighteenth- and early nineteenth-century treatises of Johann Joachim Quantz, Daniel Gottlob Türk, Johann Philipp Kirnberger, Carl Czerny, and many others are full of directions that accents should be placed on high notes, low notes, long notes, syncopated notes, chromatic notes, notes involved in modulation, and dissonances; the tradition extends into the late nineteenth century (e.g., Kullak 1893: 253–54), and even into the twentieth with Schenker's unfinished treatise (2000: 47, 55). Much ink was also spilled on sometimes elaborate taxonomies of the categories of accent, on which these theorists found it hard to agree. But to enlarge on this I shall quote briefly from two other writers on the topic, one from the eighteenth century and one from the nineteenth.

The eighteenth-century writer is C. P. E. Bach, whose *Essay on the True Art of Playing Keyboard Instruments* I mentioned at the end of Chapter 1. Bach (1974: 163) writes that 'dissonances are played loudly and consonances softly, since the former rouse our emotions and the latter quiet them', an unexceptionable statement that precisely describes what d'Albert does in, for instance, bars 15–16 of op. 90 no. 3. Here it is Bach's reference to emotion—those same 'passions' that, as we saw in Chapter 1, excited Schenker's anxious commentary—that I would like to emphasise; in the next sentence he prescribes accentuation for 'an exceptional turn of melody which is designed to create a violent affect'. And the same association of points of emphasis with affective expression recurs much closer to d'Albert's—and Schenker's—own time in the late nineteenth-century treatise by Mathis Lussy to which I have already referred, which no less an authority than Paderewski (2001) described as 'his excellent book on musical expression'.

Central to Lussy's theory of performance expression is what he calls the *accent pathétique*, and he sees this as prompted by twelve kinds of musical event: among these are—again—long notes, notes approached by leaps, changes in contour, upper neighbour notes, dissonances, and notes foreign to the key. Most of the notes that d'Albert chooses to emphasise in op. 90 no. 3 fall under one or more of Lussy's headings, and Lussy's description of the performance of the *accent pathétique* is suggestive: every time it appears, he writes, 'the soul of the musician, excited by the obstacles to be overcome, is animated, impassioned or paralyzed. The general tempo undergoes a modification: one accelerates or slows down' (Doğantan-Dack 2002: 132). Again, then, the affective dimension is crucial. And as if carrying on from where Bach left off, Lussy writes that 'it is precisely these unexpected, irregular, exceptional notes, without musical logic, which most particularly have the ability to affect the sentiment' (Green 1994: 197).

Immanent accents may then be expected, regular, the explicable product of musical structure, or they may be unexpected, irregular, illogical, in other words inexplicable except as feeling. Whereas Sapellnikoff's performance of the opening section of Schubert's op. 90 no. 3 emphasises the former, d'Albert's emphasises the latter: paradoxically, it is the exceptional notes, the notes that subvert or simply bypass structure, that become the central pillars around which d'Albert structures his performance. Or one might compare them to the pylons of suspension bridges, with the curving, weight-supporting cables corresponding to d'Albert's tempo profiles. For it is as if, in d'Albert's playing, time itself becomes shaped. Modernist music theory encourages us to think of music as something that takes place in time but is not intrinsically temporal: it is a kind of evenly gradated object best understood from what Johnson and Larson called the observer's perspective. Seen this way, time functions like air, or at least air as it appears in everyday life, a transparent and neutral medium. This is what Karlheinz Stockhausen called the 'traditional concept…that things are in time'—whereas, he continued, 'the new concept is that time is in the things' (Maconie 1989: 96). Actually Stockhausen's 'new concept' seems close to the 'qualitative' sense of time that the choral director and chant specialist Marcel Pérès sees as having co-existed since the thirteenth century with the modern, quantitative sense of time (Sherman 1997: 39–40), but history is not the point here: as in the case of Stockhausen and Pérès, so in d'Albert's hands time seems to take on a quality or even a quantity of its own. It is as if time were being shaped on the fly, pressing towards and ebbing away from expressive moments and so creating an effect of continuous inhalation and exhalation: rather than the music taking place *in* time, it is as if the music was made *of* time. I shall come back to this in Chapter 4.

This explains the characteristic way d'Albert rushes or snatches at certain passages, as at transitions between sections. Such playing has long been out of favour, and it is no doubt the principal source of d'Albert's present-day reputation for uncertain rhythmic control. As we saw, this is the same charge that Paul Henry Lang levelled at Furtwängler. And the entirely historical prejudice against mobile tempo has become so engrained that Bruno Repp, the pioneer of scientific approaches to the study of recordings (1999: 475), simply takes it for granted that for 'the basic tempo…to change during the course of a phrase' must be a fault. (I shall come back to this shortly.) If the difference between music that is *in* and music that is *of* time is at root an ontological one, based on different conceptions of what sort of thing musical time is, then it becomes possible to understand how quickly performance styles not only fall out of fashion but actually become unintelligible. Robert Philip observes that 'with the oldest generation of players on record, one sometimes gets a hint of a lost language which is no longer quite understood, as with d'Albert's unprepared lurches on to the beat' (1992: 69). It is not so surprising, then, that the unnamed author of the liner notes on the Dal Segno transfer of d'Albert's recording of op. 90 no. 3, whom one might have expected to be on d'Albert's side, refers to his 'strange rhythmic lapses', while for Harold Schonberg (1965) his recordings 'cause nothing but embarrassment…the playing is inexplicable, full of wrong notes, memory lapses and distorted rhythms' (295).

Yet this is the pianist of whom Liszt wrote 'I know of no more gifted as well as dazzling talent than d'Albert' (Schonberg 1965: 292), and whom Adorno (1984) described in 1931 as 'still the greatest of all pianists' (314). Properly understood, d'Albert's mobile tempos are an integral component of his pianistic style: a style that is predicated on the communication of moment-to-moment expressiveness, and which—in contrast to what I call the 'structuralist' style of late twentieth-century common practice—I shall refer to as 'rhetorical'.

SPOKEN MELODY, OR SUNG SPEECH

Schenker's article on Schubert's op. 90 no. 3 dates from twenty years after d'Albert's roll. It appeared in the final issue of his one-man journal, *Der Tonwille*,[11] and—like d'Albert's performance—was based on the transposed and rebarred editions that were still current (though Schenker was aware that this was not how Schubert had written it, and deplored the changes). By this time the graphing technique for which Schenker is now known was in place: indeed, just as it was in the op. 101 *Erläuterungsausgabe* that Schenker first developed his mature concept of prolongation, so the article on op. 90 no. 3 has as good a claim as any to be regarded as the first really complete illustration of Schenker's analytical method. The graph with which the article begins is a well-formed example of the $\hat{3}$-$\hat{2}$-$\hat{1}$ *Urlinie*, elaborated into five linear-harmonic layers: analytical commentary takes up the first two-thirds of the article and is organised around these layers. The last third begins with a few general comments on the performance of the piece, and thereafter consists of detailed, bar-by-bar instructions as to what the performer should do (Schenker 2005: 141–42). It is bar-by-bar performance commentaries like this which, as I said in Chapter 2, have been more or less ignored by the Schenkerian community.

It would obviously be naive to expect too close a relationship between d'Albert's piano roll (which there is no reason to believe that Schenker ever heard) and the article that Schenker wrote twenty years later. For one thing, pianists do not necessarily play the same piece the same way on successive nights, let alone across successive decades. Even if—as Leech-Wilkinson (2009b: 250) argues—most performers form their personal style early in their career and then stick to it, there is still a big inferential leap between the evidence of how d'Albert played op. 90 no. 3 on 19 May 1905 and how he might have played it in the 1890s, when Schenker wrote so glowingly about him. Then again, one might assume that Schenker's formulation between 1905 and 1925 of the theory that bears his name would have had a profound influence on his sense of how music should go. Evidence of this might be detected in the gradual cooling of his enthusiasm for d'Albert: Schenker's diaries reveal a note of criticism as early as 1897, though that relates specifically to his playing of Schenker's own music, but by 1907 the critique has become more general: his playing is 'careless, irresponsible,...frivolous' (Federhofer 1985: 63, 66). The carelessness, admittedly, might be attributable to d'Albert's career shift from performance to composition, which was widely seen as having had an effect on his playing, rather than to a change in Schenker's taste. But even so, looking for parallels between d'Albert's roll and Schenker's article is quite a long shot.

At the most general level, Schenker directs that 'The melodic line must be prominent, penetrating in tone, floating clearly above the dark accompaniment of the right and left hands', and that accented passing notes should be played more strongly than their resolutions, in the manner of 'the best singing artists'. Even

11. Published in 1925, contrary to the printed publication date of 1924 (Schenker 2005: v).

allowing for the way dynamic values were compromised in the Welte-Mignon recording process, it seems clear that this is an accurate description of what d'Albert does. But then, so do any number of other pianists, while we have seen that Schenker's directions for the playing of accented passing notes can be matched from any number of performance treatises, as can the comparison with singers. But there are some more specific points of coincidence. For instance, Schenker writes of bar 154 that 'there should be a hesitation in the first quarter, and a resumption of motion in the remaining quarter notes': that is exactly what d'Albert does. Again, Schenker specifies that

> in bar 66, the first quarter note hesitates, the remaining ones move forward more rapidly. The same holds true in bar 68, despite the closing off of the section, so that the last quarter note, d^1, moves without pause towards c^1 in bar 69. The sectional division is not to be expressed by the usual *ritardando* at the closing cadence.

D'Albert does all this; he even makes the left-hand semiquavers at bar 71 sound like a glissando, as Schenker prescribes. And as for the linking of sections without *ritardando*, that is what d'Albert does throughout most of the performance, apart from an exaggeratedly rhetorical fermata before the transfigured return of the opening theme at bar 109—transfigured because of the Lisztian octaves and spread chords. Although Schenker refers to 'the usual *ritardando*', it appears that he means not that this cadence should be treated as an exception, but that 'the usual' way of playing is wrong: as early as 1911, among the papers subsequently published as *The Art of Performance*, Schenker wrote that 'the requirement that a composition's form not be exposed too nakedly frequently demands considerably quicker playing where the seam occurs' (2000: 55).

But it would beggar belief if Schenker's prescriptions and d'Albert's playing corresponded throughout, and they don't. One obvious difference comes right at the beginning. Adopting the imperative tone that characterises his writing on performance, Schenker proclaims that

> The law of performance governing note repetitions in general demands that the two half notes of bar 2 be directed towards the whole note of bar 3, with the sort of acceleration that the accentuation in bar 3 makes obvious. The changes of pulse in bars 1–3 in this way hold the key to performance of the entire piece. All is lost if b^1 in bar 1 is more strongly emphasized than b^1 in bar 2, and if bar 2 is not directed towards bar 3 in the manner of an upbeat.... Schubert's marking < > in bar 7 demands a movement in bars 5 and 6 whose goal is b^1 in bar 7—thus one should not get lost in the quarters of bar 6.

But that is not at all how d'Albert plays the opening. Even allowing for the limited dynamic information provided by the roll, we can say that he emphasises the b^1 at bar 2 rather than the one at bar 3, accelerates through bars 3 and 4, puts a dynamic accent on the a¹ at bar 5, luxuriates ('gets lost') in the crotchets, and then slows down to the a¹ in bar 8, giving it an agogic accent. So on a literal reading all is indeed lost (though as it happens, d'Albert—who as I said frequently plays repeats differently—gets it right at bar 11, while Sapellnikoff gets it right from the start).

But this is an excessively literal way to make the comparison between d'Albert and Schenker. Both Schenker's instructions and d'Albert's performance invoke a hierarchy of tones, whose relative saliences are expressed through what Schenker terms 'changes of pulse' as well as dynamic emphasis. (In Clarke's 1988 listing of the generative sources of performance expression, this corresponds to the second and third principles for both tempo and dynamics: both can be used to accentuate particular notes, and to mark group boundaries.) Schenker and d'Albert are employing what I termed the same 'language' of rubato, but the interpretations they are expressing through this language differ. In accentuating the b¹ in bars 1–4 and the a¹ in bars 5–8, d'Albert is implicitly parsing the score in the manner of a traditional harmonic reduction, as a series of evenly paced functional harmonies (two bars each of I and VI under b¹, and of II and V under a¹). Schenker, by contrast, sees everything before bar 8 as a prolongation of the opening tonic: that is how he graphs it at the first and most detailed level of his analysis. It is not, then, as if d'Albert and Schenker are speaking different languages. Rather they are expressing different points of view in the same language.

Schenker also speaks in this passage of accelerating to the point of accentuation, whereas d'Albert characteristically creates accentuation through slowing down. But then, the psychological principle is in both cases the same: if an accent is a point that is marked for consciousness, then—as Leech-Wilkinson said—it is the fact rather than the direction of change that matters, so that accelerando will do as well as rallentando. What is crucial is that Schenker's prescriptions for performance convey the same kind of mobile tempo that is audible on d'Albert's roll. At the beginning of bar 19, for instance, Schenker says it is 'important that...the first two accompanying eighth notes, d¹ and e¹, should be played with slight hesitation; the difference should be made up by acceleration in the third quarter'. At that particular point d'Albert does the exact opposite, but it is a perfect description of the effect of faltering, of time threatening to stand still, that I described at the beginning of bar 25. Nor is this an isolated reference on Schenker's part. I count twelve specific invocations in Schenker's two-page commentary of hesitating, delaying, lingering, and pausing on the one hand, and of resuming motion, hurrying forward, pushing forward, and accelerating on the other. All this evokes the same continuous process of inhalation and exhalation that I described in d'Albert's playing. Indeed the second and third sentences of Schenker's section on performance provide a succinct summary of the way d'Albert plays op. 90 no. 3 that could hardly be improved upon: 'One should not simply announce one note after the other: rather, one should lead toward and retreat from significant notes. This results in spoken melody, or sung speech'. And again there is a resonance with something Schenker said in the 1911 papers, where, following a discussion of dynamic shading, he concludes, 'Nuances of this kind are as thoroughly undefinable as the vibrations in the rise and fall of the voice of an orator or actor and thus entirely defy a precise description' (2000: 42).

The next step in my argument is to consider the relationship between Schenker's idea of how music goes in performance, as it emerges from his commentary on op. 90 no. 3, and his theoretical thinking as embodied in the analytical section of his 1925 article. But before that, I want to explore some larger issues that are raised both by Schenker's reference to spoken melody and sung speech, and by aspects of d'Albert's playing. Roës has d'Albert say of op. 90 no. 3 that it has 'a superb voice which seems to speak', but that does not make this Impromptu in any way unique. Often seen as the tail end of a rhetorical tradition that was at its height in the seventeenth and eighteenth centuries, the idea of music as heightened speech was central to nineteenth-century opera, most obviously in the works of Wagner. But it was a commonplace of nineteenth-century writing about music in general, and whereas—as we shall see in Chapter 4—today's historically informed per-formers draw a clear distinction between the ideas of music as song and music as speech, nineteenth-century writers generally did not. In the *cantilena* or vocal style of piano performance, the Czerny pupil, pianist, and pedagogue Adolph Kullak says, 'the player must conceive the melody as a connected, orderly chain of tones, symbolically imitative of the spoken phrase.... The singing touch... is the first condition' (1893: 253). And a few lines later he refers to 'the supreme law of musical declamation', a term that is nowadays associated with a shadowy per-formance tradition deriving from, or passing through, Beethoven (Barth 1992). I shall come back to these historical perspectives in Chapter 4: what concerns me here is how far the comparison between music and speech can contribute to an understanding of the rhetorical style of d'Albert's playing—a term for which Schenker's words provide ample justification. I will first discuss aspects of per-formance in music and speech, and then the dimensions of emotion and affect that pervade both.

That there are parallels between the performance of music and speech is evi-dent, as illustrated for example by the phenomenon of phrase-final lengthen-ing (slowing down at the end of phrases). But there have been few attempts to develop these parallels in terms of style. One way this might be done is in relation to the distinction, in speech, between syllable-timed and stress-timed languages. Examples of the former include French and Italian, in which syllables occur more or less regularly, while the latter include (British) English and German, in which stresses occur more or less regularly: these stresses normally correspond to important semantic elements, and the intervening phonemes are squashed in between them as necessary. A recent article by Aniruddh Patel, John Iversen, and Jason Rosenberg accordingly drew a comparison between French speech and music on the one hand, and English speech and music on the other. Although in each case they found some evidence for the association of speech and language, the comparison was skewed in that—in yet another expression of the textualist mentality—the authors based their comparison on notated rather than performed music. At least they commented that it would be important to base future studies on performance data (Patel et al. 2006: 3038).

The absence of proper research, however, need not stop us from making a simple listening comparison between d'Albert's playing and contemporary recordings of speech. But what kind of speech might offer a fair comparison for d'Albert's playing? Like German, d'Albert's mother tongue was stress-timed, for despite his French name and virulent German cultural nationalism, he actually came from Glasgow. (So, in a bizarre coincidence, did d'Albert's principal rival as a Beethoven interpreter, who also had a European career: Frederic Lamond.) In 1876, at the age of twelve, d'Albert won a scholarship to study with Sir Arthur Sullivan, among others, at what later became the Royal College of Music; five years later he won a scholarship to Vienna, from where he progressed to become a pupil of the elderly Liszt at Weimar. It was at this time that he changed his first name from Eugène to Eugen.

The scene now shifts to Little Menlo, the leafy Surrey home of Colonel George Gouraud, who in 1887 became the British distributor of Thomas Edison's phonograph. In a prolonged publicity campaign, Gouraud invited a succession of celebrity guests to his dinner parties at Little Menlo, where he recorded them. Among these recordings is an after-dinner speech made by Sullivan on 5 October 1888,[12] in which Sullivan says he is 'astonished and somewhat terrified at the results of this evening's experiment—astonished at the wonderful power you have developed, and terrified at the thought that so much hideous and bad music may be put on record forever'. It is not always easy to make out Sullivan's words above the crackle of the cylinder, but what is plainly audible is the careful pacing of his delivery, with a series of semi-regularly placed emphases that convey the dynamics of his meaning even when you do not catch the words. If that already sounds a little like d'Albert's playing, the resemblance is that much stronger in a recording of another Little Menlo guest that Gouraud made a few months later, on 18 December: William Gladstone.[13] The recording begins with Gouraud's introduction, and when Gladstone starts to speak he is barely audible, presumably because he stood too far from the horn. But from about 1'45" he gets into his stride. He intones in a semi-monotone, the pattern of his stresses varying but on average around one a second (the average tempo in the opening section of op. 90 no. 3 as played by d'Albert is 67 MM). More formal and apparently studied than modern speech, the effect is strongly reminiscent of the singer Manuel García's description of declamatory music, which 'pays no regard to the number of bars or symmetry of cadences, or even to regularity of time', being based rather on 'prosodic accents and excitement of passion'.[14] All this reinforces the sense that d'Albert is bringing

12. Accessible at http://ia600506.us.archive.org/10/items/EDIS-SRP-0155-14/EDIS-SRP-0155-14.mp3 (details at http://www.archive.org/details/EDIS-SRP-0155-14). All web links accessed November 2012 except as otherwise stated.

13. Accessible at http://www.nps.gov/edis/photosmultimedia/upload/EDIS-SRP-0190-12.mp3 (details at http://www.nps.gov/edis/photosmultimedia/documentary-recordings-and-political-speeches.htm).

14. Quoted from *Garcia's New Treatise on the Art of Singing* in Brown (1999: 155).

not just a speech-like but a prose-like performance style—a style in which meaning and emotion play the primary shaping role—to Schubert's song-like, sym-
metrically structured composition.

This comparison between d'Albert's playing and Sullivan's or Gladstone's speech
is admittedly loose and impressionistic, but the same kind of parallels do not hold
with other, strikingly different, speech styles of the time. An example of the latter
is the more obviously dramatic declamation of Sir Henry Irving, whom Gouraud
had recorded a few months earlier (30 August), and who in his renderings of
Shakespeare was criticised for doing what I just suggested d'Albert does: turning verse into prose (Goodale 2011: 29). Even more different was what Greg
Goodale calls the 'orotund' style against which Irving's own delivery was a reaction: Goodale (27) quotes a public-speaking handbook from 1880, which directs
that 'every letter as well as every syllable in a word should be distinctly heard'. This
is a direct expression of the idea of sounded text to which I referred in Chapter 1,
and a striking though no doubt accidental anticipation of Schoenberg's description of the ideal performance as one in which 'what the composer has written is
made to sound in such a way that every note is really heard'.

My purpose in taking the idea of music as speech so literally is to make two
related points. The first is that performance is strongly shaped by social expectations that go far beyond music: Goodale (21) describes the Shakespearian declamation of the late nineteenth century as 'a style that we today would consider
bombastic and pretentious but that audiences expected', and ascribes the changes
in speech style that took place at the end of the nineteenth century to such factors
as the spread of recording technology, and an anxiety about manliness caused by
the transition from physically active to sedentary occupations. (In Chapter 6 of
this book, I make a similar attempt to set developments in musical performance
style into their broader cultural contexts.) The second point is that such changes,
whether in speech or in music, can take place surprisingly quickly, and that past
patterns of performance can quickly become, if not as Philip suggested positively
unintelligible, then at least hard to take seriously. Charles Rosen (2005) writes
that 'listening to a recording of Sarah Bernhardt intoning Racine makes one laugh
today' (9), and the same applies even to 1950s newscasters and politicians. It certainly applies to music: Robert Hill writes that 'it is hard to suppress a giggle'
(1994: 40) on hearing Alessandro Moreschi's 1902 recording of the Bach-Gounod
'Ave Maria', while Daniel Leech-Wilkinson (2010a) tries to explain why people's
first reaction to hearing early recordings today is often disbelieving laughter. The
second, he adds, is feeling threatened by them.

I said that when you listen to early recordings of speech you can grasp the
emotional dynamics even when you can't make out the words, and the idea of
music having a meaning that lies beyond specific denotation is a hallmark of
Romanticism. (It is built into the genre Felix Mendelssohn invented: songs without words.) And the effect of meaningfulness, of music being pregnant with meaning even though we can't say just what the meaning is, takes me to the second issue
I mentioned, that of emotion and affect. I have made many references to the ebbing and flowing of time in d'Albert's playing, or in that of rhetorical performance

more generally, and here a very obvious parallel can be made with contemporary music theory: I am referring to the 'energeticists', such as August Halm and Ernst Kurth, though Lee Rothfarb (2002) also includes the earlier work of Halm's friend Schenker under this category. The energeticists' aim was to understand music as the product of shaping forces that work in combination through the different parameters of music. But such thinking forms part of a longer tradition of seeing music in terms of dynamically changing patterns of energy or tension that goes back at least as far as Hanslick's 'tonally moving forms' (1986: 29), and from there can be traced through Richard Wagner, Susanne Langer, Roger Scruton, and Peter Kivy, among many others. It also resonates with current thinking about musical gesture: according to Robert Hatten (2006: 3), 'in Western musical styles a kind of virtual gravitational field or vectoral space provides an analogue to the forces working on the human body in physical space, enabling the motivated opposition of downwards grief versus upwards elation'. This is the same idea of music being shaped by an internalised sense of gravity that we have already encountered in Christiani, Lussy, Cone, and Todd.

Despite differences of interpretation, all of these writers see music as a dynamic play of forces that in some way replicates, represents, or embodies the morphologies of human feelings or emotions. It is in short a theory of musical meaning. Recent experimental research has confirmed the consistency with which people perceive changing levels of energy, tension, or intensity as they listen to music (you get similar results almost regardless of what you ask them to track); these perceptions correlate on the one hand with a variety of physiological measures, including heart beat and respiration, and on the other with 'melodic contour, note density, dynamics, harmony, tonality, and other factors' (Krumhansl 1996: 401). Moreover, changes of intensity in one such parameter are perceived as similar to changes in others (Eitan and Granoy 2007). Beyond music this approach has been applied, for example, to dance (Foster 2008), but it has been most expansively developed by Daniel Stern, whose work ranges from developmental psychology to psychotherapy. According to Stern (2004: 36), the dynamic time shapes that he terms 'vitality affects' mould everyday experiences of individual subjectivity as well as conversations and other interpersonal transactions. He sees the morphology of the musical phrase as the most direct analogue of vitality affects (26ff), but argues that they underlie the time-based arts in general, though their expression is mediated by the specific codes applicable to the art form in question (Stern 2010: 82–84).

'The feeling quality of vitality affects', Stern (2004: 64) writes, 'is best captured by kinetic terms such as, *surging, fading away, fleeting, explosive, tentative, effortful, accelerating, decelerating, climaxing, bursting, drawn out, reaching, hesitating, leaning forward, leaning backward*, and so on'. Most of these terms are directly applicable to d'Albert's playing, and several appear in Schenker's instructions for the performance of op. 90 no. 3. The shaping forces of which the energeticists spoke were composed into scores, but d'Albert's playing shows how directly Stern's 'dynamic time-shapes' can be mapped onto performance. And indeed there is a tradition of such discourse in performance pedagogy that goes back beyond, and quite possibly influenced, the energeticists: 'the breathing-process of the feeling', Kullak (1893: 268) writes at the beginning of his chapter on crescendo and decrescendo, 'consists in two movements, which, aside from any specific meaning, characterize all emotion; an outpouring from the breast, and an in-drawing into the fathomless depths of its life.... The emotional life is an undulating play of upsurging and subsidence'. John Rink's 'intensity curves', which as we saw in the previous chapter provide a summary representation of multiple musical parameters and so facilitate the real-time pacing of performance, might in this way be seen as a new development within a long established tradition.

But there is an obvious difference between the operation of vitality affects in everyday life and in music, or at least instrumental music. In everyday life, vitality affects are experienced as inseparable from the particular events or objects that prompt them or are embraced by them. Stern (2004: 12–16) provides an example that revolves round preparing and eating a slice of bread and honey while listening to the radio. (He even graphs the resulting series of intensity profiles, on a scale of 1 to 10.) The same applies to what Leech-Wilkinson (2009a: chapter 8, paragraphs 78–79) calls two 'signs of deep emotion in early 20th-century singing,... the Italian sob and the German swoop': these expressive gestures, as he terms them, are musically stylised representations of real-world emotional behaviours, giving a quality of veridicality to the love, grief, or joy specified in libretti or song texts. Instrumental music, however, gives us the intensity profile, the affect, without specifying the referents.

This takes us into territory that has been thoroughly explored by philosophers of music. Peter Kivy and Stephen Davies agree that music can express basic emotions, such as happiness or sadness, but not those 'higher' emotions that can be felt only in relation to a specific object (jealousy is an obvious example). Leech-Wilkinson (2009a: chapter 8, paragraph 122) draws on James Russell to make a similar distinction between 'core affect' and 'full-blown emotion', which resonates with the parallel but more succinct distinction between 'affect' and 'emotion' that is made by cultural theorists such as Patricia Clough and Brian Massumi. Leech-Wilkinson (paragraph 14) suggests that, in instrumental music, expressive gestures can serve to transform affect into emotion, and that among the aims of performance analysis should be 'to show how gestures in sound alter core affect' and 'what kind of emotional experiences result from these changes'. I am not sure how far expressive gestures can do that kind of denotational work, except when they have highly conventionalised meanings, and would myself see this as more the role of critical commentary and interpretation, which in a sense do the same work for instrumental music as libretti and song texts do for vocal music. However it does not greatly matter, as Leech-Wilkinson (paragraph 122) concedes that the generation of full-blown emotion is 'by no means inevitable' in instrumental music.

Either way, then, we end up with the idea that music embodies not so much emotion as a potential for emotional interpretation, indeed for multiple emotional interpretations (and as I said, it may take a particular performance to make us realise what interpretation a given piece can afford). It follows that specific emotional meaning is not inherent in the musical work but arises from the contexts of its interpretation, understanding that word in the broadest sense. And as should be clear from Chapter 1, that principle is fully in line with the performance studies approach. But it creates a practical problem for the analyst of musical performance. In his discussion of string quartet performance, Robert Martin (1994) asks whether the opening of Beethoven's op. 131 expresses 'loneliness, tragedy, religious fervour, spiritual resignation, or something else' (123), and adds, 'Many performers are uncomfortable with such questions, though they are not at all uncomfortable with emotionally expressive playing'. This is not, or at any rate not just, a matter of stiff upper lip or the fear of being thought sentimental. Adorno (2006: 77) expressed the point succinctly: 'musical expression is not the expression of a fixed intentional object. It flares up, as it were, only to disappear again'. One might say that it is more the flaring than the object that is the performer's business. And by definition, words cannot articulate what Lawrence Zbikowski calls 'a dynamic, imagistic mode of thought that is inaccessible to language' (2011: 97). Cultural theorists underline the point, widening the gap between uninterpreted affect and interpreted emotion: Clough (2007) writes that affectivity is 'a substrate of potential bodily responses, often autonomic responses, in excess of consciousness' (2), while for Massumi (1995) 'emotion and affect—if affect is intensity— follow different logics and pertain to different orders' (88).

Massumi's glossing of affect as 'intensity' is particularly suggestive in relation to performance. By this he means an irreducibly temporal experience that embodies 'the incipience of mutually exclusive pathways of action and expression that are then reduced, inhibited, prevented from actualising themselves completely— all but one' (1995: 91). Words represent the experience by specifying just that one: they cannot represent the more generic quality of potentiality that we hear in d'Albert—or in other rhetorical performances, or in performance in general— because, in representing it, they give it specific realisation. But such problems are not limited to talking about performance. Hanslick was making the same point as Adorno, only in more graphic terms, when he wrote in *On the Musically Beautiful* that music can convey 'clamor…but not the clamour of ardent combatants' (Geoffrey Payzant's less vivid translation tones this down to 'violence…but certainly not the conflict').[15] As I said in Chapter 2, Hanslick's solution was to relocate discourse from what can't be satisfactorily talked about to what can, that is, from meaning to the strictly musical structures that underlie it. Yet such strategies come at a cost. We saw how Hanslick's aesthetic theory led him to deny what, as a practising critic, he did not hesitate to believe. The same applies to Schenker, if my analysis of his dogmatic, excessive denial of C. P. E. Bach's 'passions' is correct: he was not the first theorist who, on discovering that something didn't fit his theory, denied its existence. The better course of action is to accept that, when we talk about music—and especially about performance—much

---

15. For Payzant's translation see Hanslick (1986: 9); the first, by Gustav Cohen, is from Hanslick (1957: 21). The original reads: 'das *Stürmen*…doch nicht der »Kampflust«'.

of what we want to say slips between our words, or else we say more than we mean to. That is what Charles Seeger (1977: 51) called the musicological juncture, and it is the root cause of the tension between theory and practice reflected in Christiani's table.

SCHENKER VS. SCHENKER

Returning at last to my main argument about op. 90 no. 3, I hope I have demonstrated that—while there are of course significant differences between what d'Albert did and what Schenker said—both belong within the same stylistic universe. Given the twenty years that separate them, does this mean that Schenker's analytical method built on his pre-existing sense of how music goes? Just how close is the linkage between the two parts into which Schenker's 1925 article falls, the graph and analytical commentary based on it, and the prescriptions for performance? And can we detect connections between Schenker's analysis and d'Albert's performance? The last question doesn't take long to answer. I have already mentioned the closest connection between the graph and a performance prescription: the interpretation of the opening b^1 as falling to a^1 at bar 8, not 5, as indicated in both Schenker's analytical charts and his performance directions—though as we saw d'Albert did not perform it that way. The other possible example is the converse, an analytical observation that isn't reflected in Schenker's performance instructions but is reflected in d'Albert's performance: Schenker (2005: 137) writes that the opening section concludes not with the cadence in bar 16 but with the one in bar 48, on the grounds that bars 1–48 are unified by a $\hat{3}$-$\hat{2}$-$\hat{1}$ succession. That would fit with the way in which (unlike Sapellnikoff) d'Albert marks the division at bar 49, but not those at bars 17 or 33.

But these are not very substantial connections. As we have seen, many of the performance prescriptions are concerned with the nuancing of specific notes or points in the score (mainly in terms of tempo, though also dynamics, articulation, or pedalling), but there is nothing in Schenker's graph that would explain why these particular points are selected for such treatment. And as for the commentary based on the graph, it is primarily concerned with theoretically motivated issues such as how the organisation of the middle section (round b^1 and its neighbour note c^2) compensates for the lack of neighbour-note elaboration in the initial section; how premature closure is avoided within the music's outer sections (by retaining the emphasis on $\hat{3}$ until the final descent); how E minor and C major are established as autonomous middleground keys rather than mere scale degrees of G; and the need to understand the occasionally extreme chromatic modulations 'against the norms of the diatonic system' (Schenker 2005: 141). None of these really offer opportunities for performance intervention.

There seems, then, to be a much closer relationship between d'Albert's piano roll and Schenker's description of how op. 90 no. 3 should go, despite the twenty-year time gap, than there is between the two halves of Schenker's article. Why might this be? I have two explanations to propose, the first of which, if successful, would obviate the need for the second. The first, then, is based on the particular nature of Schubert's composition. In a nutshell, it wears its structural heart on its sleeve. The first forty-eight bars parse effortlessly into three groups of sixteen bars, each entirely regular in its power-of-two construction. The middle section features three-bar phrases and elisions, but even so it is quite unambiguous, with structure clearly specified by means of melodic contour and harmony. This might suggest that Schenker chose the piece not for its analytical challenges but as a convenient demonstration of his new analytical system: in fact, the original idea of this issue of *Der Tonwille* was to devote it to music for children.

The proposal, then, is that d'Albert can de-emphasise phrase and section structure by playing through the cadences and marking non-structural points because, in this particular case, the structure has been hard-wired. That is what Carl Reinecke (1897)—an older contemporary of d'Albert of whom more in Chapter 4—said of Beethoven's 'Waldstein' Sonata (65–66), and it resonates with Cone's observation that, 'of course, the more explicitly the rhythmic form has been written into the music, the less the performance is required to add' (1968: 31). Or, in Lussy's language, d'Albert can concentrate on the *accents pathétiques*, the 'unexpected, irregular, exceptional notes, without musical logic', just because regularity and logic have been built so firmly into the composition. It is like Wason's idea of structure being 'so clear that the interpreter may occasionally phrase *against* formal segmentations of the music without placing that dimension of the music in jeopardy of total loss'. At the end of Chapter 2 I paraphrased Wason's claim as 'heads I win, tails you lose'. But in the case of Schubert's piece there is a way of testing whether or not this is the right explanation.

Basically the claim is that op. 90 no. 3 is the exception that proves the rule. If d'Albert is playing against structure because of the special compositional nature of op. 90 no. 3, and if the relationship between compositional structure and performance is as tight as structure-to-performance theorists have assumed, then we should expect non- or anti-structural performances to be the norm for this piece. In order to establish whether or not this is in fact the case, I discuss a small sample of further recorded performances, listed in Figure 3.3. Media Examples 3.3–3.8 provide bars 1–48 of each, so enabling the discussion to be followed aurally as well as verbally.[16] Four of them, dating from between 1938 and 1961, are by performers on whom Schenker left comments (Edwin Fischer, Artur Rubinstein, Emil von Sauer, Artur Schnabel); one is by a performer influenced by Schenker, Murray Perahia; and one is by an anonymous pianist dubbed HP (for Human Performer), who made a recording of bars 1–32 specifically for a study of Todd's model of phrase arching by Luke Windsor and Eric Clarke (1997).[17] All of these, of course,

16. To facilitate comparison with d'Albert's and Sapellnikoff's performance, bar numbers in Media Examples 3.3–3.8, and in the following text, follow Figure 3.2.

17. This recording was kindly made available to me by Eric Clarke and is used with the pianist's permission.

Pianist	Recording	Label and Release Date	Original Recording Date	Media Example
Eugen d'Albert	The Great Pianists Vol. 6 Masters of the piano roll series	Dal Segno DSPRCD022 (released 1992)	Welte-Mignon 422, 1905	3.1
Sapellnikoff	Private transfer by Denis Hall		Welte-Mignon 950, 1905	3.2
Edwin Fischer	The Pre-War Schubert Recordings	APR (Appian) 5515 (released 1996)	1938	3.3
Emil von Sauer	1940 Live Recordings from Amsterdam and Vienna	CD-Arbiter 114 (released 2005)	16–17 May 1940 (Austrian radio)	3.4
Artur Schnabel	Schubert: Impromptus D899 and D935	EMI Classics 724358683325 (released 2005)	1950	3.5
Artur Rubinstein	Schubert	RCA Victor-BMG 09026-63054-2	1961	3.6
Murray Perahia	Schubert Impromptus	Sony BMG Masterworks Classic Library 94732 (released 2005)	1982	3.7
HP			Private recording made for Windsor and Clarke 1997	3.8

Figure 3.3 Recordings of Schubert, op. 90 no. 3

are sound recordings, and I shall therefore comment more freely on dynamics than I did in the case of the piano rolls.

Small as it is, this sample displays a range of stylistic trends, some of them predictable. Schubert's piece is played in G major in all the recordings made before the end of the Second World War, and in G-flat major in all made thereafter. Again, the level of tempo variation drops dramatically after the 1905 piano

		Average Tempo	Standard Deviation (%)
D'Albert	1905	70	19.5
Sapellnikoff	1905	68	22
Fischer	1938	70.5	10
Sauer	1940	64	14
Schnabel	1950	70	14
Rubinstein	1961	59	13.5
Perahia	1982	61	9.1
HP	ca. 1995	75	10.3

Figure 3.4 Average tempos and standard deviations in recordings of Schubert, op. 90 no. 3. Figures are for bars 1–48, except in the case of HP's partial recording of bars 1–32. See Media Examples 3.3–3.8

rolls, thereafter remaining within a relatively narrow band: this can be seen from the normalised standard deviations in Figure 3.4. Perhaps less predictably, the table also shows that the average tempo for bars 1–48 of the four recordings from before 1945 ranges from 64 to 71 MM, whereas the later recordings all fall outside this band: Schnabel and HP are faster, Rubinstein and Perahia slower. (That runs contrary to widespread beliefs about the increasing convergence of tempos since the Second World War.) An average tempo value, however, can mean very different things in different performances.

I referred to the 'basic' tempo of Sapellnikoff's performance of the first section of op. 90 no. 3, and this term is widely encountered in empirical performance analysis. It has been discussed by Bruno Repp (1994), who makes the point that since expressive performances generally include phrase-final lengthening and caesurae, their tempo as experienced is likely to be rather faster than a simple arithmetical average would indicate. (That is, simply measuring the time a phrase, section, or movement takes and dividing it by the number of beats results in a figure with no obvious perceptual reality; Gabrielsson [1999: 540] calls this the 'mean' tempo, and distinguishes it from the 'main' tempo, which corresponds to Repp's 'basic' tempo.) Repp anticipates the argument that, in performances where the tempo is constantly changing, there might be no such thing as a basic tempo, but—as we have seen—rejects it out of hand: 'This objection can be dismissed... because even highly expressive pieces are commonly preceded by metronome indications in the score. If composers and editors think such music has a tempo, there must be a principled (if intuitive) way of following their tempo prescriptions' (1994: 158).

This is an argument based on textual authority, and as such illustrates how the paradigm of reproduction has become embedded even in relatively recent scientific writing on music. Against it one might invoke the authority of Beethoven,

who in the autograph manuscript of his song 'Nord oder Sud' wrote, '100 according to Mälzel, but this applies only to the first measures, as feeling has its own
tempo' (Taruskin 1995: 214). What is relevant here, however, is not authority—of
whatever kind—but the listening experience. To listen to d'Albert's recording of
op. 90 no. 3 is to feel the ebbing and flowing of tempo, to draw it into your own
body: when I say his tempo is mobile, I mean precisely that you do not experience
it in terms of a basic tempo, and I would claim the same of Sauer and Schnabel.
The idea that there must be a basic tempo, and that it must remain stable (so that,
as Repp claimed, for 'the basic tempo…to change during the course of a phrase'
is a fault), is a product of aesthetic ideology rather than of how performers have
actually played. It is another example of having a theory and denying what does
not conform to it, except that in this case the theory is an unconscious one and
consequently not recognised as such.

The presence or absence of a perceptible basic tempo forms a useful means of
grouping these recordings. As I said, there is a basic tempo in Sapellnikoff's playing of at least the first two eight-bar phrases, which he also articulates clearly—but
in doing so he uses a lot of tempo variation, and so ends up with the high standard
deviation shown in Figure 3.4. His playing is very old-fashioned in comparison
to Fischer's 1938 recording, a striking example of the more streamlined interpretive approach that developed between the wars and became dominant after
1945. Fischer, whose playing Schenker had criticised in 1920 for its hard touch
and lack of tone (Federhofer 1985: 229), gives a smooth, cantilena-like performance. Divisions between sections are clearly articulated, and there is even a trace
of phrase arching: Fischer gets faster and louder as he plays into bars 1–8 and
slower and softer as he comes out of them, and does the same again in bars 9–16.
There is also some trace of this in bars 17–24 and 32–40 (where he also shapes
the four-bar sequences), though not in bars 25–32 or 41–48. Only in bars 38–42,
where Fischer makes a broad decelerando from the second sequential passage
that continues into the new phrase at bar 41, is there a palpable reminiscence of
older, more mobile playing.

In general, then, Fischer's performance is forward-looking in its perceptible
basic tempo and lack of inflection. As a result, though the performance is not on
average particularly fast, it might still bring to mind Schenker's complaint from
just a few years earlier (1979: 6) that 'today one flies over the work of art in the
same manner as one flies over villages, cities, palaces, castles, fields, woods, riv-
ers, and lakes. This contradicts not only the historical bases of the work of art but
also—more significantly—its coherence, its inner relationships, which demand to
be "traversed"'. The final word is a reference to what Schenker had said earlier in
the same paragraph, and evokes the trudging and freewheeling of d'Albert's playing: 'every relationship represents a path which is as real as any we "traverse" with
our feet'. In contrast to the flattened out landscape seen from a plane, Schenker's
terrestrial image resonates with Johnson's and Larson's participant perspective—
the perspective that Lewis also associated with the performer.[18]

---

18. See Chapter 2, p. 45.

Fischer's immediately pre-war recording groups with the three most recent recordings in this small sample, by Rubinstein, Perahia, and HP. Rubinstein (whom Schenker heard in 1933, admiring his playing of Chopin but not Beethoven [Federhofer 1985: 249]) seems to set up a basic tempo around 65 MM in the first phrase, but the second is more mobile, while the subsequent phrases (bars 17–48) might suggest a basic tempo closer to 62: clearly there is not a definitive borderline to be drawn between performances that do and do not have a basic tempo. What groups this recording with Fischer's is rather its characteristically unfussy quality and clear articulation of phrases, though Rubinstein achieves this more through phrase-final lengthening than through phrase arching. (I shall have more to say on this distinction in Chapter 6.) In this much slower but again relatively uninflected performance, small expressive gestures can have a telling effect: an example is the emphasis on the second beat of bar 13, achieved through a combination of prolongation and diminuendo, and clearly prompted by Schubert's < > marking (though Rubinstein treats it more like a *subito piano*). Perahia's recording shares many of the same qualities. These include a similar average tempo, careful articulation of structure, and occasional but telling expressive interventions, among which the second beat of bar 13 again figures. Unlike Rubinstein's, there is a certain amount of phrase arching in Perahia's playing, but it is limited by the smaller amount of tempo variation (less than any of the recordings in Figure 3.4, as measured by standard deviation). The expressivity of Perahia's playing resides primarily in dynamics and tonal variation.

Finally among this group, HP's performance is much faster, to the extent that the quaver figuration verges on sounding like a written-out tremolo, but shares the same values of unfussiness and clear articulation. (In this context his minute hesitations preceding the b^1 on the first beat of bars 3 and 11, as it happens mirroring Schenker's instructions, come through strongly.) However HP's principal means of achieving articulation is phrase arching: as compared to Fischer, he is consistent in applying it on an eight-bar basis, with the addition of four-bar phrasing to bring out the sequences in bars 17–20 and 21–24 (the parallelism of which is also strong in Rubinstein's and Perahia's performances). The only real irregularity is how he maintains the slower pacing from bar 23 to the downbeat of bar 26—another echo of the treatment of bars 24–25 and 40–41 that I noted in earlier recordings. It is appealing, except for those with a strong commitment to the aesthetics of organicism, to think of such memorable moments as taking on a life of their own and circulating among performances in the manner of memes or earworms, more or less divorced from other aspects of the interpretations in which they were originally embedded.

The two recordings whose tempo I hear as essentially mobile can both be seen as compromises between the values of 'old school' performance and the more streamlined approach I have just described. Sauer, who appears in Schenker's 1895 list of respected performers, plays bars 5–7 of op. 90 no. 3 almost like d'Albert, and de-emphasises the phrase division at bars 8–9: once again, the manner in which he plays through the divisions of bars 24–25 and 40–41 preserves the memory of older playing. On the other hand he strongly articulates the division at bars 16–17 and brings out the sequences at 17–24 and 33–40, though with the novel and effective twist of a *subito piano* at bar 39. It seems appropriate to characterise this as a performance built on an 'old school' foundation but taking some account of current tendencies.

As for Schnabel, whose playing of the classics Schenker described as combining manual dexterity and intellectual grasp with the lack of any musical understanding (Federhofer 1985: 250–51), his recording immediately stands out for its radically fast tempo—even faster than HP's—and clarity of structural articulation, achieved through phrase-final lengthening: four of the five longest notes in the first forty-eight bars of his performance occur on the final beat on an eight-bar phrase (bars 8, 24, 40, and 48), with the other—actually the longest note of all, at bar 30—being a rhetorical lengthening of the cadential b¹, carrying the suggestion of a dominant thirteenth. On the other hand the mobility of Schnabel's tempo and his avoidance of any simple treatment of the sequences bear the marks of an older pianistic conception. And these two characteristics come together in what sounds like a modulation to a different temporal plane from bar 38, creating the same impression as in d'Albert's performance that time might momentarily stand still—except that Schnabel articulates the beginning of the new phrase and so creates a more disciplined effect than d'Albert's unruly playing. All this is consistent with the idea that Schnabel forged an idiosyncratic kind of modernist performance out of ways of playing that had a long history.

It is, then, as if there are two essentially distinct approaches to Schubert's op. 90 no. 3. One approach focusses on its symmetrical, balanced, and elegiacal qualities; it can result in fast or slow performances, but tends either towards a lower level of tempo and dynamic inflection, or towards organising them in terms of more or less regular patterns. This might be described as treating the music as if it was verse. The other approach treats it more like prose, organising the performance around the creation of a series of individual, irregular, and sometimes unpredictable expressive moments: performances like d'Albert's 'transcend "motive," "theme," "phrase," and "bar line"', to repeat Schenker's words from *Free Composition*, being rather organised around the music's perceived emotional content. It is tempting, and certainly not incorrect, to call the first approach modernist or structuralist performance, and the second premodern or rhetorical performance. (They also map onto what Taruskin [1995: 108–10], borrowing from T. E. Hulme, calls geometrical and vitalist performance.) But while it is true that the first became generally dominant after 1945, the dates in Figure 3.4 hint at something that will also emerge from later chapters: different ways of playing rarely succeed one another in neat historical sequence. There was an extended period when the two approaches, and a range of positions between them, represented available stylistic options.

And that takes me back to my main argument. If Schubert's op. 90 no. 3 can accommodate a range of interpretive approaches from the structuralist to the rhetorical, then it cannot be explained away as the exception that proves the rule, a piece whose unusual degree of structural overdetermination entails a non-structural realisation: it was, after all, chosen by Windsor and Clarke specifically to evaluate Todd's theory of phrase arching, the basic assumption of which is that performance is an epiphenomenon of structure. From this two consequences follow, both of which I have already suggested. First, the relationship between structure and performance is not as tight as analysis-to-performance theorists have imagined, and it is not even obvious that it makes sense to think of structure as something that compositions 'have', as opposed to affordances for the creation of structural and other meanings in performance. Second, structuralist performance, better known as modernist performance—the kind of performance in terms of which Schenker's writings on performance have been read—should be seen as a historical style, and not the paradigm for performance in general as which it has been widely represented in music-theoretical and pedagogical circles.

In this way we are forced to the second explanation for the disconnect between Schenker's analysis of op. 90 no. 3 and his prescriptions for how it should go in performance. This is, quite simply, that even as Schenker perfected his analytical method, shaving off the filigree detail of classical music in order to reveal the streamlined forms underneath, he continued to think of music in terms of the mobility of tempo and 'speaking' quality that characterised an increasingly anachronistic, rhetorical style of playing. That has two thought-provoking implications. The first is that we have been hearing Schenker's analyses wrong all this time: we have interpreted what he wrote in light of a sound image, a sense of how music goes, that is quite different from Schenker's. The second is that the relationship between theory and practice is more distant than those in the theoretical camp, at least, may have bargained for. Performers involved in the practice-as-research movement sometimes emphasise the tacit, or procedural, nature of the knowledge on which they draw in the real time of music making, contrasting it to the explicit, formalised, or tacit knowledge with which theorists deal. The former is embodied and inherently temporal; the latter is abstract and typically based on a spatial conception of time. The parallel with what Massumi called the 'different logics' of uninterpreted affect and interpreted emotion is not coincidental; this is the performance analyst's version of Seeger's musicological juncture. And if I am right, Schenker illustrates it particularly clearly.

That Schenker felt himself in many ways out of kilter with the times in which he lived is well known, and complaints about declining performance standards frequently mask nostalgia (especially when there are no recordings to contradict them). But there was more to it when in 1925—the year of his essay on op. 90 no. 3—Schenker wrote that 'anyone who has heard the performances of masterworks twenty years ago can scarcely believe how performance could become already so much worse today' (1994: 111)—and of course the twenty years take us back to 1905, the year of d'Albert's roll. For it was in those years that what we now think of as modernist performance style was solidifying, and while he did not attend concerts as regularly as in the 1890s, Schenker listened to them on the radio, and often commented on them in his diary. His views on Felix Weingartner, whom in earlier years he had criticised for exaggerating details at the expense of synthesis, are varied, but Weingartner's conducting preserved many aspects of the older style, and in 1922 Schenker comments of a performance of Brahms's

Symphony no. 1 that Weingartner is 'better at everything than Furtwängler, because closer to the tradition' (Federhofer 1985: 268). Furtwängler, despite his study with and advocacy of Schenker, comes in for detailed and surprisingly strong criticism in the privacy of Schenker's diary: he speaks like a dilettante and doesn't understand sonata form; worse, he talks of the *Urlinie* but is really a surface performer (115–16). At least, Schenker comments, he is better than Toscanini (130). Perhaps most revealingly, the conductors whom Schenker praises are often ones whose names—at least as conductors—are now generally forgotten, such Paul von Klenau and Franz von Hoesslin (161–72, 157–58).

Rosen (2005) has remarked that 'Bartók was both a composer who helped to revolutionize the music of the early twentieth century and a traditional pianist in an old-fashioned style' (7). This might suggest we should simply accept a similar disconnect between Schenker's theorising and his idea of how music should go in performance. But this is seriously problematised by his explicit and continuing intention to forge precisely such a connection, as expressed, for example, by the passage from *Free Composition* that I quoted near the beginning of Chapter 2: 'The *performance* of a musical work of art can be based only upon a perception of that work's organic coherence....Consequently, the concept of background, middleground, and foreground is of decisive and practical importance for performance'. From 1911 on—when as we saw he drafted the majority of the materials eventually published as *The Art of Performance*—Schenker repeatedly announced his intention to publish a treatise on the subject, and he continued to regard it as a live project at least until 1930 (Schenker 2000: xii). Yet it is difficult to see how he could have brought it to a successful conclusion, given the deep contradictions in his thinking.

Perhaps the most obvious of these contradictions concerns the fundamental principle I mentioned in Chapter 2, that notations specify effects, and the performer is free to choose the manner of their realisation: as long as 'the performer is fully aware of the desired effect', Schenker writes in the 1911 papers, this 'serves to justify any means he might use to produce it' (78). (In the annotated edition of Bach's *Chromatic Fantasy and Fugue* that he published the previous year, Schenker made the point more graphically: 'even the nose may assist, as long as the proper meaning is conveyed' [Schenker 1984: 69].) But it is impossible to square this with the kind of minute detail, even of precise physical gesture, that Schenker routinely included in his performance instructions: in bar 36 of op. 90 no. 3, he says, 'the hand should remain steeply angled over the keys', while on the upbeat to bar 65 'the hand is lifted, it strokes the air in an arc', and at bar 85 'the left hand should be held erect on the first eighth, and the figure...should be played lightly, almost as if one did not intend to produce actual sounds'. (Use of the nose is not specified.) The same tension appears in another guise when, at different points in the 1911 papers, Schenker (2000: 33, 77–78) writes on the one hand that, for the great composers of the past, 'the content of their work was always created according to the needs of synthesis, never merely according to those of the hand', and on the other that, for any given piece, there are specific fingerings and gestures in the absence of which 'a performer cannot possibly produce the composer's intended result'.

Schenker is at odds with himself, as well as with the changes in performance style that were taking place around him.

There are equally striking contradictions in the other unfinished treatise on performance that I have already mentioned: not Schoenberg's, which never progressed far enough to be unfinished, but Adorno's, which goes back to discussions with Rudolph Kolisch in the 1920s—as I said in Chapter 1, there was at one point an idea that they would co-author it—and which Adorno continued to regard as a live project at least until 1959 (Adorno 2006 xii–xiii). At one moment we see Adorno insisting that 'there is no reason whatsoever to consider the sensual sound of music more fundamental to it than the sensual sound of words to language'; a few pages later we read that 'in music, reading necessarily demands a sensual image, whereas literature practically forbids that of its true content' (162, 167). As with Schenker, I would argue, the contradiction is a deep one, grounded in ontology. I cannot better the diagnosis of Adorno's problems on the back cover of the paperback translation of his notes, presumably by the editor, Henri Lonitz, which takes this as its point of departure:

In the various notes and texts brought together in *Towards a Theory of Musical Reproduction*, one finds Adorno constantly circling around an irresolvable paradox: interpretation can only fail the work, yet only through it can music's true essence be captured. While he at times seems more definite in his pronouncement of a musical score's absolute value—just as a book is read silently, not aloud—his discourse repeatedly displays his inability to cling to that belief.

As I see it, the basic problem with both Schenker's and Adorno's approaches to performance, and the reason neither of their books actually exists, lies in their common reliance on the paradigm of reproduction. I see this as incompatible with any adequate theory of musical performance, but especially the kind of performance epitomised by 'old school' playing—to which Adorno, despite being thirty-five years younger than Schenker, seems to have been equally attached. Adorno's proclivities become obvious when he asserts in his notes that 'in a meaningful presentation of a work of thematic music, no 2 bars will be even chronometrically equal' (2006: 102): that is virtually a paraphrase of Leschetizky's advocacy, as formulated by Malwine Brée, of 'constant changes in *tempo* and contrasts in movement....No composition should be played in a uniform *tempo* from beginning to end' (1913: 53). (So much, again, for Repp's basic tempo.) And as we saw, Adorno describes d'Albert as the greatest of all pianists. It is equally obvious when he reminds himself that 'it must be stated clearly in the study that almost all musical interpretation today is nonsensical and wrong' (2006: 134, 145), while at another point he writes, 'Against Furtwängler and Walter—*and* against Toscanini! And Karajan'.

The point is not, then, to borrow Schmalfeldt's language, that theorist-Schenker relinquished the aim that his theory should encompass everything about music, performance included: theorist-Schenker was not in the habit of relinquishing things. It was that, in practice, this aim was unachievable on terms that were acceptable to performer-Schenker—which is presumably what also happened with his attempts in the 1920s to extend his theory to dynamic levels.[19] To be sure, as we saw, Schenker's American successors *did* succeed in combining the fragmentary theory of performance from 1911 and the analytical theory from the 1920s and 1930s into a more or less coherent whole, and in terms of institutional acceptance and the dissemination of informed performance practice it was a remarkable success. But that success was achieved on the basis of a style of performance that was fundamentally different from how Schenker believed music should go—a style of which Schenker heard the early stirrings, and did not like what he heard. It seems possible, then, that the surprisingly negative assessments in Schenker's diary of his most prestigious supporter in the world of professional performance are there not *in spite of* the fact that Furtwängler studied with Schenker and incorporated what he learned into his performances, but just *because* he did.[20]

In this way performance emerges as perhaps the most spectacular illustration of how Schenker's theory, in its passage from pre-war Vienna to post-war America, was turned inside out, adapted to aesthetic, ideological, and intellectual values as different as could be from Schenker's own, in short, modernised. That this could happen demonstrates not only the power of ideological interpretations in general, but also the peculiar malleability of discursive representations of performance—a malleability that results from the inability of words to capture the nuances of expressive performance, or the complexity of their interactions. The theorist Michael Green concludes his study of Lussy's *Traité de l'expression musicale* by saying, 'there is more to a good performance than simply knowing which surface events to respond to....It is essential that the common response to individual events be carefully controlled so that the structure is clearly articulated' (1994: 134, 145). In effect Green is turning Lussy into a period proponent of the analysis-to-performance approach, so strengthening the assumption that it is a permanent paradigm of what performance should be. And yet, on a more straightforward (that is, less ideologically loaded) reading, Lussy's most distinctive idea, the *accent pathétique*, stands for exactly the opposite. It is like the story of modernist performance being read into Schenker's words, only in miniature. And that such 180 degree swings in the meanings attributed to texts about performance can happen only dramatises the problems inherent in any attempt to reconstruct past performance styles from written documents, and hence the fragility of our knowledge of how music sounded before the age of recording.

19. See Chapter 2, p. 36.

20. In his article 'Heinrich Schenker and great performers', which was intended to show that Schenker was a real musician and not just a theorist, Oswald Jonas cites a specific example of a feature arising out of discussion with Schenker that Furtwängler attempted to incorporate into his interpretation of Beethoven's 'Pastoral' Symphony: the D-C-G in the violins at bars 275ff of the first movement, which Schenker saw as a reminiscence of the same notes (an octave lower) at bars 11–12. Jonas heard Furtwängler rehearsing this, but he couldn't get it to work: 'again and again it did not come to his satisfaction', writes Jonas, 'nor was it convincingly expressed. The author turned to a friend who was also present with the remark that one could clearly perceive the influence of Schenker in this effort' (Jonas [2003: 132]). Jonas does not draw the obvious conclusion.

4

Beyond Structure

Established music-theoretical approaches to performance, particularly in North America, assume the paradigmatic status of what I have called structuralist performance—and in calling it 'structuralist' rather than 'structural', I intend the suggestion that it may be the appearance of structure rather than the working out of defensible analytical interpretations that matters. (There is a parallel with the 'desperation' that drove Taruskin [1995: 99] to distinguish the 'authentistic' from the authentic.) It is not however structuralist performance—which I see as a style, like any other—that is the object of my critique: it is the assumption that it embodies a universal principle about how music should go in performance.

In Chapter 3 I cited Mitchell Ohriner's suggestion that structure is best seen as produced by performers within the framework of compositional affordances. Whether the term is used to refer to the affordances or to their interpretation, structure is a conditioning factor of performance and of thinking about performance. But its role is variable and depends on context. At the most general level, some music requires interpretation—whether or not of a specifically structural nature—in a way or to a degree that other music does not. John Butt writes that, in Bach, 'the performance is already there in the notation itself', and enlarges: 'It's very hard to play Bach well, but if you get the notes right it's very hard to ruin. With Handel, on the other hand, you can get the notes right and nothing else and it will sound absolutely terrible—there's nothing there at all' (Sherman 1997: 184, 174). Or it may be a matter of the individual piece: as Mine Doğantan-Dack (2008: 305) says, some pieces admit of only one structural interpretation, while others afford alternative interpretations. As we saw in Chapter 2, the starting point for Dodson's study of recordings of Beethoven's Sonata op. 81a is that the score affords alternative structural interpretations, which he identifies in Schenkerian terms, with different performances embodying different choices. Then again, structural approaches can help in steering a way through complex music, rather like finding a path through the undergrowth. An example might be bars 127–48 from the development section in the first movement of Brahms's Piano Trio op. 8 in its 1889 version: in a 1999 article I presented a bass-line reduction of this passage, and described it as 'articulating non-obvious relationships between non-contiguous points in the music and so facilitating a controlled pacing that knits together what are at first sight chaotically diversified materials' (Cook 1999b: 232–33).

However the issue is not whether structuralist approaches can be useful for performers—of course they can—but how universally applicable they are, and my bass-line reduction also included the following passage from op. 8, bars 149–76. Here, I argued, the reduction is more tenuous. The notes of which it consists do not control the harmonic and linear texture in the same way as in the previous passage: this time Brahms seems to have designed the music to befuddle what might look like straightforward analytical relationships (for example between the F# of bar 149 and the G of bar 157). Consequently, I suggested, a performance that somehow clarified this relationship, that rendered it structurally articulate, would misrepresent the intended musical effect. That of course is Rothstein's point, which I also mentioned in Chapter 2, about situations where the performer's role is precisely *not* to bring out structure. Adorno (2006) made the same point with exemplary clarity, though he characteristically added a second clause that complicates it: 'In some music, it forms part of the sense *not* to make the structure transparent—but that is then itself a part of the structure the analysis must lead us to' (71). The added clause opens the way to Wason's 'heads I win, tails you lose' argument. The more straightforward conclusion is that transparently structuralist performance is an option rather than an obligation, a style rather than a paradigm for performance in general.

And after all, why should it necessarily be the performer's job to disambiguate structure? If the opening of Mozart's A major Sonata K 331 is perfectly designed to hold readings based on $\hat{5}$ and $\hat{3}$ in balance, is it self-evident that performers must commit themselves to one or the other? The frequently made assumption that, unlike analysts, performers cannot hedge their bets derives its plausibility from the concept of performance that I discussed in Chapter 1: the composer has a specific conception which it is the performer's duty to internalise and communicate to the listener. My reservations about this communication model will become increasingly clear as the book proceeds. For now, I will simply cite the evidence of some empirical research. In the experiments into perceptions of energy and tension that I mentioned in the last chapter, Carol Krumhansl (1996) played listeners a recording by Philippe Entremont of the opening of Mozart's Sonata K 282, together with a 'deadpan', in other words nominal, MIDI version.[1] (There was also a second MIDI version that replicated the human performer's timing with deadpan dynamics, while a third was the other way round.) The results were in all cases virtually identical. If the purpose of performance is to communicate something that is already inherent in the music, then in terms of this crucial dimension of listening experience the composition speaks for itself—which

1. Entremont recorded the sonata on a Bösendorfer SE specifically for this project. (The Bösendorfer SE is an acoustic grand piano equipped with MIDI sensors, similar in principle to a Yamaha Disklavier.)

means that performance is redundant, just as Schoenberg claimed. The point, of course, lies in the conditional clause. In playing Schubert's op. 90 no. 3, d'Albert was creating energetic and tensional morphologies that could never have been predicted on the basis of analysing the score and were not in that sense inherent in the music at all. And it's revealing in this context that empirical research by Eric Clarke and Luke Windsor, admittedly based on simpler musical materials, revealed that 'music students judged the *least* structurally communicative performances...to be their most preferred renditions' (Clarke 2005a: 160). All of this, as I see it, shows the limited applicability of the structuralist paradigm.

Of course, as Clarke goes on to say, what applies to the simple musical materials used in this project may not apply to more complex materials, or maybe music students have different preferences from other listeners. But that again makes my point: the structuralist paradigm, and the communication model that supports it, applies more to some music and some contexts than to others. And a particular context in which it has, and has long had, a special role is education. In an empirical study from 1983, John Sloboda had pianists perform musical materials that had been specifically designed to be metrically ambiguous: he found that the more experienced the pianists were, the more they used expressive performance to disambiguate the meter. But what is telling is his observation that one of the pianists, whose work regularly included playing music for dictation tests, communicated the metre more effectively than another who was equally accomplished but did not do such work. The didactic context, that is to say, elicits a particular style of playing. So do other circumstances: as Eric Clarke says, 'the style of performance in a concert recital is likely to be rather different from the same performer's style at a children's concert' (1988: 24).

In his study of nineteenth-century pianism, Jim Samson (2000) traces the association of pedagogy with 'a structural—as opposed to an aesthetic or generic—sense of form' (111) back to 1840s Berlin, and the traces of this can be found in piano performance manuals from the later part of the century. Christiani (1885), for whom as for many twentieth-century theorists 'intelligent perception should precede and direct the mechanical execution', coins the general term 'periodizing' for parsing a composition into periods, phrases, and sections. He writes that 'as the reader's mind discerns these *architectonic* phrases, so should he, as interpreter, convey them to his audience through the means of metrical accentuation, at the beginning and at the proper breaks between groups' (237, 117, 137). And if this sounds like the kind of superficial understanding of form against which Schenker inveighed, then Christiani also suggests conveying to the audience another kind of structure that might seem to anticipate Schenkerian analysis: hidden melodies, and in particular those 'about which it is doubtful whether the composer premeditated them' (226). Christiani continues: 'Whether the composer intended such hidden melodies, or not, should never deter the performer from following his own interpretation, provided that it is based on sound reasoning.... Far from being a liberty taken with the composition, hardly enough of importance can be attached to the discovery and the bringing out of hidden melodic strains' (238).[2]

This is taking us onto familiar pedagogical territory. Renee Timmers observes that 'Conscious awareness of the structure of the music...helps to increase the effectiveness of practice' (2005: 674). What appears to be a 'mechanical' problem in fingering, to borrow Christiani's term, may be untangled through an analysis that sorts out what goes with what. Rothstein's analytical approach to phrase extension (1989) does the same in another domain. Joshua Rifkin talks about a chamber music masterclass where he coached an ensemble whose members 'were very capable performers, extremely gifted; any one of them could render a dazzling Brahms fiddle concerto or its equivalent' (Sherman 1997: 382). But they were playing a serenade by Max Reger, with whose idiom they were not familiar, and so they made a hash of it, 'because they didn't know where the phrases were falling, where the weight lay, and so forth. It had to be painstakingly pulled out of them by consideration of questions like, How are we going to make this palpable, and how are we going to project this?' The point then is not so much the level of the performer's skills, but the nature of what is being done. And it is in this context that Doğantan-Dack (2008) draws a clear distinction between the kind of analytical facilitation of performance exemplified in the work of Roger Chaffin and his co-workers—with which I would group the examples I have just given—and what she calls 'performer's analysis' (305), by which she means the generation of a personal performance interpretation. As I said in Chapter 2, this is a different use of the term from Rink's.

Doğantan-Dack explains what she means through the example of the second movement of Beethoven's 'Pathétique' Sonata, op. 13, a recording of which is included with the book in which her essay appeared. She begins by reviewing the various plausible interpretations of this movement that analysts have put forward, but—she says—you cannot develop your own interpretation by simply borrowing someone else's analysis. (Tim Howell [1992: 702] has said the same.) Instead the performer has to 'turn to herself', and Doğantan-Dack's starting point is what she terms the 'tempo-expression' (2008: 306) marking at the head of the movement, *Adagio cantabile*. Despite this marking, she observes, the melody 'never gains independence to "sing" on its own'. And she diagnoses the problem: 'the fingers of the right hand, which also have to take part in playing the accompaniment, cannot "grow into" the keys as they would normally do when singing on the piano; the wrist is also not free to "breathe," as in normative pianistic *cantabile* practice' (306-7). However, Doğantan-Dack continues, this changes at bar 51, when the theme comes round for the fourth time, for here the accompaniment—now in

---

2. Kullak (1893) makes a similar point: 'The singing tone is often more deeply hidden, and the player must be habituated to earnest musical reflection in order to discover the melodious point' (261). Also reminiscent of Schenker, but without the trope of concealment, is Reinecke's reference (1897) to the 'red thread which runs through the whole' (2), the grasping of which is essential for performance.

triplets—'allows the "singing" fingers playing the melody more elasticity...and the wrist more "space" to breathe' (307). There is in this way a kind of embodied narrative that progresses from constraint to relative freedom, and as such Beethoven's marking remains 'an imagined guiding force, rather than an actually, and fully, enacted one'.

Doğantan-Dack then goes on to consider various ways in which this interpretive conception might be represented in performance, the essential choice being whether to treat bar 51 as a goal or as 'an event that just comes to pass, as it were'. She prefers the former, she says, even though 'in performance this conception invariably leads me to override Beethoven's *piano* dynamic marking in bar 51 and keep the dynamic level *forte* till the coda'. That may offend proponents of *Werktreue*, she admits, but the performer's job is 'to *make* a piece work aesthetically', and 'an aesthetically satisfying performance does not necessarily rise upon the pillars of *Werktreue* ideology' (308). What Doğantan-Dack claims for the performer here is no more than what was claimed by Christiani in relation to hidden melodies, or by Kullak (1893) when he wrote that 'The entire science of rendering turns on the conception of ideas: the direction no longer suffices, that the player must heed the intention of the composer, and shape his rendering accordingly. He should follow the latter in emotion and creative energy; and even if not his equal in productive fancy, he should be his peer in aesthetic judgement' (280). The pianist and harpsichordist Wanda Landowska (1964: 407) made the same point more strongly when she imagined Rameau rising from his grave to demand changes in her performance of his 'La dauphine': 'You gave birth to it', she imagined herself saying, 'it is beautiful. But now leave me alone with it. You have nothing more to say; go away!'

It is for the epistemological clarity of her account that I have quoted Doğantan-Dack at length. All this illustrates her reference, which I quoted in Chapter 2, to the 'many different kinds of assumptions, information, images and associations' which contribute to an individual performance interpretation, and which—she continued—'do not necessarily form a hierarchy of importance'. In such performer's analysis, issues of formal structure or historical insight circulate on the same level, so to speak, as the hermeneutical scenarios keyed by the epithets that both Hans von Bülow and Alfred Cortot applied to Chopin's Preludes. These include narrative elements but might best be described as emotional story boards. Bülow pictures the E minor Prelude (op. 28 no. 4) as

one of the paroxysms to which Chopin was subject on account of his weak chest. In the left hand we hear his heavy breathing, and in the right hand the tones of suffering wrung from his breast. At the twelfth measure he seeks relief by turning on the other side; but his oppression increases momentarily.... His heart-throbs grow slower and fainter; at the chord resting on Bb (third measure from the end) they suddenly cease for a moment.... The final chord shows that he sleeps (translated in Schonberg 1965: 128).

As transmitted by Jeanne Thieffry, Cortot's scenario for this Prelude has the same corporeal and emotional dimension, though it is no longer tied to the figure of Chopin (unless, of course, the funeral is his):

> This piece must be played in the mood of a mourner, with the face dimly veiled and the eyes heavy with tears.... At the twelfth bar pass from the feeling of sadness to sudden terror.... Then the lament dies away. There is a pause—a *long* one—and then in the last chords a note of doom' (Cortot and Thieffry 1937: 46).

And again this is an interpretive tradition that can be traced in the writings of the nineteenth-century piano pedagogues. For Kullak, Beethoven's Sonata op. 110 is characterised by 'a spirit of gentle mournfulness. This is the fundamental idea, imposing moderation on the display of power, and requiring a prevailingly songful, lyrically resigned spiritualization of the harmonies' (1893: 318). The point Kullak wants to make is that the moment-to-moment variety of the music should be balanced by 'unity of meaning', and in order to convey this he tells the performer what to feel: Daniel Leech-Wilkinson (2009a: chapter 6, paragraph 49), who compares Cortot's description of the E minor Prelude to how he played it on a 1928 recording, observes that 'there is no more efficient way of communicating to a student performer how to shape a piece in a particular way than to tell her how to feel or what to imagine the music is evoking'. Kullak even details eight contrasted interpretations of Beethoven's 'Moonlight' Sonata, op. 27, by Czerny, Ubilischeff, Liszt, Marx, Köhler, Elterlein, Weber, and Cornelius, which vary from churchyards to Gothic cathedrals and moonlit visions of the protagonist's corpselike face. It is not that the music is *about* such images, he explains, but that each constitutes an alternative perspective on 'the primal source of the emotions', that is to say the music itself (1893: 327).

By listing eight hermeneutical interpretations of op. 27, Kullak makes the point that you have a choice about what to feel or imagine that the music is evoking (something that does not emerge from Thieffry's account of how the E minor Prelude 'must be played'). Doğantan-Dack said you cannot develop an interpretation by simply borrowing someone else's analysis. As I read Kullak, he is suggesting you develop your own personal interpretation of the music through bouncing it off a variety of narrative, pictorial, and emotional images: 'the very art of rendering', he says, 'consists in divining, among the different possibilities, that form of unity which corresponds either to the inclination or to the conviction of the interpreting subjectivity' (1893: 320). It is in this frank acknowledgement of subjectivity—equally the premise of Doğantan-Dack's account of the 'Pathétique' movement—that the epistemological contrast with academic approaches becomes most evident, and the more the hermeneutic process resembles academic research, the more salient the differences become.

In his *Piano Notes*, Charles Rosen (2003: 193–95) writes that 'One method of arriving at an original and yet responsible approach ... is to return to the sources, to abandon the traditional editions and look instead at the manuscripts and the original printings'. That sounds like the academic rationale for HIP. But as Rosen continues, the difference in his epistemological orientation becomes increasingly evident. 'The alien handwriting and notation can have an extraordinary effect of suggestion', he writes; 'we start to notice details of the text that have escaped us'. At this point he reminds us (as does Doğantan-Dack) that fine performances may be based on faulty scholarship, and concludes that 'in the end, it is not so much the composer or the music that benefits from the study of manuscript and original edition as the performer'—a formulation that amounts to much the same as Kullak's reference to the inclination or conviction of the interpreting subjectivity.

And Rosen's take here on historically informed performance—which is not so different from the post-Taruskin consensus—might suggest a corresponding take on 'analytically informed performance'. Whereas in HIP the interaction between scholarship and performance has always taken place in the studio, rehearsal room, and concert hall, with scholars often serving as consultants to performers, interactions between theorists and performers have tended to take place on campus, on the scholar's turf: more than HIP, what I shall term AIP has been pursued within the contexts of academic epistemologies, modes of dissemination, and criteria for evaluation. (An obvious reason for this difference is that there is not a distinctive AIP audience, in the way there is an HIP one.) Two further comparisons should reinforce the point. The first may seem rather ironic, given my suggestion in Chapter 2 that the prescriptive nature of the page-to-stage approach resulted in part from the influence of composer-theorists such as Edward T. Cone. I am now suggesting that a useful model for the relationship between analysis and performance might be found in that between theory and composition. Composers who work within the context of academia are theoretically informed, but do not simply translate theory into composition, even (perhaps especially) when it is their own theory: they use it rather to open up previously unimagined possibilities, to spark ideas off, to react against, to play with, and so to forge a conception that is both sonic and personal. Performers do all of that, and the example of composition shows that the academy is capable of supporting epistemological pluralism.

The second comparison arises out of Martin Scherzinger's argument for a kind of formalist analysis that 'opens doors of imaginative possibility' and so yields 'ideas that can be put to politically progressive use' (2004: 272, 274): he cites the imaginary example of an analysis of the first movement of Beethoven's Violin Concerto that takes seriously the 'radical peculiarity' of the D#s in bars 10 and 12, prompting consideration of theory's complicity in the narratives of organicism and teleology that place Beethoven at the end of a progression from Perotin, Machaut, Josquin, Monteverdi, and Bach, and in so doing assert the world-historical role of Western art. From a standard academic perspective this is decidedly fanciful. But Scherzinger's proposal can be seen as an application to the practice of academic writing of a composer's approach to theory (it is relevant in this context that he is a composer as well as a theorist). And seen in this light rather than that of the standard analysis-to-performance paradigm, structural analysis may be actually an under-exploited resource for the development of personal interpretation in performance.

MOZART'S MINIATURE THEATRE

My aim in the main part of this chapter is to place approaches to performance premised on the identification of music with some kind of structured object alongside an approach that still takes the score as its starting point but is based on a different premise. In Chapter 3 I set up the idea of rhetorical performance in opposition to structuralist performance, and I now wish to broaden this idea and place it within a historical context. The traditional approach to performance is to see it as a form of asynchronous communication: the already existing work is to be accurately transmitted through performance to the listener. As epitomised by the oratory of the law courts, rhetoric also involves the communication of pre-existing ideas, but the primary focus is not now on the transfer of information. Instead it is on persuasion, which is to be achieved as much through the manipulation of listeners' feelings as by the marshalling of facts. As the fortepianist Tom Beghin writes, 'in judicial oratory, being "effective" means winning one's case' (2007: 132).

Oratory, in short, is a form of performance, directed towards the other and irreducible from real time. Following the Western recovery of the classics that stimulated the Renaissance, the study of rhetoric became and remained a major focus of traditional education. So it is not surprising that it was adopted as a model for the practice and understanding of musical performance, which can equally be described as directed towards the other and irreducible from real time. According to Patrick McCreless, 'what the late eighteenth century tended to call rhetoric gradually began to be subsumed under what the nineteenth century called structure' (2002: 876), but it was only in the twentieth century that the identification of music with structure—and hence of performance with the communication of structure—achieved the status of a self-evident music-theoretical and aesthetic truth. And the result was less a theory of musical performance than a theory of music that turned performance into a mere epiphenomenon. Historically then, to the extent that such a thing as a theory of musical performance can be said to have existed, it drew on the concepts and practices of rhetoric.

For Schenker (2000), 'expressive, rhetorical performance' *is* performance, for 'a nonrhetorical performance...is no performance at all' (70). This is on the one hand a statement of stylistic allegiance, as I began to explore in the last chapter, but on the other it reflects a longstanding tradition that Schenker received through such sources as C. P. E. Bach's *Essay on the True Art of Playing Keyboard Instruments*—as well, no doubt, as through his own legal training. Much of what Schenker writes in the papers published as *The Art of Performance* could have come straight out of an eighteenth- or early nineteenth-century theory treatise: when he says that 'if our manner of speaking were continually to remain on one pitch and the syllables were the same length we would have no structure, no differentiation, and thus we would lose any possibility of communication', Schenker's thought (2000: 45) is in essence no different from Heinrich Christoph Koch's of over a century earlier ('in speech...certain syllables of the words are marked by a special emphasis, by which the content of the speech is mainly made clear to the listener'[3]). And in each case the purpose is to apply the same principles to musical performance.

The tradition of thinking of music as rhetoric goes back to the sixteenth century, but it involves a number of distinct aspects, not all of which have direct relevance to performance. For example, much of the effort of rhetorical theorists of music went into applying the formal categories of classical oratory to composition. The aspect on which I wish to focus is the tradition of rhetorical figures, which developed from the stereotypical characters and expressive types of baroque opera into the so-called topics of the classical style: an informal lexicon of recognisable musical types that reference musical genres, and through those genres the real-life situations and values with which they are associated. This is a system of representation based on specifically musical intertextuality, in the eighteenth-century writer Michel Paul Guy de Chabanon's words 'giving one song the character of another' (Allanbrook 1983: 6). In a more diffuse form, it continued into the nineteenth and twentieth centuries, and can be seen in today's popular culture (Samson 2000: 121, Agawu 2009: 42–50, Tagg 1982). My focus here, however, is on the classical period, in which, as Leonard Ratner—with whom the modern concept of topics originated—put it, the fortepiano 'brought the greater outside world of music into the home' (Ratner 1991: 616). In this way Mozart's sonatas, for example, became vehicles through which the larger world was represented, arguably taking on some of the attributes of television in today's homes. And topics played a key role in this. It is a tradition of which, according to Kofi Agawu, Schenker was well aware: when Schenker wrote of 'every change of sound and of figuration' pulling at the performer and listener, Agawu says, 'he might as well have said "every topical change"'.[4]

The Italian sob and German swoop that I mentioned in Chapter 3, stylised representations of real-world expressive vocalisation, might be thought of as purely performative topics, leaving no trace in written records. Musicologists have seen topics primarily as textual signifiers, in terms of what was played rather than how it was played, but both signifiers and signified were no doubt equally ways of playing: it is clear from contemporary treatises that topical categories, like those of genre and character, had specific implications for performance. Rather than attempt to reconstruct performance characteristics from written sources, however, I focus in this chapter on twentieth- and twenty-first-century responses to the notated topics of which the *locus classicus* is the first movement of Mozart's Sonata in F major, K 332—indeed it is so densely populated with such recognisable topical figures that John Irving (1997: 67) has suggested it was written as a model for students to emulate. The exposition section is shown in Figure 4.1. This is taken from the sonatas volume of the complete Mozart edition, edited by Brahms and published in 1878 by Breitkopf & Härtel, and the basis of many of the most commonly used editions during the century after its publication. To it I have added

---

3. Translated from Koch's *Musikalisches Lexikon* (1802) in Brown (1999: 19).

4. Agawu (2008: 55). His case is helped by his citation of the translation by Orin Grossman; William Drabkin's translation in Schenker (1996: 28) is 'every change of chord and diminution'. (The original reads 'jeder Klang- und Diminutionswechsel'.)

the topical labels that Wendy Allanbrook (1983: 6–7) applied to the first part of
the movement. Although there are some traces of what is now called topic theory
in contemporary treatises, Ratner developed it quite informally on the basis of
studying scores, and the labels are his, sometimes as transmitted by his students—
of whom Allanbrook was one. And on the basis of these labels she describes the
movement as 'a miniature theater of human gestures and actions, which is crafted
by imitating the kinds of music written to accompany these gestures'.

The theatrical analogy brings out the dramatic, visual, one might say multimedia quality of the listening that Mozart's score seems to demand, in contrast to
the audio-only contemplation mandated by modernist aesthetics. But what might
be said about its implications for the performer? 'In performance', Allanbrook
(1992) writes, 'one's conservative tendency may be to make a continuous line
out of this flashy collage of gestures and ignore the street theater, but that is our
loss' (131). Ratner concurs: 'Figures and motives would be sharply profiled and

Figure 4.1 Mozart, Sonata K 332, 1st mvmt. exposition (Breitkopf & Härtel edition,
1878), with Allanbrook's topical labels added

Figure 4.1 Continued

subtly nuanced', he says (1991: 616), writing more on the basis of imagination or common sense than from specific historical evidence, and he continues, 'they would be set against each other in relief by the performer's control of dynamics, tempo, articulation and emphasis to mark critical notes and figures for special attention'. The use of the conditional mode underlines the fact that, as so often in academic writing about music, neither Allanbrook nor Ratner is talking about any performance in particular. And a few pages later Allanbrook (1992: 136) lapses into the familiar imperative modality: the performer 'must be aware of the progress of these gestures, as few performers are today, and must articulate each one with its proper qualities'.

Pianist	Recording	Label and Release Date	Original Recording Date	Media Example
Carl Reinecke	Private transfer by Paul Tuck		Hupfeld 50634, ca. 1907	4.15
Wanda Landowska	Wanda Landowska Plays Haydn and Mozart	Pearl GEMM 9286 (released 1997)	1938	4.1
Robert Casadesus	Mozart Piano Concertos No. 24 KV 491 and No. 27 K 595, Piano Sonata No. 12 KV 332, Rondo KV 485 (1937–51 recordings)	Archipel 194 (released 2004)	1940	4.2
Glenn Gould	Glenn Gould Edition—Mozart: The Complete Piano Sonatas, Fantasias K 397 and K 475	Sony Classical 52627 (released 1972)	1966	4.3
Alicia de Larrocha	Mozart: The Piano Sonatas, Fantasias, and Rondos	RCA Victor Red Seal 82876-55705-2 (released 2003)	1989	4.4
Malcolm Bilson	Mozart: Piano Sonatas Complete	Hungaroton 31009/14 (released 2006)	1989	4.5
Geoffrey Lancaster	Mozart Sonatas for Fortepiano	Tall Poppies TP022 (released 1992)	1992	4.6
Bart van Oort	Mozart: Complete Keyboard Works	Brilliant Classics 93025 (released 2006)	2005	4.7

Figure 4.2 Recordings of Mozart, Sonata K 332

So what have performers actually done with the topics in the first movement of Mozart's K 332? In the next few pages I briefly describe a selection of seven recordings, four on the modern piano and three on the fortepiano, made between 1938 and 2005: they are listed in Figure 4.2, and their exposition sections may be accessed in Media Examples 4.1–4.7. (An eighth will follow later.) The first sound recording that I have been able to locate was made by Landowska, though it was not released owing to the outbreak of the Second World War; its 1938 date may seem surprisingly late but is not untypical for Mozart sonatas, one problem being that the movements were too long to be fitted onto a single 78 side. Landowska's performance, on a Pleyel piano, belongs to the same world of interwar classicism as Fischer's recording of Schubert's op. 90 no. 3 from the same year, but is at the other end of the spectrum. The slow tempo (crotchet = about 120) gives the playing a stately quality: it also enhances the impression of a careful literalness, with chords spread only as notated in standard editions, and at bar 29, by analogy with 25. Dynamics are understated and articulation is predominantly legato, reflecting the long slurs found in nineteenth- and early twentieth-century editions like Figure 4.1 (more on this shortly). Rubato is used only sparingly, with the exception of a huge rallentando to the cadence at bar 12 (the preceding bar lasts almost two and a half seconds). This appears again when Landowska repeats the exposition, yet again in the recapitulation, and for the final time when she repeats the second half of the piece. The effect is strange because it overshadows the beginning of the section, as well as jarring with the otherwise ubiquitous literalism; it almost sounds as if the intention was to break the sides at these points. (The first movement by itself lasts over eleven minutes.)

Robert Casadesus's recording from two years later is a better match for Fischer, a light, efficiently compact performance at a consistent crotchet = 154 and without the repeats. He plays the movement as written, but without the impression of fetishising the score that Landowska's playing sometimes creates: his pedalling of the *forte* section from bar 25, for example, creates a degree of gestural smearing that is entirely lacking in Landowska's note-by-note performance.[5] Jumping well into the post-war period and now choosing examples more or less at random, Glenn Gould's recording from 1965–66 (but first issued in 1972) is brisker still, at an aggressive crotchet = 174 and again without repeats. The general absence of pedal and characteristically dry acoustic reinforce the drive of the predominantly non-legato playing, and Gould veers between exaggerated respect for the notated articulation (he clips the crotchets in the right hand of the first three bars to bring out the one-bar slurs found in the original editions, as if to refute the nineteenth-century editors) and total disregard for it (the detaching of the left hand quavers in the same bars, or of the slurred crotchets at bars 20–22). As in some of his other Mozart interpretations, such as the following year's recording of K 331 with its exceptionally slow tempo, you have the sense that Gould is making some kind of statement about how everyone else performs it, showing how differently it can be played. So his recording makes a good foil for Alicia de Larrocha's, from 1989, which might be described as an impeccably consensual interpretation: fast but not too fast (crotchet = 140 at the opening, but slightly relaxing to crotchet = 135 for the

---

5. There is a recording from the following year (1941) by Eileen Joyce; it was unavailable when I conducted this research, but has recently been re-released on Appian APR 75012.

second theme), essentially literal but animated through understated dynamic change. She enlarges the beat almost imperceptibly to mark phrase endings, to allow space for spread chords (such as at bar 25), or to give a particularly expressive note time to work (the g^2 of bar 42). She repeats the first half of the movement but not the second. By contrast with Gould's provocatively spiky recording, de Larrocha's is a thoroughly livable modernism, with the sharp edges smoothly rounded.

In none of these recordings is there the least sign of Allanbrook's 'street theater'; the only striking characterisation of a topic is Gould's hunt calls (though they sound more like trumpet fanfares than horns), and that may be no more than a reflection of his frenetic tempo. If these performances embody the 'continuous line' that Allanbrook referred to, then they do so in very different ways, but each of them is oriented towards the expression of directed motion and overall coherence. They represent different flavours of structuralist performance, corresponding to the music-theoretical and aesthetic orthodoxies that became fully entrenched during the period they cover. They also correspond to the mainstream modernist perception of classical music that Lewis Lockwood (2002) expressed when, in response to a topical interpretation of Beethoven's String Quartet op. 132, he wrote, 'I have to admit that I have never been able to adjust my mind to this way of hearing, by "topics" and "allusions," except in cases in which the allusions are obviously and specifically planted for programmatic purposes' (87). That puts these recordings in the opposite camp from the more recent recordings made by fortepianists, for whom—as for HIP more generally—rhetoric formed a rallying call and a signifier of difference from the mainstream.

The title of Nikolaus Harnoncourt's book *Baroque Music Today: Music as Speech. Ways to a New Understanding of Music*, originally published in 1982, says it all. He rewrites the history of music in terms of a rhetorical conception that brings together performer and listener, and that extends from Monteverdi to Mozart: 'I contend that we understand Mozart just as little as Monteverdi', he writes, 'when we reduce him to the merely beautiful, which is done more often than not'. And we do this, he says, because of the sea change that came over music in the aftermath of the French Revolution, after when 'the listener was no longer a partner in a dialogue, but rather was inundated with and intoxicated by sound and so reduced to a state of passive enjoyment' (1995: 135). This perhaps opportunistic and certainly reductive interpretation of music history has been strongly criticised, for instance by Joshua Rifkin (Sherman 1997: 384–85), but whatever its merits, the result was to place Mozart at the centre of the standoff between mainstream and HIP performance. 'In the case of Mozart', writes the highly influential fortepianist and scholar Robert Levin (Sherman 1997: 320), referring to mainstream performers,

the baby was virtually thrown out with the bath water. Those very sweet, long, legato lines served the purpose of showing how tasteful and Olympian and perfectly balanced Mozart was. They did not show how his music, like Haydn's, depends on a constant amazement, a perpetual inconsistency with mercurial transformations from the flirtatious to the grand, from the grand to the teasing, from the teasing to the beseeching to the charming to the lyrical to the lamenting and back and forth—and often four or five of these things within the space of eight bars.

Not surprisingly, K 332 has been in the front line. Another highly influential fortepianist and scholar, Malcolm Bilson (1992), refers to its opening bars as 'my most frequently cited example of neglected or wrongly executed slurs' (243). Mozart's one-bar slurs, he explains, correspond to sighs, and the ubiquity of one-bar slurs throughout the movement gives it 'a strong sense of lilt' that is 'probably more important than the notes in Mozart's basic conception'. The point is that the four-bar slur at the beginning of Figure 4.1 is not Mozart's but Brahms's: in the original sources, as in modern Urtext editions, there is a slur joining the minim and crotchet of each of the first four bars, and similar discrepancies continue through the movement—and throughout late nineteenth-century editions of the classics in general. Modern editions generally reinstate Mozart's slurs. Yet, Bilson complains, 'virtually all present-day musicians are running right over such slurs with no inflection whatsoever'. What, he asks, is the point of all the musicological fussing over whether some autograph slur was intended to cover two or three notes, when nobody takes any notice of the slurs in performance?

Bilson's own recording of K 332 dates from 1989, three years before the article from which I have been quoting, and illustrates what he says about the opening bars: he emphasises the minims, playing the linked crotchets more lightly—the opposite of Gould, who instead accentuates the crotchets.[6] Bilson is of course well aware of the topical tradition,[7] and his interpretation of these slurs as representing sighs is in line with Allanbrook's identification of the singing style. It might be objected that Bilson's performance is no more singing in quality—indeed perhaps less so—than the traditionally modernist *cantabile* of, for example, de Larrocha's recording of the same year. But in response to this two points might be made. First, very sweet, long, legato lines are not possible on the fortepiano (and therefore, for what it is worth, not what Mozart had in mind); singing on the fortepiano has to be done in other ways. And second, topics, like all signs, depend on difference. What matters in Bilson's playing is not just the specific characteristics of this or that bar, but its variety and contrast—the same variety and contrast that Levin talked about.

Bilson creates a slight caesura in bar 12, and brings out the new tonal quality of the hunt calls that follow, giving them a rhythmic articulation that creates the distinct impression that he is playing a little faster than at the opening (though in fact he plays both at crotchet = about 156). All this gives rise to a change in discursive register, as if the music after bar 12 was coming from somewhere

---

6. In his article on Mozart performance, Bilson (1992: 243) specifically associates such accentuation with Schnabel.

7. See for example the discussion, in which Bilson took part, following Leonard Ratner's 1991 paper on Mozart performance.

else—which in a sense it is: as Allanbrook (1992: 13) observes, this is where the scene shifts from the salon to outdoors. Bilson's playing from bar 23 has a strongly gestural quality, with the semi-quavers of bar 25 smeared into a stylised glissando, and with a quality of dynamic attack that is hard to create on the modern piano. As Bilson says, though of K 282, 'it seems not possible to really burst forth in the *forte* on the modern piano, because the sound would be too crude' (1992: 241). At the same time the rhetorical discontinuity of his playing is coupled with the same delicacy of nuance that I noted in de Larrocha's recording, whether to mark phrase or section endings or to create expressive space (as at bars 72 and 80); again like de Larrocha, Bilson repeats the first half of the movement from K 332 but not the second. Unlike her, however, he introduces a number of unnotated ornaments in the recapitulation. He also plays c#[1] in the bass at bar 216—an expressive inflection present in the first (1784) edition of the sonata and included in modern Urtext editions, but not found in the Breitkopf & Härtel edition, or in any of the piano recordings I have been discussing.[8]

Perhaps, then, Allanbrook had not been listening to the right people when in 1992, three years after Bilson's recording, she complained about performers not articulating the gestures in K 332. As it happens, another recording of K 332 on the fortepiano came out in the same year as Allanbrook's book, by Geoffrey Lancaster, and this serves to show how fortepiano performances of Mozart sonatas were becoming a tradition in their own right. Although Lancaster's recording *sounds* very different from Bilson's, probably as much because of the recording acoustic as because of the instrument, one might describe it in very much the same terms, except that everything is slightly more so. It is a little faster, at about crotchet = 162. Lancaster introduces the same kind of expressive nuances, only just a little more so, and he too adds a few unnotated ornaments the last time we hear the music (which in his case is on the repeat of the second half, as he repeats both halves). In fact he sometimes plays the same ornaments, for example on the third beat of bar 154, and like Bilson he plays c#[1] in bar 216: in the repeat he combines it with a momentary hesitation, creating a distinctly arch effect. Finally Lancaster differentiates the discursive registers of the music, like Bilson, and he is just that bit more willing to let the large-scale shaping look after itself while he concentrates on the details (for example in his four-bar phrasing of the second theme). Agawu (2008: 55) says of topics that, by comparison with structuralist approaches, 'the labor of analysis is more productively deployed in highlighting discontinuity—we know that all is well in the background, so to speak', and the same might be said of Lancaster's performance.

 Much more different from Bilson's recording is that of his former student Bart van Oort, which was made in 2005. Van Oort does not add unnotated ornamentation, but in other respects his performance extends Bilson's approach to detail. There is almost constant nuancing: a little extra time for the leap of a sixth at bar 3, a little more for the accented passing note at the

8. It is, however, found in Eileen Joyce's recording from 1941.

beginning of bar 4, a prolongation of the first beat of bar 8 to throw weight onto the second-beat trill. At some points it might seem more appropriate to think of his timing being controlled from the level of gesture or phrase, rather than in terms of a constant underlying tempo that is subject to inflection. In such a context passages of relatively metronomic playing, such as the hunt call topic from bar 13, stand out: this is one of the ways van Oort characterises the topic. This varied pacing means that overall there is no basic tempo in Repp's sense, but at various points van Oort seems to calibrate his playing in relation to what I shall call a 'reference' tempo, meaning that he touches on rather than sustains it. And despite his confusing use of Repp's term, something of the sort is implied by van Oort's characterisation of 'true rhythmical' as opposed to 'metrical' playing: 'The most important liberty which was taken for granted in the eighteenth century was rhythmic flexibility (occasionally turning into true rubato) and, within the basic tempo, minimal fluctuations of tempo' (2003: 79). 'Minimal' might be going too far, however. Van Oort takes the opening of the movement in the general region of crotchet = 150, but he speeds up to perhaps crotchet = 160 during the *Sturm und Drang* topic from bar 23 (the general principle seems to be the rushing of the semiquaver figuration). The second subject begins with two-bar, pendulum-like motions that give expressive emphasis to the melodic leap to g^2 at bar 42 and the accented passing notes at bar 44: the combination of the rubato and the plucked quality that van Oort draws out of his instrument, together with the notated arpeggiations, is vividly evocative of guitar playing—although that does not feature among Allanbrook's topical labels (she simply calls the second theme a 'minuet'). From about bar 46, however, the tempo settles into a steady crotchet = around 140, the regular beat matching the flowing semiquavers of the melody.

Perhaps it is not too schematising to suggest that the remainder of the movement gravitates around these two reference tempos: crotchet = 150, sometimes speeding up a little, and crotchet = 140. The latter characterises the lyrical passages such as from bar 71, where the consistent lengthening of the expressive melodic points (at bars 72, 74, 78, and 80) does not detract from the sense that there is an underlying tempo. The former underlies the louder, more active topics, and here, too, patterns of fluctuation within the framework of the reference tempo are on the whole easily explicable. An example is the passage from bar 56, the first occurrence in the movement of significant metrical complexity. The look of the score suggests that there is a one-bar elision at 56 (in other words, the previous phrase concludes with, and the following phrase begins with, that bar). But the intrinsic conservatism of metrical perception—the tendency to hold onto any metrical interpretation until it proves untenable—means that it may be only in bar 60 that the elision is definitely established.

That bar initiates a cycle of fifths (C-F-B♭-E♭-A♭-D-G) that drives the music towards the dominant of C major, preparing for the lyrical melody at bar 71. At bars 64–65 there is a hemiola, which—in the manner of hemiolas, but particularly because of the cycle of fifths—represents the compression of three bars into two, with bar 66 completing the notional four-bar phrase. Bar 67 is the point where this metrical complexity is relieved, a regular four-bar prolongation of dominant harmony, with progressive fragmentation, that leads to the lyrical melody. Van Oort begins this passage at a regular tempo, but abbreviates the elided bar, 60, where the alternations of *forte* downbeats and *piano* afterbeats begin: the effect is to link bars 60 and 61 as weak and strong bars within the new metrical unit. He treats the next two bars in the same way, but less emphatically, and then initiates a decelerando that lasts until bar 67. The broadening of the tempo might be seen as compensating for the compression of the hemiola, and linking it to the last bar of the notional four-bar phrase initiated by the hemiola; the lengthening of bar 66 gives time for the a♭-g-f# to do its expressive work; and the palpably higher tempo from the downbeat of bar 67 marks the point of metric resolution, like taking your foot off the brake. Whether or not the details of my interpretation are convincing, van Oort brings a high degree of articulacy to these bars. There seems to be a reason for everything. One might describe this as rhetorical style married to structural clarity.

According to Robert Levin, the particular challenge of performing classical music is how you 'communicate the surface tension created by details, whose purposeful opposition is nevertheless integrated into the whole' (Ratner 1991: 619). Allanbrook (1992) has considered in some detail how the extreme variety of K 332's topical surface is held together, and though her focus is on the composition what she says has clear implications for performance. How, she asks with specific reference to bars 20–23, is it possible for Mozart to move in next to no time between 'two gestures that are from the opposite ends of the expressive spectrum—the neat formulaic horn calls and the passionate fantasy-like *Sturm und Drang*' (135)? As she explains, pitch, tonality, register, texture, and dynamics all change. The one thing that remains the same is the iambic rhythm (two crotchets linked across the bar line), which comes from bars 14–15 of the hunt call, features throughout the link passage, and forms the starting point for the *Sturm und Drang* passage: she refers to it as 'the "middle term" in this musical syllogism'. As in the other examples she considers, there is a kind of counterpoint of 'same' and 'other', and in each case the element of 'same' is built into the composition, in that sense hard-wired. That enables performers to align themselves with the 'other', in Agawu's terms to highlight discontinuity, and it is on the following page that Allanbrook talks about the need for performers to articulate each topic with its proper qualities.

Topics are like Wagnerian leitmotifs in that what matters about them is not so much their specific lexical content, but rather the fact of their intertextuality and what it means for the music's ontology. For the performer this translates into the opportunity, through the handling of tempo, dynamics, articulation, and tone, to create the shifts of register that I have described, and the effect is to turn music into a dramatic medium, in line with Allanbrook's 'miniature theater of human gestures and actions'. When music is called dramatic, what is most often meant is that it builds large-scale effects of tension and plays on the unexpected. But that is as characteristic of the novel as it is of the drama (and in these terms, the first movement of K 332 is a highly undramatic sonata movement: far from playing on the listener's expectations, the transition from the development to the recapitulation is highly predictable, in effect an enlarged version of the fanfares that announce the second theme in the exposition). What more significantly characterises the drama is its social dimension, its counterpointing of agencies. But perhaps a still better analogy is with role play in virtual worlds, where you create personae through performative means (quite literally you are who you say you are), and where everything you say is, by definition, in quotation marks. That after all is the defining feature of the topical universe: as Agawu says, features of the eighteenth-century European soundscape found their way, in a stylised form, into formalised compositions, so becoming musical objects 'whose identities are permanently enclosed within quotation marks' (2008: 45). Hence my reference to ontology.

Performed and heard in these terms, the very fabric of the classical style is representational. It is not just a matter of the formulaic topics, such as hunt calls, *Sturm und Drang*, the brilliant style, the learned style, the Turkish style, and the rest. It is the presence of voices in instrumental music, of bow strokes in keyboard music, the breathing that pervades music for any medium, all of which play a central a role in traditional musical pedagogy regardless of instrument, and are in this way built deeply into performers' thinking. It is the portamento that both Chopin and Schenker looked for in piano playing, or the fingerings Schenker advocated so as to create the effect of 'a *single* breath or bow stroke' (Eigeldinger 1986: 45; Schenker 2000: 26, 28). It is in the gestures specified by the sound, and in what the music says, too. 'The fortepiano', as van Oort (2003) writes, 'creates a clear musical texture, a prerequisite for rhetoric, by means of a silvery tone that doesn't sound too long, a sharp onset, and a large palette of colours' (78). And he adds: 'All of these characteristics make it easy to articulate—to speak the musical words'.

These features combine to create an imaginary domain, or magical reality, where scholarship and fantasy can work together to create and renew performance interpretation. Tom Beghin, who specialises in playing Haydn, speaks of a passage in the E-flat major Sonata Hob XVI: 49 where Haydn apparently writes himself into a harmonic dead end. Beghin compares Haydn's successive attempts to find a way out, and the virtuosic ease by which he finally achieves it, with the oratorical trope of *dubitatio*, through which the orator feigns doubt in order to dramatise the solution when it is produced. To illustrate his point he reproduces an engraving, from a contemporary treatise on dramatic gesture by Johann Jacob Engel, of an actor depicting doubt[9]: this image, Beghin writes, 'is fitting also for the keyboardist, who, at the most intense moment of doubt, stares into the emptiness of the music desk' (2007: 150). And it is at this point that Beghin summons up his own flash of virtuosity. He continues:

Engel's prose, which carefully describes the hand movement of the actor in preparation for this moment—hands at first interacting easily and smoothly with one another, their movements increasingly becoming irregular, arms

---

9. Engel's *Ideen zu einer Mimik* (Berlin, 1785) is available at the time of writing on Google Books; illustrations follow the text, and the engraving in question is on the seventh page of the illustrations.

indecisively folded and unfolded again, then coming to a halt—resonates strikingly well with Haydn's choreography of the pianist's hands.... The crossings and uncrossings...—unusual for Haydn—offer an especially intriguing analogy to the folding and unfolding of the actor's arms.

Reminiscent of Doğantan-Dack's interpretation of the second movement of Beethoven's 'Pathétique' Sonata, which also had its origin in a distinctive configuration of the performing body, this illustrates how personal performance perspectives may be generated through the marriage of historical knowledge and creative imagination. Whether and in what way such conceptions are communicated to listeners is another matter. Perhaps it is of no importance.

RHETORIC OLD AND NEW

But there may be a more strongly historical dimension to all this, and here I come back once again to Schenker. I have to admit to a minor sleight of hand when, following Agawu, I quoted Schenker's reference to every change of sound and of figuration pulling at the performer and listener. Schenker's point was that this should be resisted, that performer and listener alike should cleave to the background. That might seem to equate to a performance along, say, de Larrocha's lines. But as usual with period commentary on performance, you have to understand it in light of contemporary norms, in this case the high level of foreground characterisation represented by d'Albert and other 'old school' performers. There are also some striking resonances between Schenker's approach and those of the modern fortepianists. For example, van Oort's reference to speaking the musical words resonates with Schenker's comparison between music and speech, though as I mentioned in Chapter 3, there is a difference. In line with nineteenth-century writers such as Kullak, Schenker generally conflates the ideas of music as speech and as song—he is talking about the rhetorical nature of music in general—whereas for the fortepianists, as van Oort says, 'the fortepiano speaks, the piano sings' (78), so that the two terms represent opposed values and even serve a polemical function. There are however some much more specific parallels between Schenker and the fortepianists.

Van Oort goes on to argue that 'the long, singing tone' of the modern piano 'led to a loss of understanding of the correct execution of the slur'. This is a recurring theme in fortepianists' discourse. As we have seen, Bilson complained about modern pianists ignoring Mozart's one-bar slurs at the beginning of K 332, and van Oort is in effect saying that this is why you need to play Mozart's sonatas on the fortepiano. Playing the 'typically classical short slurs' of this passage 'with real silences on modern instrument', he writes, 'leads to a choppy style of playing: legato is the most logical touch for the modern player'. By contrast, 'the shorter decay of the fortepiano[10] makes it easier and more logical to articulate, as the silence is reached in a natural way. What results is a rhetorical statement, rather than a legato melody' (2003: 83). And as fortepianists repeatedly say, it is the anachronistic, pianistic conception of Mozart that

---

10. Van Oort actually writes 'pianoforte', which I take to be an error.

was embodied in the editorial phrasing slur, as in the first four bars of Figure 4.1. No wonder then that Robert Levin followed up his comment about the balance between details and the whole with a reference to 'the whole problem with the 19th-century editors putting all those slurs into their editions' (Ratner 1991: 619).

The point is that Schenker was making exactly the same argument back in 1925, in an article entitled 'Abolish the phrasing slur', published in the first issue of his one-man journal *Das Meisterwerk in der Musik* (in effect a continuation of *Der Tonwille*). This is the same issue in which, as we saw in Chapter 3, Schenker complained that performance was so much worse than it had been twenty years earlier: in the mid-1920s his attacks on performance practice, and on the broader cultural values he saw performance as embodying, reached a climax, and the figure of Mozart lay at the heart of both. In the second issue of *Das Meisterwerk*, published the following year, Schenker wrote that 'the performance of Mozart's works lacks all cohesiveness. It is vapid, stiff, pedestrian, forever concerned merely with the series of notes that lies immediately ahead, thus as a whole it is lifeless and untrue' (1996: 60). After reference to a few 'old school' performers to whom this does not apply (Joachim, Mühlfeld, de Andrade, all by then dead), he concluded with the rhetorical question, 'Is Mozart, therefore, dead?' Schenker had a habit of answering his rhetorical questions, and in this case the answer is no: 'the work of genius is removed from the generations and their times....Mozart lives, and will live on forever'.

But it is in 'Abolish the phrasing slur' that Schenker unfolds his critique of Mozart performance in greatest detail. The classical composers, Schenker says, knew only 'the legato slur', a musical effect modelled on the singing voice, which performers may express using any appropriate technical means of realisation. Despite the rather confusing name, the legato slur corresponds to the one-bar slurs of the opening of K 332, and more generally to the meaning-bearing figures of classical music: it arises out of the specific features of the musical material. In this it is the exact opposite of the editorial phrasing slur, which is slapped across the score without regard for its content and so 'falsifies both the legato slur and the musical form' (Schenker 1994: 21). Time and again Schenker shows how Mozart's careful delineations of the musical figures through legato slurs have disappeared under editors' phrasing slurs: 'all the details are lost', he says, for the editor 'recognizes unity only as uniformity' (22). For Schenker, unity is created through the synthesis of contrasting elements, rather in the manner of Levin's reference to the tension between detail and whole. Uniformity, by contrast, means standardisation, the elimination of contrast and variety. And this gives Schenker, who was not prone to understatement, the opportunity to claim not only that the editorial phrasing slur has felled music at a single stroke, like a tree ('There is no more Bach, no more Handel, no more Haydn or Mozart or Beethoven'), but also that it expresses 'the social and political ideology that understands unity only as uniformity'. The phrasing slur, in short, is an emblem of sociopolitical catastrophe. The fortepianists have not quite gone that far, but the basic argument is the same.

If it is the style of the phrasing slur that can be heard in modernist performances of Mozart's music from the interwar period on, then we might expect to hear in the performances of the rhetorical performers of Schenker's day something of the 'lively performance, interwoven with the most delicate contrasts in articulation and dynamics' that Schenker imputes to the age of the legato slur. We might also wonder what resemblance such performances bear to the playing of the fortepianists who stand for rhetorical performance today. But getting the evidence is not so easy. As I said, there are few early sound recordings of Mozart's sonatas, and while this no doubt reflects the limited durations of 78s, it must also reflect taste or fashion, since the same length restrictions do not apply to piano rolls and there are few of them either. In line with the encore phenomenon to which I referred in Chapter 3, however, there are a few individual movements from Mozart sonatas that were frequently recorded, and at the head of the list is the *Rondo alla turca* from K 331 (Figure 4.3). Six recordings of the Rondo, dating from the beginning of the century to the 1920s, allow us to trace the final stages of 'old school' performance, but since I want to address the stylistic relationship between these performers and today's fortepianists, I shall begin with some salient features of van Oort's 2005 recording of the same piece (made during the same sessions when he recorded K 332). All these recordings are listed in Figure 4.4, and may be accessed as Media Examples 4.8–4.14.

As might be expected, van Oort plays the Rondo in much the same way as he plays K 332. As before, time does not flow evenly in his performance but is wrapped round the compositional content, so that again it makes sense to speak of van Oort calibrating his playing to a reference tempo rather than realising it in any literal sense: here, however, there appears to be only one reference tempo, around minim = 70. (I am giving metronome values in minims rather than crotchets because I consider that to be the tactus, the principal level of identification with the tempo; more on this in Chapter 5.) On occasion the shaping of tempo reflects particular expressive emphases: an example is the diminished seventh chord in bar 20, marked *sfp* in Figure 4.3 but just *f* (followed by *p* on the second beat) in Urtext editions, which van Oort emphasises even more strongly on the repeat. But, as befits the highly repetitive nature of the Rondo, it is the characterisation of phrase and section that is the predominant feature.

Most of the pianists lengthen the ends of phrases, and particularly the ends of sections: van Oort does this, but more so, and he is remarkably systematic about how he does it. Nowhere is this more obvious than the passage from bars 33 to 56 of the score, corresponding to bars 65–112 of van Oort's recording: I shall make these references in the form 65–112 (33–56), where 65–112 refers to the recording under discussion (reflecting any repeats) and 33–56 to the score. Van Oort consistently brings out both four- and eight-bar phrases, the latter particular strongly from bar 89 (49). At certain points, such as bars 65–80 (33–40) and 89–112 (49–56), he does this by matching tempo almost perfectly to dynamics, getting louder as he gets faster, and softer as he gets slower. In other words he is employing phrase arching, but of so extreme a nature as to create an effect like a music box that runs irregularly yet somehow manages to synchronise with the beginnings and ends of phrases. It is not a performance style in the normal sense, but rather the way in which van Oort chooses to characterise this particular material. He does so in just the same sense in which he, and other fortepianists, characterise the topics of K 332—or actors and role-playing gamers characterise their personae.

Having established a baseline for the comparison, I can describe the other recordings more briefly, beginning with those from the 1920s (Eugene d'Albert, Emil von Sauer, and Ignaz Friedman). These pianists share an approach to timing that relates both to what I said about d'Albert in Chapter 3 and to what I have said about the fortepianists in this chapter: their tempos are strongly inflected by expressive accentuation, by density of musical material (for example to allow space for the spread chords from bar 25), and by phrase structure. But whereas it remains the practice today—and not just among fortepianists—to create expression through the expansion of time, these earlier pianists also routinely contract

Figure 4.3 Mozart, *Rondo alla turca* (Sonata K 331, 3rd mvmt., Breitkopf & Härtel edition, 1878)

Figure 4.3 Continued

it, especially by rushing towards cadences: we saw d'Albert doing this in Schubert's op. 90 no. 3, but in the *Rondo alla turca* particularly good examples are provided by Sauer's and Friedman's playing of bars 86–87 and 102–3 (46–7). Despite all this, it seems possible, as with van Oort, to identify reference tempos behind d'Albert's, Sauer's, and Friedman's performances. And in the first two cases, at least, the reference tempos are a crucial means by which these pianists seize upon the highly sectional and repetitive nature of the Rondo—and, no doubt, its status as an over-learned item of the repertory for both performers and listeners—as an opportunity for bold characterisation of the various contrasted materials. As shown in

Pianist	Recording	Label and Release Date	Original Recording Date (If Known)	Media Example
Carl Reinecke	Private transfer by Denis Hall		Welte-Mignon 192, 1905	4.8
Carl Reinecke	Private transfer by Julian Dyer		Hupfeld 50318, ca. 1905	4.9
Vladimir Pachmann	Wolfgang Amadeus **Mozart: The** Original Piano Recordings	Dal Segno DSPRCD 029 (rolls reproduced in 1992)	Welte-Mignon 1206, 1906	4.10
Eugen d'Albert	The Centaur Pianist, Complete Studio Recordings: 1910–28	Arbiter 147 (released 2005)	Between 1916 and 1922	4.11
Emil von Sauer	Complete Commercial Recordings	Marston/Mainly Opera MR 53002-2 (released 1998)	ca. 1923	4.12
Ignaz Friedman	Ignaz Friedman, Complete Recordings, Volume 1	Naxos Historical 8.110684 (released 2002)	1926	4.13
Bart van Oort	Mozart Complete Keyboard Works	Brilliant Classics 93025 (released 2006)	2005	4.14

Figure 4.4 Recordings of Mozart, *Rondo alla turca* (from K 331)

Figure 4.5, I shall refer to these as 'A' (bars 1–24 of the score), 'B' (bars 25–32), and 'C' (bars 33–56), with the coda (bar 97, second time bar) unfolding from the final B section.

For d'Albert, whose recording dates from some time between 1916 and 1922, each of these materials has its own reference tempo: at each of its appearances, A gravitates around minim = 64, B around minim = 60, and C around minim = 68 (also shown in Figure 4.5). Compared to his shifting tempos in Schubert's op. 90 no. 3, the tempos within each section of the Rondo are relatively consistent. This throws weight onto the disjunctions of tempo between them, which are also associated with dynamic value: played the slowest, the *forte* B section acquires a heavy, almost *pesante* quality, while d'Albert plays the C section fast and very lightly, with the A section falling somewhere in between. As can again be seen in Figure 4.5, the scheme underlying Sauer's recording, which dates from 1923, is not dissimilar to d'Albert's, though his tempo for the A material is significantly faster.[11] Sauer also

11. While d'Albert, like van Oort, takes all repeats as notated, Sauer omits the repeats of (notated) bars 65–72 and 73–88.

A	B	C	Coda
1	25	33	
	57		
65	73		96 (2nd time bar)
Formal plan (notated)			
A	B	C	Coda
64	60	68	
	60		
64	60		accel to 64
D'Albert's tempi			
A	B	C	Coda
70	60	70	
	60		
70	60		60
Sauer's tempi			
A	B	C	Coda
70	70	76	
	70		
70	70		accel to 76
Friedman's tempi			
A	B	C	Coda
58	62	67	
	67		
62	67		accel to 76
Pachmann's tempi			

Figure 4.5 Tempos in recordings of Mozart, *Rondo alla turca*

complicates matters by taking bars 33–48 (9–24 on the repeat) slower, at around minim = 65, and in addition has a habit of starting slower tempos with the final phrase or cadence of the preceding section: it is actually with the diminished seventh chord at bar 28 (20) that he changes speed, and in the same way he slows down for bars 47–48 (23–24), simply maintaining his tempo for the ensuing B section. I described Sauer's recording of Schubert's op. 90 no. 3 as essentially old-fashioned but taking some note of more contemporary tendencies, and in the same way the clean, even, streamlined quality of his playing in the *Rondo alla turca* makes the performance sound more modern than it really is.

As for Friedman's recording, from 1926, it might be described as just the reverse.[12] At a moment-to-moment level it is the most highly variegated of all three: he accelerates perceptibly through the opening sixteen bars; rushes the semiquavers at bars 17 and 33 (9); rushes towards the cadence at bar 72 (40) and hits it with a bang, creating an effect almost reminiscent of Leroy Anderson's 'The Typewriter'; and in the C section adopts the strategy 'play as fast as possible, then get faster'. When this is combined with the odd sonority of the recording—something like a pub piano played in a bathroom[13]—the effect is more one of rural festivity than of classical tradition: maybe it is relevant that Friedman was born in Podgórze, near Krakow, the son of an itinerant Jewish musician. Yet underlying the old fashioned surface is the single-tempo plan we might expect of a modern performer, whether on piano or fortepiano. It is probably relevant that, whereas d'Albert and Sauer were about the same age (born 1864 and 1862 respectively), Friedman was much younger (born 1882).

If the basis of these pianists' interpretations of the *Rondo alla turca* is strong characterisation of its contrasted materials, and if in the case of the two older pianists this is built into their tempos, then it is also built into the undisguised lurches between the tempos—for instance at bar 65 (33) of Sauer's recording as he goes straight from the heavy, *pesante* B material to the fast, even flow of the C material, or at bar 113 (57) of Friedman's, where he judderingly slams on the brakes to make the reverse transition (except the point is there is no transition). In essence these are the same means by which the fortepianists create contrasts of register between the topics of K 332. And there is one moment in the Rondo where there is a particular tradition of such registral change. This is in the coda, where the until-then-unbroken pattern of powers-of-eight-bar phrasing gives way to more irregular patterns. As notated, there is a clear six-bar phrase at bars 97–102. Then there is what starts as a literal repeat, but the right-hand grace-note-and-quaver pattern of bar 101 does not appear at bar 107, instead being postponed to bar 108. That pushes back the following bar, 109, which corresponds to the second time bar at 96—except that 96 was the final bar of a group, whereas we had assumed bar 108, not 109, was the final bar of its group. Since in terms of scansion bars 110–15 correspond to 97–102, following on from bar 109 just as the latter followed on from 96, the result is that bar 109 is left over as a kind of extra, redundant bar—a bar that does not make sense either as the end of one group or as the beginning of the next. It is also marked by the change to a stereotypical Alberti bass (something that has not previously appeared in this movement), a *piano*, and—in Figure 4.3 though not in Urtext editions—a *legato* marking, all of which clearly signify something. But what, exactly? None of this would be likely to worry a listener—it is the sort of thing that the eye picks out much more readily than the ear—but for

12. Friedman omits the repeats of (notated) bars 65–72, 73–88, and 89–97.

13. According to Evans (2009), this recording—which was coupled with a Scarlatti sonata as arranged by Tausig—was made 'on a piano with tacks stuck onto the hammers. The resulting metallic tone was a flimsy excuse for the record label's listing them as harpsichord solos, despite the obvious presence of pedalling and dynamics' (115–16).

the performer it is as if Mozart has set out to create a conundrum that forces you to stop and think, and so develop your own personal take. All these performers respond in one way or another.

Van Oort's approach is different from the others because he separates the coda from the preceding B section: he dramatically broadens the tempo, to around minim = 52, from the beginning of the second time bar at 192 (96). This is the only sustained tempo in his performance other than the main reference tempo of minim = 70, and logically speaking the change of speed might be thought to signify a one-bar elision at the notated bar 96 (or, in an even more theory-driven approach, the whole coda might be seen as an expansion of that bar). That would give rise to a seven-bar phrase at bars 192–98 (96–102), so de-problematising what we would now see as a parallel seven-bar phrase at bars 205–11 (109–15). Although this sounds like an analyst's fantasy, it corresponds quite closely to what van Oort plays. He maintains the broader tempo until bar 205 (109), where he immediately slows down radically to minim = 42 (the semiquaver figuration means this is a case where giving a metronome value for a single bar is not mis-leading); then accelerates rapidly until he hits minim = 74 at bar 208 (112); and slackens his tempo almost imperceptibly before the strongly marked beginning of the new phrase at bar 212 (116, where the marking is more Mozart's than van Oort's). The roller-coaster tempo swings continue through the final bars, with bar 217 (121) being prolonged, and then a headlong rush to the end (he touches minim = 98 at bar 221 [125], and takes the right hand at the downbeat of bar 222 [126] an octave higher than notated). In this way van Oort finds a solution for the problem of bar 205 (109), integrating it within a considered and continuous plan for the coda as a discrete section of the movement.

The approach of d'Albert, Sauer, and Friedman is fundamentally different because they all treat the coda as an extension of the final B section. That is to say, they play straight through the second time bar at 96 and hence have no strategy in place to de-problematise the extra bar, 109, when they get there. Instead each of them creates a special effect at that point, and does so in his own way. They all play much quieter at bar 109: it is what else they do that matters. D'Albert slows substantially at bars 205–6 (109–10), then speeds up through bar 206 (111) and slackens off in bar 207 (112). But the special feature of his performance is a very expressive crescendo and decrescendo that matches the accelerando and decele-rando in these bars, and is made possible through the new semiquaver figuration. From bar 212 (116) it is business as usual, and he plays straight through to the end with nothing more remarkable than a modest broadening out to bar 220 (124). Sauer also slows substantially for bar 181 (109), gradually accelerating throughout the following six bars, but what makes this moment special in his performance is a pearly, translucent sound quality that has one groping for images of fairy castles glimpsed from afar through a momentary break in the clouds. Again it is business as usual from bar 188 (116), and Sauer slows down dramatically in the final three or four bars to bring the movement to a halt. As for Friedman, although he plays through the beginning of the coda like d'Albert and Sauer, things start to change from bar 169 (105). He pulls down the dynamic level in the left hand (if he plays the spread chord it is inaudible), so that the light, semiquaver melody emerges. He plays bar 170 (106) as before, but at 171 (107) it sounds as if he plays nothing except the downbeat (presumably he does, but you can't hear it in the recording). At bar 173 (109) the immediate effect is of a return to the light, *piano* quality of bar 169 (105), but it quickly becomes evident that Friedman is doing what you knew he would do: play faster, and then faster still. And once more it is business as usual from bar 180 (116).

What we have with all three of these pianists, then, is exactly the effect of a change of register that I was describing in K 332: the sense that the music is coming from somewhere else or is spoken by a different character, an intimation of another musical world. This is a parallel in the domain of performance to the slippage into an anachronistic, Mozartean style that Beethoven composed into the final movement of his Ninth Symphony—for example at bar 810, as the choir sing 'All men shall be brothers', where as I have previously written 'the music goes into quotation marks' (Cook 1993: 104). But whereas that is a written tradition, what happens in the coda of the *Rondo alla turca* is an oral-aural tradition that overlays the written one. In a general sense, of course, that is precisely what performance within the WAM tradition is. But there are special cases where this applies with particular force, and this is one of them (we shall encounter another in Chapter 5). Mozart, as I said, has scored a conundrum, and unwritten but plainly audible traditions of interpretation have developed in response to it. You can get faster or slower, you can create new tonal or dynamic effects, but whatever you do, you must do something extraordinary. We are back at the issue of personal interpretation that I discussed earlier in this chapter.

There are also a few piano rolls of the *Rondo alla turca* that take us back to the first decade of the century, of which three are at present publicly accessible:[14] one by Vladimir de Pachmann (born in 1848) and two by Carl Reinecke (born in 1824). Pachmann's roll, which dates from 1906, displays the same stylistic features we would now expect—the various kinds of lengthening, the rushing towards cadences—and so I shall concentrate on a new interpretive feature that it illustrates. He begins at a sedate and quite metronomical minim = 58. Like d'Albert and Sauer, he has distinct speeds for the various sections, and as his reference tempos for the B and C materials are respectively around minim = 62 and 67, the effect is of a graduated increase in tempo during the first 112 bars of his performance (corresponding to bars 1–56 in the score). From this point Pachmann continues at the same tempo—but, as can be seen from Figure 4.5, that means he is now playing the B material significantly faster than he did first time round. There is a drop of tempo to around minim = 62 when the opening material returns—but that still means Pachmann is playing the music significantly faster than he did first time round. The final appearance of the B material is at the same speed as the

14. Others listed on the RPRF (Reproducing Piano Roll Foundation) 'Rollography' web page (http://www.rprf.org/Rollography.html) are by Alfredo Casella (Pleyela), José Iturbi (both Welte and Duo Art), and Raoul Pugno (Triphonola).

previous one, around minim = 67, and he continues at this speed into the coda. But as with Friedman, things soon change. Pachmann hurries into the right-hand semiquavers at bar 195 (99) and again at bar 201 (105), and as with Friedman, this sets the faster tempo at which he takes the passage from bar 205 (109), around minim = 76 (the same tempo as Friedman's, as it happens). The new, or rather old, element in Pachmann's performance is, then, what might be called the progressive tempo plan: not only does the performance fall into two blocks of increasing tempo (minim = 58, 62, 67 and 62, 67, 76), but Pachmann takes the same sections faster when they recur. As with Friedman, a comparison suggests itself with those genres of eastern European folk music that get faster and faster (Pachmann came from Ukraine), though this is so basic a musical idea that such comparisons are perhaps gratuitous.

The two rolls by Reinecke are distinctly different. One is from Welte-Mignon and dates from their *annus mirabilis*, 1905 (it was recorded on 20 January).[15] As may be seen, and heard, in Media Example 4.8, it covers the distance in much the shortest time of all the recordings I have discussed, romping home in 2'21", a clear 25 seconds ahead of Friedman. This is not just because Reinecke plays very fast, but because he abbreviates the music more radically than Friedman: he not only omits the repeats of the B, A, and B sections at notated bars 57–64, 65–88, and 89–96 respectively, but also cuts bars 103–8 and 116–21, in this way drastically truncating the coda. It seems odd he should have been in such a hurry when rolls, unlike acoustic records, did not impose tight time constraints. I shall make a few references to this recording but concentrate on the other, which was issued by Hupfeld and probably dates from around the same time. Unlike Welte-Mignon rolls, the playback speed of Hupfeld rolls was not standardised, so the overall tempo of Media Example 4.9 is based on informed guesswork—although it seems clear that Reinecke was not playing as fast as on the Welte-Mignon roll.[16] Fortunately the stylistic features on which I shall comment are to at least some extent independent of absolute tempo.

A striking aspect of Reinecke's playing of the Rondo is its wealth of detail. Just to take the opening bars of the Hupfeld roll, Reinecke accelerates through the continuous semiquavers in bars 2–3, heightening the impression of speed, and then slows down for the quavers and grace notes of bars 4–6, with the decelerando continuing into bars 7–8 for the phrase break. He repeats more or less the same pattern on the

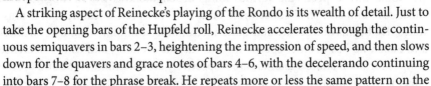

15. The transfer at Media Example 4.8 was generously made for me by Denis Hall from a roll in his personal collection; another transfer has been issued commercially on Tacet 179.

16. Hupfeld rolls bear a figure which is meant to specify playback speed (in this case 50, meaning five feet per minute), but the issue is complicated by the different formats in which Hupfeld rolls were issued. This roll has more limited temporal resolution than later Hupfeld rolls, which results in some jitter, but this should not affect the analysis. No commercial transfer is available; I am grateful to Julian Dyer for supplying me with a transfer of a roll in his personal collection, as well as for the information above. A general discussion of piano roll speeds may be found in Hall (2012).

repeat. Following a slight caesura in bar 16 (8), he plays the quavers before and at bar 17 (9) very hurriedly, slowing in bar 18 (10), and then does the same again in bars 19–20 (11–12), less exaggeratedly but still bringing out the two-bar repetition pattern. However he does not shape the repetitions in bars 21–22 (13–14) and 23–24 (15–16) in the same way, and when the opening figure comes back he plays that quite differently too: he accelerates through bars 25–27 (17–19) before relaxing to the end of the phrase, and does the same when it comes back in the repeat, so helping to create a sense of local conclusiveness. The Welte-Mignon roll is full of the same stylistic features, but I will not document them.

The level of detail is reminiscent of van Oort's playing of the Rondo, and in the Hupfeld roll Reinecke shapes the C section largely as a series of temporal waves, again like van Oort, even creating something of the same out-of-order musical box effect from bar 65 (33). But there are differences, the essential one being Reinecke's playing is much less systematic than van Oort's. Reinecke can be very responsive to the bar-to-bar or even note-to-note qualities of the musical materials, and as in the A section, he sometimes retains the inflections when materials repeat. But at other times he plays repeated materials quite differently. And whereas the Welte-Mignon roll exhibits the same stylistic features as the Hupfeld one, they don't always appear in the same places. Again, Reinecke sometimes lets his playing be dominated by caesurae between phrases, as for example at bars 49–64 (25–32), but at other times he plays across phrase breaks, or marks major sectional breaks with smaller caesurae than those between phrases within a section: examples of the latter are bar 56 (32), halfway through the first B section, and bar 160 (88), halfway through the final A section. (This, too, applies to the Welte-Mignon roll.) In short, Reinecke is not much concerned with hierarchies of phrase and section and makes little effort to be consistent in terms of his interpretation of particular points in the music. Insofar as his playing is consistent, it is at the level of overall stylistic character.

There are other differences too. Despite the constant inflections of the opening phrases which I described, one can just about think of them in terms of a reference tempo, as in the case of van Oort, and though the tempo is constantly changing when the opening figure comes back at bars 25–32 and 41–48 (17–24), it is at least within the context of an already established tempo. But that is barely the case when the opening figure comes back again at bar 129 (65), where for several bars there is no clear sense of tempo, and though Reinecke has settled down to a more regular tempo by the time the phrase repeats at bars 137, he then adopts a distinctly slower tempo for the next phrase, bars 145–52 (73–80). And when the opening figure comes back yet again, at bar 153 (81), the beat is constantly changing up until the enormous caesura at bar 160 (88)—a caesura so long as to be effectively unmeasured, although in structural terms it marks merely the repeat of the second half of the section. Nor does a clear tempo emerge in the course of that repeat. The entire A section on its second appearance, then, is characterised by mobile tempo, no less than was d'Albert's playing of Schubert's op. 90 no. 3.

The Welte-Mignon performance is also characterised by mobile tempo, though the passage corresponding to bar 81 in the score (121 in this recording, owing to the omitted repeats) is rather steadier than in the Hupfeld roll. There is however a more significant difference in terms of the relative handling of tempos as between the two rolls. In the Welte-Mignon roll, Reinecke plays the same material at more or less the same speed every time it recurs. (The figures would be something like minim = 75, 70, and 80 for the A, B, and C materials respectively, but these are calculated averages, what Gabrielsson would call 'mean' tempos rather than phenomenologically real ones: that is why I have not included the Reinecke rolls in Figure 4.5). In other words Reinecke is using contrasted tempos in the same way as d'Albert and Sauer. In the case of the Hupfeld roll, however, it is clear that—as in Pachmann's contemporaneous roll—a progressive tempo scheme is at work. Only it works the other way round from Pachmann's: when the A section comes back, Reinecke plays it slower than he did first time round, and every time the B section appears, it takes longer. As for the coda, Reinecke continues into it without changing speed, in the manner of the other early recordings, and like d'Albert and Sauer—but in contrast to Pachmann and Friedman—he slows substantially at bar 205 (109). In his case the special effect lies in the way he plays the Alberti bass, detached (that is, contrary to the *legato* marking) and rather prominently, particularly when the harmony changes at bar 209 (113): it sounds a little like a parody of Czerny's velocity project, though that is probably to read too much into the nuances of a piano roll. Reinecke's Welte-Mignon roll, by contrast, is the only one of these early recordings in which nothing special, let alone extraordinary, is done at this point. He plays quieter at bar 109 (159 in his recording), as notated, but that is it. Perhaps this is linked to the drastic truncation of the coda.

Reinecke is a particularly significant figure in this context because it was his playing of Mozart that Schenker admired above all others. Possibly the oldest Western 'art' musician to have been recorded, Reinecke was the leading exponent of the conservative pianistic tradition of Leipzig, and regularly performed with Joachim; that places him in the same aesthetic orbit as Schenker, who wrote about him repeatedly in 1896–97. 'In his truly virtuoso playing', Schenker says, for once using this word in a positive sense, 'all intentions of the artwork are in balance' (Federhofer 1990: 333, 354). Schenker adds that Reinecke's playing is characterised by a cool tone and brilliant passagework, and a tendency towards fast tempos. (We have seen that.) But most striking is Schenker's insistence (189, 354–55) that, in his brilliant passagework and readiness to introduce unnotated ornamentation, Reinecke represents Mozart's music as it would have been played in the composer's time, or even by the composer himself. It is tempting to imagine that a pianist born in the year Beethoven completed his Ninth Symphony could provide some kind of link with authentic classical performance, and Daniel Leech-Wilkinson (2009a: chapter 6, paragraph 24) wonders whether the constant upward arpeggiation of chords in Reinecke's recording of the 'Larghetto' from Mozart's Piano Concerto K 537 might not perhaps represent 'harpsichord technique surviving into nineteenth-century playing': that would be almost frightening, Leech-Wilkinson adds, 'because of the wholesale rethink it would force about everything we imagine as Classical'. It is then perhaps just as well that we are never likely to know. But in any case we need to remember that even Reinecke would have learned to play on a Chopin-era pianoforte, not a Mozart-era fortepiano (let alone a harpsichord).

Alan Dodson has remarked that Schenker's ideal in performance was a 'middle path' between 'unfeeling literalism' on the one hand and 'willful distortion of the text and its meaning' on the other.[17] Yet on the evidence of the piano rolls one might have thought that, if anyone represented willful distortion of the text and its meaning, it was Reinecke. All this provides grounds for a radical interpretation of what Schenker (2000) meant when, in the 1911 papers published as *The Art of Performance*, he followed up his claim that non-rhetorical performance is no performance at all as follows:

> Specifically the performance of Classical works must be shaped freely and expressively. All that contemporaries have reported enthusiastically about the infinitely free and colorful performances of J. S. Bach, C. P. E. Bach, Mozart and Beethoven, Mendelssohn and Brahms, all that should be taken as evidence for this fact. If one adds what can be found in essays and letters by these masters, then one cannot but become convinced that their music is performed correctly only if it is played with the utmost freedom (70).

And at this point we can return from the detour via the *Rondo all turca* and ask what such freedom might mean as applied to the street theatre—Allanbrook's term—of Mozart's topics in the first movement of K 332. The registral contrasts and wealth of detail in the recordings of the Rondo made by Reinecke and other rhetorical performers—both old and now—provide some strong hints as to the kind of playing Schenker may have had in mind. But as it happens we can go beyond hints. I have to admit to a second small sleight of hand when I said I could trace no sound recordings of that sonata before Landowska in 1938. That is true, but there exists one—and as far as I am aware, only one—piano roll of the first movement of K 332. It was again made for Hupfeld, and again by Reinecke. It is presented as Media Example 4.15.[18]

On the basis of his recording of the *Rondo all turca*, one could say there are not too many surprises in how Reinecke plays K 332. As before there are sometimes extreme lengthenings in response to phrase and section divisions, density of material (he slows down for the three-against-two passage at bars 49–50), and expressive moments; he rushes to cadences; and sometimes he pulls about the time for no apparent reason. I have no idea why he lengthens bar 14 and, apparently in compensation, abbreviates bar 15, but the suggestion sometimes advanced that such things are the result of faulty recording is not tenable: they are

17. 'Schenker's Annotated Score of Chopin's Preludes, Op. 28, and the Psychology of Artistic Performance' (unpublished paper).

18. Hupfeld Phonola 50634; no commercial transfer is available, and I am grateful to Paul Tuck for supplying me with a transfer from a roll in his own collection. Reinecke also recorded the second movement, on Phonola 50319.

ubiquitous in the recordings Reinecke made for both Hupfeld and Welte. He repeats the first but not the second half of the movement, and when materials come back he sometimes replicates these inflections, including the apparently arbitrary one at bars 14–15, but at other times he doesn't. Another apparently arbitrary feature of Reinecke's performance, which he repeats, involves the *Sturm und Drang* section: he starts playing *forte* a bar earlier than Mozart has marked it, with the second descending c^2-f^1 (third beat of bar 21). This is interesting, because it exactly fits with Allanbrook's description of this passage as the 'middle term' of a musical syllogism. As I explained, the link she identified between the hunt call and *Sturm und Drang* topics is the iambic rhythm of two crotchets across the barline. Reinecke takes it further: he links the falling fifths—which are a condensation of the melodic descent in bars 16–18—to the iambic $c\#^1$-d^1 at bars 22–23, by clothing the former in the dynamic and sonority of the latter. In other words, to borrow Allanbrook's terms, he adds extra parameters of 'same' to counterbalance the highly diversified 'other'. Whether this effect was intended by Reinecke, or is perceptible to a listener, is another matter.

But we also see the use of tempo to characterise topical materials. The plan is based around two reference tempos, and although his tempos are sometimes mobile, Reinecke establishes each of the reference tempos through passages of relatively steady playing. Because this is a Hupfeld roll, the absolute tempos in Media Example 4.15 are informed guesses. The first is crotchet = around 156 at the opening, for the second subject (bar 41), and for the second lyrical passage within the second subject area (bar 71). The second is crotchet = around 170 for the *Sturm und Drang* topic (bar 23), for the rhythmic extension of the second subject (particularly from bar 60, the point of elision where the intensification of the tempo is quite palpable), and for the cadential build-up from bar 84. And the principle underlying this is a commonplace of nineteenth-century performance pedagogy: the distinction between what Kullak calls the 'cantilena' and the 'passage'. In the latter, Kullak (1893) explains, accentuation is controlled not by metre but by 'that accent which results from the figurate constitution of the passage' (248), in other words the motive on which the passagework is based. By contrast, Kullak (1893: 253) describes the cantilena as 'a connected, orderly chain of tones, symbolically imitative of the spoken phrase'. Here the mood expressed by the melody and the accentuation required to bring out its meaning are essential: through these, Kullak explains, music 'may imitate symbolically from the outset, without being founded on words, the diversity in the expression of speech with its own full freedom' (256). It is this that he describes as 'the supreme law of musical declamation' (253).

IN TIME AND OF TIME

And the thing that I remember ... was his feeling for time.
—EDWARD SAID, on attending a Furtwängler concert
as a child, in Barenboim and Said 2003: 17

There is a sense in which topics are a red herring. At one level the Rondo represents a topic—it is a *locus classicus* of the Turkish style—but within the Rondo meaning emerges from the relationship between the characteristic materials of which it is constructed, where generic reference is a principal determinant of character. Seen this way, topics are simply characteristic materials whose generic references have condensed, through repeated usage, into a semi-codified system.[19] Or to put it the other way round, what the detour via the *Rondo alla turca* has shown is that, in terms of the rhetorical performance theorised by Kullak and Schenker, practiced by 'old school' pianists, and advocated by today's fortepianists, all characteristic materials are treated as if they were topics. And the relationship between genre and performance style is at the heart of this. As Brown (1999) says, 'Throughout most of the second half of the [eighteenth] century there was a strong connection between the type of music and the style of execution' (219). Performance style signified generic type and in this way brought connotational meaning into play—which is to say that reference is an integral dimension of rhetorical performance, whether or not topics as such are involved. Through my focus on topics, then, my aim has been to make two general points: that rhetorical performance turns on reference and is in that sense a semiotic practice, and that an approach that sees performance as a process of real-time semiosis is fundamentally different from one that sees it as the reproduction of an ideal, essentially atemporal object.

It is to the nature of that fundamental difference that I now turn. At one level, of course, it is the opposition through which HIP musicians, including fortepianists, have constructed their own identity: 'over the past century', van Oort writes, 'the classical style became noble, elegant, and singing, rather than dramatic, emotional, and speaking' (2003: 84). Each approach is constructed as the mirror image of the other. But what is at issue goes further than what might be called a modernist tendency towards monumentalisation. On the one hand we have the idea of the musical work as an ideal object more or less fixed by the score, differentiated from its environment through analytically demonstrable unity, and reproduced in performance through stylistic practices that express that unity—at one level through the 'long line' (the performance correlate of the editorial phrasing slur), and at another through the devices of structuralist performance discussed in Chapter 2. In terms of both composition and performance, the essential framework of analysis is the individual work. On the other hand we have the idea of performance as a real-time practice comparable to oratory or acting, in which meaning is produced through reference to genres or characteristic types: here the sound ideal is that of a 'lively' or 'speaking' performance, and the framework for its analysis is necessarily much broader, encompassing not only a multiplicity of genres and types but also the non-musical practices and connotational systems evoked in the act of meaning production. My excursus in Chapter 3 on turn-of-the-century speech

---

19. For further discussion, based on contemporary sources and work with leading fortepianists, see Sheila Guymer (forthcoming); it was she who gave me the idea of looking at performance in terms of topics.

patterns represented an example of the latter, and I also broached there an idea I now wish to develop: that what underlies this opposition is different conceptions of musical time.

The structuralist model is of an ideal object that is not inherently temporal but, in performance, is presented through time. Time is the medium through which the music passes, rather in the manner of its steady progression across the screen when you are playing a recording in Sonic Visualiser. Translated into performance, this corresponds to a regular tempo that is maintained, in principle and within reason, regardless of musical content: this is the source of Repp's curiously unscientific insistence, which I mentioned in Chapter 3, that there must always be an identifiable basic tempo. By contrast, the rhetorical model is one in which time is a dimension of the musical material, so that (as I put it) the music is not *in* time, as with the structuralist model, but rather *of* time. This means that music is understood to be inherently temporal—which is why phenomenologists such as Alfred Schutz (1976) insisted, with Stokowski and Kenyon, that scores are not music—and equally that it shapes temporal experience, rather in the manner of a magnetic field. Translated into performance, this gives rise to timing that is a function of sectional design, musical material (for example in terms of melodic contour, harmonic direction, rhythmic density, or texture), and expression—in other words, precisely the sort of thing I have been documenting in both 'old school' pianists and present-day fortepianists. On occasion, particularly in the case of the older pianists who were as ready to compress time as to augment it, this can result in a sense of time that is so mobile as to resist quantification.

For the musically conservative Adorno (2006: 103), tempo is 'a function of the musical *content* (*Inhalt*)', and the distinction I am making is in essence the same as that between Adorno's 'chronometric' and phenomenological time, or in Schutz's terms (1964) clock as against 'inner' time.[20] Schenker, too, insists on the difference between mechanically and musically correct timing, and this results in what is at first sight a paradoxical claim: 'true *rubato*', he says, should create 'the illusion of a strict tempo' (2000: 54). Listening to 'old school' piano playing with a moving tempo graph using Sonic Visualiser makes Schenker's point. If you focus your listening on the temporal becoming of the musical material, orienting yourself towards phenomenological rather than chronometric time, then your aural experience belies the wayward and erratic appearance of the tempo graph: to the extent that you hear the pulling and pushing of the tempo, you hear it as a dimension of the material. However in saying this I do not want to reduce Adorno's 'content' to simply material terms, as that term is normally understood. Expression and affect play a constitutive role in this kind of musical time consciousness, and here

20. For an extensive discussion of concepts of time in nineteenth-century performance, and their relationship to Beethovenian declamation, see Barth (1992). In essence Barth blames Beethoven's pupil and proselytiser, Carl Czerny, for transforming Beethoven's organic approach to musical time, based on the body, into one based on chronometric regularity. It is hard to square this with what one hears on early recordings, including of Beethoven's music—but then a long time elapsed in between.

a historical dimension comes into play. Musicologists writing on topics emphasise that a key way in which music of the classical period, defined as from the *galant* to Beethoven, differs from that of the baroque is the kaleidoscopic succession of affects, in contrast to the affective unity at which baroque music aimed. The difference is perhaps at its most obvious in opera.

In this way the rhetorical style of the 'old school' pianists offers a parallel to a basic compositional principle of classical as opposed to baroque music. But it goes further than this. One might speak of a structural primacy of affect that is evident not only in their mobile tempos, a kind seismographic tracing of the ebb and flow of what Massumi calls intensity,[21] but also in the multi-tempo plans that underlie their performances. Through these practices 'old school' performers penetrate deep into what, from a modernist standpoint, is the domain of compositional structure. By contrast, modernist performance—the product of a culture in which it is the exception for performers to be also composers—maintains a relatively fixed distinction between the domains of composer and performer. More or less constant tempos provide a structural foundation onto which expressive effects are superimposed, rather like the topping on a pizza. By repeating this metaphor, which I used near the beginning of Chapter 2, I mean to draw an analogy with the Hanslickian model according to which expression is something piled on top of structure. To a considerable degree, modernist performance is Hanslick's aesthetics turned into sound.

Now in Chapter 3 I called the difference between music understood as *in* and as *of* time an ontological one, which might suggest that we are dealing with different epistemes or mentalities, in other words mutually exclusive systems of belief. That would give rise to the style of history in which successive periods are presented as mutually foreign, even unintelligible, as illustrated by Karol Berger's *Bach's Cycle, Mozart's Arrow* (2007): Berger seeks to locate the birth of musical modernity in the eighteenth century on the basis of the new conception of linear time it embodied. The study of performance has seen a number of historical narratives based on this kind of periodisation. According to Robert Philip, who as we saw in Chapter 3 compared the playing of pianists of d'Albert's generation to 'a lost language which is no longer quite understood', recording brought about a style of performance that was optimised for repeated listening: it eliminated the untidiness and some of the excitement that had previously characterised live performance, and that we can hear on the earliest recordings, and in this way led to a narrowing of performance options, a standardisation of practice. (The periodisation is suggested in the title of his 2004 book, *Performing in the Age of Recording*.) And we have seen how the HIP interpretation of history, as set out by Harnoncourt and reflected by many other musicians and commentators, traces the evolution from a rhetorical and dramatic conception of music to one that is characterised by monumentality and passive enjoyment, and symbolised by the phrasing slur: essentially these are presented as mutually unintelligible systems.

21. See Chapter 3, p. 79.

(HIP, of course, forms the denouement of the narrative.) The same applies to the equal and opposite narrative put about by modernist performers: I referred in Chapter 1 to the Vienna Conservatory's *Stilkommission*, the mission of which was to erase the traces of nineteenth-century distortion and excess, and so reinstate what Robert Hill (1994) refers to as 'an imagined pre-romantic "classicistic" performance practice' (47). As Hill acidly comments, 'it is doubtful whether a "classicizing" performance practice of the kind invoked by modernism to lend itself authority ever existed' (52).

It is not that there is no truth in these narratives—except perhaps the last—but there are so many contradictions and exceptions that you cannot sensibly speak of a rule. Berger identifies musical modernism with a distinctive approach to time, just as I do—but for him the crucial period is the eighteenth century, whereas for me it is the twentieth. And in any case, his attempt to reduce these approaches to a simple historical narrative of before and after has been strongly criticised by John Butt (2010: 109–10) and Bettina Varwig (2012). Again, I shall discuss a counter-example to Philip's narrative of standardisation in Chapter 6, while this chapter should have made it clear that the idea of conflating classical and modernist performance is problematical, to say the least. As for HIP and the phrasing slur, the dates don't line up and people appear on the wrong sides. It is Schenker, the apostle of music-theoretical unity, who attacks the phrasing slur, which (like Levin) he blames on nineteenth-century editors—the same musicians whose wilfully Romantic legacy the *Stilkommission* was intended to stamp out. Yet as Bilson points out in relation to K 332 (1992: 243), it is in the recordings of Artur Schnabel, one of the pioneers of modernist performance, that we hear phrasing slurs fully transformed into sound. And it gets worse when Levin complains about the slurs in the Breitkopf und Härtel complete works, the distinguished editorial team for which included Brahms, Joachim, and Reinecke. As Levin says,

> every time there are sixteenth notes for one or two bars there's a slur over them, and if there are more than that it says 'legato'. Mozart never used the word 'legato' in his scores in his life; that was put in by Carl Reinecke, who edited the concertos. According to Reinecke's values Mozart had to be balanced and beautiful and well-modulated, and so he played it in the legato style (Sherman 1997: 325).

But on the basis of his piano rolls, you would think beauty, balance, and good modulation are about the last terms to apply to Reinecke's often distinctly non-legato playing. Presumably Levin was extrapolating from his editions, which once again raises the issue of how far you can make useful deductions about performance from written documents of whatever kind. It also raises a further issue: perhaps people make a basic mistake when they assume that regular patterns in notated music, whether editorial or compositional, imply correspondingly regular performance. That clearly does not apply to Reinecke. No more does it apply to Grieg, the notoriously four-square phrase structure of whose music is given the lie by the extraordinarily flexible playing revealed on the composer's recordings from

1903,[22] or to Scriabin, whose rolls exhibit equally diversified treatment of the lit-eral repetitions characteristic of his compositional style (Leikin 2011: 27, 69). It is the paradigm of reproduction that leads to the assumption that what happens on the page should be reflected on the stage. Set that aside, and it becomes as plausible to think of performers complementing the qualities of a notated script as replicating them. One might even suggest that the more regular the notation is, the less regular we should expect its intended performance to be.

However the larger point I want to make is that these periodisations are not stable, and the reason is that the approaches on which they are based are not in fact mutually exclusive. This is essentially Butt's and Varwig's point in relation to Berger: they document the co-existence of differing conceptions of time in Bach's music and more generally during his lifetime. And this becomes entirely plausible if one thinks of the conceptions of musical time to which I referred, and the other characteristics that I associated with them, as metaphors rather than belief systems. Metaphor theorists have shown how everyday discourse is conditioned by implicit metaphors, and a frequent cause of miscommunication is when people are thinking about the same thing in terms of different metaphorical constructions. When you have diagnosed this problem you have solved it: it is quite normal to slip from one metaphor to another, often unconsciously. Clearly most musicians' playing styles are not as mobile as that, but neither are they like different languages. I am suggest-ing that rhetorical and structuralist approaches represent complementary possibili-ties for construing music as thought and action, and that musicians have at various times laid more weight on one or the other, or slipped between them. That means transitions from the one to the other do not have to be explained in terms of such grand constructs as epistemes, mentalities, or historical periods.

A parallel might be drawn with a change in Haydn's keyboard sonatas that took place during the 1770s, from notations that invited co-creation by the performer, for example by indicating but not spelling out ornaments or cadenzas, to nota-tions in which all of these have been fully elaborated. It would be tempting to interpret this in terms of the evolution of the work concept, in other words a gen-eral paradigm shift reflected in local practice, but Beghin (2007) instead relates it to a purely local contingency, the emergence of a female amateur market for sheet music: as he explains, 'Haydn, from 1774 on, strove to offer his target users a complete package, including those aspects that characterize delivery by a master such as himself' (166–67). In the same way, I am suggesting that patterns in per-formance practice may reflect local contingencies, biographical circumstances, or personal taste. They may reflect micro-narratives rather than the grand narratives so readily invoked in the history of performance. It is very easy to talk airily of the history of performance style without stopping to consider how far there actually is such a thing, rather than a history of specific vocal and instrumental practices taking place in specific places or among specific social groups—or a history of

22. Leech-Wilkinson (2012: paragraph 3.8), referencing the work of Sigurd Slåttebrekk and Tony Harrison.

individual genres, or even of individual pieces. In short, there has been a tendency to erect rather lofty historical edifices on distinctly shallow empirical foundations.

But if we are talking about complementary rather than mutually exclusive possibilities of construing music, how can we explain the sense of a lost language to which Philip referred (as Peres da Costa [2012: xxviii] says, early recordings 'often sound shockingly foreign') and why do people laugh at old recordings? There is a simple and obvious answer, which is that any number of local and historically contingent performance practices may be built on the same rhetorical or structuralist foundation, and that as in any other area of culture, if you aren't familiar with the local conventions then what people do may seem bizarre. The less simple and obvious answer is that there is an asymmetry between the rhetorical and structuralist approaches, and it is at this point that we need to confront two terms which I have up to now been careful to keep out of this chapter: premodern and postmodern. As I said in Chapter 3, the structuralist approach maps almost too readily onto modernism, while the rhetorical approach can be linked to both the premodern and the postmodern. A nice illustration of how the premodern can shade into the postmodern is provided by the performance history of Webern's Piano Variations op. 27, throughout the 1950s and 1960s an icon of literalist, modernist performance. The publication in 1979 of the annotated score prepared under the composer's direction by Peter Stadlen, who had given the first performance in 1937, prompted a revisionist approach that could equally well be seen as an expression of postmodern neo-Romanticism or as a historically informed return to the premodern performance style in terms of which Webern conceived the work. Either way, the result was that pianists who had grown up with the modernist style started performing Webern's score as if it was in a foreign language—or in quotation marks.

This, however, is where the asymmetry to which I referred comes in. Until the final decades of the twentieth century, modernism was the yardstick against which other epistemes, mentalities, periods, or cultures were measured. In other words, premodern epistemes, mentalities, and the rest were conceived as being essentially the same sort of thing as modernism, only different, and the same applies to postmodernism. But there is a significant way in which modernism is not the same sort of thing, which becomes obvious if you think in terms of architecture. The nineteenth century was a time of extreme stylistic eclecticism: buildings referenced other buildings and styles, offering an obvious parallel to 'old school' pianism. By contrast, twentieth-century architectural modernism sought to eliminate such referentiality, and in its place to establish a style predicated on structural integrity. Again there is an obvious comparison with musical performance, which I shall pursue in Chapter 6.

What I want to emphasise here is that modernism drew highly selectively on what we now call the premodern (accounts of the origins of modernist architecture are basically selections of the right bits from earlier architecture), and that it set itself in opposition to the pluralism that characterised nineteenth-century culture. This applies as much to aesthetic theory as it does to architecture, or for that matter to performance: we associate such constructs as the autonomous work or the regime of musical genius with the nineteenth century, when they were indeed influential, but at the same time we ascribe to them the quality of ideological exclusivity that they developed only in the twentieth century—and perhaps not fully until after the Second World War. And it is this quality of exclusivity that characterises what I am calling structuralism, by which I mean not only the modernist style of performance that developed during the interwar period but also, and more particularly, the habits of thought associated with it—including the approaches of formalist aesthetics and music theory that I discussed in the opening chapters of this book. Structuralism presents itself as all-encompassing. Like religious fundamentalism, it denies the necessity or even the availability of alternatives. Structuralist performance excludes other styles of performance: that was the point of the *Stilkommission*. It is the style of the imperative.

By contrast, many of the constituent practices of structuralist performance are to be found within what, in the broadest sense, I am calling rhetorical performance. It is not that rhetorical performers were incapable of playing metronomically: it is that they did so only when they considered it appropriate. In other words, metronomic performance figures within the repertory of rhetorical performance practices. That is why it is not hard to find, among the earliest recorded performances, examples that are much less alien than those on which I have concentrated: my aim has not been to present a balanced overview of early recorded performers, but rather to focus on some of those who, through their difference from present-day practices, most clearly embody what a study of historical performance practice needs to accommodate. After saying that it would be almost frightening if Reinecke's playing had its origins in eighteenth-century performance practice, Leech-Wilkinson (2009a: chapter 6, paragraph 25) continues, 'we can also find among early recordings a considerable number of pianists who play in a manner much more like our own' (he cites Pugno as an example). Going back to the question with which this discussion started, then, the reason early recordings make people laugh is not that the playing on them is completely unintelligible, but that familiar sounds, gestures, and works appear in an unfamiliar and apparently incongruous guise. In particular, the rhetorical sense of time as a function of musical content distorts the temporal flow that is nowadays taken for granted, rather in the manner of a playground mirror. The effect is funny in the same way as the Trobriand Islands version of cricket, and for much the same reasons.

All the same, the performance culture of WAM is undoubtedly more pluralistic now than it was a few decades ago: we have become much more used to the idea that the same music can be played in different ways. At one level this welcoming broadening of musical horizons reflects the relaxing of modernism's grip on the concert hall, but more directly and pragmatically it is the result of the rapidly increasing dissemination of early recordings that I referred to in Chapter 2. It is unfortunate then that recent developments in international copyright law pose a threat to the continued availability of historical recordings. Absurdly, American law means that no sound recordings will be in the public domain until 2067; since only a tiny proportion of the recorded heritage has been reissued by the copyright holders, the historical study of performance has largely depended on European copyright regimes providing a fifty-year term of protection. In 2011, however, lobbying by major record companies desperate to retain income from the recordings of the Beatles and their contemporaries persuaded the European Union to raise the term to seventy years, which means that at the time of writing no recording issued after 1942 is in the public domain.[23] This is a very practical issue for the study of performance, mitigated only by the near impossibility of enforcing copyright in the age of digital media and the internet. But—as my references in Chapter 1 to the links between aesthetics and copyright law might suggest—it also bears upon conceptual and ideological issues that are highly germane to thinking about performance, including the relationship between structuralist and rhetorical approaches.

Lawrence Lessig (2008) has argued that present-day copyright regimes reflect the assumptions of what he calls 'Read/Only' or RO culture: in essence, this is the regime I outlined with specific reference to music in Chapter 1, according to which culture is structured around ownable commodities (in the case of music, works), which are more or less passively consumed by a paying public. It is a striking fact that the developments in aesthetic theory that took place during the nineteenth century, and were consolidated and fixed during the twentieth, should correspond so closely to the interests of publishers, investors, and other rights holders that lie at the heart of present-day copyright legislation. Lessig draws a distinction between the official, passively consumed RO culture and what he calls 'Read/Write' or RW culture, which is based on active participation through reworking the cultural materials that collectively constitute a shared heritage. He calls his book *Remix* in part because he sees the remixing practices of popular culture—whereby recorded music and film are reworked and recycled—as the paradigmatic contemporary example of RW culture, but also because remixing and sampling have been the prime areas within which the current copyright regime has been contested both within and beyond the courts. As Lessig (2008: 100) says, 'By default, RW use violates copyright law. RW culture is thus presumptively illegal'.

The book's central arguments are that the creative economy requires the co-existence of RO and RW cultures—this is the 'hybrid economy' of Lessig's subtitle—and that 'we need to decriminalize creativity before we further criminalise a generation of our kids' (114). But by focussing on remixing Lessig may give the misleading impression of being solely concerned with contemporary issues. In fact he claims that RW culture has always been part of the creative economy. And again he uses music to make his point, quoting the composer and band leader John Philip Sousa, in 1906, foretelling the demise of participatory musical culture as a result of recordings: 'In Sousa's time', Lessig writes, 'the creativity was performance. The selection and arrangement expressed the creative ability of the singers' (56). Traditional musical culture, then, is an obvious illustration of how the relationship between RO and RW cultures is 'complementary, not competitive'.

Lessig's book reinforces a number of the main points I have been trying to make. There are obvious affinities on the one hand between Lessig's RO culture

---

23. Unless it has already been reissued under the fifty-year rule. For further discussion of these developments on both sides of the Atlantic see Brooks (2012), Cook (2012), and Harkins (2012).

and what I called the paradigm of reproduction, and on the other between Lessig's RW culture and the intertextual and intergeneric practices I have discussed in this chapter.[24] Lessig, then, provides a model for the complementary relationship between structuralist and rhetorical ontologies of music. Then again, Lessig helps us see why the regime of the musical work was never the monolithic entity as which it has been represented. In Chapter 1 I mentioned the nineteenth-century piano cultures based on virtuoso arrangements of, and variations on, currently popular operatic arias and other materials in effect treated as musical shareware. (Mozart was an early and prolific composer of such variation sets, which would nowadays be illegal—at least in the UK—unless permissions could be obtained for reproducing the materials in question.) But the real evidence of period remixing is to be found in nineteenth-century sheet music, as listed in such catalogues as the Hofmeister *Monatsberichte*.[25] The repertory as we know it today is dwarfed by a tsunami of arrangements for every likely— or unlikely—ensemble, of which the Hofmeister category 'Music for physharmonica, harmonic flute and accordion' will have to stand as sole representative. There is a real sense in which the generally domestic participatory practices of which these arrangements form the trace, the core of nineteenth-century RW culture, were supplanted in the twentieth century by the playing of 78s and LPs, the emblematic media of RO culture: you couldn't record them, only play them back. It was also under the RO regime of modernism, particularly after the Second World War, that the whole idea of arrangement fell into disrepute. Musical participation did not cease, of course, but it was massively deflected into popular musical genres. I will come back to this at the end of the book.

But what is most important for my argument is the perspective on performance inherent in Lessig's book, which is as different as could be from the RO paradigm of reproduction. In Sousa's time the creativity was not, of course, just in the selection and arrangement: it was in the performance itself, in the interpretive practices I have described in this and the previous chapter, as well as in preluding and the extemporisation of *Eingänge* and cadenzas—referential practices which survived until much more recently than RO-dominated histories of music have generally allowed. As for the century before Sousa, reconstructing performance practices prior to the development of recording is always hazardous, but evidence that is regularly cited in relation to compositions is equally evidence of their performance. The composer and violinist Giuseppe Cambini's picturesque comment on Beethoven's first two symphonies is well known: 'Now he takes the majestic flight of the eagle; then he creeps along grotesque paths. After penetrating the soul with a sweet melancholy he soon tears it by a mass of barbaric chords. He seems to

24. I also discuss such practices in the context of digital media, specifically video mashup, in Cook (2013a).

25. Monthly or bi-monthly music catalogues published by the Leipzig music publisher Friedrich Hofmeister, issued continuously from 1829 until 1945; accessible at http://www.onb.ac.at/sammlungen/musik/16615.htm (facsimiles) and http://www.hofmeister.rhul.ac.uk/2008/index.html (searchable online repository).

harbour doves and crocodiles at the same time'.[26] When Cambini said this he had
not been studying scores: he had been at a performance (Schrade 1942: 3–4). And
what he is talking about is Beethoven's idiosyncratic development of the intergeneric references and disjunctions of register embodied in Mozart's topics and
audible in rhetorical performance.

According to Dean Sutcliffe (2003: 61), the image of Mozart's piano sonatas
'seems stuck in a time warp', mired in the cult of what Harnoncourt called the
'merely beautiful'; he mentions approaches based on topics and the use of period
instruments as ways of 'trying to ruffle their smooth surface'. We could borrow
Cambini's words and say that the doves and crocodiles Mozart composed into
his music have been erased by modernist performance from Landowska to de
Larrocha, and more generally by 'brilliant, glossy, "official" performances' that
'smooth over any discontinuities which might jolt the listener'. That is Rose
Rosengard Subotnik's paraphrase (1976: 263) of Adorno, and of course it is modernist performance he was talking about. But Schenker was saying the same as
far back as 1894. Referring to performances of mainstream classical repertory by
the virtuoso piano trio of František Ondříček, David Popper, and Anton Door,
Schenker (1990) complains that they offer 'finger engineering' in place of the
'technique of the spirit' (271–72). Everything is smoothed over: Where, he asks,
are the gaping cracks and abrupt jumps of Beethoven's music? Ironically, it is the
modernist music theory of which Schenker laid the foundations, in conjunction
with modernist aesthetics and modernist performance, that filled over the cracks,
disciplining and monumentalising the classics into perfect musical objects, perfectly reproduced.

Reproduction is performance conceived from the perspective of RO culture, or
maybe it would be better to say from the perspective of the RO dimension of our
hybrid musical culture. Seen in Lessig's terms, as a form of remixing, performance
produces meaning by signifying on what already exists. This is an idea with a
specific provenance in black cultural studies, and I shall return to it in Chapter 9.
But one might equally say that Mozart signified on popular operatic arias, and
that rhetorical performers past and present signify on Mozart. It is rather like the
relationship between pictorial representation and iconography: there are elements
of reproduction in performance, but they draw their meaning from the much
broader semiotic economies of which they form just a part. I shall be coming back
to that, too.

26. Translated in Schrade (1942: 3).

5

Close and Distant Listening

REINVENTING STYLE ANALYSIS

Scholarly editors, of music as of literature, often invoke the idea of the stemma. Like a family tree, the stemma is a representation in which time flows from top to bottom. It seeks to reconstruct the paths of transmission between the surviving texts of a given work. The original autograph, which often no longer exists, is placed at the top, and the aim of the editorial project is to recapture that text, and with it the author's conception, in the most authentic possible form. Traditional ways of thinking about performance can be seen as structured around the same kind of vertical axis: the composer's score is the starting point for the interpretation, explanation, and assessment of a given performance. This is the vertical conception to which Richard Schechner (1988b) opposed interdisciplinary performance studies when he advocated 'exploration of horizontal relationships among related forms rather than a searching vertically for unprovable origins' (28). If the page-to-stage approach moves along the vertical axis, seeking to understand a given performance in terms of the structural context of the notated work, then the horizontal axis brings into play the relationships between the performance and the universe of other performances of that work, or of related works, whether recorded, remembered, or imagined; as Lawrence Kramer (2007) says, 'A classical performance always addresses the listener against the possibility or memory of other note-for-note renditions' (82). To seek to understand performance from this perspective is to foreground the differences between performances, and to see them as producing meaning in their own right. This is the perspective of performance style.

Before I enter into more detail on the idea of performance style, how it gives rise to meaning, and how it can be studied, I would like to contextualise the relationship between the structural and stylistic dimensions of performance. As with the contrasting approaches to performance based on the ideas of structure and of rhetoric, we are dealing not with two hermetically sealed mentalities but with permanently available dimensions of performance culture whose relationship varies according to historical context. It might be helpful to begin with a visual analogue: how paintings are hung in art galleries. Today the norm is to place paintings well apart, separated from one another by plain white wall. The effect is to present each painting as an autonomous object to be understood primarily in its own terms, as the work of its creator. In this context photographs of late nineteenth-century exhibitions come as a shock: paintings are densely clustered together, a style of hanging rarely seen nowadays outside country houses. Here the effect is often to bring apparently unrelated paintings into relationship with one another, mobilising intertextual and style-oriented strategies of viewing. The style of hanging favoured today corresponds to the performance of autonomous musical works, the nineteenth-century style to the understanding of performances in relation to other performances.

Whereas the story of exhibition hanging might be told as a historical development from one understanding of art to another, that does not apply to its musical equivalent. As I said in Chapter 1, while Lydia Goehr sees the regulative concept of the autonomous musical work as having emerged around 1800, its supposed heyday embraces the period of the 'piano wars', a competitive musical culture within which virtuosi aimed to surpass other virtuosi, and were judged by audiences on the basis of their success in doing so. This provoked a neo-classical reaction that sought to reinstate the work rather than the performer at the core of musical culture, and 'work culture' has dominated aesthetic and theoretical thinking about WAM ever since. The pedagogy of performance has also emphasised the vertical dimension at the expense of the horizontal: 'Don't listen to performances!', Kolisch enjoined in 1977, 'That is not the right way, at least not for a musician, to get in touch with music. The right way is to read the text' (Quick 2010: 31). Such advice, which straightforwardly identifies the musically essential with the written, is echoed by such musicians as Pierre Boulez and André Previn (Day 2000: 224), and remains commonplace—if not necessarily heeded—to this day. Yet the competition, which represents the extreme form of horizontal listening (especially when everyone plays the same piece), has long been an integral part of musicians' career development, and with the extension of the television talent show to classical music, it has become an important mode through which that repertory is consumed.

Again, the story might be told in terms of the changed focus of the recording industry from the 1920s, when each label's aim was to cover the repertory, to the 1930s, when the star system spread from Hollywood to the recording industry. As David Patmore (2009: 128) explains, the aim was now to promote— say—Toscanini's Beethoven as against Weingartner's (the critical and marketing concept of the 'definitive' recording dates from this time), and the orientation of most record industry promotion towards performer rather than work has remained in place ever since. And Goehr (1996) herself published what was in effect a follow-up article to her 1992 book, in which she distinguished two approaches to performance. The first, which she calls the 'perfect performance of music', is the standard approach of music theory and aesthetics: it centres on the work and de-emphasises the performer. The other, which she terms the 'perfect musical performance', is just the reverse: it emphasises the performer at the expense of the work, meaning that works are 'created just to given the

opportunity to . . . performers to show their interpretive skills' (7). Two years later
these words were echoed almost literally by Small and Godlovitch, but in the
context of sweeping generalisations about the nature of music.[1] Goehr's contrast
between these opposed approaches suggests a better nuanced conclusion: we live
in a musical culture that combines the vertical and horizontal dimensions of
meaning production, with sometimes one and sometimes the other having the
upper hand. And yet it is the norm for musicology to emphasise the one at the
expense of the other.

This was not always the case. The concept of musical style has been subject
to remarkable vicissitudes since Guido Adler, in his 1885 article 'The scope,
method, and aim of musicology', divided the field into the historical and systematic approaches to music (Mugglestone 1981). Working in the shadow of
the Vienna school of art history, Adler emphasised the material dimensions of
musical culture—instruments and scores, soon supplemented by recordings—
and there was a strong empirical and comparative dimension to his conception
of systematic musicology. Turn-of-the-century pioneers such as Carl Stumpf and
Erich von Hornbostel, effectively working to Adler's agenda, brought together the
study of Western and non-Western musics on the one hand, and psychological,
ethnographical, and aesthetic approaches on the other. A particular influence on
Adler was the Viennese art historian Aloys Riegl, whose monograph *Problems of
Style* (1992) first appeared in 1893 and traced the history of decorative motifs: it
depicted style as a kind of impersonal, historical agent. Seen in Hegelian terms as
an unfolding of aesthetic destiny, the concept of style—and hence of style history
and style analysis—occupied a position of centrality within the study of music.

What seems to have changed this is the appropriation of the concept of style
by Nazi musicologists, or musicologists working in the shadow of Nazi ideologies, during the 1930s and 1940s. As the work of Pamela Potter and Ludwig
Holtmeier, among others, has shown, musicology, theory, and music psychology were all pressed into the service of racial ideology during the Third Reich.
Style was theorised in terms of racial difference, itself assumed to be biologically
grounded, and consequently became one of the targets in the process of musicological denazification that took place in the aftermath of the war. The reconstruction of German-language musicology was strongly influenced by Schoenberg, for
whom—as for most modernists—style was a kind of negative concept, the external, incidental trappings of the transcendental idea. But it was not just the concept
of style that lost its position within the musicological firmament: it was the entire
comparative project that underpinned style analysis.

If the hard-line modernism implemented at Darmstadt under a Schoenbergian
banner represented a wiping clean of the slate, then the same might be said
of the reconstruction of comparative musicology as ethnomusicology. This
might be described as a rotation from the horizontal axis to a vertical one.
Comparative musicology was condemned as a metropolitan discipline based

1. See above, p. 20.

on the European empires of the pre-war period, through which musical artefacts
and practices drawn from the colonial peripheries were compared and classified
according to taxonomies that represented the progression from savagery to modern European civilisation. It gave way to a discipline based instead on the idea of
fieldwork, stressing the need to understand musical practices in terms of their
role within the specific culture of which they formed part, in that sense vertically: making direct, horizontal links between the musical practices or artefacts of
different cultures was now seen as illegitimate, because they could have meaning
only within their own cultural context.

While the ideological motivation underlying the development of ethnomusicology is clear enough, it is less obvious in the parallel development that took
place within the sphere of music theory. But the conceptual topography was the
same. Where analysis oriented to style was based on making horizontal comparisons between musical configurations drawn from different times and places, the
post-war reconstruction of music theory—whose epicentre was North America—
again saw the making of such direct links as illegitimate, and for a similar reason: such configurations could have meaning only within their own structural
context. 'In my business', said the Princeton-based composer-theorist Peter
Westegaard (1974), ' "stylistic" and "style" are dirty words' (71). If this formulation echoed Schoenberg, then in the new project as a whole there was a resonance
with Darmstadt: the essential principle of serialism, at least in its post-war guise,
was that pitch formations derive their significance from an explicit structure, and
not from a historical tradition rendered suspect by implicit, uncontrolled values.
The control of meaning was a fundamental dimension of post-war modernism,
and this largely explains the anti-historical stance of many of the disciplines that
flourished in this environment—including music theory, ethnomusicology, and
the psychology of music.

There was a perverse consequence to this. It was in the decades following the
Second World War that computer technology began to make comparative work
based on large quantities of musical data practical in a way it had not previously been. But this happened just as the intellectual motivation for such work
atrophied. Computer-based style analysis took place: examples include, within
the field of WAM, Arthur Mendel's 'Josquin Project' of 1969, one aim of which
was to use style as a basis for settling the authorship of various works attributed
to the composer, and in the areas of folk and non-Western musics, the work of
Mieczyslaw Kolinski, Alan Lomax, and Hellmuth Schaffrath. But even in the
case of Mendel and Lomax, both of whom had high profiles, their computational
work had little impact on the discipline. And in this way what might have been a
major route for the development of performance studies in music was effectively
blocked off before it ever started. It is only in the last two decades that the cluster of approaches associated with Adler's systematic musicology—cross-cultural
comparison, style analysis, and empirical musicology more generally—has come
back onto the international musicological agenda, and even now such work tends
to be associated with cognitive musicology labs rather than mainstream departments
of music. One of the aims of this book is to ensure that, as the study of musical

performance develops, it does so within the core of music studies, rather than being ghettoised as a specialist subdiscipline.

All this helps to explain why, as I said at the end of Chapter 1, it was not in musicology or theory but in music psychology that empirical approaches to the analysis of musical performance first acquired the critical mass that makes it possible to speak of a disciplinary development. As I also said, this work was in part prompted by the development of MIDI, which made it easy to obtain pitch, timing, and dynamic data from performances recorded on MIDI key-boards.[2] MIDI code provides clean data for analysis, and considering how little information is actually encoded in the data, its ability to capture those features of piano performance that constitute style is remarkable. This made possible the foundational work of Eric Clarke and others, which for the first time began to clarify the complex interactions between the parameters involved in expressive performance.

At the same time, MIDI imposed some severe constraints on performance analysis. For one thing, since MIDI does not encode acoustic characteristics but simply feeds control data to a synthesiser, it diverts attention away from the tonal properties of particular instruments and the acoustic within which they are played, reducing performance to a kind of abstract script. Yet as I said in relation to piano rolls, what pianists play is in part determined by the particular instrument they are playing and the space they are playing in, as well as the social circumstances and purposes of the performance. Again, MIDI code was designed for keyboard instruments, and it copes highly inelegantly with instruments based on con-tinuous sound production and a full spectrum of pitches—in other words, most non-keyboard instruments and, in particular, the voice. That goes far to explain the skewing of empirical studies of performance towards the piano. A third, and for musicology crucial, issue arises out of the fact that, while Yamaha originally conceived their Disklavier as a domestic playback device—in effect a digital player piano—that market never really developed, and neither did a substantial library of commercial MIDI recordings. To work with MIDI you therefore had to take performance out of its real-world context, instead inviting research-friendly performers into your laboratory and recording them. This meant that large-scale studies involving multiple performers or performances were impractical, and of course, no historical dimension was possible.

For the performance researcher, the more than a century's heritage of com-mercial recordings presents exactly the opposite picture. Not only is the historical dimension abundantly represented, but so are all instruments, ensembles, and genres—though the recording of large-scale ensembles could be satisfactorily achieved only after the mid-1920s, when electrical recording was introduced. Rather than reducing performances to abstract scripts, recordings in principle

2. Actually it is not easy to analyse raw MIDI data: much work in this field made use of POCO, a program created by Henkjan Honing and Peter Desain which reconfigured the data into musi-cologically meaningful categories.

represent the totality of a sounded event. I say 'in principle' because, in practice, that claim needs to be heavily qualified. As I observed in Chapter 3, musicologists have tended to be excessively suspicious of piano rolls but insufficiently suspicious of sound recordings: particularly when old recordings are remastered to sound like modern CDs, they give the impression of a window on the past, the authentic sound image of a long-gone performance event. That impression is normally illusory, for a variety of reasons that I will summarise only briefly.[3]

In the case of mechanical recordings, up to the mid-1920s, there is a host of major confounds, many of which are obvious. Straightforwardly technological issues include limited frequency and dynamic range, uncertainty as to the correct playback speed (78 rpm was by no means a standard), and the different sound qualities that can result from the choice of needle. Less straightforward is the way in which the normal spatial arrangements of performance had to be reconfigured as players clustered round the recording horn, with the loudest instruments at the back; the congested conditions of such recorded sessions can be seen in Figure 5.1, one of the most famous of early studio photographs, of Elgar recording his *Carissima* with the Mayfair Orchestra on 21 January 1914. This means that dynamic balance is highly unreliable, and room acoustic to all intents and purposes absent. The disruption of normal playing arrangements must have affected ensemble, and performers unused to recording suffered from nerves (as is probably illustrated by a recording of the castrato Alessandro Moreschi made by the Gaisberg brothers in the Vatican on 3 April 1902—the one that made Robert Hill giggle).[4] Pieces for larger performing groups were generally arranged for smaller ones, and the more strident Stroh violins (in which a metal horn took the place of the wooden soundbox) replaced the normal instrument. Pieces longer than the three-to-four-minute length of a 78 side might be cut, or possibly played faster than they would otherwise have been. And the need to keep the wax soft meant the temperature in the studio had to be around 90 degrees Fahrenheit. Only piano rolls and cylinders provide evidence as to how musicians of this period played when feeling comfortable.

All this means that certain things can be safely deduced from early recordings, while others cannot. Researchers need to know which parameters can be subjected to meaningful empirical analysis. That is why the research reported in this chapter and the next is based on relative durations and, to a more limited degree, dynamics within a single recording, but places less emphasis on absolute values. You cannot be sure that two recordings were made at the same speed (nor can you safely deduce the speed from the pitch, since pitches varied and music was often transposed), while absolute dynamic values are a function of the recording processes. Many of these problems disappeared, however, with the advent in the

3. More extended discussions of discographical source criticism may be found in Leech-Wilkinson (2009a, chapter 3); Trezise (2009); and Peres da Costa (2012: 3–9, 13–24).

4. Issued in Rome as Red G & T's 54764; CD transfer released in 1987 as 'Alessandro Moreschi, the last castrato: complete Vatican recordings', Pavilion Pearl Opal CD 9823.

Figure 5.1 Elgar conducting *Carissima*, January 1914. Used by permission of Lebrecht Music+Arts

mid-1920s of electrical recording (though the 78rpm shellac disc remained, and with it the limited recording and playback time). Frequency and dynamic range improved, but the crucial innovation was the use of microphones: instead of clustering round a horn, musicians could play in a normal performance configuration. Multiple microphones were used and engineers could balance them (though that means choices about dynamics were being made by recording engineers, and may or may not correspond to what was actually played). All this meant recording became significantly more like playing for an audience: after recording his Piano Concerto no. 2 in the Academy of Music at Philadelphia in 1929, Rachmaninoff told an interviewer from *The Gramophone* that it was 'exactly as though we were giving a public performance' (Day 2000: 16). For the performance researcher the interwar period constitutes something of a golden age, because for no other period is it equally possible to draw well-founded conclusions from recordings about how music sounded in the concert hall.

Further technological developments included the 33 rpm vinyl LP (long-playing record) in the late 1940s, which increased recording times to around twenty minutes and further improved frequency and dynamic range; stereo in the late 1950; and the CD in the early 1980s. But in terms of knowing how music sounded in the concert hall, these benefits are outweighed by the introduction after the Second World War of tape editing. It rapidly became the norm for recordings to be made up of multiple takes; according to Tim Day (2000: 26), an LP might well be made up of 150 splices, and the development of multitrack and digital recording intensified the difference between what was played in the studio and what was

heard on the record—in classical as well as in popular music. Although there
was subsequently a degree of reaction—occasionally extreme—against complex
post-production, the consequence is that, since around the middle of the twentieth century, it has been essentially impossible to reconstruct performance events
from recordings: you can only reverse engineer recordings to a limited degree, and
there is generally no one performance event to reconstruct. (Even so-called live
recordings, such as those issued on the London Symphony Orchestra's LSO Live
label, contain substantial patching [Aguilar 2012: chapter 7].) What this means,
however, is not that it is pointless to analyse recordings, but that they should be
analysed *as* recordings, that is to say as cultural artefacts that embody *somebody's*
sense of how the music should go—or more realistically several people's, since
performers, producers, and sound engineers are all likely to be involved in the
decision making (Greig 2009: 26).[5] Or to put it another way, rather than thinking of a recording as the trace of a past event to be reconstructed, it is often more
productive to think of it as a product artfully designed to prompt a particular
experience when it is heard. As Peter Johnson pithily expresses it, 'recordings are
what they are' (2002c: 198). And for most of the twentieth century they were, and
in the twenty-first they remain, the normal vehicle of musical consumption. To
analyse recordings is to analyse real musical artefacts.

But having said all this, commercial recordings still represent a much less clean
source for the kind of note-to-note information that is embodied so unambiguously in MIDI code. In some cases the information is hard to extract; in others it may simply not be there to extract. And these problems are reflected in
the way the musicology of recordings—by which I mean the empirical study of
performance within a historical context—has developed. Analysts have sought
to do through recordings what they have traditionally done through scores: to
understand the real-time experience of music with the aid of visual representations that bring together events that are separated in time. In such a context there
is an obvious attraction in the idea of representing recordings in such a manner
that all information is retained and rendered visible. That is the promise of spectrograms, which represent time (from left to right), frequency (from top to bottom), and intensity (by colour or shading). But putting it that way might prompt
a comparison with Jorge Luis Borges's short story 'On exactitude in science', a
one-paragraph extract from a fictitious seventeenth-century book that speaks of
'a Map of the Empire that was of the same Scale as the Empire and that coincided
with it point for point'; not surprisingly, 'succeeding Generations came to judge
a map of such Magnitude cumberous, and, not without Irreverence, they aban-
doned it to the Rigors of sun and Rain' (1973: 141). The point of a map, after all, is
to represent important features of topography in a concise, portable format. In the
same way, the purpose of representing sound is to draw out salient features, in this
way simplifying the data and enabling the identification of patterns that cannot,
or cannot easily, be heard by the unaided ear.

5. Peres da Costa (2012: 28) makes a similar argument concerning the editing of piano rolls.

Spectrograms can be productive for a range of musicological purposes, especially in relation to vocal music: examples are the work of Leech-Wilkinson in classical music (2007, 2010b) and of David Brackett in popular music (2000). But another major approach is to extract the values of individual parameters from the recording, and to use them as a basis for exploring what are seen as key aspects of the performance. And the vast majority of such work has involved tempo. There are several reasons for this. One is the common view that it is a uniquely salient performance parameter, synthesising or summarising multiple musical processes; David Epstein (1995) describes it as 'a consequence of the sum of all factors within a piece—the overall sense of a work's themes, rhythms, articulations, "breathing," motion, harmonic progressions, tonal movement, contrapuntal activity' (99). At least as important, however, is the fact that tempo is a particularly easy parameter to capture. It can be extracted through the use of spectrograms or waveform editing programs—by identifying the note onsets corresponding to beats and measuring the distances between them—and this is the rather time-consuming procedure adopted by Bruno Repp in an extensive series of studies that laid the foundations for the empirical analysis of recordings. (It also has the advantage that you can extract the sub-beats as well, in other words capture every onset.) But musicologists generally favoured the much less laborious technique I mentioned in Chapter 2: tapping to the beats while listening to the music, with a computer logging the times of the taps. By calculating the offsets between the times and exporting the data to a spreadsheet or graphics program, you could easily create the kind of graphs that started appearing in the musicological and music-theoretical literature with some regularity from around 1990. Figure 2.1 is an example.

What is the purpose of this kind of visual representation? After all, to anticipate a conclusion that seems so obvious as hardly to need stating, informed, close listening is indispensable for performance analysis. 'I'd like to recommend the virtues of close listening, allied to notation, pencil and paper', writes Leech-Wilkinson (2009a: chapter 8, paragraphs 20–21); he goes on to emphasise that it takes practice, but 'after a time it's surprising how much detail one can hear, far more than in casual listening'. This is the kind of listening on which Robert Philip's seminal work was based. All the same, close listening has its own drawbacks. Perhaps the most insidious is its malleability: people hear what they expect, or want, to hear. In a research context, that can give rise to the kind of circularity, the recycling of supposedly self-evident truths, that—as Robert Gjerdingen (1999) has argued—can be cut through only by means of empirical approaches. Just as the use of scores can ground and enhance unaided listening, stabilising perceptions and making it easier to talk about music with precision, so, when linked to close listening, the use of tempo graphs can fulfil a similar role. It can guard against mistakes such as when an accent is attributed to dynamics but was in fact the result of an agogic (temporal) emphasis. Or to take a more complex example, Dorottya Fabian and Emery Schubert have shown in relation to Bach performance that 'While listeners may believe they respond to the "dottedness" of a rendering, their judgment seems to reflect rather a higher order construct that incorporates tempo and articulation' (2008: 198). In such cases, close listening may correctly identify the effect, yet fail to proceed from effect to cause.

At the same time the tapping method has been widely criticised. One criticism is easily disposed of, that a tempo graph presents incomplete data: of course it does, but the point of analysis is to be selective. (It is, to be sure, always important to bear this selectivity in mind, and to analyse the data in context.) Another criticism is that the method is insufficiently accurate: this has to do with such issues as the temporal resolution of computer clocks and the accuracy of ear-hand coordination. Work done this way has commonly involved tapping a piece several times and then averaging the results in order to minimise these inaccuracies, and one good thing about the method is that errors are not cumulative. But what is 'sufficiently' accurate depends on what you are using the data for, and it is not in my opinion sensible to use a straightforward tapping method for fine discrimination of single beats. (That is one reason Repp worked from spectrograms.) There is however a more complicated issue that is raised by the question of accuracy: When you tap to the music, what are you actually measuring?

If the answer is meant to be the temporal location of the beats within the acoustical signal—what Repp was measuring through his visual method—then accuracy is indeed an issue. And it is not simply a matter of ear-hand coordination. As Simon Dixon, Werner Goebl, and Emilios Cambouropoulos (2006) have argued, 'Sequences of beat times generated in this way represent a mixture of the listeners' perception of the music with their expectations, since for each beat they must make a commitment to tap...before they hear any of the musical events occurring on that beat' (196). This is as much as to say that tapping draws on the same kinds of processes and skills that, for example, a pianist employs when accompanying a singer. It involves entrainment, an embodied response to what is heard, and as such it is interpretive. This means it results in distinctly different data from visual methods for capturing tempo, which are much less influenced by context: one of the main conclusions of the study by Dixon and his co-workers was that tappers generate smoothed data, shifting individual data points in order to fit a larger profile of tempo shaping, in a way that researchers using a visual method do not.

Visual methods (and algorithmic methods, of which more shortly) are then more accurate if the aim is to extract onset times, and are more or less indispensable if the aim is to work with onsets below the level of the beats. However if the aim is to capture the experience of tempo—the feel of the music as a dancing partner, so to speak—then a real-time auditory method based on the tactus is arguably more accurate.[6] (The tactus is the primary metrical level at which listeners engage

6. This implies an answer to a further criticism of the line graphs generated through tapping: as Henkjan Honing and Peter Desain (1993: 129, 132) argue, the lines between one data point and the next constitute an interpretation, such that the onset data would be more accurately represented in the form of a scattergram. The experience of tempo, however, is precisely one of continuous motion across beats.

with the music, for example by waving their hands or tapping their feet: often this will correspond to the composer's time signature). Since in this book I am generally concerned with tempo rather than with rhythmic patterns within beats, most of the measurements on which it is based were derived from tapping. It should be added that musicologists rarely draw a distinction between these two distinct forms of timing data—but then, the difference is unlikely to matter as long as the focus is on relatively broad issues of interpretation.

A more substantial problem with the tapping method, as employed in musicological and theoretical analyses of performance from the 1990s until quite recently, has been the difficulty of forging a meaningful relationship between the analytical representation and the listening experience. What might be called the classic tapping method involved listening to the music, generating data, and drawing graphs. What I found frustratingly hard, for example in my work on Furtwängler's recordings of Beethoven's Ninth Symphony, was to complete the loop by integrating the graph into my experience of the music. The whole point of performance analysis is to work with music as experienced, yet interpreting the graph sometimes felt like analysing the score of a piece of music you had never heard and could not imagine as sound; sometimes I suspected myself of analysing the graph and not the music. The development of computer programs which combine the functions of playback and visualisation, of which Sonic Visualiser is one, disposes of this problem once and for all, for the simple reason that graphs, spectrograms, and whatever other visualisations you choose scroll as the music plays. And if at first the connection between what you see and what you hear is less than self-evident, then—as Leech-Wilkinson said about close listening—it develops with practice. In fact Sonic Visualiser can be regarded as an ideal training environment for enhancing your skills as a close listener.

It also addresses a number of the other problems inherent in the tapping method. For one thing, while it allows you to do classic real-time tapping and display tempo graphs on screen, Sonic Visualiser also allows you to edit the data. You can do this visually, for instance against a waveform representation or a spectrogram, but you can also do it aurally: set the computer to generate a click for each of the beats you have identified, and play back the music. If a beat sounds in the wrong place, drag it on screen, possibly using the waveform or spectrogram as an initial visual guide, until it sounds exactly right. (If—as in this book—the aim is to replicate the experience of tempo rather than to locate each onset, then the final decision should generally be made by ear rather than eye.) For another thing, programs such as Sonic Visualiser set timing data into the context of other parameters. Dynamic levels can be displayed onscreen along with, say, a tempo or duration graph and a spectrogram (Figure 5.2). And of course, like any audio playback program, Sonic Visualiser allows you to navigate around a soundfile, setting markers for particular points or using the tapping approach to locate and number each bar or other event. It also allows you to load a number of recordings of the same piece and synchronise them.

All this adds up to a working environment for studying recordings that replicates much of the functionality we take for granted in conventional music

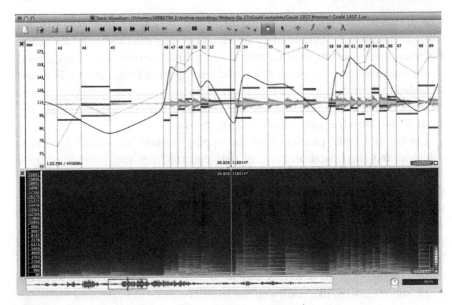

Figure 5.2 Using Sonic Visualiser to work with the middle section of Webern's *Piano Variations* op. 27, 1st mvmt., as recorded by Glenn Gould in Moscow (1957). In addition to duration (the heavier line) and dynamic graphs plus a spectrogram, event numbers and piano roll notation help you find your way around the music. The vertical axis of the upper pane represents metronome values

analysis, where you flick backwards and forwards to compare passages in a score, or compare parallel passages in different scores. Whereas in the 1990s the creation of a tempo graph seemed all too often to mark the ending point of the analysis, apart from some desultory comments based on visual inspection of the graph, it now becomes the starting point for work in which close listening is extended or augmented through technological means. That is how I wrote much of this book. And, in disseminating such research, the printed—but musically inscrutable—tempo graph can be replaced by Sonic Visualiser files to be downloaded by the reader.

Disciplinary development is conditioned not so much by what *can be done* through the expenditure of huge amounts of labour or expense, but by what can be done *practically*, within the timescales and budgets available for academic research. Programs such as Sonic Visualiser mean that the close listening approach, focussing on intensive analysis of at most a handful of recordings, is now musicologically viable in a way that has traditionally been the case of scores but not of recordings. But they also facilitate the complementary approach that Franco Moretti (2000) polemically calls 'distant listening', in effect the reinvention of comparative style analysis. As Moretti says of literary studies, and David Huron (1999) of musicology, humanities scholars have a tendency to work with very limited amounts of data regardless of what is actually available. Because only a tiny fraction of medieval polyphony has survived, that is a field where you inevitably work with limited, fragmentary, and often hard-to-interpret information. But musicologists generally work in much the same way even when a great deal of information is in fact available, for instance when studying eighteenth-century symphonies—and the same applies to recordings. Working with large quantities of material, however, demands a very different approach, normally involving some kind of reduced representation that can be analysed quantitatively. When Jean Burgess and Joshua Green (2009) wished to survey the almost unimaginable explosion of audio-video material on YouTube, for example, they adopted rigorous sampling methods together with a coding system that enabled statistical analysis.

An obvious way to work with recordings at the corpus level is to extract timing information (whether at the beat or sub-beat level), supplementing it with data from other parameters that can be readily quantified. Programs such as Sonic Visualiser accommodate a range of algorithmic plugins that detect note onsets automatically, for instance through identifying changes in spectral energy: Figure 5.2, which includes all onsets, was created this way. The quality of these algorithms has improved greatly in the last few years. With modern recordings the results can be quite clean, often requiring little more than a quick check and interpretation of events such as hand breaking, so that it may in the future become the norm to extract all onsets. (At that point the issues concerning distinct types of timing data may become more pressing.) In the case of older recordings, by contrast, a lot of editing is usually necessary, so that the labour is to a considerable extent transferred from tapping to proof listening. Nevertheless the generation of substantial quantities of data for comparative stylistic analysis is becoming an increasingly realistic proposition. And when beat or sub-beat information is matched up with the overall dynamic level—as in Figure 5.2—each musical event is defined by values in two dimensions.[7] This allows the kind of statistically based analysis of style with which this and the following chapter are concerned.

The simplest way to use data of this kind to compare aspects of performance style is through descriptive statistics, an approach pioneered by José Bowen (1996). Average tempos from multiple recordings of a given work, for instance, can be analysed as a function of the date of recording, or alternatively the performer's date of birth. (Sample findings: some pieces have slowed down over the past century while others have speeded up; modern performances generally have less tempo flexibility within sections than old ones, but contrasts between sections are often sharper; a few performers, among them Artur Rubinstein, reinvent their style during their career, but most develop their characteristic performance style by around the age of twenty and thereafter stick with it; there is a certain

---

7. Dynamic values involve a number of approximations. Those in Figure 5.2 represent overall or global dynamics, whereas the human auditory system breaks sound up into streams—for example, tune and accompaniment—and assigns a dynamic value to each. Again, Figure 5.2 shows a single dynamic value averaged across each note event; this is necessary for purposes of statistical analysis but involves a further approximation, so that for purposes of computer-assisted close listening it is usually better to use a continuous dynamic representation.

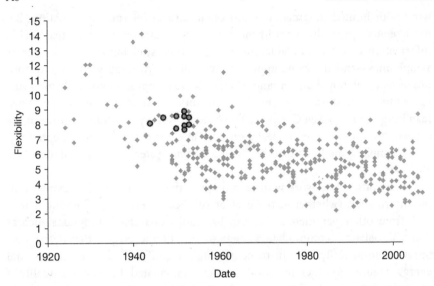

Figure 5.3 Eric Grunin's comparative measure of flexibility in recordings of Beethoven, Symphony no. 3, plotted against date of recording, with Furtwängler's recordings highlighted. Used by permission of Eric Grunin

tendency for performers to slow down with age, and a slight one for women to play slower than men.[8]) Tempo data can also be correlated with nationality, or perhaps more sensibly with the location in which performers principally trained, or again with genre or other repertorial categories. Or the analysis can be based on some measure of 'flexibility', in other words the extent to which performers vary their tempos within an individual piece or movement: a rough and ready method of doing this is to plot the standard deviation within the tempo data (as I did in Chapter 3), but a perhaps sounder method is to divide the performance into sections and calculate the relationship between the average tempo of each section and that of the whole. Figure 5.3, taken from Eric Grunin's online 'Eroica Project',[9] uses the latter method to quantify flexibility in recordings of the first movement exposition from Beethoven's 'Eroica' Symphony, and represents this as a function of recording date. I have highlighted Furtwängler's ten recordings, and as may be seen, their degree of flexibility is rather consistent.

Work of this kind might be considered attractively free of theory—indeed, once the method has been decided upon, it involves no interpretation at all—and it can be suggestive. To return to an issue on which I touched in Chapter 4, for example, Bowen's research provides sufficient counter-examples to the general tendency

8. Bowen (1996: 114–16, slower and faster, and 148, flexibility and contrast); Leech-Wilkinson (2009a: chapter 7, paragraph 31, retention of early style); Lehmann (2011: 316, age and gender).

9. Grunin's 'Eroica Project' is at http://www.grunin.com/eroica/; Figure 5.3 was taken from http://www.artforge.com/grunin/correlate.asp.

for performances to slow down over the decades, and sufficient variation between the patterns for one piece and for another, to feed doubts that performance style should be seen as Riegl saw decorative style, as an impersonal historical agent. At the same time, approaches like this are highly vulnerable to criticism on the grounds that they are so reductive as to be incapable of capturing the salient qualities of experience, or the kind of values in which musicologists are interested. For one thing, average tempo data conflate quite different kinds of musical effect: a performance that trundles along at a middling tempo may come out with the same value as one that lurches frenetically from one fermata to another. Again, the effect of a particular shaping of tempo will depend on features other than the tempo itself. As Robert Philip writes:

> A computer can measure accelerations and decelerations, but to the listener these have different *qualities*. An acceleration can seem impulsive, or uncontrolled, it can seem to be aiming precisely at a target, or to be dangerously wild. It can seem spontaneous or calculated. A deceleration can seem sluggish, calming, boring, cumulative, climactic. You can't easily measure such qualities, but they are what create the narrative of events.... Simply measuring tempo is only a starting point for understanding these things (2007: 6).

One way to address these problems is, of course, to use tempo measurement within the context of computer-assisted close listening, in other words precisely as a starting point for understanding these things. But even in the context of distant listening there are ways in which such problems can be, if not solved, then at least managed, and it is to those that I now turn. I will approach them via a rather circuitous, but I hope scenic, route.

FORENSICS VS. MUSICOLOGY

There are times when raw tempo data map quite directly onto moment-to-moment experience. D'Albert's use of mobile tempos in order to create points of arrival and departure, which I discussed in Chapter 3, is a case in point. Another, which I have discussed elsewhere, is Vladimir Ashkenazy's use of accelerando in a recording of Chopin's Mazurka op. 17 no. 4 that dates from around 1975. The expressive quality of this mazurka makes it almost unavoidable to create marked rallentandi at every transition between sections. Given the succession of disjunct phrases from which it is constructed, this presents the performer with a problem of bittiness, and to address this Ashkenazy adopts a consistent strategy: from the end of each rallentando he gradually accelerates, reaching what Repp would call his basic tempo only two or three bars into the next section. As I put it, 'The effect is to sew the sections together, while at the same time allowing the realization in full of the expressive potential of the formal cadence' (Cook 2007a: 187). One might say that in such cases tempo is operating as an essentially autonomous parameter, independent of other parameters such as dynamics and articulation—or, referring back to the discussion of intensity in Chapter 3, it might be more accurate to say that the performance embodies a tensional morphology to which tempo is the dominant input. Either way, the result is that you can see what the performer is doing in the graph.

In my 2007 article, which was an initial status report on a project I carried out with Craig Sapp at the AHRC Research Centre for the History and Analysis of Recorded Music (CHARM), I also discussed some larger-scale examples where meaningful relationships between groups of recorded performances could be read directly from tempo graphs. The project focussed on Chopin's Mazurkas, and an example is provided by his op. 68 no. 3. This mazurka falls into an A-B-A structure, with the A being about as close as a mazurka can get to a march, and the B having a markedly folkloristic character: it is often said, for example by Jean-Jacques Eigeldinger (1986: 145–46), that this is one of only two authentic folk melodies in all the mazurkas. And here again there is a performance problem. It takes the form of a curious imbalance between the two A sections, which consist respectively of thirty-two and sixteen bars, and the B section (bars 33–44), which consists of only twelve. In terms of the conventional conception of classical form, the B section is too short to counterbalance the A ones, the more so because the folkloristic material of the B section seems to demand faster playing than the outer sections, and is indeed marked *Poco più vivo*. The normal approach to this problem, as illustrated by Artur Rubinstein's highly influential recordings, is to moderate the difference in tempo: in his 1966 recording, for example, Rubinstein plays the outer sections at around 130 MM and the *Poco più vivo* at just over 158, and superimposes a variegated pattern of light and shade over the whole. The result is to de-emphasise the contrast between the A and B sections. The problem is not solved but minimised. This might be described as a strategy of damage limitation.

But there is a quite different strategy for dealing with this which is found in a small number of recordings: the first is dated from between 1950 and 1952 and ascribed to Alfred Cortot. Here the approach is exactly the opposite. The pianist pulls back the average tempo of the first section to just over, and that of the final section to just under, crotchet = 60, significantly slower than standard performance practice. On the other hand the middle section (bars 33–44) is taken at a variable tempo that averages about 225 MM, and at some points touches 300 MM: the contrast with Rubinstein's approach stands out in a tempo graph (Figure 5.4). These wildly differentiated tempos—surely not what Chopin meant by *Poco più vivo*—result in section durations of 95, 11, and 56 seconds, a level of formal disparity that it is quite impossible to accommodate within traditional conceptions of structural balance. Played this way, the *Poco più vivo* section ceases to be an element within a tripartite form: it comes across rather as a prolonged moment of recollection, or perhaps the fleeting vision of a far-off, no longer attainable world, a bucolic utopia tinged with nostalgia.

That may sound like an unfashionably sentimental way to talk about Chopin, or for that matter about performance in general, but—as we saw in Chapter 4—it is very much in line with the kind of scenario that Cortot was in the habit of creating

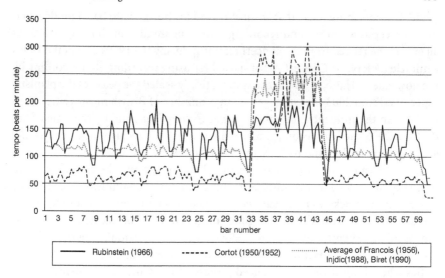

Figure 5.4 Tempo graph of Chopin, op. 68 no. 3, as recorded by Rubinstein and Cortot, together with averaged values for François, Biret, and Indjic

for the music he played or taught. It is also in line with the claim made in the liner notes of a CD by Joyce Hatto (who is supposed to have studied with Cortot) that the great pianist 'felt Chopin had embedded his own and Poland's tragedies in each and every one' of the mazurkas.[10] And Cortot's interpretations were influential. Figure 5.4 juxtaposes the recording I have been discussing with an averaged value for three other recordings that embody the same strategy, by Samson François (1956) and Idil Biret (1990)—both of whom were pupils of Cortot—as well as one by Eugen Indjic (ca. 1988), of whom more shortly. None of these other interpretations, however, are quite as extreme. Maybe there is a general pattern in performance style change for radical innovation to be gradually worn down as it becomes increasingly assimilated.

Readers with a knowledge of scandal in the world of British recording will have become suspicious during the last paragraph. The attractive and meaningful interpretation history of op. 68 no. 3 that I have recounted is complicated by the doubtful status of the recording of Chopin's Mazurkas ascribed to Cortot. It was released on the Concert Artist label, circulating in cassette form from some time around 1990, and appearing as a CD box set in 2005.[11] This label was owned by William Barrington-Coupe, the husband of Joyce Hatto and perpetrator of the celebrated hoax that bears her name.[12] Said to be a former pupil of Cortot (in

10. Liner note to Joyce Hatto, Chopin Études, 75th Anniversary Edition (Concert Artist CACD 9243-2); quoted by Ateş Orga in 'Joyce Hatto: the recordings', http://www.musicweb-international. com/classrev/2006/Jan06/Hatto2_recordings.htm.

11. Alfred Cortot, Chopin: The Mazurkas (Concert Artist CACD 9180/12).

12. For a well-researched and highly readable account of the Hatto hoax see Singer (2007), which formed the basis of Victoria Wood's television film 'Loving Miss Hatto' (2012); for details

reality it seems more likely that she just played for him), Hatto had a modest pianistic career as a concert and recording artist, apparently cut short by cancer: at all events she retired from the concert platform during the 1970s. But in the 1990s a miracle took place. Concert Artist started releasing recording after recording by the now elderly Hatto, in which she systematically scaled the peaks of the pianistic repertory. From 2003 she was taken up by a number of British music critics associated with the influential monthly journal *Gramophone*, and by the time of her death in 2006 she had become a myth: the story of the reclusive, cancer-defying artist was irresistible, and besides, the recordings were good.

That is because they were taken from existing recordings by a wide range of well-chosen professional pianists. Sometimes an entire album was copied, while at other times tracks were mixed and matched from a number of sources; often the acoustic of the recording was digitally modified, while on occasion the recordings would be slightly speeded up or slowed down. The astonishing thing is that more than a hundred Hatto CDs were issued before the fraud was unmasked. The critics who fell for it were experienced professionals, which vividly demonstrates the difficulty of retaining the details of numerous recordings in your memory, the tendency to hear what you want to hear, and consequently the danger of circularity to which I referred. Although there was muttering about the improbability of what was going on, the only query of which I am aware that was based on the recordings themselves came from horus_seth2003, a perceptive contributor to the rec.music.classical.recordings discussion list, who on 22 January 2007 posted, 'I have noticed something eerie: that the pianist playing the Mozart sonatas _cannot be_ the pianist playing Prokofiev _or_ the pianist playing Albeniz. I have the distinct feeling of being the victim of some sort of hoax'.[13] He was immediately told by another contributor to trade in his ears for another set.

It was digital technology that made the Hatto hoax possible, and it was digital technology that led to its unmasking. The media story broke after a financial analyst called Brian Ventura loaded Hatto's recording of Liszt's Transcendental Studies into iTunes, and the Gracenote software that enables iTunes to identify recordings (by matching up track durations) identified it as by László Simon. Barrington-Coupe was unlucky, in that many of the Hatto CDs would not have been recognised in this way. Gracenote would not, for example, have detected the box set of Chopin Mazurkas issued by Concert Artist in 2006,[14] which was taken from a recording by Eugen Indjic originally released in 1988: the sequence

---

of the recordings and their sources, see the Wikipedia article on Hatto (http://en.wikipedia.org/wiki/Joyce_Hatto).

13. http://groups.google.com/group/rec.music.classical.recordings/tree/browse_frm/thread/c49bc84daebb2063/9f8296c79dd6dc74?rnum=1&_done=/group/rec.music.classical.recordings/browse_frm/thread/c49bc84daebb2063/88ecd3fadff552b1?&pli=1.

14. Joyce Hatto, Chopin: The Mazurkas (Concert Artist CACD 20012); originally issued on cassette in 1993 by Barrington-Coupe's sister label Fidelio (Fidelio FED4-TC-0116/8), although there are minor differences between the two releases.

of tracks is different, and individual tracks were slightly speeded up or slowed down, or sometimes a little extra silence added at the beginning or end of a track. (In a few cases where Indjic had misinterpreted the correct pattern of repeats, Barrington-Coupe thoughtfully put it right.) But the hoax would in any case have come to light, because a quite different analytical approach we were using at CHARM had already picked up the impossible similarity between the Hatto and Indjic discs.

Sapp had extracted tempo data from a large collection of mazurka recordings, and was using Pearson correlation as one measure of the difference between performances (he also developed a series of visualisations based on this, but the discovery would have been made without them).[15] For example, for op. 17 no. 4, the average correlation for all recordings was 0.64 (1.00 would mean they were identical), but within Artur Rubinstein's three recordings (1939, 1952, and 1966) the correlations varied from 0.69 to 0.89: despite Rubinstein's reputation for having stylistically reinvented himself at least twice, each of his recordings resembles his other recordings more than it resembles any recordings by other pianists. Sometimes it happened that our collection included the same recording on multiple releases by the same pianist, which naturally generated extremely high correlation values. That happened, for example, with Rubinstein's 1966 recording of op. 68 no. 4, of which we had a release that incorrectly dated it to 1961. But we realised that something was more seriously wrong when we saw equally high correlation values between the Hatto and Indjic recordings of one mazurka, and our suspicions were confirmed when we saw the same thing with another: the figure for op. 17 no. 4 was 0.996, where the average correlation for all recordings was 0.641, while for op. 68 no. 3 the figures were 0.996 and 0.782. According to Bruno Repp (1998)—one of the few people who has previously worked in this area— 'when a correlation is higher than 0.99, it is clear that the two performances are *identical*, with the deviation from a perfect correlation being due to measurement error' (1094). However our university was still pondering the legal implications of going public when the media story broke. We posted an online article detailing our findings on the following day (Cook and Sapp 2007).

There are then ample grounds for suspicion concerning Cortot's mazurka recordings as released by Concert Artist. Other than that, Cortot never recorded the mazurkas, but there are recordings of masterclasses that he gave at the École Normale de Musique between 1954 and 1960, during which he performed sometimes substantial extracts from a number of mazurkas.[16] The longest of these extracts consists of about three-quarters of op. 30 no. 2: it does not sound at all like the recording of the same mazurka on the Concert Artist release, and the correlation value is very low (Sapp 2011: 32-33). But then, Cortot had a

15. Details of both the correlation and visualisation techniques, as well as of some of the applications described in the following pages, may be found in Sapp's doctoral dissertation (2011). Sapp also describes the extension of this technique to dynamic data.

16. Alfred Cortot: The Masterclasses (Sony Classical S3K89698).

154   BEYOND THE SCORE

reputation—though according to Leech-Wilkinson (2011) an unjustified one—for being quite variable in his performances of the same piece. And Idil Biret, who really did study with Cortot for two years, not only knows the Concert Artist recordings, but cites them as a key influence on her own playing. Her official website includes a page on her recording of Chopin's complete works, and lists 'some extraordinary Chopin recordings...which greatly inspired her': first named is 'the complete 51 Mazurkas by Alfred Cortot on three cassettes bought privately in the UK. These were recorded by Cortot in the late 1950s and never released for unknown reasons'.[17] Could Biret really not recognise her own teacher's playing? Then again, neither we nor anybody else has succeeded in matching any of the tracks on the Concert Artist disc with any other commercial recording of them. Sapp and I even wondered whether, in a masterfully ironic twist, 'Cortot' might not in fact be Hatto, and so compared the only one of the fifty-one canonic mazurkas that appears on an authentic Hatto recording, op. 68 no. 4, with the 'Cortot' recording of the same piece. Disappointingly there was little similarity between them.[18]

The jury, then, is out on the authenticity of the 'Cortot' recording of op. 68 no. 3, and hence on how far the pattern of interpretation I outlined can be explained in terms of Cortot's influence on his pupils and others. (As for the case against Barrington-Coupe, it never reached a jury, as it would have been impossible to recover the costs of litigation.) Sapp (2011), however, has gone on to use his method not only to uncover other questionable practices by Con Artist, as the now defunct label is generally known—mazurkas recorded by Biret, Anna Malikova, and Janusz Olejniczak were released under the name of Sergio Fiorentino—but also to identify questionable practices relating to piano competitions. One of the central fixtures in the world of Chopin performance is the International Fryderyk Chopin Piano Competition: it has been held in Warsaw on a five-year cycle since 1927 (broken only by the Second World War), and selected performances from it are issued on compilation CDs. A performance by Rieko Nezu from the 2005 competition turns out to be strikingly similar—not identical—to a commercial recording by Ewa Poblocka, released in 2002. And one by Nobuyuki Tsujii correlates equally closely with a commercial recording by Tatiana Shebanova (again released in 2002). What makes this interesting is the contextual information. Poblocka was joint fifth prize winner in the 1980 competition, also sharing the Polish Radio Prize for the best mazurka performance, and she served on the 2005 competition jury—but perhaps more relevantly, Nezu carried out postgraduate studies with her. As for Shebanova, she was ranked overall second in 1980. If it is not surprising that Nezu should play like her teacher, then equally it makes sense that Tsujii would model his performance on that of a previous prize winner. It may be relevant that Tsujii was born blind, and a news item dating from 1997, when he was

17. http://www.idilbiret.eu/en/?p=61. The other recordings she cites as having inspired her were by Ignaz Friedman and Raoul Koczalski.

18. Joyce Hatto, Chopin Miniatures (Delta DEP 8003), issued in 1962. This also contains two mazurkas without opus numbers, not included in the 'Cortot' collection.

nine years old, tells us that 'Because he can't read piano scores, Nobuyuki masters new pieces by listening to recordings of his teacher's performances'.[19] It seems his teacher wasn't the only person whose performances he was listening to.

The significance of all this turns on the extremely reduced representation of performances that this work was based on: simply a series of integers representing a tempo value for each beat of the music. In line with Moretti's idea of distant listening, however, the large size of the data set makes it possible to discover surprisingly interpretable relationships within it. At the same time, the value of this work might be termed forensic rather than musicological. One reason these are very different things is that the success of forensic studies of music does not depend on the perceptual salience of the data on which they are based. Indeed there is an argument that issues such as attribution are often best determined on the basis of information that is not perceptually salient. Mendel's work on Josquin, which I have already mentioned, was based on the proportion of incomplete triads, on the grounds that this is not the kind of thing that any composer consciously sets out to control. In mainstream musicology, by contrast, issues of perceptual and cognitive relevance are vital: more than anything, it is the business of musicology to explore the relationships between what musicians think and listeners hear on the one hand, and the broader cultural contexts within which music acquires meanings on the other. Yet as Repp neared the end of his foundational series of studies in the empirical analysis of recordings, he became increasingly sceptical of the ability of tempo-based models to make sense of aesthetic judgements. In 1999 he reported a particularly telling experiment in which he created MIDI versions of a number of recorded performances of Chopin's Étude op. 10 no. 3, with timing data corresponding to the source recording but all other parameters remaining constant: the correlation between his aesthetic ratings of the original recordings and the resynthesised versions was so low as to cast doubt on whether timing information, in itself, could embody musicologically useful information (Repp 1999: 473). That takes us back to Philip's observation about measuring tempo being only a starting point.

According to Honing and Desain (1993), there is a basic problem in the way empirical musicologists think of timing data. In an idiosyncratically presented article entitled 'Tempo curves considered harmful', they describe the tempo curve (what I have been calling the tempo graph or profile) as

a dangerous notion, despite its widespread use and comfortable description, because it lulls its users into the false impression that it has a musical and psychological reality. There is no abstract tempo curve in the music nor is there a mental tempo curve in the head of the performer or listener. And any transformation or manipulation based on the implied characteristics of such a notion is doomed to fail (136).

19. Accessed in March 2007 at http://web-japan.org/kidsweb/news/97-11/tsujii.html, this page is no longer accessible.

To some extent what Honing and Desain are saying about tempo graphs might be said of all graphs, which are by definition highly underdetermined representations of a more complex external reality: accordingly, as Wolff-Michael Roth and Michael Bowen say, 'to interpret graphs means to build rich situational descriptions from reductionist and transformed mathematical representations' (2001: 162). Graphs, in other words, make sense only to the extent that they are translated into real-world contexts through being linked with relevant knowledge that is not contained within them. Yet in practice they are frequently reified in much the same way that Honing and Desain say tempo graphs are: 'not only are graphs used to construct phenomena', Roth and Bowen observe, 'they also serve as existence proofs of the phenomena and, thus, are employed as rhetorical means in scientific publications' (2001: 160). It might be observed that Roth and Bowen's accounts both of how graphs signify and of how they are used, or abused, apply equally well to musical notations.

What follows from this in the context of distant listening is that, if we want to analyse performance style in a manner that usefully represents its perceptually salient qualities, then instead of analysing timing data as if they were inherently meaningful, we need to look for the real-world factors that are reflected in them—the genuinely salient factors that give rise to the data in the first place. One approach to this is to decompose the data into factors that might relate more meaningfully to the experience of music as performance. This is what Honing and Desain proposed, singling out three candidates based on (then) recent research: Neil Todd's model of phrase arching, which I referred to in Chapter 3; Manfred Clynes's concept (1995) of the 'composer's pulse', a distinctive microstructural patterning of tempo and dynamics which varies from one composer to another; and the rule-based model of expressive performance originally developed by Johan Sundberg and now generally referred to as the KTH rule system (Friberg, Bresin, and Sundberg 2006). The assumption is that each of these captures a dimension of perceptual reality in a way that tempo curves, by themselves, do not. Again, an article based on the theme from a Beethoven variation set, in which Desain collaborated with Luke Windsor and others, in effect represents a more flexible application of Todd's model of phrase arching: it is based on the assumption that expressive performance involves a combination of tempo curves with different weightings at different metrical levels, together with certain individual gestures corresponding to specific structural events (Windsor et al. 2006). The aim might be described as, through the mathematical decomposition of the timing data into these various components, to reconstruct the mental representation that is embodied in the performance.

The basic issue, then, is the same as I mentioned in relation to Grunin's 'Eroica Project', only at a more theoretically sophisticated level: separating out musically salient features that are conflated in raw timing data, and thereby achieving a higher degree of perceptual and cognitive reality. When the issue is put this broadly, it becomes obvious that a number of researchers have been exploring the same idea in different ways. In his influential study of twenty-eight recordings of Robert Schumann's *Träumerei*, Repp (1992) used factor analysis to break down his data into a number of significant but distinct components. Initially he analysed timing data for the whole piece, but the results were dominated by a single component, corresponding to the ritardandi at the ends of phrases; analysing individual sections brought to light further components that Repp saw as representing distinct performance strategies, specifically associating two of them with high-profile pianists (Horowitz and Cortot). And in a later study, again based on *Träumerei* but this time using performances by graduate students, Repp (1995) computed an average tempo profile based on all the performances under analysis, using that as a baseline against which the different—and generally more local— ways in which performances were expressively shaped might stand out. In effect he was decomposing the data into large- and small-scale components.

Two years after that, an article by Windsor and Clarke suggested using a tempo profile generated by Todd's model of phrase arching as a baseline for analysis. The advantage of this over Repp's average baseline, they observed, is that it allows you 'to quantify the extent to which a *single* performance differs from a baseline, without the necessity of collecting multiple performances' (1997: 133). The value of the approach lies not simply in the extent to which this baseline might correspond to the actual performances, but in what it leaves out: the residual data—the data reflecting factors other than phrase arching—can now be analysed in their own right. But Sapp (2011: 125–26) has explored a still easier way to achieve a comparable effect: use a mathematical smoothing function to bring out the larger features of the tempo profile, and then generate the residual data by subtracting the smoothed data from the raw data.

The implication that Repp's, Windsor and Clarke's, and Sapp's approaches have in common is that expressive performance data can be usefully separated out into a domain of larger-scale structure on the one hand, and a domain of more local events on the other, with each being analysed separately. The work that Sapp and I carried out at CHARM was based on the idea that these domains involve different relationships between tempo and dynamics—so addressing Repp's reservations about analyses based only on tempo—and have different saliences not only in a perceptual but also in a cultural sense: they represent distinct arenas within which performances afford the production of meaning. In the remainder of this chapter, then, I shall focus on local effects of accentuation in the performance of Chopin's mazurkas, emphasising the perspective of close listening. Chapter 6 also focusses on mazurka performance, but at a more macroscopic level, with an emphasis on distant listening.

PERFORMING POLAND

Welcome gems of the purest water! Welcome most precious jewels in our master's crown! Not great in extent, but rich in contents; true diamonds in which the sun of genius is sparklingly reflected in a thousand hues. Welcome, bewitching mazurkas!

—Jean Kleczynski (1912: 99)

Within the WAM tradition, the mazurka represents a highly constructed genre more or less identified with Chopin, and structured around the representation of Poland within the context of the loss of and the battle to regain national independence. As such it has been highly mythologised. For the communist regimes of the post-1945 era, the origins of Chopin's music—and above all of his mazurkas—in Polish folk culture showed, in Zdzislaw Mach's words, that 'the healthy core of the national culture was of peasant origin, and not that of a decadent élite' (1994: 67). There are then sound ideological reasons behind the quasi-official status that the composer and his works have occupied within the structures of Polish self-representation. It is twenty years since Mach (1994) wrote that 'pictures of him decorate classrooms in every Polish school, alongside those of Polish Nobel Prize winners, writers and scientists' (65). But even nowadays you hear Chopin's music over the sound system in the LOT Polish Airlines plane as you come in to land at Warsaw Chopin Airport (the name was changed in 2001, up to when it was Warsaw-Okecie Airport).

It goes back to Chopin's lifetime. In his article 'Hearing Poland: Chopin and nationalism', Jeffrey Kallberg (2004) has traced the resonances of cultural nationalism in newspaper criticisms of the early 1830s, both within and outside Poland, and in the wake of the uprising against Russian rule in November 1830 they soon acquired a more specifically political dimension. It was in 1836 that Robert Schumann famously described Chopin's works as 'cannons buried in flowers', and the less frequently quoted previous sentence explains exactly what he meant: 'If the mighty autocratic monarch of the north knew what a dangerous enemy threatened him in Chopin's works, in the simple tunes of his mazurkas, he would forbid this music'.[20] From there, as Polish liberation increasingly became a *cause célèbre* among the cultured classes of Western Europe, the political symbolism of the mazurkas became increasingly explicit, reaching a high point with Wilhelm von Lenz's proclamation, in 1868, that '*in them resided* Chopin's originality as a pianist. He represented Poland, *the land of his dreams*, in the Parisian salons under Louis-Philippe—salons which *his* viewpoint allowed him to use as a political platform. Chopin was the *only political* pianist. He *incarnated* Poland, he *set* Poland *to music!*'[21]

As Kallberg (2004: 222) says, cultural meanings are socially constructed and negotiated: 'To speak of the links between sound and culture, or of music as an expression of national ideals, is necessarily to view musical meaning as a social phenomenon shared by all participants in the sonic experience'. Meaning, he continues, cannot be reduced to 'the inherent characteristics of the music alone', and so his study focusses primarily on the recovery of the nineteenth-century contexts within which the works signified. All the same, we can reasonably ask what are the recognisable characteristics of the signifier—for without recognition there can be no signification—and what is the relationship between signifier and signified.

20. Translated in Kallberg (2004: 249).

21. Translated in Kallberg (2004: 253).

And an obvious approach to answering such questions might be through the grounding of Chopin's stylised piano pieces in the dances of Polish folk tradition: What are the specific features of the folk originals his mazurkas reference, and how do they so? Determining what these folk originals might be, however, is not a straightforward matter. As represented in dance manuals such as the *Grammar of the Art of Dancing* by Friedrich Albert Zorn (who was born ten years after Chopin), the mazurka is a professionalised and internationalised genre. Although Zorn (1905) begins by saying that 'the principal attraction in this singular dance lies in the fact that the dancer is at liberty to vary his steps at will, provided he observes the proper measure' (253), he promptly goes on to codify its steps, while the social circles with which he is concerned become clear when he remarks that 'The peasant, who accentuates the measure with his heavy iron-shod shoes, lacks neither agility nor grace; but his dance is fit only for the yard or the village inn'. By contrast, Zorn continues, 'the aristocrat executes the same steps…in a manner so elegant as to be perfectly in keeping with the brilliant company, the glistening parquet, and the magnificent decorations of his gorgeous ballroom'. To draw a contemporaneous parallel, Zorn's book relates to the peasant tradition in much the same way that Georges Escoffier's *Le guide culinaire* relates to French country cooking.

The attempt to relate Chopin's mazurkas to traditional folk dances illustrates the problems in historical interpretation of oral traditions, perhaps in a particularly acute form owing to the extent to which modern forms of such dances may reflect the impact of Chopin and the heritage industry that has grown up around him. Nevertheless there is a branch of research, originating in the work of Polish scholars but widely disseminated through writings in other languages, that attempts to identify the specific choreographic and musical features of such dances as the *mazur*, the *kujawiak*, and the *oberek*, and to line these up with comparable features in one or another of Chopin's mazurkas. While it would be silly to dismiss this scholarship, there are some deep-seated problems with it. Barbara Milewski (1999: 114) describes the idea that Chopin's mazurkas are rooted in an authentic folk tradition as 'one of the longest-standing myths in Chopin criticism'. She begins her article 'Chopin's mazurkas and the myth of the folk' by tracing back the idea that op. 24 no. 2 and op. 68 no. 3 are based on actual folk melodies to the first Polish monograph on Chopin, published in 1873 by Marceli Antoni Szule. From there it spread into other publications, being transformed in the course of this process into the accepted fact as which Eigeldinger represented it. In reality, Milewski concludes, the musical language of the mazurkas drew on codes for the representation of Polish national culture that had already developed on the urban stage, in this way reflecting a local version of the nineteenth-century project of inventing national culture under the guise of preserving it.

But there is in any case another issue. In an unpublished conference paper, Michal Podołak (2005) compared a number of recordings of the Mazurka op. 33 no. 2 in order to address the relationship between this mazurka and the various folk dances (principally the *oberek*) to which it might be related. He came up with

what, in terms of this tradition of scholarship, is a startling conclusion: depending on how the left hand part is played, op. 33 no. 2 'can become a "kujawiak,"
a "mazurka" or an "oberek"'. In other words 'the whole secret lies in the act of
performance'. And while Podołak advances this as a general principle, op. 33 no. 2
is a particularly good illustration of the extent to which, even within a written
genre, meaning emerges through the act of performance and creates traditions in
its own right (here I am taking a different route from Podołak's). Nobody claims
that op. 33 no. 2 contains literal quotations of authentic folk melodies, but it is
widely seen as among the most ethnically marked of the mazurkas, not so much
for its putative origins in the *oberek* but because of its extreme repetitiveness. As
Jim Samson (1985) says, its repetition schemes

> are designed to bring the folk model right into the foreground.... The inces-
> sant and unvaried repetitions, together with the vamping diatonic harmo-
> nies, capture something of the whirling, foot-stamping energy of the oberek.
> There are no less than twenty-four identical four-bar phrases in the outer
> sections of the mazurka, and the regularity is underlined by an harmonic
> arrangement of the phrase into six groups of four (116).

One might quibble with the description. As Samson mentions, the opening and
closing sections both comprise six pairs of four bars, cadencing respectively on
V and I, and with the third and fourth pairs transposed to the dominant. But
Chopin adds two crucial performance directions: in all editions, the eight-bar
phrases alternate dynamically—*forte, pianissimo, forte, pianissimo, fortissimo, pianissimo*—and in the *forte* and *fortissimo* sections he consistently places accents
on the third beats. Otherwise the opening and closing sections are identical,
however, except that the latter concludes with a fifteen-bar coda. So Samson's
basic point is undeniable: op. 33 no. 2 is a highly repetitive composition—and
this, as Lawrence Zbikowski (2008: 289) observes, is characteristic of music that
is designed to choreograph dances. But Chopin's mazurkas do not choreograph
dances, since they were never intended to be danced to. Rather they are sophisticated representations of dances, designed for the salon or concert hall, and in this
context the repetition structure of op. 33 no. 2 might be seen as providing a bare
canvas for equally sophisticated performative elaboration. (This resonates with
what I said in Chapter 4 about four-square phrasing in Grieg and Scriabin.) And
the key performance practice that is not represented in the score is, of course, the
mazurka rubato, the characteristic rhythmic shaping from bar to bar, often—if
not very accurately—characterised as based on the accentuation of the second or
third beat.

So what do the pianists on the records do? It is part of the oral tradition of
op. 33 no. 2 that it is a *locus classicus* of mazurka style, and so nobody omits
to characterise it as such. Many performers do this throughout, distinguishing
the alternating eight-bar phrases by dynamics, and essentially leave it at that. But
this is not the only oral tradition embodied in the recorded heritage. There is
an idiosyncratic but recent recording by the Asian/American/European pianist

Frederic Chiu, made in 1999 and characterised by a particularly strong version of the mazurka rubato; Chiu adds to its thick, earthy quality by slowing down drastically during the first bar of each *forte* in each section (that is, at bars 17, 33, 90, and 113), landing heavily on the following bar before speeding up. You can almost hear the heavy, ironshod shoes Zorn spoke of. But there is a larger narrative structure at play too. Chiu does not simply play the alternating eight-bar phrases loud and soft: he plays the *forte* ones in this heavily inflected mazurka style, but plays the *pianissimo* ones rather faster and much more lightly and smoothly—almost in the urbane, international style of Chopin's 'Minute' Waltz, op. 64 no. 1, as different as could be from the stereotypical, countrified, quintessentially Polish mazurka. (This is the musical correlate to the brilliant company, glistening parquet, and gorgeous decorations of Zorn's aristocratic ball.) Moreover there is a process of intensification both over the course of each of the outer sections, and over the piece as a whole: the mazurka rubato gets thicker and thicker, verging on self-parody by the final *fortissimo* phrase (bar 106), with the final *pianissimo* phrase accelerating into the coda.

Among other recordings with which I am familiar, the closest comparison is with those of Ignaz Friedman: two made in March 1924 and in December the following year, which are notably similar though not identical, and a third from September 1930.[22] (The role that op. 33 no. 2 played within Friedman's personal canon is indicated by his choice of its autograph for the frontispiece to his edition of the Mazurkas.) Although his tempo is significantly slower than Chiu's, Friedman has the same basic strategy. He displays his inimitable mazurka style in its earthiest form for the *forte* phrases, and plays the *piano* ones a little faster and much more smoothly (though the mazurka rubato does emerge at the half-way cadences of the *piano* phrases, as at bar 12). He also has a trick in the way he starts the main phrase of the mazurka, though it is a different trick from Chiu's. In all three recordings he prolongs the initial upbeat (which, being the initial upbeat, is effectively unmeasured), and in the two earlier ones—but particularly the 1925 one—he continues at a slow tempo, gradually putting on speed until he reaches what Repp would call his basic tempo around bar 5, though Friedman's mazurka-style rubato is so extreme that the term is barely applicable; it is like a steam locomotive lumbering into action. In other words there is a similarity between what Friedman does at the beginning of the piece and what Chiu does, more moderately, at the start of each *forte* section.

Chiu's playing of the central section has some similarities to Friedman's, too, so it is reasonable to think that he may have heard Friedman's recording; that would hardly be surprising, since Friedman is widely considered one of the outstanding mazurka players of all time. (Chiu could have heard the original records, perhaps in a private copy; he might just have heard a CD transfer of the 1924 recording

22. The first two are available on Friedman: Complete Recordings, Volume 1 (Naxos ADD 8.110684), and the third on Friedman: Complete Recordings, Volume 3 (Naxos ADD 8.110690), both released in 2003.

made by the Polish label Selene in 1998 and released the following year,[23] but not the more widely disseminated Naxos transfers, which came out four years later.) Then again, some other intermediary may have been involved. It hardly matters. Of more significance is the fact that this is one of the few mazurkas for which we can trace the story back substantially further, to 24 February 1895: that was when the music-loving businessman Julius Block made a series of private cylinder recordings of Paul Pabst, a former pupil of Anton Door who at the time of the recording was professor of piano at Moscow Conservatory.[24] In one of them Pabst plays from the beginning of op. 33 no. 2 up to a few bars into the central section; in the other, longer one he plays the second half of the opening section, and continues to the end of the piece. However he plays it in a form that is so different from Chopin's that by today's standards it would count as a transcription rather than a performance (in the track listing, Ward Marston—who both tracked down and transferred the cylinders—attributes it to Chopin-Pabst). In each of the outer sections Pabst replaces Chopin's six eight-bar phrases (paired into T[onic], T, D[ominant], D, and T, T) by seven phrases (T, T, D, T, D, T, T). In the last two phrases of each section he replaces Chopin's melody with *leggiero* scales in the highest register, perhaps derived from Chopin's final flourish (bars 135–36), so creating the initial effect of a cadenza-like *fioritura* that turns out to be a version of the principal phrase. And he ends the final section like the first, omitting Chopin's coda.

My concern, however, is with how Pabst characterises the alternate eight-bar phrases. Though he is clearly giving the opening phrase some degree of mazurka-style characterisation, it is hard to hear more than that above the inevitable rumble and crackle of Marston's transfer, especially since he is playing it fast, about the same speed as Chiu; after the beginning it is hard to hear such characterisation at all. And it would be foolish to put much faith in the dynamics on an 1895 cylinder recording. However Pabst chooses another means for differentiating the *forte* and *pianissimo* phrases, and one that the cylinder conveys reliably: register. Starting as written, he transposes the second eight-bar phrase (bars 9–16) up an octave. Then he transposes bars 17–24 down an octave, transposes bars 25–32 up an eleventh (remember he is playing this in T rather than Chopin's D), and so on. The gruff lower register corresponds to Chiu's and Friedman's heavy, earthy *fortes*, the sparkling high register to their smoother, more urbane *pianissimos*. In this way Chopin's blank canvas is again elaborated into a play of opposed musical and connotational characters, a version of the 'miniature theater of human gestures and actions' that Allanbrook identified in Mozart's K 332.

But the story does not stop here: we can trace it all the way back to Chopin himself, with about as much certainty as can be attached to any other story

23. Chopin—Friedman (Selene CD-s 9908.53).

24. These have been released as the three-CD set 'The dawn of recording: the Julius Block cylinders', Marston 53011 (2008).

about the composer.[25] Some time in the 1880s or 1890s, the pianist and later guiding force behind the establishment of the International Fryderyk Chopin Piano Competition, Aleksander Michałowski, persuaded Princess Marcelina Czartoryska—generally regarded as one of Chopin's most talented pupils and by now an elderly lady—to play for him. One of the pieces she performed was op. 33 no. 2. 'I was struck by the way she interpreted its main theme', Michałowski recalled:

> At first she played it in a brash, forthright way, with no subtlety of nuance. It was only towards the end of the piece, at the theme's second appearance, that she played it with a soft, caressing touch, utterly subtle and refined. When I asked her about this contrasting treatment, she replied that Chopin had taught it to her that way: in this piece he wanted to present the contrast between a 'tavern' and the 'salon'. That was why he wanted the same melody played so differently: at the beginning it was to evoke the popular atmosphere of the tavern, and, towards the end, the refinement of the salons (Eigeldinger 1986: 75).

If Michałowski's recollection is correct, then subsequent performance practice has transferred the contrast between the earthy and the urbane from the level of sectional repetition to that of the phrase, where it at least has the minimal support of Chopin's dynamic and accent markings. But the basic interpretive, or hermeneutical, approach remains in place. And this shows how, as also exemplified by the coda from Mozart's *Rondo alla turca* (discussed in Chapter 4), the oral traditions that are built on musical texts extend from the domain of the technical to that of semantic interpretation. WAM may be a written tradition, but its meaning floats free of the printed page and is transmitted in the oral domain: as Eigeldinger (1986) says, the interpretive tradition transmitted by Czartoryska is 'not in any musical source' (150). Cultural meaning is being produced and transmitted through the medium of performance. Indeed we could express it the other way round: WAM is an oral tradition, but one that is strongly supported by written documents. However the best way of putting it is perhaps that, as Jack Goody (1987) argued, orality is an irreducible dimension of literate culture.

Yet we are still circling around the core musical phenomenon that underlies all this cultural elaboration, the central signifier in the pianistic performance of Poland: the mazurka rubato—although another, equally appropriate term for it might be 'lilt'. As we saw in Chapter 4, this is the word that Bilson applied to the one-bar slurs at the opening of Mozart's Sonata K 332, and the parallel with the *locus classicus* of topic theory is appropriate. The mazurka is in effect a topic elevated to the level of genre: like Mozart's 'Turkish' style, it is a more or less codified sign that references a part real, part imaginary musical practice—in

---

25. Eigeldinger (1985: 150) writes that 'there is no reason to doubt its reliability, given its author's reputation'.

the case of the mazurka a cluster of highly mythologised Polish folk dances—and, through that, a range of connotations from place to people, and from nostalgia to nationalist sentiment. I will have more to say about the connotations later in this chapter, but we should first attempt a more detailed definition of the signifier. If it is not just a recurrent accentuation of the second or third beat, then what is it? Adolph Kullak (1893), who was born three years after Chopin (and seven before Zorn), classifies the mazurka style as 'a special case of irregular accentuation...carried out throughout entire compositions', and locates its essence in what we might call a conflict between rhythm and metre:

> In this dance, elevated by Chopin from its sensuous original into the most exquisitely ethereal poetry, the third quarter-note, or sometimes the second, takes the principal accent. The rhythm, however, discovers a dual aspect, for the normal accent, too, at times rises triumphant over its rival. In fact, throughout this irregular accentuation, the normal groundwork is assumed in the background and felt in advance. On such a basis a second rhythmical idea is built up, which enters on the third quarter and, running parallel to the first, maintains the sense in eager tension by its conflict with the latter. It charms by its very abnormity (244).

Contemporary accounts of Chopin's mazurka playing also focus on timing and accent, but what emerges most strongly from them is the extreme deviation from notated values: if they are to be believed, the nominally ternary metre of the mazurkas might be performed in what, as measured by a metronome, would be duple or common time (2/4 or 4/4 rather than 3/4). Among these accounts two are particularly well known. The first comes from Lenz, who studied with Chopin and records that during a lesson in which he was playing the Mazurka op. 33 no. 3, the famous opera composer Giacomo Meyerbeer arrived unannounced, and took a seat. But he did not remain silent for long:

> 'That's in 2/4', said Meyerbeer. I had to repeat it while Chopin, pencil in hand, beat time on the piano; his eyes were blazing. '2/4', Meyerbeer calmly repeated. Only once have I seen Chopin lose his temper, and it was at that moment—and what a wonderful sight he was! A faint red suffused his pale cheeks.... 'It's in 3/4', Chopin almost yelled, he who never normally raised his voice above a murmur. He pushed me aside and sat at the piano himself. *Three times* he played the piece, counting aloud and stamping out the beat with his foot; he was beside himself! Meyerbeer still held his own and they parted on bad terms (Eigeldinger 1986: 73).

The other records a more agreeable encounter and comes from the pianist and conductor (Sir) Charles Hallé, who had heard Chopin playing his mazurkas and

> ventured to observe to him that most of his Mazurkas (those dainty jewels), when played by himself, appeared to be written, not in 3/4, but in 4/4 time,

the result of his dwelling so much longer on the first note in the bar. He denied it strenuously, until I made him play one of them and counted audibly four in the bar, which fitted perfectly. Then he laughed and explained that it was the national character of the dance which created the oddity. The more remarkable fact was that you received the impression of 3/4 rhythm while listening to common time. (Eigeldinger 1986: 72)

Such accounts derive their mythopoeic value from the dramatisation of alterity. The contrast between a distinctively national experience ('It's in 3/4') and Western empiricism ('That's in 2/4') belongs in a long tradition of exoticisation or orientalisation that is predominantly the work of non-Poles: the country which joined the European Union in 2004 was seen by 1830s Parisians as the home of 'strange creatures with Oriental faces...and Asiatic outfits' (Klein 2012: 247). At the same time, these accounts are frustratingly short of concrete information on performance practice. Even the pattern of accentuation is unclear. Hallé, who does not cite any mazurka in particular, speaks of lengthening the first beat; Kullak allows for first-beat emphasis but in the context of second- or third-beat accentuation; summarising the teaching of Leschetizky (born twenty years after Chopin), Brée (1913: 70–71) explains that in the mazurka the accent falls on the first, second, or third beat. Documentary evidence, in short, underlines the extraordinary nature of the mazurka rubato, but the actual practice remains shadowy, and present-day discussions of the topic remain correspondingly speculative.

In a recent paper Jonathan Bellman has rehearsed these difficulties of interpretation and questioned the whole approach of defining the mazurka rubato as a pattern of irregular accentuation. He observes that in historical recordings any beat may be lengthened. But then he continues,

it may be that deciding which beat to lengthen is a misguided approach anyway; the metric inflection seems, at least in some cases, to be a result or the after-effect of something that is done with the melody, which means that initially focussing on the left hand may distort both the melody and the practice itself from the very beginning.[26]

And to illustrate such a case he cites a recording of the Mazurka op. 50 no. 2 made in the last year of his life by Raoul Koczalski (1884–1948).[27] Although by no means the oldest of the recorded Chopin interpreters—he was actually born two years after Friedman—Koczalski carries great authority in Chopin circles through having studied with the composer's most famous Polish pupil, Karol

26. Abstract to 'Chopin and the mazurka problem', paper presented at the 'Reactions to the Record III' conference, Stanford, 12–14 April 2012.

27. Recording date taken from 'Raul Koczalski: Chopin', Selene CD-s 9901.46 (1999), where this track is misidentified as op. 50 no. 1.

Mikuli. (The fact that Mikuli died when Koczalski was thirteen does not seem to weaken this authority—but then Koczalski was a child prodigy.) And in this recording, Koczalski appears to do something that is described in many historical sources that have a direct link with Chopin. Among these sources is the composer and pianist Camille Saint-Saëns, who claimed to have learned 'the true secret of tempo rubato' from Pauline Viardot, who in turn played duets with Chopin and received informal advice from him: 'the accompaniment holds its rhythm undisturbed while the melody wavers capriciously, rushes or lingers, sooner or later to fall back upon its axis' (Eigeldinger 49). Saint-Saëns then adds, 'This way of playing is very difficult since it requires complete independence of the two hands'. Similar descriptions come from others who studied at first hand with the composer, including Georges Mathias, Lenz, and Mikuli himself.[28] The degree of mythologisation that is routine in pianistic anecdotes and pedagogy is so great that one is generally inclined to treat such accounts with a degree of scepticism—the point is illustrated by the related theory of rhythmic compensation, ridiculed as long ago as 1928 by John McEwen—but in this case they are so consistent as to leave little room for doubt. At any rate, Koczalski's playing sounds remarkably like what Saint-Saëns and Chopin's pupils were talking about.

Musicologists have a tendency to project ways of performance audible on historical recordings back into a remote past that long predates the technology. Perhaps Koczalski's recordings provide a rare example where this can be justified, preserving as if in amber a way of playing that dates back to the first half of the nineteenth century. If so, they might be considered prime candidates for the kind of approach that Sigurd Slåttebrekk and Tony Harrison have brought to the study of Grieg's piano recordings from 1903, of which more in Chapter 8. But having said that, the way of playing that Saint-Saëns and the rest were describing was not specifically related to the mazurka and therefore cannot be seen as a generic marker. And if the core of the genre lies in performance practice, then it is not a viable topic for research based purely on documentary sources: it requires access to performances, recorded or otherwise. It follows that we are not in a position to tell the story of performing Poland through the mazurka rubato in relation to Chopin, or his pupils, or even—with rare exceptions such as Koczalski—his pupils' pupils. We can however tell it as a story about pianists born in or since the final years of the nineteenth century.

THE SAVOUR OF THE SLAV

I said that Friedman is widely regarded as one of the outstanding mazurka players, and the element of dance repeatedly comes up in accounts of his playing.

---

28. For these and many more examples see the discussion in Hudson (1994: 189–97).

According to his Australian pupil Patricia Rovik, 'It seemed as though he were dancing when he played a mazurka' (Evans 2009: 299), and Friedman apparently told another of his pupils, Bruce Hungerford, that in his early years he had danced mazurkas in the Polish villages (7). Much more than Koczalski's playing of op. 50 no. 2, Friedman's mazurka recordings from the interwar years can be characterised in terms of a pattern of irregular accentuation that has something of the autonomy of the groove in popular music, though it is more closely integrated with the melody than the groove, and more varied and flexible in its treatment. All the same, the comparison with groove is helpful in suggesting how we might describe what Friedman does.

In Chapter 3 I mentioned Cooper and Meyer's definition of the accent as a marking for consciousness of a particular point in the music, achieved through a change of state in any parameter. In mazurka performance this essentially translates to creating accentuation through dynamic emphasis (playing louder), agogic emphasis (prolonging a note or beat), and articulation (emphasising a note by clipping it): the last of these has received much less attention in the empirical literature than the first two, but plays a particularly important role in Friedman's playing. There is in addition the complication I mentioned in Chapter 3, that the effect of such emphasis may be to accentuate the note that is played louder, prolonged, or clipped, or alternatively to throw the accent onto the following beat. The general principle seems to be that the latter happens when the following beat occupies a superior position within a rhythmic or metrical hierarchy, but such hierarchies are rarely as unambiguously specified in music as the theoretical literature might suggest. Along with the fact that parameters can substitute for one another in the creation of accent, this goes far to explain the extraordinarily wide range of performance interpretations that a given score can typically afford, whether in the case of mazurkas or more generally.

But we can develop this general approach further by borrowing from Matthew Butterfield's theorisation (2006) of the groove. Butterfield's overall aim is to explain 'the forward drive of much groove-based music' (paragraph 5), and he does this primarily through invoking the idea of anacrusis. Quoting Christopher Hasty (1997: 120), Butterfield explains that 'anacrusis points forward: it is anticipatory, directed towards a future event'. It stands in opposition to the continuation of a previous event, which 'in a sense points backwards'. The key analytical decision is accordingly whether, following one note, 'one experiences the second note as simple continuation or as anacrusis' (Butterfield 2006: paragraph 11). A dynamic accent on the second beat, the use of unequal note values, and clipped articulation all inhibit the sense of continuation, he says, and therefore induce the perception of anacrusis—and these factors map onto the three parameters I identified as particularly salient in mazurka performance. Butterfield also mentions a further factor that is of special significance in this context: playing a note 'on-top' (that is, before the beat) also induces the perception of anacrusis (Butterfield 2006: paragraph 31).

We are now equipped to examine Friedman's 1925 recording of op. 33 no. 2, the first and middle sections of which may be heard in Media Example 5.1.

Bars	Beats		
	1	*2*	*3*
4	0.23	0.47	0.31
8	0.24	0.38	0.38
12	0.28	0.33	0.39
16	0.31	0.38	0.31
20	0.30	0.40	0.30
24	0.27	0.40	0.33
28	0.18	0.44	0.38
32	0.26	0.32	0.42
36	0.24	0.45	0.31
40	0.27	0.36	0.38
44	0.30	0.36	0.34
48	0.42	0.30	0.27
Average	*0.27*	*0.38*	*0.34*

Figure 5.5 Beat values as proportions of bars in Friedman's 1925 recording of Chopin, op. 33 no. 2, obtained by means of an onset detection algorithm with visual checking. Where the hands are not synchronised (e.g. bars 20, 40, 44), values are taken from the left hand

Bars 65–72 are repeated, as indicated in Chopin's score, with the repeated bars being shown in Media Example 5.1 as 73–80; as in Chapter 4, I refer to such bars as, for example, 73 (65 bis). Figure 5.5 shows the beat durations of the last bar from each group of four bars during the first section of the piece (bars 1–48), expressed as percentage proportions of the bar so that a literal performance would yield 33: 33: 33. One reason for selecting these bars is that the absence of melodic motion makes it easier to obtain accurate values, which is never straightforward with early recordings, but there is also another. Pianists do not employ the mazurka rubato consistently throughout a piece. They typically use it to characterise the beginnings of sections and other salient points, much as classical composers used thematic characterisation to mark the beginning of sections within sonata form. Just as classical themes typically peter out into fragmentation, developmental continuation, or passagework, so pianists treat mazurka rubato as a signifier: they employ it judiciously in order to reference a generic signified, just as classical composers used themes in order to reference a formal prototype.[29] (It's again like Kramer's idea of meaning being distributed in peaks and valleys.) This general principle

29. A simple visual representation of this phenomenon, derived from thirty recordings of Chopin's op. 17 no. 4, may be found in Cook (2007a: 196). Created by Sapp and based on the identification of second- and third-beat accentuation, it shows bands of intense colour, meaning that everyone is de-emphasising the first beat, at the beginnings of most (but not all) sections; there is some tendency for the same to happen every four bars, suggesting that to some degree pianists treat phrases in the same way as they treat sections.

applies to Friedman's recording of op. 33 no. 2, but he implements it in a distinctive manner, devoting particular attention to those bars where the left hand is unconstrained by melodic motion in the right and, for that reason, more exposed. This is one of those lucky cases where ease of data collection and musical significance go hand in hand.

As Figure 5.5 shows, on average these bars converge on what might be seen as a classic mazurka pattern (27: 38: 34): a short first beat and a long second beat, with an uninflected third beat—or to put it another way, the second beat is played on-top. (A convenient way to refer to this pattern is in terms of the longest, middle, and shortest beats, here 2-3-1.) But the average value is not what we hear, and the individual values of different bars vary widely. There is a much more extreme version of the 2-3-1 pattern at bar 4 (23: 47: 31): if sustained, it would almost fit into the 4/4 metre that Hallé counted out while Chopin played (**1**-**2**-**3**-**4**). The strong mazurka characterisation makes sense here, since bar 4 is the first of these exposed bars in the piece (it is also the point at which Friedman reaches his basic tempo, to the extent that he has such a thing). There is a still more extreme version of the same pattern at bar 28 (18: 44: 38). The effect is of letting in a little air after the second beat, the purpose perhaps being to counteract the smooth style of the preceding bars and assimilate them into the mazurka context. At the opposite extreme is bar 48, which marks the end of the section through a lengthening of the first beat (42: 30: 27); the closing function overrides the prevailing mazurka character, and this is the only one of these bars in which Friedman makes the first beat the longest. Somewhat comparable is bar 8, which closes the first phrase, but here the figures in Figure 5.5 (24: 38: 38) are misleading. The effect of closure derives not from the beat lengths but from the smooth articulation, illustrating the importance of this parameter in Friedman's style. It also illustrates Philip's observation, which I quoted in Chapter 5, that 'measuring tempo is only a starting point for understanding these things'.

In Butterfield's terms we would say that bars 8 and 48 function as continuation, pointing back to what has come before and so reinforcing the tonic cadence. By contrast Friedman shapes bars 4 and 28, both cadences on the dominant, in such a way as to strengthen their anacrustic character: they are directed towards a future event and so create the same forward drive that Butterfield sees as characteristic of groove. These examples also conform to an additional point that Butterfield argues in relation to groove, that such effects should be understood not simply as discrepancies with respect to nominal values, but as based on what he terms syntax. Another example of this in the mazurka context, this time an extreme example of the 3-2-1 pattern (26: 32: 42), is bar 32 of Friedman's recording. Here an explanation can be found in the linkage from the *pianissimo* of the preceding phrase to the *fortissimo* of the following one (the first appearance of *fortissimo* in Chopin's score): Friedman's broadening of the third beat, resulting in the longest of all the bars in Figure 5.5, articulates and heightens the dynamic and rhetorical transition.

At the same time, as with Reinecke in Chapter 4, it would be wrong-headed to seek an explanation for everything. I have no idea why Friedman chose to place an extreme dynamic emphasis on the third beat of bar 20, and any syntactical explanation would be questionable since he does not do the same in his 1924 or 1930 recording. Nor is this an isolated example. In the 1930 recording (and only there), for example, Friedman strikingly prolongs bar 73 (65 bis) to mark the repeat of the second half of the middle section, resulting in a variant of the 2-3-1 pattern that Meyerbeer would have pounced on (14: 58: 28). We do not, however, hear it as a (14: 58: 28) pattern. We hear it as a more normal 2-3-1 pattern with a rhetorical prolongation of the second beat, and the same might be said of the final beat of bar 32 in the 1925 recording. These are examples of the transformation of quantity into quality, to borrow Philip's term, that computer-assisted close listening makes possible.[30] But multiplying examples does not tell us why Friedman made the performance decisions he did. That question, however, begs another: whether it is necessarily helpful to think of Friedman *choosing* or *deciding* to play bar 20 with an exaggerated third-beat emphasis. Maybe he just played it that way. The terminology of choice and decision invokes the values of declarative rather than procedural knowledge, arguably representing the same prioritisation of theory over practice that we saw in Chapter 2. It is not, obviously, that performers do not make choices or decisions, but that in the real time of performance you cannot pore over each note in the way a composer or poet might. You do not have time.

At all events, as Butterfield says, playing on-top—as Friedman characteristically plays the second beats in op. 33 no. 2—creates anacrusis, provided it is not so extreme as to result in a categorical shift. If a beat is played so early that it is perceived as falling on the preceding half-beat, say, it will not be perceived as on-top at all. By contrast the passages from bar 65 and even more from 73 (65 bis), which feature extremely on-top playing, do involve a categorical shift, but here the effect is to strengthen the anacrusis. Friedman plays the first two notated beats of each bar as a single gesture in which the third quaver of the right-hand triplet is strongly emphasised while the second beat, in theory marked by a left hand chord, is virtually inaudible (at least on the recording, and it is the effect of the recording that I am talking about). Although I *know* the third triplet quaver is not the second beat, I *hear* it as if it was: the beat migrates to the triplet quaver, resulting in a particularly extreme—and this time phenomenologically real—version of the 2-3-1 pattern, in the region of 18: 50: 32. Literally then—as Meyerbeer or Hallé would count it out—the second beats during the sub-section last fully half a bar, and this demonstrates the strength of our conservative listening strategies.

You continue to hear the music in 3/4 even when it is empirically in 2/4 or 4/4, or as Hallé put it, 'you received the impression of a 3/4 rhythm whilst listening to common time'. That in turn reflects the role of the sedimented performance tradition—which is equally to say sedimented listening tradition—that is associated

30. As it happens, Butterfield (2006: paragraph 19) makes exactly this point: he remarks that swing eighths should be 'understood in terms of quality, not quantity—in terms of their effect (the feeling they engender), not their measurable appearance, which is variable and often misleading'.

with this genre. One cannot model the experience of music like this simply by tracing it back to structural principles: an irreducibly historical dimension is in play. And it is for this reason that Justin London's 'many meters hypothesis' treats the historical dimension as part of what defines a metre: 'A listener's metric competence', London (2004: 153) writes, 'resides in her or his knowledge of a very large number of context-specific metrical timing patterns. The number and degree of individuation among these patterns increases with age, training, and degree of musical enculturation'. Clearly Hallé was sufficiently enculturated to receive the impression of 3/4. But at the same time his observation that he was actually listening to common time reflects his grounding in what I termed Western empiricism, in other words, his status as a cultural outsider. As for Meyerbeer, one wonders whether he would have admitted to receiving the impression of 3/4 at all.

The passage from bar 65—and again, even more from bar 73 (65 bis)—also illustrates the characteristic role of articulation in Freidman's playing: he clips the second beats of bars 67 and 69, and again of bars 73 (65 bis), 75 (67 bis), and 77 (69 bis), which he plays quieter, in a logical though notationally unauthorised application of the *forte-pianissimo* principle from the outer sections. But a more thoroughgoing demonstration of the role of articulation within the multi-parametrical generation of anacrustic charge is provided by Friedman's playing of the first half of the middle section. In bars 54–56, and again at bars 62–64, Friedman repeatedly couples drastic clipping of the second beats with equally drastic abbreviation of the notated semi-quaver anacruses, in effect smearing them into the dotted quavers to which they lead. This runs quite contrary to Chopin's slurs, which link the second and third beats.

Butterfield (2006: paragraph 12) writes that, in groove, a clipped second note 'generates a feeling of leaping off, of springing up into the air, calling for a new event to resolve its motional energy'. That is equally apt as a description of these bars from op. 33 no. 2, but it is only part of what is happening in them. The on-top attack of the second beat combines with the clipped articulation and smeared semi-quaver to create an anacrustic charge that is thrown onto the third beat (Butterfield's 'new event'). The effect is repeated on the third beat, but here the interaction with the 3/4 metre kicks in, which means that the accumulated charge is passed on to the following downbeat, rather like the rolling over of the jackpot in a lottery. The result is what might be termed a super-charging of the downbeat, an effect unachievable either by purely compositional means or by those of more standard WAM performance practice. The super-charging accumulates even further as the bar-long patterns succeed one another, without being discharged onto a climax or structural downbeat. This is the process that, in the case of lotteries, generates national headlines.

Musical analysis often slips imperceptibly from the technical to the metaphorical or speculative, and I shall conform to this pattern. It is through metre that listening is translated into embodied experience: as London says, 'meter inheres in our attentional and motor control behaviors' (2004: 58). I suggest that, through the anacrustic processes I have described, the mazurka rubato creates a surplus of forward motion that as it were spills over from aural experience and is mapped onto the body. (You could imagine the surplus charge accumulating within the body, in the same way that toxins do.) This is responsible for the characteristically vivid sense that mazurkas induce of hearing with the body, of dancing in your seat even as you outwardly adhere to the behavioural mores of the concert hall. Here the dimension of repetition to which Samson and Zbikowski drew attention comes back into focus: dance may be characterised as an embodied practice that is more than anything conditioned by repetition. And Richard Hudson (1994: 188) writes that the mazurka rubato 'projects a special vigour or exuberance in imitation of some powerful choreographical thrust of energy'. But perhaps this does not go far enough. It is less a matter of imitation than of surrogate performance by listeners, who feel the energy of the leap (Butterfield's 'springing into the air') as their own energy, map the weight of Zorn's heavy ironshod shoe onto their own feet. One might also say that, in the mazurka rubato as in dance, embodied action is not experienced as taking place against the backdrop of a steadily flowing, chronometric time: rather time is drawn into the body, shaped by the body. Or to put it another way, it is experienced as quality rather than quantity.[31] This establishes a relationship with what, in Chapters 3 and 4, I argued was a key underlying characteristic of rhetorical performance—of which the mazurka rubato might be considered as, in a certain sense, a vestige, an isolated continuation into the present day.

Even this brief analysis should have made it clear that Friedman has no single, universal formula for playing a mazurka. He treats the mazurka rubato as a pattern of irregular accentuation but shapes it differently at different points in each of his recordings of op. 33 no. 2. And even a casual comparison with other pianists' recordings of op. 33 no. 2, let alone of other mazurkas, reveals a bewildering variety of ways of playing within the broad framework of irregular accentuation: the mazurka format supports both differing patterns of accentuation and differing ways of creating such accentuation, so creating the freedom to construct a personal performance style. London's 'many meters hypothesis' allows for the possibility that 'context-specific metrical timing patterns' might be associated with specific performers: Friedman, for example.

I suggested that Frederick Chiu's recording may reflect the direct or indirect influence of Friedman's recordings, but even here the differences are telling. Chiu uses rubato primarily for the shaping of phrases and cadences, as well as for a variety of rhetorical effects, but he does not use it as a basic means of accentuation in the way Friedman does. Instead Chiu relies mainly on dynamic emphasis for his mazurka characterisation. Indeed his strategy might be described as one of rather literal adherence to the notated third-beat accents of Chopin's score—except that

---

31. London (2004: 148) cites a quotation from John Sloboda that adds a further dimension to Philip's observation on measuring tempo, as well as Butterfield's characterisation of swing: 'we can hear rhythmic imprecision and rubato with appropriate training, but fine differences in timing are more often experienced as differences in the quality (the "life" or "swing") of a performance'.

this is a case where literal may not mean correct, if Eigeldinger (1994: 148) is right to interpret Chopin's accents (>) as agogic, as against the dynamic accents indicated by *sf* or *fz*. There is perhaps a parallel with what I said about Bart van Oort in Chapter 4: underneath a surface reminiscent of rhetorical modes of performance lie modernist values of structural coherence and adherence to the letter of the score. Perhaps one might think of van Oort as translating aspects of Reinecke's way of playing into a style that is acceptable to today's sensibilities, and of Chiu as doing the same for Friedman.

It is in the nature of signs that they can afford a virtually unlimited range of stylistic variation, provided certain basic conditions for their recognition as signs are fulfilled. That clearly applies to the mazurka rubato. I see no reason to imagine that there is a single essential criterion that defines the mazurka style, whether in terms of composition or of performance. And mazurka style is not an on-off phenomenon: some mazurka performances are more typical of the genre than others. But it is perhaps fair to say that the prototypical mazurka performance involves the creation through some kind of recurrent rubato pattern of surplus anacrustic energy, resulting in an unusually vivid sense of embodiment. In the context of the discrete historical repertory that is Chopin's mazurkas, that might be seen as the key element in referencing the range of social and cultural connotations that have accrued to the mazurkas in the first 180 years of their existence. Meaning, as Kallberg said, cannot be reduced to the inherent characteristics of the music alone, but it can be triggered by them. That is how musical signs work.

Myths, however, depend on the attribution to the sign of the qualities of the signified, and in this sphere of cultural practice essentialism reigns supreme. If the mazurka has been constructed as a signifying or ritualistic practice that embodies the quintessence of Polishness, then mythologisation clings most densely around the mazurka rubato, its central performative act. Indispensably, the belief that animates this can be traced back to Chopin himself, or rather to what those close to him reported: according to another of his pupils, Marie Roubaud de Cournand, Chopin 'often said that the French did not understand his Mazurkas, and that one had to be Polish to feel the subtleties of the national rhythm, and to render the proper local colour' (Eigeldinger 1986: 122). As exemplified by Roubaud, non-Poles have been central carriers of this tradition. Selecting quotations almost at random, the same belief is echoed some seventy years later in James Huneker's claim that 'the mazourkas, the impish, morbid, gay, sour, sweet little dances... are a sealed book for most pianists; and if you have not the savour of the Slav in you you should not touch them' (1903: 167). Another seventy years gives us a change of literary fashion, reflected in the pianist Louis Kentner's suggestion (1976) that the 'very perfection and originality' of the mazurkas 'limits, not the universality of their appeal, but the number of pianists of other than Polish nationality who could hope to approach them with the right understanding' (145–46). Then comes a flash of racy vocabulary that underlines how long ago 1976 was:

For 'understanding' in this case means not a function of the reason but one of the blood. I myself tend to keep away from the mazurkas, not from lack of affection but from respect for national affinities which must have the last word in this field of music.... So why not leave them to flower in their natural soil, rather than try to imitate the 'accent' in our clumsy foreign way?

Like Meyerbeer and Hallé, these writers assert their Western identity by opposing it to the oriental otherness of the mazurka. But pianism in the Chopin tradition serves all the more as a dimension of Polish self-identity, as illustrated by *Słownik Pianistów Polskich* (A Dictionary of Polish Pianists), an 879-page volume from Selene, who as I mentioned issue transfers of early recordings by Polish pianists. Placed before the gazetteer section are a series of impressive genealogical tables. The first of these, and the only one to be illustrated with portraits, pays homage to the greatest stars in the Chopin firmament: the composer is placed in the top left hand corner, with Czartoryska below him, and at the bottom Koczalski (Dybowski 2003: 40). But it is the arrows that do the work, for Chopin begat Mikuli, who begat Michałowski, who begat so many pupils and pupils' pupils that he has one of the densest genealogical tables all to himself (Dybowski 2003: 49). No matter that attempts to ground teacher-pupil relationships in the empirical properties of recorded performance almost always fail (Lehmann 2011: 321), presumably for the simple reason that pupils don't necessarily play like their teachers: we are talking about a symbolic plane of cultural practice, something akin to the laying on of hands that creates the apostolic succession. And the symbolic dimension is even more obvious in Michałowski's brainchild, the International Fryderyk Chopin Piano Competition—itself the subject of another, equally monumental tome from the same author and publisher (Dybowski 2005).

The competition was established in order to improve international standards of Chopin performance—'Interpretations departing too far from the original music were not allowed' (Dybowski 2005: 19)—and in this case the results appear to be empirically detectable. A study by Sapp (2011: 36–37) of recordings of op. 63 no. 3, using the same basic method that he used for Nezu and Tsujii but now expressed as a two-dimensional network, places at its centre a large group of Polish and Russian pianists, many of them associated with the competition. Then there are two distinct clusters centred round famous Polish pianists (Paderewski and Rubinstein), while other national groups (an older Russian group, a particularly coherent Hungarian group, plus a combined French and anglophone group) form a periphery. In this way the national connotations of Chopin's style are perpetuated through performance practice: the competition is not just an integral part of the 'symbolic system' of Polish national identity of which Mach (1994: 65) spoke, but a conspicuous arena for the performance of Poland. The pianist Krystian Zimerman—himself the top prize winner in 1975—has vividly evoked what all this meant for everyday life in Warsaw. In the 1960s and 1970s, as he recalled in an interview with YuanPu Chiao,

if you took a train during the Chopin Competition hours, you'd find that every passenger would be discussing the contest. Everyone would be constantly checking their watches and say, 'It's ten o'clock now; that means the

Russian pianist is playing soon'.... The train operators would even announce, 'And now we have the results of the third round of the competition. Names of the performers who have made it into the finals are as follows....' In that era, the Chopin Competition was not just a music competition, it was the life of the Polish people.[32]

And all this means that the link between musical style and meaning is best seen as inhering not in the doubtful historical origins of the mazurka genre, but in a continuously evolving tradition of performance that has been practiced on an everyday basis from Chopin's time to the present, and that continues to structure processes of social meaning production. The strange thing about this, as Daniel Leech-Wilkinson has pointed out, is the reluctance of performers to recognise their own role in these processes. It is as if they preferred to ascribe all the possible meanings that are produced in performance to the composer. 'The psychological advantages of being able to justify their choices by attributing them to the composer', writes Leech-Wilkinson (2012: paragraph 1.2), 'seem far to outweigh the uncertain likelihood of critical praise that might or might not accrue to [performers] were there no higher authority to whom they could look for support'. Yet a compelling argument might be made that, contrary to the composer-based historiographies and hagiographies that still dominate within and beyond the academy, it is performers who function as the principal motors of musical culture. Composers, after all, just write the notes.

32. Published in Chinese translation in Chiao (2007, II: 6).

6

Objective Expression

NATURE'S NUANCE

Figure 6.1 shows tempo and dynamic graphs of bars 1–32 of Chopin's Mazurka op. 63 no. 3 as recorded in 1994 by Vera Gornostaeva (Media Example 6.1). They are based on measurements at the beat level, and the standard graphs are straightforward visualisations of the data. In the smoothed graphs, a mathematical function has been applied that de-emphasises beat-to-beat change and so brings out larger trends. What I call the desmoothed graphs are generated by subtracting the smoothed values from the standard values: the larger trends are removed, so that beat-to-beat change is emphasised. The resulting graph represents the residual data to which I referred in Chapter 5. In the second half of that chapter I was mainly concerned with accentuation and the effects built around it, in particular the mazurka rubato and the signification that attaches to it. That is the level of note-to-note change that the desmoothed graph brings to prominence. Although it tells us nothing about sub-beat values and articulation, both as we have seen important dimensions of the mazurka rubato, careful examination reveals—for example—the lengthening of the second beat at bars 2, 4, 9, 10, and 14 of Figure 6.1 that is sometimes held to be the strongest single distinguishing feature of mazurka performance. Indeed in bars 2 and 10—that is, at the corresponding points in the first and second eight-bar phrases—tempo and dynamics between them constitute a sufficient explanation of the perceived second-beat accent: prolongation of the beat goes together with a louder attack (that is, there is both an agogic and a dynamic accent). The domain of accentuation is one in which the norm is for longer to go with louder, agogic emphasis with dynamic emphasis. This association of tempo and dynamics defines the world of meaning with which I was concerned in the second half of the last chapter.

In this chapter I explore the world of meaning brought into prominence by the smoothed graph in Figure 6.1. This is the domain of phrasing, in which the norm is for tempo and dynamics to be associated in the reverse way. As you play into a phrase, you typically get faster and louder; as you come out of it, you get slower and softer. That is, whereas in the domain of accentuation there is a direct relationship between duration and dynamic value, in that of phrasing there is an inverse relationship. Or to put it another way, the association is not between

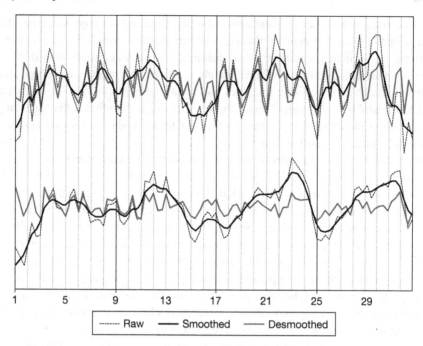

Figure 6.1 Standard, smoothed, and desmoothed tempo (top) and dynamic (bottom) graphs of Chopin, op. 63 no. 3, bars 1–32, as recorded by Gornostaeva

duration and dynamics but between tempo and dynamics. This can be clearly seen in the smoothed graph of Figure 6.1, where both parameters broadly fall into four arches of eight bars each. This is, of course, the phenomenon of phrase arching to which I have frequently referred; for instance I mentioned its employment by the anonymous pianist dubbed HP in Schubert's Impromptu op. 90 no. 3 and by Bart van Oort in the first movement of Mozart's *Rondo alla turca*.[1] I also referred to the psychologist Neil Todd's mathematical model of phrase of phrase arching, which represents one of the three factors into which Henkjan Honing and Peter Desain suggested that expressive performance might be decomposed. The idea that phrase arching is an important aspect, though not the whole, of musical expression is now the prevailing orthodoxy: Todd himself was more ambitious, giving one of his influential articles on the subject (1992) the subtitle 'A model of musical expression'.

The basic principles of Todd's model are simply stated (here I am enlarging on what I said in Chapter 3). The first principle is that music falls into phrases—a more formal term might be metrically based groups—and that this happens not at one level but at several: typically the most salient phrases will be at the level of four or eight bars, but effects of phrasing may be found at lower (e.g., two-bar) or higher (e.g., sixteen-bar) levels. That is by no means a new idea. The same

1. See Chapters 3, p. 85, and 4, p. 112.

conception, is, for example, fundamental to the thinking of Hugo Riemann, the turn-of-the-twentieth-century theorist and pedagogue whose influence remains strong in German-speaking musical cultures. The second principle is that, in performance, each phrase is normatively expressed through a temporal and dynamic arch profile. If one imagines phrases as being marked by slurs or arcs, as in the umbrella diagrams I mentioned in Chapter 2, then that is the trajectory that tempo and dynamics describe. In this way tempo and dynamics are coupled not only with one another, but also with the composed phrasing: the three elements come together to form an integrated expressive system. Moreover, because these trajectories are readily represented numerically, the model can be implemented on a computer—which is what Windsor and Clarke did, as described in Chapter 3. For a given piece of music you identify the phrases at every relevant level; you represent each phrase by a mathematical function, such as a parabola; and you add together the values. This yields a single overall profile that represents the entire piece from beginning to end, which can be graphed, or used as conducting track to control tempo and dynamic playback of a deadpan MIDI file of the piece. The major element of variability built into the model is that different weightings may be assigned to the several levels of phrasing, but it is assumed that the same numerical series will apply to both tempo and dynamics.

   In practice this last assumption makes Todd's model less effective in predicting actual performance practice than it would otherwise be. In their study of Schubert's op. 90 no. 3, Windsor and Clarke found that the best results were achieved by using quite different weightings as between tempo and dynamics. Media Example 6.2 is a MIDI realisation of bars 1–32 (in modern—or original—notation bars 1–16) of op. 90 no. 3, based on the following weightings at the eight, four, two, one, and half-bar levels respectively: tempo (1, 1, 1, 2, 4) and dynamics (4, 8, 8, 1, 1). As Windsor and Clarke (1997: 139) explain, these were the weightings that offered the best match with HP's recording (Media Example 3.8). So what is the explanation for the rigidity that Todd built into his original model? His 1985 study included data from performances by two undergraduate and two professional pianists, but his approach is not primarily an inductive one: he proposes and seeks to justify what is in essence a physiologically based theory of musical expression. As I said when discussing gravitational metaphors in Chapter 3, Todd understands the relationship between tempo and dynamics on the analogy of a physical system, but actually it goes further than analogy. He asks, 'why does artificial expression based on motion under constant acceleration sound natural?' And in reply he suggests it is because of the operation of organs of the inner ear that 'are sensitive to gravity, linear, and rotational acceleration' and in this way generate 'a percept of self-motion on the vestibular cortex'—and that have recently been discovered to be sensitive to vibration as well (Todd 1992: 3549). Tempo and dynamics are coupled, then, because the physical mechanism he is proposing means they have to be.

   To be fair, Todd nuances his claim. 'In putting forward this proposition', he says, 'we are not suggesting that this is a hard and fast rule', and again, 'the style of musical dynamics embodied in the proposition may be a kind of normative default mode of performance that a performer will adopt in the absence of any alternative instructions in the score' (3542). It is this pragmatic approach to the model that Windsor and Clarke develop: in the end, they say, its greatest value may lie in providing a more realistic baseline for empirical performance analysis than the metronomic tempo implied in a conventional tempo or duration graph. (As I said in Chapter 5, they are in effect advocating separate analysis of phrase arching and the residual data generated by the subtraction of the phrase arching, a broadly similar approach to the one I am adopting.[2]) But there is a tension between Windsor and Clarke's pragmatism and Todd's physicalism, which presents in a particularly stark form some key issues in performance analysis. However nuanced, the cash value of Todd's claim is that complex cultural phenomena can be explained in physical terms. This means that, considered as creative agents, performers disappear from the equation, just as they traditionally have in music theory: they are literally replaced by an algorithm. (One might think of Todd's model, especially as adapted by Windsor and Clarke, as representing a kind of 'expression synthesiser', a more sophisticated, pianistic correlate of the 'humanize' buttons found in programs such as EZDrummer.) It also implies that performance expression can be explained without reference to history: nobody is suggesting that the structure of the inner ear has changed on the timescales with which the history of music is concerned. Music psychology is in general insensitive to historical change—we saw this in Chapter 3, with Repp's approach to mobile tempos—but Todd's theory is a particularly clear case of this tendency.

Any self-respecting musicologist will bridle at the suggestion that cultural practices can be reduced to physiological principles, or understood in the absence of a historical perspective. (In fact most musicologists bridle at the very word 'natural'.) And while the demonstration or refutation of the first of these suggestions lies outside the province of the musicologist, questions of history lie at the core of the discipline. At the same time the question of how far phrase arching is a historical practice is hard to settle on the basis of written documents. There are basically two problems: first, that theorists, writers of treatises, critics, and performers did not talk about phrase arching, and second, that when they did, it is not clear what they meant. As to the first problem, if people didn't talk about the kind of phrase arching Todd describes, that could be because nobody was doing it—but then again, it could be because everybody was doing it, in other words, because it was too obvious to talk about. But that, of course, is only a problem if, in fact, people didn't talk about phrase arching. And there are a number of accounts dating from well back into the nineteenth century that have been cited as evidence of phrase arching. A case may be made, however, that they refer only to individual components of the integrated expressive system that Todd describes (and that we

2. In fact they come close to articulating the specific approach I am developing here: 'Timing and dynamics may be (1) positively correlated where both are used to accent discrete events, (2) negatively correlated as suggested by [Todd's] model, or (3) *either* timing *or* dynamics can be used to signal an accent or a phrase shape, but not both' (Windsor and Clarke [1997: 147]).

hear in Gornostaeva's playing). In other words, they are part of the prehistory, not the history, of phrase arching. Such accounts in particular involve trajectories in tempo or dynamics but not both; or groupings other than the metrically based phrase; or tempo and dynamic shaping that marks the ends of phrases, but without creating the continuous, controlled trajectory from beginning to end that lies at the core of phrase arching.[3]

Since I have said the evidence is inconclusive, it would be tedious to spend too long on it. Briefly, then: period treatises frequently refer to the desirability of making a break at the end of a structural unit. As early as the 1770s, Johann Georg Sulzer is writing that 'The phrase divisions are the commas of the melody which, as in speech, should be made apparent by a small pause' (Brown 1999: 139). This is the principle that, in speech, is called phrase-final lengthening, and as Dodson has written 'it has been found so consistently in the empirical literature for both music and speech that it seems to be a universal tendency'.[4] The principle may also be extended backwards within the phrase to encompass a series of notes that slow down as a cadential point is reached: Lussy—who as we saw anticipated Todd's use of the gravitational metaphor—explains this in his 1874 treatise, writing that, 'in increasing the duration of the final notes', the ritardando 'diminishes their force of attraction, their momentum. Each [note] progressively loses its attractive power, to the point that the last one is completely stripped of it'.[5] These effects represent components, but only components, of phrase arching. Then again, nineteenth-century sources embody the idea that ascending melodic contours entail an increase—and descending contours a decrease—in tempo (Thomas Lindsay's *The Elements of Flute-Playing*, first published in 1828), dynamics (Christiani 1885: 243), or both (Emil Behnke and Charles Pearce's *Vocal-Training Primer*, published in 1893).[6] Where a phrase consists of a melodic arch, this will result in phrase arching, but the phrase arching is an epiphenomenon of the contour—and in any case, many phrases do not incorporate such a contour.

But even when they do, things may not be so simple. Christiani (1885: 265–66) quotes a four-bar melody from the third volume of Czerny's *Complete Theoretical and Practical Piano Forte School* op. 500, first published in 1839: it consists of a

3. These features tend to be conflated with phrase arching proper in empirical studies such as Dodson (2011) and Ohriner (2012). (The latter is in part based on the same underlying data for op. 63 no. 3 that are used in this chapter, accessible at http://www.mazurka.org.uk/; it employs a sophisticated analytical methodology and compares performers' shaping of different sections of the piece.)

4. Unpublished paper cited in Chapter 4, n. 17.

5. Translated by Mine Doğantan-Dack (2002: 126–27), who notes that this phenomenon is rarely described in eighteenth-century treatises: 'It often happens', she comments, 'that the function of certain features universally present in human performances becomes apparent only when they are missing', a variant of the argument that people do not comment on things when they are too ubiquitous to warrant commentary.

6. Lindsay is cited in Hill (1994: 178 n. 39), and Behnke and Pearce in Philip (1992: 39).

one-bar descending phrase that is repeated in rising sequences, reaching a climax early in the third bar before falling to a cadence. The notated dynamics flow and ebb (*p dol.–cresc.–dim.–p*), and among the four temporal options proposed by Czerny, the third (*In tempo–poco accelerando–rallentando*) yields a perfect phrase arch. But there is no suggestion that this is a standard or preferred option, and Czerny goes on to say that '*accelerando* is used in ascending movements', once again associating expression with contour rather than with phrase. Then again, there is the passage from Lussy that I quoted in Chapter 3, in which he compares an ascending phrase to climbing a mountain, and in the course of which he refers to the 'inclination, which musicians have, of hastening, at the commencement of ascending phrases, and retarding towards the end'. This leads Mine Doğantan-Dack (2002: 128) to draw a comparison with Todd's model of phrase arching, but this involves a leap in the dark. For one thing, Lussy does not mention dynamics. More importantly, he presents this as an inclination against which the performer should be on guard: the passage I quoted in Chapter 3 continues, 'If, in this kind of passages, the executant, following the impulse of accelerating, does not hold back the movement, he runs the risk of being precipitated with headlong velocity' (Christiani 1885: 277).

In fact the first source to which I have traced an apparently unequivocal account of phrase arching comes from the final years of the nineteenth century. In his *Catechism of Pianoforte Playing*, Riemann (1892: 64) explicitly links tempo and dynamics ('the usual dynamic signs < and > apply also to the "agogics"'), and crucially, he links this temporal and dynamic shaping to the phrase. It is not just that he makes statements such as 'a four-bar phrase…is regularly given…with a *crescendo* for the two first and *diminuendo* for the two second bars' (69–70), which when taken together with the coupling of tempo and dynamics adds up to a phrase arch. It is that a fully worked-out theory of musical phrasing is one of the foundations of Riemann's entire system. This is based on the prototypical eight-bar period: the first four bars represent an anacrusis to the last four, within each half the first two bars represent an anacrusis to the second two, and the same principle applies within every pair of bars. Put this together with the principle that the anacrustic function is expressed through the combination of accelerando and crescendo, and you have precisely the situation that Windsor and Clarke (1997: 130) describe in relation to their implementation of Todd's model:

> At each level of the hierarchy dynamics and tempo increase to a maximum mid phrase and decrease to a minimum at phrase end. An additive function between levels means that the fastest and loudest point in the "performance" [in Riemann's case we could omit the inverted commas] will be in the middle of the phrase at the highest level of the hierarchy.[7]

7. Riemann's route to this conclusion is considerably more roundabout than my brief summary makes it appear. In particular, taken literally, his theory (unlike Todd's) would predict a climax in the final bar of the period, rather than its centre, and some convoluted argumentation involving the principle of the feminine ending is required in order to arrive at what has all the appearances of a predetermined, commonsense conclusion (Riemann [1892: 63]).

The fact that we have to wait until the dawn of the age of recording before we find such an account of phrase arching might be thought a sufficient demonstration of the historical nature, and hence the cultural constructedness, of the phenomenon. In fact I shall argue later in this chapter that the evidence is misleading, and that the style of performance which Riemann is describing—or prescribing—is very unlike that which Todd has in mind. Once again, then, the conclusion I draw is that written documents are an inadequate means of settling fundamental issues in the history of performance. Hence the recourse to recordings.

PHRASE ARCHING IN HISTORY

In what follows I focus primarily on bars 1–32 of op. 63 no. 3, but also draw some comparisons with bars 5–36 of op. 17 no. 4, omitting the four-bar introduction. The relevant score passages are shown in Figures 6.2 and 6.3, taken from the widely used edition by Chopin's pupil Mikuli that was first published around 1880, while Figure 6.4 lists the recordings discussed in this chapter.[8] Both these passages conform directly to the Riemannian model, representing a series of four harmonically closed or otherwise coherent eight-bar phrases (Riemann would call them periods, but I shall follow the sloppy anglophone practice of using 'phrase' to designate any metrically based group). These are arranged in the form of A-A-B-B in op. 63 no. 3, and A1-A2-A1-A2 in op. 17 no. 4. In the latter case, the eight-bar phrases are also defined by contour, rising to a high point in the middle and descending to the close. By contrast, the phrases of op. 63 no. 3 are more variable: the description I have just given would fit the first A and, with some adjustment (because of the modulation to E major) the second, but in terms of contour the B sections might be better described as four four-bar phrases, the first three falling from $g\#^2$ to $g\#^1$ and the last from $g\#^2$ to $c\#^2$. This groups the four-bar phrases in pairs, however, and in any case it is fundamental to both Riemann's and Todd's approaches that phrasing can operate at a number of levels, even if one of them predominates. All I want to establish is that both passages can be parsed in terms of eight-bar phrases, and are in consequence highly amenable to performance featuring eight-bar phrase arching, as in the case of Gornostaeva's recording of op. 63 no. 3.

The tempo and dynamic graphs of Gornostaeva's recording at Figure 6.1 represent the underlying data clearly enough, but that is not the same thing as bringing out salient features in a visible form. Figure 6.5 presents the same information as Figure 6.1, but in a format that is designed to elucidate phrase arching, and more specifically the way tempo and dynamics work together to

8. Details of original releases may be found in the standard Chopin discographies (Panigel and Beaufils [1949] and Kański [1986]), from which recording dates are taken where possible. Neither discography is complete, however, and in some cases data have been taken from CD documentation or other possibly unreliable sources. The recordings of op. 63 no. 3 listed in Figure 6.4 form a subset of a corpus of eighty-one recordings (seventy-nine commercial releases plus two YouTube videos, discussed in Chapter 10), on which Figure 6.18 is based.

Figure 6.2 Chopin, op. 63 no. 3, bars 1–36 (ed. Mikuli, Schirmer, 1894)

create it. The diamond shape is made up of two joined triangles, with the horizontal junction between the triangles representing the bar-to-bar succession of music, and with the black verticals dividing it into four eight-bar phrases. Each triangle is an 'arch correlation plot', generated by a program written by Craig Sapp.[9] The program steps through a series of data points, which could equally

9. On-line 'Scape Plot Generator', available at http://www.mazurka.org.uk/software/online/scape/; details may be found in Sapp's thesis (2011), especially 38–40. Figures 6.5–6.13 were generated using the Arch Correlation function with these settings: triangle; color; no gradient, flip, or smoothing.

Figure 6.3 Chopin, op. 17 no. 4, bars 1–40 (ed. Mikuli, Schirmer, 1894)

Pianist	Recording	Label and Catalogue Number	Original Recording Date	Media Example
op. 63 no. 3				
Ignaz Friedman	The Great Polish Tradition: Friedman	Selene CD-s 9908.53	1923	6.3
Sergei Rachmaninoff	Rachmaninoff Plays Chopin	RCA Victor Gold Seal 09026-62533-2	1923	6.4
Vladimir de Pachmann	The Essential Pachmann 1907–1927: Early and Unissued Recordings	Arbiter 141	1927	6.5
Ignaz Friedman	Great Pianists of the 20th Century, vol. 30	Philips 456 784-2	1930	
Ignacy Paderewski	Great Pianists of the 20th Century, vol. 74	Philips 456 919-2	1930	
Moriz Rosenthal	Moriz Rosenthal Plays Chopin	Biddulph LHW 040 (track 5)	1930	
Stanislas Niedzielski	Chopin Mazurkas	HMV B 3550	1931	6.6
Moriz Rosenthal	The Great Polish Chopin Tradition: Rosenthal	Selene CD-s 9906.51	1931	
Moriz Rosenthal	Moriz Rosenthal Plays Chopin	Biddulph LHW 040 (track 11)	1931	
Felicja Blumental	The Blumental Collection, vol. 2	Brana BR0018	1932	
Zofia Rabcewicz	The Golden Age of Polish Pianists	Muza PNCD 300	1932	
Alexander Uninsky	Fryderyk Chopin: International Chopin Piano Competitions. Best Mazurka Performances 1927–55	Muza PNCD006	1932	
Aleksander Michałowski	The Great Polish Tradition I: Michałowski	Selene CD-s 9803.39	1933	

Figure 6.4 Recordings of Chopin, op. 63 no. 3 and op. 17 no. 4 (continued)

Artur Rubinstein	Fryderyk Chopin: Mazurkas	Naxos 8.110656-57	1939	
Jakov Zak	Fryderyk Chopin: International Chopin Piano Competitions. Best Mazurka Performances 1927–55	Muza PNCD 006	1940s–50s	
Andor Földes	F. Chopin	Continental C 5032	1945	6.7
Vladimir Horowitz	Great Pianists of the 20th Century, vol. 49	Philips 456 842-2	1949	
Heinrich Neuhaus	Collected recordings, disc 3	Denon COCO-80271-281	1949	6.8
William Kapell	Chopin Mazurkas	RCA 09026-68990-2	1951	
Heinrich Neuhaus	Collected recordings, disc 4	Denon COCO-80271-281	1951	
Artur Rubinstein	The Rubinstein Collection, vol. 27: Chopin: 51 Mazurkas and the Impromptus	BMG 09026 63027-2	1952	
Halina Czerny-Stefańska	Fryderyk Chopin: International Chopin Piano Competitions. Best Mazurka Performances 1927–55	Muza PNCD 006	1953	6.9
Heinrich Neuhaus	Collected recordings, disc 10	Denon COCO-80271-281	1953	6.10
Samson François	Chopin: 51 Mazurkas, Sonates 2 and 3	EMI Classics CZS 7 67413 2	1956	
Oleg Boshniakovich	Oleg Boshniakovich Plays Chopin	Vista Vera VVCD-00022	1965	
Artur Rubinstein	The Rubinstein Collection, vol. 50: 51 Chopin Mazurkas	BMG 09026-63050-2	1966	
Alexander Uninsky	Chopin: Complete Mazurkas, Complete Impromptus, Berceuse	Philips 442 574-2	1971	

Figure 6.4 Continued

Stanislav Neuhaus	F. Chopin	Melodia C 04513-14	1972	
Vladimir Ashkenazy	Chopin: Mazurkas	Decca 448 086-2	1975	
Stanislav Bunin	Great Performers: F. Chopin	Olympia 501070	1987	
Halina Czerny-Stefańska	Chopin Mazurkas	Pony Canyon Classics PCCL-00460	1990	
Vera Gornostaeva	Frederic Chopin: Ballades, Mazurkas	Vista Vera VVCD-00064	1994	6.1
Tatiana Shebanova	Fryderyk Chopin: Complete Mazurkas	DUX 0350/0351	2002	
Stéphane Blet	Frédéric Chopin: 23 Mazurkas	Marcal MA030501	2003	
op. 17 no. 4				
Artur Rubinstein	Fryderyk Chopin: Mazurkas	Naxos 8.110656-57	1939	
Artur Rubinstein	The Rubinstein Collection, vol. 27: Chopin: 51 Mazurkas and the Impromptus	BMG 09026 63027-2	1952	
Artur Rubinstein	The Rubinstein Collection, vol. 50: 51 Chopin Mazurkas	BMG 09026-63050-2	1966	
Vladimir Horowitz	In the Hands of the Master	S3K 93039 Legacy	1971	
Vladimir Ashkenazy	Chopin: Mazurkas	Decca 448 086-2	1975	
Vladimir Horowitz	Horowitz: The Last Romantic	Deutsche Grammophon 419 045-2	1985	
Tatiana Shebanova	Fryderyk Chopin: Complete Mazurkas	DUX 0350/0351	2002	

Figure 6.4 Continued

represent tempo or dynamics, comparing them with a specified profile—in this case rising sine curves—and outputs the results in the form of a plot. Direct correlations between data and curve are represented in the plot by a light shade, sometimes with a darker centre (or, in colour versions, yellow and red), and inverse correlations by a dark shade (or blue).[10] In other words, within each triangle, light or yellow-red flame-like shapes correspond to rising arch profiles, while dark or blue flame-like shapes correspond to falling arch profiles: phrase arching accordingly appears in the form of matching pairs of lighter (yellow-red) and darker (blue) flames. Figures 6.5–6.13 are all laid out in the same format, with the upper triangle showing tempo and the lower one dynamic arching. The integrated system of phrase arching described by Todd will accordingly be distinguished by three features: regularly spaced pairs of flames; alignment of these flames with the beginning and end of composed phrases; and bilateral symmetry, marking the occurrence of the same arch shaping in both tempo and dynamics.

Figure 6.5 shows that Gornostaeva is doing something like what Todd would predict, though with some significant differences. The image tends towards bilateral symmetry: tempo and dynamics are in general working in synchrony, though the phrase arching is rather stronger in dynamics than in tempo. (That corresponds to Windsor and Clarke's findings when modelling HP's performance of op. 90 no. 3.) There are very obvious falling arches that more or less coincide with the end of the eight-bar phrases, and each is preceded by a corresponding rising arch. The strength of the falling arch at the end of the second phrase, at least as compared with that in bar 8, implies some degree of sixteen-bar phrasing. There are traces of arch shaping at smaller scales, particularly in dynamics, but it is the eight-bar level that dominates Gornostaeva's playing and provides the basic expressive framework for the performance. There is however a significant discrepancy between Todd's model and this recording, which lies in the location of the

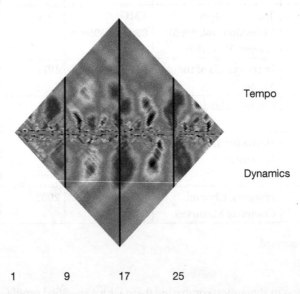

Figure 6.5 Phrase arching in Chopin, op. 63 no. 3, bars 1–32: Gornostaeva, 1994.

10. These shades are much easier to see in the colour versions of these plots than in halftone. Colour images of Figures 6.5–6.13 may be found on this book's companion website.

rising and falling arch profiles: the rising arches tend to occur later—sometimes much later—than Todd's model would predict. (It is fortunate, then, that Sapp's program makes no assumption about where arches are located, simply outputting what it finds). In fact the tendency for performance arching to occur later than composed arching appears to be widespread in recordings of op. 63 no. 3. If this is a general characteristic rather than a special feature of this particular mazurka, then it represents a further limitation of Todd's physiologically grounded model.

All this should not however obscure the extent to which the broad tendencies of Gornostaeva's playing conform to Todd's model, and this becomes obvious when comparison is made with earlier recordings. Recordings of op. 63 no. 3 do not go back as far as in the case of some other mazurkas, but there are two from 1923, shortly before the end of the era of acoustic recording. Of these, one is by Friedman. Figure 6.6 represents his playing of bars 1–32 (Media Example 6.3), and presents a quite different picture from Gornostaeva's recording. The most immediately striking feature is the major decelerando and decrescendo around bar 25, where there is a moment of delay prompted by the arpeggiated chord in the left hand (the arpeggiation is unnotated but may have been forced on Friedman by the span of a tenth[11]). But there is no preceding accelerando or crescendo. This is consequently an example of the undoubtedly historical practice of phrase-final lengthening, rather than of phrase arching as the integrated expressive system Todd describes. And the same applies, only on a much smaller scale, to the other examples of bilateral symmetry in Figure 6.6: it is generally falling

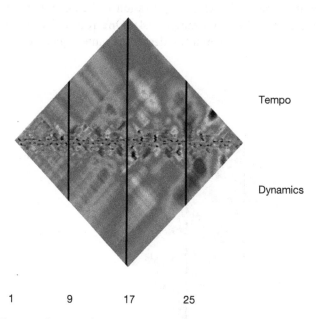

Tempo

Dynamics

1   9   17   25

Figure 6.6 Phrase arching in Chopin, op. 63 no. 3, bars 1–32: Friedman, 1923

11. According to Dr Harry Rich, who studied with Friedman during 1942–43, 'He couldn't play a ninth coherently, he had a small span' (Evans [2009: 281]). It should however be noted that 1943 is the year when Friedman retired from the concert platform as a result of neuritis in his left hand.

profiles in tempo and dynamics that coincide, again marking the end of phrases or other groups, rather than the regular, predictable, breathing-like motion that characterises Gornostaeva's playing.

An analogy from golf may help clarify the distinction. Initiating a phrase arch is like hitting a long drive: the trajectory is designed with a particular destination in view. Now Friedman actually studied piano and composition with Riemann during 1900–01 (Evans 2009: 30), and spoke appreciatively of 'Riemann's theory of phrasing—so often attacked' (26); again, Pnina Salzman, who studied briefly with Friedman in 1945, records that during lessons 'he was speaking intellectually and analyzing the music' (208). So no doubt he knew very well where the music was going. But rather like Rothstein, Friedman conceals what he knows. His playing has what Jerrold Levinson (1997) would call a concatenationist quality: its focus is on moment-to-moment expression, from the very long initial upbeat (effectively unmeasured, in that it is impossible to predict the tempo of what follows) to the equally unpredictable change of gear at bar 17. There is a little caesura on the preceding upbeat, after which Friedman hits the b# in the left hand with a quite new kind of attack. This leads to an immediately higher tempo, with the staccato left-hand offbeats and the lengthened second beat at bar 19:2 creating Friedman's characteristic mazurka feel—and then there is a sudden change back to legato at bar 21. The artistry lies in the transition from each moment to the next. This is of course an example of what I have been calling rhetorical performance, which leaves little trace in this kind of visualisation.

Robert Philip (1992: 54) describes the other recording from 1923, by Sergei Rachmaninoff, as giving 'a general impression of being straightforward in an almost modern way' (Media Example 6.4). One reason for this is suggested by Figure 6.7: there is a significant degree of quite regular eight-bar phrase

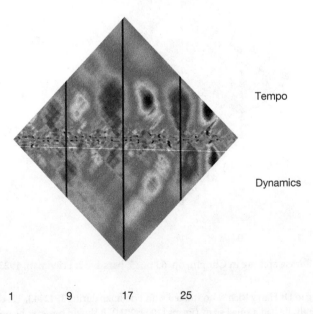

Figure 6.7 Phrase arching in Chopin, op. 63 no. 3, bars 1–32: Rachmaninoff, 1923

arching throughout. But only in the final phrase is this arching evident in both tempo and dynamics. Otherwise it occurs only in tempo, and it is perhaps this (rather than the quality of instrument, recording, or transfer) that is responsible for a certain effect of thinness, as if to modern ears the expression inherent in the tempo is not supported by the corresponding, and expected, fullness of sound. Rachmaninoff has other uses for dynamics: an obvious one is his division of the first four bars, which are linked by the linear progression $c\#^2$-$d\#^2$-e^2, as a pair of downbeats and upbeats (the effect is rather as if bars 1–2 and 3–4 represent questions, to which bars 5–8 provide the consoling answer). But even as regards tempo, there are features in Rachmaninoff's playing that are not well described in terms of phrase arching, such as the lingering over the 7–8 melodic motion at bar 15, or again over the chromatic work and broken chord in the left hand at bars 24–25. Both of these features are also found in Friedman's recording, and the sentence from Philip which I quoted at the beginning of this paragraph concludes by saying that Rachmaninoff's playing also 'contains elements of rhythmic adjustment which are characteristic of early twentieth-century piano playing', that is, rhetorical performance.

By contrast, Philip (1992: 53) writes that 'Perhaps surprisingly, Pachmann, who had a certain reputation for eccentricity [this is something of an understatement], interprets the rhythm of this piece much more literally' (the comparison is with Paderewski). Vladimir de Pachmann's 1927 recording, now from the electrical era, presents almost the reverse picture from Rachmaninoff's (Figure 6.8, Media Example 6.5). Here, unlike in Rachmaninoff's recording, there is strong, regular dynamic arching, but this time very little tempo arching. There is also an issue with the location of Pachmann's dynamic arching: in bars 9–16 and 17–24,

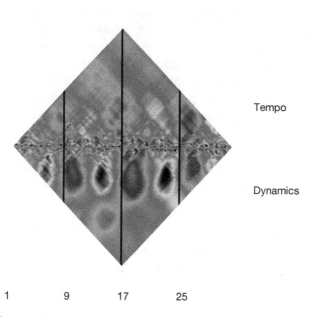

Tempo

Dynamics

1   9   17   25

Figure 6.8 Phrase arching in Chopin, op. 63 no. 3, bars 1–32: Pachmann, 1927

in particular, he plays the first half of the phrase softly, broadening out only when he reaches the second part. Although this sounds—to coin a term—perfectly natural, it is almost the opposite of what Todd's theory would suggest. One might argue that it is an extreme case of the delay between composed and performed phrasing to which I referred, but it is probably more sensible to see this purely dynamic effect as falling beyond the purview of Todd's model. Nevertheless the ebb and flow of Pachmann's dynamics give his playing the effect of fullness that Rachmaninoff's lacks, even while his timing borders on the matter-of-fact. As Figure 6.8 shows, he makes slight decelerandi between phrases, but as in the case of Friedman this is a matter of phrase-final lengthening rather than phrase arching. Like Rachmaninoff, Pachmann is using tempo and dynamics for essentially different purposes: tempo defines points of structural articulation, while the shaping of expressive form is carried by the dynamics. This separation of functions, which runs counter to the basic thrust of Todd's theory, is a feature of all the recordings of op. 63 no. 3 from the 1920s, and it is worth pointing out that though Pachmann's recording dates from four years later than Friedman's and Rachmaninoff's, it arguably reaches further back into the history of performance. Pachmann was born in 1848, earlier than any other pianist known to have recorded op. 63 no. 3.

Several lines of development can be traced during the 1930s, and I shall summarise these more briefly. The first half of the decade yields evidence of the continuing rhetorical tradition, as represented by pianists born between the 1850s and 1880s. Here age acts as a fair indicator of playing style. Perhaps the most old-fashioned is that of Aleksander Michałowski (1933), whose relaxed approach to the text and habitual hand breaking mark this as 'old school' playing: Michałowski was born only three years after Pachmann. The same features are also found in the 1930 recording by Paderewski (born 1860), who consistently turns Chopin's quaver pairs into dotted quaver and semi-quaver. Hardly less old-fashioned in their rhetorical detail are three remarkably similar recordings from 1930–31 by Moriz Rosenthal ('remarkably' because the one from 1930 is played much faster than the others but is otherwise similar). In this context the playing of the much younger Friedman (born 1882), which I have been characterising as 'rhetorical', might seem positively tidy, but it retains the defining rhetorical characteristic of a flexible tempo that is apparently driven as much by emotional as by melodic, harmonic, or textural intensity. All of these players, then, focus their attention on drawing out the expressiveness of the music's note-to-note progression.

As far as I know the first woman to record op. 63 no. 3, Zofia Rabcewicz was born in 1870, approximately midway between Paderewski and Friedman. And as might be expected, she too lingers on expressive detail at the expense of phrase shaping (for example bars 5–6 at the expense of 1–8). Yet there are features in her 1932 recording that feed into the later phrase arching style: a smoothness of dynamic control, and an even, uncluttered style of playing against which the passages of rhetorical emphasis stand out. A recording made in the previous year by a much younger player—Stanislas Niedzielski, who was born in 1905 and studied with Paderewski—displays the same features, but adds two more (Media Example 6.6). The first is the very rapid tempo, which averages about crotchet = 162 across the entire piece—the same as Rosenthal's 1930 recording, but far faster than others from the 1920s or 1930s (which fall into the range 115 to 143, with an average of 132). The second is a coupling of tempo and dynamics to create clearly perceptible arch-like shapes, although the pattern is not as regular as Todd's model would prescribe. The degree of bilateral symmetry in Figure 6.9 shows how tempo and dynamics generally work together; the blue flames are out of kilter at the end of the first phrase, however, because Niedzielski keeps the dynamics up for the end of that phrase, but then drops down for bar 10, giving it the effect of an echoed afterbeat. And more generally, tempo and dynamics do not always coincide with the composed phrasing. Bars 1–8 and 25–32 are performed in something approaching the Todd model, and Niedzielski begins the phrase at bar 9 the same way—but then he slows down to draw the expression out of bar 14, very much in the manner of the rhetorical performers, before accelerating rapidly in the following bar and continuing without a break into the third eight-bar phrase. Despite the signs of phrase arching, he is organising his performance as the rhetorical performers did: around expressive moments rather than regular phrasing.

Two other recordings from this decade take the relatively even, uncluttered playing found in Rabcewicz's and Niedzielski's playing to a new level. One is by Alexander Uninsky, only twenty-two at the time of his 1932 recording of op. 63 no. 3, whose playing reduces the detail of rhetorical playing to a kind of bas-relief achieved through a slight broadening at expressive points against a background of smooth, uninflected playing. Nevertheless the performance might still be seen as perpetuating the rhetorical conception to the extent that, as with Niedzielski,

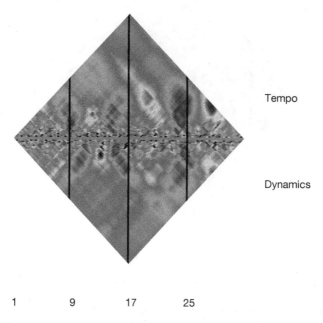

Figure 6.9 Phrase arching in Chopin, op. 63 no. 3, bars 1–32: Niedzielski, 1931

it is structured more around expressive moments than around regular phrasing. The other recording, from 1939, is by a much older player, Artur Rubinstein (born 1887 and thus only five years younger than Friedman). Everything I have said about Uninsky applies to him, but the effect is that much more radical, because of Rubinstein's unprecedentedly slow tempo. (The crotchet = 115 that I mentioned above is his, though Rubinstein achieves this largely by not speeding up for the central part of the piece: his average tempo across bars 1–32 is 124.) The result is to sweep the old rhetorical detail almost completely away, so giving rise to the same classicising purity of effect that marks Landowska's unissued recording of Mozart's K 332 from the year before. Rubinstein's playing is not without an understated expressive shaping—which stands out in the context of this highly measured playing—but its novelty and historical impact lie in what Rubinstein does not do. That impact had to be postponed, however, because at this point the Second World War intervened, and the cultural life of Europe largely came to a standstill.

By the time of the war, then, two characteristics are in place that will come together to form the post-war phrase-arching style: a clean, uncluttered playing style, and a linking of tempo and dynamics at the level of the musical phrase—although tempo, dynamics, and phrase structure are not as yet integrated in the manner that Todd describes. There are two recordings from the second half of the 1940s that could be seen as hybrids, combining characteristics of the old and the new styles of performance. Andor Földes's recording (Figure 6.10, Media Example 6.7) was made in 1945—a date that might have been unlikely in Europe, but Földes had emigrated to the United States in 1940[12] (which means

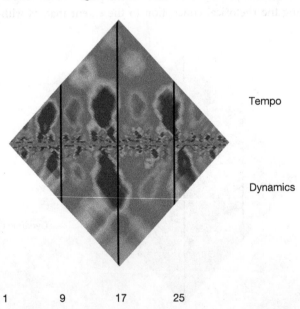

Figure 6.10 Phrase arching in Chopin, op. 63 no. 3, bars 1–32: Földes, 1945

12. As stated in Allan Kozinn's *New York Times* obituary of Földes, published on 19 February 1992 (http://www.nytimes.com/1992/02/19/arts/andor-foldes-pianist-dies-at-78-known-for-renditions-of-bartok.html).

this is probably the first recording of op. 63 no. 3 from outside Europe). As in Niedzielski's recording of fourteen years earlier, there is not only a relatively clean style of performance that preserves just a faint memory of rhetorical playing, but also a sense that the music is coming in waves and that these waves are becoming the chief locus of expression. Sometimes, however, they are not so much waves as lurches. Földes broadens his tempo dramatically at bar 5, and accelerates equally dramatically at the beginning of bar 8, rushing through the cadence in the manner—for example—of d'Albert in Schubert's op. 90 no. 3. In the second half of bar 12 he suddenly broadens the tempo, targetting the transposition of the second four-bar phrase in the following bar, the turning point for the modulation to the relative major. If that sounds a little like Niedzielski, then so does Földes's sudden acceleration to the end of the phrase and rushing through the cadence. This time he maintains a faster, though by no means steady, tempo until in bar 22 he slows down—again dramatically—for the end of the eight-bar phrase. Only in bars 25–32 does he execute something that really resembles the Todd-style phrase arch. Although tempo and dynamics in general work together, then, there is not the regular relationship between them and the composed phrasing that Todd prescribes. It is rather as if a new, wave-like style was being superimposed on an older underlying conception.

As for the second recording to which I referred, this dates from 1949 and is by Vladimir Horowitz (Media Example 6.8). As might be expected from the older player (Horowitz was born in 1903, ten years before Földes), this recording retains a much clearer memory of pre-war playing—for instance in the rushing from the g#^{2} to the end of the phrase at bars 7–8, in the Friedman-like mazurka characterisation of bar 19, and in the emphatic drawing out of expression at the phrase end in bars 22–24, as well as the occasional hand breaking. But as Figure 6.11

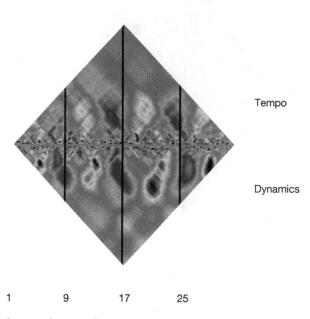

Tempo

Dynamics

1   9   17   25

Figure 6.11 Phrase arching in Chopin, op. 63 no. 3, bars 1–32: Horowitz, 1949

indicates, all this is firmly contained within phrase arching that is more systematically coordinated between tempo and dynamics than in any of the previous
recordings I have described. It is as if the old rhetoric has been rationalised
and regularised through being incorporated within a larger, structuralist
framework.

In chronological terms the next recording is another from North America, by
William Kapell (1951), and like Földes—indeed like many of the earlier pianists—he plays 25–32 as a recognisable tempo (though not dynamic) arch. Apart
from that, however, there is little evidence of phrase arching in his playing, and
so I will skip over him to two recordings, both by women, that appeared in the
next two years: those of Felicja Blumental (1932) and Halina Czerny-Stefańska
(1953). The basic character of Blumental's recording is established by its speed,
an astonishing crotchet = 187 averaged over bars 1–32—much the fastest tempo
within the entire collection of eighty-one recordings of op. 63 no. 3 on which
this chapter is based. At this speed phrases emerge as salient organisational units,
yet—like Horowitz—Blumental incorporates a range of sometimes extreme
expressive gestures derived from the rhetorical tradition. Czerny-Stefańska's
performance (Media Example 6.9) could not be more different. Her average
tempo in bars 1–32 is crotchet =110, significantly slower than the crotchet = 124
at which Rubinstein played this passage. The analytical representation of her performance (Figure 6.12) is strikingly similar to that of Horowitz's (Figure 6.11),
reflecting the same systematically coordinated phrase arching that was present in
the older pianist's performance. Yet Czerny-Stefańska's playing sounds nothing

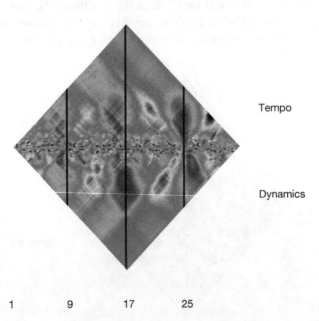

Figure 6.12 Phrase arching in Chopin, op. 63 no. 3, bars 1–32: Czerny-Stefańska, 1953

like Horowitz's. That is because in Horowitz's recording the phrase arching is heavily overlaid by rhetorical gestures, which do not show up in this visualisation; Czerny-Stefańska's recording, by contrast, sounds the way the figure looks. In short, she builds not only on Rubinstein's slow tempo but also on the clean, uncluttered quality of his playing, and adds Horowitz's systematic phrase arching to the mix.

The result of these combined factors is that, in the hands of Czerny-Stefańska, Rubinstein's classicising purity turns into an almost hygienic clarity that is at the same time tempered by the phrase arching. There is an overall expressivity that is not located at particular moments of the music, as in rhetorical playing, but rather inheres at the larger, more abstract level of structure. It embodies a new conception. Perhaps then it is no accident that four years earlier, in 1949, Czerny-Stefańska had won both first prize (jointly with Bella Davidowicz) and the Polish Radio Mazurka Prize at the Fourth International Fryderyk Chopin Piano Competition, the first to be held after the war. Indeed one could trace the emerging style of mazurka performance through the comparison between the 1949 competition and the two previous ones, when the mazurka and the overall prizes again went to the same pianist: Uninsky in 1932, and in 1937 Jakov Zak. There is a recording by Zak that combines a Rubinstein-like cleanness of playing with modest but fairly coordinated phrase arching: if this is how he played in 1937 then he would claim a significant place in my narrative. Unfortunately I have been unable to improve on the exasperatingly vague dating ('1940s/50s') that is provided in the booklet of the CD transfer.

It would be reasonable to borrow Philip's phrase, only without the 'almost', and describe Czerny-Stefańska's manner of performance as straightforward in a modern way. And given that she was in her twenties when she won the Chopin Competition and just over thirty when she made her 1953 recording, it would also seem reasonable to hear in it the sound of a new, post-war generation. There is however a complication. The most extreme example of Todd-style phrase arching that I have found in any recording of op. 63 no. 3 comes from 1953—the same year as Czerny-Stefańska's—but from a pianist then in his mid-sixties: Heinrich Neuhaus, who at one stage had a few lessons with Michałowski but was mainly self-taught (Methuen-Campbell 1981: 140). It is shown in Figure 6.13 (Media Example 6.10), and exhibits all the features I have been discussing. There is strong tempo and dynamic arching closely coordinated with the composed phrase structure, but the key to the effect is a radical straightforwardness of playing that lets the phrase arching speak unimpeded to the listener—and that results in a graphic representation so clean and symmetrical that it almost looks as if it had been painted on canvas rather than created via the elaborate detour of piano performance and computational analysis. The eight-bar phrasing dominates so completely that other structural features of the music barely impinge. The recording represents a minimalist,

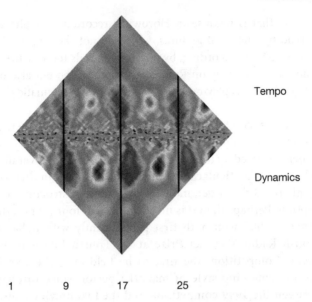

Figure 6.13 Phrase arching in Chopin, op. 63 no. 3, bars 1–32: Neuhaus, 1953

streamlined interpretation, to the extent that it hardly seems appropriate to call it an interpretation at all.[13]

The exceptional regularity of Neuhaus's 1953 recording makes it a textbook illustration of phrase arching, and many subsequent recordings follow the same pattern, if not quite such an extreme degree. There is for example François's recording of 1956, from the same complete set of the mazurkas that I mentioned in Chapter 5; as I said there, he studied with Cortot, as did Czerny-Stefańska. (In some respects, however, his performance is more like Blumental's than Czerny-Stefańska's.) There is a 1965 recording by Oleg Boshniakovitch, who like Gornostaeva was a pupil of Neuhaus, as well as subsequent recordings by other Russian pianists such as Vladimir Ashkenazy (1976) and Grigory Sokolov (whose 2001 film recording of op. 63 no. 3 I shall discuss in Chapter 10). There is even what looks like a family tradition of phrase arching: Stanislav Neuhaus, whose recording dated from 1972, was Heinrich's son, while Stanislav Bunin (1987) is his grandson.

The visualisations I have presented up to now are designed to show at a glance the extent to which tempo and dynamic arching work together. They

13. In addition to the 1953 one, there are recordings by Neuhaus from 1949 (recorded in concert) and 1951, which are similar but less extreme expressions of the phrase arching style: in combination with the fact that during the 1930s Zak was one of Neuhaus's many pupils at the Moscow Conservatory, this might suggest that Moscow was a key site in the development of the new style. After all, stylistic trends in performance develop because particular individuals do particular things under particular circumstances, although there is rarely the evidence to reconstruct such developments in detail.

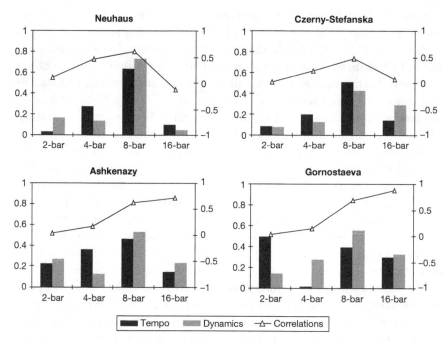

Figure 6.14 Phrase arching profiles for Chopin, op. 63 no. 3, bars 1–32, as recorded by Neuhaus, Czerny-Stefańska, Ashkenazy, and Gornostaeva

extract certain features while de-emphasising others, and in this way help to channel and stabilise a particular kind of analytical listening. It follows that alternative visualisations can represent performances from different perspectives, and Figure 6.14 represents four of the recordings I have discussed in the form of what I shall call phrase arching profiles. The underlying data are the same as before, and so is the analytical algorithm. This time, however, the purpose of the visualisation is to separate out the relative strengths of phrase arching at different levels, which were hard to make out from Figures 6.5–6.13 because they were dominated by eight-bar arching. The vertical bars represent strength of arching at the two, four, eight, and sixteen bar levels, averaged over the whole of bars 1–32 (this is why it was important to select passages with consistent, sustained phrase arching). Values for tempo and dynamics are shown separately, and it would be possible to imagine the graph as representing the 'expression synthesiser' I referred to near the beginning of this chapter, with the individual bars corresponding to mixer-style faders. I will come to the line graphs shortly.

Figure 6.14 confirms what we already know, that all four recordings—and particularly Neuhaus's—are dominated by eight-bar arching. But the contributions of the other levels are now plainly visible, and vary considerably. In fact each recording presents its own picture. In Gornostaeva's case the role of other levels is especially marked: there is significant degree of sixteen-bar phrasing in both tempo and in dynamics, of four-bar phrasing in dynamics but not tempo, and in particular of two-bar phrasing in tempo—actually higher than at the eight-bar level—but not in dynamics. (I mentioned some but not all of these in my discussion of Figure 6.5.) Although the eight-bar level provides the strongest combination of tempo and dynamic arching, the strength of the other levels might raise questions as to why the dominant impression from hearing Gornostaeva's recording is of eight-bar phrasing. The answer may lie in the line graph. This shows the degree of correlation between the tempo and dynamic arches. The relevant scale is at the right, and as usual with correlations, 0 signifies a complete lack of relationship, while 1.0 signifies identity. (−1.0 would signify a perfect but inverse relationship.) In the cases of Neuhaus, Ashkenazy, and Gornostaeva the correlation at the eight-bar level is over 0.6, which means the one parameter is a fairly good predictor of the other. The two-bar level of Gornostaeva's recording, however, shows no correlation between tempo and dynamics: that may explain why this level does not emerge strongly when the recording is heard, despite the strength of the two-bar tempo arching. Czerny-Stefańska's recording presents yet another picture: at 0.5, correlation at the eight-bar level is lower than in the other three recordings, but it is still stronger than at the other levels, and so the effect of eight-bar phrasing comes through. It looks then as if, for the listener, the experience of phrase arching results partly from the relative weighting of tempo and dynamic arches at various levels, and partly from the degree of correlation between them.

All this is consistent with Todd's basic insight that phrase arching, in its modern form, represents an integrated expressive system. But, as Figure 6.14 shows, there is a great deal of variation in how performers employ it. This emerges from a comparison between recordings of op. 63 no. 3 by the same pianist. The collection on which this chapter is based includes six sets of multiple performances: two each by Friedman, Uninsky, and Czerny-Stefańska, and three by Rosenthal, Rubinstein, and Neuhaus, with recordings being separated by a matter of decades in the cases of Uninsky, Rubinstein, and Czerny-Stefańska. The recordings by Friedman, Uninsky, Rubinstein, and Rosenthal are consistent in the negative sense that they make little use of phrase arching. By contrast, Neuhaus's 1953 recording exhibits stronger phrase arching than those of 1949 and 1951, while Czerny-Stefańska's 1990 recording exhibits significantly less than her 1953 one—though, as in the earlier recording, her limpid playing makes the phrase arching come through more strongly than a phrase arching profile might suggest.

If pianists are not necessarily consistent in how they use phrase arching in different performances of the same piece, then the same applies to their performances of different pieces. This is where the comparison with bars 5–36 of op. 17 no. 4 comes in. As I said, this thirty-two-bar section falls more unambiguously into eight-bar phrases than the passage from op. 63 no. 3: if performance can be strongly predicted from structure, then in op. 17 no. 4 we should find phrase

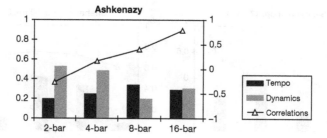

Figure 6.15 Phrase arching profiles for Chopin, op. 17 no. 4, bars 5–36, as recorded by Ashkenazy

arching even more dominated by the eight-bar level than in op. 63 no. 3. In fact the reverse is the case, for reasons that probably have to do with other aspects of the compositions. For one thing, op. 17 no. 4 is usually played significantly slower than op. 63 no. 3: in the recordings on which this chapter is based, the average tempo of these passages is crotchet = 91 for op. 17 no. 4, as against 130 for op. 63 no. 3. Linked to this is the highly ornamental melodic style of op. 17 no. 4—a style that, in Jim Samson's words, is 'so seldom found in the mazurkas that we might be tempted to question the genre' (1996: 117). This combination of features encourages even modern performers to adopt what might be characterised as a more surface-oriented approach than in op. 63 no. 3. The profile for Ashkenazy's recording (Figure 6.15) is typical, with strong dynamic arching at the two-bar level: Ashkenazy uses dynamic shaping to extract the maximum expressive charge from each two-bar phrase. And, as the comparison with Figure 6.14 shows, that means he plays op. 17 no. 4 in a drastically different style from how he played op. 63 no. 3. Much the same might be said of Horowitz, whose 1971 and 1985 recordings of op. 17 no. 4 both feature dynamic arching at lower levels, with little of the integrated phrase arching that marked his much earlier recording of op. 63 no. 3.

Yet this picture of varied practice as between op. 17 no. 4 and op. 63 no. 3 is itself varied. Figure 6.16 shows how, in Tatiana Shebanova's 2002 box set of the complete mazurkas, op. 17 no. 4 features phrase arching as strong, and as dominated by the eight-bar level, as op. 63 no. 3. As for Rubinstein (Figure 6.17), the profile of his 1939 recording of op. 17 no. 4 has some features in common with his op. 63 no. 3 from the same set, in particular the pattern of correlations between tempo and dynamics. But his 1952 and 1966 recordings of op. 17 no. 4, though fairly similar to one another, are quite different from the corresponding recordings of op. 63 no. 3: the 1966 recording, in particular, actually uses more phrase arching, featuring the highest degree of correlation between tempo and dynamics at the eight-bar level of all the recordings in this collection, with the sole exception of Shebanova. Some pianists, then, use the same kind of phrase arching in these two pieces; others, probably the majority, do not.

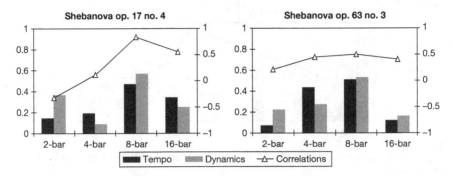

Figure 6.16 Phrase arching profiles for Chopin, op. 17 no. 4 and op. 63 no. 3, as recorded by Shebanova

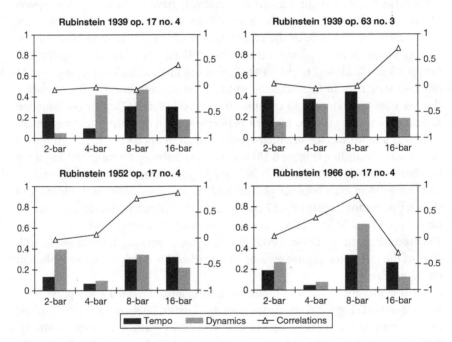

Figure 6.17 Phrase arching profiles for Chopin, op. 17 no. 4 and op. 63 no. 3, as recorded by Rubinstein

While such lack of consistency may frustrate empirical musicologists aiming to define pianistic style in terms of objective relationships between score and performance, it is consistent with an aesthetic premise to which many performers are strongly committed. As the violinist Sándor Végh said, 'Learning a work and reproducing it the same way every evening is not a productive interpretation, it is a reproduction. You must always make it new and have the courage to follow that inspiration' (Lawson and Stowell 2012: 832). While composed phrase structure affords particular patterns of phrasing in performance, it is far from determining them: the mutual entailment of composition and performance is simply not that tight. And that resonates with the idea, which underlay much of what I said in Chapters 3 and 4, that the quality of an individual performance may often reside less in the interpretation of structure—like op. 17 no. 4 and op. 63 no. 3, the pieces by Schubert and Mozart that I discussed in those chapters do not offer that much scope for different structural interpretations—than in features that do not impinge upon structure. Expressed like that, the idea is obvious, yet it is ruled out by theoretical approaches based on the mapping of performance features to score-based structure, and consequent disregard of features that do not map.

I said that the visualisations in Figures 6.5–6.13 supported a particular form of analytical listening. I would not say the same of Figures 6.14–6.17, basically because they do not represent the temporal succession of the music. They are too abstract to be easily linked to perceptual experience. But if that makes them less useful for purposes of close listening, it opens up possibilities for distant listening. Because the information in the phrase arching profiles is quantified, it is possible to deploy it in a manner that is comparable to Bowen's and Grunin's scattergrams. As we saw in Chapter 5, these typically plot durations, tempos, or measures of flexibility against date of recording, or sometimes the performer's date of birth. I said that the problem with them is that they conflate quite dissimilar musical phenomena by reducing duration, tempo, or flexibility to a single value. Phrase arching profiles are also reductive, of course. But while phrase arching represents only one dimension of performance, it is a high-level one that combines aspects of tempo and dynamics with a specific compositional context. That is why, in developing their decompositional approach, Honing and Desain identified phrase arching, in the form of Todd's model, as one of the factors that might relate most meaningfully to the experience of music as performance.

For this reason, we might reasonably expect a scattergram based on strength of phrase arching to reveal more about both the experience of performance and its cultural significance than measures based on simple descriptive statistics. At least in the case of op. 63 no. 3, plotting individual elements within the phrase arching complex—for example dynamic arching at the four-bar level—does not produce readily interpretable results. But then, we should not expect it to, because the principle underlying phrase arching is that such elements signify not on their own, but as part of the integrated expressive system to which I have repeatedly referred. Figure 6.18 is therefore based on a simple formula designed to yield an overall measure of phrase arching strength in performances of this mazurka: it reflects, first, the weighting of tempo and dynamic arching at the eight-bar level relative to other levels, and second, the degree of correlation between tempo and dynamics at that level, with the first factor receiving twice the weighting of the second.

Some health warnings are in order at this point. This formula is intended to help rough out an approach rather than, in itself, to represent a contribution to knowledge. Not only is it specifically adapted to op. 63 no. 3 in its focus on the eight-bar level, but it was also arrived at pragmatically; justifying and elaborating it on the basis of empirical tests would be a project in itself. A principal limitation

204　　　　　　　　　　　　　　　　　　　　　　　　　　　BEYOND THE SCORE

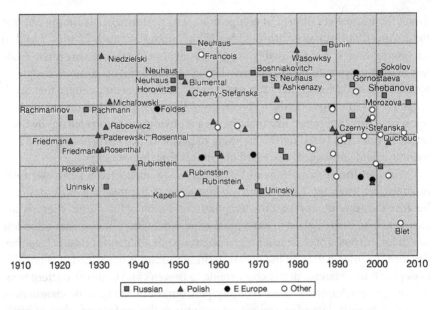

Figure 6.18 Phrase arching plotted against recording dates for Chopin, op. 63 no. 3, bars 1–32

is that while it models phrase arching in the sense of the conformance of tempo and dynamics with rising and falling sine curves as well as with one another, the perceptual experience of phrase arching depends on factors that are not embraced by the model I have been using. I said that the model sees Horowitz's and Czerny-Stefańska's recordings as similar even though they sound quite different, because it does not—and is not designed to—detect the rhetorical detail of Horowitz's and earlier recordings. Again, strong adherence to the phrase arching model at certain points within a recording may override perceptually salient discrepancies at others. An obvious example of this is Niedzielski's recording of 1931, which to my ears appears much too high up in Figure 6.18: his treatment of bars 9–24, with no account taken of the major phrase break at bars 16–17, militates against the sense of regularity and predictability that is inherent in the phrase arching style. (The same applies to Michałowski's recording of two years later, in which there is a surprisingly high degree of coordination between tempo and dynamics—which however is obscured behind his old-school, moment-to-moment rhetoric.) Conversely, one of the reasons Czerny-Stefańska's recording does not appear higher in the scattergram is that the model takes no account of her slow overall tempo, which is an essential component of what I called the almost hygienic clarity of her performance. (In Chapter 10 I shall argue the same of Irina Morozova's performance.) No doubt a more refined model of phrase arching could address some of these issues, but the basic principle is that all analytical models are reductive. Consequently the location of certain recordings in key positions in Figure 6.18 should be seen not as directly representing hard-and-fast facts about perceptual significance or musical meaning, but rather as prompts to further investigation adopting less reductive approaches. Distant listening, in short, makes it possible to work with large data sets, but is most valuable for musicological purposes when used in conjunction with strategically deployed close listening.

All the same, a number of provisional conclusions, or hypotheses, emerge from Figure 6.18. When I published an initial version of this study (Cook 2009), based on a sample of fifty-six recordings, Neuhaus's 1953 recording stood out as embodying a far higher degree of phrase arching that any previous recording, giving rise to a punchy headline story: modern phrasing arching developed after 1945, nicely illustrating Leech-Wilkinson's (2009a: chapter 4, paragraph 31) observation that 'the Second World War marked a watershed in musical performance style'. Figure 6.18, based on a significantly larger data set that includes Niedzielski's recording from 1931, reveals a more complicated situation, underlining the extent to which the elements of the phrase-arching style developed during the interwar period. Nevertheless, when allowance is made for the various confounds described in the previous paragraph, I would maintain that the underlying narrative is still broadly correct: though anticipated in a few recordings from the 1930s, the integrated expressive system of phrase arching that Todd describes is a phenomenon of the post-war period. If that is right, Todd's model is not so much 'a model of musical expression', as he called it, but rather of *some aspects of musical expression during the second half of the twentieth century*. Then again, the scattergram confirms something suggested by the names that have been recurring in connection with recordings featuring high levels of phrase arching: the pianists in the upper quartile of Figure 6.18 include 44% of those in our collection who were born or trained in Russia as against 16% of those from Poland, 13% of those from elsewhere in Eastern Europe, and 17% of pianists from elsewhere. It is remarkable that this effect persists through the second half of the century, given the extent to which performance education became internationalised during that period, not to mention the impact of recordings. And this suggests that Todd is really modelling *some aspects of musical expression associated in particular with Russian piano playing during the second half of the twentieth century*.

But the most significant conclusion to be drawn from Figure 6.18 is like the curious incident of the dog in the night-time: it has to do with what didn't happen. Though the scattergram shows an increase in phrase arching after 1945 at the upper end of the range, it shows no corresponding decrease at the lower end: there continued, and continue, to be recordings featuring very little phrase arching, at least as I have modelled it. (As it happens, the most recent commercial recording in this collection, by Stéphane Blet, has the lowest value of all, because of an inverse correlation between tempo and dynamic arching.) And this illustrates what I said in Chapter 5 about the use of informal working methods based on a small subset of the available evidence. Without Figure 6.18, my narrative would inevitably have given the impression that the development of a new kind of phrase arching brought about a general transformation in the performance of these mazurkas. As I suggested, inherited patterns of musical historiography lead us to think of style as the kind of impersonal historical agent in terms of which Riegl saw art history. We associate specific historical periods with specific stylistic norms. In Chapter 5

I expressed doubts about this approach, and Figure 6.18 reinforces them. At least in the case of op. 63 no. 3, the development of a new approach to phrase arching did not extinguish previous performance options. Existing approaches remained in currency, whether because older pianists saw no reason to change their style, or in the case of younger pianists as a result of the reissuing—at least in Europe—of many old recordings following the expiry of copyright. We cannot, then, speak of a general transformation of style; rather there was one set of stylistic practices, to which another was added. We might think in terms of a field of possibilities that expanded during the period up to the 1950s and thereafter remained essentially static.

Two more general points emerge from this, one to do with historical interpretation and the other with method. They are linked, and I can focus both around Robert Philip, to whom I have repeatedly referred—and with justification, as more than anybody else he can be considered responsible for the development of a musicology of recordings. His book *Early Recordings and Musical Style*, published in 1992, had its origins in a doctoral thesis at Cambridge (he applied to Oxford but was told that recordings were not a suitable subject for musicological research). It offered an in-depth survey of classical recordings from the first half of the twentieth century, organised around key technical features of performance, together with a brief but suggestive discussion of the implications of such work. Taken together, this amounted to a first draft of the history of classical performance during this period, and it put forward some key ideas that, over the last twenty years, have acquired the status of received truth. Prominent among these is the idea that performance style has become increasingly standardised, in part because of things like air travel and the internationalisation of music education, but particularly because of recordings.

As I said in Chapter 4, the suggestion is that, by enabling the same performance to be heard repeatedly, recording made it necessary to tidy up—or re-engineer—performance style. The kind of loose ensemble that might add to the excitement of live performance became exasperating when heard again and again, and so the sometimes very fast tempos adopted by early performers were slowed down, in accordance with what became the self-evident principle that 'a tempo must be chosen so that the shortest note-values can be played accurately and clearly' (Philip 1992: 234). That of course resonates with Schoenberg's claim, which I quoted in Chapter 1, that 'the highest principle for all reproduction of music would have to be that what the composer has written is made to sound in such a way that every note is really heard': significantly, Schoenberg wrote this around the middle of the 1920s, the decade during which recording became big business. And it is an aspect of what is widely seen as the increasing literalism of approach that became normative after the Second World War, a concern to conform to the letter as much as the spirit of the score. This implies a change in what a recording might be thought to be: it becomes less the trace of an event, and more a musical object in its own right. (I shall return to this issue in Chapter 11.) More practically, it implies two kinds of convergence: first, a narrowing of the range of acceptable tempos, as the fastest fell into disuse; and second, a more general convergence in performance style as the range of available options shrank. Seen this

way, the development of the conservatory sector, competitions, and other formalised modes of assessment have led to ever higher standards of execution, but
at the expense of diversity of interpretation.

Actually what was new about Philip's take on this was not the idea, but the extent
to which he backed it up with evidence. The idea itself forms part of a pessimistic
tradition of commentary that extends far back into the history of recording. To
cite a few examples, one of the headings in Adorno's notes (2006) for his unfinished book on performance reads, 'Standardization of performance through the
gramophone record' (23), and in an essay from 1938 he expands on this: 'Perfect,
immaculate performance in the latest style preserves the work at the price of its
definitive reification. It presents it as already complete from the very first note.
The performance sounds like its own phonograph record' (Adorno 2002: 301).
Over thirty years later, on the final page of 'The grain of the voice', Roland Barthes
(1977: 189) echoed Adorno: 'today, under the pressure of the mass long-playing
record, there seems to be a flattening out of technique; which is paradoxical in that
the various manners of playing are all flattened out *into perfection*'. (This is part
of his larger argument that Fischer-Dieskau represents the perfect, disembodied,
phonographic voice, in contradistinction to the tongue, the mucous membranes,
the physical presence, in a word the grain of Panzéra's voice.) A decade after that,
in 1985, the writer and critic Hans Keller (1990: 22) was even more damning: 'The
gramophone record's repeatability has had a disastrous and well-definable effect
not only on the sheer act of listening, but also on musical education and, thence, on
performance itself'.

The truth of these arguments is not self-evident, for several reasons. If recording
led to standardisation, it might have been for reasons other than repeated listening. Writing in 1913, the pianist Max Pauer records the horror he felt on first hearing the idiosyncrasies of his own playing, while Mark Katz (2004: 22) suggests that
the lack of the visual dimension of live performance forced studio musicians to
tighten up their timing, as dramatic pauses readily intelligible in the concert hall
ceased to make sense on record; as an extension of this argument, one might suggest that performance became more structurally oriented because visible gesture
was no longer available as a means of clarification. (I return in Chapters 9 and 10
to the role of gesture in performance.) But there may also have been factors unrelated to recording. Similar complaints were being made before recording could
have had an effect: Harold Bauer (1947), for example, inveighed against the cult
of shallow perfection at the Paris Conservatoire in the first years of the twentieth
century. Again, changes in performance might reflect the increasing separation of
the roles of composer and performer to which I referred in Chapter 4, which will
have influenced how performers saw musical texts.

And finally, it would be just as plausible to see recordings working against standardisation. As Donald Greig (2009: 27) and Michael Haas (2009: 61) say, the fact
that you can always do another take should logically promote acceptance of risks.
Similarly the growing availability over recent decades of a vast archive of recordings
should add to the range of available options, whether by provoking experimentation with unfamiliar historical styles, or simply the desire to do something different.

Narratives of a decline resulting from recordings, however, draw on many resonant cultural values: distrust of technology and the industries built on it, the standardisation that forms part of an increasingly bureaucratic society, the alienation that results from the replacement of human presence by the mechanical, and the waning or betrayal of an esteemed cultural tradition. As a result, their inherent attraction—at least to pessimists—renders them largely impervious to evidence.

But there is a further problem, which is that the evidence is not very good, and this goes back to the limitations of close listening that I mentioned in Chapter 5. As I said there, Philip's work was based primarily on close listening—highly expert close listening, reflecting his professional career as a radio producer as well as the sheer number of recordings he must have heard—supplemented where appropriate by simple measurements (for example of duration or average tempo). No doubt he also relied on extensive score annotations, notes, and memory. But the problem with even expert memory was dramatised by the Hatto hoax: it turned out that a number of prominent critics—again highly expert listeners—had reviewed the same recording in distinctly different terms depending on who they thought it was by.[14] And more than that, it took iTunes and Sapp's correlation measures to bring to light the fact that it *was* the same recording. Admittedly record reviewing and musicology are rather different things, but if you cannot even recognise recordings when you hear them again, you are likely to have difficulty in making sophisticated style-analytical comparisons between them. The point is that traditional sound reproduction technology did not provide any easy way to make direct, evidence-based comparisons between a large number of recordings: what you were actually comparing was a combination of your notes, remembered impressions, and expectations. Even with the use of current computer-based navigation environments such as Sonic Visualiser, it remains hard to keep track of the large numbers of recordings that exist of any reasonably popular classical work.

In short (and this is the second general point), the close listening approach makes it more or less inevitable that you will work with a small number of representative recordings which you come to know extremely well. But simply to say that is to point out the problem: unless you have done the research, how do you know which recordings are representative, and what they are representative of? The recordings of op. 63 no. 3 that I described in outlining the development of phrase arching were indeed representative, but what they were representative of was a particular development in phrase arching, not the totality of recordings of

---

14. An example is Bryce Morrison, who in 1992 complained of a recording of Rachmaninoff's Piano Concerto no. 3 that the soloist, Yefim Bronfman, 'lacks the sort of angst and urgency which has endeared Rachmaninov to millions', yet when presented with the same recording under Hatto's name, in 1997, acclaimed it as 'among the finest on record.... Everything is vitally alive and freshly considered' (Williams [2007: 74]). In reply to criticism, Morrison replied, not entirely convincingly, that the different tonal qualities of the recording made the effect quite different: 'Bronfman's performance has not been lifted wholesale, but altered to suggest a different quality or calibre' ('Hattogate: Bryce Morrison replies', *Intelligent Life*, http://moreintelligentlife. co.uk/story/hattogate-bryce-morrison-replies).

this mazurka. Given the ideological stakes, it would be desirable to have a fully evidence-based answer to the question of how far performance styles in WAM have converged, but that can only be achieved through the use of distant listening approaches, which would entail the generation of far more data. My study of phrase arching in op. 63 no. 3 would suggest that, in this aspect at least, there has been an expansion rather than a contraction in the range of performance styles. Nancy November (2011) draws similar conclusions from her study of a large number of Beethoven quartet recordings. And in an article specifically focussing on this question, and drawing on statistical analysis of a wide body of repertory, Dorottya Fabian (2006) found little evidence of convergence.

All this doesn't mean that there are not respects in which convergence has taken place: after all, the argument about changing constructions of musical time that I presented in Chapter 4—that a chronometric sense of time replaced a broader conception, within which the chronometric was merely one possibility—would suggest as much. But you cannot adequately support such claims by citing half a dozen examples. Advancing from Philip's first draft of performance history to anything approaching reasonable historical certainty will require a great deal more evidence than is currently available.

PHRASE ARCHING IN CULTURE

This chapter represents only a pilot study. There are a few recordings from the critical period before 1950 that I was unable to source[15]; they might have changed the story. More significantly, the results I obtained for op. 63 no. 3 and op. 17 no. 4 might or might not be replicated in further studies of Chopin's mazurkas, or Chopin's music in other genres, or nineteenth-century piano repertory more generally. And then there is the question of how far piano performance is representative of WAM performance in general. Rather than attempting further reconstruction of performance style history in the absence of adequate evidence, however, my aim in the remainder of the chapter is to extend this initial scoping exercise to issues of the relationship between performance style, as represented by phrase arching, and a range of broader contexts, both within and beyond music.

I have already mentioned the parallels between Riemann's theory of the musical phrase and the practice of phrase arching. Of course Riemann goes back to before the development of the integrated system of phrase arching, at least insofar as it can be deduced from op. 63 no. 3: the *Catechism of Pianoforte Playing*, which I cited earlier, dates from to 1892 (the German original was published in 1888), and Riemann died in 1919, four years before the first recordings in our collection. Given the depth of their penetration into music education in germanophone countries, Riemann's writings may nevertheless have had an influence on the

---

15. Other recordings by Michałowski (1930) and Czerny-Stéfanska (1949), plus recordings by Jan Ekier (1937), Edouard Kilényi (1937), and Mikhail Sheyne (1949). All are listed in Kański (1986: 47).

development of phrase arching. Peres da Costa (2012: 305) draws a link between Riemann and the first unambiguous description of phrase arching I know of, from Walter Gieseking and Carl Leimer's *The Shortest Way to Pianistic Perfection* (1972: 43); the German original dates from the same year that Friedman, Paderewski, and Rosenthal recorded op. 63 no. 3, and the year before Niedzielski's recording. But if Riemann did exert such an influence, then it was rather like Schenker's influence on the development of present-day performance pedagogy: a misinterpretation of his intentions, or an appropriation of his ideas, in either case based on a quite different conception of how music should go.

While on the one hand Riemann gives what looks like a clear description of phrase arching, on the other he prescribes playing in a highly detailed, locally oriented, in a word rhetorical, manner. It was, after all, Riemann who coined the term 'agogic', and he complains that far too little attention has been given to 'explaining the rhythmical nature of a motive (precisely through the "agogic" *nuances*)' (1892: 66). These nuances, he explains, enable 'the plastic development of the small motives'; the degree of lengthening must sometimes be 'very great', in some cases perhaps 50% (77, 65, 66). As for dynamics, he emphasises the need to accentuate single notes 'without disturbing the dynamic and agogic shading answering to the metre', and to distinguish multiple parts 'by a different quality of stroke.... The pianist... must be able not only to render three simultaneous parts audible in different degrees of strength, but he must be able to shade correctly each one for itself without losing their distinction' (78, 84–85). The multiple annotations of some of the score examples in the *Catechism* clearly convey the intricacy of the performance style he had in mind. And given his reputation as a kind of musical Mr Plod—in Allan Evans's words the inventor of 'a system of phrasing that soon became obsolete, for it required the music to conform to its rules rather than conforming itself to the music' (2009: 26)—it is striking that Riemann goes out of his way to prescribe the use of asymmetrical patterns of grouping in order to counter the tendency of phrase structure towards an undesirable regularity. All this warrants William Caplin's description (2002) of Riemann's theory of performance (as well as Lussy's, on which it was partly based) as 'rooted in a Romantic aesthetic of ultra-expressivity' (684). That lends a certain irony to Riemann's justification of his annotations in terms of historical authenticity: he hoped through them 'to prove that neither Beethoven nor Mozart, nor Bach and Händel for that matter, thought and felt in that colorless and thread-bare fashion which people now-a-days are so fond of calling classical repose and simplicity' (Vial 2008: 117). But either way, his conception of how music should go lies at the opposite extreme from the kind of simplicity represented by Czerny-Stefańska's or Neuhaus's recordings. And after all, it is Friedman, in whose highly rhetorical playing there is little evidence of phrase arching, who actually studied with Riemann.

Riemann's aim to revive authentic performance of the classics resonates with Schenker's remarks about the 'infinitely free and colorful' performance of the classics[16]—which adds a further layer of irony, given that Riemann was the principal

16. See above, p. 123.

target of Schenker's attacks on editors who substitute their own phrasing for the composer's and so reduce performance to mechanical execution. But while Schenker's own views on how music should go were no closer to the practices of post-war phrase arching than Riemann's, there is a more abstract level at which a parallel might be drawn between the development of his theory and the emerging performance practice. If op. 63 no. 3 is anything to go by, then the individual elements of phrase arching existed in the 1920s, and probably long before then: we saw them in the tempo arching of Rachmaninoff's recording from 1923, and the dynamic arching of Pachmann's from 1927. The development of phrase arching proper lies in the coordination of these elements within a single system. In the same way, as Joseph Lubben has explained, Schenker's analyses from the early 1920s, as represented in *Der Tonwille*, explore the largely independent operation of structures and parameters, for example the interaction between voice leading, melodic design, motivic organisation, and rhythm: Schenker talks about the 'synthesis' of these elements, but by that he means 'the composer's arbitration of the conflict between these independent tendencies' (Lubben 1995: 25). But by the time of *Der freie Satz*, which was published in 1935, the *Urlinie* has become the controlling factor. The analytical task is now to show how melodic design, motivic organisation, and the rest are conditioned by the *Urlinie*, and 'synthesis' now refers to the incorporation of those elements within the *Urlinie*. The *Urlinie*, in short, has become the core of an integrated expressive system. And this links to the issues of ontology that I mentioned a few pages ago, at least if we accept Adorno's view that performance under the regime of recording presents music as 'already complete from the very first note': in line with the tradition of music as writing, but now in the medium of sonic writing, its primary existence is as a quasi-spatial object. All that applies equally to the *Urlinie*. And it is of a piece with the recrudescence of a range of idealist traditions in post-war Darmstadt, most obviously in the music of Karel Goeyvaerts and Karlheinz Stockhausen. In this way it is possible to draw parallels across theory, composition, and performance.

But perhaps more revealing are the links beyond music. Here I take as my starting point a number of keywords that repeatedly occur not only in the performers' discourse of the time but also in the context of other cultural practices. The idea of the natural has cropped up several times in this chapter. Gieseking and Leimer (1972: 44) follow their description of phrase arching with the remark that such playing 'will correspond to natural musical feeling'; in fact the chapter in which it appears is entitled 'Natural interpretation'. Gornostaeva similarly writes of her teacher at the Moscow Conservatory, where she now teaches, that 'For those who listened to Neuhaus's playing it seemed that there was nothing more natural than his perception of music'.[17] Neuhaus himself invoked the concept. In his pedagogical treatise *The Art of Piano Playing* (1993), he refers to his friend Boris Pasternak's claim that 'Simplicity...is what men most need, but complexity they understand better', adding that 'precisely that which we call "simplicity" because it reminds us of

17. Quoted in the liner note to 'The Art of Henry Neighaus' (Classical Records CR-083).

nature, is in actual fact most complex' (201). At other points he employs a range of naturalistic metaphors: the rhythm of a musical composition, he writes, should be compared 'to such phenomena as pulse, breathing, the waves of the sea, the swaying of a wheat field, etc' (30). Waves come back on the following page, when he criticises choppy, impulsive playing: 'A sequence of uncoordinated moments and convulsive movements brings to mind the catastrophic nature of a seismographic record and not the majestic waves of a calm sea swayed by the wind'.

Nature, waves, coordination: it is all reminiscent not only of the stately oscillation of Neuhaus's phrase arching but also of an essay entitled 'The dancer and nature' by Isadora Duncan, which Matthew Pritchard quotes while outlining some of the new imagery for music that was introduced by German-language music theorists during the first few decades of the twentieth century:

> With the strengthening of the breeze over the seas, the waters form in long undulations. Of all movement which gives us delight and satisfies the soul's sense of movement, that of the waves of the sea seems to me the finest. This great wave movement runs through all Nature.... All free natural movements conform to the law of wave movement.... It is the alternate attraction and resistance of the law of gravity that causes this wave movement'.[18]

It is intriguing that Duncan settled in Moscow in 1921, the year before Neuhaus started teaching at the Conservatory, but not really to the point: ideas like this do not respect national boundaries. I can illustrate this through another of Neuhaus's keywords, simplicity, while moving on a further two years and changing the scene to Paris: 'Simplicity. That was the first thing. A good dress, well designed, beautifully cut, with a single idea in its construction and only such trimming as gave it character...as a rule, the simpler it was, the better. Simplicity of line, perfection of accessories...and those who were superlatively chic had taken another step, adding a bit of personal detail'.[19]

Coco Chanel's couture house remained at the heart of Parisian fashion until the outbreak of the Second World War, and her little black dress epitomises the simplicity that was already present in Rubinstein's recording of op. 63 no. 3 before the war, and that was combined with the long undulations of phrase arching in post-war recordings. ' "Simplicity," ' writes Mary Davis in her 2006 study of music, fashion, and modernism in Paris during the first half of the century, 'became a kind of shorthand for anything that was abstract, concise, and clear' (191), and the features of Chanel's fashion that *Vogue* picked out in this quotation—the single constructive idea and sparse, but telling, personal detail achieved through accessorisation—translate readily to the new simplicity of musical performance. And Chanel's most famous creation prompts Davis (165) to a succession of keywords

---

18. Quoted from 'The dancer and nature' (c. 1905) in Pritchard (2013: 148).

19. Quoted from 'Before and after taking Paris', *Vogue* (New York), 1 November 1924, in Davis (2006: 166–67).

that were equally applied to musical performance: 'the little black dress', she writes, 'offered another route to simplicity in fashion. Undecorated and architectural, it was an intense expression of the emphasis on line and structure in dressmaking that had been Chanel's focus from the outset of her career'. Another parallel between the little black dress and phrase arching is that neither has ever gone out of fashion.

But the most obvious parallel between changing performance style and the domestic environment within which music was increasingly experienced is encapsulated in the juxtaposition of Figures 6.19 and 6.20: two of Osbert Lancaster's drawings from his book *Homes Sweet Homes* (1939),[20] published two months after the outbreak of hostilities and containing blackly humorous references to the air raids to come. From the perspective of the stripped-down modernist decor of the 1930s, given an extended lease of life during the 1940s and 1950s through the 'Utility' furniture and austerity aesthetics of the post-war period, recordings like Friedman's or Rosenthal's must have sounded much the way Figure 6.19 looks: fussy, over-decorated, unstructured. (In the same year Lancaster's book came out, the Romanian critic Aladár Toth compared Friedman's playing to a salesman laying out 'all the silks, the velvets, the lace, and muslin that they have in the store', and added, 'of course one soon tires of the abundance of such formless wealth' [Evans 2009: 172].) There is also something symbolic in the contrast between the wind-up gramophone of Figure 6.19, the flamboyant horn of which forms the focal point of the drawing as well as for the family clustered around it, and the wireless tucked discreetly against the wall in Figure 6.20. In saying all this, I am seeking to place phrase arching within the context of the international modernism that swept across the arts, design, and the built environment in two successive thrusts, before and after the war. The parallels between these two thrusts can be seen particularly clearly in typography, for example in the relationship between Gill Sans (designed in 1926 and commercialised in 1928) and Univers (respectively 1954 and 1957): the values of Figure 6.20 are embodied in the streamlined, sans-serif clarity of each. But architecture allows the fullest comparison with phrase arching.

It was in 1923, the year when Friedman and Rachmaninoff recorded op. 63 no. 3, that the original French edition of Le Corbusier's *Towards a New Architecture* was published. The first illustration in the main part of the book is a photograph of the Garabit Viaduct, a compression arch bridge constructed of wrought iron and designed by Gustave Eiffel; one of the last is an airship hangar in the course of construction, a soaring arch in reinforced concrete (Le Corbusier 1946: 15, 264). Curvilinear forms also characterise Le Corbusier's Chapelle Notre-Dame-du-Haut in Ronchamp, one of the most iconic examples of post-war architectural modernism, the roof of which is a concrete shell: it was under construction when phrase arching in op. 63 no. 3 reached its peak with Neuhaus's recording. But there is more to this comparison than the coincidence of arched shapes in music

---

20. 'Edwardian' (p. 57) and 'Functional' (p. 77).

Figure 6.19 'Edwardian', from Osbert Lancaster's *Homes Sweet Homes* (1939: 57). Used by permission of Clare Hastings

and in building. Le Corbusier (31) justified the basing of architecture on such design elements in terms of both function and perception: 'Architecture', he wrote, 'is the masterly, correct, and magnificent play of masses brought together in light. Our eyes are made to see forms in light.... The essentials of architecture lie in spheres, cones and cylinders'. Accordingly the Pyramids, the Pantheon, and the Pont-Royal 'belong to Architecture', whereas the historicising confections of the Gare d'Orsay or the Grand Palais do not: in short, 'Architecture has nothing to do with the various "styles"' (32–33). This familiar modernist trope is equally characteristic of Adolf Loos and Schoenberg—though it should be noted that

Figure 6.20 'Functional', from Osbert Lancaster's *Homes Sweet Homes* (1939: 77). Used by permission of Clare Hastings

in all three there is an underlying current of classicism that is often overlooked, with classicism being understood as a timeless principle rather than a historical style. And once again the translation into terms of performance is easily made. On the one hand we have the dense referentiality and embeddedness in tradition of rhetorical performance, aligned with the historicising eclecticism of the Gare d'Orsay and Grand Palais; on the other, the simplicity and naturalism—the freedom from historical constraints, the self-evidence—of modernism, whether musical or architectural.

Ironically, however, Le Corbusier and the other European modernist architects were roundly criticised by the American engineer, inventor, and visionary Buckminster Fuller on the grounds that they were themselves no more than stylists. It was in 1955 that Fuller complained, 'The international style's simplification was...but superficial. It peeled off yesterday's exterior embellishment and put on instead formalized novelties of quasi-simplicity'.[21] In short, 'it was still a European garmentation'. Fuller's point, to which Ronchamp forms something

---

21. Buckminster Fuller, 'Influences on my work' (1955), in Fuller (1972, 64). Corbusier is not named, but on the previous page Fuller speaks of the internationalists fortifying their argument

of an exception, was that the European modernists engineered their buildings round the post and beam, design elements that went back to early traditions of timber building. It was not just that post-and-beam construction was inherently unstable, Fuller argued: it reflected the long outmoded 'belief that the earth was flat and infinite—*ergo*, all "straight lines" were open-ended, or infinite'. By contrast, he continued, 'in Nature all the lines are completely curved'.[22] Accordingly, building on the tradition of nineteenth-century engineers like Eugène Viollet-le-Duc and indeed Eiffel, Fuller advocated structures based on curved members in compression and the use of shells, and he applied the same design principles to his Dymaxion houses and cars (one of which was owned by Leopold Stokowski)—as well as his most famous invention, the geodesic dome, with its ability to encompass unprecedented spans.

In these works curved, streamlined forms become the elements of a new design conception that embraced both engineering and aesthetics. And the thinking behind Fuller's designs translates to music through the contrast between the linear organisation of rhetorical performance—in effect a series of accents or spot loads—and the integrated system of phrase arching, in which each event is uniquely positioned within an encompassing, architectonic structure. Whereas Friedman's playing can be understood as a series of expressive moments, phrase arching transferred the locus of expression from the individual moment to a larger temporal envelope, thereby creating an extended span of expectation and realisation. It contributed to the sense, as Adorno put it, of the music being complete from the first note. Just as load was distributed across the structure of a geodesic dome, so the result of phrase arching was to create an expressive stability that was as foreign to rhetorical performance as Fuller's principles were to post-and-beam construction. And, in the tradition of the international modernist aesthetic, the result was in both cases the display rather than the concealment of structure.

My purpose in drawing attention to these parallels is not, of course, to trace paths of putative influence: there is no suggestion that European musicians had heard of Fuller, at that time little known even in America. Within broad aesthetic contexts such as those of interwar and post-war modernism, ideas circulate promiscuously and chaotically, often articulated by fashionable keywords, and meanings accrue as they resonate with one another. I have been trying to suggest some of the resonances that changing styles of performance may have had in the contested circumstances of mid-century modernism. I have in short been interpreting phrase arching as an expression of modernism. Because of the relative literalism of performance today, it is easy to think of all expressive nuance, even phrase arching, as representing a survival from premodern performance. That

'by photographic examples of American silos and factories', evidently a reference to pp. 25–32 of *Towards a New Architecture*.

22. Fuller, 'Later development of my work' (1958), in Fuller (1972, 96). Carl Ruggles had the same thought: in painting, he wrote, 'There shouldn't be any straight lines. It's against nature. Did you ever see straight lines in a bunch of flowers, in the sea, on a mountain?' (Ertan [2009: 238]).

may well be true of specific elements within phrase arching, but it does not appear to be the case of the integrated expressive system that Todd describes. On the contrary: against the background of the antimacassars and knickknacks of Edwardian interiors and the clutter and subjectivity of rhetorical performance, it is easy to see how the new simplicity of post-war phrase arching took on the values of an aesthetic, expressive, and even ethical disciplining of performance. Like modernist interiors, phrase arching discarded unwanted tradition and emotional baggage now perceived as excessive and unhealthy, the result of what—in the context of musical performance—Leech-Wilkinson (2009b: 252) has termed the 'expressive inflation' that occurred during the early twentieth century.

Of course, in music as in the home, what seemed to some listeners like a breath of fresh air presented itself to others as an abandonment of tradition and meaning. For a substantial group of conservative or at least nostalgic commentators, the new simplicity in performance was a symbol of social and cultural decline. Adorno's unfinished book on performance is a treasury of vituperation on this topic, with Toscanini fulfilling the role of red rag to the bull. Among the many laconic references in his notes, there is a reference to 'The dreadful streamline music-making of Toscanini, Wallenstein, Monteux, Horowitz, Heifetz'; the word 'streamline' is in English, and links to an entry two pages earlier that defines 'streamlining' as 'fetishism of smooth functioning without musical sense and construction' (Adorno 2006: 6, 4). A few pages later Adorno speaks of 'the fetishization of reproduction, the senseless Toscanini ideal' (24). And by the time he starts his draft, Toscanini represents a regression to 'the pre-Wagnerian mechanical beating', in which 'a hundred dryly correct details are strung together through the endeavours of a technological temperament to produce escalations and explosions' (196).[23]

The central issue is the one for which Adorno blamed the gramophone: the standardisation that permeates an increasingly administered society. That of course is a complaint that could be made about many of the other manifestations of modernism I have touched on. Davis (2006) writes of the little black dress that 'Chanel proposed standardization and repetition to the extent that not even the color would set one iteration of a design apart from the next' (165). She continues, 'Registering this "assembly-line" approach, *Vogue* likened the dress to the latest developments in the industrial world, describing it as a "Ford signed Chanel"'. One wonders whether they were not also thinking of Ford's famous maxim 'Any customer can have a car painted any colour that he wants so long as it is black', surprisingly enough a genuine quotation—or at least one that Ford ascribed to himself in his autobiography, which was published in 1922, four years before the *Vogue* article (and, incongruously, the year before the Friedman and Rachmaninoff recordings of op. 63 no. 3).

And standardisation is exactly what Rosen (2003: 190) complains about in phrase arching. Curiously, he describes it as a habit that developed in Vienna,

---

23. Adorno enlarges his critique of Toscanini along these lines in his essay 'The mastery of the maestro', written in 1958 (Adorno [1999, 40–53]).

and comments that 'The continuous rise and fall of tempo articulated the music monotonously rather like a string of sausages'. (It is also curious that he expresses this in the past tense.) Rosen characterises it as 'mechanical', which it is, in the sense that it demands no greater analytical or interpretive engagement with the music than the ability to determine where the phrases begin or end (and not even that if you have a *Phrasierungsausgabe*, as Riemann never tired of telling his readers).[24] There is a comparison with vibrato in violin performance, which the oldest generation of violinists to have been recorded—such as Joachim, born in 1831—used selectively to mark expressive highpoints, but which from the generation of Kreisler (born 1875) became a permanent feature of tone production. As Leech-Wilkinson (2009b) puts it, 'A permanent wider and slower vibrato applies now to everything, regardless of the changing musical surface, as if its width and speed could signal feeling in the abstract while its regularity could guard against feeling in the moment' (252–53).

This links to another aspect of Adorno's critique of performance, his attack on 'beautiful tone', but as he does not fully develop it in the notes for his book but refers instead to a 'statement by Rudi [Kolisch]', I shall quote the famous violinist's own, more extended argument. *Beautiful tone*, Kolisch says (and the italics are his), 'is an extra-musical phenomenon in so far as no work of art music was ever written for "beautiful tone". Its exclusive cultivation substitutes a subjective-sensualist, musically indifferent aspect for all dynamic-expressive elements of musical language. Under its aegis, musical reproduction takes place outside of its true task, namely the uncovering of construction, merely as a cult of the beautiful'.[25] Phrase arching could be seen in exactly the same terms, as the masking through sensual attractiveness of a standardised product. Adorno's essential criticism of modernist performance is that it fetishises the virtuoso, who creates an impression of personal expressivity, but in reality fails to engage with the particularities of the musical content; in effect a variant of the principle that Adorno elsewhere calls pseudo-individualisation, this recalls Schenker's earlier views on both virtuosity and the phrasing slur.[26] There is also a comparison with Joachim Hartnack's characterisation of Heifetz's tone: 'the expression of a widely-accepted

24. In his *Phrasierungsausgabe* of Beethoven's sonatas, first published in 1885, Riemann explained that 'This new method of notation is a running commentary, a detailed thematic analysis of the works. It prevents a defective or faulty conception of the same and indicates instead proper expression, doing away with the need for reflection. The author offers the beginner an indispensable relief in working out phrasing' (translated in Harrison [2005, paragraph 20]).

25. Translated from Kolisch's essay 'Über die Krise der Streicher' (1958) in Adorno (2006, 255); Adorno's own critique is on pp. 99–100.

26. In his annotated edition of Bach's 'Chromatic Fantasy and Fugue', published in 1910, Schenker (1984: 69) condemned 'the school of fingering whose adherents, because of ignorance or lack of understanding, prescribe a succession of fingers wholly determined by external criteria', a position that he maintained in subsequent publications. For Schenker as for many of his contemporaries—or for that matter Christiani in his taxonomy of musicians (p. xviii)—'virtuoso' is a term of abuse.

American ideal of beauty, fulfilled in the pure aestheticism from which all impurities, but also all problems have been eliminated'.[27] If the acoustic gramophone in Figure 6.19 at least places the music at stage centre, commanding the listeners' attention, the discreetly sited wireless in Figure 6.20 hints at background music, music as décor, or in the common American phrase, beautiful music.

But whether heard as a breath of fresh air or a symptom of cultural decline, the new musical simplicity takes us onto a well-trodden path in music history. The reaction against subjective interpretation and excessive emotionalism in performance took the form of the literalist ideology of which the strapline was Toscanini's *com'è scritto* (as it is written), and the mission statement Stravinsky's (and others') *Poetics of Music in the Form of Six Lessons*, published in French in 1942, and in English translation five years later. As is well known, the approach to performance set out in the *Poetics* turns on the distinction between execution and interpretation. The first is the strict and faithful realisation of the music itself. The second is its appropriation by the Romantic performer, which lies 'at the root of all the errors, all the sins, all the misunderstandings that interpose themselves between the musical work and the listener and prevent a faithful transmission of its message' (Stravinsky 1947: 122). Despite its ethical or even religious expression (it sounds like something out of a litany), this ideology served a highly pragmatic purpose for Stravinsky: he had lost the rights in his works up to 1917 as a consequence of the Russian Revolution, and therefore had to develop a performing career during the interwar period, specialising in his own music. As the composer, the only person with inside knowledge of the music, Stravinsky could claim an authority which his far more experienced competitors (such as Monteux and Stokowski) could not. It is no accident that the ideas developed in the *Poetics* first appeared in an article published in 1924—just the time when Stravinsky was beginning to forge his career as a performer (White 1979: 574–77).

It is twenty-five years since Richard Taruskin published his famous interpretation of HIP as a variant of Stravinskian modernism, in which he advanced an even more striking claim about the nature of performance in the second half of the twentieth century: 'all truly modernist musical performance', he wrote, 'essentially treats the music performed as if it were composed—or at least performed—by Stravinsky' (1995: 114). The implication is that we should see Stravinsky's recreation of old music for the modern world through his neoclassical compositions as only half of the picture: he did the same in terms of performance. Given the extent to which twentieth-century 'art' musical culture actually meant playing and listening to eighteenth- and nineteenth-century music, this could open up an argument that Stravinsky's greatest impact on the experience of music during the second half of the twentieth century was in terms of performance rather than composition. Without quite saying that, Taruskin lends weight to such an

---

27. Cited in Leech-Wilkinson (2009a: chapter 5, paragraph 23); a line later, Hartnack compares it to 'the chrome and glass of automobiles', which Leech-Wilkinson (n. 39) suspects of being a borrowing from another of Adorno's attacks on Toscanini.

idea when he tells us a few pages later that 'Stravinsky's performance style gained an enormous prestige among progressive musicians in the 1920s and 1930s' (1995: 117). And recent work by Jeanice Brooks has thrown light on some of the processes through which this influence was exerted, as well as the role played in it by Nadia Boulanger.

In the first place, Boulanger shared a number of basic aesthetic values with Stravinsky during this period. We have already encountered many of them in this chapter—nature, simplicity, structure, the timeless—but as Brooks (2013) says, the central ideal 'was often summed up in one of the most potent words in contemporary aesthetic discourse: architecture' (43). There is a letter in which Boulanger writes to Clifford Curzon, 'You are such an inspired = architectural artist', and as Brooks says, 'Curzon's trajectory is in some ways the story of modernist performance encapsulated' (110, 86). In his early twenties he studied with Schnabel and Landowska as well as Boulanger, all of whom urged him to eliminate rubato from his playing, and the result was what the pianist himself described as the difference between 'the old and new Curzon'. In other words, Curzon made a deliberate decision to eliminate rhetorical elements from his playing, and the same may apply to the adoption of phrase arching: it was a style that people could put on in light of changing aesthetic beliefs, rather like Chanel's latest fashion, rather than necessarily being deeply embedded in their training. In Chapter 3 I mentioned Leech-Wilkinson's claim that performers generally acquire their stylistic habits early in life and then stick to them: it follows that scattergrams measuring stylistic characteristics against the performer's date of birth will generally show more interpretable distributions than those based on date of recording. But in the case of phrase arching it is the other way round. A version of Figure 6.18 based on date of birth yields no intelligible pattern.

In the second place, Boulanger clearly played a highly significant role in disseminating Stravinsky's ideas about performance, not so much through her role in coordinating publication of the *Poetics* (she does not seem to have contributed to the actual text), but rather through the extraordinary succession of performers, composers and writers on music who studied with her and went on to high-profile careers and prestigious positions. But in the third place—and this is Brooks's central claim—Boulanger 'performed much more like the Stravinsky of performance myth, created by his writings, than Stravinsky himself' (2013: 116). It is not that she was influenced by Stravinsky's performing style and then became more royalist than the king, plausible as that narrative might be. It is that she was already performing that way, whether because of the French tradition of uninflected performance that Bauer complained about, or because of her specific association with Raoul Pugno, who was her mentor, possibly lover, and certainly co-performer, and who was well known back in the 1890s for a particularly understated—as it were, modern—style of playing.

In short, as much as Boulanger disseminated Stravinsky's message, the association with him aided in the dissemination of hers: Brooks writes of the first performance of *Dumbarton Oaks*, which Stravinsky entrusted to Boulanger's direction, that it 'furnished Boulanger with opportunities to bring the composer's authority to bear on the promotion of the architectural approach she had been advocating all along, using his prestige to lend weight to the expression of her convictions' (2013: 114). And there is a larger message for the history of performance style here. If Brooks is right, then what we need to explain is not so much the creation of new stylistic elements in performance. After all, in terms of the distinction between rhetorical and structuralist (or architectural) time that I outlined at the end of Chapter 4, Pugno-style performance was always an option within the rhetorical style, something approaching a degree zero of temporal inflection. What we need to understand is how stylistic elements take on new meaning within a new aesthetic system. In terms of phrase arching, the question is not so much about its individual components, which probably predate the age of recordings, but how they came to signify within the new expressive system. I hope this chapter has suggested some possible answers.

Brooks refers to the myth of Stravinskian performance style, and it is notorious that, as a performer, Stravinsky did not do what he said. His three recordings of the *Rite of Spring* (1929, 1940, 1960) vary considerably, for example, but in all of them he plays faster or slower than his own tempos, introduces unnotated tempo changes, and even adds *Luftpausen* in the best Romantic tradition.[28] Perhaps then it was not so much a matter of treating music as if performed by Stravinsky, in Taruskin's phrase, but rather performed as Stravinsky said it should be performed. However the situation is a little more complicated than this makes it sound. In the *Poetics*, execution—literal performance of the score—is promulgated as a universally valid principle, in contradistinction to the universally sinful practice of interpretation. But in the *Conversations*, published in 1959, there is a section called 'The performance of music', in which Stravinsky draws a distinction between two musical traditions.

On the one hand, he says, there is the Romantic tradition, which 'depends strongly on mood or interpretation. Unless mood dominates the whole, the parts do not relate, the form is not achieved, detail is not suffused, and the music fails to say what it has to say'; this, Stravinsky adds, means that 'considerable fluctuations in tempo are possible' (Stravinsky and Craft 1959: 118). On those rare occasions when Stravinsky conducted Romantic music—usually because it was incorporated into one of his own compositions, such as the slightly recomposed passages from Tchaikovsky in *The Fairy's Kiss*—Stravinsky adopted a correspondingly Romantic, indeed positively old-fashioned style. On the other hand, Stravinsky continues, there is the 'classic' tradition, which demands execution and not interpretation— and, as if it was not already obvious, he adds, 'I am speaking of my music'. From this it would follow that the passages in the *Rite of Spring* to which Stravinsky brings extensive tempo fluctuation are those that most strongly betray their late Romantic lineage. And Boulanger drew a similar distinction, in practice if not in theory: as Brooks (2013) says, 'Boulanger clearly saw both Schubert and Beethoven as classics and Schumann as a romantic' (88), playing Schumann with greater elasticity.

---

28. For further discussion of *The Rite* see Fink (1999), and of Stravinsky and performance more generally, Cook (2003).

Stravinsky could get away with performing Tchaikovsky-Stravinsky as if the Russian revolution had never happened: perhaps it was as much the period performing style as Tchaikovsky's composition that Stravinsky was recontextualising in *The Fairy's Kiss*. But where did this leave those performers of nineteenth-century music—the core of the concert hall repertory, and the music I have been talking about in this chapter—who felt the need to move with the times, like Curzon, or who were 'suddenly afraid to be called romantic, ashamed of being called sentimental', as Schoenberg (1975: 320) put it in 1948? Ideologies of literalism, such as execution and *come scritto*, were not capable of literal application to such music, for reasons that have become obvious to everybody since the invention of MIDI. It is significant that Gieseking and Leimer's advocacy of phrase arching followed hot on the heels of their insistence that '*absolutely correct execution* of a composition' is the necessary foundation of good performance (1972: 43), for phrase arching squared the circle. It did not entirely eliminate the old expressive codes; even the sense of time being shaped by content survived in a vestigial form. But the elements of expression were regularised and rationalised, relocated from the plane of moment-to-moment succession to that of structure. Expression was no longer a dimension of the performer's subjectivity or a mode of address to the listener. Instead it was a dimension of the music itself. Unlike the old rhetorical pianists—or the gramophone in Figure 6.19—performers no longer buttonholed their audiences, thrusting their presence upon them and so intruding on a private aesthetic experience. And in fact the same might be said of phrase arching itself. Music in films and commercials is experienced less in its own right than through the meaning it invests in the represented narrative or advertiser's message: as Claudia Gorbman (1987) puts it, it is 'unheard'. In the same way, phrase arching is experienced in terms of an expressiveness that is attributed to the music itself. That may explain why there is so little talk about phrase arching until the development of empirical performance studies.

In short, expression remains, but it has been transformed into something objective, *sachlich*. I cite the German word because it gave its name to the *Neue Sachlichkeit*, the movement that swept across the visual arts during the interwar period as a reaction against both expressionism and futurism. More than neo-classicism or the Parisian cult of the chic, it is the *Neue Sachlichkeit* that provided the ideological background for Stravinsky's concept of execution, and for much of the rhetoric that went along with it. But there was a striking difference in the *Neue Sachlichkeit* as between the visual arts and music. In painting, photography, and architecture, the *Neue Sachlichkeit* was little more than a passing fad at a time when isms were succeeding one another with bewildering speed. In music, by contrast, it became installed as an enduring ideology of performance, for decades unquestioned because considered to be self-evident. Eventually the Stravinskian ideology of performance as embodied in the post-war mainstream was challenged by the HIP movement—but, as I said in Chapter 1, that was itself largely based on the same values and assumptions, and in this way a Stravinskian ideology in its own right. As a consequence, these assumptions became internalised to the point that they seemed to be not assumptions at all, but simply the natural way for music to go. Historical performance studies and practice as research have together chipped away at such assumptions, but they remain largely intact. The task of bringing them to consciousness and demonstrating their historical constructedness—the task to which I hope this book will contribute—is far from complete.

7

Playing Somethin'

REFERENTS AND REFERENCE

Musicological and music-theoretical approaches to performance grew out of traditional analytical practices and consequently revolved around the individual musical work, though in practice that usually meant the score. In Chapters 3 and 4, but more specifically in Chapters 5 and 6, I placed increasing emphasis on the production of meaning through performance style, a major axis of which is horizontal rather than vertical: performances create meaning in relation to other performances, and not just in relation to works. This brought a number of approaches into play—in particular empirically based distant listening, which forms a complement to the more traditional approach of close listening.

I want to underline this idea of complementarity, of both-and rather than either-or. Because musicology and aesthetics have traditionally placed such overwhelming emphasis on individual works, there has been an understandable and even justifiable tendency among some commentators to go to the opposite extreme and deny the cultural significance, or even the reality, of the musical work. George Bernard Shaw inverted the standard relationship of works and performers when, in a concert review, he wrote of a pianist whom we have already encountered that 'M Vladimir de Pachmann gave his well-known pantomimic performance, with accompaniments by Chopin' (Schonberg 1965: 313). That was an ironic comment on an individual, notoriously idiosyncratic pianist, but we saw in Chapter 1 that some academic writers have erected the same inversion into a general principle: for Small and Godlovitch the purpose of musical works is to give performers something to play, while for Martin they are fictions that allow us to speak of performances.

As usual, it is a question of steering between Scylla and Charybdis, but to do that you have to recognise Scylla and Charybdis for what they are. Bojan Bujić (1993: 137) speaks of 'composition and notation on the one hand, and performance on the other' as 'two separate phenomena', while David Wright (2012) observes that there are 'two sorts of histories dealing with the same musical culture, one about composers and one about performers and their audiences' (173).

And Peter Johnson speaks of 'the two musics' (1997: 4).[1] If on the one side we have music understood as a pure, temporal process that leaves no residue—what Christopher Small calls musicking rather than music—then on the other we have the approach that identifies music with a textual product, and transforms it from Small's verb into a substantive. This second construal of music might then be represented by the statement attributed to André Pirro that I quoted in Chapter 1 ('I never go to concerts any more. Why listen to music? To read it is enough'), and statements to the same general effect have not infrequently been made by highly trained musicians: 'It's not that I don't want a record player', Pierre Boulez said, 'I don't need it.... I prefer to read a score' (Day 2000: 222).

Figures like Pirro and Boulez symbolise the potential for scores to support an essentially literary culture, being circulated, read, and discussed in much the same way as poems and novels: E. M. Forster (1951) observed that 'Professional critics can listen to a piece as consistently and steadily as if they were reading a chapter in a novel' (126). Of course, this may be a culture of the elite, but then WAM is largely the product of an elite, and so it follows that notation is deeply built into its basic conception. It is not simply a medium for the transmission of music, but part of the music itself. 'This reification through notation', Adorno writes, 'is not *merely* external to the composition..., but rather seeps into it as an aspect in itself, as the frictional coefficient of its externality, so to speak, the resistance that strengthens it' (2006: 140). Pedro Rebelo (2010) puts it more succinctly: 'notation becomes characterized by operations on itself', and in consequence constitutes 'a generative environment' (99). Or you might say that notation shapes music in the act of representing it. However you put it, the point is that the domain of composition involves logics and historical processes that do not necessarily map directly onto the domains of performance or of listener experience, just as performance culture involves oral and aural processes that leave no trace in writing. The one cannot be reduced to the other, and so, in Johnson's words, the idea of the 'two musics... resists hegemonies, whether of composer over performer or vice versa'.

But of course the cultures of music as performance and music as writing are still intimately related, and in order to pass between Scylla and Charybdis we need an understanding of just how they articulate with one another. In this and the next chapter I ask what the idea of a musical work means from the perspective of performance, and more specifically, how scores function in performances: what will emerge from this is a focus on the social dimensions of performance, and— once again—an approach grounded in semiosis rather than reproduction. And my strategy is to begin with performances in which the role of works or scores is at a minimum, in other words with improvisation, a category of musicking that is often invoked in opposition to performance, particularly in the context of the discourses around jazz. Bruce Johnson, who includes the quote from Pirro in his

---

1. Johnson ascribes this notion to me, but the actual term 'two musics' may be found in Barthes (1977: 149), where however it refers to 'the music one listens to' and 'the music one plays'. Barthes continues: 'These two musics are two totally different arts, each with its own history, its own sociology, its own aesthetics, its own erotic'.

contribution to the *Cambridge Companion to Jazz*, does so in order to draw the sharpest possible line between jazz improvisation and classical performance. In line with today's official, institutionalised culture, Johnson insists, WAM is 'ocularcentric': centred on the notated text, it is 'a spectacle of scopic hegemony, the eye engaging with a "product"' (2002: 102). Jazz, by contrast, is 'distinguished from art-music models in the priority of the ear, in collective improvisational performance' (104). In this way it is 'a vehicle for a form of musical socialization, that is peripheral to the tradition of the artist-as-individual, as "soloist"' (106). The approach is riddled with binaries: eye is opposed to ear, compositional product is opposed to improvisational process, individual is opposed to community. And it does not take much knowledge of the role of jazz within the history of American racial politics to understand why this might be the case. Johnson's binaries map directly onto Ben Sidran's opposition of 'literate' and 'oral man', according to which 'the peculiarly "black" approach to rhythm' is linked to the 'inherently communal nature of oral improvisation' (Walser 1999: 298–99). I will argue against this oppositional conception of the relationship between performance and improvisation.

I said I would begin with performances in which the role of works or scores is at a minimum, and the limiting case is free improvisation. This term is used in the contexts of both WAM and jazz, and though its connotations are distinctly different, much the same points can be made of both. Boulez, the archetypal post-war modernist for whom improvisation was an evasion of the real challenges of creative innovation, lampooned the tradition of avant-garde improvisations that developed in the 1950s: at first there would be some excitement, he said, 'and so everybody just made more activity, more activity, louder, louder, louder. Then they were tired so for two minutes you had calm, calm, calm, calm, calm. And then somebody was waking up so they began again, and then they were tired, sooner this time, and so the rest was longer. You cannot call that improvisation' (Oliver 1999: 147). Boulez's point is that while the music may be free in the sense of avoiding overt references to established idioms or predefined musical materials, it will be structured by something, in this case banal patterns of behaviour that are not specifically musical at all. He might have added that a certain gestural lexicon developed in the context of such improvisations, particularly when the improvisers worked with one another regularly. This demonstrates that the concept of 'free' improvisation is in a certain sense self-defeating—the freedom is ultimately illusory, or at least limited—but to say this does not necessarily entail the aesthetic conclusions that Boulez drew. Jared Burrows, whose background as an improvising musician is in jazz, makes the same point, only in a positive light: the process of improvisation, he writes, creates 'its own time-dependent meanings— let's call them short-term archetypes—specific to each improvisation', and groups that frequently perform together develop archetypes that persist from one improvisation to another (2004: 10). Scores and works as traditionally defined may not be involved, then, but 'free' improvisation is both structured and constrained by specific patterns of interaction that emerge in the course of performance.

There is a story that Charles Mingus, who was associated with the free jazz tradition both musically and in terms of his civil rights activism, grew tired of

Timothy Leary's partiality to vacuous spontaneity, and told the ex-Harvard psychologist and guru of psychedelia: 'You can't improvise on nothin', man. You gotta improvise on somethin'.'[2] Scholars of improvisation have repeatedly made the same point. The ethnomusicologist Bruno Nettl almost echoes Mingus's words when he writes that 'One does not simply "sing," but one sings something', and though he is talking about music in general, he specifically applies this principle to improvisation: 'It may be stated as an article of faith that improvisers always have a point of departure, something which they use to improvise' (1983: 40; 1998: 15). And Eric Clarke concludes his discussion (1992) of the cognitive processes involved in improvisation by saying, 'Any performance depends on the performers possessing some representation of the music being played, however small-scale and short-term that representation may be' (794).

In jazz improvisation the clearest illustration of this principle is provided by one of its most canonic forms: jazz standards, in which extensive improvisation is contained with a framework frequently drawn from pre-existing songs, for example by Tin Pan Alley songwriters or from Broadway shows. In structural terms, this framework—the composed element which enables one to speak of the musicians playing 'Summertime' or 'My Funny Valentine'—may consist of no more than the series of chord changes that defines each section. Moreover these chord changes may be voiced very flexibly, to the point of being barely recognisable to listeners who lack a high degree of enculturation. The improvisation may make no discernible reference to the song melody, while on the other hand it will also incorporate elements that are not specific to the standard in question: these may range from references to solos well known from recordings to what Paul Berliner (1994: 102) refers to as the various 'ideas, licks, tricks, pet patterns, crips, clichés, and, in the most functional language, things you can do' that make up the fabric of jazz improvisation.

It was primarily in the context of jazz standards that Jeff Pressing developed his well-known schematic model of improvisation. In his original publication (1988: 160), Pressing illustrated his model through a complex diagram that, in spite of what Clarke (2005a) calls 'the rather intimidating appearance of its formalism', is 'actually not formal enough to be implemented as a testable model' (170). Perhaps then it is best to just describe it. Put simply, it shows how you get from one moment to the next. The basic idea is that an improviser responds to what he or she has just played, so the model relates each event to the previous one. The way this works is that the earlier event is decomposed into a number of distinct aspects or dimensions, and for each of these the improviser can choose, in the next event, to do something similar or something contrasting. As shown in Pressing's diagram, these all feed into a box called the 'array generator', which is where the decision-making process takes place. There is enough sophistication in

2. Barry Kernfeld's use of this quotation at the head of his chapter on jazz improvisation (1995: 119) suggests that the context was a musical one, but it was in fact the shooting of a movie (Coleman and Young [1994: 36]; Santoro [2001: 271]).

the model to account for the various transformational techniques which Berliner (1994: 186ff) terms coupling, fusion, contour crossover, overlap, truncation, substitution, and a kind of permutation of aspects from one motif to another. As Berliner puts it, 'musicians carry over the inflections and ornaments of particular phrases to embellish other phrases', so that 'virtually all aspects can serve as compositional models' (146), and this is exactly what Pressing's model represents.

But that is only part of the model, and my particular concern is with another part, which revolves around what Pressing calls the 'referent'. He defines this as 'an underlying piece-specific guide or scheme used by the musician to facilitate the generation of improvised behaviour', explaining that in jazz 'the referent is the song form, including melody and chords' (1998: 153, 152). As we have seen, the nature of such reference can be extremely flexible, involving the processes that jazz theorists refer to as paraphrase, motivic improvisation, and formulaic improvisation, but in each case reference is being made to some kind of abstract model. This is a completely different process from the protocols for event-to-event progression represented by the first part of the model, and for this reason the referent appears in Pressing's diagram as a separate box linked to the array generator. There is also a further box called 'memory', and this encompasses features that inform performance style beyond the horizon of the individual piece. These range from the personal treasury of 'licks, tricks, pet patterns, crips, clichés . . . and things you can do' that I already mentioned, to shared expectations regarding the nature and temporal shaping of solos, and the 'repertory of compositions, classic solos, and discrete phrases' (Berliner 1994: 493) that represent the jazz tradition as internalised by its practitioners. In this way improvisers refer not only to the piece-specific features in terms of which Pressing defines the referent but also to many features that are not piece-specific, and when I speak of 'reference' I shall intend the term to encompass the totality of these features.

Though set out primarily in terms of jazz standards, Pressing's model is capable of much wider application, and not just in jazz. It can, for example, be applied to the performance of Arcangelo Corelli's Violin Sonatas op. 5, which were first published on 1 January 1700 and exerted a crucial influence on violin music through much of the eighteenth century: indeed there are so many close variants of Corelli's music in the work of other composers, many of them now more or less unknown, that—like Chopin's mazurkas—op. 5 might almost be described as constituting a musical genre rather than just being a set of twelve compositions. Although it appears from contemporary documents that in performance all movements of these sonatas were subject to a variety of elaborations, paraphrases, and other transformations, I am in particular concerned with the slow movements. Corelli notated these in a skeletal form (Figure 7.1) that, if anything, resembled the renaissance-style counterpoint exercises used in the eighteenth century to teach basic principles of composition. And it is in that form, with the addition of an occasional appoggiatura, accacciatura, or mordent, that the twelve sonatas that make up op. 5 were played throughout much of the twentieth century. This kind of note-perfect performance, however, represents a confusion between Johnson's two musics. Corelli's notation represents what John Butt (2002: 117, 120) calls an

Figure 7.1 Corelli, op. 5 no. 5, 1st mvmt. (Pietrasanta, 1700)

'alternative embodiment' of the music, a version intended to be read and then translated into the quite different medium of music as performance. It is like the theatre, where 'the text is refashioned in a gestural, embodied idiom that provides the condition of its potential to signify *as* performance' (Worthen 2003: 56).

We might say that Corelli's notations are less like scores in the conventionally understood sense than like lead sheets, in that—as Bowen says of the latter—a literal performance of the notation 'would barely be considered a performance of the tune at all' (1993: 148). Or at least that is what eighteenth-century musicians would have thought, for these slow movements have also been transmitted in a multitude of contemporary notations put down on paper by players and pedagogues, which show how Corelli's skeletal melodies were transformed through violinistic ornamentation that could vary from the relatively restrained to the wildly flamboyant; sometimes the flamboyance spills over into the graphic representation (Figure 7.2). There is evidence that in the eighteenth century the violone or cello part would have been extemporised, too (Watkin 1996). As for the harmonic support, commonly provided on the harpsichord but sometimes on instruments such as chamber organ or archlute, there is a striking similarity to the practices of jazz voicing. Like other baroque composers, Corelli writes a bass line with figures indicating the harmonies. The chord symbols of jazz are not coupled in the same way with bass lines, but the processes whereby they are translated into performance are in key respects similar.

For instance, as Pressing (1998: 58) explains, a chord symbol like C9(#11) 'triggers a set of constraints on how it may function (its placement in time and register, and in relation to other notes)'. He cautions that 'The precise acts that may be considered consistent with a given chord symbol cannot be exhaustively spelled out, due to the infinite nature of variation'. But he goes on to give some examples: while register is not specified in the chord symbol, he says, there are certain expectations governing what is appropriate, and the same applies to what notes may be doubled or omitted, or to chord inversions. All this applies without modification to the realisation of Corelli's figured bass lines. And if there is not, in principle, so much difference between the practices of figured bass and jazz

Figure 7.2 Corelli, op. 5 no. 5, 1st mvmt., embellished by Johan Helmich Roman (Stockholm, Kungeliga Musikaliska Akademiens Bibliotek, Roman Collection Ms. 97). Used by permission of Musik- och teaterbiblioteket (The Music and Theatre Library of Sweden)

voicing, then in other respects too op. 5 fits Pressing's model with ease. Corelli's score is the referent, the shared framework within which the performers improvise. What they play may stick relatively close to what is written (filling in leaps with scale degrees, adding arpeggiations, and so forth), or it may strip off Corelli's melodic outline and replace it with something quite different. But in either case performers are not simply playing what Corelli wrote, but playing *with* it, or perhaps around or against it.

It might of course be objected that these supposedly improvised transformations of Corelli's scores may in reality have been pre-planned, so that the performers were actually performing pre-composed versions of the music: that is what the multitude of surviving notations suggests, and it is commonly the case today. As Peter Walls (1996) has documented on the basis of recordings, present-day performers no longer play the slow movements as notated in Corelli's 1700 score, but they frequently play them as notated in an embellished edition of the first six sonatas published in 1710 by Estienne Roger and ascribed on the title page to Corelli—an ascription that was controversial at the time, and has remained so ever since. Walls points out that this applies even to those performers who demonstrate, in the remaining op. 5 sonatas, that they have mastered the art of embellishment, and follows this up with the cynical observation that 'The conviction with which violinists can simulate improvisation suggests that—for the most part—spontaneity has always been well rehearsed' (1996: 138). But then, the same phenomenon is by no means unknown in jazz: witness the copyright deposit versions of some of Louis Armstrong's music from the mid-1920s, produced in order to comply with the law's ocularcentric conception of the musical object, which are remarkably close to the improvisations Armstrong recorded two or three years later with the Hot Five (Gushee 1998: 297–98). Written and oral transmission are inextricably linked in the performance cultures of both WAM and jazz—which fits uneasily with Sidran's essentialising distinction between literate and oral man.

But there is one element that is missing, or at least under-emphasised, in Presssing's model. Pressing conveys the image of improvisation being in essence a solo activity (as when he speaks of the referent being 'used by the musician'). Like other, earlier models of jazz improvisation, for example that of Philip Johnson-Laird (1991), he treats it as something that happens in the head of the improviser, rather than something that happens in and arises out of a social context (or the performing body, but I will come to that in Chapters 9 and 10). This individualistic approach perhaps reflects the longstanding association of genius—a concept closely intertwined with that of improvisation—with lone creation in the garret. At all events, just as the traditional model of genius is nowadays giving way to an understanding of creativity as primarily social and performative (as illustrated for example by Hargreaves, Miell, and MacDonald 2011), so in the study of improvisation the focus on the individual musician is giving way to a more social and collaborative approach. As Clarke says, 'the great majority of musical improvisation is an explicitly social activity involving sometimes complex interactions between performers, as well as between performers and audience' (2005a: 173).

The recorded heritage of jazz is full of memorable real-time interactions between improvisers. Consider, for example, the musical repartee in the 1978 recording of Dexter Gordon and Johnny Griffin playing 'Blues up and down' at Carnegie Hall (Younts 2010). The two saxophonists trade related ideas that become more and more tightly interlocked, not unlike the *stretto* section of a baroque fugue, until about ten and a half minutes into the piece Griffin breaks into an easily identifiable version of Irving Berlin's song 'Anything you can do'—or in full, 'Anything you can do I can do better, I can do anything better than you'. This is an extreme example of the kind of intertextual reference of which Berliner spoke, an important role of which—rather like such references in conversation—is social bonding. At the time of writing, this performance of 'Blues up and down' is accessible on YouTube,[3] where Docnolan53 has commented that 'You can feel the comradeship...this is what was called a "Cut Battle" back in the old days. Two great tenors Stating there ground then trading back and forth'.

But the point about the social nature of improvisation does not apply just to such spectacular examples of communal and competitive interaction: it is a much more general one. 'The melodic vocabulary of the improvising jazz soloist', writes Ingrid Monson (1996), 'must always be seen as emerging in a complex dialogue between the soloist and the rhythm section' (114). Wadada Leo Smith expresses the same idea with characteristically idiosyncratic trenchancy: 'most of the "musical analysts" who have allegedly transcribed the solo-lines of the great masters', he says, 'have misrepresented them by not transcribing the whole of the line, but by singling out, instead, only one element of the line. in the evaluation of this music, the opinion has been that the solo-line is the creation of a "soloist," and that the other improvisers involved are mere accompaniment. this is an invalid evaluation' (Walser 1999: 321). And Bruce Johnson (2002) seizes on this as another impermeable division between jazz and 'art' music, proclaiming that 'Continuous collective improvisation is...a vehicle for a form of musical socialization, that is peripheral to the tradition of the artist-as-individual, as "soloist"' (106). Yet when Monson (1996: 84) writes that, in jazz, 'To say that a player "doesn't listen"...is a grave insult', the same applies with no less force to the performers of a Corelli sonata: in either case there is a relationship of mutual dependency and co-creation between the musicians. We enter here on dimensions of musical trust, sometimes shading into personal friendship, to which I shall return in the next chapter.

Admittedly this dimension of interaction is not entirely missing from Pressing's model: he has a box bearing the legend 'Sounds from other players', again linked to the array generator where decisions are made. But the social dimension of improvisation, and of performance in general, is more than the supplement to a primarily individual practice as which Pressing's model represents it. An ensemble is not simply an aggregation of individual musicians. As the free improviser and jazz theorist David Borgo (2005) observes, 'To envision an improvising ensemble as the simple *addition* of individuals...misses the dynamic, interactive,

3. http://www.youtube.com/watch?v=hXvQDsXN3iw.

and emergent qualities of performance' (10). A useful complement to Pressing's model, then, is the model of group creativity proposed by the psychologist, educationalist, and part-time jazz pianist Keith Sawyer (2003: 86–93). As its designation implies, his model—which builds on research in conversation analysis—is intended to be quite general in application. But Sawyer develops it in relation to improv theatre and jazz, and as the model is easier to explain in the largely verbal context of improv theatre, I shall begin there.

Sawyer sets out a scenario in which one actor, Andy, walks to the centre of the stage, pulls up a chair, sits down, and moves his hands as if holding a steering wheel. Bob walks over to him and fishes in his pocket for something. In doing this Bob is working with Andy's cue that he is driving, and he is adding further definition to the implied situation. He could, for instance, have pulled up another chair and sat down next to Andy, so turning himself into a passenger in a car. Instead, his fishing in his pocket suggests that he is looking for change, and therefore that they are in a bus. Each successive action—which may of course include speech— relates coherently to the evolving situation, but at the same time contributes to shaping it in new ways. The central idea is what, following Michael Silverstein, Sawyer calls 'indexical entailment': each action constrains the range of appropriate responses to it, and the series of successive entailments forms the core of the improvisatory process. Of course, if the implications of what one actor does are so constraining that only one response is possible, then the other actor has no freedom to improvise, and for this reason the conventions of improv theatre disallow what is known as 'writing the script in your head'.

As the dialogue continues, the situation develops in directions that could not have been predicted. No individual actor can foresee how the situation will develop because it unfolds from the interaction of individuals. At a given moment in the dialogue there are multiple possibilities for continuation: as Sawyer says, 'a combinatorial explosion quickly results in hundreds of potential performances, branching out from each actor's utterance, and it is this wide range of possible trajectories that results in unpredictable emergence' (2003: 91). The evolving situation (what Sawyer terms 'the emergent'), and the meanings that attach to it, are in this way jointly produced by the actors who collaborate in the performance. And with this explanation we are in a position to understand Sawyer's concise description of what happens in improv theatre:

A performer, constrained by the collectively created emergent, originates an action with some indexical entailment; the other performers, through their responses in subsequent actions, collectively determine the extent to which this act enters the emergent; the new emergent then similarly constrains the subsequent performers. Throughout, the 'meta-constraint' of genre definition controls many properties of this interactional process: how much indexical entailment is considered acceptable [that is where writing the script in your head comes in], how performers' acts are allocated, how performers create acts which retain coherence with the emergent (2003: 89–90).

All this transfers quite directly to the context of musical improvisation. The entailments will now be defined in musical terms: Sawyer refers to 'tone or timbre, mode and scale permitted, rhythmic patterns, specific motifs, stylistic references, and references to other performances or songs' (95). As for the 'meta-constraints', they will reflect such factors as the musical genre (there is improvisation in both bebop and modal jazz, but there are obvious differences between them) and performance context (you might not do the same in Carnegie Hall as you would in a club or school concert). And the resulting model of jazz improvisation is largely compatible with Pressing's: both models are structured around the event-by-event process of decision making,[4] while Sawyer's indexical entailment corresponds to the functions of Pressing's array generator. The major difference is that whereas Pressing's improviser simply reacts to what has just been played, Sawyer's model is driven by a continuously developing emergent that is irreducibly social because jointly produced by the performers (that is why Sawyer called it 'collectively created'). Whereas Pressing's model is framed in terms of a cognitive process taking place within the individual—and in this way exemplifies what Clarke (2005a) refers to as the 'head-bound' (170) perspective of cognitive psychology—Sawyer's approach is based on an ongoing process of cognition that is distributed across all the members of the ensemble. In this book I will not enter into the concept of distributed cognition (Hutchins 1995), but we should note that, in his account of jazz improvisation, Burrows (2004: 2) invokes it in order to explain the 'subtle, web-like interplay' of social and musical relationships that develops in the course of free, collective improvisation—what, in a neat inversion of Jungian language, he terms 'the collective conscious'.

Sawyer's model has another feature in common with Pressing's, which is that it is as applicable to WAM performance as it is to jazz improvisation—or, as I would prefer to say, it helps us to locate the dimensions of improvisation that are inherent in virtually all musical performance. It is, I hope, obvious that it applies to any performance of a movement from Corelli's op. 5 in which the performers are extemporising—provided, of course, that they listen to one another. In fact Sawyer's model might be seen as representing just what it means for musicians to listen to one another. But we don't have to restrict the idea of improvisation to performances that could, as in such a case, be transcribed into staff notation.

Consider the performance of a page from a Mozart quartet (any page, real or imaginary, will do). The musicians play the music as written. Except that, of course, they *don't* play the music as written. The score shows notes that represent the fixed pitches of the chromatic scale, with proportional durations (each crotchet lasts twice as long as a quaver). Dynamics are reduced to a handful of categories ranging from *pianissimo* to *fortissimo* together with crescendo and decrescendo indications, while timbres are represented only through the designation of the instruments, apart from an occasional marking such as *pizzicato*. Tempo

---

4. Like Pressing, Sawyer presents his model graphically, and both diagrams place time on the horizontal axis: compare figure 3.1 in Sawyer (2003: 87) with figure 7.4 in Pressing (1988: 160).

is indicated impressionistically, by means of words that also say something about the general character of the music (*Allegro, Adagio, Andante cantabile*). And so on. But the musicians do not execute the score as a series of instructions, in the way a computer plays a MIDI file. In performance every one of these parameters is given a specific, nuanced value, and the crucial point is that these values are negotiated between the performers. To say that a string quartet plays in tune is to say that the players listen to one another, each accommodating his or her intonation to the others'. Rhythms and tempos are mutually agreed, largely in the course of rehearsal (though as we shall see, what happens in rehearsals is not always what happens in concerts). And the same applies to dynamic balance and timbre.[5] Although all this is happening as it were inside or between the notes in the score, in other words at the level of unnotated nuance, the process of interaction is the same as Sawyer describes, and the result is again a collectively created emergent.

Another way of putting this is that, regarded as specifications of sound, Mozart's string quartet scores are woefully incomplete, just like the scores of Corelli's slow movements. But that is not the right way to see them. Like lead sheets, Mozart's notations define frameworks within which musicians collectively negotiate the fine details of their performance. And these unnotated details are largely responsible for the quality and expressive character of the music as audiences experience it; Bruce Benson writes that 'it is precisely what is *not* to be found in the score that we often most value' (2003: 84–85), and goes on to say that interpretations by Stokowski or Karajan not only sound quite different from those of Hogwood or Pinnock, 'but may well have a radically different *effect* on us—and that effect may well cause us to choose one over the other'. Indeed. But we can develop the point in a more evidence-based way. A recent survey by Alf Gabrielsson and Erik Lindström (2010: 392) of empirical research into emotional expression in music concluded that 'Results seem most clear-cut regarding effects of tempo/speed, intensity/loudness, and timbre/spectrum'. As Leech-Wilkinson (2012: paragraph 3.2) comments, all of these are 'matters in which performance crucially determines effect'. Conversely, he continues, quoting from Gabrielsson and Lindström's study, ' "Results regarding pitch seem more ambiguous": the effect of pitches and harmonies seem to be easily inflected by tempo and loudness'. In short, contrary to the working assumptions of most critical writing on music, emotional expression appears to have more to do with what performers do than with what composers do. And that adds a further dimension to the claim that, as representations of what performers do or listeners experience, scores are drastically incomplete. This is what lies behind Robert Martin's bold suggestion that 'musical works, in the listener's world, simply do not exist' (1993: 123). His argument is that what composers write are not works but sets of instructions. Instructions can only go so far, however, and therefore 'performers collaborate with composers in the creation of performances' (122). And it is as performances that 'musical works...enter in the world of musical listeners' (124).

---

5. For an overview of empirical research in this area see Keller (forthcoming).

To summarise, composers provide a highly worked out, and often hermeneutically suggestive, framework; performers add the specific sonorous content that conditions listeners' experiences, even to the extent of eliciting their emotional responses. What in the world of listeners—and also of critics and musicologists, who after all are listeners too—we call musical works are the product of this process of collaboration between composers and performers, and indeed critics and musicologists. Moreover, as a result of the enduring qualities of scores, such collaborations can extend over centuries, during which time works accrue new meanings, as well as losing old ones: Beethoven's Ninth Symphony does not mean in 2012 what it meant in 1824, in terms of either auditory experience or social, cultural, and political connotations. This is a plausible way of thinking of the relationship between works and performances. It is what Patrik Juslin (2003) assumes when he claims that 'The ultimate goal of research on expression in music performance is to understand what, exactly, the performer "adds" to a written piece of music' (280). It is implied by the way Amazon list recordings (Franz Schubert and Murray Perahia, Frédéric Chopin and Artur Rubinstein). But for all that, there is something wrong in this image of performers finishing off what the composer left unfinished, filling in the gaps inside or between the notes. And it is something that goes to the heart of what happens in the real time of performance.

Performances do not simply reproduce scores, but neither do they simply fill them out. In a sense, to repeat Butt's term, all scores are alternative embodiments. Just as a pianist may understand the musical point made by one of Beethoven's marked fingerings, and then substitute her own, so the violinist playing one of his quartets will substitute just this F# at just this time—that is, *her own* F#—for the generic F# that appears in the score. One might say that, in taking possession of the music and making it their own, performers erase the score, and this thought has been expressed in various ways. In the notes for his book on musical reproduction, Adorno says that improvisation must lie at the heart of his theory of performance, and that it entails 'the *undoing* of reification through the musical sense that suspends the text'; elsewhere he writes that 'true interpretation *reverses* the notation' (2006: 87, 140). Alfred Schutz (1964: 169) concurs: the notes in the score belong to the prehistory of the performance, he says, being superseded in the act of making music. Monson observes that 'At the moment of performance, jazz improvisation quite simply has nothing in common with a text (or its musical equivalent, the score)'. And again her point extends far beyond the boundaries of jazz; to repeat what I said earlier, it helps us locate the dimensions of improvisation that are inherent in all musical performance. So it applies to Furtwängler (1977: 51, 36), for whom all performance was 'subject to the law of improvisation', and who saw it as essential that the performer should 're-experience and re-live the music each time anew'. Indeed it applies beyond music. As Anthony Frost and Ralph Yarrow say in the context of theatrical performance, 'It does not matter that the play has been rehearsed for a month, with every move, every nuance of speech learned and practised. In that act of performance the actor becomes an improviser' (2007: 1). There is a sense in which, in the real time of performance, everything is always being done for the first time.

The relationship between what is rehearsed and what is performed is the focus of an ethnographic study that Frederick Seddon and Michele Biasutti (2009) carried out in collaboration with the Paul Klee String Quartet. The starting point of this research was previous work by Seddon in which 'musicians describe how they listen to recordings they have made and hear themselves playing phrases they have never previously practised but that have emerged as a result of what other musicians were playing at the time' (2009: 398). That is exactly what members of the Klee Quartet said: the second violinist, for example, commented that when in performance one member of quartet plays a note unexpectedly softly, 'the other members understand his intentions and they follow him because some different things are coming out and many times are more interesting than what we did during the rehearsal' (409). At such times, Seddon and Biasutti (407) report, 'the musicians seemed to respond to each other in an atmosphere of risk taking and challenge that extended their joint creativity. They took risks with musical phrasing, timing and dynamics, and in so doing they challenged each other's musical creativity'. And again the musicians' comments bear this out: as the cellist says, 'the risks are high...you are aware that there is a risk but it is a risk that gives great joy because in that moment you are really making music'. When that happens, he adds, 'the quartet is no longer four individuals with their own individualities, their own personalities, their own knowledge: it is only a unique energy'.

All of this, then, fleshes out Borgo's reference to the 'the dynamic, interactive, and emergent qualities of performance' that make an ensemble something other than an aggregation of individuals, as well as illustrating Sawyer's emergent in action. And what gives the Seddon and Biasutti study particular relevance in this context is that it is a follow-up to a similar study of a jazz sextet. There were obvious differences: unlike the jazz musicians, the quartet were playing from scores, and as the authors write, you might expect this to severely limit the kind of interactions that could take place and the resulting emergent qualities of the performance. But that is not what they found. In essence, Seddon and Biasutti say, the processes of creative interaction in jazz and classical performance are identical. Even though they were playing the notes in front of them, 'the classical musicians in the current study were able to collectively create "spontaneous musical variations" while empathetically attuned during the concert performance' (411). They played things they did not expect to play, and perhaps did not know they could play. That is, they were improvising.

THE WORK AS PERFORMANCE

Small wonder then that, across the twentieth century and into the twenty-first, writers from musicology, jazz studies, sociology, and philosophy have insisted that improvisation is an irreducible dimension of WAM performance, or of performance in general. In an essay first published in 1951, Alfred Schutz (1964: 177) specifically spelled out the essential continuity of performance practice across jazz and WAM: 'there is no difference in principle between the performance of a string quartet and the improvisations at a jam session of accomplished jazz players'. (The parallel would have been closer if he had referred to an established jazz ensemble used to performing together, rather than a jam session.) Writing almost half a century later, Ed Sarath concurs: 'even interpretive performance of repertory', he writes, 'might be considered as a species of improvisation. For even in works entirely composed, performers will have some degree of creative options through volume dynamics, inflection, tempo, frequency of vibrato and other expressive nuances' (1996: 21). And though he is approaching improvisation primarily from the perspective of jazz, he adds that classical performers 'deconstruct personal interpretive patterns in seeking spontaneous renditions of pieces they have already played countless times'.

Again, for Carol Gould and Kenneth Keaton (2000), 'jazz and classical performers alike interpret their pieces and improvise in doing so' (143). Richard Cochrane (2000: 140) generalises the point ('The practice of improvisation in fact exists in all musical performances except those carried out solely by machines'), and in so doing echoes what Paul Bekker (1922: 300) said nearly eighty years earlier: 'The art of musical performance is in its origin and essence an art of improvisation'. (Furtwängler would have concurred.) Finally, in *The Improvisation of Musical Dialogue* (2003), Bruce Benson—in the words of the publisher's blurb—'argues for the innovative thesis that composers, performers, and even listeners are more properly seen as "improvisers"'. If the thesis still seems innovative, despite having been argued so many times before, the reason is the deep-seated prejudices, drawing on sources that range from textualism to racism, that have prevented it from taking root. As Benson (2003: 3) says, 'The claim that music is fundamentally improvisatory is hardly intuitively obvious. Rather, it may well seem simply untrue. But I think the reason we are reluctant to accept such a characterization stems more from the way in which we happen to think about music than from actual musical practice'.

After his comment on the differences between Stokowski, Karajan, Hogwood, and Pinnock, Benson poses a question: 'If performers cannot help but be improvisers, then where exactly are the limits of this improvisation to be drawn?' (2003: 85). The limits applicable to the performers of whatever Mozart string quartet you imagined are clearly different in many ways from those applicable to a jazz standard, but what makes them seem *categorically* different is not that they are less pervasive: it is that they are not captured by staff notation. The social interactions I have been talking about, and the audible nuances to which they give rise, do not register on the scale of aesthetic theory based on textualist assumptions about works and their identity. Yet while we may be able to see the potential for a certain narrative of interpersonal transactions in a score, it is only in performance that this potential is transformed into reality. Similarly it is performance that engenders distinctive sound qualities, conditions emotional responses, keeps us listening to the same music even when we know it backwards—because of course, in performance, it *isn't* the same music. But all this passes under the radar of textualist approaches predicated on the paradigm of reproduction.

Though he is coming at it from an unfamiliar direction, Benson is posing the familiar question of the relationship between works and performances, which—as we saw in Chapter 1—aestheticians have generally addressed from the perspective of ontology. The basic approach is to define the work in terms of compliance classes underpinned at some level by notation, and on the basis of that to consider what performances might or might not be considered as proper performances of that work. This approach echoes the page-to-stage approach discussed in Chapter 2 in both its own-way quality—from work to performance—and its fundamentally prescriptive conception. More productive for an understanding of music as performance, however, is an approach that works in the opposite direction, and in what follows I begin with performances—or at least representations of performances—and ask to what extent and in what way the idea of the musical work is entailed by them, and to the extent that it is, in what way it might be defined. My focus then is on what I called the work as performance, and my aim is descriptive rather than prescriptive. I conclude that, as enacted in the practice of performance, the musical work is an irreducibly social construct.

As I mentioned, in addition to Corelli's 1700 edition, and the 1710 edition that may or may not be Corelli's work, the op. 5 sonatas exist in innumerable notated versions. Most of these consist of written-out embellishments, in the manner of Figure 7.2. It is sometimes hard to be sure what they were intended for, but many of them are presumably traces of the carefully rehearsed spontaneity Walls spoke of—in other words, violinists working out their own personal performing versions. Others may have been intended as models to be copied by beginners, that is, designed for pedagogical purposes. Conceivably some represent attempts to capture a particular violinist's embellishments (Butt [2002: 117] suggests that the 1710 version may be an attempt to capture Corelli's own ornamentation). But it is not just the slow movements, which Corelli notated in skeletal form, that appear in multiple versions. There are recompositions of faster movements where Corelli's original is capable of relatively literal performance, such as those of Francesco Geminiani. His version of the second movement from op. 5 no. 9, for example, replaces Corelli's running quavers with more rhythmically inflected patterns consisting of crotchets and quavers, and consequently ends up with fewer notes than the original.

And what is the purpose of all this? I cannot improve on Hans Joachim Marx's 1975 evocation, in this context, of 'the thrill of the new, the not yet experienced, which [the eighteenth-century listener] expected even from a performance of older music' (67). Perhaps the same applies to the 'Dissertazioni del Francesco Veracini sopra l'Opera Quinta del Corelli', as the original manuscript is headed, a recomposition of all twelve sonatas from op. 5 which remained unpublished until recent times. Veracini's recomposition extends to structure—Corelli's materials are omitted, replaced, repeated, resequenced—and sometimes tightens up Corelli's relatively loose forms, giving them a coherence that is less impressionistic and more systematic than the original. (There are times, however, when it works

the other way round: Corelli writes a tightly organised movement, so Veracini
loosens it up.) And libraries are full of similar but more fragmentary manuscripts
that are probably the traces of studies in composition, exercises in the reshaping of
familiar materials.[6] Like the arrangements in the Hofmeister *Monatsberichte* that
I mentioned in Chapter 4, these are the multifarious traces of period remixing,
Lessig's RW culture.

Will the real op. 5 please stand up? Corelli's op. 5 lends weight to Aaron Ridley's
stern injunctions about the unproductive ontological fixation of philosophical
approaches to works and performances, for it proves impossible to provide a specifically musical explanation of what makes these notations variants of Corelli's
composition rather than separate works in their own right. The most straightforward way to ground work identity in musical specifics is represented by Nelson
Goodman's *Languages of Art* (1968), according to which a performance is a performance of a work only if it corresponds precisely to those elements of a score
that are capable of precise definition. It follows that a performance of Mozart's
Sonata K 332 that contains a wrong note is not a performance of K 332—whereas
a performance so slow that it lasts four hours is, since Mozart did not precisely
define the tempo. But we know that in historical terms, at least, simply playing
the notes of an op. 5 slow movement from Corelli's 1700 is a travesty, just as in
the case of a lead sheet. Or it would be like staging a four-hour performance of
a Shakespeare play based on a Folio text, ignoring the evidence that these texts
circulated and were read as literature, with abridged versions being made for stage
productions (Erne 2003). Literalism has very little place in performance.

Whereas musicians and musicologists have never succeeded in taking
Goodman's approach seriously, however, it might seem possible to reframe it in
more musically plausible terms. One of the music examples in Johann Joachim
Quantz's famous treatise on flute playing, published in 1752, is an *Adagio* with
written-out embellishments and dynamic indications. In his analytical study of
this *Adagio*, Stephen Hefling (1987) seeks to show how the embellishments project the voice leading structure, very much in the way that page-to-stage theorists
approach performance—and indeed Hefling is treating Quantz's example as the
graphic representation of a performance. As usual with this kind of writing, he
finds what he is looking for: 'the correlation between Quantz's ornamentation
and dynamics and the linear analysis of his piece is too striking to be dismissed',
Hefling concludes (217). On this basis you might expect all the variants of a particular movement from op. 5 to constitute alternative foreground elaborations
of a single middleground that can be extracted from Corelli's original notation,
which we would then see as defining the work's identity. That would set the limits
Benson was asking for, and it would do so in purely musical terms. But in practice
analysis of variants sometimes results in different middlegrounds—and sometimes these middlegrounds seem to have nothing to do with Corelli's original,
other than that they fit with his bass line. When this happens you can, of course,

6. For more extensive discussion see Cook (1999c).

retreat to a more remote middleground, looking for the communality between the variants at a still deeper level. The trouble is that by the time you have done that, you may be left with linear-harmonic patterns so basic, or archetypal, that they are shared by any number of pieces: it is like the idea that Schenkerian analysis reduces all music to 'Three blind mice'.[7] Purely musical analysis, in other words, provides no convincing reason for seeing these variants as variants at all; instead, it might equally well suggest that what we call op. 5 is actually made up of any number of separate musical works. Like Goodman's approach to work identity, it creates a theoretical reality that contradicts real-world cultural practice and is equally hard to take seriously.

The problem lies in the assumption that there must be some essential feature or structure, or set of features and structures, that identifies the musical work and distinguishes it from all other musical works. If we abandon that assumption, common sense returns. We might, for example, think of op. 5 in terms of Wittgenstein's family resemblances: not all members of a family will share Uncle Edwin's nose, but some will, and those who don't will share other features such as Aunt Alice's chin—so that looked at in the round, we can see everyone is related. (This is the conclusion at which Benson [2003: 159] arrives, via a quite different route that sees him jettison the baggage-laden term 'work' in favour of 'piece'.) Or again, we might think in terms of what Lawrence Zbikowski (2002) calls 'typicality effects'. There are various attributes that birds generally have (they have feathers, they fly, and so on), but not all birds have all these attributes, which means that some birds are more typical of the category than others: people 'view robins and sparrows as the best examples of birds', says Zbikowski (38), with 'ostriches, emus, and penguins among the worst examples'. In either case, the point is one that Charles Seeger (1977: 316) made in his study of the variants of 'Barbara Allen': 'no such entity as *the* 'Barbara Allen' tune" can be set up other than for temporary convenience.... Melodies are, by their very nature, infinitely changeable or interchangeable'. Or as Barbara Herrnstein Smith (1980) said of the 'Cinderella' story: 'For any particular narrative, there is no single *basically* basic story subsisting beneath it but, rather, an unlimited number of other narratives that can be *constructed* in response *to it or* perceived as related *to it*' (221).

All this applies straightforwardly to op. 5. Some variants are highly typical, which is to say that they incorporate the most recognisable signifiers of the tradition of writing and playing that is op. 5—and whereas those signifiers might relate to what in Hefling's terms would be seen as more structural features, then again, they might not. Others are less typical, lying at the margins of what can be reasonably identified as op. 5 (that would apply to Veracini's 'Dissertazioni'). But there is no *really* real op. 5 to stand up, because op. 5 is a tradition of writing and playing—and indeed listening—that is embodied in an indefinite number of variants whose only common feature is that they are, and presumably always were, intended and heard as variants of op. 5. And what this means is that, as enacted

---

7. I present this argument in greater detail in Cook (1999c: 201–9).

in performance, op. 5 is a social construct, a product of historical contingency, and as such incapable of strict definition in terms of either structural analysis or textualist aesthetics.

This is a principle that applies as much to genres as it does to works—the distinction between work and genre is itself socially constructed—as well as to looser concepts such as tradition (Volioti 2011). That is why, as researchers in music information retrieval increasingly recognise, you cannot satisfactorily reduce genre categories to stylistic algorithms (Craft 2012). It is also what Kallberg was talking about when he said the meaning of the mazurka cannot be reduced to 'the inherent characteristics of the music alone'. The fact that cultural categories are socially constructed does not, of course, mean that the relationship between them and their notational or auditory signifiers is simply arbitrary. You cannot hear just anything as Corelli's op. 5. There must be at least *some* signifiers of work identity to afford the hearing of a performance as a performance of op. 5, and in most cases, there will be many. But even then, an act of interpretation is involved: listening is subject to a high degree of cultural mediation. As Daniel Miller (1987) says of material culture, 'Societies have an extraordinary capacity either to consider objects as having attributes which may not appear as evident to outsiders, or else to ignore attributes which would have appeared to those same outsiders as being inextricably part of that object' (109). The same applies to music as performance.

The world of Corelli's op. 5, as I have described it, is then significantly out of kilter not only with the approaches to the musical work that are still dominant within music aesthetics, but also with the textualist and structuralist values of which those approaches are an expression. This is most obvious in terms of the openness of the work concept as represented by op. 5. On the one hand we cannot rationalise the limits of acceptable improvisation—as Benson put it—in terms of musical specifics: there is always one more version to be found. On the other, the distinction between what is and is not op. 5 becomes highly permeable. Within Corelli's output, elements of op. 5 blur into what Christopher Wintle (1982) called the 'tonal models' common to any number of his compositions, while recomposed versions of op. 5 blur into independent compositions. (That is why I said op. 5 was in some ways more like a genre than a set of compositions.) And if you cannot say where one work stops and another starts, then you cannot apply the idea of plagiarism, which—because it is the reverse side of the assumption that any art work is the product of authorial originality—is arguably as central to modernist aesthetic theory as it is to copyright law. Without barriers to its proliferation, op. 5 takes the form of loose assemblage of parallel versions, like 'Barbara Allen' or 'Cinderella'—an assemblage that is enmeshed in an equally unstructured tradition of interpretation and connotation, and that might be said to have a centre but no clearly demarcated boundaries. Corelli's published score of 1700 clearly has a privileged role within this assemblage—it might be thought of as the centre of a gravitational field—but the extent to which it anchors or regulates the work complex should not be over-stated. The composer's score is after all, as Martin said, just a set of instructions, and in the case of op. 5 an exceptionally incomplete set of instructions at that.

It would be possible to argue that Corelli's op. 5 is an extreme example of what is in reality the normal condition for musical works within the WAM tradition: Kallberg (1996: chapter 7), for example, has explored the implications for the concept of the musical work of the plurality of authorised, and unauthorised, versions in which Chopin's music exists. But that is not the reason I have discussed op. 5 at such length. I have done so on the same assumption that underlies Hefling's discussion of Quantz's *Adagio*, namely that an embellished notation represents a performance. Of course, as I have been at pains to emphasise in this book, notations of whatever kind cannot stand in for performances in any straightforward way: not only do they fail to capture many of the most salient aspects of performance, but the nature of a representation crucially depends on its purpose, and the purposes of the notations of op. 5 are often unclear. Yet the totality of the notations still discloses, in visible form, something of the topography and dynamics of the musical work as performance. The aesthetic, or perhaps I should say counter-aesthetic, values I have described are abnormal in the context of music as writing, but normal in the context of music as performance.

To put it another way, in the course of the nineteenth and twentieth centuries music as writing came to be regulated by the modernist ideologies embodied in what Adorno would call 'official' music aesthetics (this is the story that Lydia Goehr tells). But as I said, orality is an irreducible dimension of music as performance: it is no accident that I likened to it to 'Barbara Allen' and 'Cinderella', both primarily oral traditions. And as such, music in performance is not regulated in the same way or to the same extent as written music. It might be said that 'official' music aesthetics, especially in its ontological vein, is an attempt to regulate performance in line with the ideology of music as writing, but if so its success is limited. Even if a combination of recording technology, textualist ideology, and modernist institutionalisation has pulled music as performance into increasingly close alignment with music as writing, it remains the case that—as many interdisciplinary performance theorists maintain—performance resists ideology. And my claim is that this is much more the case of performance within the WAM tradition than its bureaucratic ethos and dependence on written documentation make it appear. In Sidran's terms, it remains an enclave of irreducibly oral culture within the heartlands of literacy.

Because of the continuing influence of textualist or more generally ocular-centric thinking, aestheticians, musicologists, and music psychologists have rarely theorised the musical work as performance, or indeed recognised that any such thing might exist, instead taking it to be in essence an acoustical reflection of the musical work as construed in terms of notation. In other words they have conflated the two musics. This has given rise to concepts of musical cognition that owe more to reading than to listening, and that are then expressed in thinking about performance. I have referred several times to the idea that performance is a stage within the process of communication from composer to listener. As Caroline Palmer (1997: 118–19) says, citing Roger Kendall and Edward Carterette, 'Music performance is often viewed as part of a system of communication in which composers code musical ideas in notation, performers recode from the notation to acoustic signal, and listeners recode from the acoustical signal to ideas'. And while such approaches leapfrog the 'middleman interpreter', to borrow Adorno's phrase again, the same pattern is replicated in Patrik Juslin's 'lens' model of the expression of emotion in performance: the performer intends to express anger, this is encoded within a particular weighting of expressive cues (in tempo, loudness, timbre and so on), and the cues are decoded by the listener to give rise to the percept of anger (Juslin and Timmers 2010: 472). Whereas a basic problem of such models, as I see it, is that they do not allow for the qualities of negotiation and emergence that are crucial to the understanding of performance, I am here more concerned with the underlying conception on which they are built: that music starts as a mental representation in the composer's head, and ends as an ideally identical mental representation in the listener's head. Put that together with the convergence between music psychologists and theorists that took place during the last decades of the twentieth century, based as I said in Chapter 1 on the assumption that such representations are to be found in music theory, and you end up with a conception of music as a kind of writing in people's heads.

Translated into academic language, the one-sentence summary is that perception is a process of cognitive reconstruction. This is what Eric Clarke calls the 'information-processing' paradigm that has dominated work on music perception since the 1970s, and here we come to one of the main ways psychological approaches to music have developed since that time. As Clarke (2005b) explains, the information-processing approach is based on the assumption that 'structure is not in the environment: it is imposed on an unordered or highly complex world by perceivers' (12). But, he continues, there are obvious problems with this approach. The whole idea of a mental representation is conjectural (you cannot observe mental representations, only infer them), and results in a highly complex theoretical model. 'Rather than making use of the structure that is already out there in the environment', Clarke says, 'the outside world is needlessly and endlessly internalized and duplicated' (15).

As the terms of his critique suggest, Clarke's preferred way out of these problems lies in the adoption, or adaptation, of James Gibson's ecological approach to perception. I will pursue a more circuitous route that heads in the same direction, like the old road running alongside the motorway. But Clarke provides a good starting point. An article of his from 1995 contains one of the few invocations within the empirical performance literature of a semiotic approach. Referring to HIP, Clarke remarks that 'a whole performance ideology may be connoted by one or two local performance features' (1995: 28): there are characteristic patterns of timing, dynamic change and non-vibrato that immediately locate a performance within that tradition. He then goes on to apply the same principle to structure. In Chopin's Prélude op. 28 no. 4, for example, he identifies two distinct interpretive strategies, one of which is to play the piece as two matching halves, and the other to play it as a single, prolonged gesture held together by the descent of the fundamental line. And just as in the case of HIP, you can reference one or the other interpretation by particular treatment of a few key points in the music (the handling of bars 12–13 will obviously be particularly critical).

It is worth spelling out what is at issue here. A conventional information-processing approach would assume that a performer starts off with one or other of these representations, and would then chart the processes through which the performer attempts to induce the same representation in the listener. This means understanding all aspects of the performance as shaped by the analytical interpretation; it is as if the piece had never been played or heard before, so that the representation has to be specified exhaustively, built up stage by stage from scratch. In contrast, the semiotic model short-circuits the information-processing hierarchy; it seeks out the minimal cues required to reference one interpretation or the other. An analogy may help to underline the difference. There are several styles of Chinese calligraphy, of which the 'official' and 'regular' scripts are the most explicit: every stroke within the character is shown separately. But most Chinese calligraphy does not take this form. Instead it uses a 'cursive' script, in which some strokes are run together and others omitted. That is to say that cursive scripts adopt a series of shortcuts, conventions of abbreviation that are arbitrary and hence specific to particular times and places. They rely on readers' knowledge of these conventions. Official and regular scripts, with everything explicitly spelled out, are the equivalent of the structural hierarchies modelled by music theory, and the information-processing models of performance and perception that are based on them. By contrast, cursive scripts provide a parallel to the performance of op. 28 no. 4 that Clarke describes, which does not set out to reproduce the structure literally or exhaustively. Instead, it is based on a system of abbreviations and cues, and this contributes to the irreducibly historical dimension of performance—and indeed of listening—that we call style. The one-sentence summary of *that* is that performers do not reproduce structure: rather they reference or signify it.

There are some other consequences of thinking of perception as a process of cognitive reconstruction that I will describe in less detail. In a listing of prevalent misconceptions about performance, Mine Doğantan-Dack (2008) refers to 'the idea that the performer's interpretive activity concerns local details rather than large-scale structural relationships of a piece of music' (305). And by way of example she cites the suggestion I made some years ago that 'large-scale structure is to a high degree hard-wired into music as composed, and that the performer's ability to generate musical meaning depends much more on the handling of details' (Cook 2007a: 189); similarly Leong and Korevaar (2005: paragraph 12) have speculated that 'perhaps background structure is robust', explaining that 'it is expressed in all but the most idiosyncratic performances, whereas the existence of more surface-level structures depends to some extent on how they are or are not performed'. Against such ideas Doğantan-Dack argues that if large-scale structure was hard-wired, then it 'would always be identified in the same way by different analysts'. That doesn't necessarily follow; the elements of an architectural façade are fixed, yet the design may be multiply interpretable. Nor would all performers agree with Doğantan-Dack. The pianist and teacher Alexandra Pierce, whose distinctive pedagogy blends Schenker and Dalcroze, refers to performers as 'specialists in the foreground' (1994: 117). Steven Schick (1994: 145) writes with reference to Brian Ferneyhough's *Bone Alphabet* that 'I have never worried much about projecting large-scale form. I believe—and this usually works out—that if I am very careful to render the extreme microlevel of rhythm and texture with fully fleshed-out structure and personality, the larger issues take care of themselves'.

I cannot resolve the controversy, but I think the distinction between reproduction and signification that I am now proposing helps to clarify what is at issue. According to Leech-Wilkinson (2012: paragraph 4.9), 'Performers seem to outline structures, and feel that they are, but in fact all they are doing is working from moment to moment while keeping a sense of longer-term intensity modulation: a little more here, a little less there, and so on'. (It might be more tactful to replace 'all' by 'what'.) After all, it is hard to see how there could be any direct correlate in performance to an analytical beam that lasts across fifty or a hundred bars—except perhaps through something like the huge accelerandi and arch-shaped profiles of Furtwängler's performances of Beethoven symphonies, but such examples are rare. In other words, it is hard to see how a performer might reproduce such an analytical construct, in the way phrase arching might be seen as reproducing the kind of analytical slur used in Riemann's *Phrasierungsausgaben* by mapping it onto the parameters of tempo and intensity. To the extent that performers intervene in large-scale form, then, the key mechanism must be a form of signification rather than reproduction, as illustrated by the kind of cue that Clarke described in the performance Chopin's op. 28 no. 4— which was after all an intervention in overall structure, though admittedly op. 28 no. 4 is a miniature.

But I would still maintain that large-scale structure may not be the most productive place to look for the emergence of musical meaning, in terms of performance or indeed more generally. Citing evidence that listeners do not directly perceive the large-scale tonal structures that occupy so prominent a place in score-based theory, Leech-Wilkinson (2012: paragraph 4.11) argues that 'to make structures of the sort discovered by music theory a principal focus for performance is misguided, attending to an aspect of music that is not of great import for listeners, nor amenable to perceptible expressivity nor thus to the making of musical meaning'. That is why, in this book, I focus predominantly on rather short musical passages, often from what in standard theoretical terms would be seen as rather simple pieces of music: it is in such contexts that the distinctive creative contributions of performers stand out most clearly. And it is at least arguable that the feeling many performers undoubtedly have that they must justify themselves in terms of large-scale structural interpretation derives less from the actual exigencies of performance than from pressures of aesthetic ideology—and specifically, an ideology based on the reconstruction of large-scale form conceived in the textualist terms of music theory. That in turn raises the broader question of whether, for performers who wish to seek recognition within the academic culture of practice as research, it is better to argue that performance fulfils criteria for research formulated in such textualist terms, or conversely to assert that the value of what they do is quite independent of such criteria. Such questions are highly germane in an academic funding environment where performance practice has come to occupy an increasingly important role, but I cannot do justice to them here.[8]

The claim that meaning is for the most part afforded by the musical surface links, of course, to the claim I made some pages back—again supported by Leech-Wilkinson—that emotional expression has more to do with what performers do than with what composers do. But there is a deeper issue at stake, and like so much in the aesthetics and theory of music, it can be traced back to Hanslick. I have referred several times to the Hanslickian model according to which emotional expression is understood as a superstructure, something that is supported by and can be understood only in terms of the structural fabric of the music. If Hanslick's writings had the effect of banishing emotion from serious discussion of music, they did so through what might be termed a strategy of indefinite deferral: we cannot talk sensibly about emotion until we understand everything about structure, and as we never understand everything about structure, we never talk about emotion. There is an parallel between this and the information-processing approach that Clarke criticised in cognitive psychology. As Clarke explains, the influence of that approach is felt through 'the almost ubiquitous conception of music perception as a series of stages or levels, proceeding from simpler and more stimulus-bound properties through to more complex and abstract characteristics that are less closely tied to the stimulus and are more the expression of general cognitive schemata and cultural conventions' (2005b: 12). And his figure I.1 shows this schematically: the physical level of sound, corresponding to the discipline of acoustics, is linked by successive arrows to the domains of psychoacoustics, cognition, and finally what Clarke refers to as 'Aesthetics/Sociology/Critical Theory' (13). It is only once we have ascended through the acoustic, psychoacoustic, and cognitive pizza that we arrive at the topping, where high-level issues such as style, emotion, and meaning come into play.

But as Clarke goes on to say,

> Direct experience suggests that this is wrong: if you hear a burst of music from someone's radio, for instance, it is more likely that you will be able to say what style of music it is (opera, hip-hop, Country and Western) than to identify specific pitch intervals, or its key, meter, and instrumentation. In other words, people seem to be aware of supposedly 'high-level' features much more directly and immediately than the lower-level features that a standard information-processing account suggests they need to process first (2005b: 15–16).[9]

8. I discuss them further in Cook (forthcoming).

9. Though Clarke does not cite empirical evidence in support of his claim, two articles providing such evidence appeared shortly after his book came out (Gjerdingen and Perrott [2008], and Krumhansl [2010]).

And other research points in the same direction. A study by John Sloboda, Karen Wise, and Isabelle Peretz (2005) compared the performance of congenital amusics[10] with a control group on a standard battery of tests (contour, intervals, scale, rhythm, meter, and recognition memory), and also on a newly devised test for emotional understanding, defined in terms of the ability to identify the emotion that a performer intended to convey in playing a given melody. Whereas the amusics performed much worse than the control group in the standard tests, as expected, there was no difference in the emotion test. The amusics' emotional judgements cannot have been the outcome of lower-level parametrical judgements, as the information-processing model suggests, since they were incapable of making such judgements: as with Clarke's radio example, supposedly higher-level judgements were being made in parallel with supposedly lower-level ones. Sloboda and his co-workers suggest that the amusics may have been relying on perceptual cues that apply equally to the perception of music and of speech, in which they had no deficit, and we saw in Chapters 3 and 4 that there are significant areas of overlap between speech and musical performance. All this might suggest that, in reality, performers' most significant contribution to the production of musical meaning on the large scale lies not in the area of structural articulation, but rather in that of emotional specification.

But the final problem that arises from an information-processing approach underpinned by textualist assumptions is the most obvious and the most fundamental one, and here we come back to the ontological issues that I outlined in Chapter 1, and that have repeatedly surfaced since then. Writing sucks time out of music. The music-theoretical models that music psychologists married to the information-processing approach construe music as extended in space rather than time. The Schenkerian conception of prolongation as an unfolding of structure into time is only a particularly overt version of a much more widespread way of thinking according to which music is not, at the most basic level, temporal at all. It is a way of thinking that is deeply irreconcilable with musical performance, that paradigm of artistic becoming in which the most refined temporal gradations play a foundational role. And it gives rise to the idea that performance is the reproduction of something that already exists. By contrast, to think of performance as an act of signification is not only to place it in the social context of players and listeners but also to locate it at a particular point in time. To signify is to draw upon the past in order to shape a still ongoing future, and that is precisely the conception embodied in Sawyer's emergent. And so in performance, whether of jazz standards or Mozart's string quartets, time is always of the essence. As Schutz (1964: 174–75) said in a striking anticipation of hippy language, 'performer and listener are "tuned-in" to one another, are living together through the same flux, are growing older together while the musical process lasts'.

10. Congenital amusics might be defined as people who really do have cloth ears, rather than—as in most cases—merely believing they do as a result of bad teaching or other environmental factors.

8

Social Scripts

Scores are more than just tablatures for specific actions or else some sort of picture of the required sound; they are also artifacts with powerful auras of their own.

—Brain Ferneyhough (Ferneyhough and Boros 1990: 11)

AN ETHNOGRAPHIC TURN

'Whether checkers are played with bottle tops on a piece of squared linoleum', writes Erving Goffman (1972: 19), 'or with uniformed men standing on colored flagstones in a specially arranged court square, the pairs of players can start with the "same" positions, employ the same sequence of strategic moves and counter-moves, and generate the same contour of excitement'. Playing checkers, or what the British call draughts, involves ignoring all sorts of things that would matter in other situations, which means that—as Goffman puts it—it operates according to particular 'rules of irrelevance'. As we have seen, the aesthetics of music has also been based on assumed rules of irrelevance. In essence what are seen to matter are sound structures, Hanslick's tonally moving forms, as specified in scores and embodied in performances. By contrast a wide range of other things that happen in performances are considered not to matter, and these extend from visual appearance and physical gesture, which I shall discuss in Chapters 9 and 10, to the social interactions that I discussed in the last one.

Musicologists' research methods are also conditioned by this distinction between the 'musical' and the 'extra-musical'. The primary sources are documents, and the principal methods for working with them are archival research and close reading—the same techniques on which historical and literary studies are based. The documents in question of course include scores as well as textual materials, which adds a further dimension to close reading, and a similar if more drastic extension of the techniques of close reading makes it possible to incorporate recordings within this research model without any fundamental rethinking. This is basically the approach I used in Chapters 3 and 4, and I hope that in doing so I was sensitive to a danger that this approach creates: of treating recordings as if they were texts, repositories of inherent meaning, designed for contemplation. Rather they are, as we saw in Chapter 5, the more or less partial traces of sound-producing actions, and of decisions that affect how the sounds are heard (this formulation is intended to be broad enough to cover anything from Moreschi's 1902 recording of the Bach-Gounod 'Ave Maria' to today's studio-produced classical or pop recordings). The documentary approach also creates a further danger, which I hope I averted in Chapter 6 when making use of techniques of distant reading. This is that, when you attempt to relate the music, so understood, to its social and cultural context—as in the parallel I pursued between musical phrase arching and broader issues of standardisation—you construct a binary opposition between the musical and social, as if music was simply a reflection of society. The objection to this is obvious: music is itself an intrinsic dimension of society.

That explains why, in the last chapter, I wanted to emphasise the presence of the social within the musical: performance is a paradigmatically social activity, and its effects and meaning derive in large measure from that social dimension. In this chapter I explore further aspects of musical socialities, and consider how scores can be understood in terms of the scripting of social action and interaction. In other words, I am bracketing some of the traditional rules of musical irrelevance, and in the following chapters I shall bracket some more. And this entails a broadening of research approaches, and in particular the incorporation within the musicological toolkit of the ethnographic approaches that are fundamental to such fields as anthropology, interdisciplinary performance studies, and of course ethnomusicology. Within the last few years there has been an explosion in musicologists' use of such techniques, especially by early career researchers: graduate schools are full of such work, to the extent that it does not seem exaggerated to speak of an ethnographic turn in the discipline as a whole. This promises to give a voice to performers—whether as consultants, collaborators, or researchers in their own right—in a way that is not the case of more traditional approaches dominated by reified conceptions of the musical work and performance style. It enables a more direct focus on performance as process, rather than as commodified product. And it contributes to the formulation of new research questions, in contrast to how the page-to-stage approach incorporates performance within an already established disciplinary agenda and so addresses existing questions at the expense of formulating new ones.

It would be logical to think of this ethnographic turn as having its origins in the social, or sociological, dimension which the 'New' musicologists of the 1990s aimed to incorporate within their reinvented discipline. Agenda-setting writers such as Susan McClary and Lawrence Kramer wanted to show how, despite its supposed autonomy and transcendence, classical music embodied ideological values: that was, for example, the point of McClary's interpretation of Beethoven's symphonic style as an expression of patriarchal hegemony. Indeed the claim was

that music was such a powerful vehicle for ideology precisely because of its supposed autonomy and transcendence, meaning that it naturalised ideological values, representing them as just the way things are. As McClary's analyses showed
particularly clearly, the whole approach revolved around looking for the signs of
the social within the musical text. The basic principle was pithily expressed by
Adorno, on whom the 'New' musicologists primarily drew in bringing a sociological perspective to bear on the discipline: in his 1932 essay 'On the social situation
of music', he wrote that music is able

> to express—in the antinomies of its own formal language—the exigency
> of the social condition and to call for change through the coded language
> of suffering.... It fulfills its social function more precisely when it presents
> social problems through its own material and according to its own formal
> laws—problems which music contains within itself in the innermost cells of
> its technique (2002: 393).

In this way, Adorno continues, the tensions and contradictions of society are
'defined as technical problems' (399), in that sense encoded within the score—
from which it follows that they can be decoded through analysis of musical texts.
And that is exactly what McClary was doing when she analysed Beethoven. The
result is that what was intended as—and in many respects actually was—a fundamentally rethought discipline continued to be built around some very traditional
assumptions about musical texts and how meaning is built into them. In short,
the 'New' musicology was built on music as writing, not music as performance.

What makes all this rather ironic is that, by the time the 'New' musicologists
were drawing on Adorno in order to bring their discipline up to date, sociologists
saw his approach as hopelessly old-fashioned (this was, after all, half a century
after he wrote the essay from which I have been quoting). In a memorial lecture
for Charles Seeger which he delivered in 1989—a lecture designed for an audience of music specialists—Howard Becker (1989) had Adorno in his sights when
he proclaimed that 'sociologists aren't much interested in "decoding" art works,
in finding the works' secret meanings as reflections of society. They prefer to see
those works as the result of what a lot of people have done jointly' (282). And he
went on to list some of the aspects of art that sociologists found more interesting: 'occupational organization, the development and maintenance of traditions,
the training of practitioners, mechanisms of distribution, and audiences and their
tastes'. In short, if sociologists after Adorno (the pointed title of the book that Tia
DeNora published in 2003) wanted to work with music, they didn't look for social
meaning in scores. They looked for it in the real-world activities where scores find
their place, in how people work together in the course of such activities, and in
the institutions within which their activities are structured. And although Becker
didn't specifically mention it—perhaps because he took it for granted—performance ticks all the boxes for work of this kind.

In the UK, the ethnographic turn to which I have referred might be symbolised by the relationship between two research centres, both of which worked on

musical performance, and both of which were funded by the Arts and Humanities Research Council. The first, the AHRC Research Centre for the History and Analysis of Recorded Music (generally known by the acronym CHARM) focussed—as its name implies—on recordings. Although it included a project on the history of the UK record business between the wars, its primary focus was on making historical recordings accessible to scholars (through creating a major online discography, and through establishing an online archive of digitised recordings), and on developing analytical approaches to the study of recordings; as I mentioned, the computational methods used in Chapters 5 and 6 were developed at CHARM. The centre's orientation was strongly musicological, and it was primarily interested in recordings for their potential to support a musicology oriented towards performance.

CHARM was funded through a five-year grant (2004–2009), but there was an opportunity to compete for a further five years of funding, the outcome of which was a successor centre, the AHRC Research Centre for Musical Performance as Creative Practice. As implied by the new centre's name (which regrettably yielded the acronym CMPCP), the focus was now not on recordings but on the real-time practice of performance, whether in the teaching studio, the rehearsal room, or the concert hall. While retaining its musicological foundations, the new centre was designed to interact much more than the old one with professional musicians, and the partner institutions included conservatories as well as universities. All the main research projects carried out by centre personnel involved the use of ethnographic approaches, and CMPCP mounted a series of seminars designed to identify specific techniques appropriate for performance analysis, and to disseminate knowledge of them throughout the performance research community.[1]

As this may suggest, the development of ethnographic approaches to performance has been a largely UK-based phenomenon, helped by a funding regime that has seen the forging of closer relationships between practice and research as a priority; that explains the predominance of British names in the following brief survey of work in this area, in which I focus on studies of the real-time practice of performance, rather than the larger contexts referred to by Becker. Although it is still very much a developing field, ethnographic work on performance might be classified into three at least partly distinct categories (though many researchers work in more than one). The first and most widespread involves the use of what might be called classic ethnographic techniques, carried out by researchers who normally have high-level training in performance—and whose effectiveness as researchers depends on this—but who do not necessarily participate in the performances under investigation. Data collection techniques typically include observation and interview, sometimes incorporated within a systematic methodology such as Interpretative Phenomenological Analysis or Grounded Theory.

1. Further information on CHARM and CMPCP may be found on their respective websites: http://www.charm.rhul.ac.uk/ and http://www.cmpcp.ac.uk/.

Most of CMPCP's projects fall into this category, as do projects carried out by Jane Davidson and Elaine King, both of whom have worked on rehearsal practices as well as performance as such.

The focus on rehearsal is shared by two parallel projects to which I shall return later in this chapter: Amanda Bayley's project with the Kreutzer Quartet and Michael Finnissy, and Paul Archbold's with the Arditti Quartet and Brian Ferneyhough.[2] In addition to involving new music for string quartet, both projects investigated the distribution of creativity between composer and performers; both involved close collaboration among the various parties (for example some of the outputs of Bayley's project are co-authored with Neil Heyde, the Kreutzer's cellist); and both resulted in DVDs featuring extensive rehearsal, performance, and interview footage. The use of this technology, rather than the traditional journal article, allows the integration of diverse media and facilitates dissemination to practitioners. Archbold describes the DVD 'Climbing a mountain', which documents the preparation of Ferneyhough's Sixth String Quartet, as 'an unashamedly specialist film designed to help composers and music students understand the rehearsal process, from notation to performance'.[3]

In the American context, the work of Roger Chaffin, Gabriela Imreh, and Mary Crawford offers another model of collaboration. I mentioned in Chapter 2 that Chaffin and Crawford are psychologists, whereas Imreh is a concert pianist. As Chaffin and Crawford initially conceived the project, Imreh's role was as subject: the psychologists, as experimenters, would investigate the cognitive representations she employed in learning and performing a complex repertory item (the third movement of J. S. Bach's *Italian Concerto*). But this was quite contrary to Imreh's expectation, which was—as Crawford explains—that she would participate 'as an active, thinking partner, not as a passive subject' (Chaffin et al. 2002, 15). The success of the project depended on the negotiation of a co-researcher relationship between the participants, with each bringing his or her own expertise to the project on an equal basis, as reflected in the co-authorship of the book to which the project gave rise. Ethnographical research, then, has its own problems, even though the relationship between researchers and practitioners is less hierarchical than in the work described in Chapter 2, where performers were taken out of their own context and placed on the music theorist's turf. And there is more to it than the differing perspectives and objectives of academics and practitioners, or the fact that the study of performance gets skewed towards a rather small number of research-friendly musicians. Always a concern for ethnomusicologists, problems of informants feeling

2. Both projects were part of larger research programmes also involving music by other composers; further details and links to outcomes may be found at http://www.wlv.ac.uk/default.aspx?page=19240 (Bayley) and http://itunes.apple.com/gb/itunes-u/arditti-quartet/id441504831 (Archbold).

3. http://www.kingston.ac.uk/pressoffice/news/232/27-07-2011-strings-on-screen---arditti-quartet-reveals-tricks-of-the-trade.html.

patronised or exploited by researchers—particularly, at least in the UK, when the informants are conservatory-based performers and the researchers are from universities—are something that musicologists now have to worry about, too. The trend away from informant-researcher relationships and towards collaborative research is motivated by pragmatism as well as idealism.

One way to avoid, or at least displace, such tensions is of course for the researcher and the performer to be the same person—in other words to conduct autoethnographic research, the second of the categories I mentioned. Keeping a performance diary to trace and reflect on the development of an interpretation is a learning approach used by a number of UK conservatories, and autoethnographic research projects have incorporated this approach within a larger context that may include the use of classic ethnographic techniques. There was, of course, an autoethnographic element within the Chaffin-Imreh-Crawford collaboration, and autoethnography played a prominent role in another project in which Chaffin collaborated with the singer Jane Ginsborg (who has professional qualifications in both performance and psychology). Ginsborg kept records of the stages through which she prepared a performance of *Ricercar I* from Stravinsky's *Cantata*: analysis of this material provided evidence of the structural and expressive 'landmarks' Ginsborg had internalised, and this in turn linked to her ability to recall the words and the music, not only at the time of the performance but also long after (Ginsborg and Chaffin 2011). Another example, in which autoethnography merges with the classic ethnomusicological technique of participant observation, is the work of the Marmara Piano Trio, of which Mine Doğantan-Dack is the pianist: this professional ensemble was established in 2007 for the specific purpose of advancing a programme of practice as research, with open rehearsals and workshops as a central part of its activity. A project entitled 'Alchemy in the spotlight', which like CHARM and CMPCP was funded by the AHRC, is described on the website as intended 'to represent performances and performers within the disciplinary discourse in their own terms, by articulating the characteristics of the practice of performing live on stage, where performers make performances within a temporal environment that is bound up both with the logic of indeterminacy and the necessity of uninterrupted flow'.[4] In short, the aim is to highlight the experience of the performer and to take a first step towards rectifying what Doğantan-Dack refers to as 'the absence of performers within disciplinary discourse'.

Autoethnographic approaches in turn shade into a third category of research that falls outside the bounds of ethnography as normally defined. Professional expertise in performance is again involved, but now in another way. A good example is a project by the violinist David Milsom, the aim of which was to recreate the performance styles audible on the earliest recordings by violinists of the

---

4. Mine Doğantan-Dack, 'Preparing Beethoven for Live Performance: The "Alchemy Project"', 3 (http://www.academia.edu/773163/Preparing_Beethoven_for_Live_Performance_The_Alchemy_Project).

classical German school, in particular Joachim.[5] Milsom adopted an obvious and yet unusual research method: he tried to imitate what he heard on the records, much as aspiring jazz and rock musicians do. And while Joachim made few recordings, Milsom went on to apply the style he had internalised through imitating Joachim to other music. This approach might be seen as in essence a variant of the virtuous circle between scholarship and performance that I described with reference to HIP in Chapter 1, but the incorporation of recordings adds a new element. And the autoethnographic dimension emerges with particular clarity from a project I mentioned in chapter 5, in which the Norwegian pianist Sigurd Slåttebrekk collaborated with the record producer Tony Harrison. The immediate aim was to recreate the recordings of nine of Grieg's short piano pieces that the composer made on 2 May 1903, and on the comprehensive project website Slåttebrekk and Harrison explain what this involved:

> examining the components of Grieg's playing and re-playing them: single notes, turns of phrase, longer sections, whole pieces; deconstructing, re-building, melding and forging. Understanding through imitation, and imitation through understanding. The resultant recordings were often massively edited on the computer, sometimes as an end in itself and sometimes as a bridge to further refine the performance for the next day's recording.[6]

But the larger aim was to go beyond imitation and use it as a means of internalising Grieg's performance style, thereby gaining an insider's understanding of late-nineteenth-century pianism. As with Milsom, Slåttebrekk and Harrison's ultimate aim is 'the incorporation of our new knowledge into other repertoire'.[7]

In this idea of acquiring an insider's understanding of a distant culture, work based on what might be termed the Elvis impersonation methodology approaches ethnomusicology, except that the distance to be bridged is in time rather than in space. Indeed the ethnographic turn I have been describing might be thought of as an ethnomusicologisation of Western 'art' musicology (there are also, of course, ethnographic studies of popular music, though they often focus more on contextual dimensions than on the act of performance). But it is perhaps better to see this as part of an ongoing process of transformation in both disciplines, the effect of which is to bring them closer together. Just as musicologists have increasingly adopted ethnographic approaches, so ethnomusicologists have increasingly included Western music within their purview: Kay

---

5. String Chamber Music of the Classical German School, 1840–1900: A Scholarly Investigation through Reconstructive Performance (http://www.leeds.ac.uk/music/dm-ahrc/).

6. Chasing the Butterfly, http://www.chasingthebutterfly.no/?p=25 (the quoted passage is at http://www.chasingthebutterfly.no/?page_id=75). The project also gave rise to an audio CD of the same name (Simax PSC1299).

7. http://www.chasingthebutterfly.no/?page_id=257.

Shelemay's study (2001) of the HIP scene in Boston is an example of research that could have equally well have been undertaken by a musicologist with an excellent grasp of ethnographic method, or (as was in fact the case) an ethnomusicologist with an excellent knowledge of HIP. The same applies to Stephen Cottrell's ethnographic study of professional music making in London (2004), to which I shall be referring later in this chapter. It is worth nothing that, though this project focussed on musicians' experiences and on the larger contexts of music making rather than on actual practices of performance narrowly defined, it was still based on participation, in the sense that Cottrell could not possibly have carried it out if he had not himself been a professional musician.

And after all, the sense that may at one time have existed that musicology is about 'our' music, whereas ethnomusicology is about 'their' music, is no longer plausible in an increasingly globalised world where everyone has multiple and shifting identities. Equally unrealistic, for reasons that I hope are by now blatantly obvious, are attempts to distinguish the disciplines on the basis of the kind of sources they work with, such as when George List (1979) suggested that the proper domain of musicology was scores, and that of ethnomusicology performances. In the study of WAM performance at least, these disciplinary divisions serve no purpose. It makes much more sense to think in terms of the combination of varied but connected disciplinary approaches that Laudan Nooshin (2008: 74) suggests we call 'music studies'.

SOCIALITY IN SOUND

As we saw in the previous chapter, to study performance is to study people interacting through sound: Monson observes that 'In an improvisational situation, it is important to remember that there are always musical personalities interacting, not merely instruments or pitches or rhythms' (1996: 26). Clarke also considers this issue, citing doctoral work by Matthew Sansom. Sansom recorded pairs of free improvisers playing together and then interviewed them individually, using the recordings to elicit comments about how one player had interacted with the other. 'The creative impetus in Sansom's duos', Clarke reports, is 'at least as much to do with an exploration of interpersonal dynamics as it is to do with a direct manipulation of musical materials' (2005a: 174). Clarke cites a number of the improvisers' comments in support of this, of which one will have to stand for all: 'Sometimes in this performance', Mick says, 'I get a bit worried whether Ross is . . . doing as much as he naturally, as he really wants to, whether he's kind of laying back a bit to give me space, whether he's actually doing it because that's what he wants to do'. There is, of course, nothing specifically musical about what Mick is saying. It is standard relational work that happens in this instance to be transacted through musical performance, with the transaction informing the course of the improvisation. The players' 'awareness of musical materials', Clarke comments, 'is contained within the framework of a primary attention to interpersonal dynamics'. And though he cautions that in Sansom's research the balance between musical and interpersonal dynamics varied both within individual performances and between them, Clarke draws a strong conclusion: 'the clear message is that viewing improvisation as simply a matter of pitches, rhythms, chord changes and textures would be to miss the point—certainly for this idiom, and arguably for most others too'.

I would like to expand on Clarke's final remark. WAM performance equally involves the creation of special intimacies between performers, for here, too, musical work is at the same time interpersonal work. In a recent article Mine Doğantan-Dack (2012a: 43) quotes Arnold Steinhardt, who was for forty years the first violinist of the Guarneri String Quartet, on how the musical and social blur into one another: 'I was now connected with and dependent on David, John, and Michael for a good performance', Steinhardt writes. And he continues, 'How strange! If I played out of tune, they played out of tune; if they stumbled, so did I; and if I managed to play beautifully, we would all share the credit....My future was their future; theirs was mine'. Long-term musical ensembles, such as string quartets or for that matter successful rock bands, entail long-term personal relationships. Doğantan-Dack follows up Steinhardt's words with her own observations, based among other things on her membership of the Marmara Piano Trio:

> The social dynamics among the co-performers in an ensemble are as important as the musical dynamics for a successful performance, and each live performance is in fact an opportunity to further develop and strengthen the social bonds between the co-performers....Live performance is the site where the trust and support between the co-performers get tested, confirmed and re-confirmed, and acquire their true practical meaning; the willingness and the ability to create an emotional comfort zone during the live event when co-performers need it is crucial for the success of the performance.

And whereas musicians usually speak of such relationships, and the moments of intimacy that come with them, in musical rather than emotional terms, a few quotations chosen almost at random will show how this experience of music making as an intensely interpersonal act cuts across the boundaries of musical repertories or traditions. Susan Hellauer, who performs medieval music with the *a cappella* quartet Anonymous 4, writes that achieving good tuning involves close collaborative work: 'we have to examine the way in which our individual voices work together. For example, we often have to modify one person's pronunciation or shaping of a vowel sound so that even our overtones will match' (Sherman 1997: 51). Again, describing a passage from Antoine Brumel's *Missa Victimae Paschali*, John Potter (1998: 178–82) focusses on the intimate negotiations and conjunctions between the performers that are entailed. 'The voices are setting up patterns of tension and relaxation', he writes, 'acutely conscious of each other, both seeking to accommodate each others' desires and to satisfy themselves'. At the end of the first bar, for instance, a particular dissonance 'is only a passing moment but it creates a moment of acute pleasure that they may wish to prolong' (182, 180).

Pleasure is also prominent into Elisabeth Le Guin's description of a passage from the first movement of Luigi Boccherini's String Quartet in A major, op. 8

no. 6. The pattern of interlocking repetitions in the upper parts, she says, creates a range of 'interactive opportunities: in their tradings-off there is the subtle pleasure of trying to mimic one another exactly, while their lockstep thirds raise the issue of balancing the sonority' (Le Guin 2002: 220). With 'their small frictions and overlappings', she explains, these repetitions 'direct the player's ear towards nothing beyond himself, and perhaps peripherally his colleagues, in the intimate act of playing'. In the next sentence she seems to ascribe all this to Boccherini, saying it is typical of him to place such a reflective moment in the middle of an extrovert *Allegro brillante*, but of course it takes both the composer and the performers to make it happen. (That is why Robert Martin, whom I quoted in Chapter 7, referred to performers collaborating with composers in the creation of performances.) And just in case, after all these WAM examples, it needs reinforcing that this sort of thing happens in jazz too, here is Monson (1996: 141) describing a moment in the Jaki Byard Quartet's 1965 recording of 'Bass-ment Blues'[8]: 'Dawson anticipates and reinforces Tucker's continuing triplet rhythms in measures 5 and 6 by playing a triplet-based fill between the snare, tom-toms and bass drum....Dawson could not have known for sure whether Tucker would continue with eighth notes in measure 6 but correctly anticipated that he would'. And she adds: 'Such spontaneous, fortuitous moments of coming together or hooking up are highly prized by musicians' (143).

All these intensely interpersonal moments could be understood in terms of Sawyer's model of group collaboration, as described in the previous chapter: each description revolves around the way in which the collectively created emergent structures the performers' interactions. My concern here, however, is with how intimacy, emotion, and pleasure intertwine with more conventionally musical values in performance. It would be tempting to say that all of these are different dimensions of, or different ways of describing, the same phenomenon, complementary sides of the same coin—which is more or less what Clarke says of Sansom's work. But perhaps this literal coextensivity of the social and the musical is a specific characteristic of free jazz that does not completely translate to other genres. Would we, for example, really expect to find musical correlates to the special personal relationships embodied in some string quartets, such as the Ying Quartet (which comprised three brothers and their sister from its establishment in 1988 until 2009, when the first violinist left), or the Carducci Quartet, which consists of two married couples? Then there is the case of a student quartet featured in a study by Jane Davidson and James Goode (2002). The quartet consisted of three girls and a boy, who played second violin and was the least accomplished player but tried to dominate the group: Davidson and Goode remark that 'As observers it was hard for us to resist the possibility that there was a gender dynamic to the style and content of the exchanges'. (Keith Murnighan and Donald Conlon's [1991: 169] observation is also relevant here: 'Second violinists are critical to their group's success...but they are rarely recognised'.) Under such circumstances, as

8. From The Jaki Byard Quartet Live! Vol. 2 (Prestige PR-7477).

Cottrell (2004: 89–90) explains in the course of an extended discussion of the social dynamics of small ensembles, it is important to maintain a kind of firewall between social and musical relationships, to avoid tensions or disagreements in the one domain bleeding through to the other.

Role-playing games provide a useful parallel here, and indeed resemble musical performance in a number of ways. For one thing, role playing is a paradigm of performativity: in the world of the game, as I said in Chapter 4, you are who you make yourself out to be. (The same might be said of mazurka performance. Asian/American/European as Frederick Chiu may be, one thing he isn't is Polish—until he starts playing.) Dennis Waskul explains that role play involves operating at three distinct levels: that of the 'persona' (the 'sly gnome' or whatever you represent yourself to be in the game), the 'player' (who has internalised the rules and is therefore able to play the role of the gnome), and the 'person'—the real-life individual who sits at the table in a traditional role-playing game such as Dungeons & Dragons, which is what Waskul (2006: 21) is talking about, or at the console in a videogame. And he adds that 'role-playing games can be described, explained, and understood as activities that exist in the unique interstices between persona, player, and person' (22). All this translates quite readily to music. At the level of persona your role is defined by the melody you play—or some filler material that glues the ensemble together, if you are playing the role of second violin. Then, at the level of player, you are exercising your technical and artistic skills in playing your instrument: you are a violinist. And as a person you are John or Mary, at this point tied up in rehearsal, but wondering if you will have time to get to the supermarket before picking up the kids. These roles are distinct, but what is characteristic of role playing in both games and music is that there is always potential for slippage between them: a musical example is the 'irresistible temptation to map the four parts onto the persons of the performers' that Mary Hunter (2012: 54) observes in writing about string quartets. As Waskul says, 'neat distinctions between person, player, and persona become messy: they erode into utterly permeable and interlocking moments of experience' (2006: 30). This, he adds, is equally true of the multiple roles we all play in everyday life.

That might make it sound as if games, and music, symbolise everyday life, but they do more than that. Tom Boellstorff makes this point as regards Second Life, the virtual world in which role play is again a major feature (which is why it is sometimes referred to as a game, even though there are no winners or losers). In Boellstorff's words, 'virtual worlds are not secondary representations of the actual world. They…draw upon many elements of actual-world sociality, but…reconfigure these elements in unforeseen ways' (2008: 201). This echoes Mark Johnson's formulation (2007), itself based on John Dewey, that art creates 'heightened…experiences of meaning, using all our ordinary resources for meaning-making' (208): it suggests that games and art—music included—should be seen not just as metaphorical representations of real-world sociality, though they are clearly that, but also as metonyms, little bits of reality. That applies to the musical intimacies I described, as also to Second Life, which Boellstorff (2008: 171) describes as 'a site of intimacy in its own terms'. It applies to social interactions that are contrafactual or otherwise unachievable in the real world but can be acted out in music or in Second Life, and to the constructions of identity that result (since it is primarily through relationships that we construct identity). Boellstorff quotes a claim that 'all media have always offered entrances to imagined spaces or "virtual realities," opening up symbolic worlds for transgressive experiences' (Förnas et al. 2002: 30), and both Second Life and music illustrates this. Boellstorff (2008) cites a Second Life resident who told him, 'In SL, you can get some marginal experience of what it's like to be fat, or black, or female' (249). In music, remixing technologies enable white teenagers to appropriate aspects of black musical identity even without being able to embody them in live performance, and in this way gain some marginal experience of what it's like to be black (Monson 2011). Or I could cite an example of my own from the days when I played in a recorder consort in Hong Kong: while performing a piece by Dufay where two of the lines intertwined with one another in a particularly sensual manner, I found myself making eyes to one of my male colleagues in a way I would not have dreamed of in any other context. We were both married. I was role playing, musical role playing.

All this confirms Monson's claim (1996) that musical structure has 'as one of its central functions the *construction* of social context'. As usual, Monson is talking with specific reference to jazz, but Cottrell (2004: 91) makes essentially the same point when he writes, within the context of WAM performance, 'Musical texts become sites through which social relationships are negotiated'. The new element which Cottrell introduces is the idea that music is designed and notated in order to prompt the negotiation of social relationships. While he refers to the score as a 'text', explaining that he means this in the Geertzian sense, the term has become strongly linked with the conception of music as writing, according to which scores have inherent meaning that may be interpreted through contemplation, or decoded through analysis.[9] That is the approach of literary studies. But the role of scores within the context of performance is in important ways more like that of theatrical scripts. Thinking of scores not as texts but as scripts leads one to ask, I think productively, what features of performance the score scripts, and how it does this. One might say that where the text turns in on itself, the script points outwards, bearing the promise of future action.

I can make the distinction in terms of the opening of Mozart's Quartet K 387 (Figure 8.1). A traditional musicological description (or, in the common and telling term, reading) of the first ten bars might go something like this:

A two-bar opening phrase moves from the tonic to the supertonic and is balanced by another two-bar phrase that returns through the dominant to the tonic; this pair of matched two-bar phrases leads in turn to a four-bar phrase in which a distinctive motif ascends from the viola through the second violin

9. Confusingly, in 'The death of the author', Barthes (1977) uses 'text' to signify exactly the opposite: the freedom of the reader to create meaning, precisely because it is not inherent in the text.

Figure 8.1 Mozart, Quartet K 387, opening

to the first violin. This culminates in a homophonic but deceptive cadence on the submediant, which is immediately compensated through the addition of a two-bar closing phrase that cadences in the tonic, resulting in an extension of the normative eight-bar sentence to ten bars.

This musicological language is abstract and depersonalised. Reference is made not to people making music together—the description is of 'the music', not a particular performance of it—but to what, following Waskul, we might call instrumental personae (such as 'the second violin'). Roger Graybill (2011) writes that we can 'think of each instrumental part as a role that is adopted by the performer' (221), and adds that when we speak of a string quartet as a group of equals, 'it is these roles, not the performers per se, that exhibit equal status'. Whereas performers come and go, roles endure, like Hamlet, and are in that sense timeless—which is why it seems appropriate for this kind of analytical description to be expressed in the present tense. Also in the domain of persona is the 'distinctive motif' that ascends through the instruments. The ascent takes place as a motion in the coordinates of pitch and time, but this is a time in which what is to be is already determined, as on the printed page. Again, the motif is passed from one instrument to another, handed on rather like the baton in a relay race (though a race where the outcome has always been known). In that sense it is conceived as a kind of material object. And if we ask what this object is made of, the answer will be sound structures, that is to say specific configurations of pitch classes and rhythms—but since these can only be usefully specified in notational terms, that is effectively tantamount to saying it is made of notes, of writing. This is a description of music as text.

In this book I sometimes refer to this kind of musicological approach as 'traditional'. But it is actually quite a recent tradition: thinking of music in terms of quasi-material structure is more characteristic of the twentieth century than the eighteenth or even nineteenth. Commentators from the late eighteenth or early nineteenth century were more likely to talk of the string quartet in terms of social interaction (and a trace of this is preserved in the ambiguity by which the term may mean players, work, or genre). 'A fundamental part of the rhetoric about quartets', Mary Hunter has written, was 'the notion of equal participation by all four parts', and she adds that 'writing on this topic also has a strong social, even political, cast, with "freedom" not an uncommon term' (2012: 59). A review of Beethoven's late quartets by Adolph Bernhard Marx, published in 1828, makes her point. 'We have four deeply stirred creative spirits', Marx writes, 'who soar in glorious freedom and wonderful sympathy in a quadruple brotherly embrace....If practitioners do not make an equal band of noble, equal, free and brotherly spirits, no clear appearance of the artwork is possible, and even full satisfaction of the players cannot be hoped for' (Hunter 2012: 64). And just in case anybody might miss the political connotations, Hunter spells them out: 'quartets, both as compositions and as performance, model a polity where voluntarily discharging mutual obligations on a basis of equality and respect results in freedom'.

The most familiar metaphor, however, was drawn from social interaction through speech. As early as 1777 the composer and critic Johann Reichhardt referred to the quartet as 'a conversation among four persons' (Mazzola 2011: 176). In 1835 Pierre Baillot said that its 'appealing dialogue seems to be a conversation among friends sharing their sensations, feelings and mutual affections' (Vial 2008: 81-2). But the most famous example is Goethe, who in a letter to C. F. Zelter dated 9 November 1829 described it as 'the most comprehensible type of instrumental music: one hears four reasonable people engaged in conversation with one another' (82). Goethe's words resonate in Brian Ferneyhough's reference to 'the old image of four civilized people talking to each other' (Archbold 2011: 53), but nowadays the idea of music as conversation is more familiar in the context of jazz. As Paul Berliner (1994) has comprehensively documented, it is ubiquitous in practitioners' discourse, as well as underlying the approaches to interaction between jazz musicians adopted by Sawyer and Monson, both of whom build on Silverstein's work on conversation analysis; Maya Gratier, too, explores how jazz improvisers coordinate with one another on the basis of cues—such as 'repetition, mirroring and matching, punctuation, and completion and synchronisation'— that are familiar from the study of conversation (2008: 101).

And this prompts a comparison with the theatre. After all, scripting conversation is precisely what playwrights do—just as bringing the script to life by making it appear as if it is being extemporised is what actors do. There is then an implicit theatrical analogy in the analysis Hunter offers of the idealised social interactions in Beethoven's String Quartet op. 59 no. 2. She quotes bars 11–21 of the second movement (Figure 8.2), but it is bar 16 on which her commentary centres. At first sight, she explains, there is nothing to this bar: it is just the dotted-note figure that will accompany the iteration of the chorale-like tune that begins in the following bar. But several factors throw things out of balance. It is quite different from anything heard so far, with its abbreviated notes and *sempre staccato* marking, as well as its contradiction of the *alla breve* character of the chorale tune. It is also excessively foregrounded for an accompaniment figure. It is not just that it is 'classic "second fiddle" material', only played by the first violin, Hunter (69) says; its character means that it 'completely rules the roost', and worse, 'it acts as a rigid timekeeper even as the tune in the second violin becomes more lyrical'. Yet at the same time it prejudices synchronisation between the players, since 'The silence in the middle of each crotchet beat denies the other parts any warning that the tempo might be changing, so the semiquaver pickup is the only indication to those playing the long notes of when the next beat will arrive'.

Hunter's claim is that, like a playwright, Beethoven has intentionally scripted a particular social transaction into the score: at first the accompaniment figure, the equivalent so to speak of Waskul's sly gnome, attempts to dominate the discourse in a socially and stylistically inappropriate manner, but as the movement proceeds, it is 'accommodated and eventually integrated into the texture and the thematic web of the movement' (73). This is a nice example of how, by writing notes in a score, a composer can set up the negotiation of social relationships, but it also illustrates the problems in talking about the performative qualities of music without talking about actual performances. Hunter does not cite any recordings of op. 59 no. 2, but—with a little imagination—I believe I can hear what she is talking about in a sample of post-war recordings, where this moment seems to create a certain awkwardness. By contrast, the Léner Quartet, who recorded op. 59 no. 2 around 1927 and whose playing was by that time distinctly old-fashioned, sail effortlessly through this passage (Media Example 8.1).[10]

10. Columbia L 1856/1859; reissued in 1994 on 'Ludwig van Beethoven: The String Quartets, volume 2 (Stradivarius).

264

BEYOND THE SCORE

Figure 8.2 Beethoven, Quartet op. 59 no. 2, 2nd mvmt., bars 11–21

Hunter's analysis assumes that the performers must aim at tight synchro-nisation, as the post-war quartets do: that is why she sees a problem. But tight synchronisation is not a prerequisite of the older style represented by the Léner Quartet, who were recording during the glory days of Friedman's career and had many attributes in common with the rhetorical pianists. It is not that they play this passage with rhythmic abandon, just that the loose ensemble against which Hunter wishes to guard falls within the stylistic norms of their performance style and so the passage occasions no awkwardness. Such playing is illustrated even more clearly by the Bohemian Quartet, which was also recording during the 1920s but whose members were half a generation older than the Léner's: Robert Philip (2004) writes of their recording of Dvořák's 'American' Quartet op. 96 that 'each player is functioning as an individual. Each responds to the behaviour of the oth-ers, but there is little impression of pre-planned details. They have simply got used to each other's behaviour and have learned to live with it.... They simply were not aiming at our modern notions of ensemble' (120).[11] That makes the recording less a musical object in its own right, and more the trace of a long gone event.

A more contemporary perspective from which to think of scores as scripting social action is that of management theory. Effective management means design-ing frameworks within which people can work together. On the one hand this requires a clear goal that motivates and coordinates people's efforts. On the other, it means not unnecessarily prescribing the details of what they should do. Excessive prescription demotivates and disempowers people, leading them to do things by the book. But real life is rarely like the book. That is why as many decisions as possible should be made on the ground, on the basis of local information, and in real time. Effective management, then, empowers people by harnessing their tacit knowledge and creativity. It encourages them to play by ear, while still singing from the same songsheet as their colleagues. The musical metaphors make the link with classical scores like K 387 or op. 59 no. 2. As I said in Chapter 7, such notations define frameworks within which the fine details of performance are negotiated: in this way they empower musicians. Seen in terms of the specification of sound, the notations are severely limited, which is why performances can sound so different. But this is precisely what renders them so effective as a means of scripting the social action and interaction we hear in string quartet performance.

It is what, in the architectural design process, Frank Gehry (2004: 21) calls 'stay-ing liquid': irreversible design decisions are postponed until they actually need to be made. This explains Gehry's otherwise inexplicable practice of not issuing blue-prints to building contractors engaged on his projects, who are instead expected to derive the measurements they need from a scale model of the building. The result is that, in Eric Abrahamson and David H. Freedman's words (2006), they 'work with the Gehry team in the task of translating the look and feel of the model into a full-scale structure', so realising Gehry's philosophy that 'everyone working on

11. Polydor 95084-95086; reissued in 1994 on 'The Czech Quartet Tradition' (Biddulph Recordings).

the building should keep creating throughout the construction process' (87–88). There is a parallel in the Beethoven quartet clubs described by Christian Friedrich Michaelis in 1829, as we can see if we translate Gehry's model and blueprints into Beethoven's score and parts:

> For some time musicians and friends of music have founded numerous quartet clubs [Quartettvereine], whose primary, or exclusive exercise is the study of Beethoven's quartets. It could be called more than a 'club' when some of the latest and most difficult masterworks are gone through fifty or a hundred or more times in order fully to enter into the spirit of the master, and to play him worthily. No effort is spared, the score is consulted, [with respect to] the intention of the master, the meaning of individual spots, or of the whole is earnestly discussed, every good suggestion put to a practical test (Hunter 2012: 58).

Yet the collaborative principles and values Gehry enunciates in relation to buildings, which I have been putting forward in relation to WAM, are more often associated with jazz and free improvisation, with WAM being seen as representing exactly the opposite. An example comes from Dean Rowan, who is an urban planner, though the article in question is from the journal *Critical Studies in Improvisation*. Drawing on a number of previous writers, Rowan (2004) compares the uniform, statewide procedures that at one time governed the planning of open space in Illinois to 'a classical score from which the individual cities once uniformly played' (16). Following the removal of the legal basis for these procedures, he says, 'the cities' solutions were improvised, albeit not purely spontaneous, deviations'. Rowan accordingly advocates getting away from traditional, rational planning, which 'has musical analogs in strict allegiance to the composer's score and obeisance to the hierarchical command of the conductor' (21), and instead embracing approaches that 'vibrantly accord with improvisational methods, employing practices of active listening, alleviation of oppressive hierarchy, and invitation and acceptance of differences'. The classical score is in this way seen as exactly what I have been arguing it is not: an exhaustive specification of deliverables, an explicit and accountable spelling out of what is to be done, in the spirit of the ISO 9000 family of quality management standards. The very vocabulary that Rowan employs testifies to the dense network of ideology within which WAM has become enmeshed: strict allegiance, obeisance, and hierarchical command encode the values of top-down management and political dictatorship, whereas vibrancy, alleviation of oppression, and acceptance of difference all encode the egalitarian, bottom-up values of social democracy. It is the same image of WAM that we encountered in the writing of Bruce Johnson.

Music lends itself to interpretation as social symbol, and like all symbols it is multiply interpretable, depending on what rules of irrelevance you apply to it. On the symbolic plane there is little point in arguing for or against one or another interpretation. But if we are talking about the enactment of social relationships in performance, then the argument can take a much more evidence-based form.

The quadruple brotherly embrace that Marx read into Beethoven's op. 59 no. 2 exists on the symbolic plane, that of Graybill's group of equals or Waskul's persona; it is hardly a description of the social dynamics of flesh-and-blood quartets, whether in Marx's time (Hunter [2012: 59–60] points out that Karl Möser not only led but dominated the quartet that bore his name) or today. In his discussion of the social dynamics of small ensembles, Cottrell addresses the issue of leadership, building both on Murnighan and Conlon's study of string quartets and his own experience as the leader of a saxophone quartet. The most successful model, he says, is that of 'directed democracy' (2004: 87). One person will take the lead in terms of both musical interpretation and the management of rehearsals; in a quartet it will be the first violinist, whose role extends to both the virtual world of the music and the real world of people management. And whereas decisions will have to be made that not everyone agrees with, they are made in such a way that everyone feels involved in the decision-making process. Referring to his own group, Cottrell (88) writes that 'we spend time arriving at "our" interpretation of a particular piece, an internalized image of the way the music works, how all the parts fit in with one another, what needs to be brought out where, and which corners we need to be particularly wary of'. The result is 'a relatively stable group conception of the music', a conception that is jointly owned by the group members, and in which each of them is invested. One might put this in Marxist terms and say that, in this way, each ensemble member has a share in the means of production.

Of course the dynamics of small ensembles are very different from those of large groups such as orchestras, where—as Cottrell goes on to explain—job satisfaction tends to be significantly lower. There are no doubt many reasons for this, but two stand out from Cottrell's account. One is 'a feeling that one is making a contribution to the end product which appears to be undervalued or unnoticed'(105). Linked to this is the second, the lack of a sense of ownership of what is done, as when one orchestral player told Cottrell, 'The whole nature of being an orchestral musician is that you basically subjugate your whole person, all your ideas, your own personal ideas, you have to just completely throw them away. Just say, right, I don't matter' (107). In Marxist terms, the individual player neither feels she has a share in the means of production, nor is invested in the end product. This is a definition of alienation, and explains what Mauricio Ferares, a violinist and also secretary of the Dutch Musicians' Union, told the audience at a public meeting in 1970: 'The performers, the musicians are just as alienated from their product as the workers in industry, and both take the role of wage laborers in businesses. Just as a laborer loses his freedom when he enters a business, so the musician loses his individual freedom when he goes and works in an orchestra'.[12]

Robert Adlington, who quotes Ferares in his account of the controversy over the future of the Dutch orchestras at that time, also quotes the politician, banker, and cultural commentator Jacques Attali. 'The moment labor has a goal, an aim, a program set out in advance in a code', Attali (1985: 134–35) says, the musician

12. Translated in Adlington 2007: 551.

'becomes a stranger to what he produces....Music then had a goal exterior to the pleasure of its producer, unless he could find pleasure...in his very alienation'. When he refers to a program set out in code, Attali (whose writing combines sophisticated postmodernism with a curiously naïve romanticism) is referring to scores, which he sees as an integral element in the alienated economy of the orchestra. According to him, 'The musicians—who are anonymous and hierarchically ranked, and in general salaried, productive workers—execute an external algorithm, a "score" [*partition*], which does what its name implies: it allocates their parts' (66). Some of what Attali is saying is obvious enough: the hierarchical structure of the orchestra, reinforced by conspicuous disparities in pay, has an obvious affinity with corporate structure, so making it available as a symbol of the late capitalist order. But Attali is also suggesting that alienation enters into the very fabric of the music, and this becomes clearer when, a few lines later, he says that each orchestral player 'produces only a part of the whole having no value in itself'.

Attali is not in the habit of providing concrete examples of what he is talking about, but I think I can provide one, on the basis of my experience of playing in orchestras. From the oboist's perspective, Mozart's symphonies are like an expanded version of chamber music: you are always playing a line that makes sense in its own terms, as well as in terms of the whole. By contrast, Beethoven's symphonic scores allocate your part in the way Attali describes: you find yourself patched from one layer of the texture to another, which means that though the overall orchestral effect makes perfect sense from the podium and auditorium, your individual part sometimes makes very little. In this way the notes on the page change your role within the entire sociocultural complex of the performance. Chamber music can be thought of as music played by the players for the players, but overheard by an audience (if there is one). By contrast, to play oboe in a Beethoven symphony is to carry out a professional service for the benefit of a paying audience (and if there isn't one, you call it a rehearsal). Your relationship to the audience is not fundamentally different from that of a waiter to the clientele of an expensive restaurant—a parallel that is underlined by the fact that both orchestra players and posh waiters traditionally wear dinner jackets.[13]

And as if this all too visible image of 'official' public culture was not sufficiently alienating to many potential customers of classical music, its distance from the

13. Daniel Leech-Wilkinson (personal communication) has suggested that this professionalisation of the relationship between performer and listener may be one of the underlying causes of the attenuation of expression in post-war performance: the lack of personal relationship or mutual investment in orchestral performance renders deeply felt emotion on the performer's part inappropriate, and expressive meaning is instead attributed to the composer or the work. By contrast it was primarily in chamber music contexts such as string quartets, where musicians were playing to and for one another, that highly expressive performance survived through the post-war years. This might be seen as a complementary explanation to the modernist ideologies I explored in Chapter 6, or perhaps better, the change in the relationship of performer and listener might itself be seen as a symptomatically modernist phenomenon.

concerns and values of everyday life is reinforced by the strange—even bizarre—discourses with which it is surrounded, discourses that throw a very particular light on social relationships. I referred in Chapter 1 to the language of 'authority', 'duty', and 'faithfulness' that characterises these discourses. Then there is the 'great principle of submission' to the work which, in his *Poetics of Music*, Stravinsky (1947: 127) demanded of the performer. Fred Maus has traced this idea as it appears in writings about the relationship between musical work and listener. The frequency of such words as 'submit', 'control', 'power', 'domination', and 'bound' in Edward Cone's book *The Performer's Voice* inspires him to an interpretation of the aesthetic experience based on the language, values, and experiences of BDSM: 'sado-masochists', Maus (2004: 35–36) writes, 'and the music-lovers that Cone describes, find intense pleasure in experiences structured by an extreme dichotomy between active and passive roles'. All this is just as applicable to the relationship between work and performer. And it is only underlined by the ubiquitous iconography of those in whom the authority of the work is invested, the masterful conductors who wield the baton as others wield the whip. Really it is not surprising that Rowan, Johnson, and countless others think about WAM the way they do.

But if the image of the martinet conductor[14] is the most stereotyped symbol of this authoritarian construction of classic music, it is also a good place to start deconstructing it. Murnighan and Conlon found that string quartets whose leaders were too authoritarian were less successful than those who adopted Cottrell's directed democracy, and the orchestral musicians whom Cottrell interviewed thought the same about conductors. As Cottrell (2004) says, they were 'particularly scathing about those who they perceive as being overly dictatorial' (108). They insisted that was not the way to get the best results. What a conductor 'should really be', one musician told Cottrell, 'is an enabler. He should allow all those musicians to give of their best'. Another agreed: 'I think you have to let your own voice shine. I think a good conductor does allow that'. And research on how conductors and orchestras work together carried out within management studies has come to the same conclusion. There is a widespread assumption that the globe-trotting maestro must be a prime exemplar of what in management speak is called charismatic leadership—the kind of leadership that involves a top-down relationship between leader and followers. However Yaakov Atik, a management consultant who not inappropriately specialises in conflict resolution, carried out extensive interviews not only with orchestral players but also with conductors and orchestral administrators, and found that all of these parties considered the most effective leadership style to be a transformational one. This is grounded in 'an interactive and dynamic perception of the relationship between superior and subordinate' (Atik 1994: 27), resulting wherever possible in the delegation of local decision making to individual players. One of Atik's interviewees, a former player

---

14. One of the musicians interviewed by Cottrell (2004: 108) uses this term, while a Google search on 'martinet conductor' yields 144 hits, many of them referring to George Szell.

now working as an administrator, spoke of the conductor who will 'communicate a point about something and from that point on, leave it up to the abilities that he knows the players have'. And he added: 'That is true leadership' (26).

Of course it might be objected that interview-based studies like Cottrell's and Atik's tell you what people think, or how they would like things to be, but not how they actually are. However Murray Dineen's observational study (2011) of how conductors signal the initial downbeat of a performance also tends towards the same conclusion. Dineen takes a semiotic approach, according to which, as 'the boss's tool', the baton articulates the power relationship between conductor and orchestra: in conducting, Dineen says, 'this power is never settled ultimately, but is instead the constant subject of negotiation' (2011: 139). An example of such negotiation is the process through which an orchestra decides how to read a new conductor's beat, for instance determining whether his gestures are oriented more towards the mechanical or the affective: under such circumstances, Dineen says, the players will above all 'ask themselves if the conductor's downbeats are going to be consistent and always clear, or if they will play a cat-and-mouse game with the orchestra, withholding clarity so as to keep them "on their toes" and thus fresh and focused (and invariably irritated and frustrated)' (136). While the element of negotiation means it is a two-way process, this cat-and-mouse game illustrates how conductors can be said to choreograph social relationships by means of gesture, much as composers do by means of notation. And clarity of beat, or the lack of it, plays an important role in this.

According to Leslie Lewis (2010), Valery Gergeiev does not beat time clearly when performing standard repertory well known to the orchestra: this forces the musicians to listen to one another, and the result is a tighter ensemble than is achieved by student conductors whose beat, as conventionally assessed, is much clearer. And Furtwängler was famous for his unclear beat. The leader of the Berlin Philharmonic Orchestra, Henry Holst, put it like this: 'His beat lacked that "flick of decisiveness" that will enforce precision over an ensemble. That kind of precision he did not like at all: he wanted the precision that grew out of the orchestra, from the players' own initiative, as in chamber music' (Schonberg 1968: 276–77). Perhaps this lies behind Adorno's quip that 'Furtwängler would be the greatest living conductor if he happened to be able to conduct' (2006: 86), as well as the complaints from Paul Henry Lang about his orchestral discipline that I cited in Chapter 2. But this was entirely conscious on Furtwängler's part, for Dineen (2011: 135) quotes his claim that 'There is no doubt that the sharp downbeat has its disadvantages': it results in 'a reduction of the expressive possibility that the living flow of the music demands' (Bamberger 1965: 211). Furtwängler expresses this claim in terms of abstract musical properties, but what he is talking about is social as much as it is musical. And this resonates with what I suggested at the end of the previous paragraph: Gergeiev's and Furtwängler's beats work in much the same way as Mozart's or Beethoven's crotchets.

Dineen makes further observations that reveal the social complexity of conducting. One is 'an evident delay or lag in some orchestras, a brief moment between the conductor's gesture and the sound it elicits'. Dineen's perhaps extravagant interpretation of this (2011: 142) turns on the negotiation of power: it is a tiny moment of defiance through which the orchestra declares 'both its independence and resistance to the conductor'. More relevant for my purposes is what Dineen calls the 'shadow ensemble' (140), a group of key players who maintain constant eye contact with one another, and to whom other orchestra members are highly responsive. A lexicon of small gestures, such as indicating downbeats by nodding the head, enables this group to take over direction of the orchestra at critical times (Dineen mentions a guest conductor who showed up drunk), but it also has a more permanent presence within the social dynamics of the orchestra. These observations blur into the results of Lewis's ethnography (2011) of the complex interactions of leadership that characterise chamber orchestras such as the Britten Sinfonia. Most often the Sinfonia play without a conductor, in which case there will be complex and rehearsed interactions as responsibility for coordinating or timesetting passes from one performer to another—a situation that is familiar from chamber music, and that Lewis theorises in terms of distributed cognition (as invoked by Burrows in the context of collective improvisation). On other occasions there is a conductor, but—as in the case of Dineen's 'shadow ensemble'—that does not mean the other interactions cease. Conducting is just one option within a range of flexible leadership solutions.

In short, the media image of the dictatorial maestro based on nineteenth- and twentieth-century century discourses of musical authority is a caricature of a far more variable and complex social reality. What might be called the command economy model of WAM, where all decisions are made by those in authority and simply handed down, is in reality a recipe for the disfunctional. There are exceptions, but the point is that they are exceptions. Some are intentional, such as the *succès de scandale* that Ernst Krenek achieved in 1923 with the premiere of his Second Symphony (which was attended by Adorno, then aged twenty). His biographer John Stewart (1991: 43) tells the story:

> As Krenek recalls, when the parts had been distributed, he told the players: 'Now we are going to play a piece which you will not understand one bit. Whoever thinks he has the theme please play very loud.' The players dutifully did so, and the ragged performance had a colossal effect that produced an immediate uproar in the audience. Programs and fists were waved above a tumult of shouting and shoving, and some people even came to blows.... Young Adorno was simply overwhelmed by what he took to be a vision of terror and catastrophe.

Krenek, in other words, created the musical effect he was after through constructing a social situation in which the players did not listen to or negotiate with one another—in contravention of the generally unwritten (because taken for granted) norm that, in Johann Petiscus's words, each player 'should moderate his tone, so as not to scream out above the others'.[15]

---

15. Translated from Johann Petiscus's *Ueber Quartettmusik* (1810) by Hunter (2012: 63).

Then there are the unintentional exceptions. Here an example might be the recordings of Webern's complete published works that Robert Craft made in the mid-1950s. Webern's later music was greatly admired in the immediate post-war period for the perceived objectivity of its structure, but its highly pointillistic style posed specific performance problems. Melodic fragments of just one or two notes pass from instrument to instrument, often with large registral leaps or dynamic disjunctions between them. The problem was that, as Timothy Day (2000: 179) explains, no performing tradition had come into being for this kind of music: performers were not prepared for it either by their training or by their subsequent experience. For this reason, Craft explained, he had to coach each player individually 'until he had learned his part like a cipher' (Stravinsky 1972: 95). Once again, to repeat Borgo's words, the musicians were playing as an aggregate of individuals and not an ensemble, slotting in notes mechanically, by the book as it were. Adorno (2006: 149) listened to these recordings in 1958 and sensed the problem: 'The records contain the most subtle examples of senselessness through missed links', he wrote in the notes to his unfinished book, and he continued, 'Already the opening, where the trumpet plays the final note of the flute melody, then similarly the horn. Senseless otherwise'. He clearly went on thinking about it, for on the following page he declares that 'The fundamental rule for the presentation of new music' is 'the thread of the interrupted melody'—at which point it becomes clear that he is talking about the Six Pieces for Large Orchestra, op. 6, an early example of this device.

And writing in the mid-1970s, Boulez made very much the same criticism of the way Webern's music had been performed in the 1950s. There was, he complained,

> a complete lack of continuity between the instruments. . . . So long as a player does not realize that when he has a note to play it comes to him from another instrument and passes from him to yet another, . . . he will . . . produce a note that is 'stupid', divorced from context. That is why those earlier performances of Webern had seemed idiotic to me: the musicians did not seem to understand their roles. They played stupidly, and this was reflected in the resulting sonority, which also became stupid (Boulez 1976: 79).

Boulez's solution, as demonstrated in his own recordings, was the same as Adorno's: 'You have to discover how an instrumentalist can play an isolated sound in a way that links it intelligently with what has gone before and what follows'. And as Day (2000: 183) suggests through judicious juxtaposition of quotations, Boulez was in effect replicating the more general advice offered by the famous modernist conductor Hermann Scherchen in his 1929 *Handbook of Conducting*. 'Melodies that are not given out by one soloist throughout', Scherchen writes, 'but pass, in subdivision, from one instrument to another, cannot be correctly performed unless each player sings the whole of them as they are played, and contributes his share in accordance with the conception of the whole thus formed'. This idea of collective singing may evoke something closer to the utopian connotations of Marx's quadruple brotherly embrace than the sometimes grudging professionalism of orchestral players, but it is just a slightly flowery description of what musicians do—and not only in such iconic and highly mythologised genres as the string quartet. That is why I see musical performance as sociality in sound.

PERFORMING COMPLEXITY

To see music as just a form of writing or even as the designing of sounds is, in this way, to overlook the entire social dimension of performance, from which music derives so much of its meaning. And if this is what musicology, theory, and traditional aesthetic approaches have done, then according to Nicolas Bourriaud, the same might be said of the history and criticism of the visual arts. The basis of his 'relational aesthetics' is the idea of art 'taking as its theoretical horizon the realm of human interactions and its social context, rather than the assertion of an independent and *private* symbolic space' (2002: 14). In other words, Bourriaud proposes that one of the prime functions of art is to construct social relationships among its spectators: it choreographs or scripts social interaction. And having talked at length about the nature of the social interaction involved in performance, at any or all of Waskul's levels, I will now focus in greater detail on specific ways in which scores script performances.

Up to now I have focussed on how scores create spaces for social interaction through underdetermination: the indicative, nominal values of the score leave what Adorno calls a 'zone of indeterminacy' (2006: 181) within which performers negotiate—or more accurately expressed, the just-so, negotiated values of performance augment, substitute for, or displace the notated values. But this makes it sound too much as if the score is just a low-definition version of the performance. As I said in Chapter 7, performers do more than fill in the gaps inside or between the notes. Largely because of the social dimension, the relationship between scores and performances is more indirect, more complex, and more distant from textualist models of reproduction than that would imply. And because of the difficulty of getting away from the entrenched thinking embodied in such familiar models, an effective means of making the point is to step outside music and to develop the analogy with material culture I initiated earlier in the chapter.

Frank Gehry views buildings as expressing and fostering social relationships. Because learning is a social activity, writes Kim Cameron (2003: 90), the Peter B. Lewis Building that Gehry designed for the Weatherhead School of Management in 2002 'had to foster lots of chance collisions and productive interaction patterns'. The same performative approach also characterised the design process. Gehry employed a wide range of visual aids in order to engage the many parties involved in the project. Richard Boland and Fred Collopy (2004: 11), both faculty members at Weatherhead, refer to the many models they saw as the design developed: Gehry's team 'work with their hands', they say, 'making models of the exterior and interior elements out of paper, metal, plastic, waxed cloth, or whatever material gives them both the form and feeling that they are seeking'. But perhaps most telling are the freehand sketches which Gehry produced at an early stage of the design

Figure 8.3 Early sketches by Frank Gehry for the Peter B. Lewis Building. Used by permission of Frank Gehry

process (Figure 8.3). It is obvious that these do not embody significant informational content of the kind that, for example, a quantity surveyor might wish to see: imagine pricing the contract on this basis! Rather, as Boland and Collopy explain, the sketches are 'meant to be spontaneous and evocative of both form and emotion', while for Cameron they express 'a playful sense of experimentation and right-brain thinking'. But the best insight into their function comes from Gehry himself, when he writes: 'you have to dream an idea.... Then you have to work it through the staff in my office. You have to work it through the client, all the people and the committee who have things to do with it.... There are thousands of people in the end that touch this thing' (Cameron 2003: 91). The purpose of these sketches, then, is to facilitate collaborative work, setting out a broad framework that communicates visual dynamics and emotional tone but does not preempt the innumerable concrete decisions that must be negotiated in the course of the collaboration—helping to keep the process liquid, to repeat Gehry's term.

There is an obvious parallel between Gehry's sketches and graphic scores, and indeed it would hardly occasion surprise if one were to come across Figure 8.3 while leafing through John Cage's *Notations* (1969). Pedro Rebelo, whose description of notation as a generative environment I cited in Chapter 7, describes Earle Brown's 'December 1952'—an early graphic score consisting exclusively of vertical and horizontal lines of varying lengths and widths—in terms that offer a direct parallel to Gehry's sketches: 'the score functions as a catalyst to musical collaboration, in which decision-making is distributed between composer, conductor, and performer' (Rebelo 2010: 20). There are differences, of course. In the context of a construction project, the top right and bottom left sketches of Figure 8.3 suggest the articulation of multiple volumes that is a feature of the building as ultimately constructed, and if you are familiar with the tangled, sail-like forms of its stainless steel roof then you can almost see the bottom left sketch as a stylised image of what was built. By contrast the context of 'December 1952' is much more open. Brown's notes suggest treating the score as the map of a three-dimensional space to be traversed in the time of the performance[16]: 'The composition may be performed in any direction from any point in the defined space for any length of time and may be performed from any of the four rotational positions in any sequence'. This allows an effectively unlimited number of ways in which the graphic design might be translated into sound, and Brown directs that performers should make their own interpretive decisions in real time, with only the total duration being agreed in advance (even then he adds that 'further defining of the event is not prohibited'). Just like Gehry's sketch, Brown's score is as much scripting a particular kind of social interaction as representing an aesthetic object.

One of Rebelo's own compositions, 'Exposure 4.1 for Saxophone Quartet', illustrates a different, but again highly indirect, relationship between notation and performance. This partly graphic score includes groups or clusters of notes, sometimes in simplified and sometimes in fully conventional staff notation, so prescribing finger patterns.[17] But breath articulation is specified by means of a separate graphic notation. Given the sensitivity of multiphonics to control of breath, the result is that sonic outcomes become significantly indeterminate. In essence the purpose of this notation is to prompt a rethinking of what it means to play the saxophone: as Rebelo says, it 'produces a method for revisiting the workings of the instrument while suggesting an alternative type of performer-instrument engagement that is based on articulating the separation between the keys/fingers and the mouthpiece/embouchure' (21). Although the element of indeterminacy will have implications for interactions between performers, there is a parallel with Berio's *Gesti* for solo alto recorder, at the beginning of which the performer is directed to repeatedly finger one or two bars from a Telemann sonata movement; the mouth part, by contrast, consists of a dense series of highly specific notations for degrees of lip tension, fluttertongue, singing through the instrument, and inhaling. 'Because of the frequent "contradictions" between the tension of the lips and the finger positions,' writes Berio (1966: 3), 'and because of the speed of changing patterns, the resulting sound is unpredictable....Sometimes the instrument will produce no sound at all'. In this way notation serves as a means through which conventional technique is deconstructed, the familiar defamiliarised.

In none of these cases are performers simply filling in the gaps in the notation: the score is not a low-definition version of the music as performed. Rather

16. Prefatory note to 'Folio and 4 Systems' (1954), http://earle-brown.org/images/file/media/Folio%20and%20Four%20Systems%20Prefatory%20Note.pdf.

17. The score is accessible at http://pedrorebelo.files.wordpress.com/2010/05/exposure-4-0-2011.pdf.

the notation elicits social or physical action that does not translate in any direct manner into sonic outcome. My purpose in discussing these examples is to separate out some of the quite distinct elements and processes through which scores condition performances. The point is to underline the highly mediated nature of the relationship between them, as well as its dependence on specific conventions of interpretation. Non-conventional scores bring the complex nature of this relationship into focus, but my point applies to notations in general: it is just harder to see in the case of notations that are so familiar that we do not easily distinguish the phenomenon from its representation. The complexity of the relationship will come back into focus, however, as we turn to a musical practice that is based in conventional staff notation, and that might appear above all to demand literal reproduction in performance. Yet at the same time it resists such performance, and in this both the social dimension and the reconstruction of conventional technique play an essential role. It is to this practice that the remainder of the chapter is devoted.

The composer and cellist Frank Cox has written at length about the performance practices associated with what are often called 'New Complexity' composers such as Brian Ferneyhough (Cox's teacher), though Cox simply refers to 'complex music'. Cox's starting point is the 'High-Modernist Model of Performance Practice' (hereafter HMMPP) associated with what, in Adornian manner, he calls 'official new music' (Cox 2002: 89). This, Cox explains, is based on the familiar model of 'the "communicative chain" of conception, notation, performance, and reception' (71). It understands this in terms of 'the ideal of a noise-free, "transparent" relationship between all elements of the above-mentioned chain', in which 'all the notes are correct, all the rhythms are accurately realized, all the dynamics, phrasing marks, etc., are audibly projected, and so on'. Insofar as this corresponds to an established philosophy of performance, it is Nelson Goodman's, according to which—as we saw—any performance that deviates in any of these respects should not be regarded as a performance of the purported work at all. In fact HMMPP is simply an extreme form of the traditional concept of all-purpose virtuosity that I mentioned in Chapter 2, based on the assumption that scores specify sound content and performances reproduce scores. It is the principle of music as writing taken to its logical conclusion and assumed to be universally valid (84, 95).

In the course of his critique of this model, to which I shall return, Cox remarks that he will leave it to 'non-human judges', such as computers and other electronic devices, to 'deliver absolute judgments on the correspondence between notation and realization' (103). Empirical musicologists have hardly needed such encouragement. An example of such work is a project in which I collaborated with Eric Clarke, the composer Bryn Harrison, and the pianist Philip Thomas: it was based on *être-temps*, a piano piece by Harrison that had been commissioned specifically for the project. One of the aims was to counteract the overwhelming emphasis on eighteenth- and nineteenth-century music that characterises empirical performance research; others were to involve the composer and performer as members of the research team, to focus on the process of performance preparation from

Figure 8.4 Bryn Harrison, *être-temps*, p. 4. Used by permission of Bryn Harrison

initial run-through to premiere, and to complement quantitative work with ethnography. We made both audio and MIDI recordings of Thomas's playing at various stages up to and including the premiere, recorded a joint rehearsal in which
Harrison and Thomas worked together on the piece, and conducted interviews
with both composer and performer. Like Thomas, Harrison has come to the complexity tradition via American experimental music rather than the dominant
Ferneyhough-Cox route, but *être-temps* shares many of the notational characteristics of Cox's complex music. The most obvious of these is its multilinear textures
with nested, sometimes multiply nested, irrational rhythms. Figure 8.4 shows a
representative page of the score, and Media Example 8.2 is Thomas playing it (the
page is repeated).

Predictably, we did what Cox anticipated: we compared Thomas's performances to the rhythmic specifications in the score, collapsing the multilinear texture into a single series of timepoints and correlating that with the MIDI files. As
detailed by Clarke in the joint article that resulted from this project (Clarke et al.
2005: 48–52), the results we obtained for the top system in Figure 8.4 suggested
that Thomas did not perform very accurately at all. This might fuel cynicism as
to the value of the elaborate notation: as Cox says, critics have not infrequently
claimed that 'the entire domain of complex music is merely a manneristic result
of notational development, and the performance practice for this music consists
largely of fakery' (2002: 78). At this point, however, we recalled what Thomas had
told us about how he learned this and similar passages. As he expressed it in his
contribution to the article,

> I felt that the only way to learn this was to get to know each line on its own,
> and then in pairs before putting them all together, much like Bach coun-
> terpoint....When putting everything together I would then find points that
> I could identify as markers, such as a downbeat in one voice which the other
> voices could respond to, always trying to hear the individual energy of each
> line as learned on its own (Clarke et al. 2005: 40).

Maybe then the place to look for accuracy was within each individual line?
Re-analysed on this basis, the data showed that Thomas's performance was
strikingly accurate; the contrast between this and our original measurements
suggested he was expressing his contrapuntal conception of the music through
a slight desynchronisation between textural layers—a technique usually associated with early twentieth-century pianism. There is an important lesson here. We
had begun with an analysis that was mathematically right but musically wrong,
in that it was not adapted to Thomas's performance strategy. Inadvertently we
had fallen into the same trap as Binet and Courtier, who (as I said in Chapter 1)
assumed that the point of performance was to reproduce the score. And we
discovered this only because we supplemented our quantitative approach with
an ethnographic one. Because of the multi-dimensional nature of performance,
it always makes sense to combine approaches where possible, and the combination of measurement and ethnography is a prime example.[18] I shall return to this
in Chapter 10.

Actually the charge of fakery, while understandable, betrays ignorance as well
as cynicism. Performers of complex music fuss a great deal about accuracy. The
topic cropped up repeatedly in Thomas's interview, and especially in the joint

---

18. For a particularly ambitious combination of quantitative and ethnographical approaches
see Volioti (2012), a study of performance traditions in Grieg's piano music that uses the
self-organising maps approach adopted in Rink, Spiro, and Gold (2011), but triangulates it with
performer interviews. Volioti (2010) offers a more general discussion of the relevance of empirical and ethnographical approaches in the definition of tradition.

rehearsal. And Thomas made use of a number of techniques in order to achieve accuracy that have become sufficiently widespread among specialists in this area of performance, and sufficiently well documented in their writings, to be called an established performance practice. These techniques include, for example, converting polyrhythms into a uniform temporal series by taking their least common multiple (Schick 1994: 138), and converting complex textures into spatial grids in order to clarify the relative placement of events—whether as between different lines or instruments, or in relation to the conductor's beat (Cox 2002: 97). Again, a common device for handling irrational rhythms is tempo conversion: instead of attempting to play six in the space of five, you temporarily increase the tempo by 20%. As Cox (97) says, this necessitates 'a high level of ability to memorize and accurately and instantly reproduce absolute metronomic speeds', but that is a skill that performers of this repertory (like conductors specialising in film scores) have developed. One preparation technique that I have not seen mentioned in the complexity literature is the use of synthesised 'reference' recordings; it will shortly become obvious why this might be.[19]

As can be imagined, the use of these techniques entails extensive preparation. Thomas describes using a calculator to sort out a particularly complicated example of tempo conversion,[20] while Irvine Arditti explains that a 'kitchen table pre-rehearsal analysis of the piece' is indispensable when playing the music of composers like Ferneyhough. The result of all this preparation is that when music of this kind is performed, the musicians are frequently playing from something quite different from the published parts: Bayley and Heyde (forthcoming) refer to the 'very often elaborate hybrids in which extensive additional material (often cues in various forms) has been added by the player'. It is a curious thought that a musicologist of the future, working on the basis of published scores and recordings, might be quite unable to reconstruct the processes through which this kind of music was actually played.

As our analysis of Thomas's playing indicates, the net effect of these techniques is that something remarkably close to literal reproduction can be achieved. When they talk and write about their playing, however, performers tend to be more ambivalent. Thomas apparently underestimated his own accuracy, telling Clarke,

19. Actually I know of little documentation of this practice at all; for a rare example see Nigel Morgan's blog 'Blaze—the Reference Recordings', 10 January 2012, http://www.soundingthedeep.co.uk/2012/01/10/blaze---the-reference-recordings/.

20. 'The initial tempo in *être-temps* is set at quaver = 104. Using this as my control tempo, I was able to treat the rhythmic ratios as slightly faster or slightly slower than this reference point. I tabulated a literal metronome mark for all the differing tempi, so that I could be sure of the correct relativities of tempo; this also enabled me to establish the degree of difference between relatively simple ratios, such as 8:7, and more complex ones, like a triplet within a 7:6 ratio. One particularly complex relationship, found on page 7, needed a calculator to reveal that the speed of a quaver in one bar (bar 136) corresponded to 114 MM, while in the next it was 121—a difference of only 6%' (Clarke et al. [2005: 40–41]).

'hearing it on the Disklavier, if someone was going to really meticulously see the timings of that, then it would be different every time. I'm not going to be, it's not going to be exact'. Again, Cox (2002: 99) points out that interaction between parameters means that mathematical accuracy in timing 'bears no absolute relationship to perception'. And the pianist Ian Pace (2009: 190) roundly asserts that asking whether Ferneyhough's rhythms can be played accurately is the wrong question. All of this, of course, could be seen as an insurance or pre-emptive strike against the threat posed by empirical musicologists. But I would rather put it down to a fundamental contradiction between the reproduction-based approach of Cox's HMMPP and a way of thinking that is definitive of what I shall call the culture of complexity.

In an interview with James Boros from 1990, Ferneyhough distinguished between two types of performers. One, he says, is 'the "gig" musician…who, in a couple of rehearsals, is justly proud of producing a "professional" realization of just about anything' (Ferneyhough and Boros 1990: 6–7). Writing for this type of musician entails the absorption of 'whole chunks of conventional wisdom in terms of musical thinking', Ferneyhough continues, 'since ease of realization is frequently a function of expectation or applicability of already present manual patterns'. The other type is 'the performer who's willing to spend six months or so really trying to penetrate to the roots of a style, to focus in on the mental development of the composer during the act of creation so as to be able to actively counterpoint this against his own personal learning and reproduction dynamic'—and this, he adds, is the sort of performer with whom he prefers to work.

Elsewhere Ferneyhough has said, 'We should never forget that contemporary music wouldn't exist today I think without dedicated ensembles' (Archbold 2011: 54). The culture of complexity depends on long-term relationships in which professional collaboration and shared commitment shade into friendship. But what exactly is in it for the performers? 'Most performers worth their salt', writes the pianist Stephen Drury (1994: 194), 'relish a composer's challenge and prefer to sink their teeth and digits into a musical stew rich enough to require hours of study and repeated performances with new and changing flavors, insights, and experiences'. Cox (2002) puts it more strongly: 'All players who have seriously attempted to master the challenges of radical complex music can testify to the transformative effects these challenges have on one's relationship to the instrument' (128). Cox's formulation touches on one of the fundamental values of this culture, which is a commitment to transcending the 'conventional wisdom' to which Ferneyhough referred, a process of self-development as both musician and person that is structured around the constant re-evaluation of what it is to play your instrument. Of course this is not something unique to complexity culture. We saw the idea of disassembling and reassembling technique with Rebelo and Berio. And in his unfinished book, Adorno (2006) wrote that 'the habituality of each player'—which we might gloss as the all-purpose technique of Ferneyhough's 'gig' musician—is 'negated, and sublated by the specific insights arising from each work. This marks the transition to true interpretation' (131). As usual with Adorno, these ideas have deep roots: in Chapter 6 I mentioned the parallel between his and Schenker's views on virtuosity, which are not so far from Cox's on HMMPP.

But composers and performers of complex music have perhaps developed this way of thinking more radically than any others, transforming it into the performance equivalent of Frankfurt-School critical theory. The point can be made by juxtaposing three quotations of increasing temperature, so to speak. The clarinettist Roger Heaton (2012a) complains that conservatory-trained performers of contemporary music 'find it impossible to suppress an impulse derived from earlier styles to "phrase" or "shape"' (97, 96), in other words to play 'musically' where the criterion of musicality is a nineteenth-century expressivity (or perhaps we should say a present-day understanding of nineteenth-century expressivity). By contrast, he continues, 'The role of the performer is to identify with the work using a number of different strategies that hold the key to a performance stimulated by creativity and imagination rather than observance of tradition'. The Adornian flavour comes closer to the surface in Cox (2002: 79), for whom performers who cannot be bothered to master complex notations instead use them 'as a "cue-sheet" for their musical habits', and he continues:

> When freedom is defined as merely the negative of responsibility the content of the freedom will usually sink to the adolescent level of the definition—at worst, a generic narcissism. Bare intuition deprived of challenges tends to be extremely conservative, and the freedom of the individual interpreter can only be meaningfully realized when all his/her abilities are directed toward meeting and realizing new tasks at least sufficient to them, or even better, beyond their present reach.

And with Pace, the Adornian agenda becomes quite explicit. In Morton Feldman's *Bunita Marcus*, for example, Pace recommends a strategy of 'working *against* the assimilation of this music into a notion of "tradition"'—even, he adds, 'if this makes the music less amenable to what might be called a "chill-out" form of listening' (2009: 175). By the final page of his article he is speaking of 'a strategy of *resistance* in performance: resistance towards certain ideological assumptions that entail absorption of musical works into the culture industry' (192).

Yet there is something paradoxical in this culture. The percussionist Steven Schick commissioned Ferneyhough's *Bone Alphabet* (1991), and it was in the course of preparing it that he developed the tempo conversion and other techniques I referred to earlier (as did other performers at other times and places). But, he tells us, the composer was not happy: 'In rehearsal Ferneyhough clearly expressed his desire that the performer not translate polyrhythmic composites into shifting tempi', on the grounds that 'polyrhythms seen as shifting tempi imply a reorientation of the overall metrical point of view' (Schick 1994: 139). In recommending these techniques, Schick therefore justifies their value 'as a stage in the learning process', adding, 'Eventually such passages should be heard by the performer in the original tempo' (140). Cox (2002: 98) concurs: despite 'their great value as preparation for practice or as methods of checking for accuracy', he says, all these conversion techniques are 'insufficiently responsible to the notated tasks'. He concurs with Ferneyhough too, adding that tuplets are 'most productively conceived of as temporary counter-meters existing in a precise dissonential relationship to the meter and other strata'.

And two pages later he launches another attack that seems to undermine the 'great value' of these techniques in preparation. In adopting them, he argues, 'one is not practicing the individual tasks themselves (as indicated by the notation)....One is not learning the tuplet itself' (100). Conversion techniques, after all, run counter to the basic principles of the culture of complexity. They consist of the grafting of new capabilities onto established techniques, the extension into new areas of what Heaton similarly refers to as 'a kind of "utility musicality" which may have nothing to do with the specific piece or its radical nature' (2012b: 786). They make it possible to reproduce complex scores understood as sound design, but not to realise their potential for transformation. In short, they enable 'gig' musicians to play Ferneyhough. The defamiliarised becomes familiar. Yesterday's Parnassus becomes tomorrow's audition piece. Or to put it another way, a new musical tradition defined in opposition to HMMPP and its 'naïve fetishization of the text' (Cox 2002: 131) ends up by simply raising the professional bar and leaving the reproduction of the text in place. It becomes the new establishment.

To what extent, then, does the culture of complexity attribute creative agency to the performer in the interpretation of these complex scores? Ferneyhough has often been asked why he notates his music as he does, even by sympathetic performers such as Arditti (Archbold 2011: 57), and consequently a number of responses are on record. Sometimes his approach to the performer seems quite depersonalising, sometimes it is a theorisation of the performer's freedom, and sometimes it contrives to be both at once. Ferneyhough's *Time and Motion Study III* (1974) uses the International Phonetic Alphabet to break down and recompose the texts on which it is based, and it sounds as if something similar is happening to the performers when Ferneyhough (1995: 94) refers to 'notating the tension of the throat muscles, position of the tongue and the shaping of the lips, etc. as separately-rhythmicized parametric strands'. That takes Rebelo's and Berio's approach to the next level. It is as if the composer is bypassing the singer as a person and instead scoring directly for his or her vocal organs. But then Ferneyhough adds that, in this way, 'I was implying to the performer that he or she think themselves into the dynamics of the simultaneity as such, not reproduce a more or less complex action. I was, above all, looking to generate a form of "mental polyphony" in the interpreters' minds'. There is a similar ambivalence in Ferneyhough's statement with reference to his 1974 flute composition 'Unity Capsule', that 'performers are no longer expected to function solely as optimally efficient reproducers of imagined sounds; they are in themselves "resonators" in and through which the initial impetus provided by the score is amplified and modulated in the most varied ways imaginable' (100). This is an assertion of the performers' agency, but in the depersonalised form of 'resonators' (and note that he says 'in and through which', rather than 'whom').

Much clearer, however, is the rationale Ferneyhough (1990: 10–11) provides in the 1990 interview with Boros, where he directly addresses accusations that his notational 'over-specification' leaves performers without decision-making potential of their own. 'What might arguably upset a performer even more', he acidly observes, 'is not knowing why they're doing something', and he explains that his method of notation attempts 'to suggest to the player relevant methods and priorities wherewith the material can usefully be approached'. And drawing a comparison with conventional scores—those that are not over-specified—he adds that 'Suggesting contexts of this sort via notation allows the player a different but no less important "free space" within which to move'. In short, Ferneyhough is arguing that what Cox would call the freedom of responsible performance lies not in executing a series of instructions, however impeccably, but in possessing one's own understanding of the music, and expressing that through performance. It is exactly the argument that Schenker made against the performing editions published by editors such as Riemann (who, as we saw in Chapter 6, justified his *Phrasierungsausgaben* on the grounds that they did away with the need for reflection). Indeed it is an argument with a much longer lineage. In his *Contribution to the Study of Ornamentation*, published in 1903, Schenker (1976: 46) attacked Bülow's editions of C. P. E. Bach's keyboard music (in which phrasing and dynamics were specified and embellishments written out) for encouraging just such an ignorant, mechanical approach, and he quoted Bach's own injunction in his *Essay on the True Art of Playing Keyboard Instruments*: the performance of such embellishments, Bach says, 'requires a freedom of performance that rules out everything slavish and mechanical. Play from the soul, not like a trained bird!' (1974: 150) And this links to what I said in Chapter 7 about the slow movements of Corelli's op. 5. The original notations do not tell performers what to play, but instead present them with a version of the music that is designed for the intelligent eye, that embodies 'its own logic of sequence and motivic consistency' (Butt 2002: 120)—and leaves to them the challenging task of recreating it as performance.

Both Harrison and Thomas are committed to the creative agency of the performer. Thomas writes that 'performers take an active role in the creative act of forming the composition' (Clarke et al. 2005: 41), while in interview Harrison concurred: 'I wouldn't want to feel I was one of those composers who feel that there's no flexibility in terms of what the player can bring to a piece, I think that's where the sort of human aspect comes in and I think that that's the really, really important part of music-making as far as I'm concerned'. He went on to explain that, when he started getting performances and attending rehearsals, he would feel he had to immediately have the answer to any question the performers might ask, whereas now he thinks it important to trust the players' judgements. In this way Harrison, like Robert Martin, sees the creative process as not terminating when the score is finished, but continuing as performers bring the music to the stage, and it is clear from the DVDs of Ferneyhough working with the Arditti Quartet and Finnissy working with the Kreutzer Quartet that they think the same way. But perhaps the most tangible way to make the point is in terms of how Thomas thought of Harrison's complex notations. I have described the measures he took to ensure that he got them right through preparation and calculation. In interview he described himself as 'counting like mad' during a page that consists of irregularly repeated chords. And yet he repeatedly denied that, in performance, he was executing the specifications of the score in a straightforwardly mathematical sense. He referred, for example, to Harrison's use of changing bar lengths and nested tuplets in one passage as 'a classic kind of notational device to prompt the performer to respond in ways which will always keep it floating and never rooted in anything, always keep it changing'. And he remarked of a passage near the end when the hands are playing in different tempos, 'It's not highly calculated stuff, it's more a way of just inspiring the performer to do certain kinds of thing'.

Of course, given the preparation that had gone into this performance, you might suppose that Thomas had internalised the piece as sequence of actions and sounds that he was then able to reproduce in performance: that could explain the apparently relaxed approach suggested by his references to the score prompting or inspiring a particular response (or, as he said on other occasions, encouraging or nudging him). Seen this way, complex music might be thought to encourage an over-learned approach that would be prejudicial to the kind of flexibility and ongoing decision-making that is valued within the culture of complexity. But that is not at all how either Thomas or Harrison saw it, as became clear from one of their exchanges during the joint rehearsal. As usual, Thomas was worrying about whether he was really playing accurately.

PHILIP THOMAS: How does it feel the last section, when it's more complicated rhythm between the two hands?
BRYN HARRISON: You can feel the change from something that is in one metre to two, definitely, you get a slight feeling of acceleration as well, which is nice.
PHILIP: Do you think it's accurate? I think I'm pretty accurate.
BRYN: As far as I can tell, I'm struggling to tell.
PHILIP: You kind of do it so much, I've practised it, and then you get used to it, and it gets compromised again, so I've got to keep kicking myself in the arse to kind of take it apart again, I think that's the problem, I've got to keep unravelling it.
BRYN: Otherwise you get used to the sound and keep imitating yourself in a slightly inaccurate way really.

For Thomas, what is crucial is not that you accurately reproduce the intended sound design. Or put more precisely, it is crucial, but as a means rather than as an end. The end is a kind of energy that is created through the act of complex performance, a manifestation of real-time presence. That is why he has to take the music to pieces and put it back together every time he plays it, in that sense playing it always as if for the first time. (I am reminded of Frost and Yarrow's claim that, despite the intensive rehearsal that leads to it, every dramatic performance is improvised.) In his contribution to the article, Thomas explained that this energy is already implicated or prefigured in the process of learning the music. He is speaking of the passage consisting of irregularly repeated chords where he had to count like mad:

> As I devise a strategy for counting, a certain energy is created in my mind which impacts upon the articulation of the gestures. Page 5, for example, consists very simply of the same three-note cluster repeated at different dynamics, with slightly different durations, and positioned irregularly throughout the page. The complexity of the counting needed to measure accurately the lengths of the intervening rests is, of course, unheard by the listener; but the impact of that counting upon the articulation of the cluster across time is such that each sound has its own energy. If Bryn had notated this using either a simpler rhythmic strategy, or space-time notation, that energy would, I suggest, be noticeably lacking (Clarke et al. 2005: 39–40).

Cox talks in a similar way of energy, but he pushes the idea a stage further. He speaks of 'that intangible performative energy which arises in the gap between what is learned, what is earnestly striven-for, and what can be achieved in responsible performance of any music' (97). His basic point, then, is one about performance in general. But it has a particularly direct relevance to 'radical complex music', he continues, where 'this energy is often built into the tasks of the piece and is a substantial part of the musical content'. And it is here that he goes beyond Thomas. For Cox (103), this energy is itself not so much an end as a means. The end is ultimately an ethical one: 'The measure of performative responsibility ought to be grounded less on the external threat of punishment of mistakes (absolutely equated with failure[21]), than on a Kantian positive striving to live up to *self-acknowledged* moral imperatives for responsible interpretation in confrontation with the musical tasks and musical substance'. Mathematically correct reproduction of complex rhythms is not then the point, nor does it matter 'whether any hearer can judge the difference between "correct" performance or not' (Cox 2002). What matters is the sincerity with which the attempt is made. In short, the score scripts a process of personal development, a form of *Bildung*, and this is another dimension of performative meaning that is overlooked when music is seen as a form of writing or as sound design.

When, in the seventeenth century, Western musicians first came to the High Qing court, the Chinese were particularly struck by their ability to play music at sight, even transcriptions of Chinese melodies (Jia 2012: 32). This is something that traditional Chinese notations, and indeed most non-Western notations, are not designed for. For example, creating a performance on the basis of the character-based tablature used for the *qin* or long zither, traditionally the preferred instrument of scholars, involves an extended process of technical and

---

21. By 'absolutely' he means in terms of HMMPP.

hermeneutical interpretation, known as *da pu* (Yung 1985); both in the time it takes and in the personal interpretation to which it gives rise, the process has obvious similarities to the interpretive practices of complexity performers. And more than anything it is the ability to play at sight, represented at its highest level by Ferneyhough's 'gig' musicians, that creates the impression that the music is all there in the score and only requires skilled reproduction—in other words that notation is transparent, just a stage in the communicative process from composer to receiver. (It would be quite impossible to think of *qin* tablature in such a way.) And that, of course, is the ideology of Cox's HMMPP, and of the textualist paradigm more generally. Graphic and complex scores, as well as *qin* tablature, make the limitations of that ideology self-evident, but they only present in a more obvious form something that is also true of conventional notations such as those of Mozart's and Beethoven's string quartets.

In short, as I said in Chapter 7, notation shapes music in the act of representing it, and so the relationship between writing and playing or hearing can never be direct and unmediated. For one thing, while there are elements of the iconic in conventional notations—elements that map more or less directly from the score onto actions or sounds—they are both limited and channelled by symbolic elements, that is, elements whose meaning is contextual and historically contingent. An icon is after all a sign, and as such part of a larger semiotic economy. (I shall return to this in Chapter 11.) We have also seen that the nominal values on which scores are based under-specify the particularities of performance, and in this sense it might be said that there is no such thing as a performing score. In place of the communicative chain presupposed by HMMPP, Cox (2002: 103) argues for understanding the relationship of score and performance as one of 'translation' between qualitatively different domains:[22] this is, of course, translation in the strong sense in which Benjamin and Rosenwald saw it as a process through which meaning is produced. If it is easy to mistake this for a relationship of one-to-one correspondence, that is because of the excessive familiarity of staff notation as used in Mozart's and Beethoven's string quartets, and because of the invisibility of the tacit knowledge—Ferneyhough's 'conventional wisdom'—that informs its use. And finally, to see music as a form of writing or as sound design is to overlook the role of scores in scripting both social interaction and personal development, and so to ignore whole swathes of the meaning that emerges in the act of performance.

But there is one last point that remains to be made about Thomas's performance of *être-temps*. Just as there can in a sense be no such thing as a performing score, so within the WAM tradition there is in a sense no such thing as a solo performance. In saying this I don't simply mean that performance involves interaction with an audience; you can after all perform to yourself, though to do so is in a certain sense to construct another self to perform to. Nor do I simply mean that the sound of performance is an inherently public medium, in that my knowledge of what I play is not privileged over yours: in that sense, performance can never

22. I developed a similar argument in Cook (1999d).

be merely, or fully, subjective. What I mean is that there is a process of interaction taking place between Thomas on the one hand, and Harrison's score on
the other (and I would argue that this might be the case even if Thomas chose
to play without the music, as we revealingly put it, in the manner of the traditional virtuoso.) I say 'interaction' because this is not a purely one-way relationship, as assumed by the 'communicative chain' model of performance, but rather
a form of dialogue. The score speaks back to Thomas as he takes it apart and
puts it together: that is how it cuts through the temptation for him to imitate
himself slightly inaccurately. It keeps him, so to speak, on his toes, in the manner of Dineen's cat-and-mouse-playing conductor. The score, in short, acts as an
non-human agent, in precisely the sense in which Bruno Latour (2005: 71) defines
this concept: it makes a difference in the course of Thomas's action.

In this way, music embodies agency and so becomes an interlocutor. Lonnie
Hillyer compares jazz improvisation to 'a guy having a conversation with himself'
(Berliner 1994: 192). In his autoethnography of jazz piano performance, David
Sudnow refers to the notes 'speaking back' to him and makes the observation—
which might seem uncanny if it were not a familiar experience—that when he
plays, 'the fingers are making the music all by themselves' (1978: 64, xiii). And
in the case of classical performers such intimate interactions of self and other
can reach far into the past: '*Most* of what I know about myself', writes the pianist Jonathan Biss (2012), 'I have learned from playing Schumann'. The ghostly
presence of the dead becomes palpable in the relationship with Luigi Boccherini
(1743–1805) that Elisabeth Le Guin experiences as she plays his Cello Sonata in
E♭ major—a relationship that she insists is not only very tender and searchingly
physical, but also 'somehow reciprocal' (2005: 14). As she plays, 'I become aware
of a poignance of presence, the unmistakable sensation of someone here—and
not only here, but inhabiting my body' (25). Boccherini choreographs her physical motions, tells her how to feel, while conversely she acts out 'the connection
between parts of someone who cannot be here in the flesh. I have become, not
just his hands, but his binding agent, the continuity, the consciousness' (24). In
short, Le Guin is in a relationship – and it is a relationship scripted by the notes
on the page. There is then a sense in which you are never alone with music. And
it is because of the 'concealed social character of solo performance' (Clarke et al.
2005: 31) that, in talking about the scripting of social interaction, I have been
talking not just about ensemble performance, but about performance in general.

9

The Signifying Body

When Jimi Hendrix came on stage I . . . found myself less than four feet from his Marshall stack. Maybe it was exhaustion, maybe it was the chaos of his equipment failures or maybe it was just the fact that off form or not Hendrix was still Hendrix, but I found myself lying on the stage staring up at this wild afro and thinking it can't get any better than this!!

—ANDY DUNKLEY

I stayed on to see Hendrix. I went down into the arena and fell asleep waiting. When I woke there was this terrible tuneless racket coming from the stage, so I decided to go, thinking I had missed Hendrix. Only later did I realise that it was Hendrix I had heard when I woke up.

—BENJAMIN HORRENDOUS*

31 AUGUST 1970, 3.30 AM

It was the time Hendrix split his pants in the middle of a song. In his biography of the guitarist, Carles Shaar Murray (1989: 8) describes Hendrix's appearance at the 1970 Isle of Wight Festival as follows:

After an unconscionably protracted delay, he sauntered on stage and grimly muscled his way through a set of his best-known tunes, padded out with meandering jams. Hendrix and his accompanists—bassist Billy Cox, drummer Mitch Mitchell—seemed to be operating in parallel but separate universes, never meshing, only sporadically catching fire. The electronic demons, once so effortlessly summoned from his wall of Marshall amplifiers and controlled and tamed with his guitar, now mocked and evaded him. . . . Shivering in the damp chill night, the crowd willed him on—he was,

*Both from 'The Isle of Wight festivals 1968–70', http://www.ukrockfestivals.com/vftmud-iow.html.

after all, the reason they were there—but to no avail. He seemed exhausted, tormented, trapped. His death, less than three weeks later, seemed hideously appropriate. On the festival stage, Hendrix had already seemed three parts dead.

The tone of this account is partly shaped by Murray's larger narrative, but the circumstances of the festival were not easy. There had been wrangles with local residents and the council about the site, and the festival had ended up located next to a hill, meaning that many attendees watched the music without paying. The organisers erected a corrugated metal wall to keep out those without tickets, but then declared the festival to be a free event, infuriating those who had already paid. Most of all, the sheer numbers overwhelmed the organisers' ability to cope with them: the audience was estimated at six hundred thousand, bigger than the legendary Woodstock Festival that had taken place the previous year in upstate New York. The day after the Isle of Wight Festival ended, one of the promoters, Ron Fouke, supposedly said, 'This is the last festival, enough is enough, it began as a beautiful dream but it has got out of control and become a monster'[1]—and indeed there was not to be another Isle of Wight Festival until 2002.

Nor were things easy for the performers. Billy Cox, who had replaced Noel Redding as the Jimi Hendrix Experience's bassist at Woodstock and stayed with the band, recalled the lack of both organisation and camaraderie that characterised the festival: for hours he, Hendrix, and drummer Mitch Mitchell huddled together in a trailer on the night of Sunday 30 August, waiting to be called to the stage.[2] In any case, according to Murray (1989), Hendrix had no wish to be there at all: 'economic pressures caused by financial mismanagement', Murray writes, 'had forced him back out on the road to play a tour in which he had no artistic interest whatsoever' (9). Like many artists whose success is built on a highly distinctive image, Hendrix had come to feel trapped by audience expectations, and increasingly it was Electric Lady, the sixteen-track recording studio he had created in New York earlier that year, on which his musical interests focussed. Given the circumstances, it is not surprising that the prevailing view of those who posted their reminiscences on the 'Isle of Wight festivals 1968–70' website is that Hendrix was by no means at his best—but, given his death eighteen days later, they are thankful they went.[3] I wondered about going, but had been to the Bath Festival in June, which had a perhaps even better lineup, and there was bound to be another chance to see Hendrix. Fortunately the documentary director Murray

1. http://www.ukrockfestivals.com/iow1970menu.html.

2. *Blue Wild Angel: Jimi Hendrix Live at the Isle of Wight* (MCA/Experience Hendrix, 2002), DVD booklet, 6.

3. http://www.ukrockfestivals.com/vftmud-iow.html.

Lerner filmed the entire festival, and though financial problems meant that none of this footage appeared until the 1990s, a film of Hendrix's performance was released in 1997 under the title *Blue Wild Angel*.

Delays piled up and it was after two on Monday morning by the time the Experience finally got on stage; many of those who *had* gone to the Isle of Wight to see Hendrix slept through his performance. The set included many of Hendrix's concert standards. And among them was 'Foxy Lady',[4] which had featured on the band's debut album, *Are You Experienced* (1967). The lyrics are addressed to the eponymous protagonist (a strutting bimbo—Murray's [1989: 73] term—who has been identified with several women in Hendrix's life at that time), and basically say he wants to take her to bed. There is no readily identifiable melody, especially given Hendrix's raspy, semi-spoken vocalisation. In fact, regarded in conventional terms as a song, there is hardly anything there. Hendrix's manager and the producer of *Are You Experienced*, Chas Chandler, recalled that 'If we had a constant row in the studio...it was where his voice should be in the mix. I mean he always wanted to have his voice buried and I always wanted to bring it forward'.[5] Hendrix's preference nicely symbolises how the textual and vocal dimension serves less as the focus of his performance of 'Foxy Lady'—whether at the Isle of Wight or elsewhere—than as the frame within which performative meaning is produced.

Indeed if we return briefly to the issue of work identity, it becomes clear that the song as traditionally defined is just one, and hardly the most significant, of the features that characterise the many performances collectively known as 'Foxy Lady'. Of course any performance of 'Foxy Lady' is haunted by the shadowy figure of the lady herself, rather as Beethoven's middle-period *oeuvre* is haunted by his Immortal Beloved, but Hendrix treated the lyrics with considerable abandon. When different performances of 'Foxy Lady' are compared it can be seen that he changes the words, drops lines, adds interpolations, or reconstructs the verses: at the Isle of Wight the second half of his second verse is actually a repetition of the corresponding section of the first verse, and it is not obvious that we should see it as a mistake rather than simply what Hendrix did on that occasion. Far more important for the song's identity, in the sense that it spells instant recognition, is its riff and the dominant seventh sharp ninth chord—a variant of the so called 'Hendrix chord'—on which it based: colouring the sound of 'Foxy Lady' as a whole, this chord can be heard, in Rob van der Bliek's words, as 'a coalescence of a significant portion of the characteristic pitch configuration used in the blues idiom' (2007: 360). Even here, however, Hendrix was not quite consistent. Of the filmed recordings listed at Figure 9.1, taken from a mixture of official recordings

---

4. Often referred to as 'Foxey Lady', owing to a misspelling on the original North American release of *Are You Experienced*.

5. Transcribed by Myles Eastwood from *The Jimi Hendrix Experience: Electric Ladyland* DVD (MCA/Experience Hendrix, 2004).

Monterey, California	18 June 1967
Royal Albert Hall, London	18/24 February 1969
Woodstock, New York	18 August 1969
Atlanta, Georgia	4 April 1970
Randall's Island, New York	17 July 1970
Maui, Hawaii (Rainbow Bridge)	30 July 1970
Isle of Wight	31 August 1970

Figure 9.1 Filmed performances of 'Foxy Lady'

and bootlegs,[6] the first three feature an opening riff that begins F#-F#-A, whereas those from 1970 begin E-F#-A. (Curiously, the published transcription of the song has E-E-A.[7]) But *pace* Goodman, it hardly matters. Everybody can recognise the song straight away whatever the first note is. It is probably only guitarists and musicologists who notice the difference.

The riff is obviously part of the song, but there are other things that might be thought of as aspects of performance yet are, if not invariant, then at least typical features of 'Foxy Lady'. (The resonance with my discussion of Corelli's op. 5 is intentional.[8]) Many of them are also shared with other songs as Hendrix performed them, but their clustering becomes a distinguishing feature of 'Foxy Lady'. The nearest thing to a genuine invariant is the long first note, building from nothing to a *fortissimo*, and generated through feedback. Hendrix created it by fingering E^2, $F\#^2$, and $A\#^2$, playing the $F\#^2$ with an exaggerated vibrato, and then gradually turning up the volume knob on his guitar to create the feedback.[9] In earlier recordings, such as the one on *Are You Experienced* and at Monterey, you hear all three notes in a kind of tremolo effect before the feedback takes over,

6. Sources used were as follows: *The Jimi Hendrix Experience: Live at Monterey* (Universal 2007); http://www.youtube.com/watch?v=5tRh67AlthQ (Royal Albert Hall, no longer at this URL as this volume goes to press but accessible at http://www.dailymotion.com/video/x6ym30_jimi-hendrix-foxy-lady-royal-albert_music); *Jimi Hendrix Live at Woodstock Definitive 2 DVD Collection* (Universal Island, 2005); http://www.youtube.com/watch?v=JchAOH4KCuk (Atlanta, no longer at this URL but accessible at http://vimeo.com/65972143); http://www.youtube.com/watch?v=u2-m6QRiEO0 (Randall's Island); http://www.youtube.com/watch?v=U9AL0p8t-Ww (Rainbow Island); *Blue Wild Angel: Jimi Hendrix Live at the Isle of Wight* (MCA/Experience Hendrix, 2002).

7. *Experience Hendrix: The Best of Jimi Hendrix* (Seattle: Experience Hendrix), 169: curious because the original recording on *Are You Experienced* begins with two F#s. As explained later, Hendrix normally detuned his guitar by about a semitone, which means that 'Foxy Lady' sounds as if it was in F minor. However I shall refer to it as in F# minor, since that is the key in which Hendrix and Cox were playing.

8. See Chapter 7, p. 241.

9. As explained in *Experience Hendrix*, 169.

and at Monterey Hendrix actually called attention to this little bit of magic: 'Foxy Lady', he announced, 'My fingers won't move, you won't hear no sound, but dig this'. In later performances, by contrast, you hear the feedback from the start, and the note lasts much longer. At the Isle of Wight it lasted so long that Hendrix made extensive dedications over it, but he didn't announce the song itself. There was no need; everyone recognised it.

As this opening note conveys no sense of time, Hendrix had to cue in the other players. By the time the feedback had kicked in he didn't need his picking hand, so he could have used it to cue them. But that is not how Hendrix performed 'Foxy Lady'. Instead, at the Monterey performance from 1967, he jumped up and down to set the tempo, and this jumping became another characteristic feature of the song, as did sinking to his knees and sometimes pointing with hand outstretched during the second or sixth bars of the opening riff (the Rainbow Bridge and Isle of Wight performances illustrate this). On occasion—as at the Royal Albert Hall, Randall's Island, and again the Isle of Wight—he would repeat both of these gestures at the beginning of the final riff, creating something akin to the effect of recapitulation in a classical composition. Steve Waksman (1999: 203) comments that 'Perhaps he experienced each performance as a unique, spontaneous act, but the repetition of gestures over time suggests a more conscious and more complicated process'. A simpler way of thinking about this is that, for Hendrix, these gestures were as much part of the song as the words.

And then there is the ending. In the original recording on *Are You Experienced*, the song ends with the final riff. In live performance, however, Hendrix added what might be called an outro, but he developed it into such a significant section of the song that I shall use the classical term 'coda' for it. Like the initial note, it is relatively brief in the Monterey performance, but the essential elements that Hendrix built on in later performances are already there. As in the opening feedback there is no measured tempo, and the other musicians create a sustained pad of sound over which Hendrix plays freely. He plumbs the depths of the guitar's range, playing only with his right hand (more on this shortly), raising or wheeling his left hand, and building to a closing gesture that is expressed in both physical and sonorous terms. In subsequent performances this coda becomes increasingly sustained and distinctive—and never more so than at the Isle of Wight.

Hendrix may have made free with the words, but songs do imply some degree of form. Except that there is no coda in the version on *Are You Experienced*, all the performances in Figure 9.1—with the sole exception of the last—follow the recording. After the introductory feedback and riff, Hendrix sings the first verse, followed after a repetition of the riff by the second; the ends of the verses are articulated by a moment's silence and an interjection along the lines of 'ooh—Foxy Lady' (with the 'ooh' in falsetto). Then there is an extensive solo, followed—except at Rainbow Bridge—by a further half verse, normally the second half of either the first or second verse. And then there is the coda. The total length varies from about three and a half to five and a half minutes. But against this background, the Isle of Wight performance stands out as strikingly anomalous. It lasts over seven minutes, and has an oddly straggling form: the standard plan I have just outlined is augmented by meandering jams—Murray's phrase—between its sections, largely featuring Mitchell, though Hendrix drifts in and out, while there is an additional improvised section between the half verse and the coda.

This is one of those cases, beloved by music analysts, where there is a single hermeneutic key that unlocks the form and so explains what might otherwise appear inexplicable. This key is the fact that Hendrix split, or at least thought he split, his pants, presumably as a consequence of the particularly extravagant split—now using the word in its other sense—that he performed at the beginning of the opening riff. After the first verse, Hendrix keeps playing in a rather perfunctory way as he walks to the back of the stage. Mitchell attempts to fill the gap as Hendrix confers with a roadie, who checks his pants and apparently okays them, as Hendrix returns to the front of the stage for the second verse, flashing a rather sheepish smile at Cox. After the verse, Hendrix starts soloing but is apparently not happy, for he returns to the back of the stage, again leaving Mitchell to fill the gap as best he can. There are further to-ings and fro-ings, and it is not until nearly five minutes into the song that it gets firmly back on track.

Hendrix's split pants stand for a general principle: all sorts of things that lie beyond the traditional musicological purview—that are excluded by traditional rules of irrelevance—affect the nature and meaning of music in performance. The Isle of Wight performance of 'Foxy Lady' is the node at which an indefinitely extended network of potentially significant factors meet, of which the song is just one. Others include its relationship to Hendrix's innumerable other performances of 'Foxy Lady', as well as his performances of other songs that feature shared elements; the position of the song about two-thirds of the way through a gruelling two-hour set; the layout of the stage; the Fender Stratocaster guitar which, as Waksman (1999: 5) says, Hendrix 'manipulated…onstage to accentuate his physical presence'; and his ongoing relations with Mitchell and Cox, both socially and musically. There is nothing unique about this. Eric Clarke (2006) is speaking quite generally when he describes musical works as 'a particular kind of environment that affords certain kinds of performing opportunities' (31), whereby 'the meaning of a performance arises from a potentially large number of interacting sources'. And in another context he uses an example from Hendrix to make the point. This is the iconic performance of the 'Star-spangled banner' at the Woodstock Festival, the meaning of which Clarke—like Rebecca McSwain (2000: 206–8)—explains by relating the subversive acoustic qualities of Hendrix's guitar playing to another and much broader element in the network of signifiers from which meaning emerges: the expectations and values of the late 1960s as symbolised by the American national anthem. As Clarke concludes, Hendrix was 'playing *with* the anthem rather than playing it'—though of course he was doing that too (2005b: 54).

But my prime focus in this chapter is on a further crucial element within this network of signifiers, and one that I have already touched on: the role of Hendrix's almost constantly moving body, which represents the dominant element of the music's visual dimension. This is not simply an aspect of the 'physical presence' that Waksman referred to, but—for those who were there in 1970, or see Hendrix's

performance on DVD or YouTube today—a basic dimension of the overall multimedia experience. By this I do not, of course, mean that 'Foxy Lady' cannot be
appreciated from an audio-only CD (though it is hard to see how a CD listener
could make sense of the straggling form of the Isle of Wight performance): it is
to say that what Hendrix did with his body was an integral part of what he was
understood to be as an artist. The most obvious way to illustrate how sound and
sight fuse in the Hendrix experience is in terms of what might be called the musi-
calisation of the body, that is to say how it is incorporated as a parameter of the
music.[10] And the opening riff (0'42"[11]) makes a good example.

Marc Leman (2010) speaks of the way in which 'dancers may embody different layers of musical meter through the movements in different body parts' (53),
and that is what is happening here. Borrowing a term from Lawrence Zbikowski
(2004: 279), we can say that different metrical levels serve as targets onto which
specific body motions are mapped. What in published transcriptions is notated
as the crotchet beat is taken at around 104 MM in the Isle of Wight performance,
and consequently becomes the tactus. It is this beat and its multiples—particularly
the minim—that Hendrix targets in his head nods (every crotchet), steps (every
crotchet, but with the alternation of feet grouping the crotchets into pairs), and
the motion of his guitar (largely on the backbeats, that is to say in a syncopated
minim pattern). Other apparent regularities, such as the matching knee-drop
and circular arm motion on the third beat of bars 2 and 6,[12] are built on these
units. This means that physical movement is inscribed into the groove, or to put
it the other way round, the groove is expressed through Hendrix's body as much
as through sound. Not only is this music for the eyes, then, but—coming at the
beginning of the song—it helps to draw the audience into the internal dynamics of the riff and therefore the song as a whole. Susan Fast (2001) writes in her
book on Led Zeppelin that 'Riffs comprise rhythm, melodic shape, harmony, and
timbres that are related to one another in specific ways' (116): they present the
rhythmic, textural, and affective tenor of the music in its most compact form.
(This is rather like van der Bliek's point about the 'Hendrix chord'.) And given that
Led Zeppelin's music was mainly riff-based, and that they too had a conspicuously exuberant guitarist in the shape of Jimmy Page, it is not surprising that Fast's
account of Page's stage behaviour offers many parallels to Hendrix's.

In physical terms Hendrix was not a free agent on stage. He was tied to the
microphone while singing: under such circumstances the main way he could create easily visible periodic motion was through flexing the knees, as he can be seen
doing between the first and second lines of the second verse in the Isle of Wight
performance of 'Foxy Lady' (2'52"). And when soloing, his movements were constrained not only by the cable connecting his guitar to the amplifier—though like

10. Further discussion of this approach may be found in Cook (1998) and Cook (2013).

11. Timings are counted from the beginning of the long opening note.

12. I am counting from the beginning of the riff (the transcription in *Experience Hendrix* precedes this with two effectively unmeasured bars).

most lead guitarists he used long, coiled cables for maximum flexibility—but also by the requirements of feedback. That entailed playing in front of the massive speakers, which were consequently arranged as a kind of wall behind him; he can also be seen repeatedly adjusting the amplifiers, which were positioned on top of the speakers. In this way there is a kind of conceptual box within the larger stage area (what, following Rudolf Laban, is sometimes called a kinesphere[13]) within which Hendrix's performance is contained: it becomes perceptible in the sense that, when he leaves it, he is moving out of his own zone. That is of course what happened when he went to confer with the roadie over his pants, and it is when he returns to his own zone that the song gets back on track.

The final constraints on his embodied practice are what are sometimes called the ergonomic dimensions of playing the electric guitar, in other words what you need to do to get the sounds you want out of the instrument. Specifically, you need to carry its weight and have sufficient freedom of movement in each hand. Here however Hendrix's idiosyncratic playing technique gave him an exceptional degree of freedom. Holding an electric guitar normally creates a topography structured round three points: left hand, right hand, and neck (almost everybody uses a strap when playing the instrument in a standing position). Hendrix, however, often took the weight of the guitar in his large hands, lifting the instrument clean off his shoulders, and so creating a less constrained topography structured round two points. But what was more important was what one would normally think of as his idiosyncratic left-hand technique—except that Hendrix played the guitar left-handed, so we are talking about what he did with his right hand. Despite playing left-handed, however, he used ordinary, right-handed guitars, holding them upside down and stringing them in reverse.[14] That means that instead of the bass strings being shorter from the bridge to the tuning peg than the higher strings, as normal, the higher strings were shorter. That in turn means they were at lower tension, and on top of that, Hendrix most often detuned his guitar so that it sounded about a semitone below standard pitch (as was the case at the Isle of Wight). The enhanced possibilities this gave of pulling the notes around worked together with a further key element of Hendrix's playing: his extensive use of the hammer-on and pull-off techniques subsequently popularised by guitarists such as Eddie Van Halen, Steve Vai, and Joe Satriani. These involve sounding as well as stopping the string with the fingerboard hand, so that the plucking hand need not be used. That is how Hendrix could solo for quite extensive passages using only his right hand, releasing his left hand for a variety of expressive purposes, in

13. Jensenius et al. (2010: 20).

14. Right-handed guitarists aiming at an authentic Hendrix style accordingly need to use left-handed guitars, and for this market Fender has produced a '68 Reverse Special version of the Stratocaster: 'close reproduction of one of Jimmy's favorites gives us an alder body with a maple neck and a fast maple cap fingerboard. The vintage-gauge fret wire is of the exact type you'd expect to find on an instrument of this year—as are the pressed-steel bridge saddles, which connoisseurs believe are tonally superior to cast units' (Leadley [2002: 57]). Only, of course, as compared to the guitars Hendrix actually played, everything is back to front.

particular the raising or wheeling motions I have already mentioned—gestures which Hendrix frequently used to mark significant points in the music, such as the transition from verse to solo improvisation, or changes in affective register (often these are the same thing). These techniques must also have facilitated the various showman's tricks that he picked up on the Chicago club circuit and sometimes incorporated within his solos, such as playing with his teeth or tongue, or behind his back, or between his legs.[15]

Fast (2001: 147) refers to the 'codified traditions of...body technique that are used in rock music performances', and the comparison between Hendrix's and Page's gestures confirms how quickly the rock lexicon of extravagant stage practice seems to have come into being. Like those who research gesture in classical music, notably Jane Davidson (2007a: 114), Fast (2001: 152ff) draws on the taxonomy of gestures developed by David McNeill for the analysis of gesture in speech.[16] These categories apply equally well to Hendrix. Gestures are *metaphorical* when they reference some abstract idea; this would apply to the raised arm that marks a point of structural transition, and corresponds closely to the use of such gestures in speech. *Iconic* gestures, by contrast, have a resemblance to some aspect of their target (this usage is similar to Peirce's). An obvious example, found in Page as well as Hendrix, is tilting or jerking up the guitar for a high note (6'28"); where this involves a thrusting motion, it also exemplifies what Waksman calls an 'overtly phallic style of performance' (1999: 188), bringing another dimension of iconicity into play. The remaining categories of gesture, *beat* and *deictic*, can both be illustrated by what Hendrix does halfway through the second bar of the opening riff (0'46"). He drops to his knees, so marking a particular point, which is what beat gestures do; and he flashes out his arm and forefinger in a gesture of address, which is what deictic means.[17]

Hendrix regularly used deictic gestures such as pointing or nodding his head in order to cue his co-performers; in fact there is rather more of this than usual in the Isle of Wight performance of 'Foxy Lady', owing to the need to recover from sartorial disruptions. But, as in the opening riff and at many other points, he also uses the same gestures when no such cuing is involved. The gesture continues to be one of address, but now it is addressed to the audience, the key element in the semiotic network that I have not so far mentioned, and this brings a further dimension of embodied signification into play. Jeffrey Kallberg (1996) has influentially argued that compositional genres should be seen as representing a kind

15. Even a perfunctory web search reveals ongoing controversy about how far Hendrix really played with his teeth or tongue. Several YouTube videos show that both are possible (the knack in playing with your teeth is to use the upper jaw, and to move the guitar rather than your head), but it is not clear from the films that Hendrix actually did this.

16. Davidson, among others, also draws on another taxonomy developed by Paul Ekmann and Wallace Friesen: a description and illustration may be found in Kurosawa and Davidson (2005).

17. Fast actually refers to 'deitic' gestures, but the standard spelling (as used by McNeill) is deictic.

of contract between composer and listener: as he puts it, 'the composer agrees to use some of the conventions, patterns, and gestures of a genre, and the listener consents to interpret some aspects of a piece in a way conditioned by this genre' (5). The idea of generic contract is all the more applicable in performance, and Philip Auslander (2013) has adopted this approach in order to cut through the interminable disputes about where improvisation stops and performance starts. He sees improvisation in terms of a 'social contract between jazz musicians and their audiences' (57), something that is not inherent in the music but rather constructed in the relationship between musician and listener. As he puts it, 'the audience experiences jazz improvisation first and foremost as a social characteristic of jazz performance rather than an ontological characteristic of the music'. Or to put it another way, improvisation becomes a function or dimension of subject position.

As performed by Hendrix, 'Foxy Lady' does not fall unequivocally into either of Auslander's categories: relatively precomposed and relatively improvised sections alternate in accordance with the song structure. The same of course applies to most jazz improvisations, which carries the implication that subject positions can change during the course of a performance. That is what happens in 'Foxy Lady'. Normally, as I said, Hendrix would play a single, extended passage of improvisation leading to the half-verse and coda. But at the Isle of Wight he played one passage of improvisation before singing the half verse, and then a second one before the coda, which was itself improvised on the basis of the features specifically associated with this section. And although this can hardly have been pre-planned, he characterised these three passages of improvisation in very different ways. By comparison with the opening riff, where as we saw Hendrix's body motions were embedded within the musical texture, the improvisation before the half verse is much more inward, more subjective, in its orientation. This is the point where Hendrix returns to his zone and the song gets back on track: Hendrix uses his head to cue Cox into the riff, and then begins to solo.

There is an immediate change of register (4'56"). He juts his jaw forward, and as if to draw a line on the preceding shenanigans, his face assumes a serious countenance. He works his mouth, as if chewing. As he coaxes increasingly vocal wails out of the guitar he holds it higher, twisting it up for the high notes, and then he starts moving his head in time with the glissandi. But the crucial signifier is Hendrix's closed eyes, the classic expression of interiority. The effect is one of withdrawal from the presence of the stage: it is as if Hendrix is accessing some invisible world from which he draws the music, acting more as a medium for a higher source than a creative agent in his own right. To use a word that Auslander shares with Waskul—and to which I shall return in the next chapter—he is constructing a persona, that of the inspired musician, and one of the means by which he does this is what Auslander calls 'guitar face': the serious countenance to which I referred is succeeded by a series of expressions that connote deeply felt emotion, providing the audience with what Auslander (2006: 112) calls 'external evidence of the musician's ostensible internal state while playing'. After the initial dedications there are no audience shots during the 'Foxy Lady' sequence of *Blue*

Wild Angel, but similar improvisations in other performances evoke an attitude of wrapt absorption, sometimes accompanied by restrained head motions. This is the Hendrix I would have come to the Isle of Wight to experience.

This is the part of the Isle of Wight performance that most resembles the extended improvisations found in other performances of 'Foxy Lady', though more in terms of how it sounds than how it looks. At the Albert Hall in 1969 Hendrix walked a few steps forward and then back at the beginning of his improvisation, but thereafter remained rooted to the same spot, just as he did in the shorter improvisation I have just described: he kept his pelvis still and limited his movement to a swaying of the upper body. This gives both these improvisations a serious, even auratic quality. By contrast other improvisations, although not dissimilar in auditory terms, incorporate elements of the showman's tricks I referred to. At Monterey he played briefly with the instrument between his legs (this is a particularly phallic episode, followed by masturbatory motions on the fingerboard). At Atlanta he briefly used his teeth and tongue, and he did the same in a more extended way at Rainbow Bridge—evidently a particularly light-hearted occasion, judging by the expressions on both Hendrix's and the audience's faces. It is easy to see why this might have been, especially from the audience's point of view: it was a free concert put on as part of the making of the film of the same name, directed by Chuck Wein, and was attended by just 'a few hundred island hippies, surfers, and students', so providing exceptionally intimate access to the star.[18]

At the Isle of Wight, Hendrix rolls out the party tricks during the improvisation following the half verse—the extra improvisation, by comparison with the normal song form (5'56"). He sinks to his knees (the roadie looks over the top of the speaker to see what is going on) and rises slowly, screwing up his face and shaking his head as he plays a tremolo, so conveying intimations of shamanic possession. After a couple of bars of the riff he lifts the guitar to his face, and plays an extended passage with his teeth, his tongue, and then his teeth again. He lifts and crooks his left leg and plays the guitar behind it for a few seconds. Then he lifts it again to his face, but seems to think better of it and resumes more standard playing. And though there are no more party tricks in this episode, the rest of the solo gives a distinct impression that Hendrix is wheeling out one cliché after another in rapid succession. To me the episode seems curiously half-hearted, bringing to mind Hendrix's sense of being boxed in by his fans' expectations and Murray's comment about his having no interest in the tour. It is almost as if, to borrow Bryn Harrison's words from Chapter 8, Hendrix was imitating himself slightly inaccurately.

At all events this improvisation positions Hendrix as the showman, and the audience as spectators: if they weren't sitting on the ground, one might call this an edge-of-seat attitude. It might be compared to watching a spectator sport, particularly one where each competitor performs individually. Or it might be

18. http://en.wikipedia.org/wiki/Rainbow_Bridge_%28film%29.

compared to a magic show, in line with the way Hendrix introduced 'Foxy Lady' at Monterey. And it is the Monterey set that provides the paradigm case of this spectacular subject position, a relationship between musician and audience that is distanced in comparison to the absorption prompted by the preceding Isle of Wight improvisation. This paradigm case is, of course, the guitar-burning episode at the end of 'Wild Thing', as recorded on Donn Pennebaker's film *Monterey Pop*, and familiar though it may be, it is worth revisiting in this context. Hendrix lays his guitar down on the stage floor: no longer a phallic extension, its prone position and pelvic curves figure it as a woman. He squats on her, talks to her, rides her, his head and upper body shaking with what could equally well be read as sexual or shamanic possession (or both). Then he goes backstage to fetch the lighter fluid, returns, stands over the instrument as he rhythmically spurts the fluid over her belly, and bends down to give her a gentle kiss before lighting the match. He conjures up the flames, and then, holding her by the fingerboard, smashes her repeatedly against the floor. On the fourth blow she begins to emit an electronic hum, a pathetically inarticulate sound compared to the expressive arabesques and pyrotechnics of the previous set, but it is only with the sixth blow that the hum becomes terminal. Redding and Mitchell keep up a sustained din while Hendrix tosses the fingerboard out into the audience and hunts for the other debris before tossing them out too.

It is at this point that we see a succession of audience shots. One girl stares wide-eyed at the stage, just her eyes moving to take in what is happening. Another clasps her face, rather as if she had toothache, and then turns to catch someone's eye. They look grim, disoriented, as people do when faced with an unforeseen natural catastrophe or fatal accident. Introducing 'Wild Thing', Hendrix had said what he was going to do, but elliptically ('I'm going to sacrifice something here that I really love, okay'), and it looks as if neither of the girls kept up with the music press. Hendrix had first tried burning his guitar in London three months earlier, ending up in hospital for treatment of hand burns.

THE WHITE MAN'S BLACK MAN

In his Isle of Wight performance of 'Foxy Lady', then, Hendrix used his body for the quite different purposes of drawing the audience into the music during the opening riff, playing the inspired musician in the improvisation preceding the half verse, and in the following improvisation constructing himself as showman and the audience as spectators. That leaves the end of the song, where his body signifies in ways that are disputable and, to me, disturbing.

One can describe the coda (from 6'46") quite simply. Hendrix gives what might be mistaken for a rather half-hearted final bow, speaking inaudibly, but immediately starts playing a tremolo. This turns into the right-hand playing in the low register that featured in the codas of the other performances, rising in register and then falling again, at which point Hendrix makes another, more emphatic showman's bow (7'15"). But again he continues playing, a series of wails or laughs shaped by the whammy bar that culminate in another, and this time final, bow. Most of this featured in the previous performances of 'Foxy Lady'; even the wailing and laughing was anticipated in the performance at Atlanta a few months earlier, although at the Isle of Wight it takes on an eerier quality, perhaps not so much laughing as cackling. But in other respects the performance at the Isle of Wight is quite unlike any of the previous performances. The effect of shamanic possession returns as the guitar howls in descending glissandi (7'08"): Hendrix's open mouth and head motions in time with the howling create an uncanny effect of ventriloquism, as if it is his voice we are hearing. It would be easy to think that at such times Hendrix is drawing on the connotations of voodoo, as he did more explicitly in what Waksman (1999: 187) calls the 'savage guitar rites' of 'Voodoo Child (Slight Return)'. The same might be said of Hendrix's sacrifice of his guitar at Monterey.[19]

It is the final few seconds of 'Foxy Lady' (from 7'15") that I find most uncanny. The repeated sweeps up the fingerboard and feedback add up to an easily readable auditory coding, or in Clarke's term specification, of extreme experience. But as Hendrix starts playing higher notes, shaping them as I said into wails and cackles by means of the whammy bar, so he starts grimacing in time with the music, and then flops his head to the left (as we see it). As high, falling glissandi squirt out of his guitar, Hendrix juts his head forward and turns to the right—but I can't find the right words for what happens during the four seconds from then until the final bow, and you will have to watch it for yourself. However I can make some more general points about this final phase of the song. The flopping head and unnatural movement of the upper body create a sense of disarticulation, as if Hendrix had become a rag doll, though his woolly hair and red pants might suggest another word that was still current in 1970. (Astonishingly it was not until 31 years later that the British firm Robertson's removed the golliwog symbol from their jams and closed their badge collection scheme.) And the point about rag dolls is that they lack the articulation of the living body: this is the equivalent in terms of embodiment to the disintegration of the music into more or less chaotic noise. It also creates maximal contrast with Hendrix's highly articulated body movements in the opening riff.

I called the final moments of this performance disturbing, and that was the immediate impression they made on me when I watched the DVD. Attempting to rationalise it in retrospect, I see the source of that impression in a racial discomfort that would have been that much sharper in 1970. The headline act of the Isle of White Festival was a black artist playing before six hundred thousand white fans, the black artist who made his reputation with two white sidemen,

19. In 1998 Fender introduced a 'Jimi Hendrix Voodoo Stratocaster', designed, in the words of their 29 January 1998 press release, to recreate 'the sound made famous by the voodoo music master himself—Jimi Hendrix—for the righthanded player', but discontinued it the following year owing to 'a Hendrix family request'. The '68 Reverse Special Stratocaster mentioned in n. 14 above, introduced in 2001, was essentially the same instrument minus the Hendrix neckplate (http://www.glennsguitars.com/guitars/others/page64/page64.html).

in short, Hendrix the white man's black man. According to Paul Gilroy (1993), Hendrix had been 'reinvented as the essential image of what English audiences felt a black American performer should be: wild, sexual, hedonistic, and dangerous' (93–94). Gilroy also speaks of 'the updated minstrel antics of his stage shows', asking whether his performance should be seen as 'parodic of the minstrel's role or undeniable confirmation of its enduring potency'. And his reference to 'Hendrix's neo-minstrel buffoonery' seems particularly pertinent to the final stages of 'Foxy Lady' as Hendrix performed it at the Isle of Wight. After all, Florence Kate Upton's original, red-trousered Golliwog came straight out of the 'darkie' iconography of the blackface minstrel tradition, one of the stock characters of which provides an obvious parallel with the red, flared pants and wide-sleeved, multicoloured top of Hendrix's stage presence: the dandy or coon, often known as Zip Coon, the blackface image of the overdressed black man who can either be seen as aping or as parodying the white man. And nineteenth-century prints often portrayed Zip Coon as a musician.

Here a long history and deep cultural tropes come into play. As to the history, Richard Middleton (2006) places Hendrix at the end of his narrative of the creation of a racially marked black music out of the encounter between black and white: Hendrix, he says, played up to 'his hysterical media reception as "the wild man from Borneo", performing out gestures of rapacious but ever so cool and dandified sexual power' (87). As to the deep cultural tropes, Waksman—who explores the subject in greater detail than I can, and on whom I draw heavily—interprets Hendrix's self-representation in relation to an idea originally put forward by Frantz Fanon (1967): white male identity is constructed in relation to a black other perceived as possessing a transgressive prowess that figures whiteness as lack. As Waksman (1999: 192) puts it, 'White men wish to possess such qualities themselves even though they have been taught to associate such bodily excess with "Other"-ness'. He links this to the blackface tradition when he analyses a photograph of the Jimi Hendrix Experience published in the June 1968 issue of *Life* magazine—actually a Google search will reveal that there is a whole genre of such images—in which, as Waksman (1999: 195) says, 'so many symbols of black masculinity, and specifically of Hendrix's masculinity, are visible on Redding's body that the process of literally "blacking up" is no longer necessary'. And that in turn resonates with an observation made by John Szwed in the 1970s and quoted by Eric Lott (1995: 8) in his historical study of American blackface: 'The fact that, say, a Mick Jagger can today perform in the same tradition without blackface simply marks the detachment of culture from race and the almost full absorption of a black tradition into white culture'.

Like the invocation of an autonomous 'white culture', so 'the detachment of culture from race' is questionable in this context. As Lott sees it, the racial cross-dressing that was institutionalised in blackface simultaneously expressed 'a nearly insupportable fascination and a self-protective derision with respect to black people and their cultural practices' (1995: 6). Like Robertson's golliwogs, blackface survived until astonishingly recently on both sides of the Atlantic: in Britain, the BBC's Black and White Minstrels show lasted until 1978, eight years after the Isle of White Festival. Jacob Smith (2008: 116) complains that minstrel show recordings, with the acoustic evidence they provide of the speech patterns associated with blackface, have been neglected in favour of printed sources. But the same cross-racial desire found expression in the vocal practices of rock performance that developed as blackface waned. Consider, for example, Jerry Lee Lewis, whose racially marked performances from the late 1950s encompassed both the visible body—most obviously in his signature standing piano playing—and the audible body in the form of what, following Smith (2008: 138), I shall call blackvoice. Bernard Gendron quite explicitly places Lewis's 'Whole lotta shakin'' in 'the tradition of black-faced minstrelsy', and explains how the white Lewis had to construct his musical blackness through 'a coarsely outlined cartoon of what it means to sing black. That is, the result had to be a caricature' (1985: 7, 9).

But then there was a further twist: black artists began to caricature themselves in the same way. Gendron (1985: 10) goes on to explain that, as Chuck Berry, Ray Charles, and Little Richard (with whose band Hendrix at one time played[20]) increasingly performed before white audiences, 'they accelerated their singing speeds, resorted to raspy-voiced shrieks and cries, and dressed up their stage acts with manic piano-pounding or guitar acrobatics'. It is a kind of double role play: the audible body becomes a medium through which black performers *masquerade* at being black. Or as Simon Frith acidly puts it, 'Thanks to rock 'n' roll, black performers now reached a white audience, but only if they met "the tests of 'blackness'—that they embody sensuality, spontaneity, and gritty soulfulness"'.[21] Ratchet that up a notch and you have Gilroy's description of the 'wild, sexual, hedonistic, and dangerous' Hendrix that was invented for the English market.

This also ties in with the mythologisation of Hendrix's blackness. Waksman (1999) quotes a classic statement of this from the white guitarist Michael Bloomfield:

> Jimi was the blackest guitarist I ever heard. His music was deeply rooted in pre-blues, the oldest musical forms, like field hollers and gospel melodies. From what I can garner, there was no form of black music that he hadn't listened to or studied, but he especially loved the real old black music forms, and they just poured out of his playing (197).[22]

Waksman goes on to comment that Bloomfield, like other white musicians who modeled themselves on Hendrix, 'had something at stake in claiming Hendrix's blackness', but I want to draw out the suggestion that, in seeking out those forms of music that had been mythologised as oldest and blackest, Hendrix was setting out to authenticate himself, to produce and distil his own musical ethnicity. And by the final stages of his life, at least, there was a better reason he might

20. Floyd (1995: 291).

21. Frith (1996: 131), quoting Alice Echols.

22. Waksman (1999: 197, 'pored' changed to 'poured').

have wished to do this than any identity issues resulting from his mixed ancestry (European and Native American as well as African American).

It emerges from his curiously defensive patter when he introduces 'Wild Thing' at Monterey: there's this story that we couldn't make it here so we went to England, he says, 'and America doesn't like us because, you know, our feet's too big, and we got fat mattresses, and we wore golden underwear'. As the musician who performed at Monterey not just with two white but two *English* sidemen and who had been taken up by the smart set in London, Hendrix's blackness met the most exacting white criteria, but came under scrutiny in other circles: 'when he returned to play in the United States', writes Gilroy (1993: 93), Hendrix 'was denounced as a "white nigger" by some of the Black Power activists who could not fathom his choices in opting to cultivate an almost exclusively white, pop audience that found the minstrel stance a positive inducement to engage with his transgressive persona if not his music'. And as for the music, Waksman suggests that its artificially constructed ethnicity leaves 'blackness...as an empty category. Hendrix may indeed be asserting his blackness, but only if he can live it according to his own rules' (1999: 187).

But the circumstances of 31 August 1970 were equally conditioned by the English audience, whose reception of Hendrix positioned him uncomfortably in a venerable procession of exotic savages brought to the imperial metropole for exhibition to a curious public. The English, after all, have traditions of their own. Stan Hawkins (2009) describes Hendrix as 'an adopted British dandy' (16), and places him in a lineage that ranges from Oscar Wilde, W. H. Auden, and Noël Coward within the broader field of culture to David Bowie, Pete Doherty, and Robbie Williams within popular music. Then again, the English have their own tradition of racial sensibility, their own tradition of blackface—and their own tradition of blackvoice, from Jagger to Lennon, and from Eric Burdon to Amy Winehouse. But whereas, in America, white blackvoice involved a single level of impersonation, for the English it involved two: not only representing yourself as black, but as American and black. If there is an authenticity deficit in Norman Mailer's image (1957) of the American hipster who—in a reversal of the Zip Coon stereotype—draws upon black signifiers of authenticity, then for the English hipster there is a double deficit.

Ulrich Adelt (2010: 8, 59) draws on Mailer in order to characterise the leading English guitarist Eric Clapton, who, he says, 'turned to a problematic construction of black masculinity that he was unable fully to identify with'. Adelt goes on to deliver the harsh judgement that 'Clapton felt it legitimate to identify as a "white negro" and take everything but the burden from "black" culture'. ('White negro' is virtually what the Black Power activists called Hendrix, though the meaning is reversed.) But the harshest judgement, because it is a self-judgement, comes from Pete Townshend. When he and Clapton went to see Hendrix, Townshend told Murray (1989), it was as if Hendrix was saying

'You've taken this, Eric Clapton, and Mr Townshend, you think you're a showman. This is how *we* do it. This is how we can do it when we take back what you've borrowed, if not stolen. I've put it back together and *this* is what it's all about and you can't live without it, can you?' And the terrible truth is we *couldn't* live without it (91).

And despite all that has changed since 1970, these issues remain live in Britain today. On the one hand there is the example of the youngest exponent of black-voice I mentioned. Amy Winehouse's set at the Glastonbury 2008 Festival offered a neat reverse image of the Jimi Hendrix Experience. She performed with two black, besuited dancers, and the relationship between them and Winehouse's pale, increasingly vulnerable body produced racial as well as sexual frisson. The physical tension that crackled throughout her hour-long set erupted in the widely reported incident just before what had been intended as the last song, ironically enough 'Rehab': Winehouse scuffled with a fan, was hauled away by security personnel, and was admitted into a clinic immediately afterwards. (There is also, of course, a terrible symmetry in Hendrix's and Winehouse's deaths.) And on the other hand, as I write this, a controversy is raging over the footballer Rio Ferdinand, who used Twitter to describe his England team-mate Ashley Cole as a 'choc ice', a term that precisely corresponds to what the Black Power activists called Hendrix.

What then did the uncannily self-exoticising role play that took place in the final moments of Hendrix's Isle of Wight performance of 'Foxy Lady' mean, and what might it mean to us today? Performative meaning—the meaning produced through vocal timbre, instrumental nuance, or the signifying body—resists spelling out. It operates by locating points of sensitivity, values that are vulnerable or open to negotiation, apparent certainties that unravel under scrutiny, or dissonances between knowledge, belief and sentiment. All of these are relevant to what happened on 31 August 1970, substantiating Waksman's claim that 'Hendrix on stage . . . signified a complex history of racial representations' (1999: 169). And Waksman's choice of terminology is intentional. He goes on to claim that, 'With this confluence of the musical and bodily, Hendrix enacted a rather sophisticated version of what Henry Louis Gates has called "Signifyin(g)" ' (203).

As is well known, Gates (1988: xxiv) coined this term in the context of black traditions of writing, in order to propose an aesthetic of 'revision, or repetition with a signal difference' that could stand against the white aesthetic canons of modernism. As Susan McClary (2001) says, his theory explains 'why African American writers often prefer to reinhabit conventional structures rather than treat formal innovation as the be-all-and-end-all of literary value, as it is for many European-based artists and critics' (36). But a principal source of Gates's idea of signifying is the practices of jazz: 'There are so many examples of signifying in jazz', he says, 'that one could write a formal history of its development on this basis alone' (63). Waksman (1999: 204), too, uses the term in both a broader cultural and a more narrowly musical sense when he writes that 'With his body, [Hendrix] "Signified" upon the preexisting text of black male potency and hypersexuality, and with his music, he "Signified" upon the various traditions that contributed to his own style'. And although—unlike Samuel Floyd[23]—Clarke doesn't use this word or reference Gates in his description of Hendrix's Woodstock performance of 'The Star-spangled banner', his suggestion that Hendrix was not playing but playing *with* the anthem embodies precisely the same idea. It is also, of course, how I have read the Isle of Wight performance of 'Foxy Lady'.

In short, building on the trope of oral as opposed to literary man which I associated with Ben Sidran, Gates is proposing a model of creative practice that does not draw on the textualist values of traditional European culture. Robert Walser (1993) underlines the difference when he defines the standard Western concept of signification through its assumption that 'meanings can be absolute, permanent, and objectively specified' (346), in contrast to Gates's concept (variously referred to as Signifying, Signifyin(g), or Signifyin'), which 'respects contingency, improvisation, relativity—the social production and negotiation of meanings'. But here two points need making. The first is that Gates developed his model in the context of black literary culture, and as illustrated by Floyd's and Walser's work, its application to music has also been in the context of black cultural practices. And in this context it is an inherently political concept, connoting an ironic relationship between subaltern and dominant culture and in this way constituting a mode of resistance. But Gates goes out of his way to define signifying—whatever the orthography—more broadly: it is 'a principle of language use and not in any way the exclusive province of black people' (90).

The second point turns on the difference between literary and musical culture. In the literary context, Gates sees Signifyin(g) as a 'black linguistic sign' that is in some ways similar to but in others 'remarkably distinct' from ordinary signification (44–45). Building on what I said at the end of Chapter 7, however, I would argue that what in literature is oppositional to dominant aesthetic values is simply the normal condition of performance—and never more so than in the case of repertory-based performance practices such as those of the Western 'art' tradition, where works are predetermined and overlearned, and the emphasis is consequently on what performers do with them. In such a context, reinhabiting existing structures rather than focussing on formal innovation is the standard modality of creative practice: it is what performers *do*. Yet the same aesthetic values that have held sway in literature—the values that create a binary opposition between creation and reproduction—have given us ways of thinking about performance that misrepresent and impoverish it through assimilating it to modernist and rationalist principles. Nick Kaye (1994) characterises performance as 'a primary postmodern mode' (22), tracing how the performance-oriented practices of artists such as Foreman, Cunningham, and Cage subvert the 'discrete or bounded "work of art"' definitive of modernism (32); for Fred Moten, as summarised by Griffith Rollefson, 'black artistic performance holds the potential of expressing an immanent critique of

23. Floyd (1995: 202) refers to the Woodstock performance of 'Star spangled banner' as 'one of the most Signifyin(g) events in American-music history'.

Western rationality'.[24] But I would extend the claim from 'black artistic performance' to performance in general. In this way the performative critique of textualist models of meaning that I have sought to articulate in this book might be understood as not only colour-blind but also in its own way political, a mode of resistance to Winn's 'pale of words'.

As I said in Chapter 7, eighteenth-century violinists played Corelli's op. 5, but they also played *with* it, signified on it. As Jim Samson (2000: 119) observes—and he specifically relates this to Gates's usage, though without specifying him by name—nineteenth-century composer-pianists signified on a wide range of pre-existing materials. I have tried to show how twentieth-century pianists and fortepianists signify on Mozart's and Chopin's texts. All of these illustrate the sense in which WAM performance is repetition: it is inherently an intertextual act, an act of reference. But it is repetition with a signal difference, and with the difference distinguishing performance from reproduction. And whereas reproduction is a yes-or-no term, such that asking how a performance reproduces a work delimits the possibilities of response and so closes down discussion, the idea of signification extends all the way from parody (what Gates [xxvi] calls 'motivated' signification) to pastiche ('unmotivated' signification). In this way it opens up questions of the particular nature of meaning production in any particular instance. The same can be said of Serge Lacasse's concept of 'transtylisation', meaning the degree of transformation involved in any intertextual practice: this runs the gamut from parody and travesty at one extreme to the near-literal reproduction which Lacasse terms 'copy' at the other (a tribute band 'aims at a *degré zéro* of transtylization',[25] as does a note-perfect rendition of Corelli's original score of op. 5).

Signifying, then, embraces a multitude of performance practices, and on the basis of Hendrix's innumerable stage appearances it might be possible to illustrate practically all of Michael Baxandall's litany of the alternative forms that artistic agency can take. As an art historian, he is speaking of alternatives to the threadbare notion of influence, but his virtuoso listing of the ways in which one artist's work can relate to that of another is equally applicable to the relationship between a performer and a text or tradition. It is possible, he says, to

> draw on, resort to, avail oneself of, appropriate from, have recourse to, adapt, misunderstand, refer to, pick up, take on, engage with, react to, quote, differentiate oneself from, assimilate oneself to, assimilate, align oneself with, copy, address, paraphrase, absorb, make a variation on, revive, continue, remodel, ape, emulate, travesty, parody, extract from, distort, attend to, resist, simplify, reconstitute, elaborate on, develop, face up to, master, subvert, perpetuate,

24. Rollefson (2008: 106); 'imminent' changed to 'immanent'.

25. Lacasse (2000: 54). Lacasse coins the idea of transtylisation specifically in relation to recorded music, but it is capable of much broader application.

reduce, promote, respond to, transform, tackle...everyone will be able to think of others (1987: 59).

The point Baxandall wants to make is that to respond to another artist or artwork is not—as the grammar of influence implies—something passive, in the sense that one billiard ball is hit by another. To be influenced is to take up a position; it is an act of agency. This is the insight that Floyd (1995) translates directly into Gates's language when he writes that 'in Signifyin(g), the emphasis is on the signifier, not the signified' (95). It is only, in Baxandall's example, if you think of what Picasso did to Cezanne rather than the other way round that all this varied terminology can enter into play, and that you can understand what he calls the 'actively purposeful element' of this cultural transaction (1987: 61). All this translates directly to musical performance. It is the difference between thinking of performance as reproduction and as signification.

10

Everything Counts

Whatever else music is 'about' it is *inevitably* about the body.
—RICHARD LEPPERT (1993: XX)

All music-making is about the mind-in-the-body.
—SIMON FRITH (1996: 128)

PLEASURES OF THE BODY

'Contemporary music theory and psychology', complains Mine Doğantan-Dack (2011: 245), has 'conceptualized musical experiences almost exclusively in mental terms', and as a result, 'the input of the body proper to music cognition has been neglected'. This is as much as to say that theorists and psychologists have generally framed their work in terms of the mind-body split I discussed in Chapter 2. They have seen the actions of the body as the outcome of mental processes based on the kind of structural representations with which music theory deals, giving rise to what Clarke and Davidson (1998) call 'a tendency to regard motor control as the handing down of a collection of progressively more concrete "instructions"—i.e. as a predominantly top-down process strongly associated with the much-favoured generative approach to music performance' (76).

As I suggested, this is a reflection of deeply embedded cultural and aesthetic assumptions about the relationship between the mental and the physical. And as Simon Frith explains, the mind-body binary has been mapped onto a variety of other binaries: WAM versus popular music, high art versus low art, high class versus low class, white versus black. As regards the first of these binaries, per-haps the starkest judgement quoted by Frith (1996: 125) comes from the pages of the *British Journal of Aesthetics*, where in 1962 Frank Howe wrote that '"The brain"...is associated with art music; "brainlessness" with pop'. But it is in the con-text of audience behaviour that these aesthetic ideologies become most palpable, because of the long-standing tradition of telling people how they ought to listen. 'A good classical concert', Frith (1996: 124) writes, is 'measured by the stillness it commands, by the intensity of the audience's mental concentration, by the lack of any physical distraction....A good rock concert, by contrast, is measured by the audience's physical response, by how quickly people get out of their seats, onto the dance floor, by how loudly they shout and scream'. And what Frith intends as social description turns into aesthetic prescription with the American critic Leo Stein, who writes that 'music requiring bodily motion on the part of the listener for its complete enjoyment, like much popular dance music, is by that token artistically imperfect'.[1] That was written in 1927, the heyday of the music appreciation movement—or as Virgil Thomson (2002: 38) called it, 'the Appreciation-racket'—and nowadays it has an old-fashioned feel. Yet, as I suggested with my reference in Chapter 8 to dinner jackets, surprisingly little has changed in terms of classical concert etiquette.

Given the association of the mind-body split with entrenched aesthetic, social, and racial values, my choice of Jimi Hendrix to illustrate the role of the performing body might be seen as an unfortunate reinforcement of entrenched stereotypes—especially given my juxtaposition of the black, ultra-physical Hendrix in Chapter 9 and the white, ultra-cerebral culture of complexity in Chapter 8. Actually things are not so simple. Musicians associated with complexity culture put considerable emphasis on the performing body. Frank Cox (2002) ends the long essay on performing complex music that I discussed in Chapter 8 by calling for what he terms 'a new form of "corporal thinking"' (129). The aim of this, he explains, is on the one hand to transcend the mind-body split that underlies the idea of all-purpose virtuosity, including Cox's HMMPP; and on the other to combat 'the tendency to fetishize the text of music', that is, the textualism on which HMMPP is based. In this way, he concludes, 'The notion of corporal thinking...forces attention onto the human element of music-making' (132). And Steven Schick spells out some of the specific forms such corporal thinking can take in the performance of complex music. He had originally thought of Ferneyhough's music as 'cerebral in the extreme', he says, but as he worked on *Bone Alphabet* he came to realise that 'physical gesture was not the simple by-product of performance, but an integral part of a growing interpretive point of view' (Schick 1994: 147, 137). By the time he had mastered the piece, he had come to think of its form in physical terms: 'a confluence of bodily movements, extruding limbs, sudden muscularity or the silent tableaux of a freeze frame....Intelligence is packaged and expressed in the form of the human body' (147). In a phrase that echoes Furtwängler on rubato,[2] Schick concludes that 'Meaningful gesture is the ultimate measure of a committed performance, a kind of Richter Scale of the musical tectonic forces underlying the composition' (152).

This chapter, then, follows up my study of Hendrix with a selective overview of the signifying body in WAM, before embarking on a case study of pianistic gesture organised around the relationship between musicology and

1. As summarised by Cone (1968: 17).

2. See Chapter 2, p. 53.

interdisciplinary performance studies. I begin by returning to Barthes's seminal essay 'The grain of the voice'. Published in 1972, it is a partisan contribution to the competing aesthetics of German and French song, as respectively represented by the dominant singer of *Lieder* at that time, Dietrich Fischer-Dieskau, and the once almost equally distinguished though now little known exponent of the *mélodie*, Charles Panzéra. By 'grain'—a term which he uses in a rather similar sense to the pioneer of *musique concrète*, Pierre Schaeffer[3]—Barthes (1977: 188) means 'the body in the voice as it sings'. And his complaint against Fischer-Dieskau is that he doesn't hear it. 'I seem only to hear the lungs', Barthes complains, 'never the tongue, the glottis, the teeth, the mucous membranes, the nose' (183).

The essay, then, is a paean to the audible body, to the physicality of sound, and as such it is relevant to know something that Barthes does not tell us in the essay: he studied singing with Panzéra in the late 1930s (Allen 2003: 116). Moreover, as a successful teacher, Panzéra authored a textbook on singing, published in 1945, which—as explained by Jonathan Dunsby (2009: 120)—includes 'chapters on breath, vocal apparatus and bodily resonance, complete with anatomical drawings and advice on general physical preparation'. In his references to tongue, glottis, teeth, mucous membrane, and nose, says Dunsby, in fact in the sheer physicality of Barthes's approach to the voice, 'we can certainly discern the disciple of the Panzéra creed'. Dunsby also comments that this highly physical approach is not unique to Panzéra, but 'something that is entirely familiar to singers'. In other words, Barthes acted as a conduit through which some of the commonplace discourse of vocal pedagogy entered into cultural theory and criticism: it is not his defense of the *mélodie* tradition but rather the physicality of his language that has made Barthes's essay so influential in thinking about performance. Probably most of those who cite 'The grain of the voice' have never heard a recording of Panzéra. (At the time of writing there are several on YouTube.)

There is a small but developing literature by singers that attempts to develop this approach by documenting the role of the body in performance interpretation. An example is a conference paper by Päivi Järviö (2010), in which the author focusses on the first appearance of Messaggiera in Monteverdi's opera *Orfeo*, a cry of anguish from offstage that is repeated four times. 'I think about all the pain I have experienced in my life', writes Järviö,

> and try to find the most suitable vowel color for crying out. Experimenting with different a-vowels finally produces one: my upper lip turns slightly upwards, my soft palate is markedly elevated, I can feel a big space at the back of my pharynx, my mouth is only moderately open. The crying out

---

3. Schaeffer uses 'grain' (the word is the same in English and French) to refer to the 'surface details' of a sound, 'analogous with the tactile sensation of a physical object's surface' (Dack 2009: 282–83). Schaeffer explains this in his *Traité des objets musicaux*, published six years before 'The grain of the voice', but the ideas in his book largely go back to the 1940s.

of this vowel makes me feel as if I were pushing something away, rejecting something. It reminds me of the feeling of nausea, being on the verge of vomiting—a form of rejection, too.

And she goes on to make some more general reflections on embodiment in singing:

The singing body is a body skilled in interior movement. The singer works with this interior movement and the resistance she feels in her body, which she connects to the whole of her singing body, to all her experience with and knowledge of the repertoire she is working on. For the singer reading the score, the signs on the page instantly turn into interior movements of her body and, if she decides to sing, into a voice that others can hear. Further, all her theoretical knowledge of the repertoire becomes flesh in her living body, thus blurring the split between theory and practice, between mind and body.

Järviö also recognises that this discourse, and the experiences it attempts to convey, will not be wholly intelligible to readers who do not share her first-hand experience of the professionally trained, singing body: 'the singer's embodied reading of the score reveals aspects that might be out of reach to a non-singer—many of which are invisible in the notation. A non-singer reading the score would probably not be able to detect them'.

The issue here is not simply the familiar difficulty of framing embodied experiences in words: it's one of communicating to people who don't share the bodily experience in question. This is a problem that Mine Doğantan-Dack has raised in relation to piano performance. Watching a video of her performance of Schubert's Piano Trio op. 100 with the Marmara Piano Trio, she writes,

I start wondering how an empirical musicologist or music psychologist might analyse and make sense of the sounds of this performance. What if they measure the acoustical data in term of currently measurable expressive parameters and perhaps fit the result into such contexts as performance traditions in chamber music or listener responses? What kind of knowledge would this analysis reveal about what happened musically—and perhaps socially as well—in that particular performance that evening? (Doğantan-Dack 2012a: 41).

And the role of the body in these issues becomes clear from an earlier article in which Doğantan-Dack (2011) compares the kind of knowledge gained by such empirical approaches with the pianist's experience of touch. She draws a contrast between scientists such as Otto Ortmann and James Jeans, who measured piano sound qualities and on this basis demonstrated to their own satisfaction that the phenomenon of pianistic touch has no objective reality, and the embodied knowledge possessed by pianists: 'a pianist's conception of "touch" does not involve reference to the absolute speed of the piano keys', she writes, 'but first and foremost to the pianist's own kinaesthetic sensations, and their relationship with the resulting sounds' (256).

Much the same might be said of another construct of pianistic discourse, the 'singing' hand. The core of this, Doğantan-Dack (257–58) explains, lies in the way 'the fingers and the hand assume a fixed position before striking the keys', a gesture that is 'guided by an aural image of the desired tone'. Her argument proceeds in two steps. The first is that 'it is not the attack that produces the sound, but the gesture bringing about the attack' (259). The second is that listeners hear music in terms of the performance motions that it specifies, a claim for which there is considerable empirical evidence (and to which I shall return shortly). That means the crucial event is the initiation of the gesture, not the sound to which it gives rise. And from this it follows that, in measuring onset times from recordings and trying to build the resulting data into larger interpretive frameworks, empirical musicologists and psychologists are missing the point in much the way that Ortmann and Jeans did: they are extracting the wrong kind of data.[4] 'To understand music *as* performance', Doğantan-Dack concludes, 'requires taking the experience of performing as the basis of an epistemology of music' (260, 247). And since that is not what current performance research does, 'the argument that the idea of *music-as-work* has given way to that of *music-as-performance* is difficult to sustain'.

Clearly, as in many other fields, there is an epistemological gap between phenomenological approaches based on embodied experience on the one hand, and empirical approaches based on measurement on the other: they give rise to different kinds of knowledge. (Marc Leman [2010: 59] would call this the difference between a first- and third-person perspective.) The same can be said more generally about approaches based on the production of art, and those based on its reception. My own view is that the kind of performer-centred phenomenology proposed by Doğantan-Dack—the particular nature of which of course will vary substantially according to what instrument, or voice, is under discussion—represents one of an indefinite number of approaches each of which contributes a complementary perspective on the inherently multidimensional phenomenon of musical performance. After all, listeners may hear performers' gestures, but they hear the notes too: perception is not monolithic. It is true that the perspective represented by Doğantan-Dack has been under-represented in performance studies, for the simple reason that few musicologists—myself included—are in a position to undertake it properly: it takes a professional musician to do what she is doing and so, as she says, 'bring to light what is physically involved in making music and what this entails for musicology' (260). But I would be reluctant to claim priority,

---

4. Godøy (2010: 110) makes a similar criticism: 'In cultivating notation, we could claim that Western musical thinking often tends to ignore the fact that any sonic event is actually included in a sound-producing gesture, a gesture that starts before, and often ends after, the sonic event of any one single tone or group of tones'.

epistemological or otherwise, for any one of these approaches as against the others. What makes Jeans's position offensive is not his measurements as such, but his assumption that the kind of knowledge gained from them is the only valid kind of knowledge.

The parallel with Järviö also extends to the role of the body in the development of an interpretation. To illustrate this I need merely refer back to Doğantan-Dack's account of how she plays the second movement of Beethoven's 'Pathétique' Sonata, or for another example Tom Beghin's discussion of Haydn's E-flat major Sonata Hob XVI: 49, both of which I cited in Chapter 4. One might describe what they are talking about as the operation of a body skilled in *exterior* movement. And what they describe is in effect a discovery process that inheres in the interaction between body and instrument. As a keen but non-professional pianist, Adorno's notes for his abortive book on performance record his reflections on these issues. 'All genuine presentation', he writes, 'has a certain sense of hewing the sound out of the piano, of playing corporeally, as it were inside the piano. This is what defines a pianist, and this is precisely what I lack' (2006: 113). And a few pages later he is thinking about the 'frictional' dimension of performance—the 'resistance' that Järviö spoke of—and the 'dialectical' relationship to the sound material that results from it (Adorno 2006: 130). 'The piano', he writes, 'does not do what I would like it to, but at the same time it is always saying: this is how it can be, this is how it should be'. Push the dialectic a stage further and you arrive at the idea that 'the instrument comes alive and starts to have a life of its own', as the improvising saxophonist Evan Parker writes (Borgo 2005: 51). A more extravagant example of this is the relationship between B. B. King and Lucille, as he called his guitar—or guitars, as there was a succession of Lucilles. 'Lucille is real', King once said, 'I'd be playing sometimes and as I'd play, it seems like it almost has a conversation with me': for Philip Auslander (2009: 605–6), this illustrates how 'musicians displace their own agency onto the instruments they play in ways that constitute those instruments as (semi-)autonomous entities to which they relate as performing partners rather than just tools'. The dialectical element in this relationship is the same as in that between Philip Thomas and the score of *être-temps*, as discussed in Chapter 8, and the suggestion I made there that the score might be seen in Latour's terms as a non-human agent applies all the more obviously to instruments.

The examples of Järviö, Doğantan-Dack, Beghin, and King show how the relationship between mind and body, and between body and instrument, is much more a matter of creative interaction than of the top-down process to which Clarke and Davidson referred. The jazz pianist Vijay Iyer uses the same word as Adorno when he describes improvising as 'a dialectic between formal/symbolic and situational/embodied constraints' (2002: 409). And as if he had just been reading Clarke and Davidson, he comments that 'the often implied characterization of the symbolic as high-level and the embodied as low-level is misleading, for these functions may interact with one another bilaterally. In particular, one should *not* claim that the high-level processes "direct" the low-level, for in some cases it is not clear that there is any such hierarchical organization' (408). But there are also more concrete ways in which, contrary to its mentalistic aesthetics, WAM reveals itself as in reality not just an embodied but a radically embodied practice.

Learning an instrument, particularly at an advanced level, can be one of the most rigorous of all modes of disciplining the human body. Elisabeth Le Guin sets this in historical context when she explains how, following developments in the pedagogy of dance, the late eighteenth century saw 'a huge increase in the production and publication of instructional treatises for every instrument. Here mechanical processes, not just of instruments but of the bodies operating them, began to be conceptualized and systematized' (2002: 243). Le Guin notes that this forms part of the larger development in the idea of discipline as analysed by Michel Foucault in *Discipline and Punish*. In order to achieve maximum control of the body and efficiency in its work, Foucault writes, 'the act is broken down into its elements; the position of the body, limbs, articulations is defined; to each movement are assigned a direction, an aptitude, a duration; their order of succession is prescribed' (1979: 152). Exercises are designed in order to reconfigure the body into a desired state.

All this can be illustrated in terms of the piano pedagogy of Ludwig Deppe (1828–1890), widely seen as the critical figure in the development of modern piano technique. As Reginald Gerig (1974) explains, the basic principle underlying Deppe's pedagogy is that 'the whole body in all its complexity must be involved in an adequate technical system' (254). This illustrates the mechanical conceptualisation to which Le Guin referred: it is rather like an old-fashioned clock, which can tell the time only if the system is operating satisfactorily as a whole. In the same way, the key consequence of the satisfactorily operating pianistic body is that, in Deppe's own words, tone production develops not through a forcible striking of the keys, but 'solely through the weight of the hand, through simple movements of lifting and falling, with quiet, relaxed fingers' (253). And this translates into numerous pedagogical prescriptions. Deppe specifies a sitting position relative to the piano such that 'the forearm from the elbow to the wrist will be slightly raised'. Again, Elisabeth Caland—one of Deppe's pupils and herself the author of a short book on his pedagogy—specifies a hand position such that 'the line *formed by the fifth finger, the outside of the hand, and the fore-arm should* be a straight one' (Gerig 1974: 253, 258). There is also a rigorous regime of exercises both at and away from the instrument. Caland was required 'to exercise with dumb-bells and even carried one about during her daily walks' (257).

The obvious comparison is with sport, equally an arena within which the body—and specifically the juvenile body—is reconfigured in line with culturally constructed ideals (and although Foucault did not himself work on sport, Pirkko Markula-Denison and Richard Pringle [2006] have analysed it in terms of Foucauldian discipline). Both music and sport involve a prescriptive and highly repetitive regime of training, preferably initiated at a tender age, and so demanding as to mandate a system of specialist education. (Recall my reference in Chapter 2 to the immersive education Rachmaninoff received from Nikola Zverev; today we have talent schools.) Both involve not just working within the body's constraints, but discovering what those constraints are and indeed renegotiating them: the four-minute mile is not what it was before 6 May 1954 because there has been a continuous process of reconfiguring the body since then, evident in steadily diminishing times.[5] Both involve a culture of competition, with the excitement of pushing the body to its limits being communicated to spectators. Perhaps most importantly, each is a culture of pleasure in the body, something that can hover on the edge of addiction. Roger Bannister, who broke the four-minute barrier in 1954, describes the experience of running in terms that could easily translate to musical performance: 'a fresh rhythm entered my body. No longer conscious of my movement, I discovered a new unity with nature'. And Andrew Blake (1996), who quotes this in his cultural analysis of sport, observes that successful sport practitioners repeatedly describe a 'feeling of transcendence, often expressed as a feeling that the player is actually observing the performance. In this account sport becomes a way of escaping from the common limits of humanity and the body. The wish to achieve this state is one of the most powerful of the utopian fantasies. It drives many musicians' (193).

This sense of transcendence clearly relates to what Mihály Csíkszentmihályi (1996) calls flow, the sense of immersive and motivated focus that can develop when there is a good balance between the challenges of a task and the skills one has to carry it out. Performers are familiar with this phenomenon, whether as theorised by Csíkszentmihályi or not. But in general the sheer pleasure of performance is conspicuously under-represented in the disciplines around music. There are some exceptions. I mentioned some performer-writers speaking of pleasure in Chapter 8, a pleasure that I take to be both social and physical. There is an essay by Clarke (2006: 26) that discusses the topic at some length, referring for example to a pianist taking part in a study of fingering who 'described how he particularly enjoyed the feeling of using his thumb', such that 'he found ways specifically to use it even when it wasn't the most obvious "ergonomic" solution'. And Charles Rosen (2003: 22) talks about the 'musical pleasure' he takes in a passage from a mazurka that includes a canon intended to be played with one hand: it is evident that Chopin 'wished not only to hear the canon, but to feel the two-part counterpoint in one hand', Rosen writes, and the pleasure disappears if both hands are used. Even those who find the piano does not do what they would like it to do experience this pleasure at times, and indeed, if playing an instrument did not engender some kind of pleasure even in the early stages it is hard to think that anyone would persist with it. Music is more than anything else a culture of pleasure, though you mightn't guess it from the academic literature.

---

5. The nearest musical equivalent might be the Royal College of Music's 'Piano Fever' event, staged in London during March 2010, which included a competition for the fastest performance of Chopin's 'Minute Waltz': the winner got it down to 53 seconds. If the competition were repeated periodically, and provided of course that there was sufficient financial or other incentive, we might expect to see the same steadily decreasing times ('Five days of Piano Fever at the Royal College of Music', http://www.piano.or.jp/report/02soc/london/english/rcm.html).

But it's not just a matter of the role of the performing body in developing an interpretation and the regimes of instrumental or vocal training, or of coordinated physical movement in achieving the fine-grained socialities of performance I talked about in Chapters 7 and 8.[6] It's also the role of the body in the discourses around performance. I began with Barthes's appropriation of the embodied language of singing pedagogy. This is in part a language of objective observation, as keyed by Panzéra's anatomical drawings. But because of the interiority of the singing body to which Järviö referred—because singing is not simply dealing with observables—the language of anatomy slips into a language of metaphor, the physical body into the imagined body, and it is not always easy to say where the one stops and the other starts. As Jane Davidson says, 'Allusions to space, motion, and emotions aid in training specific interior physical actions' (2007a: 110). And she cites a number of examples, of which one must stand for all. Rehearsing a community choir in Hong Kong, Paulina tells them:

Keep your conscious attention focused forwards, with your head and neck in an aligned, long position; then as you take your breath to sing, feel as though your lungs are filling like spreading wings [arm and hand movements illustrate the opening]. Make the sound in the line of focused attention [hand gestures, at eye level, a forward pointing action], and then direct your voice towards the back of the hall. Let me hear your voice fill the room like an angel opening giant wings.[7]

This example, like the others quoted by Davidson, also illustrates a second point: how gesture is incorporated within this discourse. Researchers into musical performance sometimes use the term 'ancillary' for such gestures as are not necessary to create sound.[8] I avoid it on the grounds that the meaning produced through gesture is an essential part of the music, and it would certainly not be the right word for the relationship between words and gestures in vocal and instrumental pedagogy. The two work together. Zbikowski (2011) explains why this is: 'gesture offers a dynamic, imagistic resource for conveying thoughts that would be cumbersome to express through language' (89). A few pages later he expresses it more strongly: 'gesture gives access to a dynamic, imagistic mode of thought that is inaccessible to language' (97). And this fused discourse of the vocalising and moving body enters the public sphere in the form of the masterclasses and open coaching sessions that have become increasingly significant elements of a musical culture the public face of which was at one time almost completely limited to

6. Overviews of work on the embodied dimensions of ensemble performance may be found in e.g., Williamon and Davidson (2002), King and Ginsborg (2011).

7. 'Speading' corrected to 'spreading'.

8. See e.g., Wanderley and Vines (2006); for an introduction to the study of performers' gestures, in which ancillary gestures are divided into communicative and sound-facilitating movements, see Goebl, Dixon, and Schubert (forthcoming).

concerts. My notes of a session held in the Cambridge Faculty of Music on 17 May 2011, in which Alfred Brendel coached the Szymanowski Quartet, illustrate how gesture, speech, and singing work together in such situations. They were playing Beethoven's Quartet in A minor, op. 132.

> Brendel sits at the side of the quartet. When he wants to intervene he leans forward and reaches out with his left hand, as if to literally grasp the players' attention. As he speaks, his hand signifies, mainly through movements whose energetic profiles translate iconically to dynamics, contour, or portamento, but occasionally through conventional gestures (for instance when he turns up his palm in a conductor's gesture to say there is more to come). Sometimes Brendel gets up to conduct: he towers over the first violinist, underlining the unequal relationship between the almost mythical pianist and the up-and-coming Polish quartet. Sometimes he offers more or less technical comments. It's important to emphasise the rest at the beginning of a phrase or melody, he says, and there is a point where he remarks, rather wistfully, that some singers would use *portamento* here. But often he is simply asking for greater warmth, or just for 'more'. And at one point he says, 'Tell yourself: I will now play this upbeat even more wonderful'. I feel what he has in mind is the sort of performance a pre-1945 Viennese quartet might have given, and he knows he is not going to get it.
>
> But what he says counts for less than what he sings, and how he sings it. He vocalises, too-ro-ro-ro-ro-te-ta. It might be a melodic motif or the bass line, but the pitches are barely perceptible (all you can be sure of is whether the notes go up or down). There is strong, expressive tremolo, and the tone quality is exaggeratedly breathy, resulting an oddly intimate version of Barthes's grain. Depending on what he wants to communicate, there may be again exaggerated dynamic changes, or an exaggerated emphasis on rhythm or articulation. This expressive croaking seems to come from deep within Brendel's body. There are of course elements of iconicity between what he sings and what he wants to hear, but overall the one stands for the other through a more complex form of representation: it makes me think of a caricature, in the sense that a particular, salient element is drawn out and foregrounded, writ large. His singing leaves out everything except the expression. Sometimes, when he sings as they play, you have the impression the quartet members are providing the notes and Brendel is providing the expression, rather like playing a pianola.

And the role of the body in WAM goes further than this. By itself and in its interaction with instruments, the body contributes to the formation of musical styles, and to the formation of the patterns of thinking that underlie styles. The experience of singing, part of everyone's experience at least as a child, creates great sensitivity to the tensional and expressive shaping from moment to moment that underlies many cultures of music making, even those in which instruments play a dominant role; consider, for example, Doğantan-Dack's 'singing' hand. Instruments in turn structure this vocal sensibility (octave equivalence is not specified in the physiology or phenomenology of the voice, but is directly represented in the topography of keyboard and most woodwind instruments). Ergonomic considerations channel the creation of music in particular directions. Folk blues guitar playing, for example, makes much use of open strings, with the left hand most often in first position: as John Baily and Peter Driver (1992) explain, this 'ties the music down to certain configurations and explains the differing characters of the various keys' (66), in contrast to other guitar styles in which open strings are avoided.[9] Iyer, who referred to the 'dialectic between formal/symbolic and situational/embodied constraints', explains what he means in more detail:

> in the midst of an improvisation, the temporally situated pianist is always making choices. These choices are informed not simply by which note, phrase or gesture is 'correct', but rather by which activities are executable at the time that a given choice is made.... In this way, for example, the improvising pianist is more likely to choose piano keys that lie under her current hand position than keys that do not (Iyer 2002: 408–9).

The element of dialectic enters because there is a trade-off between what is wanted to be played and what is wanted to be heard.

By comparison with the style of folk blues guitar playing, what is wanted to be heard in WAM is heavily conditioned by staff notation. This heightens the dialectic. 'Musical patterns are remembered and executed not solely as aural patterns but as sequences of movements', Baily and Driver (1992: 62) write, so that the music is 'represented cognitively in terms of movement patterns which have visual, kinaesthetic, tactile, as well as auditory repercussions'. And there is no straightforward relationship between these embodied gestures and the individual notes specified by staff notation. In jazz piano playing, David Sudnow writes, 'the "major triad" is not a collection of isolatable notes with their sounds. It is an arena at hand for configurationally distanced maneuvers' (1978: 74). That is also one of Doğantan-Dack's points: 'the singing touch does not affect a single note', she says, 'but a group of notes' (2011: 257), and that is why the individual note attacks that empirical musicologists are so busy measuring do not connect with the pianist's own experience. As Rolf Inge Godøy (2011) writes, 'it is not obvious that atom events in the form of notes are primordial to phrases' (71), and so one might say that notation deconstructs the performative gesture, breaks it down into atoms of

---

9. This is just one example of a small but growing literature on the relationship between the body, instruments, and musical style. In addition to ongoing work on blues and rock guitar by David Marquiss and Jill Halstead, this includes studies by Baily of the Afghan *dotar* (Baily 1985) and by Bell Yung (1984) of the *qin*. Of particular promise are approaches based on computer modelling of the body-instrument interface, such as those of Guerino Mazzola and Stefan Müller on the pianistic hand (Mazzola 2011: 126–29) and David Huron and Jonathan Berec (2009) on the trumpet.

sound: these can be reconfigured within the symbolic domain (that is what composers do), and then translated back into the terms of the body. Pedro Rebelo was
talking about this when he said that 'notation becomes characterized by operations on itself', and it underlines the claim I made in Chapter 7 (when I quoted
Rebelo) that the logic of composition does not necessarily translate easily into the
logics of performance or listening.

In this way, while WAM is no exception to the principle that all music is
grounded in the body, it is in the case of WAM a body disciplined and reconfigured by notation. As a consequence, whereas folk blues as a genre is to some considerable degree constituted by a particular interfacing of the body and the guitar,
in WAM the clearest traces of Cox's corporal thinking are to be found at the level
of idiolect: in Domenico Scarlatti's keyboard sonatas, for example, in which 'rapid,
repeated hand-crossings and very wide leaps across space in each hand' mean that

> the harpsichordist's eyes and attention must be so fiercely focused on the
> keyboard. This focus, vital to pitch accuracy, makes it plain how tightly har-
> nessed and controlled that bodiliness must be. Thus these sonatas make the
> body flamboyant and constrain it at the same time, pressing gesture into
> the service of a rapidity, profusion, energetic repetitiveness, and redundant
> precision so marked and exuberant to constitute a topos of mechanism—
> including, in its range of cheerfully frenetic effects, its prevailing hopefulness
> as a view of the world (Le Guin 2002: 247–48).

As much as any recording, then, Scarlatti's sonatas represent the traces of a distinctive embodied practice, a characteristic mode of engagement between body
and instrument, while at the same time they function as scripts through which
that embodied experience can be to some degree reconstructed and re-experi-
enced in the twenty-first century. Iyer (2002: 388) writes that 'every culture "constructs" the human body differently', which comes to much the same as saying that
every culture has its own music. It follows that both the history and the geography of music could in principle be documented in the form of a narrative of the
performing body.

BODIES IN SOUND

In striking contrast to the disembodied aesthetics of WAM, then, music emerges
as a paradigm case of embodied cognition. In place of the handing down of progressively more concrete instructions from mind to body, thinking about music
is shaped by bodily experience: as Godøy puts it (2010), it represents an extreme
example of 'the idea of body-based cognitive schemata and categories emerging from massive experience of being and acting in the world' (108). And while
the role of corporal thinking in performance is self-evident (at least when seen
without the debilitating prejudices of autonomist aesthetics), what might be less
self-evident is its role in perception and imagination.

From the phenomenological standpoint, Sudnow articulates this when he writes that 'When I say I know what a note will sound like, I mean that I am engaged in a *course that provides for that note's sound*....I do not know a note's sound apart from the context of a handful course in which its sound will figure' (1978: 69). From the standpoint of recent scientific research, Daniel Leech-Wilkinson (2012: paragraph 2.2) says that 'imagining music engages, in experienced musicians, neural networks also involved in performance', while the discovery of mirror neurons indicates more generally that—in Godøy's words (2010)—'to perceive an action is equivalent to internally simulating it' (109).[10] This, Godøy adds, 'may explain why listeners are so readily induced to move to musical sound'. In short, we hear with our bodies. Susan Foster illustrates what this means when she quotes (2008: 48–49) an account by the *New York Times* dance critic John Martin of the 'inner mimicry' involved in watching dance, written incidentally in 1939, long before anyone had heard of mirror neurons. We 'cease to be mere spectators', he says, 'and become participants in the movement that is presented to us, and though to all outward appearances we shall be sitting quietly in our chairs, we shall nevertheless be dancing synthetically with all our musculature'. This of course is what I was talking about when, in Chapter 5, I spoke of the surrogate dancing of listeners to Chopin's mazurkas who map the weight of Zorn's heavy ironshod shoes onto their own feet.

In a way, then, aestheticians and critics such as Leo Stein who insisted on disembodied listening were whistling in the wind. However you listen, the body is involved. It would be hard to find a better image of ostensively disembodied listening than E. T. A Hoffmann's account (2004) of a concert-master 'who has a string quartet at his house every Thursday. In the summertime I can hear their gentle sound, since in the evening, when the street has become quiet, they play with the windows open. On such occasions I sit down on the sofa, close my eyes, and listen in a state of profound bliss' (149). But even with his eyes closed he surely heard the musicians playing their instruments, for as Godøy says, 'massive ecological knowledge of sound production means that listeners...have a repertoire of sound-producing gestures so that in situations where there are no visible musicians..., the listeners may mentally recreate the choreography of sound-producing gestures' (2010: 106). (That was one of the foundations of Doğantan-Dack's argument.) In other words, the recumbent Hoffmann was listening to the musicians' bodies, and listening with his own body.

Stravinsky (1962: 72) inveighed against listening to music with closed eyes, on the grounds that 'the sight of the gestures and movements of the various parts of the body producing the music is fundamentally necessary if it is to be grasped in all its fullness'. But there is a sense in which, or a degree to which, you grasp the gestures

10. Godøy is quoting from an article by Vittorio Gallese and Thomas Metzinger. Arnie Cox (2001: 199) succinctly summarises one of the key studies of motor neurons: 'In one study, a monkey performs a certain grasping gesture, and there is corresponding neural activity in a specific part of the monkey's brain. This monkey then observes the same gesture performed by the experimenter *and the same firing pattern recurs in the monkey's brain*.'

and movements of the body even with your eyes shut, and so it seems unnecessary to erect a personal preference into an ideological principle. Writing in 1835, Pierre Baillot, the violinist whom I quoted in Chapter 8, took a more balanced view:

> Sometimes during the performance of slow pieces, we even see a listener seek to imbue himself more deeply with the feeling the composer wished to paint by putting his hand in front of his eyes so that nothing will distract him. But this is an exception, for the sense of sight seems to come to the aid of the sense of hearing in conveying to the listener more completely the expression of the accent through that of the physical motions (1991: 463).

That resonates not only with common sense but also with the findings of present-day writers coming at the issue from a scientific perspective. Sofia Dahl and her co-researchers, for example, write that, although you do not have to see a musical performance to understand it,

> being able to see the movements of a performer obviously contributes a great deal of information that, in turn, adds to the experience. That may explain why we as listeners also are eager to get seats that allow us to see the performance. The visual gestures give us a richer experience and establish a sense of community in which we as audience participate more fully (Dahl et al. 2010: 61).

And it is evident that many, if not all, concert-goers concur: Why, if not for the pleasure of watching the signifying body, do the seats on the left side of an auditorium always fill up first at piano recitals?

Even at a basic perceptual level, people hear things differently depending on what they see. Michael Schutz and Fiona Manning (2012), for example, have demonstrated through experiment that listeners experience a marimba note as lasting longer when they see it coupled with a long gesture than with a short one, even when there is no difference in the acoustic signal. People also hear things differently at a more global level. A study by Klaus-Ernst Behne and Clemens Wöllner (2011) showed that listeners thought they were hearing a different performance when they were in fact hearing the same one accompanied by different body movement. A study by Jennifer Huang and Carol Krumhansl showed that more active stage behaviour led novice listeners to rate what they heard more highly, with the researchers concluding that 'non-musicians attending a concert…may base their judgement more on what they see than what they hear' (2011: 362). And it is not just novice listeners who are affected. A series of studies summarised by Marilyn Boltz (2013: 215–16) shows that musically experienced listeners judge performances more highly when they can see as well as hear them, particularly when the performers are attractive. The shocking thing about this last finding is that attractive performers are consistently rated more highly even under audio-only conditions. The obvious explanation is that they receive more attention and encouragement from their teachers.

It should not, then, come as a surprise that what performers wear matters too. Like Hendrix, if less extravagantly, WAM performers signify through their clothing. As Bruno Nettl (1989: 12–13) has observed, there is an entire semiotics of musicians' dress—formal dress for orchestral players, coloured tops for early or contemporary music, and so on—and tampering with these codes is an obvious way of making a statement. The strength of the values associated with musicians' dress became evident in the public furore over Bond, the British/Australian crossover string quartet who dress like pop stars—though it was when they dropped their clothes altogether that the shit really hit the fan. (The nude shot was supposedly intended for the cover of their first album, though it may have simply have been a publicity stunt [Victoros 2009: 119–23].) But we don't have to rely on that kind of anecdotal evidence. An empirical study by Noola Griffiths (2008: 283) showed that four female violinists were rated as more technically proficient when wearing conventional concert attire than when wearing a nightclubbing dress.

Then there are visual signals that performers send to the audience because they cannot be transmitted acoustically. An obvious example is when conductors lay down the baton or close the score to convey to the audience that a piece has finished. Cottrell (2004: 158) explains some of the strategies his saxophone quartet adopted, consciously or otherwise, to reinforce the sense of an ending, for example freezing for a few moments before relaxing and putting down their instruments. He adds that such strategies are likely to be particularly important with contemporary music, where listeners cannot tell from the sound that the piece has finished (in Cottrell's diplomatic words, 'the musical language may be so complex as to make it difficult for the audience to follow the musical logic'). That neatly indicates the continuity between visual and acoustic signifiers in performance.

But the visible can penetrate far more deeply into the listening experience than these examples might suggest, and the best way to make the point is through WAM's most spectacular example of the signifying body: the conductor. According to Bruce Johnson (2002), the 'particular form of regimentation' that characterises WAM 'centralises the inviolable and completed score, the object of visual-mental focus for every musician either directly or as conducted from a central "altar"' (102). Following this line one might say that developments in nineteenth- and twentieth-century concert hall design placed conductors in a perfect position to exercise surveillance over the orchestra (the original title of Foucault's book is *Surveiller et punir*)—but more relevantly in this context, it placed them at the centre of the audience's line of vision. And this gave rise to a kind of reverse-view choreography, though nowadays the televising of concerts also gives us close-ups of conductors' facial expressions. Schoenberg (1975: 342) had a jaundiced view of 'the dances the modern conductor performs before a spectacle-loving public': the reason 'why so many present-day conductors conduct from memory', he continues, is that 'to look at the score could only disturb and hinder their display of the mimetic arts which they command to so high a degree'. (A few lines later he refers to having 'learned at his own expense what a conductor of genius is capable of'.) But we can equally phrase this in a positive light by saying that, like Hendrix, conductors repurpose modes of address by directing them to the audience, and in this way—like Hendrix in the first riff of 'Foxy Lady'—engage listeners in the sonorous fabric of the music.

Murray Dineen (2011) remarks that 'one of the principal outcomes of a well wrought conducting style is to lend a visual component to the primarily aural phenomenon of music, a stylistic visual component that is largely superfluous to functional style' (143). For instance he writes of Raphael Kubelick, conducting a Bruckner symphony with the New York Philharmonic Orchestra, that 'his gestures seemed to have little to do with the customary mechanical needs of the orchestra, but instead seemed designed to trace a *sympathetic* path reflecting the intensity—the volume, the length of line, the nature of the articulation—of the work at any given moment. This kind of aesthetic engagement resembles that of choreographed dance' (145). But of course, no conductor can visually represent everything that is going on in an orchestra at a given point. Instead the conductor's dance represent a glossed version of the musical fabric, what I would like to call the *virtual body* of the music.

Speaking of people's spontaneous movements as they listen to music outside the concert hall, Godøy writes that musical gesture can involve 'a translation from one instrumental or vocal medium to bi-manual movement, e.g., from quite complex musical textures to simplified bi-manual movements as a kind of "piano reduction"' (109). But that is not quite the sort of glossing I mean. When you listen to Chopin's mazurkas, even if you are sitting on the wrong side of the auditorium or listening to a recording, you hear gesture, movement, dance. It isn't so much the pianist's actual, visible gestures that you are responding to: what you map onto your body and feel as your own movement is, rather, the kind of kinesthetic or energetic profile that I described in Chapter 5 with reference to Chopin's op. 33 no. 2. In the same way, conductors give visible expression to the motional qualities that Godøy (2010) has in mind when he speaks of 'ecologically founded "energy schemata" at work in the perception and cognition of musical sound' (112), or that Zbikowski (2011: 97) has in mind when he speaks of music and gesture drawing on 'the same pool of cognitive resources to create analogical representations of dynamic processes'. We are of course talking about the same morphologies of feeling—Stern's vitality affects—that I discussed in Chapter 3; ongoing work in this area by researchers such as Godøy and Leech-Wilkinson (forthcoming) is likely to have an increasing impact upon the study of music as performance, demonstrating how comprehensively its meaning is grounded in bodily experience. But for now I shall simply say that Dineen's description of Kubelick will mean all the more if we understand his reference to 'intensity' in Massumi's sense.

According to Marc Leman (2010), it is 'through corporeal mediation that it is possible to engage in a behavioural resonance with music, so that personal subjective feelings, moods, flow experiences, and feelings of social bonding can be activated and exchanged' (48). That applies as much to listening as to performance, as illustrated by such practices as dancing, playing air guitar, or the 'shadow conducting' that had already become a feature of gramophonic listening by the 1920s (Katz 2004: 59). But it also means that the immobile listening of the concert hall is in its own way an embodied practice. And if Stein's idea of disembodied

Figure 10.1 Michelangeli about to play the first note of Chopin's Mazurka op. 33 no. 4, from a 1962 television film (RAI Turin recording, Opus Arte OA 0940 D)

listening amounts to whistling in the wind, then the same can be said more generally of the aesthetic ideal of autonomous listening, that is to say, listening that is purged of such extra-musical dimensions as the visual and the verbal. If music is an intrinsically embodied and multimodal phenomenon through which meaning emerges in real time, then there is no *a priori* way of drawing a line between what does and does not matter in its performance. For the drama theorist Baz Kershaw (1992), it is 'a fundamental tenet of performance theory... that no item in the environment of performance can be discounted as irrelevant to its impact' (22). Hendrix's pants make the point. Of course that does not mean everything is always relevant. (Hendrix's pants make that point too.) But there is nothing that *may* not affect the meaning of a performance. There are no rules of irrelevance. Everything counts, until proved otherwise.

BUILDING BRIDGES

There is a television film of Arturo Benedetti Michelangeli playing Chopin's Mazurka op. 33 no. 4, made in 1962,[11] which shows the pianist's elaborate preparations before he begins playing. As can be seen in Media Example 10.1,

11. 'Michelangeli plays Chopin', Opus Arte DVD OA 0940 D (2006).

Michelangeli wipes the keyboard up and down with his handkerchief, and then mops his cheeks. He puts his handkerchief down, and then clasps his hands together with the washing-like motion traditionally associated with clergymen and the best butlers. He rubs his right hand on his thigh, and then, with his wrist bent down, brings it smartly up to a position a few inches above the keyboard. He flicks his fingers forward and out to create what looks like Doğantan-Dack's 'singing' hand (Figure 10.1), before letting it fall in a measured descent to the keyboard to sound the first note. Traditional musicological thinking would label everything up to this point as extra-musical: that is, it has nothing to do with the music, where 'music' is understood as a text reproduced in performance. The performance studies approach, by contrast, recognises no such distinction.

How then might we understand Michelangeli's performance up to the first note? Philip Auslander, the performance studies scholar who has given the most sustained attention to music, has an approach that not only makes sense of what Michelangeli is doing, but also highlights the contrast with the traditional musicological approach. His starting point is that musicologists see musical performances as performances of musical works. But seen from the perspective of performance studies, he argues, that is a very narrow understanding of what 'performance' might mean:

> it does not necessarily follow that simply because the verb *to perform* demands a direct object, that the object or performance must be a text such as choreography, a dramatic text, or a musical work. Many other things can be understood as performative constructs: personal identity may be seen as something one performs, for instance. One can speak of performing a self in daily life just as readily as one speaks of performing a text in a theatre or concert hall. In short, the direct object of the verb to perform need not be some-*thing*—it can also be some*one*, an identity rather than a text (2006: 101).

But in saying this, Auslander is not thinking of the performance of everyday identity. He is thinking, in fact, in a rather similar way to Waskul on role playing, though his immediate source is Simon Frith. As Auslander explains in an earlier article (2004: 6), Frith distinguishes three levels on which pop singers operate: as a human being, as a star, and as a 'song personality', that is, in terms of the character constructed by the song. These respectively correspond to Waskul's person, player, and persona but, confusingly, Auslander refers to them as real person, performance persona, and character. From now on I shall use the term 'persona' in Auslander's sense, to denote an identity as a performer that is constructed through the act of performance, or more typically through successive acts of performance.

As Frith's term 'star' might suggest, the idea of persona is obviously applicable to popular music: artists such as Madonna and (the one previously known as) Prince have a stage identity that persists across their performances, subject to occasional or continuous reinvention, and that has no necessary relationship to their everyday identities. But there are stars in classical music too, and Michelangeli was one of them. That is why the term 'legendary' so easily attaches itself to him: one might say he was the only artist to have advanced his career through his equally legendary concert cancellations—which only added to his romantic mystique, his quality of unattainability. In this context, Michelangeli's performance up to the first note of Chopin's op. 33 no. 4 is all about persona. His elaborate preparations heighten anticipation of the performance to follow. They have a ritualistic quality, aligning the playing of op. 33 no. 4 with the performance of some religious office, and presenting the pianist as the celebrant, as the representative of a higher power. Layers of meaning are unfolded in real time, and converge upon the persona that the performance sustains. In terms of the impact to which Kershaw refers, it is clear that the performance began long before Michelangeli played the first note.

In the remainder of the chapter I use gesture as a means of focussing on the relationship between the different approaches of musicology—in particular empirical musicology—and of interdisciplinary performance studies. In this book I have repeatedly stressed the epistemological gulf between approaches premised on the paradigm of reproduction, most obviously in the form of the analysis-to-performance or page-to-stage approaches of structuralist music theory and the communication model more generally, and those based on the idea of meaning being produced in the real time of performance: while the latter is the approach of interdisciplinary performance studies, it is also the basis of the semiotic perspective that I have been developing in relation to the rhetorical tradition, the practices of intertextual and stylistic reference, Pressing's idea of the referent, Sawyer's idea of the emergent, and Gates's idea of Signifyin(g). Given the extent to which the paradigm of reproduction is built into musicological thinking, can it make sense to draw at the same time on approaches that embody such different assumptions about the nature of musical meaning? To narrow the question down and sharpen its focus, I stage an encounter between two approaches that would seem to have nothing in common: on the one hand the abstract, data-driven approach of distant listening as set out in Chapters 5 and 6, and on the other the event-oriented, embodied, and determinedly non-technical approach of performance studies. I begin, however, by positioning the empirical methods that inform distant listening in relation to a number of neighbouring areas of research.

Like other work emanating from CHARM and now CMPCP, the mazurka studies reported in Chapters 5 and 6 of this book are essentially motivated by a very traditional musicological question—how music relates to culture more generally—and aim to show how new answers to an old question may emerge from the study of performance and in particular from the use of quantitative approaches. This work adopts some methods normally associated with scientific enquiry, but, like the rest of the book, it is grounded in a humanities epistemology. In Wilhelm Dilthey's terms its aim is more one of understanding than of certainty, more one of elucidation than of explanation. That distinguishes it from a large body of research on musical performance that seeks to answer very different questions and is grounded in scientific epistemology. Much of this would be classified as empirical musicology, though it spills over into music psychology and music information retrieval.[12]

---

12. For further discussion of these issues see Cook (2002) and Cook (2006).

One measure of this difference is the fact that in this book I do not talk about the highly influential projects led by Gerhard Widmer, a computer scientist who has pioneered data mining approaches to very large sets of piano performance data in order to model the distinctive styles of leading pianists. His current project, based on a series of live recordings of Chopin's complete works that Nikita Magaloff made on a Bösendorfer SE reproducing piano in 1989, addresses such issues as how the pianist's playing changed through successive performances, the nature of the errors found in it, Magaloff's use of hand breaking, and the shaping through tempo and dynamics of bar-length patterns consisting of sixteen successive quavers (Flossmann et al. 2010). It is no criticism of the project, which in any case is still ongoing, that these topics cannot be readily linked to the issues of music and cultural meaning that concern most Anglo-American musicologists. Another measure is provided by Guerino Mazzola's 2011 book *Musical Performance, A Comprehensive Approach: Theory, Analytical Tools, and Case Studies*, the title of which may be justified through the very wide range of empirical approaches to performance that it covers. Despite some introductory references to historical composers and theorists, however, and many references to Adorno, there are remarkably few points of contact with what Anglo-American musicologists would see as the mainstream discipline. From the empirical side, then, much of work presented in this book might easily be interpreted—or, as I would say, misinterpreted—as insufficiently scientific.

To date, however, the attacks have tended to come from the musicological side. The Wagner specialist John Deathridge, for example, writes in his back-cover endorsement of Adorno's *Towards a Theory of Musical Reproduction* that 'In his refreshing antidote to the mere collection and measurement of data that too often passes for research into the practice of music, Adorno effectively declares war on the impoverishment of musical performance in the modern era and the shallow empirical investigations that unwittingly reflect it'. Deathridge's position reflects Adorno's own hostility to the use of empirical and more generally scientific methods in the social sciences, which set the pattern for similar internecine conflicts within the study of music. One example was the splitting off of music theory from musicology in the 1970s (the [American] Society for Music Theory was established in 1977); another was Joseph Kerman's 1985 vilification of musicological positivism—by which he meant the mere collection and measurement of data that Deathridge refers to.

Kerman attacked music theory for its formalism, its emphasis on abstraction, and its spurious objectivity, and Richard Taruskin (1995: 24) targetted a similar critique at the analysis of performance when he wrote that 'turning ideas into objects, and putting objects in place of people, is the essential modernist fallacy—the fallacy of reification, as it is called. It fosters the further fallacy of forgetting that performances, even canned performances, are not things but acts'. Perhaps the most sweeping objections, however, came from Carolyn Abbate, who advanced a perspective within musicology that is closely related to Peggy Phelan's in performance studies.[13] In essence Abbate (2004) claimed that the experience of live performance is the only authentic musical reality, and that coming to terms with it means 'avoiding the tactile monuments in music's necropolis—recordings and scores and graphic music examples' (510). In particular, she says, we cannot engage with the drastic qualities of performance—its strangeness, uncanniness, and defiance of the rational—by 'turning performances or performers into yet another captured text to be examined for import via a performance science' (509). Particularly cutting is her comment that performance 'has been seen, analyzed, acknowledged, but not always listened to' (508).

I find it hard not to feel a sneaking sympathy with all these criticisms, even when I think they are wrong-headed. Abbate, in particular, articulates many of the beliefs that motivate this book. I critique the page-to-stage approach because, like Abbate, I distrust its over-confident mapping from text to performance, and see it as seeking to domesticate an experience that is unruly, embodied, and resistant to the practices and values of academic formulation. I also think that 'the experience of listening to a live performance solicits attention more for the performers and the event and far less for the work than is perhaps generally admitted' (512). I agree that performances signify as what they are, and not because they 'conceal a cryptic truth to be laid bare' (536), which is as much as to say that I share Abbate's suspicion of the 'New' musicologists' appropriation of Adorno. And I love the idea of a musicology whose starting point will be things like '*doing this really fast is fun*'[14]: as Abbate continues, 'Between the score as a script, the musical work as a virtual construct, and us, there lies a huge phenomenal explosion, a performance that demands effort and expense and recruits human participants, takes up time and leaves people drained or tired or elated or relieved' (533). These are of course some of the things that ethnographers and autoethnographers of performance are concerned with (and such work has mushroomed since 2004). But I wonder whether, in declaring recordings—as well as scores and graphic music examples—off limits, Abbate is not throwing the baby out with the bathwater.

That there is bathwater to be thrown out is not in doubt. I said in Chapter 5 that at times I suspected myself, when working on Furtwängler's recordings of Beethoven's Ninth Symphony, of analysing the graph and not the music, in other words—Abbate's words—of seeing, analysing, acknowledging, but not listening to

13. Phelan's key claim is that 'Performance's only life is in the present. Performance cannot be saved, recorded, documented, or otherwise participate in the circulation of representations *of* representations: once it does so, it becomes something other than performance. To the degree that performance attempts to enter the economy of reproduction it betrays and lessens the promise of its own ontology' (1993: 146).

14. In his critique of Abbate's article, Karol Berger (2005: 496) comments, 'It is encouraging to see such hedonistic notions as beauty and pleasure regain academic respectability after decades of moralistic neglect'.

the performance. That is tantamount to treating the graph as a new form of text, to be dealt with on more or less the same terms as music analysts have long dealt with other texts. It makes it possible to do what dodgy builders do: carry on the old business under a new name. But then, I continued by explaining how software environments such as Sonic Visualiser make it possible to integrate analysis with the listening experience in a way that wasn't possible in 2004. And more generally, it seems to me that the important question is not *whether* or not one works with recordings, but *how* one does so.

You don't have to treat recordings as texts, for example by looking for cryptic truths concealed in them. You can treat them as the traces of how past performances went, or usually more realistically—as I said in Chapter 5—as the traces of how someone, or more likely several people, thought a performance should go. You can also treat them as artefacts the role of which is to prompt particular experiences when they are heard. In either case you are attempting, as far as possible, to work *through* the medium of recording *to* the experience for which it stands—which is also, of course, what analysts do, or try to do, when working with scores or graphic music examples.[15] In other words, you do what people do when they hear human gestures specified in musical sound, or what Ingrid Monson did when listening to Jaki Byard's 'Bass-ment Blues': you attempt to understand them in terms of what people have done or can do, in other words as embodying human acts and not just as things or objects. (Note my repeated references to 'attempting' or 'trying': I didn't say it was easy.) And that is my response to Taruskin, though I also note his pejorative reference to 'canned' performances, which places him in a long but questionable tradition of disparaging the technology that brought music to audiences across the world who could never otherwise have experienced it. As for Deathridge, of course there are examples of 'naively empirical research on expression' (the phrase is Clarke's [1995: 52]), but what is puzzling is that he sees empirical musicology and Adorno as attempting to do the same job. At least, why otherwise would he set them up against one another as he does? Why can't we do empirical musicology *and* Adorno?

But the question I set out to address is whether we can do empirical musicology *and* performance studies, and in order to do this I return to Chopin's Mazurka op. 63 no. 3, but now focussing on a number of video performances. Grigory Sokolov performed this mazurka on 4 November 2002, at a packed concert in the Théâtre des Champs-Elysées, Paris (where it was the first of five encores), and

---

15. Doğantan-Dack (2012: 40) makes a parallel argument when, having argued against musicologists' excessive emphasis on recorded rather than live music, she finds herself having to justify her own use of recordings: 'a necessary starting point for any contemporary research on live performance is an audio-visual documentation of it. In a certain ontological sense, of course, this kind of representation turns the live performance into a recorded one, so that we are actually able to study only the recorded event and never the live performance itself. The methodological way out of this apparent impasse is to contextualize the live event through multi-modal means so as to implicate its liveness'.

there are essential aspects of his performance that would be absent in a CD. A film
of the concert was in fact issued on DVD,[16] and the director, Bruno Monsaingeon,
writes in the liner notes that, at the start of concert, 'suddenly a massive shadow
appears who moves swiftly over to the keyboard, the only brightly lit surface to
stand out from the large coffin-like box in the centre of the stage'. This sense of
the massive, almost Russian bear-like form with the fluid movements and delicate
touch is part of the experience you carry away from the performance, even on
DVD. Someone ripped this track to YouTube, where many viewers posted com-
plimentary comments until it was removed as the result of a copyright claim. But
one of the few critical postings came from vtpiano7 and had to do with the way
Sokolov's hands fly up after he plays certain notes, almost like a marionette:

> Is a pitty a pianist who sometimes play wonderful, but sometimes his kind
> of "maniac" way to play the piano(Technicaly) makes hime to make some
> musical mistakes,specially that one of make some values shorter than they
> really are, owed to his "mania" of quit hands so fast from keyboard. I don´´t
> understand some very good artists who have a so big lack of self control.[17]

A more positive way to make the same point would be that Sokolov uses visible
gestures to make musical points. And indeed, to some extent all pianists do this.
A significant amount of research has been devoted to the body motions of pianists, in particular an extensive series of studies by Jane Davidson (summarised in
Davidson 2007b). Without going into unnecessary detail, the main features are a
global body sway that emanates from the hips (in contrast to electric guitarists or
Jerry Lee Lewis, the classical pianist's kinesphere is obviously constrained by the
seated posture), and a variety of more localised gestures, such as lifting the hands
and tilting or nodding the head. To a limited—but only a limited—degree these
are linked to the structure of the music that is being played. Gestures tend to be
interchangeable, but there is considerable consistency in the points at which they
occur. Individual performers may develop a repertory of distinctive gestures, and
listeners can read performers' expressive intentions from them.

But as the YouTube posting indicates, Sokolov takes this gesturing further than
most pianists. The 'quit hands' gesture (Figure 10.2) is just one example of this.
Sometimes Sokolov uses it as a form of articulation: the gesture clips the note visually in the same way that it can be clipped aurally, in either case creating an accent.
(There are precedents for this. In his *Letters to a Young Lady on the Art of Playing
the Pianoforte*, Czerny [1840: 31] notes that some pianists 'after every short note,
suddenly take up their hands as if they had touched a hot iron', while, according to
his pupil William Sherwood, Liszt did this when playing waltzes: he 'had a habit
frequently of dashing the wrist abruptly from the chord at the second beat of the
measure,... sometimes almost prematurely' [Hudson 1994: 187].) More often, like
a momentary caesura, the gesture serves to mark the break between groups of

16. 'Grigory Sokolov: Live in Paris' (Naïve DR 2018 AV 127, 2003).

17. http://www.youtube.com/watch?v=LOpW8hlvZzk (accessed 28 March 2008).

Figure 10.2 Sokolov performing Chopin's Mazurka op. 63 no. 3 (Ideale Audience International Naïve DR 2108 AV 127)

notes, such as a phrase or half phrase.[18] Then again, Sokolov shapes notes after he has played them: on the first right-hand note of bar 7, for instance, he keeps his finger on the depressed key while he twists his palm to the right and back again, so lending it a visual quality of sustained shaping that—as in the case of Schutz's and Manning's study of the marimba—is cross-domain mapped to the auditory sphere. (Doğantan-Dack [2011: 254n.] suggests that this is what Liszt intended when he wrote 'vibrato' into his piano scores; Harry Rich recalls how Friedman, with whom he studied in 1942–43, did the same [Evans 2009: 283]. And Rosen [2003: 31] notes Arrau's habit of 'simulating a vibrato on the more expressive long notes', describing it as 'a psychological aid, that perhaps even convinced members of the audience that the note had extra resonance'.) The effect of sound and sight working together in this way is to create an effect of lyricism that is none the less real, none the less *musical*, for being visible rather than audible.

At the same time, these individual gestures are knitted into a continuous choreographic display that is based on the standard features of pianistic movement, but exaggerates and stylises them. The 'quit hands' gesture appears more in the right hand than the left, whether because it is associated with the melody or just because the sustained nature of the mazurka accompaniment tends to tie up the left hand, but at times it alternates between the hands, creating an effect of continuous motion that is reminiscent of the 'puzzling interweavingness' Sudnow (1978: 87) talks about in the context of jazz piano playing. Sokolov sways as he plays, usually from side to side but sometimes forward and back or in a circular motion. He nods his head for emphasis (occasionally for each of a series of

18. This corresponds to the use of hand lifts to denote the end of phrases observed by Elaine King (2006: 159).

particularly important notes). And he maintains what by analogy with Auslander's 'guitar face' one might call 'piano face': not as extreme as you expect to see in a rock star, of course, but all the same evocative of absorption and deep feeling. Sometimes he mouths as he plays (though not in obvious synchrony), and occasionally he breathes through his mouth. There is the impression of a slow, relaxed cycle of inhalation and exhalation.[19] It is a perfect picture of Csíkszentmihályi's flow. The overall effect is one of extraordinary fluency, expressed in the combination of highly controlled gestural shaping and at the same time attention to and expression of the smallest details of the music.

That is a good description of how Sokolov's playing sounds, too. And there is considerable mutual entailment of physical and auditory gesture. It is not that he makes exactly the same gesture every time a passage repeats: often he does—for example the 'quit hands' appears after the first beat of bars 1 and 9, and at the end of bars 2 and 10—but sometimes he doesn't. It is that he uses the same repertory of gestures, and uses them in essentially the same way, throughout all the pieces on the DVD—and not in particular, as one might perhaps expect, the encores, party pieces that he has presumably played on countless previous occasions. It is, in short, how he plays. The music would make perfect sense on a CD, but that does not mean that the effect would be quite the same: you can watch a colour film in black and white, but that does not mean that nothing is lost. Only the lingering effect of textualism and autonomist aesthetics could motivate a distinction between the musical and the extra-musical aspects of this performance based simply on whether you hear something or see it. On the contrary, in line with Kershaw's principle that 'no item in the environment of performance can be discounted as irrelevant to its impact', it may be said that the concept of the extra-musical is simply inapplicable to performance.

How do other performers of this mazurka use gesture, and how does it fit in with the broader musical characterisation of their performances? There are a number of videos on YouTube that have not been ripped from commercial recordings, of which I shall discuss two, by Irina Morozova and Julien Duchoud. The Morozova video is from a solo recital that she gave at the Mannes College of Music, New York, in January 2008, where she teaches in the Preparatory Division.[20] Morozova uses much the same gestures that are familiar from research on the topic—sway, hand lifts, and the rest—and she uses them with the same restrained balance and fluency that characterises other aspects of her playing. The effect is one of sensibility rather than passion, full of feeling yet classical in the sense of conveying a certain Apollonian detachment, and at times dream-like. What particularly underlines this is how, at significant moments, Morozova lifts her gaze upwards, as if that is where the music is coming from. (Examples include bar 2, bar 6—which she

19. King's 2006 pilot study of pianists' breathing suggests that slower breathing patterns are associated with greater experience.

20. The video is at http://www.youtube.com/watch?v=e8BQc5wwQGU; Morozova's biography is at http://www.newschool.edu/mannes/facultyPreparatoryDivision.aspx?mid=4810.

plays with particularly strong *rubato*—and bars 29–30, the turning point where the descent into the cadence at bar 32 begins.) Jane Davidson (2007a: 127) notes the association of this gesture with thoughtfulness, reflection, and contemplation, all of which seem applicable here. But lifting one's gaze is also an established signifier of the sublime, as seen on any number of record sleeves: a classic example is the image of Kathleen Ferrier on her recording of Mahler's *Das Lied von der Erde*, her hair touched by a celestial light.[21]

Different again is a performance by Julien Duchoud, given in June 2007 at the Chateau de Ripaille, Haute Savoie (France). An audience member posted a comment on YouTube: 'It was a wonderful concert in the old French castle! The public was touched by emotions, no one seemed to be indifferent. Everyone could appreciate such a splendid, sensual and bright playing! Chopen's mazurka sounded very nostalgically and its polish motives were performed with the special skill by this young pianist'.[22] The intimacy of the occasion can be both heard and seen on the video. The audience sit close to the pianist, who is playing from the score; though the room is dimly lit, an ordinary desk lamp, placed on the piano, throws a pool of light on it. The fact that Duchoud is not playing from memory, as Sokolov and Morozova do, immediately separates him from the virtuoso tradition—although in this respect it is not a very long tradition: as Kenneth Hamilton (2008: 73–81) explains, playing from memory became the norm only in the later part of the nineteenth century.

Reading from the score also constrains the extent of Duchoud's body sway. That throws more weight onto the occasional large upper-body motion, as at bar 48: he hunches his shoulder and turns his head towards it, grimacing slightly as he does so, and in this way projects this point as the emotional fulcrum of the piece—just as he does through the steadily increasing tempo that precedes this point and markedly slower tempo from bar 49. Similarly he plays for the most part with his hands close to the keys, which means that his occasional hand lifts come over as individual, self-contained gestures. There is neither the same sense of sustained interweaving that I commented on in relation to Sokolov, nor the restrained fluency of gesture of Morozova's performance. And again this links with the way his playing sounds. At an average tempo of crotchet = 122 MM, he takes the piece significantly faster than either Sokolov (102 MM) or Morozova (113 MM), and, by contrast with their playing, Duchoud's creates an effect of spontaneity, of focussing on the here and now. Adorno's idea that modern performance presents the music 'as already complete from the very first note' may have some purchase on Sokolov's and Morozova's way of playing, but it has little on Duchoud's. You have the impression, correct or otherwise, that he might play the piece quite differently next time, or if the audience responded differently. In short, Duchoud's playing has a

21. Decca LXT 5576, reproduced in Cook (2000: 34).

22. Posting by rozanasnegu at http://www.youtube.com/comment_servlet?all_comments&v=UflK-veX7Fk&fromurl=/watch%3Fv%3DUflK-veX7Fk; the video is at http://www.youtube.com/watch?v=UflK-veX7Fk.

moment-to-moment quality, a certain unpredictability, that has something in common with the rhetorical style of pre-war players like Friedman, even if the way he achieves it is different.

And this is where empirical analysis comes into play. Refer back to Figure 6.18, the scattergram of phrase arching in op. 63 no. 3, where the recordings of Sokolov, Morozova, and Duchoud are all picked out in the far right column. As it happens, Duchoud learned the piece after hearing Sokolov play it in concert,[23] but Figure 6.18 reinforces the impression that the two pianists do not play it in at all the same way. Duchoud appears in the middle of the chart because there are elements of both tempo and dynamic phrase arching in his playing—much more so than in Friedman's—but they are not strongly coordinated, particularly at the eight-bar level. By contrast, as I said in Chapter 6, Sokolov exemplifies the Russian tradition of phrase arching; so does Morozova (both she and Sokolov trained at the St. Petersburg Conservatory), and though she comes considerably further down in Figure 6.18, the classical understatement of her playing means that, as with Czerny-Stefańska, the phrase arching comes through more strongly than the scattergram might suggest. And this ties together the features of their playing on which I commented. Phrase arching lies behind, or is linked to, the effects of fluent, controlled shaping I mentioned in both the auditory and the visual domains. (Perhaps then the impression of regular inhalation and exhalation that I observed in Sokolov's playing was really a cross-domain mapping of the phrase arching.) The phrase arching gives their playing a quality of predictability, but I do not mean this in a negative sense: the effect is to prolong and solemnise the present moment, by contrast with the immediacy of Duchoud's playing.

At the same time, phrase arching plays a quite different role in Morozova's and Sokolov's performances. I referred to the quality of classical detachment in Morozova's playing, and that illustrates what I explained in Chapter 6: how phrase arching relocates the locus of expression from the moment-to-moment surface that Duchoud emphasises to the larger, more architectonic level of phrase structure. The expression remains, but it is now projected less as an expression of Morozova's subjectivity than as a quality of the music itself (which fits with her upward gaze, suggesting like Hendrix's closed eyes that the music is coming from somewhere else and she is its medium). In Lydia Goehr's terms (1996), all this aligns Morozova with the perfect performance of music, and gives a sense of formality to the occasion that contrasts with the intimacy of Duchoud's performance. The Mannes College recital hall is not a large space, but Morozova's playing makes it seem larger than it is, creating a distance between performer and listener that is as much musical as architectural.

Sokolov, of course, is playing in a far larger space than either Duchoud or Morozova. But as in the Mannes College recital hall, the relationship between pianist and audience is not simply defined by the built environment: it is also defined by the virtuoso tradition that is specified in the very fabric of Sokolov's playing.

23. Information provided by Duchoud to Craig Sapp, February 2009.

Virtuosity, like improvisation, can be seen as a form of social contract between performer and audience,[24] and it is social as much as physical distance that marks Sokolov's presence with the signs of the unattainable, the mythical; the difference between Sokolov and Michelangeli, of whom I said the same, is that if you buy a ticket you can rely on seeing Sokolov play. And if Sokolov, like Morozova and Michelangeli, is to be seen as music's medium, then this time the image that comes to mind is of his presiding over some rite seen from afar in a great cathedral. Or if that is to take it too seriously, then it is like watching an acrobat in the big top, for Sokolov is, after all, putting on a show (especially given that this is an encore). Either way, the effect is to structure the experience around Sokolov's charismatic presence, turning the event into something close to Goehr's perfect musical performance.

And although the effect is quite different as compared to that of Morozova's performance, phrase arching again lies at the heart of it. As Figure 6.18 shows, Sokolov is quite an extreme exponent of phrase arching. That means that, in his playing, the slow, predictable oscillation of tempo and dynamics, synchronised with one another and with the formal patterning of the music, creates an immensely strong framework of expectations, as it were a geodesic dome in sound. In their performances of op. 63 no. 3, other—even more extreme—phrase archers, such as Wasowski and Bunin, use this framework to support sometimes arbitrary expressive nuances: the nuances can afford to be arbitrary because the phrase arching takes care of the structure. It is much the same with Sokolov, except that what he superimposes on it is a choreography of at least the complexity and expressive effect of Kubelick's. Moreover it is a choreography closely related to the sound of his playing—indeed an integral dimension of his playing, but one that in the absence of the firm foundation of phrase arching might easily seem confused, self-indulgent, or plain irritating. Apart from vtpiano7, that is not how YouTube commentators respond to Sokolov's playing, and in Europe (though not for some reason North America) he is among the most active and successful of all concert pianists.

Or to put it another way, phrase arching grounds Sokolov's persona: not just that of the virtuoso, but a virtuoso with distinctive characteristics that set him apart from other virtuosos. In short, the elaborate and highly expressive choreography is a central component of the Sokolov brand, a means of product differentiation in the overcrowded market of international pianism. It brings together the qualities of which I spoke earlier: massivity, fluidity, delicacy. And it is just these qualities that are keyed in the official biography on his agent's website: 'Sokolov has gained an almost mythical status amongst music-lovers and pianophiles throughout the world.... Sokolov has amazed everyone again and again with the enormous breadth of his repertoire and his huge, almost physical musical strength.... His interpretations are poetic and highly individual, and his rhythmic freedom and elasticity of phrase are perhaps unequalled among pianists today'.[25]

24. See Chapter 9, p. 297.

25. http://www.amcmusic.com/eng/bio/bio_grigory_sokolov_eng.pdf (Artists Management Company, Verona, Italy).

Auslander (2006) concludes the article in which he sets out his idea of performance persona by saying that 'to think of music as performance is to foreground performers and their concrete relationship to audiences rather than the question of the relationship between musical works and performance' (117). Given Auslander's primary interests in popular music and improvisation, this formulation is understandable: all performance involves a performer, and hence a persona, regardless of whether there is such a thing as an identifiable musical work, or what expectations there might be of the relationship between work and performance. But the 'rather than' becomes harder to justify in contexts that are more strongly conditioned by musical works, and after all, if it is undeniable that Sokolov is performing Sokolov, then it is equally undeniable that he is performing Chopin's Mazurka op. 63 no. 3 (and a variety of other things as well, such as a particular image of Polishness, his own lineage within the procession of Russian pianists, his embeddedness in a ritualised tradition of high art, and so on: there is always one more thing any given performance can be said to be a performance of). To focus on persona or on work is to take up a different perspective on what I called the inherently multidimensional phenomenon of musical performance. The approaches of interdisciplinary performance studies and of empirical musicology provide complementary views of performance, and are likely to reveal more when used together than when deployed separately.

Following the Battle of Blenheim in 1704, a grateful nation presented its victor, the Duke of Marlborough, with the site on which Blenheim Palace was erected. Designed to be a national monument and political powerhouse, the southern façade of the palace consists of a series of nine state rooms, the doors of which are aligned in such away that you can see down the full extent of the building. This feature was exploited to grand effect when receiving guests. In this way the physical structure of the building afforded performances of social and political power, and in Gibsonian theory such affordances are seen as objective attributes of the environment. An architectural understanding of the building as a material object grounds understanding of its role in the maintenance of established hegemonies, while conversely an understanding of its social and political use throws light on the considerations that informed grand eighteenth-century architecture. In the same way, I have tried to show how an approach oriented to real-time experience can help to clarify *what* performances mean, while an approach oriented to the grounding of that experience in texts, sounds and actions can help to clarify *how* it is that performances mean what they mean. There is no need, in adopting one approach, to rule out the insights that may accrue from another, and a musicology into which performance is deeply thought will as a matter of course take advantage of every method at its disposal. That is because, in performance, everything counts.

11

The Ghost in the Machine

The 'live' has become little more than a 'sound' produced and consumed in private. The domestic space has become one of the primary sites of these new technological practices—a private and increasingly isolated site of musical production and consumption.

—PAUL THÉBERGE (1997: 241)

MUSIC EVERYWHERE

Imagine Beethoven's Fifth Symphony—as recorded by Felix Weingartner and the London Philharmonic Orchestra—thundering through an open window into the darkness of the Dorset countryside. T. E. Lawrence, Lawrence of Arabia, had completed the first draft of his *Seven Pillars of Wisdom* by the time he enlisted in the Royal Tank Corps, arriving at Bovington Camp, near Wareham, in March 1923. By November that year he had purchased and started to refurbish Clouds Hill, a small, isolated cottage within a few miles of the camp. Lawrence ate and slept at the camp, so Clouds Hill was dedicated to writing, reading, and exploring the world of music through the gramophone, whether by himself or with his friends. One of the upstairs rooms became his work room, where he completed the published text of his book. But a corner of it was dominated by a succession of top-quality gramophones, the one shown in Figure 11.1 (taken shortly after Lawrence's fatal motor-cycle accident in May 1935) being made by E. M. Ginn of Soho Square, London.[1]

1. Properly speaking, the term 'gramophone' refers to the disc player invented in 1887 by Emil Berliner, and the term 'phonograph' to the cylinder recorder invented by Edison ten years earlier. British writers tend to call everything gramophones, while North Americans tend to call everything phonographs. In this book I use the terms interchangeably to refer to the disc player.

Figure 11.1 Clouds Hill, Music Room in 1935

In a memorial volume edited by Lawrence's brother, one of these friends, the
dentist Warwick James (1937), recorded how seriously Lawrence took his gramophone: he 'devoted meticulous care to every mechanical detail rendering his
machine as perfect as possible. He used wooden needles and found by experiment
to obtain smoothness that dusting the surface of the record with graphite powder
gave the best result' (467). James also painted a verbal portrait of Lawrence in the
act of listening: 'he seemed to relax his muscles', James (467–68) wrote, 'although
his face always expressed alertness. Two positions were common to him: he often
put one hand to his cheek and supported the elbow with the other, or just placed
his hands together'. James tells us something else about the importance of records
in Lawrence's life, too, though it takes a little decoding. He joined the Tank Corps,
James says, in order to establish a regular rhythm in his life,

> and it would seem that he used music—apart from the pleasure it gave him—
> for the same purpose. Those who knew him were aware of the gradual change
> which he effected. At the time of his death he had become a much more
> normal individual in his relationship with others…he no longer avoided
> the ordinary individual as previously he seemed almost to make a point of
> doing (464).

Lawrence had in fact been close to a mental breakdown at the point when he went
to Bovington Camp, the result of wartime privations, involvement in political

campaigns for Arab self-determination, and the fame—or notoriety—that had been sparked off by photos of him dressed as a Bedouin, and fanned by the media.

Figure 11.1 also shows Lawrence's record library, housed beneath the gramophone, and James provides a list of what it contained at the time of Lawrence's death. That is how we know Lawrence had Weingartner's recording of the Fifth Symphony, and Beethoven appears to have been his favorite composer—although, curiously, James's list only includes three symphonies. Lawrence's brother, the classical art historian A. W., notes this, saying that as early as 1924 T. E. had possessed all nine: perhaps Beethoven 'appealed less to him in later years', he suggests (James 1937: 470), or perhaps it was specifically the symphonies that appealed less to him, since genres such as the string quartet—preferably played by the Léner Quartet—are strongly represented. In addition to Beethoven, Lawrence's personal canon included the core classical composers—Bach, Haydn, Mozart, and Brahms—together with contemporary English composers (especially Elgar and Delius) and a smattering of other modern composers (such as Milhaud and Stravinsky, about whom he said he wasn't sure).[2] More unexpected is the strong representation of early music, not only Gabrieli and Byrd but also Josquin, Okeghem, and Dufay: Lawrence subscribed to the early music record series *L'Anthologie sonore*. There is no trace of Arab music, recordings of which existed in considerable numbers by the 1930s.

Commenting on the catholicity of his listening, James (466, 465) adds that 'As with so many his pleasure was enhanced by repetition of the works he knew', and on another page he reinforces the point: 'his gramophone provided all he needed', James (465) observes, 'and (most important of all) he could listen alone, uninterrupted, select what he wanted and repeat the performance as often as he wished'. To a modern reader that sounds completely unremarkable; it's what we do with recordings. Yet James seems somehow uncomfortable about the whole issue:

> Here was a man making a study—an intelligent and careful study—of music through the medium most accessible to him—the gramophone—a medium which the true musician would almost despise—in fact many of them would probably deny the possibility of acquiring a true knowledge in this manner. Yet a man of the intelligence and sensitivity of T. E. adopted this procedure. It was the most convenient to him and that was sufficient, but it must have been a compromise, for always as far as he was able he pursued what he felt to be the best (465).

And James ends his reminiscences by saying that 'There is no doubt music gave him pleasure; where he stands as an appreciative listener matters little, it is sufficient that it meant much to him' (468–69).

This little cameo of Lawrence and his gramophone illustrates many of the features that made mechanical reproduction so remarkable to music lovers

2. As recorded by Lawrence's Royal Tank Corps colleague Alec Dixon (1937: 334).

in the first decades of the twentieth century: indeed, just as Andrew Blake
(2004: 479) says that, through sound recording, 'a new category of human subject, "the listener", was created', so the same might be said about the music lover.
Sound reproduction relocated music, not only from the city to the countryside,
and from public event to private enjoyment, but also from the past to the present (how else could you have heard Dufay in Dorset?). It made music something
you could collect, and through collecting it, define who you were, even regulate
your life. On the one hand the gramophone was a medium of pleasure and of
self-improvement; on the other it was a focal point of domestic life, not only
physically but also behaviourally. It became the object of what Evan Eisenberg
(2005: 43) calls the 'phonographic rites' of cleaning and adjustment, and at the
same time brought a new form of everyday activity into being, the musical
equivalent of reading a novel. At the same time the comparison with the novel
throws into relief an apparent discomfort occasioned by solitary listening. In
short, the relationship between live and mechanically reproduced music problematised taken-for-granted assumptions about performance, listening, and the
nature of representation.

One symptom of this is the role that gramophones play in detective stories
of the period, with the controverting of normal expectations being exploited
for criminal purposes. In 'Mr Ponting's alibi', Austin Freeman (1965: 531) has
Dr Thorndyke say, 'It has often occurred to me that a very effective false alibi
could be worked with a gramophone or a phonograph—especially with one on
which one can make one's own records'.[3] In this story the alibi turns on a witness protesting at his neighbours' loud music making, and as Dr Thorndyke
says, 'it was practically certain that a blast of "music" would bring him out'.
(Of course it was only a gramophone playing, and the scare quotes round
'music' draw attention to its problematic status.) Another symptom is the
uncanny quality of mechanical sound reproduction on which early listeners
often commented, perhaps even more in the case of the radio than the gramophone, because here the sound literally came from nowhere. Felix Eberhard
von Cube said as much in a letter to his friend Henrich Schenker written on
26 March 1929:

> How strange it is that, at the moment I begin to write this letter, Handel's
> Judas Maccabeus can be heard so loudly and clearly from my father's big
> receiver that it is as if I were myself sitting in the great hall of the Vienna
> Musikverein. I can thus imagine that, for me and my thoughts to reach you,
> I only have to travel from Lothringerstrasse down the Rennweg. At pres-
> ent I am sitting in Duisburg, and the radio waves magically bring Vienna,
> the hall of the Musikverein, and the Maccabeans right into the house. The

3. 'Mr Ponting's alibi' was first published in the February 1927 issue of *Pearson's Magazine*. In
order to record, the criminals would have needed a cylinder recorder, a technology in its last
gasp by that date (commercial manufacture of cylinders ceased in 1929).

technology has indeed made enormous progress; the quality of the sound of our apparatus is so perfect that there is almost something uncanny about it.[4]

The solitary listening in which Lawrence and von Cube indulged needs to be set into its historical context. With the exception of singing or playing to yourself—particularly on the piano—music was necessarily a social activity in the days before mechanical sound reproduction, and early gramophonic listening inherited the behavioural forms of its predecessors. An advertisement in the April 1914 issue of the *Strand Magazine* (p. 43) spells this out: 'Melba gets the applause as heartily as at Covent Garden. You cannot refrain from applauding the *diva* when you hear her in your drawing room. "My drawing room"—you say? Yes, when it is equipped with 'His Master's Voice' Gramophone...Covent Garden complete bar the scenery!' And in his 'material history of classical recording' (in fact as much a history of the discourses around recording), Colin Symes (2004: 26) discusses an advertisement issued by the Columbia Graphophone Company in February 1915, shown in Figure 11.2. In the foreground we see two children crouching on the stairs—presumably they have crept down in their night clothes—and looking down at their parents, who are sitting next to their Columbia Grafanola 'Mignonette' (equipped with the exclusive Columbia Individual Record Ejector and retailing for a hefty $110). The telling point, as Symes says, is that the parents are wearing formal clothes—dinner jacket and long dress. The children on the stairs mean that it is evening, so what we are seeing is a concert that has been relocated to the home. This does not mean that people really dressed up to listen to the gramophone, of course, but it does tell us something about how they thought of it. Even when it took place in the home, the new, technologically mediated listening was initially framed within the existing social and aesthetic institution of the public concert.

What now seems the strange idea of the gramophone concert was surprisingly long-lived. Samuel Chotzinoff recalls that in 1951, following the death of Arturo Toscanini's wife Carla, he arranged parties for the conductor's friends that were organised like concerts: there was a set programme of Toscanini's own records, lasting about an hour and a half. Everyone listened in silence, apart from 'exclaiming "oh" and "ah" rapturously (and sincerely) at certain moments, greatly to the old man's delight. He himself sat upright in a chair and conducted the music with the vigour and passion he displayed at rehearsals and performances' (Eisenberg 2005: 60). More commonly, however, such concerts were staged by gramophone societies, and here the dimension of self-improvement comes to the fore. A letter published by *The Gramophone* in 1929 recounts how the author established a 'club for the study of symphonic and chamber music through the gramophone' in Schenectady, New York: a complete analysis of each work was given, illustrated

---

4. Translated in *Schenker Documents Online*, http://www.schenkerdocumentsonline.org/documents/correspondence/OJ-9-34_16.html; the original letter is in the Oswald Jonas Memorial Collection, University of California at Riverside (OJ 9/34 [16]).

Figure 11.2 Advertisement for Columbia Grafonola 'Mignonette', published in *McClure's Magazine*, February 1915 (p. 4)

Figure 11.3 Photograph from *The Illustrated War News*, 30 December 1914 (p. 34)

at the piano (Morgan 2010: 154). Such record clubs again proved longer lived than might be expected, and a few survive to this day. Eric Clarke records attending one in 2002, at which 'chairs were set out in rows in the living room of a local piano teacher, facing the sound system (and piano). The recordings were listened to in attentive silence; during an interval, tea, coffee and cakes were served in a separate room; and at the end of it all there was applause for the evening's "performer"' (Clarke 2007: 63).

Of course, not all social listening took the form of gramophone concerts. It could be practiced is less formal situations, especially as the pre-electric technology was portable: you could take gramophones into the garden or on picnics. This portability also made a possible a very different site of musical listening that was contemporaneous with the affluent surroundings of the Columbia Graphophone advertisement, but on the other side of the Atlantic: gramophones were widespread in the trenches, supplied as part of the war effort and helping to bridge the gap between the front and home (Connor 2008). Figure 11.3, reproduced from the 30 December 1914 edition of *The Illustrated War News*,[5] was taken in the trenches east of the Aisne, in north-eastern France, and shows the gramophone in its role as an instrument of community. (The caption reads 'Underground, with gramophone, white table-cloth, and flowers: French soldiers in a "home-like" bomb-proof trench'.) It fulfilled the same role in the Second World War, too. In the upstairs hall of Hemingford Grey Manor, one of the oldest continuously inhabited houses in Britain, visitors admire the imposing horn of a 1929 E.M.G. gramophone[6]: this is where the then owner, Lucy Boston, used to entertain pilots from

5. P. 34, accessible at http://www.gutenberg.org/files/18334/18334-h/18334-h.htm.

6. See http://www.greenknowe.co.uk/gallery6.html. The initials E.M.G. stand for E. M. Ginn, who made Lawrence's gramophone—but Ginn left E.M.G. to set up his own firm in the early 1930s.

the neighbouring U.S. bomber base with tea and classical music. As Simon Jenkins (2003: 343) writes, 'The response was at first hesitant, but the invitations soon became popular. Eventually, Boston had to import old car seats for the crowds of young men eager to escape the tedium and stress of the bomber base'. Examples could easily be multiplied, but the point is sufficiently obvious. In the first decades of the twentieth century, social listening to the gramophone was the norm.

'Solitary listening', writes Mark Katz (2004: 189), 'impractical without recording, is perhaps now the dominant type of musical experience in most cultures'. And as Eisenberg (2005) says, records can serve to cut people off from one another: 'They are well suited to a society where everyone is off pursuing his own dream' (26). The reason I have been placing so much emphasis on social listening in the early days of recorded music is that thinking about recordings nowadays tends to emphasise its role as an instrument of subjectivity, the extreme form of which—and certainly the most common—is headphone listening. Associating recorded music with solitary listening in turn leads us to associate live music with social listening, from which it is only one further step to criticise recorded music for its destruction of music's social dimension and consequent reduction of music to a commodity. Today we can easily feel awkward listening to recorded music in company, at least if the music is foregrounded: closing your eyes is rude, says Clarke, and making eye contact is worse, and so you end up with 'eyes fixed to the floor or the elevated middle distance' (2007: 64). It was the other way round in the early days of gramophonic listening. And if it seems extravagant to suggest Lawrence's solitary listening was the cause of Warwick James's embarrassment, an article published in the inaugural issue of *The Gramophone* and discussed at some length by Katz (2004: 16–17) confirms that this was indeed a live issue during the interwar period. The article dates from 1923, and the author, the essayist Orlo Williams, asks how you would react if you discovered a friend listening to music by himself: 'you would look twice to see whether some other person were not hidden in some corner of the room,' he says, 'and if you found no such one would painfully blush, as if you had discovered your friend sniffing cocaine, emptying a bottle of whisky, or plaiting straws in his hair' (Williams 1923: 18).

Williams's article is self-consciously flippant—he is sending up the idea you shouldn't listen to music alone—but what is significant is that the idea was there to be sent up. Solitary listening is figured as deviant because, unlike the domestic concert pictured in the Columbia Graphophone advertisement of nine years earlier, there is no culturally approved context within which it can happen. And whereas that imaginary concert clearly took place in the evening, the gramophone opened up the possibility of another form of deviant behaviour: listening to music in the morning. Williams addresses this issue too, painting a picture of your friend Wotherspoon, who lights a 'large but mild' cigar after breakfast and calls for his butler to set up the gramophone. You expostulate, but in vain, and once word gets round that Wotherspoon is 'the sort of feller who plays the gramophone after breakfast', his reputation is ruined.

Williams explains that he personally admires Wotherspoon, 'if such a man exist': he sees nothing wrong with the idea of 'a gentleman tastefully attired,

smoking in an easy but not too soft a chair, while at ten o' clock on a sunny morning, he listens to the voice of Caruso issuing from a little cupboard in a mahogany
cabinet'. And others agreed. Six years later, Compton Mackenzie, the novelist who
was also first editor of *The Gramophone*,[7] cited the possibility of listening to music
in the morning as an argument for the gramophone:

> It is easy to believe that he who has not heard a Mozart quartet played in the
> freshness of dawn has never enjoyed his music to the full, and since it might
> puzzle even a millionaire to rouse his private quartet at such an hour and
> make the players sit in the dews beneath his bedroom window, the gramo-
> phone becomes indispensable for such an occasion (Eisenberg 2005: 40).

And more generally, the differences between concert and gramophonic listening
began to be put forward as arguments in favour of the latter. In a letter published by
The Gramophone in 1925, Lionel Gilman wrote, 'You can shut your eyes and imagine yourself at the Queen's Hall, but a Queen's Hall without rustling programmes
or anyone discussing their servants or illnesses in a seat behind you' (Morgan
2010: 156). Seven years later, an unnamed writer was more sweeping: 'Alone with
the phonograph, all the unpleasant externals are removed: the interpreter has
been disposed of: the audience has been disposed of: the uncomfortable concert
hall has been disposed of. You are alone with the composer and his music' (Katz
2004: 17). The only problem, of course, is that while the interpreter had been disposed of, his or her interpretation was still inscribed into the record. And after a
further three years, in 1935, the music educator W. R. Anderson addressed this,
too, arguing that 'We want the music, the whole music, and nothing but the music'
(Morgan 2010: 151). Performances, he complains, 'continually come between us
and the music as the composer left it', and this will remain the case as long as the
making of recordings is in commercial hands. The answer, he concludes, is to
put recording in the hands of 'a supreme, non-commercial board of musicians'.
Pushed to its logical conclusion, as Schoenberg and Adorno realised,[8] this line of
thought leads to mechanical reproduction of the score.

Here, then, is a conception of the recording quite distinct from the one illustrated in the Columbia Graphophone advertisement but equally grounded in
established aesthetic premises. Emancipated from the concert paradigm, the
recording now aspires to a condition of autonomy based on another, even more
long-standing premise: in effect it becomes a form of sounded writing. Seen this
way the gramophonic experience is independent from, and perhaps superior to,
the concert. But listening to recorded music also developed in ways that divorced
it from traditional aesthetic assumptions, most obviously in relation to the explosion of popular music that was driven by the same technology. I would like to make
this point through a brief survey of changing patterns of musical consumption in

7. Nowadays *Gramophone*; 'The' was dropped from the title in 1969.

8. See Chapter 1, p. 17.

the form of successive passes that focus on sites of listening, control over the listening environment, and interactive playback.

The first element in this story, then, is the migration of listening from public spaces to a succession of increasingly private ones. The Columbia Graphophone advertisement illustrates a trend that had begun in 1906 with the rival Victor Company's Victrola: the prominent horn that was the most striking visual feature of earlier machines, and that continued on high-end machines like Lawrence's and Boston's, was folded downward and concealed within a floor standing cabinet. At a stroke this transformed the gramophone from a kind of scientific instrument into a piece of furniture. An advertisement from the September 1915 issue of *Strand Magazine* (p. 15) tells us that the Cabinet Grand Gramophone, produced by His Master's Voice, could be had in mahogany for forty pounds and in circassian walnut for an additional ten pounds. The gramophone was domesticated not only visually, but acoustically too, as the option to open or close the doors at last provided a degree of volume control. Acoustic gramophones could be very loud, as indeed they needed to be for the social uses I have described.

'In the functional salon', Adorno wrote in 1927, 'the gramophone stands innocuously as a little mahogany cabinet on little rococo legs. Its cover provides a space for the artistic photograph of the divorced wife with the baby' (2002: 273). Adorno's contempt sets the pattern for enduring, and frequently gendered, tensions between the demands of home decor and those of audiophilia: the late 1950s stereogram, even when finished in genuine teak, severely compromised the stereo image, and Keir Keightley has explored in depth how, during that decade, hi-fi became one of the battle lines in the struggle between the sexes for control of the American suburban home. As Keightley says, 'wives of fidelity fanatics watched their living rooms evolve into professional sound studios with giant speakers peering from corners where once graciously reigned Queen Anne wingback chairs' (1996: 158), and it was not unknown for them to express views on this. (It is a frequently observed fact that audio fetishism, as symbolised by Eisenberg's Saul and Clarence—respectively an audiophile and a collector—is an almost exclusively male practice.) By the end of the century, surround sound systems helped to turn sitting rooms into the marginally more acceptable form of home cinemas, and became part of the built environment as they were increasingly integrated into penthouse flats, executive homes, and upscale mill conversions at the design stage. Sound reproduction also migrated from the house to its mobile counterpart: predictably, so called 'jeep beats' first developed in Los Angeles, and by the final decade of the twentieth century popular music production was increasingly targetting multi-speaker in-car systems. Indeed the hip-hop genre Dr Dre called G-Funk was driven specifically by the demands of the automotive listening environment (Williams forthcoming).

At the same time, the progressive miniaturisation of sound reproduction technology created a host of other ways in which music became more intimately embedded within the fabric of everyday life. The compact record player of the LP era was still relatively bulky as a result of the 12-inch format; it depended on a power supply (unlike its mechanical counterpart), and it could not be played on the move. All three limitations disappeared with the transistor radio and cassette recorder, but personal stereo took the integration of music into everyday life to a new level. By feeding sound directly to the ears—the nearest approach to intravenous music—the Walkman, iPod, and iPhone make your musical experience independent of other people's even in congested situations, at the same time creating the phenomenon that Paul Fahri called the 'Walkman dead': 'The eyes flicker with consciousness, but they don't *see*. They're somewhere else'.[9]

In Miriam Simun's words (2009: 930), mp3 listeners 'utilize music to carve out personal spaces as they navigate the physical spaces, places, and people encountered during the commute': one of her interviewees told her, 'I listen to it to get a bit more space in London'. As Simun continues, people use music 'to assert agency in configuring their experiences and actions', and that gives them 'real control in organizing their thoughts and emotions' (936). Personal stereo, in short, helps to make the cityscape your own, which is why it has been celebrated as an example of how individuals can 'refuse the neat divisions and classifications of the powerful and, in doing so, critique the spatialization of domination'.[10] And at the same time that technology enables you to mark the outside world with your own sonic signature, it can bring music into your body. Music is felt as well as heard in the Repose E2000 Home Entertainment Chair, which incorporates not only 5.1 surround sound but also 'Sub-sonic "Bone rattler" technology'.[11] Finally music enters the most private spaces with the Ann Summers iGasm, a vibrator that hooks up to your iPod and operates in time to the music. The result, according to the advertisement, is to 'take your appreciation of music to a whole new level'. (Or at least it was; introduced in 2007, the product was withdrawn following a legal claim by Apple.)

But it is not just a matter of new sites for experiencing music. Applications of recording technology have given people previously unattainable control over their musical environment. From the start the gramophone gave its user the ability to 'select what he wanted and repeat the performance as often as he wished', as James said of Lawrence. The LP autochanger, primarily designed for uninterrupted listening to multi-disc recordings of opera, also allowed you to programme a series of records in any sequence you chose, while CD players allowed you to do the same with individual tracks. In the mean time listeners had taken advantage of cassette technology to create compilation tapes, the predecessors of today's playlists; Brian Eno recalls the compilations he and his friends made of tracks that would create and sustain a particular mood (whereas commercial compilations were always based on contrasting moods), and sees that as the origin of ambient music.[12] With the arrival of the internet, not only could music be bought, or otherwise acquired,

9. Quoted in Katz (2004: 18). Foundational studies in this area include Bull (2000 and 2007).

10. Cresswell (2006: 47), paraphrasing Michel de Certeau.

11. http://www.reposechair.com/products.html.

12. Brian Eno on *Front Row* (BBC Radio 4), 2 April 2010.

BEYOND THE SCORE

at any time, but the single track became the individual unit of purchase. This created great consternation among record companies, as it became clear that industry profits had depended on selling consumers albums consisting mainly of tracks
they didn't want. Online music libraries such as Spotify, at the time of writing
still a free service unless you pay to avoid the advertisements, turned music into
a kind of utility, in Symes's words (2004)—though not referring specifically to the
internet—putting music 'as much on tap as water or electricity' (3).

While accessing music was easy, however, especially if you were not too concerned about legality, finding what you wanted was not. The result was the development of a new engineering discipline, music information retrieval, and the
implementation of a range of alternative music recommendation systems such
as last.fm and Pandora: though they work differently, each suggests music you
might like on the basis of your previous choices. And once you have your playlist, or a set of playlists for different situations and moods, you can use the shuffle
feature incorporated in iPods and iPhones, which plays tracks from your music
library in randomised order. In an article for the *New Yorker*, the music critic Alex
Ross (2004) explained that he had transferred about a thousand tracks from his
CD collection onto his iPod, and continued: 'There is something thrilling about
setting the player on Shuffle and letting it decide what to play next. Sometimes
its choices are a touch delirious—I had to veto an attempt to forge a link between
György Kurtág and Oasis—but the little machine often goes crashing through barriers of style in ways that change how I listen'. Or if that sounds too challenging,
Microsoft's web tool MixShape will sort your playlist into a structured sequence
based on tempo and mood, in effect automating the art of the DJ.[13] If tracks in
your playlist won't fit, then MixShape will source replacements from Spotify that
match your taste.

In this way the relocation of listening afforded by technological change extended
to the construction of personal musical environments. But equally important was
he development of interactive playback. This is typically seen as a contemporary
phenomenon: in 2008—the year he was named one of *Time* magazine's hundred
most influential people—Alex Rigopulos (the co-founder of Harmonix Music
Systems, which developed the video games Rock Band and Guitar Hero) claimed,
'we're at the beginning of a . . . revolution of music now where playing with music
[rather than listening to it] is what people are going to expect to do with music that
they love' (Moseley 2013: 282). But again it has a long history. In the mid-1910s
the phonograph manufacturer Aeolian marketed a device called the Graduola,
which according to the distinctly overblown advertising copy allowed listeners to
feel rather than merely hear the music, and so discover their own natural musicianship: it was in fact just a device for volume control attached to the phonogram
by a cable (Katz 2004: 59–60). But there is tantalising evidence that users of early
gramophones thought it quite normal to intervene more drastically in playback.

13. http://www.mixshape.ie/.

Early gramophones allowed adjustment of speed, a necessary facility given that recording and hence playback speeds were not standardised (a so-called 78 might in reality be a 75 or an 82). But the facility was evidently used for other purposes too, as becomes evident from a complaint made by Louise, the niece of Adelina Patti, the soprano whom Hanslick so admired that he forgot his own aesthetic theories. Speaking of an after-dinner gramophone performance at which Adelina was present, Louise exclaims, 'How unsatisfactory it is that when you want a thing in a high key it alters the tempo so that things go at a terrific speed, and to lower it everything must drag'. Were they singing along with the music, in an early version of karaoke, adjusting the speed to suit their voices? Or suiting the music to their mood? After quoting Louise's letter, which dates from 8 April 1906, Simon Trezise (2009) comments that 'the records were regarded as flexible in terms of their realisation' (207). Perhaps listeners like Louise were thinking of the gramophone along rather similar lines to the pianolas I mentioned in Chapter 3, where the machine took care of the notes and the pianolist provided the expression: more, that is, as a musical instrument than a device for the delivery of ready-made musical experiences. And indeed the idea that the gramophone was a musical instrument was a staple of advertising copy until the interwar years. The Cabinet Grand Gramophone from His Master's Voice, for instance, was described as 'THE ARISTOCRAT among musical instruments'.[14]

Edison's advertisements made great play of the fact that their cylinder recorders gave customers 'not only the best renditions of the world's best entertainers, but also the opportunity for home record making'.[15] Following the demise of this technology—largely because cylinders could not be mass produced as efficiently as discs—there was no consumer format that allowed recording as well as playback of sound until the development around 1950 of tape and by the mid-1960s of cassette recorders. This is an important difference as compared to still and motion photography, both of which generated extensive participatory cultures during this period. Perhaps that is why gramophonic listening was criticised for its passive quality. In an essay dating from 1941, for example, Adorno (2002) complains that listeners 'are forced to passive sensual and emotional acceptance of predigested yet disconnected qualities' (266–67). One should however be careful about taking such claims at face value: the argument being made here about the transition from live to reproduced music had previously been made about the transition from a participatory musical culture to one based on concert attendance, for example in late nineteenth-century Vienna (Botstein 1992).[16]

14. *Strand Magazine*, September 1914, 10.

15. *Saturday Evening Post*, 12 November 1910 (reproduced in Thompson [1995: 141]).

16. In other words, the argument advanced in favour of A against B is subsequently advanced in favour of B against C. Another example is Benjamin Britten's argument—summarised by Symes (2004: 47)—that concerts demanded 'effort and sacrifice', resulting in a 'moral dividend', whereas 'the record made music *too* accessible'; this has been recycled as an argument in favour of physical recordings and against downloads (Bergh and DeNora [2009: 110]).

All the same, the idea clearly spread that faithful reproduction was engineered into the recordings, and should be accepted for what it was—that is, passively—by listeners. Alf Bjornberg (2009: 114) quotes a striking example of this: a hardware review from the Swedish technology magazine *Teknik för alla*, published in 1952, which states that 'the frequency range is specified as 50–10,000 c/s. In order not to let this fine frequency graph be destroyed by persons who like so-called soft sound, the tone control has sensibly enough been eliminated'. In other words the engineers had got it right, so there was no reason for the listener to interfere. It was left to a reader to point out, in a letter, that one reason users might want to adjust the tone quality from its optimally engineered value was that they wanted to talk over the music. Another article from the same journal, this time from 1959, refers to the human ear as 'the weakest link in the reproduction of sound' (122), so underlining the extent to which the emerging ideology of hi-fi built on the values of scientific expertise; it is reminiscent of Seashore's claim that 'We hear but little of what actually exists, and that little is greatly distorted in hearing'.[17] In Chapter 4 I called 78s and LPs the emblematic media of Lessig's RO culture, the high point of which Lessig (2008: 263) himself locates in the 1970s, and hi-fi listening might be regarded as the definitive enactment of the paradigm of reproduction.

As early as 1964, however, Glenn Gould (1987: 93) was speculating that it would not be long until 'a more self-assertive streak is detected in the listener's participation'—for example, until ' "do-it-yourself" tape editing is the prerogative of every reasonably conscientious consumer of recorded music'. (Commenting positively on Gould's ideas just three years later, the producer John Culshaw [1967: 266] extended them to film: 'Equipped with some machine-of-the-future, the opera lover at home could not only adjust the sound to his precise requirements, but also "produce" the opera visually in whatever way he liked'.) In the event it took the replacement of tape by digital technology to make this happen, and it happened almost entirely in the sphere of popular—or as the Swedish magazines called it, 'loudspeaker'—music. Internet sites such as Indaba Music offer precisely the functionality that Gould envisaged, among many others, and in addition support a virtual community of users who comment on one another's remixes. Bands like Nine Inch Nails and Radiohead have released songs as GarageBand multitrack files, meaning that users of this popular (and free) Apple application can remix them, while in 2012 Beyoncé held a competition in which entrants downloaded, remixed, and uploaded her single track 'End of time'.[18] There are just a few classical parallels. As early as 2006, the Canadian Broadcasting Corporation initiated a series of remixing competitions, the first being based on Richard Wagner's 'Ride of the Valkyries' (Sinnreich 2010: 81). And in 2010 Steve Reich, in conjunction with Indaba Music and Nonesuch

---

17. See Chapter 1, p. 30.

18. http://endoftime.beyonceonline.com/.

Records, staged a competition to remix the third movement of *2 X 5*, attracting more than two hundred entries.[19]

More recently, smartphones have emerged as the favoured technology for new ways of interacting with recorded music. One example is RjDj,[20] an iPhone app developed by Michael Breidenbruecker (who previously set up last.fm). This combines input from the phone's microphone with music 'scenes' and dynamic sound processing, so delivering a customised sound environment to the user's headphones: it 'detects ambient sounds, rips out samples or mutates them into harmonies, then intelligently mashes them up with what's playing' (Burton 2010). A huge range of music scenes is available, sourced in collaboration with such major labels as Atlantic Records, Warner Music, and EMI, while consumers are encouraged to upload their own, so building a community of RjDj users. And while the focus of RjDj is on the interaction between music and environment, another iPhone app, Anthony Pitts's musicGPS, focuses on self-documentation, creating an inventory of your musical experiences and linking them to the environment in which they occurred. The app keeps a log of what you listened to where and when, linking this information to maps, and allowing the addition of notes and photographs: these can be automatically uploaded to Facebook.[21] The strapline on the musicGPS website is 'the soundtrack of your life', as if you were starring in your own personal movie.

Here, then, music is being used as an instrument of identity construction, as it is by all who exploit the cavernous memories of today's mp3 players in order to create a personal musical environment that travels with them wherever they go. And as illustrated by Simun's commuters who use it to gain control over their thoughts and emotions, music serves as a means not only of self-construction but also of self-regulation. All this illustrates the efficacy of recorded music as what Arild Bergh and Tia DeNora (2009: 109) call 'a technology of the self'.

ORIGINAL AND COPY

Digital technology gives spectacular form to uses of recorded music for purposes of the definition and the regulation of the self that go back to its earliest days: after all, I spoke of the 'personal canon' represented by T. E. Lawrence's changing collection of 78s, while James spoke of Lawrence's use of the gramophone to establish a regular rhythm in his life after his near mental breakdown. Such uses of music obviously fall outside the traditional framework of Hanslickian aesthetics, as does much else that I have described in the preceding pages, but that is just part of the challenge that recording presented to traditional ways of thinking about performance.

19. http://www.nonesuch.com/journal/steve-reich-2x5-remix-winners-announced-2010-12-07, where the winning and runner-up remixes may be heard.

20. http://rjdj.me.

21. http://www.musicdna.info/musicGPS.aspx.

The paradigm of reproduction construed the recording as the copy of an original, a substitute for the real thing, in a word (Taruskin's word), as 'canned' music. The use of this term in relation to music goes back to the earliest days of phonographic culture. Its first appearance seems be in the article by Sousa on which Lessig drew when talking about the creativity of performance,[22] which was published in 1906 under the title 'The menace of mechanical music'. Once, Sousa recalls, people used to sit out in the summer woods and sing songs round a camp fire. But now 'the ingenious purveyor of canned music is urging the sportsman, on his way to the silent places with gun and rod, tent and canoe, to take with him some disks, cranks, and cogs to sing to him as he sits by the firelight, a thought as unhappy and incongruous as canned salmon by a trout brook' (Sousa 1906: 281). There is even a drawing of this deplorable scene (Figure 11.4).

By contrast, the antonym of 'canned' music—not 'fresh' but 'live' music—did not enter the vocabulary until several decades later, and one might ask why. Auslander (2002: 16–17) traces the term back to 1934, but this is in the context of radio broadcasting and refers to recorded material in general.[23] (As we will see, that is where he finds the answer to the question.) Jonathan Sterne (2003: 221) follows Sarah Thornton, according to whom the word became commonly used in relation to music only in the 1950s: one of the contexts for this was the emerging hi-fi culture, so one could argue that it was the development of increasingly sophisticated sound reproduction technologies—technologies that could be mistaken for the real thing—that made it necessary to distinguish live from recorded performances. (We will see however that the issue of mistaking recordings for the real thing predates the 1950s; in fact we have already seen it with 'Mr Ponting's alibi'.) At all events, the issue of liveness—to which I shall return at the end of the chapter—lies at the heart of the tensions regarding the relationship between recorded and live performance that I observed in James's reminiscence of Lawrence, and that continue to characterise discourses about recordings to this day, not least within musicology.

As I said, recording technology drove an unprecedented development in the production and consumption of popular music. At the same time, coupled with the radio and much later the internet, it revolutionised the dissemination of classical music. As Eric Clarke writes, 'Prior to the invention of recording, access was constrained by a whole range of factors, including class, money, and geography' (2007: 51); by contrast, recordings offer 'almost unlimited access, and a familiarity and intimacy with a particular performance...that was scarcely possible through the unique experiences of pre-recording listening'. In short, recording represented a sea change in the democratisation of high culture, and for most consumers,

22. See Chapter 4, p. 132.

23. It first appears in the 1934 edition of the *BBC Yearbook*, complete with the scare quotes that commonly identify neologisms: 'Listeners have...complained of the fact that recorded material was too liberally used...but...transmitting hours to the Canadian and Australasian zones are inconvenient for broadcasting "live" material' (quoted in Ayto [2006: 97]).

"Incongruous as canned salmon by a trout brook."

Figure 11.4 'Incongruous as canned salmon by a trout brook' (Sousa 1906: 279)

music—classical or otherwise—is recorded music. Yet even in the twenty-first century there is a continuing reluctance on the part of musicologists to accept recorded music as a musical phenomenon in its own right rather than an ersatz form of something else.

We saw in Chapter 10 that Abbate (2004) draws an impermeable distinction between live and recorded music: on the one hand there is 'real music, music-as-performed...the event itself' (532), on the other a monument in music's necropolis. Lawrence Kramer (2011: 275) is less intemperate but broadly agrees: classical music is first and foremost an event, he says, and 'For this reason live performance remains the essential basis of classical music despite the primacy of recordings in the lives of most latter-day listeners'. And writing from the performer's perspective, Mine Doğantan-Dack stresses both the difference between live and recorded performance, and the normative role of the former: 'there is ample anecdotal evidence that for performing musicians there are significant phenomenological, aesthetic and indeed existential differences between the experiences of performing live and in the recording studio', she writes, and 'performing for audiences in live contexts...remains as the gold standard in evaluating one's expertise and musicianship' (2012: 36). That, she adds, makes it 'particularly important to articulate the significance of live musical performance as the ultimate norm in classical music practice, at a time when performances recorded and edited in the studio provide the context for an overwhelming majority of musical experiences'.

As the term 'canned' emphasises, such thinking is intrinsically hierarchical. The idea that live performance is the original, and the recording a copy, establishes what, in *The Audible Past*, Sterne (2003: 284) calls the 'discourse of fidelity' that has accompanied recording from its earliest days; the application of the term 'fidelity' to sound recording goes all the way back to 1878 (221). But the values implicit in this discourse, together with a sense that recordings are increasingly transgressing against them, emerge with particular clarity from an article by Pierre Boulez that first appeared almost a hundred years later, in the 6 May 1977 issue of the *Times Literary Supplement*:

> Techniques of recording, backing, reproduction—microphones, loudspeakers, amplifying equipment, magnetic tape—have been developed to the point where they have betrayed their primary objective, which was faithful reproduction. More and more the so-called techniques of reproduction are acquiring an irrepressible tendency to become autonomous and to impress their own image of existing music, and less and less concerned to reproduce as faithfully as possible the conditions of direct audition (1978: 60).

As Sterne (2003: 218) argues, the discourse of fidelity judges sound reproduction according to the degree to which it erases itself—to which it becomes transparent—and this means that all differences between live and recorded music are figured as deficiencies.[24] And this is not just a matter of acoustic characteristics. Despite his apparent discomfort over solitary listening to the gramophone, James recognised that, for Lawrence, one of its special advantages was the possibility of unlimited, identical repetition. Katz tells us that in interwar America, where the phonograph was seen as a vehicle for both musical and moral education, repeatability 'was believed to be the key to understanding and developing a taste for

---

24. Emily Thompson (1995: 144) quotes a nice illustration of this from a trade paper for Edison dealers, which in 1915 suggested a sales pitch for the new Edison Diamond Disc phonograph. The shopper has asked how its tone compares with that of some lesser model:

MR. BROWN: The Edison has no tone.

SHOPPER: No tone?

MR. BROWN: Exactly that. Mr. Edison has experimented for years to produce a sound re-creating instrument that has no tone—of its own....If a talking machine has a distinctive tone, then such tone must appear in every selection, whether band, orchestra, violin, soprano, tenor or what not. In other words, there is a distortion of the true tone of the original music.

"good music"' (2004: 53), serving in particular to separate the wheat from the chaff—that is, classical from popular music. Again, Bergh and DeNora (2009) see repetition as the basis of 'a new form of listening experience involving anticipation, premeditation in choosing music for listening, and the fulfilment of expectation on re-experiencing "the same" musical event' (109). Yet as we saw in Chapter 6, this is the very feature Hans Keller seized on as late as 1985 in order to denounce the gramophone's 'disastrous' effects on musical listening, education, and performance. And of course, it is the need for recorded music to support repeated listenings that commentators from Adorno and Barthes to Robert Philip have blamed for the increasing standardisation of post-war performance.

Sterne's aim in *The Audible Past* is to place the discourse of fidelity in a broad cultural context, and his explanation of it draws heavily on the technology and conditions of early recording. He is less concerned to situate it in the context of different musical genres or subsequent developments. The prioritisation of live performance is general in classical music, and is reflected in the imperceptibility of the editing that routinely goes into classical recordings—as also in the discomfort that many performers feel about it. As Donald Greig (2009) says, 'Though commonly used, edits and patching are regarded by many classical performers as "cheats"' (23), a frequently cited example being the dubbing of Elisabeth Schwarzkopf's high Cs into Kirsten Flagstad's recording of Wagner's *Tristan und Isolde* (Chanan 1995: 133). And more generally there is a tension between performers who favour long takes (Peter Hill [2009: 14] writes that 'Long takes or complete performances...enable one to lose oneself in the music, to forget the intimidating gaze of the microphone, and...to start to create') and producers who are cynical about them. Michael Haas refers to 'the oft-cited "great arc" that mysteriously disappears in takes, sapping all force from once-animated performances' (2009: 61), and describes it as 'a lazy misconception that misses the central reality of today's listener'.[25]

Prioritisation of live performance was also general in jazz at least until 1970, when Miles Davis released *Bitches Brew*: Davis and his producer, Teo Macero, employed a great deal of quite perceptible editing—an example is the successive repetitions of the same one-second fragment in 'Pharaoh's dance'—and the resulting controversy is a measure of the extent to which the discourse of fidelity was at that time embedded within jazz culture. But within popular music the situation is different and more complicated. There are bands like Rush, whose concerts sound like their records because their records sound like their concerts. In other words, their collective persona is that of a gigging band. Then there are bands like the Pet Shop Boys, whose vocalist, Neil Tennant, said of their lip-synching at the American Music Awards, 'I quite like proving we *can't* cut it live. We're a pop group, not a rock

25. Writing in 1974–75, Glenn Gould (1987: 355–56) refers to a broadcast in which 'the very distinguished and very venerable British conductor Sir Adrian Boult' explained his opposition to 'patching', on the grounds that 'at all costs I must have the long line intact'. Gould comments: 'He's wrong, of course—splicing doesn't damage lines. Good splices build good lines'.

and roll group'. The headline story, then, would be that rock (like classical music and, at least until relatively recently, jazz) prioritises live music whereas pop prioritises the recording.

But as is argued by Philip Auslander (who quotes Tennant's statement[26]), the picture is not that simple, for two reasons. One is a number of notorious scandals in which pop musicians have been held to rock criteria of fidelity; Milli Vanilli are the most famous example, though Auslander (2008b: 125) also mention Ashlee Simpson. (In both cases the scandal arose because the artists were discovered to be lip synching.) The other reason is that the identification of rock with the prioritisation of live performance is itself over-simplified. As Auslander explains, rock has always been disseminated and consumed primarily through the medium of recordings, so that official studio releases carry something of the same authority as Urtext editions in classical music: he approvingly quotes Theodore Gracyk's claim that 'studio recordings have become the standard for judging live performances' (75). It is, then, reasonable to speak of the recording of 'Bohemian Rhapsody' on Queen's 1975 album *A Night at the Opera* as the definitive version, and indeed the song was translated only with difficulty, and over a period of time, to live performance. (The key problem was the studio-produced chorus of the middle section, which Queen could not perform live, since they had only three singers—or four if you count John Deacon. The band eventually arrived at a format whereby a recording of the operatic section was played on a darkened stage, flanked by live performance of the outer sections.) According to Auslander, live performance still has a special role in rock, but now it is one of authentication: 'The visual element of live performance', he explains, 'the fact that those sounds can be produced live by the appropriate musicians, serves to authenticate music as legitimate rock and not synthetic pop' (91). In other words, live performance shows that the band are capable of replicating the recording.

Although much more could be said on this subject—and both Auslander and others have said it[27]—the point I want to make is a simple one. Despite the differences, all these genres share a hierarchical way of thinking that treats one side of the equation between live performance and recording as the original, the real thing, and the other as a copy or substitute. But it is not a given that the relationship between live and recorded music should be seen this way. Arved Ashby (2010) makes the point through a comparison with the visual arts: 'Photography', he says, 'was long thought parasitic to painting because of the way it pursued and propounded beauty, and it took decades for the discipline to achieve the resourcefulness and critical respect that eventually qualified it as an art form' (194–95). That last clause contains the crucial difference.

Nowadays we see photography and painting as quite distinct cultural practices, and are not tempted to see the one as a copy of, or as inferior relative to, the

26. Auslander (2008b: 91).

27. For another take on the relationship between live performance and recording in rock, again from a performance studies perspective but resulting in a different interpretation, see Shumway (1999).

other. The conceptual transformation that took decades in the case of photography has hardly happened at all in the case of recording, which is not generally seen an art form in its own right. An even more telling comparison can be made with film, with which—as David Patmore and Eric Clarke (2007) explain—sound recording has striking affinities: 'both media were founded upon the idea of "the image" (aural, visual, or both) "captured" on a moving ribbon.... In both cases the intended version of "reality" was pieced together through a process of repeated takes and editing' (283). But again what makes the comparison telling is the differences. One, to which I shall return, is the nature of the diegesis that is involved. The difference that is relevant here, however, is that it occurs to nobody to think of a film as a copy or ersatz replica of a theatrical performance. It is the same as with photography and painting: we think of film and theatre as what Henry Jenkins (2008: 14) would call different cultural systems, not different delivery systems for the same cultural content. We do not place them in a hierarchy.

An obvious way forward, then, might be to apply the same thinking to music, and recommendations that we do just that come from many directions. For Eric Clarke, drawing a comparison with classical performance, 'a recording can be regarded as a particular and specific way of "sounding" music, one for which rather different cultural and listening expectations are appropriate—as well as performing practices' (2005: 165). From the performer's perspective, but now with a specifically contemporary slant, comes Roger Heaton's statement (2009) that 'a recording and a concert are two entirely different endeavours' (217). From the perspective of jazz improvisation, Derek Bailey (1992) writes that 'Records simply supply a different listening experience to listening "live"; for the majority of people, apparently, a preferable one' (104). And from the producer's perspective, we can choose between Culshaw, who worked primarily in opera (and for whom communicating with a live audience was 'an entirely different exercise from communication through a microphone to a domestic audience'), and the rock producer, engineer, and writer Albin Zak ('recordings assert their own versions of acoustic reality').[28] Clearly there are important differences as between live and recorded music in terms of both production and consumption, and treating them as separate cultural systems has the great advantage that each can be considered on its own terms, without potentially distorting or irrelevant interference from the other.

All the same, live and recorded music are so closely entangled with one another that I believe it makes more sense to encompass them within an enlarged concept of performance, and then deal with the divergences between them. One argument for this more integrated approach is that treating live and recorded music as distinct cultural systems creates irresolvable boundary disputes. Where do live recordings fit? When a New York Philharmonic Orchestra concert comes with live-feed video close-ups, in the manner of stadium rock concerts, is that still live? and when the Nashville Opera makes commentary by the director and cast available via iPod, in the manner of additional material on DVD or digital

28. From Culshaw's autobiography, quoted in Day (2000: 52); Zak (2009: 308).

television?[29] What if the opera is relayed to an overflow space? or to a remote location as a simulcast? Does it matter if the network connection delays the sound by a second or two? or if it is relayed the following day? If the last of these is a recorded performance, just where did the transition from live to recorded music take place? Auslander would argue that, while the extent of mediatisation clearly varies as between performances, all are to some degree subject to what he calls 'media epistemology' (2008b: 36). Consequently, he says, 'there can be no such thing as technologically unmediated performance' (2008a: 117).

But there is also a quite separate argument against treating live and recorded music as distinct cultural systems, and this has to do with training and career paths. The techniques of photography and painting are so different that they are almost invariably pursued as separate careers, each with its own pattern of training and professional accreditation. There is a certain degree of overlap between stage and screen actors (as also between theatrical producers and film directors), but there are still very significant differences in technique, and most people specialise in one or the other. In the case of music, however, whether classical or popular, that is only true to a very limited extent: almost everybody who records also plays live, and there are not separate training programmes for performers of live and recorded music. I would claim that in terms not only of training and career paths, but also of reception and underlying values, live and recorded performance are mutually entailed to the extent that they constitute a single cultural system within which there is a range of varied practices. Indeed I would sign up to the very broad definition of performance that Aaron Ridley (2004) sets out as part of the attack on ontological approaches to performance that I mentioned in Chapter 1: 'By "performance"', he says, 'I will mean not only the playing of a work by an individual or group before an audience, but also recordings, transcriptions, arrangements, versions and, in general, renditions of every kind' (111).

SIGNIFYING SOUND

In the remainder of this chapter I pursue a circular path that will twice bring me back to Ridley's position, the aim being on the one hand to substantiate it, and on the other to link it to the larger argument of the book. In my view, much of the confusion in thinking about recorded music has its source in an inadequate or inappropriate concept of reproduction. The advertisement shown in Figure 11.5 dates from around 1914, like Figure 11.2, and shows an Aeolian 'Vocalion' gramophone, an equally home-friendly rival to the Grafonola 'Mignonette'[30]: the female

---

29. These examples are drawn from Auslander (2008b: 26).

30. Day (2000), whose figure 2 reproduces this image, states that it is from the *Strand Magazine*, 1914, but I have been unable to locate it there. A very similar image, but showing a harpist and with a couple in the foreground, appears near the beginning of a publicity booklet entitled *The Aeolian-Vocalion*, which carries the date 1915 (though someone has inserted '1914' by hand);

Figure 11.5 Advertisement for Aeolian 'Vocalion', ca. 1914

listener, the fact that she is working at her embroidery, and the reference in the text to the machine's freedom from stridency all key the domestication of the gramophone to which I referred. This time, however, the listener is alone—except that she is *not* alone, for she shares her room with the performers on the disc. They hover beside and above the gramophone, a spectral presence like the angels whose celestial song Palestrina, and Pfitzner, attempted to reproduce (Figure 1.1). The same trope of reproduction that is so familiar from the culture of performance, then, extends into that of recorded sound.

Sterne emphasises the deep cultural roots of the discourse of fidelity, but its affinity to the traditional discourses of performance is particularly striking. Goehr (1992) employs two of the principal keywords of recording ideology when she refers to the ideal of performance under the regime of the musical work as 'transparency through fidelity' (236). The concept of *Werktreue* revolves around performers' duty of faithfulness to the work, and their associated obligation to efface themselves, to act as a transparent medium for the communication of the musical work. In precisely the same way, the discourse of fidelity in recording revolves around a faithfulness to the performance that is again expressed in terms of transparency, a complete correspondence between original and copy—but a complete correspondence that, as Sterne (2003: 286) says, can never be achieved. And if in the culture of recording the discourse of fidelity is one of deficiency, then exactly the same can be said of the culture of performance. In short, performance is to work as recording is to performance. There is even a further stage in this chain of similitude, when transfers of old recordings are judged on the basis of their faithfulness to the original recording (although they may also be judged in terms of fidelity to the original performance, as remastering can sometimes bring out qualities that were in the performance but hidden in the original recording). While I will not enter into transfer engineering here, it is—as much as recording—a practice that is informed by aesthetics and ideology, a form of interpretation in its own right, in which the basic tension is between faithful reproduction of the original—whatever that original may be—and the creation of a sound that is accessible and attractive to modern ears conditioned by CDs or mp3s.[31]

Predictably enough, my critique of the concept of reproduction as applied to sound recordings is much the same as in the case of performances: what is in reality a complex process of semiosis is misconstrued as one of literal replication. Georgina Born (2009: 294) advocates thinking of recording not in terms of reproduction but rather in terms of representation, which is surely correct. Yet to think of it in terms of a semiotic relationship, so that recordings reference, signify, or signify on performances, perhaps sharpens the point. It allows us, for example, to

the next illustration shows two men and two women seated on a sofa, wrapped in deep contemplation, with the ghostly image of a tuba player emanating from behind the gramophone. See http://memory.loc.gov/service/gdc/scd0001/2012/20121121012ae/20121121012ae.pdf.

31. Discussion of these aspects of transfer engineering may be found in Trezise (2009: 201–3) and Ashby (2010: 149–55).

acknowledge that the relationship between recordings and performances can be massively iconic, while at the same time reminding us that—as I said near the end of Chapter 8—an icon is still a sign, and operates within a larger semiotic economy. One way to make this point is in terms of the historicity of gramophonic listening. As Sterne (2003: 14) says, 'Many theorists and historians of sound have privileged the static and transhistorical, that is, the "natural", qualities of sound and hearing'. (So does the advertising copy in Figure 11.5.) This would imply that listening is a constant, with changes in the gramophonic experience being simply a function of technological change. But that is obviously incorrect. We hear the same technology quite differently from how it was heard in the early years of the twentieth century.

Advertisements for early gramophones were not known for understatement, and their glowing accounts of the listening experience have to be taken with more than a grain of salt.[32] However there is a well-known account of gramophonic listening in Thomas Mann's novel *The Magic Mountain*, the German original of which appeared in 1924 and is set in a Swiss sanatorium before the First World War. During the course of the narrative, the sanatorium acquires a gramophone. Eisenberg (2005: 47–50) and Clarke (2007) have discussed this topic in some detail, but a single quotation will suffice for my purposes. The sanatorium residents are listening to an Offenbach overture:

> They listened, their lips parted in smiles. They could scarcely believe their ears at the purity and faithful reproduction of the colour of the wood-wind. A solo violin preluded whimsically; the bowing, the *pizzicato*, the sweet gliding tone from one position to another, were all clearly audible.... The vivid, consummate piece of music was reproduced in all the richness of its light-hearted invention (Mann 1952: 637).

This is supposedly happening around 1912, but of course Mann could have been writing with the sound image of later gramophones in mind. The crucial point however is that the novel was published in 1924, the year *before* electrical recording reached the market place: Mann is talking about an acoustic recording, and more than that, an acoustic recording of orchestral music. Today such records are the

---

32. The booklet for the Aeolian Vocalion mentioned in n. 30 describes the opening of Schubert's 'Unfinished' Symphony, as recorded by the Russian Symphony Orchestra, as follows: 'Suddenly through the silence sound the great, bass notes of the tuba, voicing the opening theme [perhaps this explains the second image to which I referred]. How smooth, how wonderfully true are these tones! Surely they come from the great horn itself—this marvelous phonograph has but reflected them through intervening time. The appealing, string (*sic*) beauty of the violins opens in agitated rhythm. The wood-winds rise to the militant crash of the full choir of brasses. And, as the majestic measures unfold the pallid-pure voices of the flutes, the rich, suave tone of the 'cellos, the plaintive sweetness of the wood-winds, the sweeping staccato of the harps, the assertative majors of the brasses—sound and resound, answer and reanswer through the polyphonic mazes of gorgeous tonal harmony'.

classic signifiers of historical distance and nostalgia for a lost world, because their noisy surface and shrill tone is instantly recognisable: to us, the sound of the recording is so deafening that it takes effort, or experience, to hear the musical content embedded within it.

Of course *The Magic Mountain* is a novel. But there is still more striking evidence of the verisimilitude that characterised period experiences of acoustic recordings. The story begins with concerts mounted by the manufacturers of reproducing pianos,

> at which Cortot or Moiseiwitsch would perform a piece, and then the same work would be reproduced from the roll that the artist himself had made, so that direct comparison could be made. Rolls were played in which parts of the work had been left blank, and the live performer would fill in the missing bars. Responsible critics like Ernest Newman confessed themselves unable to tell when the man stopped and the machine took over (Gueroult 1966: 24).

And the composer and critic Deems Taylor records a similar exhibition involving Friedman that took place in 1921: shutting his eyes, Taylor found it impossible to tell Friedman and the mechanical piano apart—until there came a passage 'played with the tremendous power and sonority that only human fingers can produce' (Evans 2009: 104). Taylor confidently opened his eyes—and 'there sat Friedman with his hands in his lap, gazing idly out into the audience'. All this is interesting in relation to present-day debates about how well reproducing pianos captured the distinctive qualities of individual pianists—something which contemporary listeners were much better placed to judge—but it is not entirely surprising: the tonal quality of a reproducing piano is, after all, that of a real instrument heard live, the issue being more one of temporal and dynamic nuance.

However similar concerts or demonstrations were mounted by the Edison company (and to a lesser degree others) from 1915 until the mid-1920s, and here the results are more surprising. They were called 'tone tests' and varied from high-profile events—Emily Thompson (1995: 131) mentions one held at Carnegie Hall in 1916 that had an audience of two and a half thousand—to much more modest events held in small-town locations. Typically they involved a female singer, an accompanist, and a gramophone (in Edison's terminology, a disc phonograph). At some point there would be an episode when the lights were dimmed, or a curtain might be drawn, or listeners might even be blindfolded. The singer would start the performance, but it would end with just the gramophone; sometimes the singer would steal offstage—as the audience would see when the lights came up. They were invariably fooled. Or so the newspapers said. A *Boston Evening Transcript* review of a tone test involving the singer Christine Miller, from 1915, reported that you could only tell singer and recording apart by watching Miller's lips, while a report from the same year in the *Des Moines Times* claimed that 'Not a person in the audience was able to say whether Miss Miller was singing or the new Diamond Disc phonograph was playing' (Thompson 1995: 156–57).

The importance of the tone tests is twofold. In the first place, they are a dramatic illustration of how the discourse of fidelity was translated into practice. Sterne (2003: 215–16) explains that in the years leading up to Edison's tone tests, the Victor Company ran a series of advertisements that juxtaposed the image of a singer (such as Enrico Caruso or Geraldine Farrar) and either a gramophone or a record: in each case the images are roughly the same size, and the caption is either 'Which is which?' or 'Both are X' (where X is the singer's name). In this way the advertisements suggest that live performance and recording are equivalent to one another: they might be said to be competing for the same slot. In the same way, Sterne says, 'the tone tests expressly sought to establish for their audiences an equivalency between live performance and a sound recording.... The most important result was in convincing audiences that one was comparable to the other' (261, 263). And Thompson (1995: 160) links this to the fact that—as we saw in connection with Patti's niece—phonographs, like reproducing pianos, were marketed as musical instruments: 'Tone tests...equated listening to records with listening to musical instruments and to live vocal performance'. Given the duration, scale, and impact of the tone test campaign, then, it could be seen as a major factor in explaining how the paradigm of original and copy became so deeply entrenched in thinking about recorded sound. According to Thompson (132), 'by equating phonographic recordings with live performances of music, the tone test advertising campaign of the Edison Company helped to transform musical culture in America'. Sterne goes even further: it helped to 'define the way in which sound fidelity has been thought down to the present day' (2003: 263).[33]

It is however the second respect in which the tone tests are important that primarily concerns me here: the implications of audiences' inability to tell live from recorded performance. We should not be too naïve about this. Sterne (247) emphasises the extent to which, from the start, sound reproduction 'required a certain level of faith in the apparatus': early listeners willed the technology to work, connived in its illusions. Again, Thompson points out that, if tone tests were designed to show how perfectly gramophone replicated singers, then equally the singers were trying to sound like the gramophones. (Anna Case, who performed in the very first tone test as well as many others, recalled that 'I gave my voice the same quality as the machine so they couldn't tell' [Milner 2009: 7].) And the Edison publicity machine generated press releases and coordinated advertising campaigns in order to secure optimal press coverage. Perhaps money changed hands. But the scale of these events, and of the coverage of them in the newspapers and elsewhere, as well as the ten-year period during which they took place, means that the responses to them cannot simply be discounted.

33. Symes (2004: 79) also mentions that the same techniques reappeared in the 1950s: events were held at high-profile venues such as the Royal Festival Hall (London) in which live performances and LPs were juxtaposed. And the same thinking was embodied in a well known advertising slogan from the 1970s: 'Is it live or is it Memorex?'

What makes it hard to believe that 'they couldn't tell', as Anna Case put it, is the fact that the tone tests were based on acoustic recordings. As Thompson (1995: 159) comments, 'Modern listeners, attuned to digitally recorded and reproduced stereo sound, may find it hard to believe that audiences were unable to distinguish between the artist and the record'. Indeed Symes (2004) states baldly that the claims must have been hyperbolic, since 'The sound that was actually achievable on record was subject to severe constraints and fell far short of being the absolute last word in reproduction' (64). But his 'actually' is rather too reminiscent of the scientific criteria adopted by the Swedish hi-fi ideologue who described the human ear as the weakest link in the reproduction of sound, and of course, those who attended the tone tests had not themselves heard 'the absolute last word in reproduction' (whatever that might be). I prefer to think that those who participated in the tone tests experienced what they said they experienced, and to see them as illustrating Sterne's claim that 'every age has its own perfect fidelity' (2003: 222). All this underlines the extent to which, as I said in Chapter 7, listening is culturally mediated.

And this is where we come back to iconicity. Recordings are like live performances in the same sense that a drawing of a horse is like a real horse. But that is not at all a straightforward sense. Taking their cue from Umberto Eco, Roth and Bowen (2001) write that 'the apparent visual similitude between the outline drawing of a horse and some living horse is produced, consistent with some cultural decision, and therefore has to be learned' (187). To see a drawing as a horse, they continue, involves knowledge of the 'rules and conventions' that govern 'geometric similitude and topographical isomorphism'. If people aren't aware of this—if they think the drawing simply looks like a horse—that is 'because of their familiarity with the representations that have become transparent in their activities'. The point becomes easier to appreciate if, instead of the realistic depiction of a horse, we think of a pony—and specifically one of Thelwell's cartoon ponies.[34] There is no literal or statistical sense in which any real pony looks like a Thelwell cartoon. The relationship between pony and cartoon is not one of literal resemblance but one of signification. The cartoon abstracts a rather small number of key features that we are able to translate back into the real world, so seeing the cartoon as a pony. We might say that these key features specify the pony, and through this Gibsonian term we can forge a link with Clarke's interpretation (2007) of the tone tests. 'From an ecological perspective', he writes, 'it is the events that are *specified* by the stimulus information rather than the stimulus information itself that is important—which makes the phenomenon much easier to explain. As long as the signal preserves sufficient information to specify the appropriate invariants, the listener will hear the music' (60).

At first sight this might seem like a rehabilitation of the supposedly 'natural' qualities of sound and hearing that Sterne critiqued, but that is where we need to factor in the dimension of learning to which Roth and Bowen referred. This is something that Sterne (2003: 256) stresses: 'sound reproduction', he says, 'required

34. A selection may be viewed at http://www.thelwell.org.uk/images/ponies/index.htm.

the development of audile technique'. He defines this as 'a particular kind of listening for detail and a particular relation between listener and instrument', and claims that 'audile technique is prior to the possibility of any "faithful" relation between sounds' (223). Seen in this light, the entire tone test campaign might be interpreted as a kind of aural training programme, designed to teach people to hear recorded sound in accordance with discourse of fidelity. And in the context of post-war Sweden and the developing culture of hi-fi, Bjornberg (2009) similarly emphasises the importance that was attached to 'ear training', by which he means 'a purposeful training of the ability to listen to reproduced sound in order to develop sensitivity to distinctions in quality of sound and to the degree of fidelity to the original' (60). The training in question is partly technical in nature, as when a review of a wire recorder from 1950 refers to distortion being perceptible only to 'a small number of trained ears' (114). But it also extends to training of a much broader nature. In 1959 you are told to 'relax, sit still and comfortably', and to enjoy stereo 'in small doses' (114–15). Eleven years later an article states that 'in order for the musical experience not to become merely the sum of the details, an active effort by the listener is required. He [sic] should be interested and devoted, enter into moods and emotional trajectories, analyse logical connections if he likes to, make findings, observations and interpretations'.

This is beginning to sound like Virgil Thomson's 'Appreciation-racket', and the association between recording and the music appreciation movement goes back at least to the First World War. According to Megan Prictor (2000), Sir Walford Davies 'first put the gramophone to use to teach and encourage British troops during his YMCA-sponsored work in France in 1916–17' (214); in 1922 he recorded a series of 'Melody Lectures' on disc, combining speech with musical examples, and he also issued lists of recommended records for use in Welsh schools. Again, in 1924 Percy Scholes published his *First Book of the Gramophone Record*, in effect a history of music in fifty records, with a *Second Book* appearing in the following year. And in 1927 the American radio manufacturer Federal-Brandes released a sixty-page pamphlet that, in Sterne's words, 'explained how to listen and what to listen for in both the music and the medium' (2003: 280–81). Its author, the music educator Sigmund Spaeth, cautioned that 'Many people who are listening to music are really not listening at all', and argued that if you can distinguish the sounds of your environment, then you can distinguish musical instruments (281). The kind of music appreciation promulgated by Davies, Scholes, and Spaeth stands in a tradition that predated the broad dissemination of mechanical reproduction, as represented for example by Hermann Kretzschmar's *Führer durch den Konzertsaal* (1887–1890): its essence is that it gives you things to listen for, creating a prefabricated repertory of associations to which the music can be matched.

There are several ways in which we might understand this nexus of education, technology, and commerce. An obvious one is a desire on the part of the listening public for self-improvement or social advancement, a desire for cultural capital that gramophone and radio manufacturers sought to translate into economic capital. Then again, going back to Clarke's Gibsonian terminology, we could say that having things to listen for sensitised you to a particular, culturally approved, set of invariants: it directed attention away from the medium and towards the message. In this way it was a method for improving signal-to-noise ratio, only in the domain of encultured listening rather than audio engineering. Finally, and more speculatively, this entire approach might be seen as driven by the sensory gap that opened up as recorded music increasingly stepped into the slot previously occupied by live music, in which—as I argued in Chapters 9 and 10—the visual plays a prominent role. As early as 1905 two devices appeared on the market in apparent anticipation of Windows Media Player, the Stereophone and the Illustrated Song Machine: when attached to a cylinder recorder, they 'rotated images in time with the music'. Katz (2004: 19), from whom I draw this information, quotes from a trade journal that described the Illustrated Song Machine as 'just what the public has wanted since the first automatic machine [i.e., phonograph] was placed on the market, and the listener drew a mind's picture as the words and music were repeated to him'. And in his study of the National Gramophonic Society, which was set up by Compton Mackenzie to create and disseminate recordings of classical chamber music, Nick Morgan (2010) cites a member who in 1925 advocated listening with a score, even if you didn't read music: 'a knowledge of "notation" is not indispensable', he wrote, for 'The eye readily follows the movement of each instrument as it becomes prominent and one soon learns to associate sound and notes' (152). In both of these cases sound is complemented by sight in a literal sense, but music appreciation did the same thing in an imaginative sense: it provided a set of stable, intentional objects through which the inchoate experience of musical sound could be anchored—or as Abbate would say, domesticated.

Audile technique, then, is something learned, culturally constructed, and therefore historically contingent: that is why, for Sterne, 'Sound reproduction is historical all the way down' (2003: 23). But we can add further flesh to the bones through pursuing the comparison with cinema. There are frequently cited accounts of the audiences from 1895 who saw the Lumière Brothers' *L'arrivée d'un train en gare de la Ciotat* and jumped to get out of the way of the oncoming engine: though there are some doubts as to how authentic these accounts are (Huhtamo 1997), the early date suggests that the issue here was a lack of filmic literacy on the audience's part. But the issue of literacy goes further than that, and revolves around the understanding of cinematic time. It would be possible to describe a film—or a studio sound recording—as the reproduction, in a scrambled sequence, of a series of events that took place in the studio. But to say that would display as fundamental a misunderstanding of the genre as complaining that the events in a novel didn't really happen. Neither films nor sound recordings signify as traces of real-world events. They signify by prompting acts of interpretation by listeners, through which those events are understood as elements in an unfolding, imaginatively constituted reality. That is what diegesis means—a term that is well established in film criticism, and that I see as equally useful for the theorisation of sound recordings.[35]

35. As does Simon Trezise (2009: 207), who writes that 'a recording does not "show" a performance to us, for the performance that generated the recorded artifact is hidden: the relationship is not mimetic; rather, we may regard a record as forming a diegesis with and within its domestic or other environment'.

However there is a basic difference between diegesis in films and in sound recordings. As a genre, film is based on narrative diegesis, meaning we experience the events that unfold in the two hours or so over which the film plays as if they were unfolding over a period that could be hours, months, or decades, and not necessarily in the same sequence as they are presented (for example where there are flashbacks). To understand what happens at any moment in a film is to map it onto the unfolding story. In contrast, musical diegesis takes place in the real time of listening: we experience the music as a continuously unfolding event in which we recover the signs of the body from the sound, map them onto our own bodies, feel the music's movement as our movement. That is to say, we hear recordings as performances. But we should note that the real-time nature of musical diegesis does not make the experience of recorded music more 'natural' than that of film: the fictive is built into each genre. Simon Frith (1996: 211) makes this point in relation to rock and pop, but his point is just as applicable to classical recordings: 'I listen to records in the full knowledge that what I hear is something that never existed, that never could exist, as a "performance", something happening in a single time and space; nevertheless, it is now happening, in a single time and space: it is thus a performance and I hear it as one'. Hearing, in short, is believing, even when you don't believe what you hear.

Musical diegesis, the experience of music as performance, is then a listening practice rather than a function of the recording process. You might be listening to an acoustic recording, say Elgar's *Carissima* (Figure 5.1): this piece for small orchestra was designed to fit on a single side of a 78 rpm disc, and no editing was possible with acoustic recordings, so what we hear is a trace of what was played in the studio, unfolding in (more or less) the same time. Then again, you might be listening to a symphonic LP from the 1950s, consisting of 'a composite of takes and inserts recorded over a period of time and spliced together'[36]: here multiple performance times are fragmented and interpolated in a manner that cannot now be reconstructed, except in the unlikely case that the spliced master tape has been preserved. Or you might be listening to a 1970s rock song like 'Bohemian Rhapsody', assembled through multi-tracking: here both time and space are comprehensively reconstructed, the latter through the close miking of individual tracks with reverberation being added in post-production, resulting in a temporal and spatial tightness that Queen could never match when they performed the song live. (This reconstruction of space is not limited to rock: as Symes [2004: 82] says, the concert hall sound of classical recordings is 'an engineering construct'.) It makes no difference how the record was produced. In each case you hear the music in terms of diegesis, of continuous temporal unfolding, in short, as performance. Auslander (2004) concurs and draws the obvious conclusion: 'Regardless of the ontological status of recorded music, its phenomenological status for listeners is that of a performance unfolding at the time and in the place of listening. Sound recordings of musical performances should therefore be considered legitimate objects for performance analysis...alongside live musical performances, documentation of live performances, and music videos' (5).

36. Thomas Frost, quoted in Day (2000: 26).

That brings us back, for the first time, to Ridley's generous definition of musical performance. And all this applies equally to contemporary studio pop created using Pro Tools, with sounds being sculpted into high relief, or rationalised through quantisation, pitch correction, and the removal of breaths and other signs of the audible body. The result is a contrafactually clean sound that forms the exact equivalent of the equally contrafactual fashion photographs created through computer enhancement. Digital post-production and digital air-brushing both mould female bodies into size 0 fantasies, as do deodorants, depilation, liposuction, and cosmetic surgery. Like the spherified peas of molecular gastronomy—real peas that have been disassembled and then reconstructed into idealised peas—the voice is reconstructed, re-engineered: as the producer and recording engineer Steve Savage (2011: 56) writes, 'What is never really possible is a simple reproduction of what actually happened inside the singer's mouth'. Or it is like Thelwell's pony, broken down into its signifiers and then reconfigured contrafactually in a manner that imbues it with the signs of humanity, creating a pony optimised for human perception—a graphic pony that, for us, is more like a pony than the real thing, just as spherified peas pack a taste punch that no real pea can match.

In short, digitally produced pop is an extreme example of what Steven Pinker calls 'auditory cheesecake' (1999: 534). Pinker is addressing the issue of how and why music evolved:

> We enjoy strawberry cheesecake, but not because we evolved a taste for it. We evolved circuits that gave us trickles of enjoyment from the sweet taste of ripe fruit, the creamy mouth feel of fats and oils from nuts and meat, and the coolness of fresh water. Cheesecake packs a sensual wallop unlike anything in the natural world because it is a brew of megadoses of agreeable stimuli which we concocted for the express purpose of pressing our pleasure buttons. Pornography is another pleasure technology.... The arts are a third (Pinker 1999: 525).

And Patrik Juslin (2011: 123) has made a rather similar proposal in relation to musical instruments: 'they are reminiscent of the human voice'—that is, they press the same hedonic and affective buttons that have evolved in parallel with the voice—but at the same time 'they go much further in terms of their expressive features'. They are then 'super-expressive voices', voices that are more voice-like than real voices.

All this helps to explain how recorded music can sound more like live performance than live performance does. It creates the sound image against which audiences measure live performance, driving the tendency—to which I shall return in the final chapter—for concerts to increasingly resemble recordings. Sterne (2003: 245) observes that as early as the 1920s the aim was 'realism, not reality itself.... The point of the artifice is...to construct a realism that holds the place of reality without being it'. He says this with specific reference to the broadcasting of live sporting events, but I think his point applies to mechanically reproduced sound in general. Only it might be stated more strongly. The discourse of fidelity leads us to think of recordings as reproducing a musical reality, as the copy of an original that lies outside the recording. But the business of recordings is less to reproduce an existing reality than, under the cloak of reproduction, to create a new one. Their motivating principle is not so much realism as hyperrealism.

Sterne (2003) puts his finger on the central problem with the discourse of fidelity when he describes it as 'an impossible vantage point from which to assess the fidelity of the machines to a fictitious external reality' (285). In contemporary studio-produced pop, it is self-evident that recording is structured around Pinker's pleasure buttons far more than around mimesis. But that should not be taken as an opportunity to draw a line between today's manufactured artifice and yesterday's unmediated naturalism. Again it is Sterne (2003: 235–36) who makes the point that, from the earliest days of recorded sound, 'People performed for the machines....Recording did not simply capture reality as it was; it aimed to capture reality suitable for reproduction'. Figure 5.1 provides an illustration, not only in terms of the reconstruction of performance practice outside the studio but also in its carefully staged poses and composition. In the same way, photographs of Victorian children almost invariably show them freshly caught, scrubbed, and clothed. The photographs represent how children were meant to be and not how they were.

It is again a matter of the 'familiarity with the representations that have become transparent' of which Roth and Bowen spoke. All recordings work through signification rather than reproduction, it is just that we are too used to them to be aware of it and so mistake the signifier for the signified. That is what gives rise to scandals such as those over Milli Vanilli and Ashlee Simpson, which—following Auslander—I described in terms of pop artists being held to rock criteria of fidelity. But what happened could be described more simply in terms of an excessively naive conception of the nature of live performance in a mediatised age. And this is not something that applies just to music. Much the same might be said about the controversy over Robert Capa's 'The falling soldier', formerly known as 'Loyalist militiaman at the moment of death, Cerro Muriano, September 5, 1936' and the most iconic photograph of the Spanish Civil War, which appears to have been staged some thirty-five miles from the battle site of Cerro Muriano. Perhaps there will be another such controversy when it comes out that most of the animal sound effects in David Attenborough's natural history films are so called Foley sounds, humanly generated sounds created in the studio. Hearing, in short, is believing, even when you aren't hearing what you believe you are.

I said I would return to the issue of liveness. Turning on the categorical distinction of original and copy, the discourse of fidelity constructed liveness as a yes-or-no ontological characteristic. Performance was either live or it was recorded. And as Thornton (1995) has explained, a series of aesthetic judgements were built on this ontological distinction: the term liveness 'accumulated connotations which took it beyond the denotative meaning of performance....The expression "live music" gave positive valuation to and became generic for performed music. It soaked up aesthetic and ethical connotations of life-versus-death, human-versus mechanical, creative-versus-imitative' (42).

Conceived this way, the ontological conditions of liveness might be said to be co-spatiality and co-temporality: performers and listeners need to be in the same place at the same time. In this context, however, it is striking that—as Auslander says—the first known use of the term 'live' as the antonym of 'recorded' arose in the context of radio broadcasts. It is not that people did not know whether they were listening to something happening around them or to a broadcast. It is that they did not know whether what they were hearing on the radio was being broadcast as it happened or had been recorded. As Auslander (2002 17) argues:

> Unlike the gramophone, radio does not allow you to see the sources of the sounds you're hearing; therefore, you can never be sure if they're live or recorded.... The possibility of identifying certain performances as live came into being with the advent of recording technologies; the need to make that identification arose as an affective response specifically to radio, a communications technology that put the clear opposition of the live and the recorded into a state of crisis. The response to this crisis was a terminological distinction that attempted to preserve the formerly clear dichotomy between two modes of performance, the live and the recorded, a dichotomy that had been so self-evident up to that point that it did not even need to be named.

That is Auslander's answer to the question of why the idea of 'live' music did not arise until so much later than that of 'canned' music. In this context, however, 'live' refers to co-temporality, but not—since we are talking about a broadcast—co-spatiality. That is consistent with Auslander's view (2008a) that the former counts for more in judgements of liveness than the latter: 'spatial co-presence has become less and less important for a performance to be defined as live', he observes, 'while temporal simultaneity has remained an important characteristic' (112). But as I said earlier, where there is no co-spatiality, even the co-temporality criterion becomes blurred, as illustrated by 'live' relays with a slight (or not so slight) time lag.

That, however, is not the crucial point that emerges from this early use of the term 'live'. The crucial point is that—as Auslander explains it—listeners were unable to tell the difference between live and recorded material by simply listening to it. Understood in ontological terms, liveness subsisted in something you *knew*, or at least believed, about what you were hearing, and not in what you actually heard. Like an antique dealer's certificate of authenticity, the label 'live' was necessary because otherwise you couldn't tell the difference. But understood this way, the concept of liveness becomes hopelessly thin. Liveness is seen as making the difference, in Thornton's words (1995: 42), between 'the truth of music, the seeds of genuine culture' on the one hand, and recordings, those 'false prophets of pseudo-culture' on the other. But if you can't actually tell the one from the other, then liveness is reduced to a dogma, a value-judgement without empirical content. If it was just a matter of aesthetic theory, we might write off the whole concept of liveness as the product of obsolete ways of thinking. A parallel might be made with the study of virtual communities. The value-laden concept of liveness that Thornton documents is linked to the belief—still as widespread in performance studies and media studies as in musicology—that face-to-face interaction is the sole authentic basis of community. And in his book on YouTube communities, Michael Strangelove (2010) writes that 'By using the false starting point of envisaging community as based in face-to-face relations, we end up unnecessarily problematizing the lack of face-to-face interaction in cyberspace' (104). Seen in such terms, the problem of liveness is not so much a problem as a misunderstanding.

But it's not just a matter of aesthetic theory. The concept of liveness is one that people who make, listen to, or talk about music use and find meaningful. As Paul Sanden (2013) says, 'The fact that liveness still exists for many musickers even in situations that are not live (according to traditional definition) is a testament to its power as a concept through which meaning is interpreted' (4). The way to rescue the term, then, is to find an alternative grounding for it, and that is what both Auslander and Sanden attempt. After surveying uses of the term, Auslander writes, 'It is clear from this history that the word "live" is not used to define intrinsic, ontological properties of performance that set it apart from mediatized forms, but rather is a historically contingent term' (2008b: 60). In another publication he adds a little more detail: the qualities that constitute liveness are 'phenomenological (as opposed to ontological)', he says, 'in the sense that they are not characteristics of the performance itself but things experienced and felt by performers and spectators' (2008a: 108). And he sees the sense of community associated with live as opposed to recorded music as having far more to do with the listeners than with what is happening on stage: it 'arises from being part of an audience, and the quality of the experience of community derives from the specific audience situation, not from the spectacle for which that audience has gathered' (2008b: 65). In short, Auslander redefines liveness in ways that apply as well to recorded as to concert music.

Sanden also grounds liveness in listener experience, but puts flesh on the bones by emphasising the specific stimulus properties that afford the experience of liveness. His basic thesis is that 'Liveness represents a perceived *trace* of that which *could be live*';[37] the point is not that it *is* live in the face-to-face sense, but that it can be heard that way. This translates to the claim that 'the perception of liveness depends…on the persistent perception of *characteristics* of music's live performance', and on this basis Sanden distinguishes a number of aspects of live performance in respect of which any music, regardless of the extent of its mediatisation, may exhibit a greater or lesser degree of liveness. Particularly relevant to my argument are Sanden's categories (2013: 11) of corporeal liveness ('Music is *live* when it demonstrates a perceptible connection to an acoustic sounding body'), interactive loudness ('Music is *live* when it emerges from various interactions between performing partners and/or between performers and listeners/viewers'), and virtual liveness: 'music can be *live* in a virtual sense even when the conditions for its liveness (be they corporeal, interactive, etc.) do not *actually* exist'.

---

37. Sanden (2013: 6); his formulation echoes what Savage (2009: 33) calls the 'it could have happened' aesthetic, and Savage's article provides a practical example of the operation of the idea of liveness in a studio production context.

Sanden gives an example of virtual liveness: 'if I believe I hear the sound of a hand hitting a drum, even if what I actually hear is a sound completely synthe-sized by electronic means, that sound may still convey to me a very real corporeal liveness' (2013: 42–43). In other words, corporeality and hence liveness are speci-fied in the sound. That is the point I was making when I spoke of recovering the signs of the body from the sound, mapping them onto our own bodies, and so feeling the music's movement as our movement. Physical and affective motion are specified in the sound, and in this way the phenomenological qualities that define corporeal liveness are present as much in recorded music as in what we hear at a concert. In the same way, the social dimensions of music with which I was con-cerned in Chapters 7 and 8—the negotiation of what might be called temporal and dynamic grain in light of the developing context of Sawyer's collectively cre-ated emergent—are specified in the sound: as Ian Cross (2009) says, 'even physi-cally inert but intent listening, even to recorded music, might best be thought of as covert interaction with the traces of human behaviour that are evidenced in the sonic surface of the music' (77). In this way interactive liveness, like corporeal liv-eness, is as much present in recorded music as at a concert. And at the same time, to the extent that the conditions for the music's corporeal and interactive liveness do not *actually* exist in recorded music, its liveness is virtual.

'Liveness is ultimately perceptual', Sanden (2013: 32–33) remarks, 'and there-fore dependent on imagination'. Another way to say the same thing is that live-ness is a product, or a dimension, of musical diegesis: it is part of what it means to hear music as performance, recorded or otherwise. To extend the concept of liveness to recorded music in this way is not, of course, to minimise the obvi-ous differences between the production and the reception of music of different genres and in different situations. It is not to deny that, for performers such as Doğantan-Dack, performing for an audience and in the studio are quite distinct things (though, according to Day, 'Many musicians...have insisted that there is no difference between giving live concerts and performing for the microphone', among them Fischer-Dieskau[38]). It is rather to say that the binary distinction between what is conventionally called live and recorded music is not the only, and perhaps not even a particularly important, fault line in the topography of musi-cal performance: Sanden observes that 'ontological distinctions that were once fiercely defended between live and recorded modes of musical reception seem to mean little any more' (2013: 6). In encompassing the music of both concert hall and recording studio within an expanded concept of performance, then, I am not only arriving back for the second and last time at Ridley's generous definition of musical performance, but also agreeing with Auslander (2008b: 5) when he says—of performance in general—that he is 'treating live and mediatized performance as parallel forms that participate in the same cultural economy'.

There is in essence no difference between the paradigm of reproduction, as I have called it in relation to works and performances, and Sterne's discourse of

---

38. Day (2000: 53); Fischer-Dieskau's name is not mentioned in the text but appears in n. 245.

fidelity in the relationship between concert hall and recording studio. Each is based on the same concept of original and copy, and each is a thoroughly inadequate way to think about music. The result has been a skewing of academic studies away from the concerns and realities of musical cultures both in the past and in the present day. But worse, each has served to constrain the practice of music, and together they go far to explain the parlous position of classical music in the early years of the twenty-first century. And that sets the stage for my final chapter.

12

Beyond Reproduction

THE BEST SEAT IN THE HALL

In the previous chapter I argued against the idea that recordings reproduce performances, on the grounds that this is to misconstrue the complex operation of recordings in processes of musical meaning production. That was in essence a theoretical argument. But this way of thinking has also had significant consequences for the practice of classical recording. As in the case of performance, so in that of recording: the conceptual constraints of the reproduction paradigm have been built into creative practice, or rather into practice that has in consequence been less creative than it might have been. Musicological assertions of the primacy of performance in concert have found a real-world correlate in the 'Keep Music Live' or similarly named campaigns that have been mounted by musicians' unions since the 1950s in North America—according to Sarah Thornton (1995) one of the first uses of the term 'live' in a specifically musical context—and since the mid-1960s in the UK (41–42). As Simon Frith (2008) explains, the Musicians' Union was 'exercised over the years…by the suggestion that sound technicians (engineers, record producers, sound mixers) could be considered music-makers like conventional instrumentalists': this is the exact equivalent, translated into terms of people, of the hierarchy implicit in Boulez's claim about 'the so-called techniques of reproduction…acquiring an irrepressible tendency to become autonomous and to impress their own image of existing music'.

Another real-world correlate of the ontological distinction academics have drawn between concert and recorded performance may be found in the criteria set up by the Official Charts Company (OCC), which is responsible for the published sales charts of recorded music in the UK. The OCC maintains a number of separate charts based on genres, one of which is called the Classical Artist Album Top 50 Chart. This is meant to cover mainstream classical releases, and the eligibility guidelines for this chart exclude releases that would not be 'capable of live performance in a concert setting' (Victoros 2009: 35). This stipulation is well intentioned: the aim is to prevent what the music industry calls 'core' classical releases being crowded out by commercialised crossover artists such as Bond, whom I mentioned in Chapter 10, and whose releases appear in the main album chart. (As it happens, Bond's debut album *Born* was mistakenly placed within the

Classical Artist Album Top 50 Chart, going straight in at number two, but being expelled the following week—which created a golden publicity opportunity that their record company was quick to exploit.[1]) Nevertheless the criteria pursue this worthy end by identifying the WAM tradition with—and limiting it to—concert performance, in other words through enforcement of the paradigm of reproduction: more creative exploitation of the media technologies through which it might reach a broader audience is ruled out. As so often, there is a tension between maintaining the heritage and making it accessible.

Since the introduction of the vinyl LP in the 1950s, discourses around classical record production have been dominated by the ideology encapsulated in Walter Legge's famous maxim, 'I want to make records which will sound in the public's home exactly like what they would hear in the best seat in an acoustically perfect hall' (Schwarzkopf 1982: 73). That precise formulation appeared only in the memoir of Legge that his wife, the singer Elisabeth Schwarzkopf, published in 1982, three years after his death, but its key phrase was already current during the early years of the hi-fi era. Symes (2004) illustrates an advertisement for the Pye Mozart HF 10 amplifier that appeared in the November 1957 issue of the *Gramophone*: the strapline is 'The finest seat in the house' (74). On the other side of the Atlantic, but at exactly the same time, Harmon Kardon issued a brochure for their 1957 range of audiophile equipment, the cover of which bore the words 'The best seat in the concert hall!'[2] And the longevity of both concept and strapline is demonstrated by a brochure produced by the German headphones manufacturer Sennheiser in 2008, which says that 'As soon as you put on your Sennheiser audiophile headphones you will think you are in the best seat in the concert hall'.[3] Of course, as we saw in Chapter 11, the basic idea was built into Jonathan Sterne's discourse of fidelity and goes back far into the acoustic era. But electrical recording technology—and more particularly the introduction in the late 1940s of tape recording—greatly expanded the options available within the recording process, both technically and interpretively, and so brought into being a new figure in the process of music making: the record producer.

Legge, who began his career with HMV (subsequently EMI) in the late 1920s but whose career peaked in the post-war years, penned an autobiographical sketch that was included in Schwarzkopf's memorial volume. Its first words are: 'I was the first of what are called "producers" of records' (Schwarzkopf 1982: 16). Two sentences later Legge explains what this means by drawing a distinction between himself and his predecessor at HMV, Fred Gaisberg, who—he says— had told him, 'We are out to make sound photographs of as many sides as we

1. Victoros (2009: 116–19).

2. Scans of this fourteen-page brochure may be found at http://www.hifilit.com/hifilit/Harmon-Kardon/harman-kardon.htm.

3. 'Art of Sound: Headphones 2008', formerly at http://www.sennheiser.co.uk/ie/icm.nsf/resources/Headphones_ArtOfSound_08.pdf/$File/Headphones_ArtOfSound_08.pdf (accessed August 2012).

can get during each session'. Legge continues: 'My ideas were different. It was my aim to make records that would set the standards by which public performance and the artists of the future would be judged—to leave behind a large series of examples of the best performances of my epoch'. These records would be exemplary in the sense that they embodied the finest performances that could be achieved by the best artists working under ideal conditions. And that is where new possibilities created by post-war technology came in. As writers such as Sterne and Théberge make clear, technology affords but does not determine cultural practices: production might be seen as the series of interpretive choices through which Gaisberg's sound photographs were transformed into the experience of being in the best seat in an acoustically perfect hall that lay at the heart of Legge's ideology of recording. Symes refers to the image of the best seat in the hall (hereafter BSH) as the 'keystone' discourse of classical sound recording, and it is in effect the translation of Sterne's discourse of fidelity—and hence the paradigm of reproduction—into the terms of post-war studio practice.

If the BSH ideology represented a choice, then it was equally a ruling out of other possible choices. This becomes obvious from a comparison between the production processes of classical and popular music, where quite different approaches to production became the norm: the key date in this development is 1966, when the Beatles announced they were giving up touring and immediately started work on *Sgt. Pepper's Lonely Hearts Club*, which relied heavily on studio techniques. (There is a classical parallel in Glenn Gould's decision just two years earlier to retire from the concert platform and devote himself to work in the recording studio, the difference being that Gould had virtually no influence on classical recording culture as a whole.) In this way it is the BSH ideology, not the technology of recording, that consigns recorded music to the subordinate role I documented in Chapter 11. One of my aims in this chapter is, then, to review some of the faltering steps that have been taken towards different approaches to the recording of classical music.

What makes this important, given current concerns about the position of classical music in contemporary culture, is the way the BSH ideology of recording interlocks with an ideology of concert performance that is, so to speak, its mirror image: an ideology that renders the concert hall experience as similar as possible to that of recorded music, through repressing—or at least not taking advantage of—the visual, corporeal, and social dimensions afforded by concert performance. In short, recordings imitate the concert hall, while concerts imitate recordings, and it is at this ideological level that we might speak most convincingly of a convergence between them and a homogeneity of practice across the larger field of classical performance. While I see concert and recorded music as 'part of the same cultural economy', to repeat Auslander's words, that is no reason for uniformity of practice. So in this chapter I shall talk about some ways in which recordings might be less like concerts, and concerts less like recordings.

If standard histories of WAM have tended to marginalise performers, they have to an even higher degree marginalised recordists (a term that encompasses both producers and sound engineers, and is useful because the dividing line between them is variable and often fuzzy). Arved Ashby makes the acute observation that

'In the classical music realm…lingering notions of text and work have compelled musicians to classify recording as a technological rather than artistic-aesthetic process' (2010: 18): recordists, in other words, are viewed as technicians rather than musicians, just as the musicians' unions claimed.[4] It is not just that—like those equally silent musicians who came into being during the previous century, conductors—recordists 'make music', as Andrew Blake (2009: 53) says (and what is telling is that he needs to say it). It is that they have exerted a massive influence on how music sounds and how we expect it to sound, as much in the case of classical as of popular music. These changes in sound image have barely registered in musicology, which is not entirely surprising, given that the discipline has never been good at dealing with things that can be heard but not seen. What musicologists are much better at is tracing the creative contribution of key individuals to musical developments, and there has recently been a drive on the part of recordists for academic and artistic recognition, more or less along the lines of that accorded to film directors. This drive, it should be said, comes primarily from rock and pop producers, an increasing number of whom are moving on to second careers in higher education.[5] In contrast, it seems, the paradigm of reproduction has led classical producers and engineers—like performers—to underestimate their own role in processes of musical change.

Albin Zak describes the idea of the producer being an *auteur* as 'controversial' (2001: 179). Zak is approaching the issue from the direction of bands who may be more or less willing for the producer to stamp his or her own signature on a project, in the way that Phil Spector did ('did' because he has been in jail for murder since 2009). But from a more specifically academic point of view there are two issues over adopting the concept of *auteur* in this context. One has to do with the nature of the producer's work. For Legge, production involved the creation and implementation of an aesthetic ideology, as I said, but like all producers, he was also a hustler, a fixer, and a people manager. (An impressive listing of the many things producers may be called on to do is provided in Blake: 36–38.) More than anything, production might be called a relational practice, in some ways comparable to fashion photography, though the pop producer and studio owner Rick Hall has compared himself to the manager of a basketball team (Zak 2001: 179).

4. The same kind of schismatic categorisation is found even within recording. According to Charles Rosen (2003: 148–49), in one of the restrictive practices historically rife in the music industry, U.S. union regulations forbade recording engineers to read music, even when they in fact had this skill: that made it necessary for producers to replay the tape and signal where a cut was to be made, though it would have been much simpler for both parties to say 'bar 80, third beat'. Even today sound engineers working in popular music complain of lack of recognition (Izhaki [2008: 4–7]).

5. This is embodied in the title as well as the activities of the Association for the Study of the Art of Record Production, which holds regular international conferences and publishes the *Journal on the Art of Record Production* (http://www.artofrecordproduction.com/).

At one extreme, pop production can be inseparable from the process of song-writing: Mike Howlett (2009), who during the early 1980s produced a series of hits by such New Wave bands as Martha and the Muffins, Orchestral Manoeuvres in the Dark, and A Flock of Seagulls (and who now teaches in higher education), has documented how essential features of their songs developed only in the studio. At the other extreme, the producer of a recording of Beethoven's piano music is likely to act as an interlocutor, an additional pair of ears, in some ways standing in for the absent audience. But in either case production is a social activity, located within a highly segmented context of collaboration: John Culshaw (1967)—of whom more shortly—referred to the essential role of 'the administrators, the accountants; the tape editors and the men who take such pains to transfer the sound from tape to disc in such a way that the two are indistinguishable; the factory technicians who strive to maintain that quality through a process of mass-production; the promotion men and the representatives who get the records into the shops' (16).

It makes sense then that, in the context of popular music as a whole, Stan Hawkins writes of 'the entire teams of people who work to construct the *auteur*' (2009: 13). And in his long essay 'The prospects of recording' (written for *High Fidelity* and first published in 1966), Gould (1987) saw in studio recording the potential for a musical practice in which the traditional 'class structure within the musical hierarchy—distinctions that separated composer and performer and listener—will become outmoded': as a result, he says, 'the nature of... authorship will become very much less imposing' (351–52). The problem with the idea of producers as *auteurs* is in this way not a problem over producers as such, but a more general one: music making is by definition collaborative, so the ideology built on the concept of *auteur* is neither a realistic nor a productive approach to understanding it. By contrast the second issue to which I referred relates more specifically to producers. Virgil Moorefield's 2005 book *The Producer as Composer* traces the development of popular music production away from the BSH paradigm, and towards a conception of the song—or track—within which production is a fully integrated dimension (hence the title). I do not intend criticism when I observe that this book falls effortlessly into the mould of a traditional musicological study that proceeds more or less chronologically, focusses on key figures with close readings of exemplary works, and embraces its topic within a teleological evolution of the role of the producer 'from that of organizer to auteur' (as the publisher's blurb puts it).

In short, the second issue with the *auteur* approach is one that it shares with musical historiography in general: it places undue emphasis on innovative but not necessarily influential practitioners—to borrow Thomas Kuhn's terms (1962), on paradigm change at the expense of normal practice. Figures such as Culshaw and Gould, neither of whom had much influence on other producers of their time, constantly reappear in the literature, at the expense of the large number of highly talented and professional practitioners whose technical explorations and careful work within the BSH paradigm have been responsible for our basic ideas of how music should sound. Yet if, as Katz says, recording 'shapes the very way in which we *think* about music' (2004: 47), then these are the people who have done the shaping.

ACOUSTIC CHOREOGRAPHY

It is a little embarrassing in view of what I have just said that I shall now talk about Culshaw and Gould, but then my aim is essentially the same as Moorefield's, only transposed into the field of classical music: not to outline the field of classical record production as a whole, but—as I said—to trace some of the faltering steps towards alternatives to the BSH ideology. And the introduction of stereo in the 1950s is a good place to start.

An article published in 1943 by D. C. Somervell and entitled the 'The visual element in music' explored a number of situations in which salient elements of music cannot be conveyed through sound alone. Somervell's point was that this created problems for radio listeners that do not exist in the concert hall, but what he said applied equally to the gramophone. He gave the example of a passage from a Beethoven quartet where a run of semi-quavers passes from the first violin to the viola to the cello: in a good performance, he says, you don't hear the points of transition, but at a concert—unless, of course, you close your eyes—you see them, and that is part of what makes the music meaningful. Then again, in a concerto by J. S. Bach for two pianos (this *is* 1943), you can see the interaction between the two pianos even though you can't distinguish them if you close your eyes. For these effects to work on the radio, he says, either it is necessary for the listener to follow the score, or—in the case of the Bach—pianos with distinguishable tone qualities could be used. Reality, to borrow Sterne's words, needs to be made suitable for reproduction.

But Somervell was writing before the development of stereo, which created a much more obvious way to achieve the necessary differentiation: by separate placement of the instruments in the virtual space of the recording. The introduction through stereo of a new parameter into the gramophonic experience prompted controversies about its use in which the BSH ideology came into question. The location within his autobiographical sketch of Legge's famous formulation of the BSH ideology is telling. He goes on to say that stereo gave him new opportunities of realising it, but this brought him into conflict with EMI's technical and sales departments:

> They believed that the public wanted the 'gimmick' of stereo—would like to listen to the left and right extremes which in these days left a hole...in the space between the loudspeakers. It took a long time for me to induce these people that their ideas of stereo were the very opposite of what musicians and the musical public wanted (Schwarzkopf 1982: 73).

And two sentences after that he is explaining his decision—admittedly not until 1963—to leave EMI. But the controversies about the use of stereo extended beyond EMI. The very name of Phase 4 Stereo, the audiophile label introduced by EMI's British rival Decca in 1961, reflects them: early liner notes explained that Phase 1 meant the use of stereo to replicate concert layout, Phase 2 referred to the kind of gimmickry Legge objected to, and Phase 3 was the use of stereo to create effects of movement within the stereo space. In contrast, as Decca explained, Phase 4—which involved the use of ten- and later twenty-channel recording consoles—meant 'new scoring concepts incorporating true musical use of separation and movement. In this phase, arrangers and orchestrators re-score the music to place the instruments where they are musically most desired at any particular moment and make use of direction and movement to punctuate the musicality of sounds'.[6] Scores were prepared in which separate musical staves denoted separate channels, with the music being renotated across them; after recording, the multiple channels were mixed down to stereo. In this way the new technology was being used not to recreate the spatial dimension of concert performance, but in accordance with a form of musical logic, for example to heighten the contrast between textural elements. In short, it was being used for just the kind of purposes Somervell was thinking about a decade before stereo came in.

As at EMI, so at Decca the possibilities of stereo provoked institutional dissension. Tony D'Amato was brought over from New York to mastermind Phase 4 Stereo, and was duly seen as an American interloper imposing brash American values (MacKenzie 2006). As D'Amato explained in an interview published in 1997, Phase 4 was commercially successful in America and in Asia (especially Japan), but not in the UK. At one stage, he says, two separate masters would be made of each recording, 'one for England with a bit less emphasis on the "levels", because you know the British don't care much for gimmicks', and one for the rest of the world (Green 1997). D'Amato had trained at the Juilliard School, and while most Phase 4 recordings were of popular or light music, together with various kinds of novelty recordings, a dedicated 'Concert series' was introduced in 1964. This was weighted towards the lighter end of the classical spectrum, but included, for example, Beethoven sonatas and symphonies. Several of the latter were conducted by Stokowski, who was now in his eighties but had been pushing the boundaries of recording since the 1930s; Symes (2004) describes him as 'never an ardent defender of the idea that the classical record should defer to the acoustic conditions of the live concert' (55).[7] Decca's best known contribution to the innovative exploitation of stereo in the classical repertory, however, lay not in Phase 4 Stereo but in the recordings of operas by

6. Information on Phase 4 Stereo is taken from Tony Maygarden, 'London Phase 4 Stereo', where an 'arranger's control sheet' is reproduced (http://www.endlessgroove.com/issue4/lp4s.htm).

7. Unsurprisingly there was extensive discussion of this in the last of Gould's three interviews with Stokowski, which took place in 1970 and extracts from which appear in Gould (1987: 258–82). During the 1930s Stokowski took part in a research collaboration with the Bell Telephone Laboratories, outcomes of which included the development of the sapphire stylus and, on an experimental basis, some of the earliest stereophonic recordings (McGinn [1983]). For a brief but penetrating discussion of Stokowski and recording see Ashby (2010: 46–49).

Richard Strauss and—most famously—Wagner that Culshaw produced in the decade from 1957 to 1967. Indeed, given the relative timing, Phase 4 might be seen as an attempt to build on and commercialise the approach that Culshaw had already initiated in his recordings of the third act of *Die Walküre* (1957), *Das Rheingold* (1958), and *Tristan und Isolde* (1960). Perhaps Culshaw's most influential recording, however, was that of *Götterdämmerung*, released in 1964, the year that the Phase 4 'Concert series' was introduced.

In *Ring Resounding*, his account of the recording of the *Ring* cycle, Culshaw repeatedly stresses the centrality of stereo to his entire project. He describes stereo as 'the break-through we had waited for in order to record complete operas in a way that might bring the home listener into closer contact with the drama' (1967: 21). And on the next page: 'Until stereo, a record was a document of a performance, and one could not really expect it to be more' (this is reminiscent of Legge on Gaisberg, though for Legge it did not depend on stereo). And two pages after that: 'A stereo opera recording is not a transcription of a performance, but a re-creation of the opera in aural terms quite different from those of the opera house'. In the recordings up to *Tristan*, Culshaw's focus is mainly on the use of stereo to convey spatial movement and so to create, through purely aural means, something of the missing dimension of physical staging. In Act I of *Tristan*, for example, Culshaw conceived the staging 'with the ship in which the future lovers were travelling located diagonally onstage at an angle of about forty-five degrees to the audience' (Patmore and Clarke 2007: 278): this was as far as possible conveyed through the sound, involving the effects of movement that in Decca's terminology defined Phase 3 in the development of stereo. And a sketch of the set design was included in the leaflet that accompanied the recordings in order to guide the listener's imagination. But Culshaw also employed special effects to translate other aspects of the staging to the medium of the gramophone. An early example was the adjustment of Gustav Neidlinger's voice at the point in *Das Rheingold* where, as Alberich, he puts on the Tarnhelm. A related but more sophisticated effect—of which Culshaw (187) declined to provide a technical explanation—appears in *Götterdämmerung*, where use of the Tarnhelm allows Siegfried (Wolfgang Windgassen) to disguise himself as Gunther (Dietrich Fischer-Dieskau): Windgassen's tenor voice was given a baritone coloration, so creating an aural representation of his disguise, but reverted to its normal tone at the point when he removes the Tarnhelm.

In their article on Culshaw's opera recordings, David Patmore and Eric Clarke (2007) outline the BSH ideology and then say that 'Culshaw's philosophy of recording was directly opposed to this view of the purpose of recording' (285). This could use a little nuancing. As much as Legge, Culshaw was working within a realist aesthetic. The issue is how far this aesthetic is to be understood in terms of reproduction of the acoustic properties of a concert hall or opera house, as against the translation or recreation of the experience in specifically phonographic terms. Culshaw (279) made the difference clear when, in the leaflet for *Tristan*, he wrote that 'The idea furthest from our minds was to copy, on records, what is heard in the average opera house; instead we tried to ensure that the intense emotional experience of *Tristan und Isolde* should survive the transfer to a medium unknown to the composer, and use to the full whatever advantages that different medium could bestow'. There is a parallel with Michel Chion's distinction (1994: 109) between reproduction and rendering in film sound: 'The film spectator recognizes sounds to be truthful, effective, and fitting not so much if they reproduce what would be heard in the same situation in reality, but if they render (convey, express) the feelings associated with the situation'.

On another occasion Culshaw wrote, with reference to the same recording, that 'What you have to do is to make stereo convey in a way that I think has never been possible on record before, the intensity of feeling in this opera' (275). And he frequently remarked on the lengths to which he went in order to create emotional effects through acoustic means, such as the fear and isolation that Gutrune (Claire Watson) feels in Act III of *Götterdämmerung*, which in the opera house might be conveyed through dim lighting (281). The aim, then, is realism—emotional realism—and it is achieved not through the impossible attempt to reproduce the means by which this emotion would be represented in the opera house, but rather through a directly phonographic representation. Or to put it more generally, the aim is not to recreate the opera-house performance of the work, but to recreate the work itself. It is in this sense that, as the record critic Edward Greenfield wrote, 'The recording of the *Ring* set the seed for what in effect was a new concept in recording as an art-form distinct from live performance' (286).

In *Ring Resounding*, which was published three years after Gould quit the concert stage, Culshaw (1967: 265) paid a warm tribute to 'the distinguished pianist Glenn Gould, who is an extremist in his conviction that the future of music lies entirely in the home'. (It is later in the same paragraph that he builds on Gould's futuristic speculations about do-it-yourself tape editing by suggesting that users will be able to 'produce' operas visually in whatever way they like.) And the feeling was mutual. In 1966 Gould (1987) wrote that 'the "Ring" cycle as produced by a master like John Culshaw for Decca/London attains a more effective unity between intensity of action and displacement of sound than could be afforded by the best of all seasons at Bayreuth' (334). Commentators often couple Culshaw's and Gould's philosophies of recording, which is reasonable to the extent that—to repeat Greenfield's word—both saw recording as an artform independent of the opera house or concert hall. Like both Legge and Culshaw, Gould's starting point was that a recording 'is not a picture postcard of a concert' (Mach 1981: 92). And if there is a parallel between Phase 4 Stereo and Culshaw's approach to phonographic realism, then the parallel with Gould's interpretive approach to recording is all the closer. In effect, Gould developed the idea that recording technology could be deployed on the basis of musical logic. That is the basic principle behind what Gould called 'acoustic choreography', which took him in a direction quite different from Culshaw's.

In 'The prospects of recording' Gould recounts something that had happened the previous year, and that embodies his approach to recording in a nutshell. He was recording the A minor fugue from the first volume of Bach's *Well-Tempered Clavier*, he explains, and had attempted eight takes, the sixth and last of which he and his producer had considered satisfactory: take 6, Gould says, was played 'in a solemn, legato, rather pompous fashion', while take 8 was staccato and skittish (1987: 338–39). At the subsequent editing session, however, both these takes were found to be too monotonous. 'At this point', Gould continues, 'someone noted that, despite the vast differences in character between the two takes, they were performed at an almost identical tempo'—and that quickly gave rise to the solution: use take 6 for the opening and concluding sections of the fugue, and take 8 for 'the episodic modulations with which the center portion of the figure is concerned'.

The particular point Gould wants to make in telling this story is that the result was a much better performance than could have been achieved with a single take, and that post-production allows one to 'transcend the limitations that performance imposes upon the imagination'. But the idea of creating—composing—the final recording out of palpably different recorded materials, and doing so on the basis of the musical structure, is also a general illustration of how Gould conceived of record production as an interpretive act in the same sense that performance is, and more than that, conceived of piano playing and post-production as complementary parts of an integrated performance practice. An interview from 1971 underscores the distance between this conception and the BSH ideology. Gould remarks, 'The tacit assumption in the record business has been that a piano is sitting more or less in front of you, and if you hear the first note in that position you are going to hear the last note accordingly. Nothing upsets a producer more than trying to mingle perspectives' (381). In other words the assumption is that the recording reproduces the performance. The difference between this and Gould's approach is the difference between realism understood in two entirely distinct senses: on the one hand as representing what happens in a concert hall, and on the other as representing the music itself.

Gould's acoustic choreography elaborated this basic conception on the analogy of cinematography. That is how Gould himself described it, with reference to a recording of Sibelius's piano music that he made in 1977 (the only example of his acoustic choreography to be released in his lifetime[8]). All the music was recorded on eight tracks, he explains, comprising four stereo pairs, which could then be mixed in the studio, like the stops of an organ. And he continues:

It's like photographing the music sonically, as though you treated the microphone like a camera. You 'shoot' the score from different angles, so to speak. For example, for the closest of the perspectives, we placed microphones right

8. It was released in November 1977 under the title 'Glenn Gould: Sibelius, 3 Sonatines op. 67—"Kyllikki" op. 41' (Columbia M 34555), re-released on CD within the Sony Classical Glenn Gould Edition, and included on the CD that comes with Bazzana (1997; track 24). A brief account of its making has been left by Andrew Kazdin (1989: 144), who collaborated with Gould on many of his project but notes that 'the Sibelius project was thought up by Glenn alone'. Kazdin (138–39) was also responsible for the technical description provided in the liner notes.

inside the piano—virtually lying on the strings—not unlike a jazz pick-up. The next perspective was my standard one which, for many tastes, is a bit too close for comfort. The third perspective was a sort of discreet Deutsche Grammophon-style European sound, and the fourth and last was back-of-the-hall ambiance[9] (Mach 1981: 97).

The result, Gould adds, is that 'you very often sense that a particular statement, a particular theme, is suddenly much further away from you without at the same time necessarily getting softer'. And these contrasting sonic and spatial qualities are deployed in accordance with musical structure. Kevin Bazzana, who has made a study of the original sources for these recordings, quotes the script of a radio talk from 1978, in which Gould explained his procedure. In the last of the three lyric pieces *Kyllikki*, Gould says, the outer sections are in B-flat major and minor, while the central section is in G-flat major,

> and there's absolutely no modulatory preparation between the two harmonic areas. So, it seemed to me that the way to characterize that transition—or lack of transition—was through a 'zoom shot'. The outer segments, which are virtually identical, are also 'shot' identically—hard cuts only, very bright colours, very tight perspectives—but the moment we hit the G flat major segment, we go to a sort of crow's nest pick-up (Bazzana 1997: 250).

As with Phase 4 Stereo, then, structural aspects of the music are mapped onto the parameters of the recording, just as they might be mapped onto the parameters of piano performance: as Bazzana (252) says, 'For Gould, acoustic choreography was simply a recording artist's extension of such performance practices'. Or to put it in a more traditional way, Gould as both pianist and producer—as performer—is in the business of expressing structure. If I am reverting to the language of page-to-stage theory, that is because Gould's thinking was strongly marked by the premises, if not the methodologies, of structuralist analysis.[10] One of the telling differences between Culshaw and Gould is that the former was fastidious in his consideration of the composer's expressive markings and intentions, whereas Gould—as Bazzana puts it—'treated all scores as if they had been written by Bach, as collections of pitches and rhythms with no firm guidelines as to how they were to be realized in performance'.[11] Gould made his own performance decisions according to what he saw as purely musical criteria. While that does not necessarily mean they are susceptible to straightforward analytical explanation,

9. Spelling of 'Grammophon' corrected.

10. For further discussion see Bazzana (1997: 87–97).

11. Patmore and Clarke (2007: 286); Bazzana (1997: 37), perhaps echoing Taruskin's claim (1995: 114) that modern performance, including HIP, treats all music as if it were composed by Stravinsky.

it helps explain why Gould is one of the most frequently cited performers in the music-theoretical literature.

Up to the 1970s, then, it is possible to tell a story that represents some sort of classical parallel to Moorefield's narrative of popular music production. And there is a little more to tell. The development of quadrophonic sound in the early 1970s prompted a rash of experiments with the use of acoustic space for purposes beyond the BSH paradigm, but there was little takeup—a story that looks like being replicated forty years later in the attempts to transform 5.1 surround round into a major consumer format for music. Then there were Herbert von Karajan's experiments with specifically phonographic effects. Ashby (2010: 52–53) devotes detailed consideration to two of these, a 1975 recording of Schoenberg's Variations for Orchestra op. 31, the chamber-like scoring of which prompted Karajan to reseat the orchestra for each variation, and his 1981 recording of Saint-Saëns's Symphony no. 3, where a large cathedral organ was overdubbed to overwhelming effect in postproduction: each uses the recording process to create a listening experience that, in terms of the BSH paradigm, is frankly contrafactual. But after that the trail runs cold. The controversies that raged in classical recording at that time did not have to do with the BSH paradigm as such, but rather with the ways of realising it—such as the minimalist approach adopted by Nimbus Records, among others, using a single point array of microphones and minimal editing, in contrast to the multi-microphone layouts and complex post-production techniques adopted by the majors. Again, digital technology was embraced in the recording of classical as much as popular music, prompting further controversies over digital versus analogue sound, but was duly assimilated into the BSH paradigm.

But I referred to the BSH paradigm as an ideology, that is, a system of belief that represents artifice as nature. The BSH paradigm embodies a choice, but is not seen that way: rather it is taken for granted, as simply the way things are. In line with Sterne's discourse of fidelity, faithful reproduction is transparent, it effaces itself. Or to put it another way, the semiotics of representation that I discussed in Chapter 11 is naturalised, in much the same way as classic cinematic representation: just as, to repeat Gorbman's word, Hollywood film music aims to be 'unheard', perceived not in itself but in the shaping of narrative or the sharpening of character, so audio production within the BSH paradigm aspires to inaudibility. But at the same time, ideological representations of how things are frequently mask quite divergent practices, and this applies to classical recordings. Despite Legge's maxim and the advertisers' straplines, mainstream production practice has in reality been concerned more with creating the effect of transparency than with literal reproduction of concert hall experience.

A telling illustration of this is a production practice that Adam Krims has presented as a move away from the representation of concert experience. His starting point is classical crossover. Recordings made by the British singers Sarah Brightman and Charlotte Church around 2000, Krims explains, 'tended to frame the voice in a highly resonant space, in which the voices seem to float ethereally,

losing their traces of corporal production: breaths, any reedy timbre, the shaping
by bodily production of vocal sound effects, often against the singer's will—
all recede in the beautified haze of floating, resonant sound' (2007: 136).
But, he continues, these production values have not been restricted to the
hybrid genre of classical crossover; they also appear in what, in terms of repertory and performance practice, must be regarded as mainstream classical
recordings. The description I have just quoted also takes in the recordings of
Anonymous 4, the *a cappella* ensemble specialising in medieval music, whose
commercial success is built on solid scholarly foundations (and a member of
which is Susan Hellauer, whose comments on the matching of vowel sounds
I quoted in Chapter 8).

Other artists whom Krims specifically mentions include Yo-Yo Ma and, in particular, Christine Schornsheim, whose 1997 recording of C. P. E. Bach's *Organ
Concerto* Wq 34 with the Akademie für Alte Musik (issued—like Anonymous 4's
recordings—on the highly respectable label Harmonia Mundi) he describes in
some detail. Through 'the combination of close microphone placement, spacious
stereo imaging, and highly resonant space', Krims says, this recording creates a
sound image in which instrumental detail emerges in high relief, but is located
within a cavernous, resonant space. The result is the creation of

> an *abstract musical soundstage*, not mimetically referring to any achievable
> live concert experience and not audible outside the mediating presence of
> the recording itself.... Such a playback space suggests a new manner of con-
> ceiving and constructing the recorded-music listening situation, diverging
> from the traditional notion of concert realism (which, however, in a continu-
> ation of older concert discourses, continues occasionally in classical record-
> ing advertising to this day) (2007: 144).

But what Krims presents as a new, anti-realistic practice of production might well
be seen as falling within the established practices of mainstream classical production at the turn of the twenty-first century.[12] While the discourses of BSH pro-
claim the paradigm of reproduction, studio practices have been directed at the
reconstruction of reality, in this way pursuing what in Chapter 11 I described as
an aesthetic of hyperrealism. The BSH paradigm has conditioned classical record
production, but in terms of transparency and self-effacement rather than the
actual reproduction of concert experience. It is in terms of the frankly interventionist production exemplified by Culshaw and Gould—the creation of a phonographic experience that proclaims its difference from concert experience—that, as
I said, the trail has run cold.

There are just a few exceptions. One is a double CD of piano music composed
in 1908–09, entitled *Remixing Modernism* and released in 2010 under the aus-
pices of the Queensland Conservatorium Research Centre (which has become

---

12. I owe this point to Myles Eastwood.

a centre for practice as research both within Australia and internationally).[13] Based on concerts prompted by the centenary of these works, this CD was a collaboration between pianist Stephen Emmerson and recordist Paul Draper, both of whom are on the conservatorium's academic faculty. As described in the CD booklet, Emmerson originally envisaged a standard studio recording, and indeed the CD as released includes this on the first, so-called horizontal disc. In discussion, however, the idea emerged of a more interventionist approach based on the combination of multitracking and contrasted microphone placements, in line with Gould's acoustic choreography. However, as Draper explains, 'this primary sonic palette proved to be surprisingly limited and so we increasingly drew upon modern popular music production techniques including the automation of DSP plug-ins for equalisation, pitch, reverberation, stereo field, distortion and compression' (2009: 18). The intervention is sometimes subtle and sometimes overt, the first of Schoenberg's Three Piano Pieces op. 11 providing an example of the latter: movement between four groups of microphones and additional DSP (digital signal processing) effects heighten the musical detail, in Draper and Emmerson's words 'responding to the kaleidoscopic musical gestures' (2011). In the case of Berg's Sonata op. 1, by contrast, the emphasis is more on underlining the structural divisions and smooth transitions of the sonata form. It is this interventionist production that is presented on the second, 'vertical' disc (so named after the visual appearance of the multiple tracks in Pro Tools).

Though Draper's and Emmerson's use of digital effects greatly extends the techniques that Gould used, the conceptual resonances are strong. Like Gould, Draper and Emmerson underline the collaborative nature of the project ('a collaboration between very different sets of ears that were brought to bear upon every aspect and every decision involved in the process' [2011]), and the extent to which 'insights attained in post-production may lead to concepts for the music that were not evident earlier' (2008: 35). Again, they emphasise that the purpose of their interventions was 'not to impose sound effects on the music, but to magnify the interpretations' (32): production decisions 'reflected the nature of the work's musical language', whether in terms of structural articulation or expressive content (2011). It might, of course, be hard to claim anything else within an academic milieu where structurally or otherwise discursively defensible interpretation is valued above personal taste or idiosyncrasy.

The institutional context is perhaps also responsible for a certain diffidence that pervades the representation of the project. Gould, as we saw, had little concern with composers' intentions: he simply worked with the notes. Draper and Emmerson (2011), by contrast, invoke statements by Schoenberg to the effect that each age has its own interpretive ideas, and that parameters such as dynamics, tempo, and timbre are not fixed elements of the work but rather resources

13. Stephen Emmerson, *Remixing Modernism: Berg, Schoenberg, Bartók* (1908–09), Move Records MD 4431 (2010). The omission of Draper's name from the CD sleeve is inexplicable; who, after all, did the remixing?

to be employed by the performer: it is as if they felt the need to seek his permission before intervening in his music. Defensiveness also emerges from their
acknowledgement that their approach is 'potentially provocative and challenges
some deeply embedded assumptions about Classical music'. Finally it is revealing that there was clearly considerable disagreement and soul searching about
how the project might finally be disseminated. We learn from the 2008 paper
that at this stage Emmerson favoured a DVD that would allow users to choose
between production treatments (which sounds very like Gould's speculations
about do-it-yourself tape editing). Draper, however, regarded that as a mere novelty project, and favoured the twin CD approach—which Emmerson saw as 'an
ill-conceived commercial stance given a limited audience' (2008: 35). Evidently
Draper won the argument.

If Schoenberg represents one principal strain of modernist composition and
(through Kolisch and Steuermann) performance practice, then Stravinsky represents the other, so it is fitting that two further examples of radically interventionist production involve *The Rite of Spring*. Of these, the one that is closer

to Draper and Emmerson's approach is an experimental remix of 'Jeu de rapt'
(Media example 12.1), created in 2006 by Steve Savage and Lolly Lewis for
a CHARM workshop entitled 'Creative production for classical music'. This was
based on the multitrack master files from a commercial recording of *The Rite* that
the San Francisco Symphony had recently made, and the basic idea was to subject
them to the kind of DSP treatment that Savage uses in his professional practice
as a pop producer. Compared to Draper's and Emmerson's work, that of Savage
and Lewis exploits more aggressive effects designed, for example, for guitar amp
distortion or rock and roll drum processing. The overall philosophy is perhaps
less like Gould than like an augmented version of Phase 4 Stereo, and at times
less like Phase 4 Stereo than like Culshaw. As in the case of Culshaw's Wagner
productions, so one of Savage's and Lewis's primary aims was 'to heighten the
violent subtext' of 'Jeu de rapt' (Savage 2006: 1), in other words, to create emotion
through directly phonographic means. In Chion's language, this is rendering, not
reproduction.

The other recording of *The Rite* to which I referred comes from a quite different direction, but makes an interesting comparison for just that reason. Stefan
Goldmann is a Berlin-based DJ and electronica composer who, in 2009, released
an edited version of *The Rite* made up of '146 individually treated segments' from
'over a dozen' (apparently fourteen) commercial recordings of the work.[14] 'At
first listen', Goldmann writes, 'you hardly recognise it's been edited at all. Every
couple of seconds though you find yourself in a different room, listening to a
different orchestra under a different conductor. A journey through microphone
positions and mixdown decisions. Each time a different world in the headphone.'

---

14. 'Igor Stravinsky, *Le Sacre de Printemps*, Stefan Goldmann edit', Macro M10 (2009). Details
and the following quotes from Goldmann are taken from his web site, http://sgoldmann.word-
press.com/2009/06/30/igor-stravinsky-le-sacre-du-printemps-stefan-goldmann-edit/.

The effect is subtle, perhaps too subtle, even on headphones. Or perhaps that it the point: precisely because it *almost* sounds like an ordinary recording, it creates an effect that becomes increasingly unsettling as you listen. Colin Shields describes it on the Little White Earbuds website:

> Goldmann's edit combines subtle layers of tone in ways that jar and frustrate, because no orchestra should be able to combine them in one sitting. Goldmann's track is creepy. The familiar feeling of hearing an orchestra perform, subverted minute by minute by a collision of sounds that shouldn't quite be with one another, gets under the skin...the wonderfully subtle feeling of standing on wobbly ground Goldmann creates here is a real treat (2009).

On his website Goldmann makes a reference to 'the great Tonmeister-tradition and the "invisible editing" techniques employed in classical music where the utmost goal is to keep engineering inaudible', and the obvious way in which to interpret this recording is as a Brechtian critique of the idea of transparency that underlies the BSH ideology. That, at any rate, is the clear implication of the quotation from the mastering engineer Bob Katz that Goldmann places prominently on the web page for this CD: 'I'm so paranoid I sometimes believe I can hear edits at live concerts'. It is also uncannily reminiscent, if in a rather distorted way, of another of Gould's speculations about do-it-yourself tape editing: 'you could snip out these measures from the Klemperer edition and splice them into the Walter performance.... There is, in fact, nothing to prevent a dedicated connoisseur from acting as his own tape editor' (1987: 348).

The examples of Draper and Emmerson, Savage and Lewis, and Goldmann hardly add up to a coherent trend, but at least they enable us to pose a question: Might such explicitly phonographic approaches create new options for the presentation of classical music within a culture increasingly attuned to the values of digitally mediated sound? Draper and Emmerson broach this issue. 'Initial reactions to the "vertical" album have been uniformly strong', they say (2009: 4). One the one hand, some people are 'outraged that we should interfere in such ways against the "Viennese tradition"'. (Andrew Kazdin [1989: 143], the producer and sound engineer who collaborated with Gould on most of his recordings, notes that some critics reacted to Gould's Sibelius disc in the same way: 'the most outraged of the reviewers suggested that this recoding was either a joke on Kazdin by Gould, or a joke on Gould by Kazdin, or a joke on everyone else by Kazdin and Gould'.) On the other hand, Draper and Emmerson continue, some people 'are so enthralled that they rewind, discuss, and listen again to uncover more meaning'. They conclude, optimistically, that 'our early approaches to DSP orchestration are beginning to offer a promising route for audiences to experience and reinterpret classical music recordings as virtual artworks in their own right'. And in his paper, Savage writes: 'Might this kind of mixing open up this music to ears that are steeped in the hyperreal sound of pop music recordings? Could mixes such as these help to reinvigorate the classical music market? I can't answer these questions' (2006: 12).

Nor of course can anybody else, but it is worth considering the larger context to which Savage refers. In 2003, Bill Holland, at that time divisional director of Universal Classics and Jazz, was quoted as saying that the classical music industry had 'no option but to break down barriers and respond to modern tastes.... Everything you would ever want to record in the way of broadstream repertoire has been recorded. How many versions do you need of standard works?'[15] Now a standard business response to the kind of saturated market Holland describes is to make your product different from the others. And, if you are producing records, then using production techniques to create distinct and distinctive phonographic experiences—whether or not along the lines of the work I have described—might seem an obvious route to explore. Judging by the responses Draper and Emmerson received, some people are receptive to such approaches, and if others aren't, then that is in the nature of markets: you offer different products to different consumers. That is after all what happened in the days of Phase 4 Stereo, which as D'Amato said was a commercial success outside the UK.

There is also a further consideration related to patterns of consumption. Peter Hill (2009) questions the record industry's 'axiomatic belief that flaws that would go unnoticed in a concert become irritants with repeated listening' (14), and the same objection might well be made to the kind of highly interventionist recordings I have been describing. But the practice of repeatedly listening to the same disc is a function of people building their own record collections, which for most of its history was the economic basis of the record industry. As consumers increasingly access music via streaming services such as last.fm and Spotify, however, this becomes an increasingly irrelevant criterion: the pattern now becomes one of renting music rather than owning it, and the consequence is that consumers are no longer locked into hearing the same recording over and over again. It seems likely that one of the root causes of the record industry's historical reluctance to grasp new opportunities offered by changing technologies has been what lay behind the outraged responses of some listeners to Draper's and Emmerson's 'vertical' recording, or for that matter the critic Thomas Heinetz's description of Stokowski's Phase 4 recording of Rimsky-Korsakov's *Scheherazade* as 'a hideous crime' (Symes 2004: 76): the entrenched way of thinking I have variously described as the paradigm of reproduction, the discourse of fidelity, and the BSH ideology—a way of thinking that rules out alternatives while not even acknowledging that there are alternatives to be ruled out.

It is as if the conceptual model of original and copy suffused and constrained the industry's business practices as much as its production approaches. The key

---

15. Ian Burrell, 'Record giant spends £6M on operatic quintet hailed as saviours', *Independent*, 5 July 2003. The context of this remark was the contract offered by BMG to Amici Forever, a relatively unknown group of classically trained singers operating on the borders between opera and pop.

innovations in marketising these opportunities, after all, have come from outside a music industry now—with Universal's acquisition of EMI—reduced to three global corporations. While the majors were busy suing peer-to-peer file-sharing services and lobbying politicians in order to perpetuate an obsolete business model based on sale of physical copies, Apple captured the music retail market: introduced in 2003, the iTunes store became the biggest music vendor in the United States in 2008, and in the world two years later. It is also striking that among the various founders of last.fm and Spotify, not one came from a background in the music industry. They came from deejaying, games, computer engineering, and internet marketing.

RETHINKING THE CONCERT

The recordings I described in the last few pages might be described as classical remixes, but the term is generally applied to another genre that draws on the same technologies but combines classical materials with the approaches of hip-hop and other RW cultures based on sampling. The genre might be traced back to Steve Reich's album *Remixed* (1998), in which various of Reich's concert pieces were remixed by the likes of Coldcut,[16] but in the UK the classical remix is particularly associated with the London-based Nonclassical record label established by Gabriel Prokofiev: grandson of Sergei, Prokofiev is a composer of contemporary classical music and electronica, as well as a record producer. Rather like *Remixing Modernism*, many Nonclassical releases combine conventionally produced instrumental recordings with remixed versions. The difference is that—unlike *Remixing Modernism*—the Nonclassical remixes do not retain the timeline of the original. Prokofiev's own String Quartet no. 2, for example, appeared in 2007 on a CD that includes not only the four-movement original played by the Elysian Quartet but also remixes of individual movements by a variety of artists with backgrounds in electronic and dance genres (including Prokofiev himself).[17] The remix of the second movement by the dubstep duo Vex'd, for instance, incorporates fragments of Prokofiev's often post-Stravinskian writing within textures whose connotations range from avant-garde to ambient to electronica.

Four of the remixes (including Prokofiev's and the Vex'd one) are also released as a 12-inch vinyl album, which provides a clue to one of the purposes for which they are intended. Nonclassical is not just a record label: it is a larger project to disseminate contemporary classical music in non-classical surroundings (hence the name), in particular through club nights held at the time of writing at The

16. In fairness it should be noted that *Remixed* was released by a Warner label, Nonesuch—which also co-promoted the remixing competition based on Reich's *2 X 5* (pp. 350–51).

17. 'The Elysian Quartet/Gabriel Prokofiev/String Quartet no. 2/With Remixes by/Hot Chip/Vex'd/The Earlyman/Conboy/Starkey/Marcus Lancaster & Eric Shinn', Nonclassical (2007).

Macbeth in Hoxton, East London. The 'About' page on the Nonclassical web site pulls no punches:

> At each event, innovative and virtuosic classical musicians blow away audiences with their incredible musicianship and new compositions. The success of the night partly stems from the fact that it presents Classical as if it were Rock or Electronic music. Bands play through the pub's PA, everyone has a pint in their hand and perhaps most importantly there are DJs playing throughout the night. Even the most sceptical visitors to the club can't help but be stimulated by being so close to the high-quality musicianship presented at NONCLASSICAL. Classical music can be part of everyone's lives and this night is part of rediscovering its relevance.[18]

The remixes, then, feature in the DJ sets with which club nights begin. As Prokofiev explains, 'The idea of a DJ is that there's background music that uses the sound of classical contemporary music, primarily through remixes, to get people in the zone, so that by the time the performers come out the audience are warmed up and have a real sense of anticipation' (Battle 2010). Once again there is a resonance with Gould, who argued for the neglected potential of background music to give listeners familiarity with a wide range of styles (1987: 350–51).

There is a long tradition of classical music being staged at alternative venues ranging from stately homes to art galleries, and Nonclassical is just one of many recent ventures to bring music of the classical tradition to new places and to encourage the socialised listening practices conventionally associated with jazz clubs rather than concert halls. I will not attempt a general survey, but just to make the point, similar initiatives in London alone include Classical Revolution, the London operation of an international movement that began in San Francisco in 2006, which in particular features jam sessions; Limelight, which operates at The 100 Club—a basement venue that in the past hosted B. B. King and the Sex Pistols— and whose strapline is 'Classical music in a rock 'n' roll setting'; the Little Proms ('These "Concerts" are more like Indie gigs, We mic it up, drink beer and have a thoroughly great night'); the Yellow Lounge Classical Club, a concert series held in the arched tunnels at the back of Waterloo station; Multi-Storey, which promotes orchestral concerts in the (former) Peckham Rye Multi-Storey Car Park; Carmen Elektra (not to be confused with the actress and glamour model), which specialises in opera clubnights consisting of short, contemporary operas interspersed with DJ sets; and the Orchestra of the Age of Enlightenment's Night Shift pub crawls, which again feature DJ sets.[19] Some of these, such as Limelight and Multi-Storey, are oriented towards a more general classical repertory, whereas others specifically focus on

---

18. http://www.nonclassical.co.uk/?page_id=2.

19. http://www.classicalrevolutionlondon.org/; http://www.londonlimelight.co.uk/; http://www.remotegoat.co.uk/event_view.php?uid=23366; http://www.multi-story.org.uk/; http://carmen-elektra.com/about.html; http://www.oae.co.uk/thenightshift/.

new and experimental repertory (including Nonclassical, though it does hold occasional 'Historical nights' celebrating figures like Schoenberg and Cage). And Carmen Elektra's strapline is 'Opera underground', perhaps expressing more than the fact that some of its performances take place in cellars.

But the movement in general is receiving support from some of the big beasts of the classical music establishment. In the august pages of the *Telegraph*, the critic Ivan Hewitt writes of the Yellow Lounge Classical Club that 'One could feel the pack-ice of the concert format cracking, and the heat was coming from a new sort of interaction between people, space and music'.[20] In the pages of the *Observer*, a discussion took place between the composer Jonathan Harvey and the cellist Julian Lloyd-Webber, in which Harvey advocated the use of amplification in classical concerts to create a more relaxed environment in which people could come and go; Lloyd-Webber argued that a better way to encourage new audiences is to relocate performances to venues like nightclubs, adding 'I think that can work very well' (Thorpe 2010). And in his Royal Philharmonic Society Lecture of the same year, which took place in London's Wigmore Hall, Alex Ross made the same point as Lloyd-Webber. The non-electronic nature of the concert hall, he argues, is 'the most distinctive quality of the place', but at the same time he refers to 'the encouraging trend in contemporary classical performance...to bring musicians out of their accustomed, "official" settings and place them in more intimate environments' (2010). He makes specific reference to Prokofiev.

What Harvey, Lloyd-Webber, Ross, and Prokofiev all share is unease about the institution of the classical concert, not least because—in Lawrence Kramer's words (1995)—its audiences are 'shrinking, graying, and overly pale-faced' (4). If the aim in disseminating classical music should be to use to the full whatever advantages a given medium can bestow, as Culshaw said of his gramophone operas, then how far can the medium of the classical concert be said to do that? I would argue not very far, and once again I would blame the paradigm of reproduction, this time in its guise as the aesthetics of autonomy. Conceived in terms of the aesthetic values that developed during the nineteenth century and were consolidated into early twentieth-century modernism, the classical concert is designed to recreate, as far as is possible within the context of an event funded by a paying public, the subjective experience illustrated by Fernand Khnopff's painting *Listening to Schumann* (Figure 1.2). It is a system for the delivery of musical works to individual listeners built, in Small's words, on 'the assumption that a musical performance is a system of one-way communication' (1998: 26). Hence a seating arrangement that orients each listener towards the stage, in contrast with the social interaction designed into the boxes of traditional theatres: according to Small, 'The auditorium's design not only discourages communication among members of the audience but also tells them that they are there to listen and not talk back' (127). Again compared with a traditional theatre, décor is restrained to avoid visual interference. In a cultural

20. *Telegraph*, 6 December 2011 (http://www.telegraph.co.uk/culture/music/classicalconcert-reviews/8937872/Yellow-Lounge-Classical-Club-Old-Vic-Tunnels-review.html).

rather than acoustic sense the hi-fi concert hall is a low-grade anechoic chamber. Reduced as far as possible to sound alone, music is decontextualised, presented as an ideal sound object to be apprehended on its own terms and for itself.

Small's interpretation of the Western classical concert is overwhelmingly negative, emphasising the extent to which it serves to maintain social hegemonies. My criticism is different. I have no wish to denigrate the strong experience of music, to misquote Gabrielsson's phrase (2011), that is connoted by Khnopff's painting. In line with my discussion in Chapter 10 of the listening body, music heard with closed eyes—what Kivy (1990) called music alone—is a visual and kinesthetic experience as much as an auditory one, an experience of being kinetically and emotionally moved that is perhaps the more vivid for being virtual rather than actual. In Clarke's words, the 'emphasis on abstraction and ineffability' to which the concert aspires can lead to 'a particularly intense kind of auditory attention and involvement' (2007: 50). And under such circumstances the social dimension of music is as irrelevant as the visual dimension, or more accurately, both are liabilities to be mitigated by any available means.[21] But as a justification for the concert, the problem with this is obvious. As Sennheiser are well aware, if that is your aim, then it is nowadays much better achieved by listening through high-quality headphones to a high-quality recording, preferably in a darkened room. That is actually what Clarke was referring to, and it is a much more satisfactory realisation of traditional aesthetic ideals of transcendence than any concert hall can provide.

The basic thesis of Ashby's 2010 book is that 'absolute music and its attendant cultures have in important respects been embodied—even encouraged—by recording' (55), and it is precisely for this decontextualised, desocialised experience of music that listeners have valued the gramophone. That applies as much to Lionel Gilman in 1925 or Katz's unnamed writer of seven years later, who spoke of the hall, audience, and performer being disposed of,[22] as it does to the composer Milton Babbitt ('I can't believe that people really prefer to go to the concert hall under intellectually trying, socially trying, physically trying conditions, unable to repeat something they have missed, when they can sit at home under the most comfortable and stimulating circumstances and hear it as they want to hear it'),[23] or to Glenn Gould:

> as far as I'm concerned, music is something that ought to be listened to in private. I do not believe it should be treated as group therapy or any other kind

---

21. Including concerts in the dark: the 2013 Bristol Proms offered an example of this niche phenomenon, with the Fitzhardinge Consort performing a programme that included Gesualdo's Tenebrae Responsories 'in complete darkness. Proper darkness. Darkness so dark you can't see your hand in front of your face…in which exquisite choral music and harmony glow like light' (http://www.bristololdvic.org.uk/bristolproms.html#singing).

22. See Chapter 11, p. 345.

23. Quoted in Gould (1966, the original version of 'The prospects of recording', which contained quotations from other musicians omitted when it was reprinted in Gould [1987]).

of communal experience. I think that music ought to lead the listener—and, indeed, the performer—to a state of contemplation, and I don't think it's really possible to attain that condition with 2,999 other souls sitting all around (Mach 1981: 102).

So what kind of rational cost-benefit calculation might lead people to go to a concert? The answer, clearly, has to do with the things that are not delivered by even the highest-quality headphones. One obvious example is the visual dimension. In Chapter 10 I cited Dineen's admiration for the dance that Kubelick performed before the orchestra, and also Huang and Krumhansl's study showing the positive effect of stage behaviour on the experiences of novice concert goers; Melissa Dobson and Stephanie Pitts (2011: 366) replicated Huang's and Krumhansl's results with British audiences. Given this, it is testimony to the perverse influence of the paradigm of reproduction that the visual dimension of concert performance is not given greater emphasis in musical practice, education, and criticism. Today's novice concert goers are after all tomorrow's classical audiences.

There are signs of change. As in stadium concerts and the opera house, so in the concert hall the combination of live performance with screen images is increasingly common. The publicity for a concert by the pianist Jan Lisiecki at the 2013 Bristol Proms, for example, promised 'an up-close and personal performance' that was 'filmed from every angle and projected on a single screen behind the performer'.[24] And it is not just a matter of presentation: there are a small number of classical musicians who build a considered and creative approach to the visual dimension into the very act of performance. An example is the Chicago-based chamber ensemble eighth blackbird, who specialise in contemporary music. In a tradition that echoes the Kolisch Quartet, eighth blackbird memorise their core repertory. Unlike the Kolisch Quartet, however, eighth blackbird use the resulting liberation from fixed music stands to move around as they play. As has long been standard practice with pop singers, especially since the development of the wireless microphone,[25] choreography becomes an interpretive dimension of performance, with effects that range from the projection of structure to the production of narrative or dramatic meaning. The real space of the stage is in this way used in a manner analogous to the virtual space of Gould's recordings. It is possible to gain some idea of eighth blackbird's approach from YouTube,[26] but tellingly, the experience is not the same. It is partly that you lose the auditory dimension of

24. http://www.bristololdvic.org.uk/bristolproms.html#angles. The performance was also relayed in real time to an adjacent venue, where images derived from multiple cameras and motion detection technology contributed to an 'augmented and experimental event, which will attempt to expand and explore the concept of liveness' (http://www.watershed.co.uk/whatson/4235/jan-lisiecki-from-every-angle/).

25. For a rare example of musicological analysis of the use of stage and auditorium space in performance, see Heinonen (2010).

26. See, for example, their performance of Derek Bermel's *Tied Shifts* at http://www.youtube.com/watch?v=PJaC1tVoSm4.

the movement on stage. But more important is how the combination of acoustic, visual, and kinesthetic movement carries the music beyond the stage to suffuse the social as well as physical space of the auditorium. This is performance that uses to the full the advantages of the classical concert medium, within the constraints of traditional concert hall seating.

As Small argues, the crucial dimension of the concert experience is the sense of occasion, of being part of a community of shared experience. This is a dimension of sociality that is different from, as it were built on top of, the sociality that is inscribed within the sound of music, recorded or otherwise. Dobson and Pitts found that for novice concert goers 'the engagement of live listening is closely connected with feeling comfortable, welcome, and engaged amongst an audience of regular attendees' (2011: 370); too bad then that some aspects of concert etiquette—in particular the ban on clapping between movements, which is a twentieth-century invention (Ross 2010)—seem calculated to rebuff new audiences. Again, the sense of community is one of the things that motivate the exodus of classical music from the concert hall to the nightclub. And it is central to Lawrence Kramer's nostalgic memories (2007) of the outdoor concerts in New York City that he attended as a teenager: 'Some of my most vivid memories of the time involve summer nights in a stadium filled with people from all walks of life, from all over the city. The acoustics were terrible; the pleasure was overflowing; the ovations were long and noisy' (2). Yet in the concert hall, according to Leon Botstein (2003: 297), the communal dimension has been in retreat since 1950, or even as far back as 1914. Perhaps in setting the latter date Botstein is thinking of Vienna's much loved Bösendorfer-Saal, which was demolished just before the First World War and so became a symbol of the world that had disappeared: in another context Botstein quotes Oscar Teuber's description of it as a ' "family space", the scene of intimate music-making....The audience were always aware who was in attendance, bowing and greeting one another, much like a family'. Ironically, the nearest contemporary equivalent to this that I know is Second Life.[27]

To be sure, traces of the concert as the shared experience of a community of listeners survive in the age of digital sound and the internet, even in the largest venues. An obvious example is the Proms[28]: as Hewitt (2007) has described, there is a strong sense of community among the promenaders, and the last night (which largely consists of obligatory standards such as Elgar's 'Pomp and Circumstance' March no. 1 and Henry Wood's *Fantasia on British Sea Songs*) is a national institution. You go to participate in a collective performance of ritual in the sense that Rita Felski defines the term: activities gain value, she says, 'because they repeat what has gone before. Repetition, understood as ritual, provides a connection to ancestry and tradition; it situates the individual in an imagined community that

27. For further details see Cook (2013b).

28. The Henry Wood Promenade Concerts, presented annually by the BBC at London's Royal Albert Hall. A principal feature is the standing areas in the arena and gallery: 'promenading' or 'promming' tickets for these areas are much cheaper than those for reserved seating.

spans historical time. It is…the means of transcending one's historically limited existence' (1999: 20). The Proms have run continuously since 1895—even through the two world wars—and while they are nowadays at the cutting edge of digital dissemination and outreach (Lawson and Stowell 2012: 819), they might also be said to preserve certain aspects of premodern concert behaviour in aspic.

Then again, people go to concerts because they want to witness—to have seen in their lifetime, to have grown older in the presence of—a charismatic performer. That is what I missed out on at the Isle of Wight Festival in 1970, and—as Kenneth Hamilton (2008) explains—it is a motive for concert attendance that was built into the structure of Liszt's concerts in large venues (262). When he played in the vast Hall of the Nobility in St Petersburg, Hamilton says, Liszt had a small stage erected in the very centre of the hall. He

> entered the hall for the first recital on the arm of one of the most prominent of the Russian noblemen, made his way through the chattering audience, then positively leapt up onto the platform, deliberately ignoring steps that had been set up to make his ascent easier (and to take him directly past the view of the royal box). He then took off his white gloves and threw them theatrically under one of the pianos.

The breach of etiquette resulted in a stunned silence, broken as Liszt began to play. As with Michelangeli's television film of Chopin's op. 33 no. 4, Liszt's performance began long before he played the first note. People also go to concerts because they value the kind of interaction with the artist that is possible in the concert situation—provided, of course, that it is the right concert situation. In Liszt's smaller concerts, Hamilton says,

> There would have been pauses in which he chatted to friends in the audience or even addressed the entire public. The programmed works would have been further separated by improvised preludes (no doubt designed to offer some contrast with what had gone before). In other words, Liszt's recitals were structured by improvisation and social activity, all bound together by the magnetism of the performer (2008: 261).

The point is not, of course, to revive premodern concert conventions in any literal sense, complete with white gloves tossed under the piano. Hamilton's account of Liszt's concerts, which draws on the contemporary testimony of Vladimir Stasov, appears in the course of a revealing discussion of his own attempts, at the request of the Istanbul International Festival, to 're-create' the concerts Liszt gave in the city during 1847. In order to do that you have to factor in modern audience expectations, he says—and of course, it helps to be Liszt.

If anybody fulfils *that* criterion today, it is the Chinese pianist Lang Lang, whose concerts might be seen as translating Liszt's into the terms of the twenty-first century. Thomas Grube's film *Lang Lang Live at the Roundhouse* is based on an all-Liszt concert from July 2011 that drew heavily on the conventions of pop

BEYOND THE SCORE

performance. Lang Lang emerges from a cloud of dry ice, and a one point paper petals fall from above. Like Sokolov, Lang Lang choreographs the music with his body, but unlike Sokolov, his version of what I called 'piano face' comes straight out of the world of rock guitar performance. After nailing the Sixth Hungarian Rhapsody, Lang Lang punches the air, tells the audience 'Love you guys', and adds, 'Well, that was a workout'. Audience members respond by waving their hands above their heads, sometimes with their forefingers pointing outwards, just as they might at the Glastonbury Festival. The point is not, however, the dry ice and paper petals as such, any more than it was Liszt's white gloves. It is that the concert is conceived as a social occasion rather than a music delivery system. That resonates with the key conclusion Botstein (2003: 299) draws from his analysis of the orchestral concert today: 'the conductor', he writes, 'must forge a construct of meaning that confronts the reality that every concert is a civic and political event'. He then goes into considerable detail about what that might mean in practice.

If classical concerts and recordings rarely use to the full the advantages that their respective media bestow, the reason is the entrenched ways of thinking that I have documented in this book—ways of thinking that drew on earlier elements but condensed during the first half of the twentieth century, and especially during the interwar years, into the exclusive aesthetic system known as modernism. As a result, the post-war years saw a degree of consensus about how classical music should go that had not previously existed: symptoms range from closer adherence to the score to the sense of musical time being a neutral medium rather than a dimension of content. And though this consensus was challenged by HIP, especially as the latter began its steady march towards modern times, what was not challenged—or has only more recently started to be challenged—is the idea that there is in essence a right way to play music, and that to play it otherwise is to do wrong. (The issue that divided the early HIP ideologues and the proponents of the mainstream was not whether there was a right way to play the music, but what it was.) And when I say 'do wrong', I intend the moral connotations. In this book I have repeatedly referred to the ethically charged vocabulary that surrounds the performance of music, which came to the fore in the debate around HIP but is equally embedded in the ideas of *Werktreue*, faithfulness to composers' intentions, and high-fidelity recording. Equally a keyword of the discourses around WAM and rock, the idea of authenticity reaches into all of these domains, and adds the dimension of personal sincerity.

As we saw in Chapter 1, this kind of language, and the imperative tone that goes with it, date back at least as far as the days of Schoenbergian modernism, and they have much in common with modernism in other arts during the interwar period. The most obvious comparison is with Le Corbusier (1927). There is his denial of style ('The "styles" are a lie' [9]), in essence a covert claim that how you think things should go is the only way they can possibly go. There is his emphasis on aesthetic purity, which shades into megalomania and at times—as in his dealings with Mussolini (Weber 2008: 359–60)—totalitarianism. But above all there is his relentlessly moralistic tone, with its constant message that there is one right way to build, and that other ways are not just aesthetically but ethically wrong. I suggested in Chapter 6 that it was, in particular, through Stravinsky that the positivist values of the *Neue Sachlichkeit* became entrenched in the sphere of music as an enduring philosophy of performance, long after other arts had left it behind it as a passing fad. At all events, the idea that cultural choices are a matter of right and wrong endured in music long after it had waned, if not disappeared, in other fields.[29] And, as Leech-Wilkinson (2012: paragraph 3.3) argues, there are structures in the world of classical music that maintain this status quo: 'performers who dared to offer a radically different view', he writes, 'would be slapped down by performance police (teachers, critics, bloggers) and spurned by potential employers (agents, conductors, ensembles, venue managers, record and radio producers). Where is the incentive to innovate when maintaining traditions is the very focus of everyone's professional engagement with music?'

As I suggested in Chapter 1, the point is simply made by comparing the practices and discourses of WAM with those of the theatre or even opera. Worthen writes that 'throughout its stage history the ongoing vitality of Shakespearean drama has depended on the ability to fashion Shakespeare's writing into the fashionable behavior indigenous to the changing tastes of the stage' (2003: 24). Again, Peter Sellars's productions of the Mozart–Da Ponte operas—for example with *The Marriage of Figaro* set in a luxury apartment at New York's Trump Tower—have provoked plenty of controversy: even critics favorably disposed to them, writes David Littlejohn (1992), 'admit to being unhappy with some of his grosser inconsistencies, and with his dark and narrow visions of the Mozart–Da Ponte worlds. But', Littlejohn continues,

> they have little or no trouble with his contemporary American restagings, which they regard (I am paraphrasing) as viable starting points for explorations of the emotional life of these operas in overtly modern terms. They praise the operas' cultural immediacy and passionate vitality....Above all, they praise the theatricalism, the high-spirited intensity, and the ensemble finesse (142).

Yet the music in such productions continues to be performed according to a quite different aesthetic that prioritises faithfulness to the text, to tradition, and to the composer's intentions or expectations. Taruskin (1995: 24) calls this a 'pseudo-ethics, born of a misplaced sense of obligation', and adds: 'A performer cannot please or move the ancient dead and owes them no such effort. There is no way we can harm Bach or Mozart any more, nor any way that we can earn their gratitude'. Kivy (1995: 151) agrees. And more generally, Kramer (2007) suggests that, if classical music 'seems stuffy and outdated to too many people', one of the reasons is that 'we insist on walking on eggshells in its vicinity. We talk about it too timidly when we talk about it at all, and we listen to it too ceremoniously' (78–79).

29. Though not in television talent shows: witness the authoritarianism embodied in the titles as much as the practices of the popular BBC programmes *Maestro* and *Masterchef.*

But more than that, we perform it as if we were walking on eggshells. I would suggest that classical music is much tougher, much more resilient than the majority of classical musicians, critics, and musicologists give it credit for being. It continues to make sense when arranged for ensembles wildly different from that for which it was written, when imported into entirely different stylistic idioms such as those of rock and pop, or when recontextualised in cigar commercials.[30] It stands to reason, then, that it also continues to make sense when played in the innumerable ways that are made possible by the multiplicity of available performance parameters and the complex interactions between them. Daniel Leech-Wilkinson and Mine Doğantan-Dack have recently been experimenting with what might be seen as perverse performance practices, such as playing repertory pieces two or three times faster or slower than would normally be considered acceptable— which inevitably has knock-on effects for other parameters.[31] It seems to be hard to create a performance that does not make *some* kind of sense, though the sense may well be very different from what we are used to. It may also be hard to predict, suggesting that the only way to know what kinds of sense a piece might make in performance is to try them out. That should not be so surprising: after all, HIP is a triumphant demonstration of how new performance approaches can discover unsuspected meanings in old pieces. All this sits uncomfortably with the kid gloves that Leech-Wilkinson's performance police require performers to wear when playing classical music, as if they were handling unique, fragile manuscripts.

A further consideration follows on from this. As I said, Moreschi's Vatican recordings of 1902 reveal a performance practice that sounds bizarre to modern ears: it is impossible to be sure how much is to be understood as ornamentation and how much as nerves, but at all events the performance style could not possibly have been predicted on the basis of documentary sources. As I have repeatedly claimed, performance practices fall through the gaps between words; they are like the soft tissues that disappear when animals are fossilised. Consequently glib assumptions that we have any secure understanding of how music sounded in past centuries cannot be sustained. But at the same time there are practices which we know were at one time common yet which present-day orthodoxies exclude from the performance of music from that period. Just to cite one example, I referred in Chapter 4 to the remarkably late survival—almost as late as clapping between movements—of the practice of preluding in piano concerts. As Hamilton (2008: chapter 4) explains, it served to create transitions between individual pieces or to introduce the sound world of what is to follow, rather like the DJ sets at Nonclassical's club nights: Artur Balsam recalled how in recitals from 1937

---

30. 'Happiness is a cigar called Hamlet' is the strapline of a series of commercials featuring J. S. Bach's *Air on a G String*, played by Jacques Loussier and his trio, which aired on British television from 1966 until 1991, when tobacco advertising was banned.

31. For example, in a joint presentation entitled 'How creative can a musical practice be?' CMPCP/IMR Performance/Research Seminar, London, 24 June 2013.

or 1938, Friedman 'never stopped playing. If a piece ended in C minor and the next was in G major he would make a little modulation between the pieces, always, but always, in good taste' (Evans 2009: 163). Despite the solid historical foundation of the practice, however, attempts to revive preluding—while not completely unknown—lie altogether outside the mainstream of today's performance culture. All this creates a strong suspicion that what is really being policed is current performance practice, propped up by claims of historical authenticity that are selective at best and self-seeking at worst. But the real question is not how well supported these claims are. It is why in music, and apparently only in music, we should make so strong—though selective—an assumption that, if something went one way then, it must go the same way now. Hamilton observes that 'Just because Chopin probably envisaged a fairly flowing op. 10 no. 3 or Liszt recommended a gentle *Feux follets* does not mean that other approaches are not possible or effective' (2008: 273). A claim like that would seem almost too obvious to make in other fields of cultural practice. In music it still carries more than a whiff of heresy.[32]

Hamilton's discussion of nineteenth-century concert practices (2008: 259) is explicitly designed to provoke thought about concert practices today, and his key observation is perhaps that 'Virtually the entire spectrum of playing styles were heard and applauded somewhere, from our standard sober renditions of pieces to versions which we would without hesitation classify as transcriptions' (or possibly travesties, I am inclined to add). He continues: 'the key word is variety'. This is closely related to the point I made with reference to performance style when, in Chapter 6, I spoke of Pugno-style performance representing a degree zero of temporal inflection within the total range encompassed by rhetorical performance. It is the same as with Liszt's white gloves. The value of studying the stylistic features of what Hamilton calls the 'golden age' of pianism does not lie so much in rehabilitating specific stylistic practices. It lies in recapturing the pluralism that was so prominent a feature of nineteenth-century musical culture: a pluralism as conspicuous in terms of aesthetic epistemology—basic beliefs about what performance is—as in terms of stylistic practices. Hamilton (281) begins the final paragraph of his book by identifying what he sees as the fundamental question: 'is the composer's voice the only one worth listening to when devising performance approaches?' The answer, of course, is no.

But the even more fundamental question, to which I would also answer no, is whether we should be looking for generally applicable answers to questions about

---

32. For Hamilton (2008: 261, 280, 281), the heresy is against musicological dogma. He refers to musicologists regarding 'performance ideas not derived from or associated with the composer [as] at best irrelevant or at worst corrupting'; again, he speaks of nineteenth-century performers' editions being 'treated in scholarly quarters with embarrassment or derision', or even 'shunted off to the old-folks' home of anachronistic attitudes by the forward march of musicology'. Of course there are specific branches of musicology which concern themselves with the reconstruction of Urtexts and period performance practices. But as I said in Chapter 1, over the last generation, critical and historical musicology have been reshaped by reception theory and related approaches to the extent that I have difficulty recognising the mindset Hamilton evokes. It is as if musicologists and performers each blame the other for the inflexibility of today's performance practices.

performance at all—as if, for example, we should as a matter of principle favour Goehr's perfect musical performance over her perfect performance of music, or vice versa. It is not obvious that there is a limit on the number, or nature, of viable performance options, whether these are informed by historical precedent, structural interpretation, rhetorical effect, or personal taste. In every instance there will be some reasons for doing it one way, and some for doing it another. Each will have its own consequences, which can be explored and evaluated. There are lots of ways of making sense of music as performance, and lots of senses there for the making. It really is as simple, and as complicated, as that.

MAKING MUSIC TOGETHER

Plato's curse lies at the root of the situation I have described, but of course it isn't just that. Sheer economics threaten the concert performance of WAM, at least in its grand public guises. Even if it wasn't for the shrinking, graying, and pale-faced audiences, the demand—despite Harvey—for non-amplified sound rules out the economies of scale that have turned rock and pop performance into the economically most viable sector of the UK music business since the mid-1990s.

But it isn't just that either. It is also the inexorable tendency for costs in labour-intensive sectors of the economy to rise relative to consumer products and services subject to progressive manufacturing efficiencies and productivity gains. This is the general economic principle called Baumol's cost disease or the Baumol effect, and its originators—William Baumol and William Bowen—used string quartets as an example: you cannot enhance productivity by cutting the workforce to three, or getting through the work in half the time.[33] And there is a further consideration that is particularly relevant to large musical ensembles. There is not an arithmetical relationship between the number of performers, for instance in an orchestral concert as against a piano recital, and what consumers expect to pay for their tickets. Given all this, it probably takes an unreasonable amount of faith in the chances of greying audiences being renewed as the rock generation get their bus passes, or in the future of state subsidies for WAM, to be confident that the large classical ensembles, whether in the concert hall or opera house, can in the long run be maintained at their present levels—at least outside the classical-music heartlands of East Asia. (The 'W' in WAM has become increasingly ironic.)

There is a great deal of talk about classical music being in crisis. This is anything but new. Culshaw (1967: 261) did not expect the opera house to survive the twentieth century ('simple economics and the expansion of private forms of communication like records and television will see to that'), while Charles Rosen has remarked that 'The death of classical music is perhaps its oldest continuing tradition'. Ross (2010), who quotes this, says he is sanguine about the music itself, but

---

33. Baumol and Bowen (1968); for a wide-ranging discussion of this principle in relation to music see Botstein (2004: 55–59).

that its institutions are another matter, with which Gould would have agreed: 'the fate of the public event is incidental to the future of music—a future deserving of far greater concern than is the fiscal stability of the concert hall' (1987: 332). And in the concluding chapter of their *Cambridge History of Musical Performance*, Colin Lawson and Robin Stowell (2012) write that 'Various recent surveys have pointed to an ageing and diminishing audience for mainstream classical music, giving rise to description as a niche activity rather than an enlightened, beneficial and indispensable part of society' (824). Their formulation contains some clues for nuancing the prevailing doom and gloom.

For one thing, they are speaking of 'mainstream' classical music, but there are areas within the larger culture of classical music that attract audiences of a different demographic: early music is one, contemporary music—which has rebuilt at least some of the audience it lost in the 1970s and 1980s—is another. (Nonclassical is an expression of this.) Again, classical concerts retain much of their popularity in contexts when they have strong community foundations. That includes its grand public forms where there is a local tradition that associates them within civic pride and identity: it can be hard to get tickets for the Chicago Symphony Orchestra. More typically it applies to smaller-scale concerts in churches or schools, perhaps organised by local music clubs. But Lawson's and Stowell's most important clue lies in the word 'niche'. If one's expectation is that classical music should occupy the role it did a hundred years ago, in a far more monolithic culture than today's and in the absence of a global popular music industry, then the picture must be one of irreversible decline. A more reasonable expectation is that classical music should be a *successful* niche culture, or set of niche cultures—a role that is not inconsistent with being enlightened, beneficial, or even indispensable.

The crisis in classical music, then, is a strangely patchy one. After all, on any professionally certified measure, standards of performance have never been so high, and Western conservatories are buoyed up by the East Asian market. Through technological mediation, classical music has never been so accessible to so many people as it is today. In terms of total listening hours across the globe it must be more widely disseminated than it has ever been. If levels of consumption fall far short of those for popular music, that is because of the unparalleled expansion of the latter rather than the decline of the former; the consumption of music is not a zero sum game. Then again, there are constant complaints about the decline in active musical participation, just as there were in late nineteenth-century Vienna (Botstein 1992: 143), but any parent with teenagers knows otherwise—and while most of it is admittedly in popular musical genres, the classical music making that goes on at this level is often at an amazingly high standard.

Perhaps, then, the sense of crisis is in part generated from within the microculture of classical music, part of the same phenomenon of walking on eggshells to which Kramer referred. That at any rate is the view of Marcas Lancaster, one of the remixers featured on the Nonclassical CD of Prokofiev's String Quartet no. 2. 'Speaking as an outsider on classical music', he says, 'it appears to me to be a preoccupation with people within it to think it exhausted and in need of revitalising but from where I'm standing it's such an incredibly rich and proud tradition. Many insiders are kind of over it, whereas almost everybody else is still blown away by it, generally'.[34] And while Lancaster sees initiatives like Nonclassical as playing an important role in combatting the institutionalisation and ossification of the classical tradition, he adds, 'I still sometimes think the notion of invigorating it is almost demeaning to the whole canon of classical music because it doesn't appear to need it'.

Mixed as the overall picture may be, the large classical ensembles that flourished under the post-war funding regime are still at the sharp end of the economic pressures on classical music. But then, the Baumol effect, which bears so dramatically on orchestras, applies only to fully professionalised music making. There is a possibility that, in an age when most music—both classical and popular—is consumed in an increasing variety of technologically mediated forms, any decline in professionalised orchestral performance may be counterbalanced by an increase in non-professional activity, comparable to the situation that currently obtains in choruses. And here there is a historical dimension to be brought into play. In the postwar period, arts management and funding policies prioritised professional performance. A telling illustration of this is a row that developed during the planning of the 1951 Festival of Britain over Handel's *Messiah*, and has been documented in a doctoral thesis by Jonathan Tyack.[35]

Messiah had become an emblem not only of Britishness but also of choral participation, resulting in a nineteenth-century tradition of performances with massed choirs and correspondingly enlarged orchestras—a tradition that was particularly strong in the north of England. Planning for the 1951 festival was however controlled by the newly founded Arts Council of Great Britain, which aimed to project a modern, professional image of British music, at the same time informed by recent scholarship. The festival programme included one concert featuring a massed Yorkshire choir, which wanted to perform *Messiah*, but the organisers vetoed this, permitting them to perform only selections from *Messiah* alongside other items. The festival's complete performance of *Messiah* was instead given by John Tobin with the London Choral Society, a small, selective chorus whose official aims included 'the performance of contemporary works and the revival of earlier works in the style of their period', with the orchestral accompaniment in its original, eighteenth-century form. And the prioritisation of professional quality over participation extended to the physical design of the Royal Festival Hall, which was built for the festival and included only very limited space for choral singers. This duly attracted controversy, and an editorial in the *Musical Times* spelled out a viewpoint that was shared with both the decision makers at the Arts Council and the BBC's Third Programme, itself established in 1946:

> we find it objected that the Festival Hall has no room for a very big choir; and the objectors seem to assume that the omission was a careless oversight on the part of the designers. Perhaps 'foresight' is the apter word....Musicians

34. Private communication, 14 September 2012.

35. The following paragraph is based on Tyack (2007, chapter 4).

now tend to be more and more satisfied with the tone, flexibility and keener human utterance of the smaller and more teachable body.

The decisive victory of the proponents of professionalism over those of participation inaugurated a pattern of prestige-led public funding for the arts in the UK that lasted for more or less the remainder of the century, and that was broadly mirrored by public funding in Europe and by private funding in North America. This at the same time supported, and was supported by, a recording industry kept buoyant by the successive waves of technological innovation—coupled to a rhetoric of ever greater fidelity—that led consumers to repurchase their music collections over and over again: first on LP, then stereo LP, and finally CD. Unfortunately for the record industry, most consumers decided that CDs, which became commercially available in 1982, were good enough, and subsequent technological innovations prioritised mobility and access rather than sound quality. Once the boom stimulated by the CD had subsided, the record industry entered into long-term decline. Together with pressures on both sides of the Atlantic towards smaller government and a succession of financial crises, the result was the undermining of the post-war settlement without anything fully taking its place. In the long run, this policy-based professionalisation of classical performance at the expense of its participatory basis—which presents a glaring contrast to the massive participatory cultures supporting semi-professional and professional rock and pop—may be seen to have been a wrong turn.

Certainly it is striking that, in this mediatised age, classical music has achieved many of its highest-profile successes in precisely those domains of the social that are excluded from serious consideration by the aesthetics of autonomy and the paradigm of reproduction. I shall make the point by drawing examples first from choruses, which represent the long tradition of participation rebuffed in 1951, and then from the mainly post-war phenomenon of the youth orchestra. Long seen by both arts managers and academics as of peripheral significance, community-based choral singing was catapulted into the UK media spotlight in 2006 with Gareth Malone and the prime-time BBC television programme *The Choir*. In all four series of this programme, Malone brought choral singing to people who had never previously had the opportunity, or indeed the desire, to sing—in a comprehensive school, for example, or a deprived outer London suburb. The final series focussed on the workplace, and in the second episode (first broadcast on 27 September 2012) Malone created a choir at the Bristol branch of the Royal Mail.

This was a business in trouble, repeatedly restructuring itself and shedding jobs to cope with the decline in postal business and the spectre of looming privatisation. And from the start the episode exhibited a blurring between the world of the workplace and that of the music. As one of the choir's songs, Malone chose the Beatles's 'We can work it out', and the lyrics struck resonances with the postal workers: 'sometimes I sort of feel that the managers aren't really listening to what we are saying', one said, 'and that first line, "Try to see it my way", is actually really quite relevant at the moment'. But it was Tim Barber, a member of the management team but also of the choir, who set out music's potential for social transformation most clearly.

Addressing a meeting of forty regional managers on the eve of the choir's first performance in front of their workplace colleagues, Barber said:

> As a choir, we work together brilliantly. We help each other. We support each
> other. We put up with each other's mistakes. And actually, when we get it all
> right, it sounds fantastic. Why doesn't that translate to the workplace? What
> is it we're missing? There's a belief and there's a passion in our people that we
> don't know about, because we don't ask them. Gareth has asked them, and
> I think Gareth was pretty stunned, and I was certainly quite stunned, about the
> response that he got. Actually, there's a real buy-in to our business and it's in
> people's blood.

And he introduced Peter, a shop floor worker ('one of my bass-line colleagues'), who
told the managers:

> It doesn't make a difference who you are, because you're all after the same object
> at the end of the day. All we are is singers. And it's like that, the choir's kind of
> brought us all together and instead of being individuals, we actually end up as a
> team. We all look forward to actually singing together.... We're all thinking the
> same way choir-wise, but also work-wise as well.

In each episode of *The Choir* there is a narrative trajectory from the apparently
impossible task of setting up a community choir where such a thing is unknown,
through the hard work and inevitable hiccups of getting it off the ground, to ultimate success. Music becomes a medium through which human relationships are
fostered and through which identities are negotiated: the programme is in essence
about the power of performance to build community. While this phenomenon
has clearly owed much to Malone's charismatic personality and camera-friendly
manner, it has also embedded the value and values of communal singing in public consciousness: the BBC set up a dedicated website on choral singing,[36] and
research into its health and wellbeing benefits hit the headlines. At the same time
it should be emphasised that all this did not happen in a vacuum. Until 2009,
Malone directed the youth choir and community choir at LSO St Lukes, a former
church that is the base for the London Symphony Orchestra's extensive education
and outreach programme. In part through the initiative of arts funding bodies in
the closing years of the twentieth century, such work has become an important part
of classical performance culture today, and that is why it is so important to resist the
negative stereotyping that opposes WAM to the community values of other musical
traditions—as exemplified by Dean Rowan, whom I quoted in Chapter 8.
      Just as high-profile as *The Choir*, but now in the international domain, are
the classical youth orchestras linked to projects of social reconstruction or conflict transformation. As I began to draft this chapter, in April 2009, London's
Royal Festival Hall hosted Gustavo Dudamel and the Simón Bolívar Orchestra,

36. http://www.bbc.co.uk/sing/.

the topmost rung of El Sistema, the National System of Venezuelan Youth and Children's Orchestras; they played Tchaikovsky and Bartók. 'It is the orchestra most countries would love to have', Mark Brown (2009) wrote in the following morning's *Guardian*, 'a product of a system most countries would love to emulate'. And indeed there are UK-based initiatives aiming at precisely that: one was established in the Raploch district of Stirling in 2008, and another in England the following year ('In Harmony', a government-backed organisation led by Julian Lloyd-Webber and targetting deprived areas of Lambeth, Liverpool, and Norwich). Then in August, the West-Eastern Divan Orchestra—the media-friendly creation of Edward Said and Daniel Barenboim which brings together young Arabs and Jews (and Spaniards) to play side by side—performed a programme of Berlioz, Liszt, and Wagner at the Proms, in addition to a late-night programme of Mendelssohn and Berg. The inclusion of Wagner was, of course, significant in view of the ban on public performances of his music in Israel, against which Barenboim has famously protested. It was one of the relatively small proportion of concerts from the 2009 Proms to be televised live.[37]

Both orchestras regularly attract rapturous reviews, partly because of their intrinsic quality, but also because of what they stand for. Guy Dammann's review of the final concert (Beethoven's Ninth Symphony) from the West-Eastern Divan Orchestra's return to the Proms in 2012 exemplifies the tone: 'As for Barenboim, concluding a week of extraordinary concerts by shaking the hand of every member of the orchestra, his old-fashioned musical and political ideas once again proved themselves both noble and necessary, and he made the Proms' unofficial preamble to the Olympics both an honour, and a joy, to behold'.[38] These orchestras epitomise a dream—of creating paths out of social deprivation, of forging social cohesion, of bridging deep cultural divisions. But is it just a dream, or can music really bridge deep cultural divisions?

Some light was thrown on this by a project that took place within six Oslo schools between 1989 and 1992: called the 'Resonant Community' project, it featured performances from a range of immigrant cultures represented within the Norwegian population. This project is cited as a success in the small but growing literature on music and conflict transformation.[39] However a series of interviews with project participants, conducted thirteen years later by Arild Bergh, raised questions about the nature and extent of this success. The problem, as Bergh (2007: 147) analyses it, is that while the participants enjoyed the performances, 'they never made a link at the time of the performances, between the music and the performers, and the children in their class who had an immigrant background or the immigrant population at large'. Bergh (149, 151) concluded that listening was not enough: 'it is among musicians, rather than the audience,

37. http://www.guardian.co.uk/music/2009/aug/23/proms-48-49-barenboim-review.

38. http://www.guardian.co.uk/music/2012/jul/29/prom-18-barenboim-review?INTCMP=ILC NETTXT3487.

39. See, for example, Castelo-Branco (2010: 250) and Grant et al. (2010: 191).

where music most reliably builds new relationships', he proposes, and again, 'This project clearly showed the difference in being a relatively passive listener or being a fully involved participant'. In other words, music may act as a symbol of inter-cultural understanding, but as long as its operation remains solely in the symbolic domain, its practical effect is limited.

This pessimistic assessment can be turned around into the optimistic idea that, through the act of performing together, music may have the power to go beyond symbolisation and become a real enactment of understanding across cultural and political divisions. For Salwa Castelo-Branco, 'music can be a catalyst for imagin-ing conflict resolution', and again, 'performance can constitute a "new reality" that can be shared by factions in strife, a neutral space for denouncing conflict and violence as well as for reconciliation and healing in postconflict divided com-munities' (2010: 243, 249). This is in essence what Tim Barber was saying about the Royal Mail Bristol choir, only ramped up by an order of magnitude, and it is this utopian conception that lies behind both the Simón Bolívar Orchestra and the West-Eastern Divan Orchestra. For Dudamel, 'an orchestra is a little commu-nity, but the perfect community, because you need to listen [to] the other musi-cians'.[40] Barenboim says the same: 'An orchestra requires musicians to listen to one another; none should attempt to play louder than the next, they must respect and know each other'.[41] That in turn resonates with what Johann Petiscus said in 1810 about string quartet performance, as quoted in Chapter 8: 'Each [player] should moderate his tone, so as not to scream out above the others'. And it shows how the ideas of music and community that I am here presenting in a present-day context resonate with the much longer, and hardly less utopian, tradition of musically scripted community that I discussed in that chapter.

The original thinking behind the West-Eastern Divan Orchestra was more com-plex and dialectical, not to say paradoxical, than Barenboim's formulation might suggest. In Ben Etherington's words (2007), it was 'to draw together musicians from various places in the Middle East without trying to artificially dissolve the political antagonisms involved. Music as a non-representational medium provides an arena in which communication is possible without immediately veering into hostility' (125). In other words, through its autonomy, instrumental music pro-vides the 'neutral space' of which Castelo-Branco spoke. As Etherington goes on to say, it is one of the many ironies of the West-Eastern Divan Orchestra that Said should invoke the distinctively Western ideology of aesthetic autonomy as a step on the way to Middle Eastern reconciliation, but the basic idea is not a new one. Writing in the first half of the twentieth century, the Viennese critic David Josef

40. Gustavo Dudamel interviewed by Verity Sharp on *The Culture Show* (BBC Two, trans-mitted 10 June 2008): extended interview accessible at http://www.bbc.co.uk/cultureshow/videos/2008/06/s5_e2_dudamel_extra/.

41. Barenboim's acceptance speech for the Prince of Asturias Award for Concord 2002, http://www.fpa.es/en/prince-of-asturias-awards/awards/2002-daniel-barenboim-y-edward-said.html?texto=discurso.

Bach wrote that, unlike programme music, absolute music can speak to all classes because of its 'soulful' rather than 'intellectual' nature (Berkley 1988: 50). And speaking of the playing of chamber music between the wars within the German Jewish community, Philip Bohlman writes that 'the absence of specific meaning within the text allowed meaning to accrue only upon performance, thus empowering any group—for example, an ethnic community—to shape what it will from absolute music' (1993: 259). It is however in the form of Barenboim's simpler and more marketable conception of playing for peace that the West-Eastern Divan Orchestra has captured the imagination of both media and general public.

Yet there is a problem that has been building up over the last few pages. The idea of young musicians working and playing together, melding their individual voices through a kind of ventriloquism into that of Beethoven, Tchaikovsky, or some other great composer of the Western tradition, is perfectly calculated to elicit the same kind of uncritical mythologisation that enabled the Hatto hoax to succeed for so long (and that turned *The Choir* into a media sensation). In another context, Bergh (2011) complains about 'the amount of hyperbole surrounding music in general, and music and conflict transformation more specifically' (364). Because of its intangibility—its lack of resistance to whatever claims are made of or through it—music is an ideal medium for wish fulfillment, and sweeping claims are made on the basis of flimsy evidence: a few pages later, Bergh (368) remarks that 'there tends to be a leap of faith from anecdotal/empirical data to general claims about music's power with little grounded discussion'. If reconciliation is really enacted through making music together, how long does it last after the music stops? Can youth orchestras really deliver where political and economic initiatives fail? In the end, do they amount to more than a distraction?

Castelo-Branco (2010: 246) remarks that 'we must question whether cultural initiatives can occupy the place of political and social intervention'. There are good reasons for believing that the Simón Bolívar Orchestra plays an important role within an effective programme of social mobility, but that is because it forms the top layer of an extensive network of local youth orchestras that goes back to the 1970s and includes an associated instrumental training programme. The long-term success or otherwise of similar ventures in the UK and North America, where the same kind of integrated national infrastructure does not exist, will be telling. As for the West-Eastern Divan Orchestra, a number of ethnographic studies—in particular by Rachel Beckles Willson—have documented the extent to which its young musicians see the orchestra as offering an opportunity to build careers away from the troubles of the Middle East, and the counter-productive impact that the orchestra has sometimes had on the spot: the parachuting in of international celebrities and media teams sucks attention and funding away from more local and sustainable initiatives. In short, making music together can undoubtedly play a role in projects of reconciliation, but what is less obvious is how far that is because of some special power that music possesses—because, in Bergh's words it acts as 'a quick working "magic bullet"' (2011: 371)—or simply because performance provides a social framework that helps people from different backgrounds to work closely together. Seen that way, classical music functions in essence like football, except that it is less obviously competitive and comes with more highfalutin connotations. In which case the greatest value of music in the creation of community and the bridging of cultural distance may, after all, lie not in its directly transformative potential—what Bergh refers to as '"the power of music"' (373)—but rather in the symbolic capital it brings to such projects.

Or has a healthy scepticism concerning the hype attracted by such iconic ensembles as the Simón Bolívar Orchestra and the West-Eastern Divan Orchestra led us to move too fast and too far? The same issues arise in relation to iconic genres such as the string quartet or free jazz. Such genres are iconic in two related but distinct senses. They are iconic in terms of the particular symbolic capital, as I put it, that attaches to them. But they are also iconic in Peirce's sense: they embody microsocial structures that are readily scaled up to become models of social and even political organisation. If the orchestra is a little community, as Dudamel said, then—as Julian Johnson writes—'To watch a string quartet perform [and even more, I would add, to listen to it] is to witness a complexity and refinement of interaction that is matched by very few human activities.... It has to do with a quality of mutual care, respect, and understanding, with being part of a collective and yet independent' (2002b: 127). And we saw in Chapter 8, not least from Dean Rowan, how free jazz has in the same way been read as the model of a better society. Indeed the seven-year, $4 million Improvisation, Community, and Social Practice project—which is based in Guelph (Canada) and publishes the journal *Critical Studies in Improvisation*—is based on the premise that musical improvisation is a productive 'model for social change': its mission, as explained on the project home page, is to play 'a leading role in defining a new field of interdisciplinary research to shape political, cultural, and ethical dialogue and action'.[42]

Perhaps unkindly, Alan Stanbridge has used the pages of the Improvisation, Community, and Social Practice project's own journal to point out some of the basic problems inherent in the idea of musical improvisation as a model for social change. He cites some of Jacques Attali's and Susan McClary's more hyperbolic claims on the subject. Then he acidly points out that 'more challenging forms of contemporary jazz and improvised music remain resolutely minority tastes, which tends to circumscribe rather severely the utopian and far-reaching claims made regarding the development of "new social relations" or "the transformation of societies" based primarily on free jazz and the avant-garde' (Stanbridge 2008: 10). And now he targets his attack more pointedly:

> In their editorial for the inaugural issue, the editors of *Critical Studies in Improvisation* acknowledged the need to 'assess the (often utopian) claims made for the social and cultural impact of improvisation'..., although the continued deference to Attali's highly problematic work in the discourses that inform the various Guelph research projects tends to severely compromise any such level-headed assessment. Perhaps it is time for these projects

42. http://www.improvcommunity.ca/.

to move beyond the idealized visions of outmoded political rhetoric, à la Attali, or the romanticized celebrations of 'marginality', à la McClary, in favour of a considerably more pragmatic—and considerably more realistic—perspective on contemporary music-making, acknowledging not only the positive sociopolitical potential of improvisatory creative practice, but also its social and political limits.

The problem may be that there has been too much focus on iconic ensembles and genres—that is, on the domain of the symbolic—and too little on the everyday processes through which music might achieve the social effects that are imputed to it. And here there is recent research that provides a lead. The basic premise of this work is that, as Ian Cross (2009: 190) puts it, 'music has all the attributes of a communicative system that is highly adapted to facilitate the management of the uncertainties of social interaction'. (As the word 'adaptive' indicates, Cross is suggesting that music has been selected for in evolution, in opposition to Pinker's 'cheesecake' model.) Central to this approach is what Cross (183) calls 'floating intentionality'. Through its temporal morphologies, Cross argues, music shapes affect—this is the same idea we encountered in Stern and Massumi, among others—and in doing so it enables the coordination of people's emotional states, even when individuals understand it in disparate ways: as Cross says, 'the meaning of a specific musical piece or act may be experienced quite differently by different participants at the same time' (182–83). That in turn links with Etherington's, Bohlman's, and Bach's idea that it is the non-representational nature of music, the absence of specific meaning within the text, that enables it to forge communication across cultural divisions.

As Cross (189) sees it, while the communicative functions of music operate at a number of levels, the most basic one is entrainment, that is to say the tendency for musicians to 'regulate the temporal alignment of their musical behaviours by engaging in continual processes of mutual adjustment of the timing of actions and sounds'. (That lies at the core of the temporal negotiations in ensemble performance that I talked about in Chapter 8, negotiations that are at once cognitive and embodied.) Cross continues, 'even those who appear engaged in "passive listening" to music will be modulating their attention'—an idea that he later develops into the suggestion I quoted in Chapter 11, that listening might be thought of as 'covert *interaction* with the traces of human behaviour' (2010: 77). And he links this with neuroscientific evidence of the links between perception and action (75), in line with what I said in Chapters 5 and 10 about listening with the body.

But there are two particular aspects of entrainment that are crucial to my argument. The first is that everyone seems able to entrain effortlessly with a beat that lies within, and preferably centrally within, a range of some 200 to 2,000 milliseconds, the range of the tactus (London 2004): that is what one would expect of an adaptive trait (31–33). Even more revealingly, there is evidence that we entrain more readily with a pulse that entrains with us, as opposed to a mechanically regular series of beats (Cross 2010: 74–75). This reinforces the idea that the adaptation is a social one, and perhaps suggests that rubato builds social relationship into music, figures it as the listener's partner. If that is the case, it underlines my argument in Chapter 8 that we are never alone with music. The second aspect of entrainment is the near ubiquity, across times, places, and styles, of music that is structured in such a way as to afford entrainment. In other words music's communicative potential—its ability to enact openness to the other—does not depend on the symbolism of iconic repertories. It is built into practically all musical performance and listening. And an extended project by Cross's co-researcher Tal-Chen Rabinowitch has translated this theorisation of potential into demonstration of effect: an experimental study, based on a battery of measures for empathy, showed how children taking part in a year-long programme involving games-based musical participation outperformed a control group that participated in similar games but without the music component (Rabinowitch, Cross, and Burnard 2013). We should note that empathy has been identified as a key element in conflict transformation (Laurence 2008). Maybe music does, after all, have the edge over football.

'Unless sounds are held by the memory of man', wrote Isidore of Seville around the turn of the seventh century, 'they perish, because they cannot be written down' (2006: 95). But what was impossible in Isidore's day became possible: memory was supplemented and in time supplanted by script, and the paradigm of reproduction became the basis for the plethora of aesthetic, academic, commercial, or legal practices and institutions that have been built on the permanence of music as writing. And by inscribing the evanescence of sound even more comprehensively into the material artefact, the technology of recording added a further dimension to this monumentalisation of music. It is telling that, although no material trace survived of Edison's intoning of 'Mary had a little lamb' into his prototype phonograph in 1877, the inventor saw fit to recreate this historic moment in the form of another recording fifty years later.[43] And among the uses he saw for his invention was preserving the voices of great men.

But perhaps the most evocative examples of the twentieth century's condensation of musical performance into enduring artefact are two conspicuous, public acts of communication directed at unknown cultures. The first was the burial at the Paris *Opéra*, on Christmas Eve 1907, of two lead-lined urns containing a total of twenty-four shellac discs of vocal and instrumental music, largely though not exclusively by French composers and performers: canned music in the most literal sense, and only a year after Sousa coined the term. In June 1912 a further twenty-four discs were added, together—thoughtfully—with a gramophone and spare needles.[44] It was specified that the urns should not be opened for a hundred years. The second was NASA's inclusion with the two Voyager deep space probes

43. A recording made by Edison in 1927, in which he recounts this, may be accessed at http://www.archive.org/details/EDIS-SCD-02.

44. 'Les voix ensevelies' (http://expositions.bnf.fr/voix/index.htm). This was a PR coup by The Gramophone Company, which supplied the records and gramophone. They were not in fact buried but placed in a basement storage room. In 1989 it was discovered that the contents of one of the urns, and the gramophone, had been stolen.

in 1977 of a golden disc containing an eclectic selection of classical, popular, and world musics, together with words addressed by Jimmy Carter to an alien (but, it is to be hoped, English-speaking) audience:

> This is a present from a small distant world, a token of our sounds, our science, our images, our music, our thoughts, and our feelings. We are attempting to survive our time so that we may live into yours. We hope someday, having solved the problems we face, to join a community of galactic civilizations. This record represents our hope and our determination and our goodwill in a vast and awesome universe (Torricelli and Carroll 1999: 324).

One is reminded once again of Beethoven's inscription on the score of the *Missa Solemnis*: 'may it go from the heart to the heart'—that is, if aliens have hearts.

On the one hand, then, a mythologisation of musicking as human process; on the other, a monumentalisation of music as enduring product. Both verge on bathos. But between the two extremes and all too easily squeezed out from our thinking lies a world of performance that encompasses professional musicians, amateurs, and listeners alike, and that combines the pleasures of social interaction, embodied practice, sensory gratification, and private fantasy. Music is not just the 'extreme occasion' as which Said (1991: 17) described the Western classical concert: it is a ubiquitous feature of everyday life. Beneath the bathos, then, beneath the hype, the human value of musical performance subsists in its very ordinariness.

REFERENCES

Abbate, Carolyn. 2004. 'Music—Drastic or Gnostic?' *Critical Inquiry* 30, 505–36.

Abrahamson, Eric, and David H. Freedman. 2006. *A Perfect Mess: The Hidden Benefits of Disorder*. London: Weidenfeld and Nicolson.

Adelt, Ulrich. 2010. *Blues Music in the Sixties: A Story in Black and White*. Rutgers University Press.

Adlington, Robert. 2007. 'Organizing Labor: Composers, Performers, and "The Renewal of Musical Practice" in the Netherlands, 1969–72'. *Musical Quarterly* 90, 539–77.

Adorno, Theodor. 1984. *Gesammelte Schriften*, Rolf Tiedemann, ed., in collaboration with Gretel Adorno, Susan Buck-Morss and Klaus Schultz, vol. 19 (Musikalische Schriften VI). Frankfurt am Main: Suhrkamp.

Adorno, Theodor. 1999. *Sound Figures*. Rodney Livingstone, trans. Stanford, CA: Stanford University Press. (First published 1978)

Adorno, Theodor. 2002. *Essays on Music*. Richard Leppert, ed. Berkeley: University of California Press.

Adorno, Theodor. 2006. *Towards a Theory of Musical Reproduction: Notes, a Draft and Two Schemata*. Henri Lonitz, ed., Wieland Hoban, trans. Cambridge: Polity Press. (First published 2001)

Agawu, Kofi. 2008. 'Topic Theory: Achievement, Critique, Prospects'. In Laurenz Lütteken and Hans-Joachim Hinrichsen, eds., *Passagen: IMS Kongress Zürich 2007—Fünf Hauptvorträge*. Kassel: Bärenreiter, 38–69.

Agawu, Kofi. 2009. *Music as Discourse: Semiotic Adventures in Romantic Music*. New York: Oxford University Press.

Aguilar, Ananay. 2012. *Recording Classical Music: LSO Live and the Transforming Record Industry*. PhD diss., Royal Holloway, University of London.

Allanbrook, Wye Jamison. 1983. *Rhythmic Gesture in Mozart: Le Nozze di Figaro and Don Giovanni*. Chicago: University of Chicago Press.

Allanbrook, Wye Jamison. 1992. 'Two Threads Through the Labyrinth: Topic and Process in the First Movements of K.332 and K.333'. In Wye Jamison Allanbrook, Janet Levy, and William Mahrt, eds., *Convention in Eighteenth- and Nineteenth-Century Music: Essays in Honor of Leonard G. Ratner*. Stuyvesant, NY: Pendragon, 125–71.

Allen, Graham. 2003. *Roland Barthes*. New York: Routledge.

Archbold, Paul. 2011. *Performing Complexity: A Pedagogical Resource Tracing the Arditti Quartet's Preparations for the Première of Brian Ferneyhough Sixth String Quartet* (http://events.sas.ac.uk/uploads/media/Arditti_Ferneyhough_project_documentation.pdf).

Ashby, Arved. 2010. *Absolute Music, Mechanical Reproduction.* Berkeley: University of California Press.

Atik, Yaakov. 1994. 'The Conductor and the Orchestra: Interactive Aspects of the Leadership Process'. *Leadership and Organization Development Journal* 15/1, 22–28.

Attali, Jacques. 1985. *Noise: The Political Economy of Music.* Brian Massumi, trans. Manchester: Manchester University Press. (Originally published 1977)

Auslander, Philip. 2002. 'Live from Cyberspace: Or, I Was Sitting at My Computer This Guy Appeared He Thought I Was a Bot'. *PAJ: A Journal of Performance and Art* 24/1, 16–21.

Auslander, Philip. 2004. 'Performance Analysis and Popular Music: A Manifesto'. *Contemporary Theatre Review* 14/1, 1–13.

Auslander, Philip. 2006. 'Musical Personae'. *Drama Review* 50/1, 100–119.

Auslander, Philip. 2008a. 'Live and Technologically Mediated Performance'. In Tracy Davis, ed., *The Cambridge Companion to Performance Studies.* Cambridge: Cambridge University Press, 107–119.

Auslander, Philip. 2008b. *Liveness: Performance in a Mediatized Culture.* 2nd ed. London: Routledge. (First published 1999)

Auslander, Philip. 2009. 'Lucille Meets GuitarBot: Instrumentality, Agency, and Technology in Musical Performance'. *Theatre Journal* 61, 603–16.

Auslander, Philip. 2013. 'Jazz Improvisation as a Social Arrangement'. In Nicholas Cook and Richard Pettengill, eds., *Taking It to the Bridge: Music as Performance.* Ann Arbor: Michigan University Press, 52–69.

Ayto, John. 2006. *Movers and Shakers: A Chronology of Words That Shaped Our Age.* Rev. ed. Oxford: Oxford University Press.

Bach, C. P. E. 1974. *Essay on the True Art of Playing Keyboard Instruments.* William J. Mitchell, ed. and trans. London: Eulenberg. (First published 1753 [Part I] and 1762 [Part II])

Bailey, Derek. 1992. *Improvisation: Its Nature and Practice in Music.* London: British Library National Sound Archive.

Baillot, Pierre. 1991. *The Art of the Violin.* Louise Goldberg, trans. Evanston: Northwestern University Press. (First published 1834)

Baily, John. 1985. 'Music Structure and Human Movement'. In Peter Howell, Ian Cross, and Robert West, eds., *Musical Structure and Cognition.* London: Academic Press, 237–58.

Baily, John, and Peter Driver. 1992. 'Spatio-Motor Thinking in Playing Blues Guitar'. *World of Music* 34/3, 57–71.

Bamberger, Carl. 1965. *The Conductor's Art.* New York: McGraw-Hill.

Barenboim, Daniel, and Edward Said. 2003. *Parallels and Paradoxes: Explorations in Music and Society.* Ara Guzelimian, ed. London: Bloomsbury.

Barrett, Sam. 2008. 'Reflections on Music Writing: Coming to Terms with Gain and Loss in Early Medieval Latin Song'. In Andreas Haug and Andreas Dorschel, eds., *Vom Preis des Fortschritts: Gewinn und Verlust in der Musikgeschichte.* Vienna: Universal Edition, 89–109.

Barron, Anne. 2006. 'Copyright Law's Musical Work'. *Social and Legal Studies* 15, 101–27.

Barth, George. 1992. *The Pianist as Orator: Beethoven and the Transformation of Keyboard Style.* Ithaca, NY: Cornell University Press.

REFERENCES 417

Barthes, Roland. 1977. *Image-Music-Text*. Stephen Heath, trans. London: Fontana Press.

Battle, Laura. 2010. 'Redefining Classical Music Conventions'. *FT.com/Arts*, http://www.ft.com/cms/s/2/4655daa0-384d-11df-8420-00144feabdc0.html#axzz2f45OZjYs.

Bauer, Harold. 1947. 'The Paris Conservatoire: Some Reminiscences'. *Musical Quarterly* 33, 533–42.

Baumol, William, and William Bowen. 1966. *The Performing Arts: An Economic Dilemma*. Cambridge, MA: MIT Press.

Baxandall, Michael. 1987. *Patterns of Intention: On the Historical Explanation of Pictures*. New Haven, CT: Yale University Press.

Bayley, Amanda, and Neil Heyde. Forthcoming. 'Communicating Through Notation: Michael Finnissy's Second String Quartet from Composition to Performance'. *Music Performance Research*.

Bazzana, Kevin. 1997. *Glenn Gould: The Performer in the Work*. Oxford: Oxford University Press.

Becker, Howard. 1989. 'Ethnomusicology and Sociology: A Letter to Charles Seeger'. *Ethnomusicology* 33, 275–85.

Beghin, Tom. 2007. ' "Delivery, Delivery, Delivery!" Crowning the Rhetorical Process of Haydn's Keyboard Sonata'. In Tom Beghin and Sander Goldberg, eds., *Haydn and the Performance of Rhetoric*. Chicago: University of Chicago Press, 131–71.

Behne, Klaus-Ernst, and Clemens Wöllner. 2011. 'Seeing or Hearing the Pianists? A Synopsis of an Early Audiovisual Experiment and a Replication'. *Musicae Scientiae* 15, 324–42.

Bekker, Paul. 1922. 'Improvisation und Reproduktion'. In Paul Bekker, *Gesammelte Schriften, vol. II, Klang und Eros*. Stuttgart and Berlin: Deutsche Verlags-Anstalt, 294–307.

Benson, Bruce. 2003. *The Improvisation of Musical Dialogue: A Phenomenology of Music*. Cambridge: Cambridge University Press.

Berger, Karol. 2005. 'Musicology According to Don Giovanni, or, Should We Get Drastic?' *Journal of Musicology* 22, 490–501.

Berger, Karol. 2007. *Bach's Cycle, Mozart's Arrow: An Essay on the Origins of Musical Modernity*. Berkeley: University of California Press.

Bergh, Arild. 2007. 'I'd Like to Teach the World to Sing: Music and Conflict Transformation'. *Musicae Scientiae*, special issue, 141–54.

Bergh, Arild. 2011. 'Emotions and Motion: Transforming Conflict and Music'. In Irène Deliège and Jane Davidson, eds., *Music and the Mind: Essays in Honour of John Sloboda*. Oxford: Oxford University Press, 363–78.

Bergh, Arild, and Tia DeNora. 2009. 'From Wind-Up to iPod: Techno-Cultures of Listening'. In Nicholas Cook et al., eds., *The Cambridge Companion to Recorded Music*. Cambridge: Cambridge University Press, 102–15.

Berio, Luciano. 1966. *Gesti for Alto Recorder*. Vienna: Universal Edition.

Berkley, George. 1988. *Vienna and Its Jews: The Tragedy of Success, 1880s–1980s*. Cambridge, MA: Abt Books.

Berliner, Paul. 1994. *Thinking in Jazz: The Infinite Art of Improvisation*. Chicago: University of Chicago Press.

Berlioz, Hector. 1918. *Mozart, Weber, and Wagner, with Various Essays on Musical Subjects*. Edwin Evans, trans. London: W. Reeves.

Bernstein, Leonard. 1959. *The Joy of Music*. London: Weidenfeld and Nicolson.

Berry, Wallace. 1989. *Musical Structure and Performance*. New Haven: Yale University Press.

Bilson, Malcolm. 1992. 'Execution and Expression in the Sonata in E flat, K 282'. *Early Music* 20, 237–43.

Biss, Jonathan. 2012. *A Pianist Under the Influence* (Kindle Edition). New York: Rosetta Books.

Bjornberg, Alf. 2009. 'Learning to Listen to Perfect Sound: Hi-fi Culture and Changes in Modes of Listening, 1950–80'. In Derek Scott, ed., *The Ashgate Research Companion to Popular Musicology*. Farnham: Ashgate, 105–29.

Blake, Andrew. 1996. *Body Language: The Meaning of Modern Sport*. London: Lawrence and Wishart.

Blake, Andrew. 2004. 'To the Millennium: Music as Twentieth-Century Commodity'. In Nicholas Cook and Anthony Pople, eds., *The Cambridge History of Twentieth-Century Music*. Cambridge: Cambridge University Press, 478–505.

Blake, Andrew. 2009. 'Recording Practice and the Role of the Producer'. In Nicholas Cook et al., eds., *The Cambridge Companion to Recorded Music*. Cambridge: Cambridge University Press, 36–53.

Bliek, Rob van der. 2007. 'The Hendrix Chord: Blues, Flexible Pitch Relationships, and Self-Standing Harmony'. *Popular Music* 26, 343–64.

Boellstorff, Tom. 2008. *Coming to Age in Second Life: An Anthropologist Explores the Virtually Human*. Princeton, NJ: Princeton University Press.

Bohlman, Philip. 1993. 'Of Yekkes and Chamber Music in Israel: Ethnomusicological Meaning in Western Music History'. In Stephen Blum, Philip Bohlman, and Daniel Neuman, eds., *Ethnomusicology and Modern Music History*. Urbana: University of Illinois Press, 254–67.

Boland, Richard, and Fred Collopy. 2004. 'Design Matters for Management'. In Fred Collopy and Richard Boland, eds., *Managing as Designing*. Stanford, CA: Stanford University Press, 3–18.

Boltz, Marilyn. 2013. 'Music Videos and Visual Influences on Music Perception and Appreciation: Should You Want Your MTV?' In Siu-Lan Tan, Annabel Cohen, Scott Lipscomb, and Roger Kendall, eds., *The Psychology of Music in Multimedia*. Oxford: Oxford University Press, 217–34.

Borges, Jorge Luis. 1973. *A Universal History of Infamy*. Norman Thomas di Giovanni, trans. London: Allen Lane. (First published 1935)

Borgo, David. 2005. *Sync or Swarm: Improvising Music in a Complex Age*. New York: Continuum.

Born, Georgina. 2009. 'Afterword. Recording: From Reproduction to Representation to Remediation'. In Nicholas Cook et al., eds., *The Cambridge Companion to Recorded Music*. Cambridge: Cambridge University Press, 286–304.

Botstein, Leon. 1992. 'Listening Through Reading: Musical Literacy and the Concert Audience'. *Nineteenth-Century Music* 16, 129–45.

Botstein, Leon. 2003. 'The Future of Conducting'. In José Bowen, ed., *The Cambridge Companion to Conducting*. Cambridge: Cambridge University Press, 286–304.

Botstein, Leon. 2004. 'Music of a Century: Museum Culture and the Politics of Subsidy'. In Nicholas Cook and Anthony Pople, eds., *The Cambridge History of Twentieth-Century Music*. Cambridge: Cambridge University Press, 40–68.

Boulez, Pierre. 1978. 'Terminology and the Composer'. *Leonardo* 11/1, 59–62.

Boulez, Pierre. 1976. *Conversations with Célestin Deliège*. London: Eulenberg Books.

Bourriaud, Nicolas. 2002. *Relational Aesthetics*. Simon Pleasance and Fronza Woods with Mathieu Copeland, trans. Paris: Le Presses de Réel. (First published 1998)

Bowen, José. 1993. 'The History of Remembered Innovation: Tradition and Its Role in the Relationship Between Musical Works and Their Performance'. *Journal of Musicology* 11, 139–73.

Bowen, José 1996. 'Tempo, Duration, and Flexibility: Techniques in the Analysis of Musical Performance'. *Journal of Musicological Research* 16/2, 111–56.

Brackett, David. 2000. *Interpreting Popular Music*. 2nd ed. Berkeley: University of California Press. (First published 1995)

Brée, Malwine. 1913. *The Leschetizky Method: An Exposition of His Personal Views*. New York: University Society.

Brendel, Alfred. 1976. *Musical Thoughts and Afterthoughts*. London: Robson Books.

Brendel, Alfred. 1990. *Music Sounded Out: Essays, Lectures, Interviews, Afterthoughts*. London: Robson Books.

Brooks, Jeanice. 2013. *The Musical Work of Nadia Boulanger: Performing Past and Future Between the Wars*. Cambridge: Cambridge: University Press.

Brooks, Tim. 2012. 'The Association for Recorded Sound Collections and the Movement to Reform Copyright in the United States'. *Popular Music and Society* 35, 683–89.

Brown, Clive. 1999. *Classical and Romantic Performance Practice 1750–1900*. Oxford: Oxford University Press.

Brown, Mark. 2009. 'Gustavo Dudamel: A Maestro and His Magic Simón Bolívar Orchestra'. *Guardian*. 15 April 2009. Accessible at http://www.theguardian.com/music/2009/apr/15/dudamel-simon-bolivar-orchestra-southbank-venezuela.

Bujić, Bojan. 1993. 'Notation and Realization: Musical Performance in Historical Perspective'. In Michael Krausz, ed., *The Interpretation of Music: Philosophical Essays*. Oxford: Oxford University Press, 129–40.

Bull, Michael. 2000. *Sounding out the City: Personal Stereos and the Management of Everyday Life*. Oxford: Berg.

Bull, Michael. 2007. *Sound Moves: iPod Culture and Urban Experience*. London: Routledge.

Burgess, Jean, and Joshua Green. 2009. *YouTube: Online Video and Participatory Culture*. Cambridge: Polity.

Burkhart, Charles. 1983. 'Schenker's Theory of Levels and Musical Performance'. In David Beach, ed., *Aspects of Schenkerian Theory*. New Haven: Yale University Press, 95–112.

Burrows, Jared. 2004. 'Musical Archetypes and Collective Consciousness: Cognitive Distribution and Free Improvisation'. *Critical Studies in Improvisation*, 1/1. Accessible at http://www.criticalimprov.com/article/view/11/36.

Burton, Charlie. 2010. 'Mod Your Sounds with RjDj'. *Wired UK Magazine*, January 2010. Accessible at http://www.wired.co.uk/magazine/archive/2010/01/play/mod-your-sounds-with-rjdj.

Butler, Judith. 1990. *Gender Trouble: Feminism and the Subversion of Identity*. New York: Routledge.

Butt, John. 2002. *Playing with History: The Historical Approach to Musical Performance*. Cambridge: Cambridge University Press.

Butt, John. 2010. *Bach's Dialogue with Modernity: Perspectives on the Passions*. Cambridge: Cambridge University Press.

Butterfield, Matthew. 2006. 'The Power of Anacrusis: Engendered Feeling in Groove-Based Musics'. *Music Theory Online* 12/4.

Cage, John. 1969. *Notations*. New York: Something Else Press.

Cameron, Kim. 2003. 'Organizational Transformation Through Architecture and Design: A Project with Frank Gehry'. *Journal of Management Inquiry* 12/1, 88–92.

Caplin, William. 2002. 'Theories of Musical Rhythm in the Eighteenth and Nineteenth Centuries'. In Thomas Christensen, ed., *The Cambridge History of Western Music Theory*. Cambridge: Cambridge University Press, 657–94.

Castelo-Branco, and Salwa El-Shawan. 2010. 'Epilogue: Ethnomusicologists as Advocates'. In John Morgan O'Connell and Salwa El-Shawan Castelo-Branco, eds., *Music and Conflict*. Urbana: University of Illinois Press, 243–52.

Chaffin, Roger, Gabriela Imreh, and Mary Crawford. 2002. *Practicing Perfection: Memory and Piano Performance*. Mahwah, NJ: Erlbaum.

Chanan, Michael. 1995. *Repeated Takes: A Short History of Recording and Its Effects on Music*. London: Verso.

Chiao YuanPu. 2007. *The Colors Between Black and White*. 2 vols. Taipei: LinKing Books.

Chion, Michel. 1994. *Audio-Vision: Sound on Screen*. Claudia Gorbman, trans. New York: Columbia University Press. (First published 1990)

Christiani, Adolph. 1885. *The Principles of Expression in Pianoforte Playing*. New York: Harper & Brothers.

Clarke, Eric. 1988. 'Generative Principles in Musical Performance'. In John Sloboda, ed., *Generative Processes in Music: The Psychology of Performance, Improvisation, and Composition*. Oxford: Oxford University Press, 1–26.

Clarke, Eric. 1992. 'Improvisation, Cognition and Education'. In John Paynter, Tim Howell, Richard Orton, and Peter Seymour, eds., *Companion to Contemporary Musical Thought*. Vol. 2. London: Routledge, 787–802.

Clarke, Eric. 1995. 'Expression in Performance: Generativity, Perception and Semiosis'. In John Rink, ed., *The Practice of Performance: Studies in Musical Interpretation*. Cambridge: Cambridge University Press, 21–54.

Clarke, Eric. 2005a. 'Creativity in Performance'. *Musicae Scientiae* 9/1, 157–82.

Clarke, Eric. 2005b. *Ways of Listening: An Ecological Approach to the Perception of Musical Meaning*. New York: Oxford University Press.

Clarke, Eric. 2006. 'Making and Hearing Meaning in Performance'. *Nordic Journal of Aesthetics*, 33/34, 24–48.

Clarke, Eric. 2007. 'The Impact of Recording on Listening'. *Twentieth-Century Music* 4/1, 47–70.

Clarke, Eric, and Jane Davidson. 1998. 'The Body in Performance'. In Wyndham Thomas, ed., *Composition-Performance-Reception: Studies in the Creative Process in Music*. Aldershot: Ashgate, 74–92.

Clarke, Eric, Nicholas Cook, Bryn Harrison, and Philip Thomas. 2005. 'Interpretation and Performance in Bryn Harrison's Être-Temps'. *Musicae Scientiae* 9/1, 31–74.

Clough, Patricia. 2007. 'Introduction'. In Patricia Clough with Jan Halley, eds., *The Affective Turn: Theorizing the Social*. Durham, NC: Duke University Press, 1–33.

Clynes, Manfred. 1995. 'Microstructural Musical Linguistics: Composer's Pulses Are Liked Best by the Best Musicians'. *Cognition* 55, 269–310.

Cochrane, Richard. 2000. 'Playing by the Rules: A Pragmatic Characterization of Musical Performance'. *Journal of Aesthetics and Art Criticism* 58, 135–41.

Coleman, Janet, and Al Young. 1994. *Mingus/Mingus: Two Memoirs*. 2nd ed. New York: Limelight Editions. (First published 1989)

Cone, Edward. 1968. *Musical Form and Musical Performance*. New York: Norton.

Connor, John Michael Gómez. 2008. 'Gramophones in Trenches'. Paper presented at Cultures of Recording: 5th CHARM Symposium. Egham, Surrey, 10–12 April 2008.

Cook, Nicholas. 1993. *Beethoven, Symphony No. 9*. Cambridge: Cambridge University Press.

Cook, Nicholas. 1995. 'The Conductor and the Theorist: Furtwängler, Schenker and the First Movement of Beethoven's Ninth Symphony'. In John Rink, ed., *The Practice of Performance: Studies in Musical Interpretation*. Cambridge: Cambridge University Press, 105–25.

Cook, Nicholas.1996. 'Music Minus One: Rock, Theory, and Performance'. *New Formations* 27, 23–41.

Cook, Nicholas. 1998. *Analysing Musical Multimedia*. Oxford: Clarendon Press.

Cook, Nicholas. 1999a. 'Analysing Performance and Performing Analysis'. In Nicholas Cook and Mark Everist, eds., *Rethinking Music*. Oxford: Oxford University Press, 239–61.

Cook, Nicholas. 1999b. 'At the Borders of Musical Identity: Schenker, Corelli, and the Graces'. *Music Analysis*, 18, 179–233.

Cook, Nicholas. 1999c. 'Performing Rewriting and Rewriting Performance: The First Movement of Brahms's Piano Trio, Op. 8'. *Dutch Journal of Music Theory* 4, 227–34.

Cook, Nicholas. 1999d. 'Words About Music, or Analysis Versus Performance'. In Nicholas Cook, Peter Johnson, and Hans Zender, *Theory into Practice: Composition, Performance and the Listening Experience*. Leuven: Leuven University Press, 9–52.

Cook, Nicholas. 2000. *Music: A Very Short Introduction*. Oxford: Oxford University Press.

Cook, Nicholas. 2001. 'Theorizing Musical Meaning'. *Music Theory Spectrum* 23, 170–95.

Cook, Nicholas. 2002. 'Epistemologies of Music Theory'. In Thomas Christensen, ed., *The Cambridge History of Western Music Theory*. Cambridge: Cambridge University Press, 78–105.

Cook, Nicholas. 2003. 'Stravinsky Conducts Stravinsky'. In Jonathan Cross, ed., *The Cambridge Companion to Stravinsky*. Cambridge: Cambridge University Press, 176–91.

Cook, Nicholas. 2006. 'Border Crossings: A Commentary on Henkjan Honing's "On the Growing Role of Observation, Formalization and Experimental Method in Musicology"'. *Empirical Musicology Review* 1/1, 7–11.

Cook, Nicholas. 2007a. 'Performance Analysis and Chopin's Mazurkas'. *Musicae Scientiae* 11/2, 183– 207.

Cook, Nicholas. 2007b. *The Schenker Project: Culture, Race, and Music Theory in Fin-de-siècle Vienna*. New York: Oxford University Press.

Cook, Nicholas. 2009. 'Squaring the Circle: Phrase Arching in Recordings of Chopin's Mazurkas'. *Musica Humana* 1/1, 5–28.

Cook, Nicholas. 2012. 'Sound Law and the Scholar'. *Popular Music and Society* 35, 603–15.

Cook, Nicholas. 2013a. 'Beyond Music: Mashup, Multimedia Mentality, and Intellectual Property'. In Claudia Gorbman, John Richardson, and Carol Vernallis, eds., *The Oxford Handbook of New Audiovisual Aesthetics*. Oxford: Oxford University Press, 53–76.

Cook, Nicholas. 2013b. 'Music and the Politics of Space'. In Georgina Born, ed., *Music, Sound, and Space: Transformations of Public and Private Experience*. Cambridge: Cambridge University Press, 224–38.

Cook, Nicholas. Forthcoming. 'Performing Research: Some Institutional Perspectives'. In Mine Doğantan-Dack, ed., *Artistic Practice as Research in Music: Theory, Criticism, Practice*. Aldershot: Ashgate.

Cook, Nicholas, and Craig Sapp. 2007. 'Purely Coincidental? Joyce Hatto and Chopin's Mazurkas'. Accessible at http://www.charm.rhul.ac.uk/projects/p2_3_2.html.

Cooper, Grosvenor, and Leonard Meyer. 1960. *The Rhythmic Structure of Music*. Chicago: University of Chicago Press.

Corbusier, Le. 1946. *Towards a New Architecture*. Frederick Etchells, trans. London: Architectural Press. (First published 1923)

Cortot, Alfred, and Jeanne Thieffry. 1937. *Alfred Cortot's Studies in Musical Interpretation*. Robert Jaques, trans. London: G. G. Harrap & Co.

Cottrell, Stephen. 2004. *Professional Music-Making in London: Ethnography and Experience*. Aldershot: Ashgate.

Cox, Arnie. 2001. 'The Mimetic Hypothesis and Embodied Musical Meaning'. *Musicae Scientiae* 5/2, 195–212.

Cox, Frank. 2002. 'Notes Toward a Performance Practice for Complex Music'. In Claus-Steffen Mahnkopf, Frank Cox, and Wolfram Schurig, eds., *Polyphony and Complexity*. Hofheim: Wolke Verlag, 7–132.

Craft, Alastair. 2012. *The Role of Culture in Music Information Retrieval: A Model of Negotiated Musical Meaning, and Its Implications in Methodology and Evaluation of the Music Genre Classification Task*. PhD diss., Goldsmiths College, University of London.

Cresswell, Tim. 2006. *On the Move: Mobility in the Western World*. New York: Routledge.

Cross, Ian. 2009. 'The Evolutionary Nature of Musical Meaning'. *Musicae Scientiae*, special issue, 179–200.

Cross, Ian. 2010. 'Listening as Covert Performance'. *Journal of the Royal Musical Association* 135, 67–77.

Csíkszentmihályi, Mihály. 1996. *Creativity: Flow and the Psychology of Discovery and Invention*. New York: Harper Perennial.

Culshaw, John. 1967. *Ring Resounding: The Recording in Stereo of Der Ring des Nibelungen*. London: Secker & Warburg.

Czerny, Carl. 1840. *Letters to a Young Lady, on the Art of Playing the Pianoforte, from the Earliest Rudiments to the Highest Stage of Cultivation: Written as an Appendix to Every School for the Instrument*. J. A. Hamilton, trans. London: R. Cocks and Co.

Dack, John. 2009. 'From Sound to Music, from Recording to Theory'. In Amanda Bayley, ed., *Recorded Music: Performance, Culture and Technology*. Cambridge: Cambridge University Press, 271–90.

Dahl, Sofia, Frédéric Bevilacqua, Roberto Bresin, Martin Clayton, Laura Leante, Isabella Poggi, and Nicolas Rasamimanana. 2010. 'Gestures in Performance'. In Ralf Inge Godøy and Marc Leman, eds., *Music Gestures: Sound, Movement, and Meaning*. New York: Routledge, 36–68.

Davidson, Jane. 2007a. 'The Activity and Artistry of Solo Vocal Performance: Insights into Investigative Observations and Interviews with Western Classical Singers'. *Musicae Scientiae*, special issue, 109–40.

Davidson, Jane. 2007b. 'Qualitative Insights into the Use of Expressive Body Movement in Solo Piano Performance: A Case Study Approach'. *Psychology of Music* 35, 381–401.

Davidson, Jane, and James Goode. 2002. 'Social and Musical Co-ordination Between Members of a String Quartet: An Exploratory Study'. *Music Psychology* 30, 186–201.

Davis, Mary. 2006. *Classic Chic: Music, Fashion, and Modernism*. Berkeley: California University Press.

Day, Timothy. 2000. *A Century of Recorded Music: Listening to Musical History*. New Haven: Yale University Press.

DeNora, Tia. 2003. *After Adorno: Rethinking Music Sociology*. Cambridge: Cambridge University Press.

Desain, Peter, and Henkjan Honing. 1993. 'Tempo Curves Considered Harmful'. *Contemporary Music Review* 7, 123–38.

Dineen, Phillip Murray. 2011. 'Gestural Economies in Conducting'. In Anthony Gritten and Elaine King, eds., *New Perspectives on Music and Gesture*. Aldershot: Ashgate, 131– 58.

Dixon, Alec. 1937. Contribution to A. W. Lawrence, ed., *T. E. Lawrence by His Friends*. Garden City, New York: Doubleday, Doran, 323–35.

Dixon, Simon, Werner Goebl, and Emilios Cambouropoulos. 2006. 'Perceptual Smoothness of Tempo in Expressively Performed Music'. *Music Perception* 23, 195–214.

Dobson, Melissa, and Stephanie Pitts. 2011. 'Classical Cult or Learning Community? Exploring New Audience Members' Social and Musical Responses to First-Time Concert Attendance'. *Ethnomusicology Forum* 20, 353–83.

Dodson, Alan. 2008. 'Performing, Grouping, and Schenkerian Alternative Readings in Some Passages from Beethoven's "Lebewohl" Sonata, Op. 81a'. *Music Analysis* 27, 107–34.

Dodson, Alan. 2009. 'Metrical Dissonance and Directed Motion in Paderewski's Recordings of Chopin's Mazurkas'. *Journal of Music Theory* 53, 57–94.

Dodson, Alan. 2011. 'Expressive Timing in Expanded Phrases: An Empirical Study of Recordings of Three Chopin Preludes'. *Music Performance Research* 4, 2–29.

Doğantan-Dack, Mine. 2002. *Matthis Lussy: A Pioneer in Studies of Expressive Performance*. Bern: Peter Lang.

Doğantan-Dack, Mine. 2008. 'Recording the Performer's Voice'. In Mine Doğantan-Dack, ed., *Recorded Music: Philosophical and Critical Reflections*. London: Middlesex University Press, 293–313.

Doğantan-Dack, Mine. 2011. 'In the Beginning Was Gesture: Piano Touch and the Phenomenology of the Performing Body'. In Anthony Gritten and Elaine King, eds., *New Perspectives on Music and Gesture*. Aldershot: Ashgate, 243–65.

Doğantan-Dack, Mine. 2012a. 'The Art of Research in Live Music Performance'. *Music Performance Research* 5, 34–48.

Doğantan-Dack, Mine. 2012b. ' "Phrasing—The Very Life of Music": Performing the Music and Nineteenth-Century Performing Theory'. *Nineteenth-Century Music Review* 9, 7–30.

Draper, Paul. 2009. 'Foreign Objects and the Art of Interpretation'. Paper presented at the Second International Conference on Music Communication Science. Sydney, Australia, 3–4 December 2009. Accessible at http://www98.griffith.edu.au/dspace/ bitstream/handle/10072/30770/58001_1.pdf?sequence=1.

Draper, Paul, and Stephen Emmerson. 2008. 'Music, Recording, and the Art of Interpretation'. Paper presented at AUC CreateWorld 2008, Brisbane, 7–10 December 2008. Accessible at http://www98.griffith.edu.au/dspace/bitstream/handle/10072/ 29122/52637_1.pdf?sequence=1.

Draper, Paul, and Stephen Emmerson. 2011. 'Remixing Modernism: Re-imagining the Music of Berg, Schoenberg and Bartók in Our Time'. *Journal on the Art of Record Production* 5. Accessible at http://arpjournal.com/1121/remixing-modernism-re-imagining-the-music-of-berg-schoenberg-and-bartok-in-our-time/.

Dreyfus, Laurence. 2007. 'Beyond the Interpretation of Music'. *Dutch Journal of Music Theory* 12, 253–72.

Drury, Stephen. 1994. 'A View from the Piano Bench or Playing John Zorn's Carny for Fun and Profit'. *Perspectives of New Music* 32/1, 194–201.

Dunsby, Jonathan. 2009. 'Roland Barthes and the Grain of Panzéra's Voice'. *Journal of the Royal Musical Association* 134, 113–32.

Dybowski, Stanisław. 2003. *Słownik Pianistów Polskich*. Warszawa: Selene.

Dybowski, Stanisław. 2005. *Laureaci Konkursów Chopinowskich*. Warszawa: Selene.

Eigeldinger, Jean-Jaques. 1986. *Chopin: Pianist and Teacher as Seen by His Pupils*. Roy Howat, ed., Naomi Shohet with Krysia Osostowicz and Roy Howat, trans. Cambridge: Cambridge University Press. (First published 1970)

Eisenberg, Evan. 2005. *The Recording Angel: Explorations in Phonography*. 2nd ed. New Haven: Yale University Press. (First published 1987)

Eitan, Zohar, and Roni Granot. 2007. 'Intensity Changes and Perceived Similarity: Inter-Parametric Analogies'. *Musicae Scientiae* Discussion Volume 4A, 39–75.

Elder, Dean. 1986. *Pianists at Play: Interviews with Leading Piano Virtuosos*. London: Kahn and Averill.

Epstein, David. 1995. *Shaping Time: Music, the Brain, and Performance*. New York: Schirmer.

Erne, Lukas. 2003. *Shakespeare as Literary Dramatist*. Cambridge: Cambridge University Press.

Ertan, Deniz. 2009. 'When Men and Mountains Meet: Ruggles, Whitman, and Their Landscapes'. *American Music* 27, 227–53.

Etherington, Ben. 2007. 'Instrumentalising Musical Ethics: Edward Said and the West-Eastern Divan Orchestra'. In Margaret Kartomi and Kay Dreyfus with David Pear, eds., *Growing up Making Music: Youth Orchestras in Australia and the World*. Melbourne: Lyrebird Press, 121–29.

Evans, Allan. 2009. *Ignaz Friedman: Romantic Master Pianist*. Bloomington: Indiana University Press.

Fabian, Dorottya. 2006. 'Is Diversity in Musical Performance Truly in Decline? The Evidence of Sound Recordings'. *Context: A Journal of Music Research* 31, 165–80.

Fabian, Dorottya, and Emery Schubert. 2008. 'Musical Character and the Performance and Perception of Dotting, Articulation and Tempo in 34 Recordings of Variation 7 from J. S. Bach's Goldberg Variations (BWV 988)'. *Musicae Scientiae* 12/2, 177–206.

Fanon, Frantz. 1967. *Black Skin, White Masks*. Charles Lam Markmann, trans. New York: Grove Press. (First published 1952)

Fast, Susan. 2001. *In the Houses of the Holy: Led Zeppelin and the Power of Rock Music*. Oxford: Oxford University Press.

Federhofer, Hellmut. 1985. *Heinrich Schenker: Nach Tagebüchern und Briefen in der Oswald Jonas Memorial Collection, University of California, Riverside*. Hildesheim: Georg Olms Verlag.

Federhofer, Hellmut. 1990. *Heinrich Schenker als Essayist und Kritiker: Gesammelte Aufsätze, Rezensionen und Kleinere Berichte aus den Jahren 1891–1901*. Hildesheim: Georg Olms Verlag.

Felski, Rita. 1999. 'The Invention of Everyday Life'. *New Formations* 39, 15–31.

Ferneyhough, Brian, and James Boros. 1990. 'Shattering the Vessels of Received Wisdom'. *Perspectives of New Music* 28/2, 6–50.

Ferneyhough, Brian, and James Boros. 1995. *Collected Writings*. James Boros and Richard Toop, eds. Amsterdam: Harwood.

Fink, Robert. 1999. "Rigoroso ($\flat$ = 126)": *The Rite of Spring* and the Forging of a Modernist Performing Style'. *Journal of the American Musicological Society* 52, 299–362.

Flossmann, Sebastian, Werner Goebl, Maarten Grachten, Bernhard Niedermayer, and Gerhard Widmer. 2010. 'The Magaloff Project: An Interim Report'. *Journal of New Music Research* 39, 363–77.

Floyd, Samuel Jr. 1995. *The Power of Black Music: Interpreting Its History from Africa to the United States*. Oxford: Oxford University Press.

Förnas, Johan, Kajsa Klein, Martina Ladendorf, Jenny Sundén, and Malin Sveningsson. 2002. 'Into Digital Borderlands'. In Johan Förnas et al., eds., *Digital Borderlands: Cultural Studies of Identity and Interactivity on the Internet*. New York: Peter Lang, 1–47.

Forster, E. M. 1951. *Two Cheers for Democracy*. New York: Harcourt Brace Jovanovich.

Foster, Susan. 2008. 'Movement's Contagion: The Kinesthetic Impact of Performance'. In Tracy Davis, ed., *The Cambridge Companion to Performance Studies*. Cambridge: Cambridge University Press, 46–59.

Foucault, Michel. 1979. *Discipline and Punish: The Birth of the Prison*. Alan Sheridan, trans. New York: Knopf Doubleday. (First published 1975)

Freeman, Austin. 1965. *The Famous Cases of Dr Thorndyke: Thirty-seven of his Criminal Investigations as Set Down by R. Austin Freeman*. London: Hodder and Stoughton.

Friberg, Anders, Roberto Bresin, and Johan Sundberg. 2006. 'Overview of the KTH Rule System for Expressive Performance'. *Advances in Cognitive Psychology* 2/2–3, 145–61.

Frith, Simon. 1996. *Performing Rites: On the Value of Popular Music*. Oxford: Oxford University Press.

Frith, Simon. 2008. 'Musical Practice'. Lecture delivered within the Royal Holloway-British Library Lectures in Musicology series *Rock and British musical culture 1995–2005*. 6 February 2008.

Frost, Anthony, and Ralph Yarrow. 2007. *Improvisation in Drama*. Basingstoke: Palgrave Macmillan.

Fuller, Buckminster. 1972. *The Buckminster Fuller Reader*. James Meller, ed.. Harmondsworth: Pelican Books.

Furtwängler, Wilhelm. 1977. *Concerning Music*. J. L. Lawrence, trans.. Westport, CT: Greenwood Press. (First published 1953)

Furtwängler, Wilhelm. 1985. 'Heinrich Schenker: A Contemporary Problem'. Jan Emerson, trans. *Sonus* 6/1, 1–5. (First published 1954)

Furtwängler, Wilhelm. 1991. *Furtwängler on Music: Essays and Addresses*. Ronald Taylor, ed. and trans. Aldershot, Hants: Ashgate.

Gabrielsson, Alf. 1999. 'The Performance of Music'. In Diana Deutsch, ed., *The Psychology of Music*. 2nd ed. San Diego, CA: Academic Press, 501–602.

Gabrielsson, Alf. 2011. *Strong Experiences with Music: Music Is Much More Than Just Music*. Oxford: Oxford University Press.

Gabrielsson, Alf., and Eric Lindström. 2010. 'The Role of Structure in the Musical Expression of Emotions'. In Patrik Juslin and John Sloboda, eds., *Handbook of Music and Emotion: Theory, Research, Applications*. Oxford: Oxford University Press.

Gál, Hans. 1974. *Franz Schubert and the Essence of Melody*. London: Gollancz.

Gates, Henry Louis Jr. 1988. *The Signifying Monkey: A Theory of Afro-American Literary Criticism*. New York: Oxford University Press.

Gehry, Frank. 2004. 'Reflections on Designing and Architectural Practice'. In Fred Collopy and Richard Boland, eds., *Managing as Designing*. Stanford, CA: Stanford University Press, 19–35.

Gendron, Bernard. 1985. 'Rock and Roll Mythology: Race and Sex in "Whole Lotta Shakin' Going On"'. University of Milwaukee Center for Twentieth Century Studies Working Paper no. 7, Fall. (Reprinted in Simon Frith, ed. 2004. *Popular Music: Critical Concepts in Media and Cultural Studies*. New York: Routledge.)

Gerig, Reginald. 1974. *Famous Pianists and Their Technique*. Washington: Robert B. Luce.

Gerling, Cristina Capparelli. 2011. 'Creative Performance Within the Boundaries of the Score'. Paper presented at CMPCP Performance Studies Network International Conference. Cambridge, 14–17 July 2011.

Gieseking, Walter, and Karl Leimer. 1972. *Piano Technique*. New York: Dover. (First published 1932 [*The Shortest Way to Pianistic Perfection*] and 1938 [*Rhythmics, Dynamics, Pedal and Other Problems of Piano Playing*])

Gilroy, Paul. 1993. *The Black Atlantic: Modernity and Double Consciousness*. London: Verso.

Ginsborg, Jane, and Roger Chaffin. 2011. 'Performance Cues in Singing: Evidence from Practice and Recall'. In Irène Deliège and Jane Davidson, eds., *Music and the Mind: Essays in Honour of John Sloboda*. Oxford: Oxford University Press, 339–60.

Gjerdingen, Robert. 1999. 'An Experimental Music Theory?' In Nicholas Cook and Mark Everist, eds., *Rethinking Music*. Oxford: Oxford University Press, 161–70.

Gjerdingen, Robert, and David Perrott. 2008. 'Scanning the Dial: The Rapid Recognition of Music Genres'. *Journal of New Music Research* 37, 93–100.

Godlovitch, Stan. 1998. *Musical Performance: A Philosophical Study*. London: Routledge.

Godøy, Rolf Inge. 2010. 'Gestural Affordances of Musical Sound'. In Rolf Inge Godøy and Marc Leman, eds., *Musical Gestures: Sound, Movement, and Meaning*. New York: Routledge, 103–25.

Godøy, Rolf Inge. 2011. 'Coarticulated Gestural-Sonic Objects in Music'. In Anthony Gritten and Elaine King, eds., *New Perspectives on Music and Gesture*. Aldershot: Ashgate, 67–82.

Goebl, Werner, Simon Dixon, and Emery Schubert. Forthcoming. 'Quantitative Methods: Motion Analysis, Audio Analysis, and Continuous Response Techniques'. In Dorottya Fabian, Renee Timmers and Emery Schubert, eds., *Expressiveness in Music Performance: Empirical Approaches Across Styles and Cultures*. Oxford: Oxford University Press.

Goehr, Lydia. 1992. *The Imaginary Museum of Musical Works: An Essay in the Philosophy of Music*. Oxford: Clarendon Press.

Goehr, Lydia. 1996. 'The Perfect Performance of Music and the Perfect Musical Performance'. *New Formations* 27, 1–22.

Goffman, Erving. 1972. *Encounters: Two Studies in the Sociology of Interaction*. New York: Penguin.

Goodale, Greg. 2011. *Sonic Persuasion: Reading Sound in the Recorded Age*. Urbana: University of Illinois Press.

Goodman, Nelson. 1968. *Languages of Art: An Approach to a Theory of Symbols*. Indianapolis: Hackett.

Goody, Jack. 1987. *The Interface Between the Written and Oral*. Cambridge: Cambridge University Press.

Gorbman, Claudia. 1987. *Unheard Melodies: Narrative Film Music*. London: BFI.

Gould, Carol, and Kenneth Keaton. 2000. 'The Essential Role of Improvisation in Musical Performance'. *Journal of Aesthetics and Art Criticism* 58, 143–48.

Gould, Glenn. 1966. 'The Prospects of Recording'. *High Fidelity Magazine* 16/4, April 1966, 46–63. Accessible at http://www.collectionscanada.gc.ca/glenngould/028010-4020.01-e.html.

Gould, Glenn. 1987. *The Glenn Gould Reader*. Tim Page, ed. London: Faber.

Grant, M. J., Rebecca Mollemann, Ingvill Morlandsto, Simone Christine Munz, and Cornelia Nuxoll. 2010. 'Music and Conflict: Interdisciplinary Perspectives'. *Interdisciplinary Science Reviews* 35, 183–98.

Gratier, Maya. 2008. 'Grounding in Musical Interaction: Evidence from Jazz Performances'. *Musicae Scientiae*, special issue, 71–110.

Graybill, Roger, 2011. 'Whose Gestures? Chamber Music and the Construction of Permanent Agents'. In Anthony Gritten and Elaine King, eds., *New Perspectives on Music and Gesture*. Aldershot: Ashgate, 221–41.

Green, David. 1997. 'A Fireside Chat with Phase Four Producer Tony D'Amato'. *Laser Tribune*. January 1997. Accessible at http://www.bernardherrmann.org/articles/interview-damato/.

Green, Michael. 1994. 'Matthis Lussy's "Traité de L'expression Musicale" as a Window into Performance Practice'. *Music Theory Spectrum* 16, 196–216.

Greig, Donald. 2009. 'Performing for (and Against) the Microphone'. In Nicholas Cook et al., eds., *The Cambridge Companion to Recorded Music*. Cambridge: Cambridge University Press, 16–29.

Griffiths, Noola. 2008. 'The Effects of Concert Dress and Physical Appearance on Perceptions of Female Solo Performer'. *Musicae Scientiae* 12/2, 273–90.

Gritten, Anthony. 2005. 'Alibis, and Why Performers Don't Have Them'. *Musicae Scientiae* 9/1, 137–56.

Gueroult, Denys. 1966. 'The Ampico Rolls on Disc'. *Gramophone*, July 1966, 24.

Gushee, Lawrence. 1998. 'The Improvisation of Louise Armstrong'. In Bruno Nettl with Melinda Russell, eds., *In the Course of Performance: Studies in the World of Musical Improvisation*. Chicago: University of Chicago Press, 291–334.

Guymer, Sheila. Forthcoming. 'Eloquent Performance: The Pronuntiatio of Topics'. In Danuta Mirka, ed., *The Oxford Handbook of Topic Theory*. New York: Oxford University Press.

Haas, Michael. 2009. 'Broadening Horizons: "Performance" in the Studio'. In Nicholas Cook et al., eds., *The Cambridge Companion to Recorded Music*. Cambridge: Cambridge University Press, 59–62.

Hall, Denis. 2012. 'Piano Roll Speeds'. *Pianola Journal* 22, 3–9.

Hamilton, Kenneth. 2008. *After the Golden Age: Romantic Pianism and Modern Performance*. New York: Oxford University Press.

Hanslick, Eduard. 1957. *On the Beautiful in Music: A Contribution to the Revisal of Musical Aesthetics*. Morris Weitz, ed., Gustav Cohen, trans. Indianapolis: Bobbs-Merrill. (First published 1854)

Hanslick, Eduard. 1963. *Music Criticisms 1846–99*. Henry Pleasants, ed. and trans. Harmondsworth: Penguin.

Hanslick, Eduard. 1986. *On the Musically Beautiful: A Contribution Towards the Revision of the Aesthetics of Music*. Geoffrey Payzant, ed. and trans. Indianapolis: Hackett. (First published 1854)

Hargreaves, David, Dorothy Miell, and Raymond MacDonald, eds. 2011. *Musical Imaginations: Multidisciplinary Perspectives on Creativity, Performance and Perception*. Oxford: Oxford University Press.

Harkins, Paul. 2012. 'Extending the Term: The Gowers Review and the Campaign to Increase the Length of Copyright in Sound Recordings'. *Popular Music and Society* 35, 629–49.

Harnoncourt, Nikolaus. 1995. *Baroque Music Today: Music as Speech. Ways to a New Understanding of Music*. Mary O'Neill, trans. Wayne, NJ: Amadeus Press. (First published 1983)

Harrison, Daniel. 2005. Review of Alexander Rehding, *Hugo Riemann and the Birth of Modern Musical Thought. Music Theory Online* 11/2.

Harrison, Max 2006. *Rachmaninoff: Life, Works, Recordings*. London: Continuum.

Hasty, Christopher. 1997. *Meter as Rhythm*. New York: Oxford University Press.

Hatten, Robert. 2006. 'A Theory of Musical Gesture and Its Application to Beethoven and Schubert'. In Anthony Gritten and Elaine King, eds., *Music and Gesture*. Aldershot: Ashgate, 1–23.

Hawkins, Stan. 2009. *The British Pop Dandy: Masculinity and Culture*. Farnham: Ashgate.

Heaton, Roger. 2009. 'Reminder: A Recording Is Not a Performance'. In Nicholas Cook et al., eds., *The Cambridge Companion to Recorded Music*. Cambridge: Cambridge University Press, 217–20.

Heaton, Roger. 2012a. 'Contemporary Performance Practice and Tradition'. *Music Performance Research* 5, 96–104.

Heaton, Roger. 2012b. 'Instrumental Performance in the Twentieth Century and Beyond'. In Colin Lawson and Robin Stowell, eds., *The Cambridge History of Performance*. Cambridge: Cambridge University Press, 778–97.

Hefling, Stephen. 1987. '"On the Manner of Playing the Adagio": Structural Levels and Performance Practice in Quantz's Versuch'. *Journal of Music Theory* 31, 205–23.

Heinonen, Yrjö. 2010. 'Crossing the Implicit Barrier: The Use of Stage and Auditorium Space in Arja Koriseva's Anniversary Concert'. Paper presented at the Embodiment of Authority conference. Sibelius Academy, Helsinki, September 2010. Accessible at http://www.siba.fi/en/web/embodimentofauthority/proceedings/heinonen.

Henderson, Mack, Joseph Tiffin, and Carl Seashore. 1936. 'The Iowa Piano Camera and Its Use'. In Carl Seashore, ed., *Objective Analysis of Musical Performance*. Vol. 4. Iowa City: University of Iowa Press, 252–62.

Herrnstein Smith, Barbara. 1980. 'Narrative Versions, Narrative Theories'. *Critical Inquiry* 7, 213–36.

Hill, Peter. 2009. 'A Short Take in Praise of Long Takes'. In Nicholas Cook et al., eds., *The Cambridge Companion to Recorded Music*. Cambridge: Cambridge University Press, 13–15.

Hill, Robert. 1994. '"Overcoming Romanticism": On the Modernization of Twentieth-century Performance Practice'. In Bryan Gilliam, ed., *Music and Performance During the Weimar Republic*. Cambridge: Cambridge University Press, 37–58.

Hoffmann, E. T. A. 1989. *E. T. A. Hoffmann's Musical Writings: Kreisleriana, the Poet and the Composer, Music Criticism*. David Charlton, ed., Martyn Clarke, trans. Cambridge: Cambridge University Press.

Howell, Tim. 1992. 'Analysis and Performance the Search for a Middleground'. In John Paynter, Tim Howell, Richard Orton, and Peter Seymour, eds., *Companion to Contemporary Musical Thought*. Vol. 2. London: Routledge, 692–714.

Howlett, Mike. 2009. *The Record Producer as Nexus: Creative Inspiration, Technology and the Recording Industry*. PhD diss., University of Glamorgan.

Huang, Jennifer, and Carol Krumhansl. 2011. 'What Does Seeing the Performer Add? It Depends on Musical Style, Amount of Stage Behavior, and Audience Expertise'. *Musicae Scientiae* 15, 343–64.

Hudson, Richard. 1994. *Stolen Time: The History of Tempo Rubato*. Oxford: Clarendon Press.

Huhtamo, Erkki. 1997. 'From Kaleidoscomaniac to Cybernerd: Towards An Archaeology of the Media'. *Leonardo*, 30/3, 221–24.

Huneker, James. 1903. *Mezzotints in Modern Music: Brahms, Tchaïkowsky, Chopin, Richard Strauss, Liszt and Wagner*. 3rd ed. New York: Scribner's.

Hunter, Mary. 2012. '"The Most Interesting Genre of Music": Performance, Sociability and Meaning in the Classical String Quartet, 1800–1830'. *Nineteenth-Century Music Review* 9, 53–74.

Huron, David. 1999. 'Lecture 3. Methodology: The New Empiricism: Systematic Musicology in a Postmodern Age'. (From the Ernst Bloch Lectures, 1999.) Accessible at http://csml.som.ohio-state.edu/Music220/Bloch.lectures/3.Methodology.html.

Huron, David, and Jonathan Berec. 2009. 'Characterizing Idiomatic Organization in Music: A Theory and Case Study of Musical Affordances'. *Empirical Musicology Review* 4/3, 103–22. Accessible at http://hdl.handle.net/1811/44531.

Hutchins, Edwin. 1995. *Cognition in the Wild*. Cambridge, MA: MIT Press.

Irving, John. 1997. *Mozart's Piano Sonatas: Contexts, Sources, Style*. Cambridge: Cambridge University Press.

Isidore of Seville, Saint. 2006. *The Etymologies of Isidore of Seville*. Stephen Barney, W. J. Lewis, J. A. Beach, and Oliver Berghof, trans. Cambridge: Cambridge University Press.

Iyer, Vijay. 2002. 'Embodied Mind, Situated Cognition, and Expressive Microtiming in African-American Music'. *Music Perception* 19, 387–414.

Izhaki, Roey. 2008. *Mixing Audio: Concepts, Practices and Tools*. Oxford: Focal Press.

James, Warwick. 1937. Contribution to A. W. Lawrence, ed., *T. E. Lawrence by His Friends*. Garden City, New York: Doubleday, Doran, 463–78.

Järviö, Päivi. 2010. 'Music Moves in Me—The Singing Body as Interior Movement'. Paper presented at the Embodiment of Authority conference. Sibelius Academy, Helsinki, September 2010. Accessible at http://www.siba.fi/web/embodimentofauthority/proceedings/jarvio.

Jenkins, Henry. 2006. *Convergence Culture: Where Old and New Media Collide*. New York: New York University Press.

Jenkins, Simon. 2003. *England's Thousand Best Houses*. London: Allen Lane.

Jensenius, Alexander, Marcelo Wanderley, Rolf Godøy, and Marc Leman. 2010. 'Musical Gestures: Concept and Methods in Research'. In Rolf Godøy and Marc Leman, eds., *Musical Gestures: Sound, Movement, and Meaning*. New York: Routledge, 12–35.

Jia Shubing. 2012. *The Dissemination of Western Music Through Catholic Missions in High Qing China (1662–1795)*. PhD diss., University of Bristol.

Johnson, Bruce. 2002. 'Jazz as Cultural Practice'. In Mervyn Cooke and David Horn, eds., *The Cambridge Companion to Jazz*. Cambridge: Cambridge University Press, 96–113.

Johnson, Julian. 2002. *Who Needs Classical Music? Cultural Choice and Musical Value*. Oxford: Oxford University Press.

Johnson, Mark. 2007. *The Meaning of the Body: Aesthetics of Human Understanding*. Chicago: University of Chicago Press.

Johnson, Mark, and Steve Larson. 2003. 'Something in the Way She Moves: Metaphors of Musical Motion'. *Metaphor and Symbol* 18/2, 63–84.

Johnson, Peter. 1997. 'Music Works, Music Performances'. *Musical Times*, August 1997, 4–11.

Johnson, Peter. 2002. 'The Legacy of Recordings'. In John Rink, ed., *Musical Performance: A Guide to Understanding*. Cambridge: Cambridge University Press, 197–212.

Johnson, Peter. 2007. 'The Influence of Recordings on Critical Readings of Musical Works'. Paper presented at the CHARM/RMA Musicology and Recordings Conference. Egham, Surrey, 13–15 September 2007.

Johnson-Laird, Philip. 1991. 'Jazz Improvisation: A Theory at the Computational Level'. In Peter Howell, Robert West, and Ian Cross, eds., *Representing Musical Structure*. London: Academic Press, 291–325.

Jonas, Oswald. 2003. 'Schenker and Great Performers'. Alan Dodson, trans. *Theory and Practice* 28, 127–35. (First published 1964)

Judd, Charles. 1896. Review of *Recherches Graphiques sur la Musique*. *Psychological Review* 3/1, 112–13.

Juslin, Patrik. 2003. 'Five Facets of Musical Expression: A Psychologist's Perspective on Music Performance'. *Psychology of Music* 31, 273–302.

Juslin, Patrik. 2011. 'Music and Emotion: Seven Questions, Seven Answers'. In Irène Dèliege and Jane Davidson, eds., *Music and the Mind: Essays in Honour of John Sloboda*. Oxford: Oxford University Press, 113–35.

Juslin, Patrik, and Renee Timmers. 2010. 'Expression and Communication of Emotion in Music Performance'. In Patrik Juslin and John Sloboda, eds., *Handbook of Music and Emotion: Theory, Research, Applications*. Oxford: Oxford University Press, 453–89.

Kallberg, Jeffrey. 1996. *Chopin at the Boundaries: Sex, History and Musical Genre*. Cambridge, MA: Harvard University Press.

Kallberg, Jeffrey. 2004. 'Hearing Poland: Chopin and Nationalism'. In Larry Todd, ed., *Nineteenth- Century Piano Music*. New York: Routledge, 221–57.

Kański, Józef. 1986. *Dyskografia Chopinowska: Historycny Katalo Nargań Płytowych*. Warszawa: Polskie Wydawnictwo Muzyczne.

Katz, Mark. 2004. *Capturing Sound: How Technology Has Changed Music*. Berkeley: University of California Press.

Kaye, Nick. 1994. *Postmodernism and Performance*. London: Macmillan.

Kazdin, Andrew. 1989. *Glenn Gould at Work: Creative Lying*. New York: Dutton.

Keightley, Keir. 1996. '"Turn It Down!" She Shrieked: Gender, Domestic Space, and High Fidelity, 1948–59'. *Popular Music* 15/2, 149–77.

Keller, Hans. 1990. *Keller Column: Essays by Hans Keller from 'Music and Musicians Magazine', 1984–5*. Robert Matthew-Walker, ed. London: Alfred Lengnick.

Keller, Peter. Forthcoming. 'Ensemble Performance: Interpersonal Alignment of Musical Expression'. In Dorottya Fabian, Renee Timmers and Emery Schubert, eds., *Expressiveness in Music Performance: Empirical Approaches Across Styles and Cultures*. Oxford: Oxford University Press.

Kentner, Louis. 1976. *Yehudi Menuhin Music Guides: Piano*. London: Macdonald and Jane's.

Kenyon, Nicholas. 2012. 'Performance Today'. In Colin Lawson and Robert Stowell, eds., *The Cambridge History of Musical Performance*. Cambridge: Cambridge University Press, 1–34.

Kerman, Joseph. 1985. *Contemplating Music: Challenges to Musicology*. Cambridge, MA: Harvard University Press.

Kernfeld, Barry. 1995. *What to Listen for in Jazz*. New Haven: Yale University Press.

Kershaw, Baz. 1992. *The Politics of Performance: Radical Theatre as Cultural Intervention*. London: Routledge.

King, Elaine. 2006. 'Supporting Gestures: Breathing in Piano Performance'. In Anthony Gritten and Elaine King, eds., *Music and Gesture*. Aldershot: Ashgate, 142–64.

King, Elaine, and Jane Ginsborg. 2011. 'Gestures and Glances: Interactions in Ensemble Rehearsal'. In Anthony Gritten and Elaine King, eds., *New Perspectives on Music and Gesture*. Aldershot: Ashgate, 177–201.

Kivy, Peter. 1990. *Music Alone: Philosophical Reflections on the Purely Musical Experience*. Ithaca, NY: Cornell University Press.

Kivy, Peter. 1995. *Authenticities: Philosophical Reflections on Musical Performance*. Ithaca, NY: Cornell University Press.

Kleczynski, Jean. 1912. *Chopin's Greater Works (Preludes, Ballads, Nocturnes, Polonaises, Mazurkas): How They Should be Understood*. London: William Reeves.

Klein, Michael. 2012. 'Chopin Dreams: The Mazurka in C Sharp Minor, Op. 30, No. 4'. *Nineteenth-Century Music* 25, 238–60.

Kramer, Lawrence. 1995. *Classical Music and Postmodern Knowledge*. Berkeley: University of California Press.

Kramer, Lawrence. 2007. *Why Classical Music Still Matters*. Berkeley: University of California Press.

Kramer, Lawrence. 2011. *Interpreting Music*. Berkeley: University of California Press.

Krims, Adam. 2007. *Music and Urban Geography*. New York: Routledge.

Krumhansl, Carol. 1996. 'A Perceptual Analysis of Mozart's Piano Sonata K. 282: Segmentation, Tension, and Musical Ideas'. *Music Perception* 13, 401–32.

Krumhansl, Carol. 2010. 'Plink: "Thin Slices" of Music'. *Music Perception* 27, 337–54.

Kuhn, Thomas. 1962. *The Structure of Scientific Revolutions*. Chicago: University of Chicago Press.

Kullak, Adolph. 1893. *The Aesthetics of Pianoforte-Playing*. New York: Schirmer.

Kurosawa, Kaori, and Jane Davidson 2005. 'Nonverbal Behaviours in Popular Music Performance: A Case Study of The Corrs'. *Musicae Scientiae* 9/1, 111–36.

Lacasse, Serge. 2000. 'Intertextuality and Hypertextuality in Recorded Popular Music'. In Michael Talbot, ed., *The Musical Work: Reality or Invention?* Liverpool: University of Liverpool Press, 35–58.

Lancaster, Osbert. 1939. *Homes Sweet Homes*. London: John Murray.

Landowska, Wanda. 1964. *Landowska on Music*. Denise Restout, ed. New York: Stein and Day.

Lang, Paul Henry. 1978. 'The Symphonies'. In *The Recordings of Beethoven as Viewed by the Critics from High Fidelity*. Westport, CT: Greenwood Press, 1–25.

Latour, Bruno. 2005. *Reassembling the Social: An Introduction to Actor-Network-Theory*. Oxford: Oxford University Press.

Laurence, Felicity. 2008. 'Music and Empathy'. In Olivier Urbain, ed., *Music and Conflict Transformation: Harmonies and Dissonances in Geopolitics*. London: Tauris, 13–25.

Lawson, Colin, and Robert Stowell. 2012. 'The Future?' In Colin Lawson and Robert Stowell, eds., *The Cambridge History of Musical Performance*. Cambridge: Cambridge University Press, 817–33.

Leadley, Marcus. 2002. 'Micro Test: Fender Strat '68 Reverse Special'. *Guitar Magazine* 13/4, 57.

Leech-Wilkinson, Daniel. 1984. 'What We Are Doing with Early Music Is Genuinely Authentic to Such a Small Degree That the Word Loses Most of Its Intended Meaning'. *Early Music* 12, 13–16.

Leech-Wilkinson, Daniel. 2007. 'Sound and Meaning in Recordings of Schubert's "Die Junge Nonne"'. *Musicae Scientiae* 11/2, 209–36.

Leech-Wilkinson, Daniel. 2009a. *The Changing Sound of Music: Approaches to Studying Recorded Musical Performances*. London: AHRC Research Centre for the History and Analysis of Recorded Music. Accessible at http://www.charm.rhul.ac.uk/studies/chapters/intro.html.

Leech-Wilkinson, Daniel. 2009b. 'Recordings and Histories of Performance Style'. In Nicholas Cook et al., eds., *The Cambridge Companion to Recorded Music*. Cambridge: Cambridge University Press, 246–62.

Leech-Wilkinson, Daniel. 2010a. 'Listening and Responding to the Evidence of Early Twentieth-century Performance'. *Journal of the Royal Musical Association* 135, 45–62.

Leech-Wilkinson, Daniel.2010b. 'Performance Style in Elena Gerhardt's Schubert Song Recordings'. *Musicae Scientiae* 14/2, 57–84.

Leech-Wilkinson, Daniel.2011. 'Making Music with Alfred Cortot: Ontology, Data, Analysis'. In Heinz von Loesch and Stefan Weinzier, eds., *Gemessene Interpretation: C omputergestützte Aufführungsanalyse im Kreuzverhör der Disziplinen*. Mainz: Schott, 129–44.

Leech-Wilkinson, Daniel.2012. 'Compositions, Scores, Performances, Meanings'. *Music Theory Online* 18/1.

Leech-Wilkinson, Daniel. Forthcoming. 'Shape and Feeling'. In Daniel Leech-Wilkinson and Helen Prior, eds., *Music and Shape*. New York: Oxford University Press.

Le Guin, Elisabeth. 2002. ' "One Says That One Weeps, But One Does Not Weep": Sensible, Grotesque, and Mechanical Embodiments in Boccherini's Chamber Music'. *Journal of the American Musicological Society* 55, 207–54.

Le Guin, Elisabeth. 2005. *Boccherini's Body: An Essay in Carnal Musicology*. Berkeley: University of California Press.

Lehmann, Andreas. 2011. 'Expressive Variants in the Opening of Robert Schuman's Arlequin (from Carnaval, op. 9): 54 Pianists' Interpretations of a Metrical Ambiguity'. In Irène Dèliege and Jane Davidson, eds., *Music and the Mind: Essays in Honour of John Sloboda*. Oxford: Oxford University Press, 311–23.

Leikin, Anatole. 2011. *The Performing Style of Alexander Scriabin*. Farnham: Ashgate.

Leman, Marc. 2010. 'An Embodied Approach to Music Semantics'. *Musicae Scientiae* Discussion Forum 5, 43–67.

Leong, Daphne and David Korevaar. 2005. 'The Performer's Voice: Performance and Analysis in Ravel's Concerto Pour la Main Gauche'. *Music Theory Online* 11/3.

Leppert, Richard. 1993. *The Sight of Sound: Music, Representation, and the History of the Body*. Berkeley: University of California Press.

Lerdahl, Fred, and Ray Jackendoff. 1983. *A Generative Theory of Tonal Music*. Cambridge, MA: MIT Press.

Lessig, Lawrence. 2008. *Remix: Making Art and Commerce Thrive in the Hybrid Economy.* London: Bloomsbury.

Lester, Joel. 1995. 'Performance and Analysis: Interaction and Interpretation'. In John Rink, ed., *The Practice of Performance: Studies in Musical Interpretation.* Cambridge: Cambridge University Press, 197–216.

Levinson, Jerrold. 1997. *Music in the Moment.* Ithaca, NY: Cornell University Press.

Levinson, Jerrold. 1993. 'Performative vs. Critical Interpretation in Music'. In Michael Krausz, ed., *The Interpretation of Music: Philosophical Essays.* Oxford: Clarendon Press, 33–60.

Lewis, Eric. 2007. 'Ontology, Originality and the Musical Work: Copyright Law and the Status of Samples'. In Faculty of Law, McGill University, ed., *Meredith Lectures 2006: Intellectual Property at the Edge: New Approaches to IP in a Transsystemic World.* Montréal: Editions Yvon Blais.

Lewis, Leslie Anne. 2006. 'The Conductor as Analyst'. M.Mus. diss., Royal Holloway, University of London.

Lewis, Leslie Anne. 2010. 'Outside in and Inside Out: The Implications of "Leadership from Within" on the Modern Conductor's Role'. Paper presented at The 'Orchestra' from Symphony to Sustainability: Communities, Environments, Education, Technologies Conference. London, 23 April 2010.

Lewis, Leslie Anne. 2011. 'The Impact of Shared Leadership, Memory, and Cognition on Orchestral Performance: The Britten Sinfonia as a Case Study'. Paper presented at CMPCP Performance Studies Network International Conference. Cambridge, 14–17 July 2011.

List, George. 1979. 'Ethnomusicology: A Discipline Defined'. *Ethnomusicology* 23, 1–4.

Littlejohn, David. 1992. *The Ultimate Art: Essays Around and About Opera.* Berkeley: University of California Press.

Lockwood, Lewis. 2002. 'Recent Writings on Beethoven's Late Quartets'. *Beethoven Forum* 9, 84–99.

London, Justin. 2004. *Hearing in Time: Psychological Aspects of Musical Meter.* New York: Oxford University Press.

Lott, Eric. 1995. *Love and Theft: Blackface Minstrelsy and the American Working Class.* Oxford: Oxford University Press.

Lowe, Bethany. 2003. 'On the Relationship Between Analysis and Performance: The Mediatory Role of the Interpretation'. *Indiana Theory Review* 24, 47–94.

Lubben, Joseph. 1995. *Analytic Practice and Ideology in Heinrich Schenker's Der Tonwille and Cantus Harmonia Mundi.* PhD diss., Brandeis University.

Lussy, Matthis. 1874. *Traité de l'expression Musicale: Accents, Nuances et Mouvements dans la Musique Vocale et Instrumentale.* Paris: Heugel et cie.

Mach, Elyse. 1981. *Great Pianists Speak for Themselves.* London: Robson.

Mach, Zdzislaw. 1994. 'National Anthems: The Case of Chopin as a National Composer'. In Martin Stokes, ed., *Ethnicity, Identity and Music: The Musical Construction of Place.* Oxford: Berg, 61–70.

MacKenzie, Colin. 2006. 'Tony D'Amato: Mantovani's Record Producer' (obituary). *Independent.* 27 July 2006. Accessible at http://www.independent.co.uk/news/obitu-aries/tony-damato-409398.html.

Maconie, Robert. 1989. *Stockhausen on Music: Lectures and Interviews.* London: Marion Boyars.

MacQueen, Hector, Charlotte Waelder, and Graeme Laurie. 2008. *Contemporary Intellectual Property: Law and Policy*. Oxford: Oxford University Press.

Mailer, Norman. 1957. *The White Negro*. San Francisco: City Lights.

Mann, Thomas. 1952. *The Magic Mountain*. H. T. Lower-Porter, trans. London: Vintage. (First published 1924)

Markula-Denison, Pirkko, and Richard Pringle. 2006. *Foucault, Sport and Exercise: Power, Knowledge and Transforming the Self*. New York: Routledge.

Martin, Robert. 1993. 'Musical Works in the World of Performers and Listeners'. In Michael Krausz, ed., *The Interpretation of Music: Philosophical Essays*. Oxford: Clarendon Press, 119–27.

Martin, Robert. 1994. 'The Quartets in Performance: A Player's Perspective'. In Robert Winter and Robert Martin, eds., *The Beethoven Quartet Companion*. Berkeley: University of California Press, 111–41.

Marx, Hans Joachim. 1975. 'Some Unknown Embellishments of Corelli's Violin Sonatas'. *Musical Quarterly* 61, 65–76.

Massumi, Brian. 1995. 'The Autonomy of Affect'. *Cultural Critique* 31, 83–109.

Maus, Fred. 2004. 'The Disciplined Subject of Musical Analysis'. In Andrew Dell'Antonio, ed., *Beyond Structural Listening? Postmodern Modes of Hearing*. Berkeley: University of California Press, 13–43.

Mazzola, Guerino (in collaboration with Sara Cowan, I-Yi Pan, James Holdman, Cory Renbarger, Lisa Rhoades, Florian Thalmann, and Nikolai Zielinski). 2011. *Musical Performance. A Comprehensive Approach: Theory, Analytical Tools, and Case Studies*. Heidelberg: Springer.

McClary, Susan. 2001. *Conventional Wisdom: The Content of Musical Form*. Berkeley: University of California Press.

McCreless, Patrick. 2002. 'Music and Rhetoric'. In Thomas Christensen, ed., *The Cambridge History of Western Music Theory*. Cambridge: Cambridge University Press, 847–79.

McEwen, John. 1928. *Tempo Rubato: Or, Time Variation in Musical Performance*. London: Oxford University Press.

McGinn, Robert. 1983. 'Stokowski and the Bell Telephone Laboratories: Collaboration in the Development of High-Fidelity Sound Reproduction'. *Technology and Culture* 24, 38–74.

McSwain, Rebecca. 2000. 'The Social Reconstruction of a Reverse Salient in Electric Guitar Technology: Noise, the Solid Body, and Jimi Hendrix'. In Hans-Joachim Braun, ed., *'I Sing the Body Electric': Music and Technology in the 20th Century*. Hofheim am Taunus: Wolke, 198–210.

Melrose, Susan. 1994. *A Semiotics of the Dramatic Text*. London: Macmillan.

Mendel, Arthur. 1969. 'Some Preliminary Attempts at Computer-Assisted Style Analysis in Music'. *Computers and the Humanities* 4, 41–52.

Methuen-Campbell, James. 1981. *Chopin Playing: From the Composer to the Present Day*. London: Gollancz.

Middleton, Richard. 2006. *Voicing the Popular: On the Subjects of Popular Music*. New York: Routledge.

Milewski, Barbara. 1999. 'Chopin's Mazurkas and the Myth of the Folk'. *Nineteenth-Century Music* 23, 113–35.

Miller, Daniel. 1987. *Material Culture and Mass Consumption*. Oxford: Blackwell.

Milner, Greg. 2009. *Perfecting Sound Forever. The Story of Recorded Music*. London: Granta.

Monsaingeon, Bruno. 2001. *Sviatoslav Richter: Notebooks and Conversations*. Princeton, NJ: Princeton University Press.

Monson, Ingrid. 1996. *Saying Something: Jazz Improvisation and Interaction*. Chicago: Chicago University Press.

Monson, Ingrid. 2011. 'Recirculating Jazz'. Keynote paper presented at Renew, Reuse, Recycle: From Quotation to Remediation in Art and Popular Music Conference. Cambridge, March 2011.

Moorefield, Virgil. 2005. *The Producer as Composer: From the Illusion of Reality to the Reality of Illusion*. Cambridge, MA: MIT Press.

Moretti, Franco. 2000. 'Conjectures on World Literature'. *New Left Review* 1, 54–68.

Morgan, Nick. 2010. '"A New Pleasure": Listening to National Gramophonic Society Records, 1924–31'. *Musicae Scientiae* 14/2, 139–64.

Moseley, Roger. 2013. 'Playing Games with Music (and Vice Versa): Ludomusicological Perspectives on Guitar Hero and Rock Band'. In Nicholas Cook and Richard Pettengill, eds., *Taking It to the Bridge: Music as Performance*. Ann Arbor: Michigan University Press, 279–318.

Mugglestone, Eric. 1981. 'Guido Adler's "The Scope, Method, and Aim of Musicology" (1885): An English Translation with an Historico-analytical Commentary'. *Yearbook for Traditional Music* 13, 1–21.

Murnighan, Keith, and Donald Conlon. 1991. 'The Dynamics of Intense Work Groups: A Study of British String Quartets'. *Administrative Science Quarterly* 36, 165–86.

Murray, Charles Shaar. 1989. *Crosstown Traffic: Jimi Hendrix and Post-War Pop*. London: Faber.

Narmour, Eugene. 1988. 'On the Relationship of Analytical Theory to Performance and Interpretation'. In Eugene Narmour and Ruth Solie, eds., *Explorations in Music, the Arts, and Ideas: Essays in Honor of Leonard B. Meyer*. Stuyvesant, NY: Pendragon Press, 317–40.

Nettl, Bruno. 1983. *The Study of Ethnomusicology: Twenty-nine Issues and Concepts*. Urbana: University of Illinois Press.

Nettl, Bruno. 1989. 'Mozart and the Ethnomusicological Study of Western Culture (An Essay in Four Movements)'. *Yearbook for Traditional Music* 21, 1–16.

Nettl, Bruno. 1998. 'Introduction: An Art Neglected in Scholarship'. In Bruno Nettl with Melinda Russell, eds., *In the Course of Performance: Studies in the World of Musical Improvisation*. Chicago: University of Chicago Press, 1–23.

Neuhaus, Heinrich. 1993. *The Art of Piano Playing*. Trans. K. A. Leibovitch. London: Kahn and Averill.

Newlin, Dika. 1980. *Schoenberg Remembered: Diaries and Recollections (1938–76)*. New York: Pendragon Press.

Nimmer, Melville, and David Nimmer. 1997. *Nimmer on Copyright*. Albany, NY: Matthew Bender.

Nooshin, Laudan. 2008. 'Ethnomusicology, Alterity, and Disciplinary Identity; or "Do We Still Need an Ethno-?" "Do We Still Need an -ology"?' In Henry Stobart, ed., *The New (Ethno)musicologies*. Lanham, MD: Scarecrow Press, 71–75.

Norris, Geoffrey. 1993. *Rachmaninoff*. London: Dent.

November, Nancy. 'Performance History and Beethoven's String Quartets: Setting the Record Crooked'. *Journal of Musicological Research* 30, 1–22.

Ohriner, Mitchell. 2012. 'Grouping Hierarchy and Trajectories of Pacing in Performances of Chopin's Mazurkas'. *Music Theory Online* 18/1.

Oliver, Michael. 1999. *Settling the Score: A Journey Through the Music of the Twentieth Century*. London: Faber.

Oort, Bart van. 2003. 'To Speak or to Sing: Mozart and Beethoven on the Fortepiano'. In Arie Peddemors and Leo Samama, eds., *Mozart and the Netherlands: A Bicentenarian Retrospect*. Zutphen, Neth.: Walburg Pers, 77–88.

Pace, Ian. 2009. 'Notation, Time and the Performer's Relationship to the Score in Contemporary Music'. In Darla Crispin, ed., *Unfolding Time: Studies in Temporality in Twentieth-Century Music*. Leuven: Leuven University Press, 151–92.

Paderewski, Ignacy. 2001/1909. 'Tempo Rubato'. *Polish Music Journal* 4/1. Accessible at http://www.usc.edu/dept/polish_music/PMJ/issue/4.1.01/paderewskirubato.html (first published 1909).

Palmer, Caroline. 1996. 'On the Assignment of Structure in Music Performance'. *Music Perception* 14, 23–56.

Palmer, Caroline. 1997. 'Music Performance'. *Annual Review of Psychology* 48, 115–38.

Panigel, Armand, and Marcal Beaufils. 1949. *L'Œuvre de Frédéric Chopin: Discographie Generale*. Paris: Editions de la Revue Disques.

Parncutt, Richard. 2003. 'Accents and Expression in Piano Performance'. In K. W. Niemöller, ed., *Perspektiven und Methoden einer Systemischen Musikwissenschaft*. Frankfurt am Mein: Peter Lang, 163–85.

Patel, Aniruddh, John Iversen, and Jason Rosenberg. 2006. 'Comparing the Rhythm and Melody of Speech and Music: The Case of British English and French'. *Journal of the Acoustical Society of America* 119/5, 3034–3047.

Patmore, David. 2009. 'Selling Sounds: Recordings and the Record Business'. In Nicholas Cook et al., eds., *The Cambridge Companion to Recorded Music*. Cambridge: Cambridge University Press, 120–39.

Patmore, David, and Eric Clarke. 2007. 'Making and Hearing Virtual Worlds: John Culshaw and the Art of Record Production'. *Musicae Scientiae* 11, 269–93.

Peres da Costa, Neal. 2012. *Off the Record: Performance Practices in Romantic Piano Playing*. New York: Oxford University Press.

Phelan, Peggy. 1993. *Unmarked: The Politics of Performance*. London: Routledge.

Philip, Robert. 1992. *Early Recordings and Musical Style: Changing Tastes in Instrumental Performance, 1900–1950*. Cambridge: Cambridge University Press.

Philip, Robert. 2004. *Performing Music in the Age of Recording*. New Haven: Yale University Press.

Philip, Robert. 2007. 'Studying Recordings: The Evolution of a Discipline'. Keynote paper presented at the CHARM/RMA Musicology and Recordings conference. Egham, Surrey, 13–15 September 2007. Accessible at http://charm.cchcdn.net/redist/pdf/R.Philip_keynote.pdf.

Pierce, Alexandra. 1994. 'Developing Schenkerian Hearing and Performing'. *Intégral*, 8, 51–123.

Pinker, Steven. 1999. *How the Mind Works*. London: Penguin Books.

Pirie, Peter. 1980. *Furtwängler and the Art of Conducting*. London: Duckworth.

Podołak, Michal. 2005. 'Selecting from the Epoch: The Art of Selecting. A Researcher's Brief Guide to Vera Rerum Vocabula'. Paper presented at the Fifth International Conference of the Fryderyk Chopin Institute. Warsaw.

Potter, John. 1998. *Vocal Authority: Singing Style and Ideology*. Cambridge: Cambridge University Press.

Pressing, Jeff. 1988. 'Improvisation: Methods and Models'. In John Sloboda, ed., *Generative Processes in Music: The Psychology of Performance, Improvisation, and Composition*. Oxford: Clarendon Press, 129–78.

Pressing, Jeff. 1998. 'Psychological Constraints on Improvisational Expertise and Communication'. In Bruno Nettl with Melinda Russell, eds., *In the Course of Performance: Studies in the World of Musical Improvisation*. Chicago: University of Chicago Press, 47–67.

Prictor, Megan. 2000. *Music and the Ordinary Listener: Music Appreciation and the Media in England 1918–39*. PhD diss., University of Melbourne.

Pritchard, Matthew. 2013. '"A Heap of Broken Images"? Reviving Austro-German Debates over Musical Meaning, 1900–1936'. *Journal of the Royal Musical Association* 138, 129–74.

Pryer, Anthony. Forthcoming. 'Re-Reading Hanslick: Musical Performance and "The Music Itself"'.

Quick, Miriam. 2010. *Performing Modernism: Webern on Record*. PhD diss., King's College London.

Rabinowitch, Tal-Chen, Ian Cross, and Pamela Burnard. 2013. 'Long-Term Musical Group Interaction Has a Positive Influence on Empathy in Children'. *Psychology of Music* 41, 484–98.

Ratner, Leonard. 1991. 'Topical Content in Mozart's Keyboard Sonatas'. *Early Music* 19, 615–19.

Rebelo, Pedro. 2010. 'Notating the Unpredictable'. *Contemporary Music Review* 29/1, 17–27.

Reigl, Aloïs. 1992. *Problems of Style: Foundations for a History of Ornament*. Evelyn Kain, trans. Princeton, NJ: Princeton University Press.

Reinecke, Carl. 1897. *The Beethoven Pianoforte Sonatas: Letters to a Lady*. London: Augener.

Repp, Bruno. 1992. 'Diversity and Commonality in Music Performance: An Analysis of Timing Microstructure in Schumann's "Träumerei"'. *Journal of the Acoustical Society of America* 92/5, 2546–68.

Repp, Bruno. 1994. 'On Determining the Basic Tempo of an Expressive Music Performance'. *Psychology of Music* 22, 157–67.

Repp, Bruno. 1995. 'Expressive Timing in Schumann's "Träumerei": An Analysis of Performances by Graduate Student Pianists'. *Journal of the Acoustical Society of America* 98/5, Part I, 2413–27.

Repp, Bruno. 1998. 'A Microcosm of Musical Expression. I. Quantitative Analysis of Pianists' Timing in the Initial Measures of Chopin's Etude in E Major'. *Journal of the Acoustical Society of America* 104, 1085–1100.

Repp, Bruno. 1999. 'A Microcosm of Musical Expression. III. Contributions of Timing and Dynamics to the Aesthetic Impression of Pianists' Performances of the Initial Measures of Chopin's Etude in E Major'. *Journal of the Acoustical Society of America* 106/1, 469–78.

Ridley, Aaron. 2004. *The Philosophy of Music: Theme and Variations*. Edinburgh: Edinburgh University Press.

Riemann, Hugo. 1892. *Catechism of Piano Playing*. London: Augener.

Rink, John. 1990. Review of Wallace Berry, *Musical Structure and Performance*. *Music Analysis* 9, 319–39.

Rink, John. 1999. 'Translating Musical Meaning'. In Nicholas Cook and Mark Everist, eds., *Rethinking Music*. Oxford: Oxford University Press, 217–38.

Rink, John. 2002. 'Analysis and (or?) Performance'. In John Rink, ed., *Musical Performance: A Guide to Understanding*. Cambridge: Cambridge University Press, 35–58.

Rink, John, Neta Spiro, and Nicolas Gold. 2011. 'Motive, Gesture and the Analysis of Performance'. In Anthony Gritten and Elaine King, eds., *New Perspectives on Music and Gesture*. Aldershot: Ashgate, 267–92.

Rollefson, Griffith. 2008. 'The "Robot Voodoo Power" Thesis: Afrofuturism and Anti-Anti-Essentialism from Sun Ra to Kool Keith'. *Black Music Research Journal* 28, 83–109.

Rosen, Charles. 2003. *Piano Notes: The Hidden World of the Pianist*. London: Allen Lane.

Rosen, Charles. 2005. 'Playing Music: The Lost Freedom'. *New York Review of Books*, 3 November 2005, 52/17. Accessible at http://www.nybooks.com/articles/18400/.

Rosenwald, Lawrence. 1993. 'Theory, Text-Setting, and Performance'. *Journal of Musicology* 11, 52–65.

Ross, Alex. 2004. 'Listen to This: A Classical Kid Learns to Love Pop—And Wonders Why He Has to Make a Choice'. *New Yorker*, 16 February 2004. Accessible at http://www.newyorker.com/archive/2004/02/16/040216fa_fact4.

Ross, Alex. 2010. 'Hold Your Applause: Inventing and Reinventing the Classical Concert'. Royal Philharmonic Society Lecture, 8 March 2010. Accessible at alexrossmusic.typepad.com/files/rps_lecture_2010_alex-ross.pdf.

Roth, Wolff-Michael, and Michael Bowen. 2001. 'Professionals Read Graphs: A Semiotic Analysis'. *Journal for Research in Mathematics Education* 32/2, 159–94.

Rothfarb, Lee. 2002. 'Energetics'. In Thomas Christensen, ed., *The Cambridge History of Western Music Theory*. Cambridge: Cambridge University Press, 927–55.

Rothstein, William. 1984. 'Heinrich Schenker as an Interpreter of Beethoven's Piano Sonatas'. *Nineteenth-Century Music* 8, 3–28.

Rothstein, William. 1989. *Phrase Rhythm in Tonal Music*. New York: Schirmer.

Rothstein, William. 1995. 'Analysis and the Act of Performance'. In John Rink, ed., *The Practice of Performance: Studies in Musical Interpretation*. Cambridge: Cambridge University Press, 217–40.

Rothstein, William. 2005. 'Like Falling off a Log: Rubato in Chopin's Prelude in A-Flat Major (Op. 28, No. 17)'. *Music Theory Online* 11/1.

Rowan, Dean. 2004. 'Modes and Manifestations of Improvisation in Urban Planning, Design, and Theory'. *Critical Studies in Improvisation* 1/1. Accessible at http://www.criticalimprov.com/article/view/10/34.

Said, Edward. 1991. *Musical Elaborations*. London: Chatto & Windus.

Samson, Jim. 1985. *The Music of Chopin*. London: Routledge.

Samson, Jim. 1996. *Chopin*. Oxford: Oxford University Press.

Samson, Jim. 2000. 'The Practice of Early-Nineteenth-Century Pianism'. In Michael Talbot, ed., *The Musical Work: Reality or Invention?* Liverpool: University of Liverpool Press, 110–27.

Sanden, Paul. 2013. *Liveness in Modern Music: Musicians, Technology, and the Perception of Performance*. New York: Routledge.

Santoro, Gene. 2001. *Myself When I Am Real: The Life and Music of Charles Mingus.* New York: Oxford University Press.

Sapp, Craig. 2011. *Computational Methods for the Analysis of Musical Structure.* PhD diss., Stanford University. Accessible at http://purl.stanford.edu/br237mp4161.

Sarath, Ed. 1996. 'A New Look at Improvisation'. *Journal of Music Theory* 40/1, 1–38.

Savage, Steve. 2006. 'Creating the Hyperreal in Classical Recordings'. Paper presented at CHARM/WestFocus seminar Creative Production for Classical Music. London, June 2006. Accessible at http://charm.cchcdn.net/redist/pdf/wf3Savage.pdf.

Savage, Steve. 2009. ' "It Could Have Happened": The Evolution of Music Construction'. In Nicholas Cook et al., eds., *The Cambridge Companion to Recorded Music.* Cambridge: Cambridge University Press, 32–35.

Savage, Steve. 2011. *Bytes and Backbeats: Repurposing Music in the Digital Age.* Ann Arbor: University of Michigan Press.

Sawyer, Keith. 2003. *Group Creativity: Music, Theater, Collaboration.* Mahwah, NJ: Erlbaum.

Schechner, Richard. 1988a. 'Performance Studies: The Broad Spectrum Approach'. *Drama Review* 32(3), 4–6.

Schechner, Richard. 1988b. *Performance Theory.* 2nd ed. London: Routledge. (First published 1977)

Schechner, Richard. 2006. *Performance Studies: An Introduction.* 2nd ed. New York: Routledge. (First published 2002)

Schenker, Heinrich. 1976. 'A Contribution to the Study of Ornamentation'. Hedi Siegel, trans. *Music Forum* 2, 1–139. (First published 1903)

Schenker, Heinrich. 1979. *Free Composition (Der freie Satz).* Ernst Oster, ed. and trans. New York: Longman. (First published 1935)

Schenker, Heinrich. 1984. *J. S. Bach's Chromatic Fantasy and Fugue.* Hedi Siegel, trans. New York: Longman. (First published 1910)

Schenker, Heinrich. 1992. *Beethoven's Ninth Symphony: A Portrayal of Its Musical Content, with a Running Commentary on Performance and Literature as Well.* John Rothgeb, ed. and trans. New Haven: Yale University Press. (First published 1912)

Schenker, Heinrich.1994. *The Masterwork in Music: A Yearbook, Vol. 1 (1925).* William Drabkin, ed., Ian Bent et al., trans. Cambridge: Cambridge University Press.

Schenker, Heinrich.1996. *The Masterwork in Music: A Yearbook, Vol. 2 (1926).* William Drabkin, ed., Ian Bent et al., trans. Cambridge: Cambridge University Press.

Schenker, Heinrich. 2000. *The Art of Performance.* Heribert Esser, ed., Irene Schreier Scott, trans. New York: Oxford University Press.

Schenker, Heinrich. 2005. *Der Tonwille: Pamphlets/Quarterly Publication in Witness of the Immutable Laws of Music, Offered to a New Generation of Youth, Volume II: Issues 6–10 (1923–1924).* William Drabkin, ed., Ian Bent et al., trans. New York: Oxford University Press.

Scherzinger, Martin. 2004. 'The Return of the Aesthetic: Musical Formalism and Its Place in Political Critique'. In Andrew Dell'Antonio, ed., *Beyond Structural Listening? Postmodern Modes of Hearing.* Berkeley: University of California Press, 252–77.

Schick, Steven. 1994. 'Developing an Interpretive Context: Learning Brian Ferneyhough's Bone Alphabet'. *Perspectives of New Music* 32/1, 132–53.

Schmalfeldt, Janet. 1985. 'On the Relation of Analysis to Performance: Beethoven's Bagatelles Op. 126, Nos. 2 and 5'. *Journal of Music Theory* 29, 1–31.

Schmalfeldt, Janet. 2011. *In the Process of Becoming: Analytic and Philosophical Perspectives on Form in Early Nineteenth-Century Music*. New York: Oxford University Press.

Schoenberg, Arnold. 1975. *Style and Idea: Selected Writings of Arnold Schoenberg*. Leonard Stein, ed., Leo Black, trans. London: Faber & Faber.

Schonberg, Harold. 1965. *The Great Pianists*. London: Gollancz.

Schonberg, Harold. 1968. *The Great Conductors*. London: Orion.

Schrade, Leo. 1942. *Beethoven in France: The Growth of an Idea*. New Haven: Yale University Press.

Schutz, Alfred. 1964. 'Making Music Together: A Study in Social Relationship'. In Arvid Broderson, ed., *Alfred Schutz: Collected Papers II. Studies in Social Theory*. Den Haag: Martinus Nijhoff, 159–78. (First published 1951)

Schutz, Alfred. 1976. 'Fragments on the Phenomenology of Music'. Fred Kersten, ed. In Joseph Smith, ed., *In Search of Musical Method*. London: Gordon and Breach, 5–71.

Schutz, Michael, and Fiona Manning. 2012. 'Looking Beyond the Score: The Musical Role of Percussionists' Ancillary Gestures'. *Music Theory Online* 18/1.

Schwarzkopf, Elisabeth. 1982. *On and off the Record: A Memoir of Walter Legge*. London: Faber and Faber.

Seashore, Carl. 1936. 'The Objective Recording and Analysis of Musical Performance'. In Carl Seashore, ed., *Objective Analysis of Musical Performance*. Vol. 4. Iowa City: University of Iowa Press, 5–11.

Seddon, Frederick, and Michele Biasutti. 2009. 'A Comparison of Modes of Communication Between Members of a String Quartet and a Jazz Quartet'. *Psychology of Music* 37, 395–415.

Seeger, Charles. 1977. *Studies in Musicology, 1935–1975*. Berkeley: University of California Press.

Shaffer, Henry. 1980. 'Analysing Piano Performance: A Study of Concert Pianists'. In George Stelmach and Jean Requin, eds., *Tutorials in Motor Behavior*. Amsterdam: North-Holland, 443–55.

Shelemay, Kay Kaufman. 2001. 'Toward an Ethnomusicology of the Early Music Movement: Thoughts on Bridging Disciplines and Musical Worlds'. *Ethnomusicology* 45, 1–29.

Sherman, Bernard. 1997. *Inside Early Music: Conversations with Performers*. New York: Oxford University Press.

Shields, Colin. 2009. 'Igor Stravinsky, Le Sacre du Printemps (Stefan Goldman edit)'. Little White Earbuds, 11 June 2009. Accessible at http://www.littlewhiteearbuds.com/review/igor-stravinsky-le-sacre-du-printemps-stefan-goldmann-edit/#.Ujh6r2Sid7Q.

Shirakawa, Sam. 1992. *The Devil's Music Master: The Controversial Life and Career of Wilhelm Furtwängler*. New York: Oxford University Press.

Shumway, David. 1999. 'Performance'. In Bruce Horner and Thomas Swiss, eds., *Key Terms in Popular Music and Culture*. Malden, MA: Blackwell, 188–98.

Simun, Miriam. 2009. 'My Music, My World: Using the MP3 Player to Shape Experience in London'. *New Media & Society* 11/6, 921–41.

Singer, Mark. 2007. 'Letter from England: Fantasia for Piano'. *New Yorker*, 17 September 2007. Accessible at http://www.newyorker.com/reporting/2007/09/17/070917fa_fact_singer.

Sinnreich, Aram. 2010. *Mashed Up: Music, Technology, and the Rise of Configurable Culture*. Amherst: University of Massachusetts Press.

Sloboda, John, and Andreas Lehmann. 2001. 'Tracking Performance Correlates of Changes in Perceived Intensity of Emotions During Different Interpretations of a Chopin Piano Prelude'. *Music Perception* 19, 87–120.

Sloboda, John, Karen Wise, and Isabelle Peretz. 2005. 'Quantifying Tone Deafness in the General Population'. *Annals of the New York Academy of Sciences* 1060, 255–61.

Small, Christopher. 1998. *Musicking: The Meanings of Performing and Listening.* Middletown, CT: Wesleyan University Press.

Smith, Jacob. 2008. *Vocal Tracks: Performance and Sound Media.* Berkeley: University of California Press.

Somervell, D. C. 1943. 'The Visual Element in Music'. *Music & Letters* 24, 42–47.

Sousa, John Philip. 1906. 'The Menace of Mechanical Music'. *Appleton's Magazine* 8, 278–84. Accessible at http://www.phonozoic.net/n0155.htm.

Stanbridge, Alan. 2008. 'From the Margins to the Mainstream: Jazz, Social Relations, and Discourses of Value'. *Critical Studies in Improvisation* 4/1. Accessible at http://www.criticalimprov.com/article/download/361/959.

Stein, Erwin. 1962. *Form and Performance.* London: Faber.

Stern, Daniel. 2004. *The Present Moment in Psychotherapy and Everyday Life.* New York: Norton.

Stern, Daniel. 2010. *Forms of Vitality: Exploring Dynamic Experience in Psychology and the Arts.* Oxford: Oxford University Press.

Sterne, Jonathan. 2003. *The Audible Past: Cultural Origins of Sound Reproduction.* Durham, NC: Duke University Press.

Stewart, John. 1991. *Ernst Krenek: The Man and His Music.* Berkeley: University of California Press.

Strangelove, Michael. 2010. *Watching YouTube: Extraordinary Videos by Ordinary People.* Toronto: University of Toronto Press.

Stravinsky, Igor. 1947. *Poetics of Music in the Form of Six Lessons.* Cambridge, MA: Harvard University Press. (First published 1942)

Stravinsky, Igor. 1962. *Igor Stravinsky: An Autobiography.* New York: Norton.

Stravinsky, Igor. 1972. *Themes and Conclusions.* London: Faber.

Stravinsky, Igor, and Robert Craft. 1959. *Conversations with Igor Stravinsky.* London: Faber and Faber.

Subotnik, Rose Rosengard. 1976. 'Adorno's Diagnosis of Beethoven's Late Style: Early Symptom of a Fatal Condition'. *Journal of the American Musicological Society* 29, 242–75.

Sudnow, David. 1978. *Ways of the Hand: The Organization of Improvised Conduct.* Cambridge, MA: Harvard University Press.

Sutcliffe, Dean. 2003. 'The Keyboard Music'. In Simon Keefe, ed., *The Cambridge Companion to Mozart.* Cambridge: Cambridge University Press, 61–77.

Symes, Colin. 2004. *Setting the Record Straight: A Material History of Classical Recording.* Middletown, CT: Wesleyan University Press.

Tagg, Philip. 1982. 'Analysing Popular Music: Theory, Method and Practice'. *Popular Music* 2, 37–68.

Taruskin, Richard. 1995. *Text and Act: Essays on Music and Performance.* New York: Oxford University Press.

Théberge, Paul. 1997. *Any Sound You Can Imagine: Making Music/Consuming Technology.* Hanover, NH: Wesleyan University Press.

Thompson, Emily. 1995. 'Machines, Music, and the Quest for Fidelity: Marketing the Edison Phonograph in America, 1877–1925'. *Musical Quarterly* 79, 131–71.

Thomson, Virgil. 2002. *A Reader: Selected Writings 1924–1984*. Richard Kostelanetz, ed. New York: Routledge.

Thornton, Sarah. 1995. *Club Cultures: Music, Media, and Subcultural Capital.* Cambridge: Polity Press.

Thorpe, Vanessa. 2010. 'Turn up the Volume to Save Classical Music'. *Observer.* 5 September 2010, 10.

Timmers, Renee. 2005. Review of Aaron Williamon, ed., *Musical Excellence: Strategies and Techniques to Enhance Performance. Music & Letters* 86, 673–75.

Todd, Neil. 1985. 'A Model of Expressive Timing in Tonal Music'. *Music Perception* 3, 33–57.

Todd, Neil. 1992. 'The Dynamics of Dynamics: A Model of Musical Expression'. *Journal of the Acoustical Society of America* 91, 3540–50.

Tomlinson, Gary. 2012. 'Musicology, Anthropology, History'. In Martin Clayton, Trevor Herbert, and Richard Middleton, eds., *The Cultural Study of Music: A Critical Introduction.* 2nd ed. New York: Routledge, 59–72. (First published 2002)

Tong, Jennifer. 1994. *Separate Discourses: A Study of Performance and Analysis.* PhD diss., University of Southampton.

Torricelli, Robert, and Andrew Carroll, eds. 1999. *In Our Own Words: Extraordinary Speeches of the American Century.* New York: Kodansha America.

Toynbee, Jason. 2006. 'Copyright, the Work, and Phonographic Orality in Music'. *Social and Legal Studies* 15, 77–99.

Trezise, Simon. 2009. 'The Recorded Document: Interpretation and Discography'. In Nicholas Cook et al., eds., *The Cambridge Companion to Recorded Music.* Cambridge: Cambridge University Press, 186–209.

Tyack, Jonathan. 2007. *Rehabilitating the Canon: A History of Handel's Messiah in Performance.* PhD diss., Royal Holloway, University of London.

Varwig, Bettina. 2012. 'Metaphor of Time and Modernity in Bach'. *Journal of Musicology* 29, 154–90.

Vial, Stephanie. 2008. *The Art of Musical Phrasing in the Eighteenth Century: Punctuating the Classical 'Period'.* Rochester, NY: University of Rochester Press.

Victoros, Poly. 2009. *Repositioning Classical Music: Crossover in Contemporary Britain.* PhD diss., Royal Holloway, University of London.

Volioti, Georgia. 2010. 'Playing with Tradition: Weighing up Similarity and the Buoyancy of the Game'. *Musicae Scientiae* 14/2, 85–114.

Volioti, Georgia. 2011. *Tradition, Agency, and the Limits of Empiricism: Perspectives from Recordings of Grieg's Piano Music.* PhD diss., Royal Holloway, University of London.

Volioti, Georgia. 2012. 'Reinventing Grieg's Folk Modernism: An Empirical Investigation of the Performance Practice of the Slåtter, Op. 72, No. 2'. *Journal of Musicological Research* 31/4, 262–96.

Wagner, Richard. 1895. *Prose Works, Volume 5: Actors and Singers*, William Ashton Ellis, trans. London: London: Kegan Paul, Trench, Trübner and Co.

Waksman, Steve. 1999. *Instruments of Desire: The Electric Guitar and the Shaping of Musical Experience.* Cambridge, MA: Harvard University Press.

Walls, Peter. 1996. 'Performing Corelli's Violin Sonatas, Op. 5'. *Early Music* 12/1, 133–42.

Walser, Robert. 1993. 'Out of Notes: Signification, Interpretation, and the Problem of Miles Davis'. *Musical Quarterly* 77, 343–65.

Walser, Robert. 1999. *Keeping Time: Readings in Jazz History*. New York: Oxford University Press.

Wanderley, Marcelo, and Bradley Vines. 2006 'Origins and Functions of Clarinettists' Ancillary Gestures'. In Anthony Gritten and Elaine King, eds., *Music and Gesture*. Aldershot: Ashgate, 165–91.

Waskul, Dennis. 2006. 'The Role-Playing Game and the Game of Role-Playing: The Ludic Self and Everyday Life'. In Patrick Williams, Sean Hendricks, and Keith Winkler, eds., *Gaming as Culture: Essays on Reality Identity and Experience in Fantasy Games*. Jefferson, NC: McFarland, 19–38.

Wason, Robert. 1987. 'Webern's "Variations for Piano", Op. 27: Musical Structure and the Performance Score'. *Intégral* 1, 57–103.

Watkin, David. 1996. 'Corelli's Op. 5 Sonatas: "Violino e Violone o Cimbalo"?' *Early Music* 24/4, 645–63.

Weber, Nicholas Fox. 2008. *Le Corbusier: A Life*. New York: Knopf.

Westegaard, Peter. 1974. 'On the Notion of Style'. In Henrik Glahn, Søren Sørensen, and Peter Ryom, eds., *The International Musicological Society: Report of the Eleventh Congress, Copenhagen, 1972 (2 vols.)*. Vol. 1. Copenhagen: William Hansen, 71–74.

White, Eric Walter. 1979. *Stravinsky: The Composer and His Works*. 2nd ed. London: Faber and Faber. (First published 1966)

Williamon, Aaron, and Jane Davidson. 2002 'Exploring Co-Performer Communication'. *Musicae Scientiae* 6/1, 53–72.

Williams, Justin. Forthcoming. '"Cars with the Boom": Music, Automobility, and Hip-Hop "Sub" Cultures'. In Sumanth Gopinath and Jason Stanyek, eds., *Oxford Handbook of Mobile Music and Sound Studies*. Oxford: Oxford University Press.

Williams, Orlo. 1923. 'Times and Seasons'. *Gramophone*, June 1923, 18–19.

Williams, Rod. 2007. 'The Great Classical Piano Swindle'. *Intelligent Life*, Autumn 2007, 66–74. Accessible at http://moreintelligentlife.co.uk/files/completehatto.pdf.

Windsor, Luke, and Eric Clarke. 1997. 'Expressive Timing and Dynamics in Real and Artificial Musical Performances: Using an Algorithm as an Analytical Tool'. *Music Perception* 15, 127–52.

Windsor, Luke, Peter Desain, Amandine Penel, and Michiel Borkent. 2006. 'A Structurally Guided Method for the Decomposition of Expression in Music Performance'. *Journal of the Acoustical Society of America* 119, 1182–93.

Winn, James. 1998. *The Pale of Words: Reflections on the Humanities and Performance*. New Haven: Yale University Press.

Winter, Robert. 1990. 'Orthodoxies, Paradoxes, and Contradictions: Performance Practices in Nineteenth-century Piano Music'. In Larry Todd, *Nineteenth-Century Piano Music*. New York: Schirmer, 16–54.

Wintle, Christopher. 1982. 'Corelli's Tonal Models'. *Quaderni della Rivista Italiana di Musicologia* 4, 29–69.

Worthen, William. 2003. *Shakespeare and the Force of Modern Performance*. Cambridge: University of Cambridge Press.

Wright, David. 2012. 'Music and Musical Performance: Histories in Disjunction?' In Colin Lawson and Robin Stowell, eds., *The Cambridge History of Performance*. Cambridge: Cambridge University Press, 169–206.

Younts, Jason. 2010. 'Anything Dexter Gordon Can Do Johnny Griffin Can Do Better and Vice-Versa: An Analysis of Communication in Performance'. Paper presented at the Embodiment of Authority conference, Sibelius Academy, Helsinki, September 2010.

Yung, Bell. 1984. 'Choreographic and Kinesthetic Elements in Performance on the Chinese Seven-String Zither'. *Ethnomusicology* 28, 5–17.

Yung, Bell. 1985. 'Da Pu: The Recreative Process for the Music of the Seven-String Zither'. In Anne Dhu Shapiro, ed., *Music and Context: Essays in Honor of John Ward*. Cambridge, MA: Harvard University Press, 370–83.

Zak, Albin. 2001. *The Poetics of Rock: Cutting Tracks, Making Records*. Berkeley: University of California Press.

Zak, Albin. 2009. 'Painting the Sonic Canvas: Electronic Mediation as Musical Style'. In Amanda Bayley, ed., *Recorded Music: Performance, Culture and Technology*. Cambridge: Cambridge University Press, 307–24.

Zbikowski, Lawrence. 2002. *Conceptualizing Music: Cognitive Structure, Theory, and Analysis*. New York: Oxford University Press.

Zbikowski, Lawrence. 2004. 'Modelling the Groove: Conceptual Structure and Popular Music'. *Journal of the Royal Musical Association* 129, 272–97.

Zbikowski, Lawrence. 2008. 'Dance Topoi, Sonic Analogues and Musical Grammar: Communicating with Music in the Eighteenth Century'. In Danuta Mirka and Kofi Agawu, eds., *Communication in Eighteenth-Century Music*. Cambridge: Cambridge University Press, 283–309.

Zbikowski, Lawrence. 2011. 'Musical Gesture and Musical Grammar: A Cognitive Approach'. In Anthony Gritten and Elaine King, eds., *New Perspectives on Music and Gesture*. Aldershot: Ashgate, 83–98.

Zorn, Friedrich Albert. 1905. *Grammar of the Art of Dancing: Theoretical and Practical*. Alfonso Sheafe, ed.. New York: Burt Franklin.

Vasari, Giorgio, 11
Végh, Sándor, 202
Ventura, Brian, 152
Veracini, Francesco, 239, 241
Vex'd, 391
Viardot, Pauline, 166
vibrato, violin, 218
Vienna Conservatory, 27, 56, 128
Vienna Philharmonic, 28
Viollet-le-Duc, Eugène, 216
virtual body, 323
vitality affects, 77–78
voodoo, 300
Voyager space probes, 412–13

Wagner, Richard, 38, 77, 350, 355, 381,
    388, 407
Waksman, Steve, 292, 293, 300, 301, 302,
    303, 304
Wallenstein, Alfred, 217
Walls, Peter, 231
Walser, Robert, 305
Walter, Bruno, 89, 389
Waskul, Dennis, 259, 261, 267, 273,
    297, 325
Wason, Robert, 54–55, 81, 92
Wasowski, Andrzej, 335
Watson, Claire, 382
Weber, Carl Maria von, 96
Webern, Anton, 54–55, 130, 272
Wein, Chuck, 298
Weingartner, Felix, 87–88, 136,
    337, 339
Werktreue, 13, 21, 26, 95, 360, 398
West-Eastern Divan Orchestra, 407–410
Westegaard, Peter, 138

Westenra, Hayley, 9
Widmer, Gerhard, 327
Wilde, Oscar, 303
Williams, Orlo, 344
Williams, Robbie, 303
Windgassen, Wolfgang, 381
Windsor, Luke, 32, 81, 86, 93, 156, 157,
    178, 179, 181, 188
Winehouse, Amy, 303, 304
Winn, James, 16, 306
Wintle, Christopher, 242
Wise, Karen, 248
Wittgenstein, Ludwig, 241
Wöllner, Clemens, 321
Wood, Sir Henry, 396
Woodstock Festival, 289
Worthen, W. B., 24, 399
Wright, David, 224

Yamaha Disklavier, 29, 139
Yarrow, Ralph, 236, 284
Yellow Lounge Classical Club, 392, 393
Ying Quartet, 258
YouTube, 147, 232, 310, 330, 333, 335,
    371, 395

Zak, Albin, 357, 377
Zak, Jakov, 197
Zbikowski, Lawrence, 79, 160, 172, 241,
    294, 316, 323
Zelter, C. F., 262
Zimerman, Krystian, 1776
Zip Coon, 301
Zorn, Friedrich Albert, 159, 161, 164,
    172, 320
Zverev, Nikola, 34, 314

Printed in the USA/Agawam, MA
June 20, 2018

677116.005